ITALY'S NOBLE RED WINES

Nicklas
12/87

ITALY'S NOBLE RED WINES

Sheldon & Pauline Wasserman

 Sterling Publishing Co., Inc.   New York

This book is dedicated to Giorgio Grai, "L'Ombra,"
and Alfredo Currado di Vietti,
two of the world's finest people
as well as two of the world's finest winemakers,

and to the numerous other fine Italian winemakers
who made this book possible
by creating these noble red wines.

Library of Congress Cataloging-in-Publication Data

Wasserman, Sheldon.
  Italy's noble red wines.

  Reprint. Originally published: Piscataway, N.J.:
New Century Publishers, c1985.
  Bibliography: p.
  Includes index.
  1. Wine and wine making—Italy.   I. Wasserman,
Pauline.   II. Title.
[TP559I8W36   1987]   641.2'223'0945   87-7064
ISBN 0-8069-6632-7 (pbk.)

1   3   5   7   9   10   8   6   4   2

First published in paperback in 1987 by
Sterling Publishing Co., Inc.
Two Park Avenue, New York, N.Y. 10016
Original edition published in hardcover by
New Century Publishers, Inc.
Copyright © 1985 by Sheldon and Pauline Wasserman
Distributed in Canada by Oak Tree Press Ltd.
% Canadian Manda Group, P.O. Box 920, Station U
Toronto, Ontario, Canada M8Z 5P9
Distributed in the United Kingdom by Blandford Press
Link House, West Street, Poole, Dorset BH15 1LL, England
Distributed in Australia by Capricorn Ltd.
P.O. Box 665, Lane Cove, NSW 2066
Manufactured in the United States of America

Table of Contents

Acknowledgments

To Giacomo Bologna, "Italy's Grand Ambassador of Wine," who said that it would be sufficient thanks for him if we wrote about the wines themselves, making known what quality and greatness Italian wines can achieve, we offer our heartfelt thanks nevertheless, for taking us under his wing and giving us our first real introduction to the fine wines of Piemonte, generously sharing his time, his hospitality, and his ready welcome at the *cantine* of some of the finest producers; for his patience and willingness to repeat and carefully rephrase every explanation, when we could barely speak the language; for the many doors he opened and the many bottles as well, of rare and excellent wines, not only Piemontese, and not only Italian.

A special thanks to Mario Cordero, who cheerfully offered his most valuable services and without whose help we would no doubt still be in Piemonte trying to finish our research.

Our thanks to Renato Ratti, Mr. Nebbiolo, who built the foundation with his historical and original research and work on the crus of Barolo and Barbaresco, which were so useful; also for his time and advice, both invaluable to this work.

We are obliged to Angelo and Piero Solci, for the opportunity they gave us to discover some remarkable Italian wines and for their very valuable assistance in the office with our attempts to arrange and rearrange our *programma*.

A special note of appreciation goes to the irrepressible Giannola Nonino, a lovely lady who offered warm hospitality and arranged a superb itinerary for us in Friuli.

We also thank Claudia and Tonino Verro, who made the lovely La Contea available to us whenever we needed a place for an interview or a tasting in the area, as well as for all the too-good meals that gave us the strength to forge ahead and never let us forget the quality and dedication to be found in Italian wine and the people connected with it.

We want to thank Luigi Veronelli for introducing us to some fine wines and some fine producers.

To Ronald T. de Blis, who brought our attention to some wines which might not have otherwise been included, our thanks for his enthusiasm and encouragement.

To Bud Simon, once again, we offer our thanks for his thoughtfulness in introducing us to our fine publisher.

Our thanks to Angelo Charles Castelli, who not only opened many fine Italian wines for us and offered enthusiastic encouragement but also provided the fine, and much appreciated, translation for the preface.

A special word of gratitude to Harry Foulds for his encouragement and invaluable aid during our extended research on this project.

We also want to thank Augusto Marchini of the Italian Wine Center for the important information he provided and also for his invaluable assistance; the Tuscan section in particular was much improved thanks to his efforts.

Barbara Edelman, formerly of the Italian Wine Center, furnished us with difficult to obtain up-to-date DOC information.

We want also to thank Carlo Bertolotti, Silvana Genero, and especially Beatrice Mavaracchio of Torino Esposizioni, who was a great help at the VI.PI.85 fair, which did much to refine our Piemontese section.

"Cicci" Boccoli Frigerio gave willing and enthusiastic assistance in the field.

Riccardo Riccardi provided us with valuable information and a chance to taste some lovely wines.

We also thank Silvano Piacentini of the Istituto Enologico Italiano, who opened some splendid bottles which increased our knowledge and appreciation of Italian wines.

And we'd like to thank our publisher, Charles Walther, who not only made this book possible but, as a knowledgeable winelover, offered us helpful advice and suggestions that we feel contributed to making this a more interesting and valuable book.

Many thanks to the many importers who gave us much needed cooperation and much appreciated assistance. The list is long, so we thought it better and more practicable to attempt to thank all as a group rather than individually. And, considering the number of years involved in this project, we doubt we could remember them all anyway. You know who you are. *Mille grazie.*

There are so many producers who deserve special mention that we decided not to add another whole section to the book trying to list them all here. Instead, we hope the book itself will serve as a small way of saying *grazie tantissimo di cuore* and to let them know that we do indeed appreciate their generosity, their time, and the opportunity they gave us to know their wines better. Without them this book on Italy's noble red wines would not have been possible.

Preface

Writing a preface for my friends Pauline and Sheldon Wasserman is not an easy task. Many prefaces are done routinely with a description of the subject matter, but such is not possible in this case.

This book is very rich in content. The words and images deal with an area that is very important and meaningful to Italian agriculture and to the Italian economy. The Wassermans, with their customary professionalism and broad knowledge, have succeeded in putting together a complete and comprehensive treatise that will satisfy the most exacting epicurean. For these reasons, the book in itself has the ability to sustain any preface, thus relieving me somewhat of the responsibility of presenting it.

I will note, however, the feeling of panic that assailed me when I first read the Wassermans' notes, how I felt left behind, as a neophyte, at the unusual competence with which our Italian wines were not only described but also throroughly understood by them from their thousands, nay millions, of serious and very professional tastings; and they went even further, delving into an understanding of the people themselves responsible for the history of the wine and the preservation of its tradition.

Alert and objective critics that they are, the Wassermans have understood the evolution that is taking place in Italian enology for the past decade, how Italian wine in this recent metamorphosis has graduated into a class that compares favorably with the wines of other countries touted for their great wines.

In our country two larger productive categories of wines have gradually emerged. The first is made up of the great wines, those that intimately satisfy us in their most praiseworthy sensations and which contain cultural, historical, and artistic aspects of immense interest. These are notably different and superior to the second category of daily table wines, whose main function is to satisfy the simple need of quenching thirst.

It is this first category of wines that Pauline and Sheldon describe in great depth. Those who are familiar with this dedicated couple know that they write together; they write constantly. Even at the table they continue to taste and record in minute detail every sensation, every label.

They never turn down a tasting or walk away from a discussion or debate on wine, nor do they bring with them any preconceived attitudes in the quest to satisfy their insatiable curiosity.

The frenetic pens of this couple have now spawned many books that deal with the worldwide panorama of wines, not to mention the numerous articles written for newspapers and magazines. This book is another journey among the wines of Italy, but it is not a simple catalog or a classification of one of those erudite Solons that judge with pretensions of infallible taste to guide the unenlightened. Theirs are intimate impressions of two civilized and refined individuals who share their wide experience with us.

Pauline and Sheldon travel throughout the Italian peninsula in search of our magnificent wines. They take us by the hand and initiate us into both an old and a new art form, that of recognizing the wines, appreciating the wines, and becoming a friend of the wines. The work makes very enjoyable reading and, in my opinion, can be more useful than many other publications, didactic and encyclopedic, in getting to the heart of the matter of wine. It can also be beneficial to those who would venture, with minimal ease, among the many names and labels, the most complicated indications which are becoming ever more difficult for those in the modest search for a good glass of wine, and perhaps even in putting together a personal wine cellar, modest but with the stamp of character and imagination.

Their story is always one that begins with the land, the places, with recollections of traditions and human events. This is indeed the preparation required to understand the various crus, the environment, the people, and their way of life, the gastronomic customs and their proper matching with the wines.

I encourage you to read this book with confidence. You will learn many things you were previously unaware of, but above all you will learn to know and to love the good wine lying in the "religious" silence of your small *cantina*.

Angelo Solci
Milano, Italia

Introduction

All the world's wines can be divided into two broad categories: wines *di personalità*, with personality, and wines *senza personalità*, which lack that quality.

The wines in the second category are beverage wines, pure and simple. They are meant to be drunk in draughts to quench thirst and to go with food—no more, no less. If they're well made, they serve their purpose well. They are not wines for contemplation or discussion. At their best they are balanced, clean, and fruity, simple, easy, and undemanding—*non impegnativo,* as they say. Italy, like all of the wine-producing countries of the world, has its fair share of these wines.

Italy also has many wines with personality and character.

A wine of personality tells you something about itself; its nature reflects the soil, the climate, and the grape variety it comes from, perhaps even the hand of the winemaker who created it. And the finer the wine, the more definite and more complex its character, its personality, its style.

A Noble Heritage

Most of the world's fine wines have a noble heritage; they are from the favored regions and vineyard sites capable of producing grapes of character, warm enough to ripen the grapes fully and cool enough to ripen them slowly, bringing out a panoply of nuances in aroma and flavor. The grape variety itself is often also of noble stock.

The noble characters of cabernet sauvignon and pinot noir, despite the fickle nature of the latter, have long been recognized by winelovers. Few have noted that Italy is the home of noble varieties as well, varieties capable of producing great wines given an auspicious combination of nature and man.

The Italians have seldom spoken or written of their grape varieties as being noble. As high as the regard for some varieties may be among winemakers and *buongustaii,* they seem better at making or appreciating their viticultural treasures than they are at spreading the word about them. We, as serious students of wine, experienced with wines from all over the world, propose to do that for them, in recognition of Italy's noble varieties and noble wines, which have gone too long unheralded. In appreciation also of the nobility of spirit of Italy's finest producers, we devote this book to their discovery.

Italy has three indigenous varieties capable of producing wines of breed and character. These noble varieties are nebbiolo, sangiovese, and aglianico. We devote a section of this book to each.

To fully appreciate these wines, it is important to understand a little background on them, some of their history, and something about the people who produce the wines, their methods in the vineyards and the cellars, and the winemaking philosophies of some of the best of them.

Vintage Wines

Vintages are also important; these fine wines are not wines that are turned out every year one like the other. They come from varieties sensitive to changes in each aspect of their environment. And interesting though it is to know how the vintages were regarded initially, it is even more important to know how the wines are now. Should you buy, hold, drink, or dump them today?

We discuss both aspects and have asked many producers to evaluate vintages for their wines in particular, as different vineyards and microclimates can vary significantly. The character of the same variety changes not only from region to region but also from vineyard to vineyard. Knowing something about the specific crus also tells you something about the wines. The vineyards and the crus can play a significant role in the character of the wines they engender.

In this regard it is interesting to note that the differences between the top vineyards and the lesser ones are more pronounced in the lesser years and less evident in the better years. In the better years the sun shines on all the sites, and the drainage is less important because rain is not a problem. But in the lesser vintages the advantage of the extra sun gained in vineyards with better exposure helps the grapes to ripen more fully, and the better drainage prevents the grapes from becoming diluted by heavy rains.

Our Rating System

In our evaluation of the vintages, we have used a rating system ranging from four stars to zero: excellent, very good, average, poor. Brackets around a rating indicate a tentative judgment when we felt that our experience was too limited to be more definite or that the vintage was too young to assess fully. For example, as we haven't had the opportunity to taste a wide range of 1984 Chiantis as yet and since those we have sampled were at such an early stage of development, we give the vintage only a tentative evaluation, a possible star, [★].

The style and the quality of the wine itself, how it will taste in the glass, is a matter of major importance. We have evaluated the wines of numerous producers in an effort to provide a useful picture for the wine drinker. Specifics are also helpful, such as actual tasting notes on the wines. As André Simon so aptly put it, "The only way to learn about wines is to taste them, and there is no substitute for pulling a cork."

Our tasting notes for the most part are fairly current. In some cases we have gone back as far as five years. Beyond that we have very rarely included our *schede,* feeling that they are no longer relevant to the discussion of the wines. Whenever possible we have tasted a wine more than once, and, although for the most part we give our most recent tasting note we've relied on previous experiences in making our estimation on drinkability. Tasting notes give the name of the producer, and vineyard, with the number of times tasted and date of the most recent tasting in parentheses, followed by the description, and the rating. In the case of a wine which offers promise of future development, we have given, in parentheses following the rating, the potential increase in the assessment of the wine given sufficient maturity. When its development was in doubt, that was indicated by a question mark. Where we rated a wine ★★(★), for example, we felt it deserved ★★ for the present, but given time could, and probably would, merit ★★★.

As an example:

1978 Vietti, Rocche *(10 times 2/85).* Dense color; bouquet reveals an enormous richness and fragrance with hints of liquorice, flowers, tea, tobacco and cherries; incredible concentration of rich, ripe fruit; so well balanced that the tannin hardly seems evident at first; very young but even now a wine of meditation.★★★(★)

We use the same four-star system in evaluating individual wines and rating the producers.

The ratings on the *aziende,* or producers, are based on overall quality. One bottle from a given producer could merit four stars, while another is worth only one; his rating reflects both. The producers are evaluated for the particular type of wine under discussion—Barolo, Chianti, Cabernet, or whatever. If he makes multiple kinds and we only rank one, the quality of his other wines is not taken into consideration in that assessment.

In evaluating the producers we relied on our notes about wines tasted since 1972, with the exception of a few rare cases. Where our impressions were based on older tasting notes, we point that out. In some cases we find that a producer's quality has changed. In that case we give him 2 ratings: one based on our evaluation of wines before a specified time and the other on wines produced since. In some cases the quality of the wines has improved; in others it has declined.

There is naturally a subjective element in tasting wine, but recognizing that, we've tried to be as fair as possible. Whenever there was a question in our minds, and in cases where our experience was limited, we gave the producer the benefit of the doubt and opted for the higher category, up to three stars. On the ratings higher than two stars, however, we have been more conservative, and to give top marks (four stars) there could be no shadow of a doubt whatever in our minds. Any wine or producer awarded three stars or more was a clearcut three stars or more; a doubtful three stars got ★★★ − or slightly less, ★★ + .

To be fair to those who will make use of these appraisals in selecting wines, we have been cautious. In cases where we have only tasted one or perhaps two vintages, or only a few unfinished wines from cask, even if the wines were quite impressive we have hesitated to score the *azienda* overall as highly as the individual wine or wines. There is an exception to that rule. In cases when we have tasted one wine, but that from a great vintage, and that wine proved mediocre nonetheless, we felt that the one example was sufficient proof of the producer's lack of ability or commitment, and he was scored down. Given one consideration and another, a critic's job is not an easy one.

Our rating system:

★★★★	Great, superb, truly noble
★★★	Exceptionally fine
★★	Very good
★	A good example of its type, somewhat above average
0	Acceptable to mediocre, depending on the context, drinkable
+	Somewhat better than the star category it is put in
−	Somewhat less than the star category it is put in
()	Potential increase in the rating of the wine given sufficient maturity

Our Role As Critics

As critics, we cannot be totally objective; taste is, after all, a subjective matter. In making a serious assessment, though, it is necessary to have a knowledge of the grape variety and experience with the wines. It is also essential to maintain a sense of fair play.

From some wines you expect more; the possibility is there. Others are more limited; it's not possible for them to rise above a certain level. But if they are honest, well-made wines, although we may not find them to our personal taste, we must admit that they are good for their type. Wines from some varieties, notably the better and noble varieties have a recognizable character. If a wine displays this, it is a plus for that wine—in fact, if it doesn't, it is a fault. If the wine's character happens to be one that we personally don't care for, it's a wine not to drink but not to score down for that reason.

In judging the producers we have considered wines, not personalities. Our opinions of the wines are admittedly affected by our personal tastes, but we cannot and do not let our personal reactions to the people color our opinion of their wines.

While it is true that some of the finest producers have become our friends—it is always a pleasure to be in the company of people of integrity who care sincerely about quality—we have been, if any thing, a bit more critical of their wines than we would have been otherwise, to offset the natural tendency to want to be generous with friends. And we have a few friends who produce wines that are merely ordinary, from grapes or regions from which excellence is not possible. We've rated their wines as such, in person and in print, and they have never tried to influence our judgment. If their reaction had been otherwise, they wouldn't be our friends.

In this regard it is perhaps worthwhile to relate three stories.

A few years ago we were introduced to a producer and his wife, a very nice couple we both enjoyed meeting. They invited us to come back to spend an afternoon, to come for lunch or dinner. We never did. We found their wine rather mediocre, and we would not have enjoyed being in the position of wanting to be nice to the people yet not being able to say anything nice about their wine, which they were hoping to hear good things about.

While researching an earlier book, we visited a producer who was inhospitable—in fact, downright rude—so much so that we almost left before our interview. When our book was published both the producer and their importer bought a number of copies. They apparently felt that our judgment of their wines was fair.

On our last trip to Italy we visited more than four dozen producers in four weeks, which included nearly one week for the Vinitaly wine fair, and we tasted more than 1400 wines. Needless to say, upon our return we were rather beat. A few days after we got home, the Italian Wine Center invited us to a tasting. We were already familiar with all of the producers represented, but we went. There were three at the tasting to whom we had given 0 marks, and we wanted to give them one more chance to be upgraded if possible.

We emphasize that our ratings are our own personal judgments, and we recognize that personal tastes vary; you may agree with us, or you may not. We have tried to be as fair as possible. We have noted our preferences and partialities—for firm acidity and tannin, richness, also elegance, personality, and so on—which will give you, our readers, a better idea of our standards.

We also evaluate wines for interest, but basically we focus on those aspects of wine judging that can be considered standards for any good, well-made wine: balance, soundness, absence of off-odors or flavors, varietal character.

An International Character

On a slightly different note, we are of the opinion that it's a pity more and more of the wines produced in the world today are beginning to take on a sameness of character, perhaps becoming more international but in the process losing their individuality. The trend for producing wines for early drinking, for blending in some cabernet sauvignon, and for aging in *barriques,* seems unfortunately to be spreading.

While we love Bordeaux, Burgundy, and Champagne, California Cabernet and

Chardonnay, New York State Riesling, Sereksia, and Pinot Gris, Port, German Auslesen, and many others of the world's fine wines, we don't want one wine to taste like another. Tuscan wines should taste like Tuscan wines, and not imitation Bordeaux; Piemontese wines should have the character of Piemontese wines, not copy-cat Californian.

Our Role As Journalists

We have been researching this book for thirteen years. In that time we have made many trips to Italy and have spent many hours talking with producers, tasting wines, and taking copious notes. We have checked and rechecked our facts and figures. And when we began writing the book in earnest about a year ago, we designed a questionnaire to get more, and we hope more accurate, information from people not being asked to come up with facts and figures off the tops of their heads and to ensure that our information was as up-to-date as possible.

We have a profound respect for facts and have made every possible effort to ensure that the least possible margin of error could creep in. We realize that some of our information differs from what has been published previously, even recently, so we feel that it is worth pointing out that, except for history and where we cite the sources of certain information, all of our material is based on first-hand sources.

Producers sometimes gave different figures when asked the same questions more than once, and figures do change. To the best of our ability, however, we have been accurate and have turned to the most verifiably reliable sources for our information.

A Salute to Quality

We believe in quality regardless of the source, which is one of the reasons we wrote this book, to give you a greater familiarity and more appreciation for the great red wines of Italy, wines that deserve more recognition. Charles Gizelt, one of the first people we met who really cared about Italian wine, used to say, "Great wine knows no borders." He was right. We believe that in the future Italy's great wines will be rated with the other great wines of the world, recognized for the excellence they represent.

We personally would like to salute those producers who have given their best effort and have never cut corners in their efforts to turn out the finest wines possible, although the fruit of their labors may have often gone unnoticed and unappreciated by the vast majority of wine drinkers, even wine writers. They have supplied us not only with the material to write this book but also the inspiration to do so.

PART I

Nebbiolo

Chapter 1

Nebbiolo

The early history of the vine in northwestern Italy is lost in the mists of time. When the Greeks arrived in the fifth century B.C., wild vines are believed to have been growing there. The newcomers, though, brought their own vine cuttings as well as their own wine, which was much appreciated by the Liguri Rossi who inhabited the area. They learned from the Greeks how to cultivate the vine, training the plants like small bushes low to the ground and pruning them to concentrate the vine's strength into fewer grape bunches yielding riper, more concentrated fruit, to produce a sweeter, more alcoholic beverage than the thin wine obtained from their own unpruned vines.

After the Roman conquest in the second century B.C., viticulture and winemaking practices felt a new influence. The vines were trained in the Etruscan manner high on trees or tall poles. The Romans built cellars below ground and into the hills to store the wine. Originally the wine was stored in amphorae as it was in the south, but they also made use of the wooden casks made in the region, which seem to have been a Celtic invention.

Pliny noted in his *Natural History* that good wines were produced in the area of Alba and Pollentia, west of Alba near the Tanaro river (now Pollenzo). The fame of the wine of Pollentia spread at least as far as central Italy; amphorae stamped with that name have been unearthed in Rome and the region of Romagna.

In his writing on the wines of this region, Pliny makes note of a vine he called *allobrogica,* a late-ripening and cold-resistant black grape. This describes the *nebbiolo,* a variety that buds early and ripens late, the harvest taking place when the valleys are filled with morning mists, *nebbia,* from which the vine takes the name that it is most commonly known by today. Earlier it was referred to as *vitis vinifera pedemontana,* later *nubiolum.*

Renato Ratti, who has done extensive research on the wines of Piemonte, the Nebbiolo in particular, notes references to the "nibiol" in documents from the 1200s.[1] In his *Chronicles,* Oggerio Alfieri recorded that the nebbiolo was being cultivated in 1268 in the area around Rivoli in Piemonte. In 1340, the vine comes in for praise from Pier di' Crescenzi, who refers to the "nubiola" vine in his *Ruralium Commodorum,* describing it as a "marvelously vinous" variety that "makes an excellent wine, very strong, and one to keep."

It was then, as it is now, a highly regarded variety. In 1511, in the local statutes of La Morra, the nebbiolo is referred to as a precious variety, one to be particularly protected.

Barolo Discovered

Giovan Battista Croce, court jeweler to Victor Emanuele I and a knowledgeable amateur viticulturist who wrote a treatise on the subject, considered the nebbiolo the "queen of the black grapes." Its wines were much appreciated by the house of Savoy. It wasn't long after they had added Piemonte to their domains that they sent for these wines to be supplied to the court. Records show that in 1631 they received six *carra* (132-gallon, or 500-liter casks) of the best Barolo.

Such was their esteem that the dukes of Savoy sent a shipment of Barolo to Louis XIV of France, reputed to be a lover of the wines of Burgundy and Champagne. The Marquis of St. Maurice recorded that the king and his prime minister, Colbert, were both favorably impressed with the wine, pronouncing it "excellent."

In Milano, Gattinara was much appreciated at the court of the dukes of Sforza.

In the early 1700s, the nebbiolo wines of Piemonte were discovered by English merchants seeking an alternative for the wines of Bordeaux, England being involved in a war with France at the time. Old records show that they ordered the wines of Barolo and Gattinara. But the problems of transportation proved insurmountable, and the trade was lost. The tariffs levied by the Genovese republic on such shipments were exorbitant, and the only Piemontese port, Nizza, could be reached only via tortuous mountain tracks not passable by oxcarts laden with the ponderous casks of wine. So the wine continued to be basically unknown outside its own region.

During the struggle for domination of northern Italy, Piemontese wine was singled out for recognition by the Austrian general, Melas (remembered best by opera lovers for the splendid opportunity he provides for the tenor in **Tosca** to hit a dramatic high note in a triumphant cry of "Vittoria! vittoria!"). Melas ordered supplies of "nebbiolo of Barbaresco" to celebrate a victory over the French in 1799.

Barolo was also accorded recognition by a man of peace when Monsignor Chiaramonti (later Pope Pius VII) visited the Abbazia dell'Annunziata at La Morra in the early years of the nineteenth century. The prelate is reported to have been so impressed with the wine of the abbey that he asked to be supplied with some bottles on an annual basis.

Marchesi Falletti di Barolo

The most important assist to the recognition of these wines came from the efforts of the Marchesi Falletti di Barolo. According to the famous story, Marchesa Giulia Vittorina Colbert Falletti di Barolo responded to a comment from Carlo Alberto of Savoy, who had expressed an interest in tasting the wines of Barolo by dispatching a train of oxcarts transporting 300 *carra* (39,625 gallons, 1500 hectoliters) of Barolo from the Falletti vineyards in Barolo and Serralunga.

The duke was duly impressed—so much so, in fact, that he purchased a hunting lodge at Verduno as well as a *cantina* at Pollenzo where he installed the best enologist of the day, General Stangone, to oversee the vineyards and the winemaking on the estate. His son and successor, Vittorio Emanuele II, also bought vineyard property in the zone, at Fontanafredda.

The Marchesa Falletti also deserves credit for changing Barolo, in about 1840, into the dry wine that it is today. A Frenchwoman herself, she brought in enologist Count Oudart of Reims to make the Falletti wines. Previously the wines of the Langhe—and most other viticultural regions—had always contained some residual sugar left from the fermentation. In the 1800s, tastes were beginning to change in Europe, and dry wines, first produced in Bordeaux in 1805, began to gain favor over the sweet or semisweet styles that had been preferred previously.

At Castello di Grinzane, Italy's future prime minister, Conte de Cavour, a cousin of the Marchesa, ran a model farm where he planted experimental vineyards and made a serious study of agriculture. Count Oudart introduced new vinification methods as well as innovations in the vineyards, which were considered the most advanced in the Langhe. Cavour worked in collaboration with the Marchesa and Oudart to improve the quality of the wine of the zone and to develop the new dry style.

According to Renato Ratti, who has made a valuable study of the history of the region, Barolo was the first wine of the Langhe to be made as a completely dry wine, followed by Barbaresco, Dolcetto, Barbera, Grignolino, Bonarda, the white Erbaluce and Cortese, Gattinara, Carema, Boca, Sizzano, and, finally, more than a century later in the 1950s, Nebbiolo d'Alba. Passito di Caluso, of course, and Asti remained sweet.

In 1873, at the International Exposition of Vienna, the Piemontese wines won eleven medals, seven of them for Barolo, and some praise from foreign experts. Henry Vizetelly, an English journalist, wrote that "Italy, with all its natural advantages, has not yet learned how to produce a truly fine dry wine. With the exception of a limited number of special quality, like the Barolo of Piemonte..."

Domizio Cavazza and the Emergence of Barbaresco

The reputation of Barbaresco seems to have always been in the shadow of Barolo. In fact, it wasn't until late in the last century that Barbaresco was sold under that name, previously being known simply as Nebbiolo or Nebbiolo di Barbaresco.

At Barbaresco, enologist and professor Domizio Cavazza, who was to be the first director of the vinicultural school founded in Alba in 1881, worked on improving the quality and the reputation of the Nebbiolos of that zone. It was he who turned Barbaresco into a dry wine, suitable for aging. Vinifiers at Alba who bought grapes from the zone followed his example first, however, before the small growers of Barbaresco.

The local growers weren't generally vinifying their own wines. Wineries at Bra made most of the Barolo in the area.

Cavazza founded the first *cantina sociale,* or cooperative winery, in the Langhe in about 1894. In the cellars of the castle of Barbaresco he aided the members in improving their wines. Today there are 19,000 producers in Piemonte who belong to 75 *cantine sociale.*

The Vineyards

The vineyards in this area tended to be very small and fragmented among many small growers, who also had to have land for grain and other produce for their families and their livestock to live on. The vine wasn't a specialized culture, but only a part of the agriculture of the farmers in Piemonte, a situation that existed up until this century in some areas.

It is even today a region of small farms. Of the 130,000 farms in Piemonte today, 110,000 own less than 2.5 acres (one hectare). There are still many small growers in the region, and many sell their grapes or sell their wine *sfuso* to wineries who bottle it under their own labels.

The change took place here later than in many regions. Although there was some recognition, especially for Barolo, the wines of the region were not well known or available outside their own area. When more markets opened up for the wines, vine culture became more specialized as well. The best varieties for making fine dry wine were given more importance, and those for red *frizzante* or slightly sweet red wines such as Freisa and Brachetto became less important. Planting an *uvaggio* or mix of grape varieties in a single vineyard was also phased out, though there are still a few left, like the Fioretto vineyard of Vietti in the Scarrone district. As the vineyards were replanted the vines were all of the same variety.

The Regia Scuola Enologica at Alba recommended the Guyot system of training the vines on wires for dry red wines and the moscato for Asti. This method, which replaced the earlier Roman, or Etruscan, system, is used throughout the region today.

There are different grape varieties grown on the same hillside, but the nebbiolo is generally planted on the slopes with a southern exposure and at the top of the hill, where it gets more sun and where frost and dampness are less of a problem. On the lower slopes, dolcetto, barbera, and the white grapes that can be less ripe are cultivated.

The climate in this region is temperate—fairly warm in summer, humid and cold in autumn. In the Langhe in the fall, the leaves of the various grape varieties form a colorful patchwork on the hillsides—the deep bluish purple of the dolcetto, the gold of the moscato, the rich red of the nebbiolo.

Ninety percent of the vines in Piemonte are concentrated in the hilly regions of Cuneo, Asti, and Alessandria. The nebbiolo has pride of place among grape varieties, but the others are much more common. By far the most widely planted is barbera, which makes up a full 52 percent of the total acreage under vines. Next is dolcetto with 15 percent, followed by moscato at 11 percent. Nebbiolo accounts for 5 percent, or 9145 acres (3700 hectares). Freisa with 4 percent, and cortese (another white grape) and grignolino follow with 2 percent each.[2] Of the 125 million gallons (4.7 million hectoliters) of wine produced in Piemonte annually, Nebbiolo accounts for about 3.5 million (178,000).[3]

The nebbiolo is also grown in Lombardia, in the Valtellina, and in parts of the Oltrepò Pavese and Franciacorta, where it is blended with other varieties. There are small amounts planted in Liguria and Umbria as well as on the islands of Sicilia and Sardegna.

Growing Conditions

The nebbiolo is a very demanding grape variety, requiring good drainage and a sunny exposure. Soil is another important consideration. The nebbiolo fares best when planted in calcerous marly soil with admixtures of sand, low in alkalinity and high in phosphorus, potassium, and magnesium. It is relatively resistant to frost, dampness, and fog. Nebbiolo is the earliest variety in the region to bud and the last to ripen. It requires a lot of care and is a shy bearer, but it produces excellent-quality fruit. The nebbiolo grapes are generally harvested in mid-October or later.

In the Middle Ages the date of the harvest was regulated by the local authorities, who set the opening day of the harvest, announced in the *bando della vendemmia,* a regulation that none dared anticipate. This rule remained in effect until the first years of the present century, and the tradition continued to be followed in some of the more remote areas up until the 1950s although the rule was no longer enforced.

Nebbiolo and Its Subvarieties

In the various regions where the nebbiolo is grown, it has different local names. In Aosta and Torino, it's picotener or pugnet; in Novara–Vercelli, it's called spanna; in the Valtellina it is known as chiavennasca; in the Langhe–Monferrato, it is the nebbiolo. And then there are the subvarieties, or clones.

The nebbiolo is very sensitive to variations in soil and microclimates, and it clones relatively easily. The cobianco and corosso of Ghemme are believed to be clones of the nebbiolo, as is the prunent of Valvigezzo. In the Langhe there are a number of nebbiolo clones.

Three are accepted in the officially recognized DOC *(Denominazione di Origine Controllata)* wines. *Michet, micot,* in piemontese dialect, so named for its small, compact form, which is likened to a small loaf of bread, is the most esteemed subvariety. It produces a small quantity of high-quality fruit but fares best only in those areas with the most favorable soils and microclimates.

Lampia has longer, more loosely composed clusters. This is the most widely planted subvariety. It has a greater production, of consistent quality. Its wines are noted for their elegance and perfume.

There is very little of the *rose* subvariety planted. This nebbiolo is similar in appearance to michet but generally produces a wine with less color and less body than the other two. The Vietti Barolo from the Briacca vineyard (100 percent rose) and the Barbaresco from Pajorè in Treiso, including the mighty Podere de Pajorè of Giovannini–Moresco, would seem to contradict this opinion. But it may be a vine that must be especially well suited to a particular site to produce its best-quality—in these cases superb—fruit. (And, of course, in the hands of a talented winemaker...)

Besides these three, there are other less esteemed offshoots, including bolla, rossi, and san luigi.

In the province of Torino and the neighboring region of Valle d'Aosta, nebbiolo wines are produced from three local varieties: nebbiolo spanna, picotener, and pugnet.

The names differ and the appearances of the vines vary, but the wines are all recognizable as coming from the nebbiolo grape which is the hallmark of a noble variety. It has a unique, recognizable character, which subtle variations in the wines do not obscure.

The Nebbiolo Wines

The nebbiolo is a noble grape variety. Its vines produce some of the finest wines of Italy, wines that rank among the world's greats.

They are deeply colored, robust wines, high in tannin and hard, even harsh, in their youth. Their deep ruby color turns to garnet, taking on a brickish hue with maturity which shades to orange and then to onionskin. The youthful aroma of cherries takes on a floral aspect, hinting of violets or roses and with age developing a complexity of nuances—tobacco, licorice, camphor, tartufi (the white truffles of Piemonte), and a particularly characteristic note of goudron, or tar.

Chapter 2

The Wines of the Langhe

The Langhe region, in the southern part of Piemonte, is made up of a series of long hills—from which it gets its name, *lingue* in Latin—ranging in altitude from 490 to 1970 feet (150 to 600 meters). The towns, often clustered around medieval castles or towers, are situated on the summits of the hills, whose slopes are blanketed in vines. This region, in the northeastern corner of the province of Cuneo, forms a long triangle around the city of Alba, bordered basically by the Tanaro River and the ridges of the Roero hills on the west and the Bormida River on the east.

The most important grape varieties here are nebbiolo, dolcetto, barbera, and moscato. There are also plantings of arneis and favorita, and a small amount of freisa, even a little pinot bianco, chardonnay, and cabernet sauvignon. There are three important nebbiolo DOCs in the Langhe: Barolo, Barbaresco, and Nebbiolo d'Alba. Nebbiolo accounts for 11 percent of the vines; 32 percent is barbera, 31 percent dolcetto, and 17 percent moscato; the remaining 9 percent is made up of the other minor varieties.

The soil here is of maritime origin. The Tanaro River, where it veers east near Bra to flow south and east of the city of Alba, divides the region into two zones. To the left of the Tanaro, in the Roero zone, the soil is yellowish sand with admixtures of limestone and marl. To the right, in the Langa, the soil, grayish or amber in color, is composed of limestone, lightly sandy with some clay.

The hills in Roero form a continuous series of crests with steeply graded slopes which make cultivation of the vine difficult. In this zone are the vineyards of three DOC wines: Nebbiolo d'Alba, Barbera d'Alba, and the newly recognized Roero.

The vineyards for Barbera d'Alba and Nebbiolo d'Alba extend into the Langa zone on the right bank of the Tanaro. The gentler slopes of the Langa hills are more eroded, their crests forming long, almost horizontal summits. In the northeastern corner of this zone are the vineyards of Barbaresco, Moscato d'Asti, Barbera d'Alba, Dolcetto d'Alba, and Dolcetto di Diano d'Alba. In the southern part of the triangle are the dolcetto vineyards of the Langa Monregalese and Dogliani.

Production Methods

Over the years production methods in the Langhe have undergone a number of changes. This has led some journalists to categorize the producers as either traditional or new wave (modern), dividing them into two camps, which sometimes becomes more misleading than informative. We've tried to sort them out ourselves, and, in fact, it's not all that easy. What characterizes a producer as a modernist? What does it mean to be traditional?

Traditional Winemaking

In the old days wine in the Langhe was made by hand and by foot. There were no machines. Up until the 1950s, the grapes were commonly brought on oxcarts to the cellars, where they were crushed by men who trod them with their bare feet. The whole grape bunches were dumped into the *tini;* stalks and seeds were not broken up in the crushing process.

The must fermented in the open *tini,* upright wooden, vats, for about two weeks to a month. The stalks helped to aerate the must, and the cap was punched down

11

periodically.

When the fermented wine was drawn off its lees, which were pressed and the juice combined, it was transferred to large, generally old, wooden casks of local chestnut or Slavonian oak, where it was periodically racked until it was clear, a relatively short period of from one to five years depending on the vintage and the producer. Then the wine was drawn off and bottled in very large bottles—demijohns or *brente*—for further aging.

Luciano Rinaldi, of Francesco Rinaldi, told us that fifty or so years ago the wines were aged for at most five to six years in cask, then put into *damigiani,* which were stored *sotto portico,* under the eaves, for another two to three years. Today it has become too expensive and is rarely done anymore. In the winter of 1929, temperatures dropped so low that half the *brente* and demijohns broke—a doubly tragic loss, as these bottles are no longer being blown.

Giacomo Bologna, of Enoteca Braida, who has a prized collection of old blown-glass *brente,* asks his favorite producers to bottle their best vintages and crus in them for him for long aging. It's a great occasion when Giacomo decides a wine is ready and unstoppers a *brenta* to enjoy with friends (and with as many friends as Giacomo has, a *brenta*—13.2 gallons or 50 liters—is none too large).

The Advent of Mechanization

During the 1930s, machines for crushing were introduced into the zone, although many small producers continued to crush the grapes in the time-honored fashion even into the 1950s. Bartolo Mascarello, of Cantina Mascarello, said that their entire 1952 harvest was crushed by treading; they didn't buy a crusher until about 1955. Luigi Pira's wine continued to be crushed by foot up until his last vintage in 1979.

With the changeover to machines, other modifications were also made in fermentation methods. The crusher-stemmers eliminated the stalks before crushing the grapes to avoid adding the acid and astringency from the green stems to the wine. The fermentation time was lengthened to about two months to obtain more tannin and extract from the grapeskins, which were held submerged under a layer of wooden slats.

The temperature of the wine in the closed fermentors was controlled—if that is the word—by opening the windows and the doors of the *cantina* to let in the cool autumn air. If the season was an Indian summer, more imaginative measures were called for. In 1961, in many cellars in the Langhe, huge chunks of ice were dropped into the fermenting vats in a desperate attempt to cool down raging fermentations that threatened to spoil the product of a year's hard work.

The producers were making wines meant to be aged for many years in wooden casks to soften the harsh tannins, but not infrequently it was the fruit that was the first to fade. The best of them were big, dense, tannic wines requiring many years of bottle age to become drinkable. We are reminded of the observation of a fellow wine drinker who lamented that "these wines never do become ready. When they're young the fruit is covered up by such formidable tannin it takes years to soften; by the time it does, the fruit is gone." It takes a fine vintage, a dedicated winemaker, and severe selection in the vineyards to produce an excellent Barolo or Barbaresco in this style.

A More Drinkable Style

In the late 1960s, some producers, following the example of Renato Ratti, started making a different style of Barolo, a softer, fruitier, less tannic wine which developed earlier and was more approachable overall.

Fermentation time was shortened; the must spent less time in contact with the skins.

The temperature of the fermentation was lowered and regulated by heat exchangers in the vats or by the use of temperature-controlled stainless steel tanks to reduce the risk of volatile acidity and other problems that confront the traditional producer.

Malolactic fermentation was encouraged, even induced, shortly if not immediately after the first fermentation was complete, to convert the sharp malic acid into its softer lactic form.

The wines were given much briefer wood aging. Filters were often employed to clear the wines. And the bottles were released for sale earlier. This style of wine is ready for early consumption; it doesn't need long bottle aging, though the better ones can improve with some time in bottle.

And so the pendulum swung. Some wineries went so far as to turn out wines so streamlined they were nearly unrecognizable, resembling more a simple Nebbiolo than a Barolo or Barbaresco. These wines have caused a number of producers who use modern techniques to wince when referred to as modernist and to protest that they are traditional in results, as least, if not in methods.

Fermentation Techniques

There are a variety of winemaking methods used in the Langhe today. As a general rule the more traditional producers believe in a long fermentation—on the skins—commonly from thirty to sixty days, and they frequently employ *cappello sommerso* (submerged cap) to obtain fruit, color, and extract from the grapes.

There are, however, notable exceptions. Giuseppe Colla, winemaker and coproprietor at Prunotto, who is recognized as one of the most confirmed of the old guard, ferments the grapes for his Barolo and Barbaresco in glass-lined cement tanks for only ten to twenty days at about 77° F (25° C). Giovanni Conterno, of Giacomo Conterno, one of the most staunch traditionalists, macerates his grapes before crushing to extract more fruit and color. He uses *cappello sommerso* and a twenty-eight- to thirty-five-day fermentation, which he follows day and night to be sure the temperature doesn't exceed 86° F (30° C). Mauro Mascarello, of Giuseppe Mascarello, another traditionalist, ferments his wine for a full sixty-five days on the skins.

Among the modernists, Paolo Cordero di Montezemolo ferments his Barolo in stainless steel tanks for twenty-five to thirty days at controlled temperatures, doing the *rimontaggio,* or pumping over, twice a day. He also uses *cappello sommerso.* Renato Ratti, the leading spokesman for the new methods, generally ferments his Barolo for eight to twenty days on the skins; in lesser years he reduces the time, in better years he gives it longer. Ratti uses a temperature-controlled fermentation and was, in fact, one of the first to do so. Marcello Ceretto ferments his wine for seven to ten days in temperature-controlled stainless steel tanks.

Elvio Cogno, of Podere Marcarini, ferments for as long as two months in contact with the skins, though generally thirty-five days is the limit; during phase two he holds the cap submerged. Cogno also adds some uncrushed whole berries and stems to the fermenting must. Alfredo Currado of Vietti, leaning more toward the traditional style though utilizing some modern advances, ferments his Barolo for thirty-five to sixty days; his Barbaresco for thirty to fifty. He uses selected yeast for the fermentation in vats of stainless steel or glass-lined cement. After the initial fermentation, lasting up to three weeks, the cap is held submerged and the wine is churned twice a day.

Other producers:
Barale—15 to 20 days
Bersano—6 to 8 days
G. Borgogno—2 weeks followed by *cappello sommerso*
Bovio—20 days
Cappellano—15 days
Castello di Neive—10 to 15 days
Cavallotto—20 to 25 days followed by *cappello sommerso* for 15 to 20 days more
Cigliuti—25 days
Aldo Conterno—up to 60 days, usually 30
Contratto—10 to 20 days
Einaudi—15 days
Franco Fiorina—Barolo 40 to 50 days, Barbaresco 40 days, both with *cappello sommerso*
Fontanafredda—15 days in temperature-controlled stainless steel
Marchese Fracassi—15 days
Gaja—8 to 14 days
Grasso—40 to 60 days
La Spinona—15 days
Bartolo Mascarello—15 days
Massolino—20 days
Palladino—15 to 23 days in Slavonian oak
Punset—8 to 10 days
Francesco Rinaldi—15 to 30 days
Giuseppe Rinaldi—10 days
Roagna—20 to 40 days
Scarpa—30 days for Barolo, 25 days for Barbaresco
Alfonso Scavino—15 to 20 days
Paolo Scavino—15 to 20 days in temperature-controlled stainless steel vats
Seghesio—20 days
Sobrero—15 days

Malolactic Fermentation

The malolactic fermentation in the old-style wines occurred naturally in the spring, when the temperatures warmed sufficiently to prompt the process, unless for some reason—such as, ironically, too high acidity in the wine—nature didn't take its course.

Modernists make sure the malolactic fermentation takes place as soon as possible after the first fermentation by heating the cellars, warming the wine, or inoculating it if necessary.

All of the producers today recognize the importance of the malolactic fermentation and know what to do to bring it about. The only difference among them seems to be not whether, but when, the malolactic takes place. Bartolo Mascarello, Contratto, and Aldo Conterno's Barolos undergo malolactic in the spring; Renato Ratti, Ceretto, Currado, and Cogno ensure that it takes place no more than a month after the first fermentation.

Wood Aging

The biggest difference between the traditional and the new wave producers is probably in the length of time they age their wines in wood. There is no question that the modern producers believe in giving their wines less time in cask. Renato Ratti feels that wine made in the new style is better balanced, has more fruit and more style. Ratti ages his Barolo for the minimum period in wood required by DOC law, two years. Marcello Ceretto ages his Barbaresco for the minimum, one year in cask, but his Barolos for up to three years, depending on the vineyard and the vintage.

Traditionalist Bartolo Mascarello ages his Barolo three to four years in old oak (and a few chestnut) casks, most fifty years old with a capacity of 660 to 925 gallons (25 to 35 hectoliters). In the better years he puts some of his Barolo in *bottiglione* of 0.5 to 0.8 gallons (2 to 3 liters) for further aging. Bruno Giacosa ages his Barolo for five to six years in cask and his Barbaresco for three to four, although his 1964 Barbaresco was in oak for seven to eight years. Giovanni Conterno wood ages his regular Barolo for at least six years, his Monfortino no less than eight years. In November 1984, we tasted 1970 Monfortino from cask.

Alfredo Currado keeps his Barolos for two to four years in 1190- to 1585-gallon (45- to 60-hectoliter) Slavonian oak—the better the vintage, the longer in wood. His Barbarescos are given from one to three years.

Other producers:
Barale—3 years in Slavonian oak, then to demijohn
Aldo Conterno—up to 3 years in 290- to 1795-gallon (11- to 68-hectoliter) casks
Contratto—7 to 8 years in 50-year-old casks of 795 to 1585 gallons (30 to 60
     hectoliters)
Luigi Einaudi—8 to 10 years in Yugoslavian oak
Franco Fiorina—Barolo 3 to 4 years
Fontanafredda—Barbaresco 2 to 3 years, Barolo 2 to 4 years
Giuseppe Mascarello—3 to 4 years in 17- to 22-year-old 265- to 3170-gallon (10- to
     120-hectoliter), mostly 2115-gallon (80-hectoliter), casks
La Spinona—at least 2 years in 185- to 1585-gallon (7- to 60-hectoliter) Slavonian
     oak
Giuseppe Rinaldi—5 to 6 years in oak and chestnut, some 100 years old; in great
     vintages, perhaps up to 8 or 9 years
Alfonso Scavino—3 to 5 years
Paolo Scavino—2½ to 4 years
Seghesio—4 years
Sobrero—at least 4 years in old 55- to 130-gallon (2- to 5-hectoliter) Slavonian oak
     casks
Vaijra—minimum of 3 years in oak and chestnut casks

Winemaking Styles

It's interesting to see how the producers arrive at their final product. Some winemakers who take advantage of modern technology to produce their wines claim that, although they have made changes from the old-fashioned methods to ensure better control over every phase of the winemaking process, they are nevertheless producing a traditonal-style Barolo or Barbaresco. Some, like Alfredo Currado and Elvio Cogno, *are* producing grand wines worthy of the best of the old traditions, wines with, in fact, more richness and depth than some others that would be classified as traditional.

Although some of the traditional producers make wines of monumental proportions, knife-and-fork wines in their youth, others produce wines that are less imposing in their tannin content and strength but no less impressive in their pedigree. Giacomo Conterno's Monfortino needs a long time to come around, but, if stored properly, it is definitely worth the wait, becoming a wine of character and style. Bartolo Mascarello's Barolo is more drinkable when young, but with age, it develops exceptional quality. Renato Ratti's 1978s and 1979s are excellent drinking right now but, with time, will take on further nuances of bouquet and flavor.

The basic styles can be defined, but there are still many variations and differences within the categories, as well as many gradations in between. We are dealing with individuals here—hard-headed farmers, college-trained technicians, market-sensitive businessmen, and, in some cases, artists.

Even in the past, when less options were open to them and winemakers learned from their fathers and uncles, styles of wines varied, not only from one vineyard area to another but also from cousin to cousin and neighbor to neighbor. All had their own ways of doing things. When producers meet on the piazza and chat over a cup of espresso, it isn't necessarily winemaking techniques that they feel impelled to discuss and compare. Soccer is a much more likely topic of debate.

The Quality in the Bottle

The differences in the methods of production are less important than the differences in the wines themselves. To say that a producer is traditional or modern only gives a general idea of what kind of wine it is—in terms of style, that is, it tells you nothing about its quality.

Of the best Barolo and Barbaresco that we have tasted, some were made by traditional producers, others were produced by modernists, and still others were from winemakers who take advantage of some methods from each. In the final analysis the important thing is, of course, not how the wine is produced but how it tastes.

Aging in *Barrique*

Traditionally the wines of Barolo and Barbaresco are aged in *botte,* large chestnut or oaken casks, most commonly today of Slavonian oak. But many producers in Italy are trying a new technique. Taking a page from the book of the French producers in Burgundy and Bordeaux where aging in *barrique* is traditional, and from producers in California where the art of barrel aging has taken on the dimensions of a practical science, producers in many regions of Italy are experimenting with small-barrel aging for their wines. Piemonte is no exception. Quite a number of producers are putting their Barolos and Barbarescos into *barrique,* for varying lengths of time and with various degrees of success.

Without question the most successful is Angelo Gaja, whose achievement, both in the high quality of the wines produced and in the high prices he is able to get for them, has undoubtedly added impetus to the growing trend.

Gaja wasn't the first to try *barrique* aging in the Langhe. A few producers made experiments in the 1950s; Giuseppe Colla tried new oak barrels for aging the wines at Prunotto. Tests were also done in the cellars of Giacomo Borgogno. The resulting wines were not considered to have benefited from the system, however, and it was abandoned.

The traditional casks used in Piemonte are much larger than the *barriques* and many years old. Over the course of time, the wood tannins and flavor components in the wood are drawn out, producing a basically neutral receptacle for the wine which allows a limited exchange of oxygen through the pores of the wood. The surface of wine exposed to the wood in these casks is in a much smaller proportion to the total volume than that in the 60-gallon (225-liter) *barriques.* The wine in the *botti* can be, and is, aged for a much longer period. When new or nearly new small barrels are used, the situation is quite different.

Barrique aging changes the character of the wine, and to be done to advantage it requires a lot of care and not a little experience. What does the new oak add to the wine, and what does it take away? The wood adds tannin to the wine. It can also create a roundness and a suppleness of texture. The oak also adds its own character, contributing a vanilla aspect to the aroma and flavor of the wine, which if subtle provides a note of complexity but when strong can be overbearing and obscure the character of the grape variety.

We've tasted some *barrique*-aged Barolo and Barbaresco that were practically unidentifiable as nebbiolo. We find that Barolo and Barbaresco aged in *barrique* nearly always exhibit more of the character of the oak than of the grape variety, although there are exceptions, Gaja's Barbarescos being the most notable.

Angelo Gaja has learned to control the oakiness, to keep the influence of the *barrique* in the background—gajafying the wine, you might say—to produce a Barbaresco recognizable as a Barbaresco but with a suppleness and another layer of complexity. However, the nebbiolo being an excellent variety of notable character and structure, it is just possible that we might prefer the Gaja Barbarescos without the influence of the oak. But obviously, we couldn't say for certain, not having the chance to compare wines of the two styles against each other.

We must admit also that since the 1978 vintage, when Pio Boffa introduced *barriques* into the Pio Cesare cellars, his Barolos have been of a higher quality. But was it the barrels, or was it the other changes he made—cooler fermentation temperatures, reduced skin contact, immediate malolactic, and considerably shortened wood aging. *Barrique* aging may have added an extra dimension to the wines, but we're inclined to believe that the other changes had a more significant impact on improving the quality.

Colla and Borgogno were dissatisfied with the results of their *barrique* experiments in the 1950s because of the unnecessary tannin added to the already tannic nebbiolo and because of the way it changed the character of their wines. Others have also tried and abandoned *barriques*. Many producers who were not convinced that *barrique* aging had anything to add to their Barolos or Barbarescos have tried it as a test, either to prove to themselves that they were right or to prove to others that their minds were not closed to the possibility, however remote, that it might contribute something worthwhile. The Cerettos are among this group. Marcello Ceretto was dissatisfied with, though not surprised at, the results of his tests with *barriques*.

Other producers, such as Alfredo Currado, of Vietti, who has no interest whatever in changing the character of his Barolo and Barbaresco, has made some tests with *barrique* for his Fioretto. He says that while he is using some *barrique* aging for this wine—a nebbiolo–dolcetto–barbera–neirano blend—he will never use them for his Barolo or Barbaresco.

Many are influenced by market pressure, which appears to demand Barolo and Barbaresco in *barrique*, although the producers would personally prefer their wines without it. Aldo Conterno said that while he has given his 1982 Barbera some time in *barriques* of Limousin oak, he does not plan to put his Barolo in small barrels, as he feels it would take away the personality of the nebbiolo, changing its character as well as adding unneeded tannin. He didn't totally rule out the possibility, however. Armando Cordero, the enologist at Franco Fiorina, opposes *barrique* aging for the nebbiolo, pointing out that this variety has a personality of its own; it has no need of the added flavor or tannin that the oak would provide.

The general feeling among the better producers we have spoken with is that while the *barrique* may be well suited to some grape varieties, such as the chardonnay, pinot noir, and cabernet sauvignon, the nebbiolo doesn't need it. And while *barriques* are turning up in *cantina* after *cantina* in Piemonte, there are still producers like Bartolo Mascarello, who says he feels no need to prove to others his firm conviction that the nebbiolo is an excellent variety that can stand on its own; he isn't interested in making experiments. A similar view is expressed by Giovanni Conterno, another who has not bowed to the pressure even to make tests with the small barrels.

What can the *barrique* do for the nebbiolo? Can the wines be improved by barrel aging in new oak, or is it only their standing in the international marketplace, where they might frequently be judged by the standards of foreign tasters more accustomed to the oak-aged wines of Bordeaux, Burgundy, or California? In our opinion, based on the rather considerable experience we've had with the wines of Barolo and Barbaresco, as well as the nebbiolo wines from other areas, *barrique* aging doesn't make any significant improvement to these wines. Most often what it adds merely detracts from the character of the wine, making it seem more like a California, French, or internationally anonymous wine than like one from Piemonte, a region rich in its own unique winemaking tradition.

If the Piemontese producers want to take advantage of the current marketing demand for oaky wines, we suggest they put their barberas in *barrique*. This grape produces a fruity wine high in acid and low in tannin. Here they have more to gain than to lose. Giacomo Bologna, who aged his 1982 Barbera from the Bricco dell'Uccellone vineyard in *barrique,* produced a resounding success.

The nebbiolo is a noble variety, with a unique and well-defined personality. It doesn't need the added character of new oak to produce a wine of depth and complexity.

Barolo

Barolo is the most majestic of the nebbiolo wines. At its best it is unsurpassed by any other Italian wine and challenged by very few. It is a powerful wine, rich and robust, yet complex and harmonious. In its youth it is hard and austere; with age it takes on a velvety texture, developing a depth of flavor and a grandeur equaled by few wines. This is Barolo at its best; regrettably it doesn't attain these heights often. Too frequently it is lacking in character and structure. Its name is cheapened by a handful of mediocre manufacturers whose wine bears little or no resemblance to a true Barolo, or even a lesser nebbiolo wine.

When the names of wineries such as Luigi Bosca, Cossetti, Kiola (now F.lli Dogliani), Giovanni Scanavino, and Villadoria are better known than those of the fine Barolo producers, as they unfortunately are in many markets, it is not difficult to understand why many wine drinkers do not recognize Barolo as one of the world's great wines. The rocky road to recognition is made all the more difficult when truckloads of products such as these create a bottleneck at its access. But when the true winelover, open-minded and persistent in his or her search for quality, discovers the Barolos of producers such as Bartolo Mascarello of Cantina Mascarello, Marcello Ceretto, Elvio Cogno, Aldo Conterno, Giovanni Conterno of Giacomo Conterno, Alfredo Currado of Vietti, Bruno Giacosa, Giuseppe Rinaldi, and Luciano Rinaldi of Francesco Rinaldi, they may find themselves listing the three Bs of wine as Burgundy, Bordeaux, and Barolo.

Barolo is a robust wine that compliments hearty, flavorful dishes. It goes well with roast red meat, especially game such as venison.

Village	Growers	Hectares	Max. Prod. Hectoliters	%
Barolo	144	176.1035	9,861.80	14.11
Castiglione Falletto	98	102.9358	5,764.40	8.25
Cherasco	2	1.8600	104.16	0.15
Diano d'Alba	10	6.4307	360.12	0.52
Grinzane Cavour	58	33.7155	1,888.07	2.70
La Morra	408	449.4648	15,170.03	36.02
Monforte	189	172.1909	9,642.69	13.80
Novello	65	49.1370	2,751.67	3.94
Roddi	22	9.1840	514.30	0.74
Serralunga d'Alba	162	196.3805	10,997.30	15.74
Verduno	84	50.3006	2,816.84	4.03
Total	**1242**	**1247.7033**	**69,871.39**	**100.00**

Source: Regione Piemonte (1984).
Notes: 1 hectare = 2.4711 acres.
　　　1 hectoliter = 26.42 gallons or 11.11 cases.

Barolo is produced in an area of approximately 3085 acres (1248 hectares) southwest of Alba, in all or part of eleven *communes*. First is La Morra, with over one-third of the total acreage. Following in decreasing order are Serralunga d'Alba, Barolo, Monforte, Castiglione Falletto, and parts of six other villages.

DOC/DOCG Requirements

	Minimum Age (years) cask	total	Minimum alcohol	Maximum yield (gallons/acres)
DOC Regular	2	3	13%	599
Riserva	2	4	13%	599
Riserva Speciale	2	5	13%	599
DOCG Regular	2	3	13%	599
Riserva	2	5	13%	599

Barolo has been granted DOCG *(Denominazione di Origine Controllata e Garantita)* status under Italian wine law, which regulates its production, both in the vineyard and the cellar, and supposedly guarantees its authenticity. Bureaucrats and "there-ought-to-be-a-law" lobbyists notwithstanding, in the real world there is only one real guarantee for a product: the integrity of the producer. The next best indication of the quality of a wine is the vintage, then the vineyard. Let's not forget that the garish red DOCG band stuck over the bottle capsule appears also on some rather abysmal bottles of Barolo.

Producers like Bartolo Mascarello, Giovanni Conterno, Bruno Giacosa, and Alfredo Currado, just to name a few, don't bottle wines unworthy of their names. When some of the wine of a particular vintage doesn't meet their personal standards, they declassify it to Nebbiolo delle Langhe; or if they feel that it is not even up to that level, they will not bottle it under their own label at all, but sell it off *sfuso*. In the worst cases they may judge the grapes are not even worth picking. We have no doubt that rejected grapes from Giovanni Conterno's vineyard, left on the vines by harvesters under strict orders not to pick any grapes that don't meet his standards, have provided anonymous improvement to many barrels in neighboring cellars.

Naive consumers may delude themselves into believing that the government can legislate quality into existence, but there will always be those producers who, though they may squeeze under the government umbrella, will provide the most blatant evidence to prove that you cannot outlaw mediocrity.

Rating: Barolo★★★★

The Crus of Barolo

The *crus* (single vineyards) of Barolo have recently received a lot of attention. More and more bottles now carry, besides the name of the production zone and the producer, the name of the vineyard plot where the grapes were grown. It is the latest trend, and the trend is growing.

But this is not a new concept or even a new practice. Much more common, yes, but novel, no. Among the oldest bottles of Barolo still in existence are two labeled simply "1752 Cannubi," the most famous vineyard in the zone. In the cellars of Barolo the wines from the various locations are usually vinified separately and held in different casks marked with the names of the vineyards, even parts of vineyards. This has been done for many years. Bruno Giacosa notes that his grandfather handled the wines from the various plots individually in the cellar although he didn't bottle them under the vineyard names.

When we taste the wines from cask in the cellars, the producers will frequently name the vineyard, chalked in abbreviated form on the casks, often offering more than one sample from a particular vintage so that we can note the differences among them, which are sometimes striking.

In the old days, when the oxcarts of grapes from the various locations arrived at the winery, the grapes were fermented as they came in, then pressed in small basket presses and each batch aged separately. A winemaker would naturally want to know which vineyards provided the best fruit, and in the hands of a fine winemaker the grapes from the various plots would be handled differently in vinification and aging to bring out the best in the individual wines. Private customers no doubt selected their wine from the casks they preferred.

But up until recently the wine in the bottle was rarely labeled with the name of the vineyard. If the producer made wine from only one vineyard, the distinction might not have seemed necessary, as that is what his name on the bottle represented. If a small producer made wine from various small plots, it would hardly be worth the extra effort to have many different labels for the various crus, unless his wine was from a particularly well-known and highly regarded vineyard, such as Cannubi, in which case it was worth drawing attention to the fact.

There aren't a lot of crus in that category, however. A few have long been recognized, but today we see a multitude. Vineyards previously little known outside the zone are popping up like mushrooms after a rainstorm, and just when you think you've got them down a plethora of subcrus appear on the marketing horizon—crus within the crus, little known outside the immediate neighborhood, some it seems outside the immediate family of the vineyardists themselves. Are these distinctions justified by the differences in the wines?

A significant impetus to labeling the crus separately came from Luigi Veronelli, a writer with a major influence on Italian wine. He encouraged the producers to bottle their best vineyards under cru names, most notably in a major article written in the mid-1960s which had an important impact. Obviously the producers agreed that it was a good idea. Cru labeling emphasizes the special qualities of a particular bottling. The marketing benefits are clear, but perhaps even so it can be carried too far. We are reminded of Baker's law: A difference is a difference only if it makes a difference.

Even among the producers who disagree with the concept of cru bottlings there is a recognition that the wines from the various zones within Barolo have their own characteristics. At Franco Fiorina, Pio Cesare, and Giacomo Borgogno, for example, they point out that it is because of these variations that they make their objection, maintaining that the best Barolos are those made from a balanced blend of wines that takes advantage of the particular attributes of the different areas, the wine from one zone providing structure and firmness to the blend, that from another adding body, another contributing delicacy and perfume, and yet another permitting longevity.

These variations in the wines are derived from various aspects of the land—the composition of the soil, the exposure to the sun, and the incline of the slope, even the particular subvariety of the nebbiolo grape cultivated. The best vineyards naturally have the best exposure to the sun, which enables the grapes to ripen more completely. Which ones they are can readily be seen after a snowstorm. We could confidently point out the best locations in the zone last winter as we observed the vineyards where the snow had already melted. These obviously received more of the benefit of the sun's warming rays. In some of the less favored spots, as Mario Cordero of Vietti put it, "you'd have to bring down the sun in a basket" to fully ripen the grapes. The best vineyards invariably also have good drainage. This is a twofold benefit: the vines absorb less water after a storm or during a rainy period, and the roots of the vines must dig deeper into the earth in search of moisture where they have a more constant environment.

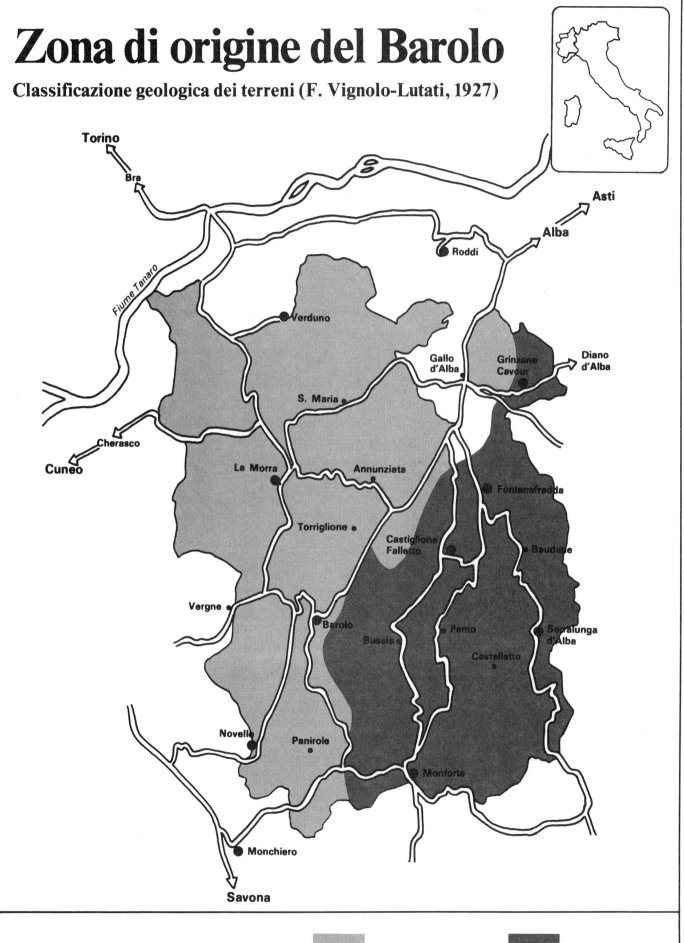

Zona di origine del Barolo

Classificazione geologica dei terreni (F. Vignolo-Lutati, 1927)

La linea ——— circoscrive la zona del Barolo. **TORTONIANO** **ELVEZIANO**

Major Subdivision

There are two main valleys in the Barolo production zone: the Barolo valley to the west and the Serralunga valley to the east. La Morra and Barolo itself are the major villages in the western valley, which also encompasses Novello and Verduno. In the Serralunga valley, Serralunga d'Alba, Castiglione Falletto, and Monforte are the major towns; Grinzane Cavour is also included in this district.

The soil in the Barolo production zone is of marine origin, rich in limestone with a high concentration of microelements. According to Renato Ratti, who has made a thorough study of the viticultural region, the terrain is divided into two types: tortonian and helvetian. In the Barolo valley the soil is tortonian, with a basic composition of limestone and marl; in the Serralunga it is characterized by conglomerates of limestone and sand.

As a general rule the wines of the *Barolo* valley are noted for their perfume and delicacy; they are lighter in body and develop sooner than those from the Serralunga valley. The wines of the *Serralunga* valley are richer, fuller in body, more tannic and robust; they take longer to come around and are longer-lived.

Ratti details the nuances noted in the wines of the various areas: the wines of the Serralunga valley have suggestions of licorice and tar; the Barolos of Serralunga itself display camphor and mint; those from Castiglione Falletto have a pronounced licorice characteristic and nuances of spice, mint, dried peaches, and prunes; those from Monforte recall spices, mint, hazelnuts, and almonds. The wines from the Barolo valley bring up underbrush and tartufi as well as licorice. Those from the village of Barolo have less of a licorice character but more suggestions of underbrush, truffles, and mint. Those from Cannubi display notes of tartufi, underbrush, raspberries, and black cherries. The wines of La Morra, especially from the slopes, combine nuances of tartufi, mint, tobacco, spices, cherries, and blackberries.

Ratti lists the major vineyard districts of the Barolo valley as Brunate, Cannubi-Boschis, Cannubi-Muscatel, Cerequio, Collina Cannubi, Conca dell'Abbazia dell'Annunziata, Le Turnote, Monfalletto, Rocche di La Morra, Rocchette, and Sarmazza. The major vineyard areas of the Serralunga valley are Baudana, Brea, Bussia Soprana, Bussia Sottana, Cerretta, Cucco, Fontanile, Gabutti-Parafada, Lazzarito, Marenca-Rivette, Momprivato, Pian della Polvere, Pugnane, Rocche di Castiglione Falletto, Santo Stefano di Perno, Vigna Arionda, and Villero. Within these areas are the single vineyards, or crus.

Gianfranco Oberto, a regarded authority in Barolo, divides the vineyards of the zone into six major areas. In the *commune* of Barolo, he puts Cannubi, Cannubi-Muscatel, and Cannubi-Boschis. In the area between Barolo and La Morra are Cerequio and Brunate; in La Morra are Rocche, Rocchette, Conca dell'Abbazia dell'Annunziata, Le Turnote, Monfalletto, Ciocchini, Serre, and Ornata. In the Serralunga d'Alba district are Brea, Cucco, Lazzarito, Vigna Rionda, Marenga e Rivette, Gabutti-Parafada, and Cerretta. In the area of Monforte are Bussia Soprana, Bussia Sottana, Costa di Rose, Fontanile, Pian delle Polvere, and Santo Stefano. And in the Castiglione Falletto district are Baudana, Momprivato, and Villero. Except for two vineyards, Oberto's six zones agree with the general view. The two exceptions are Baudana, which others put in Serralunga d'Alba, and Costa di Rose, which is on everyone else's list as being in Barolo. It is also surprising that he lists the Rocche vineyard of La Morra and omits the Rocche of Castiglione Falletto, which is considered to be the most important vineyard of that village.

Carta del Barolo
Renato Ratti
Antiche Cantine della
Abbazia dell'Annunziata
LA MORRA (CUNEO - ITALIA)

Torino
Asti
Fiume Tanaro
Alba
Bra
Pollenzo

MARCENASCO
MONFALLETTO
Roddi
FONTANAFREDDA
ZONCHETTA
MONTANELLO
Verduno
Gallo Grinzane
Grinzane Cavour
S. Maria
Diano d'Alba

MONFALLETTO
LE TURNOTE
MOMPRIVATO
CONCA DELL'ABBAZIA DELL'ANNUNZIATA
VILLERO
ROCCHETTE
BAUDANA
ROCCHE
La Morra
Annunziata
CERRETTA
Castiglione Falletto
BRUNATE
ROCCHE
CEREQUIO
GABUTTI - PARAFADA
SARMAZZA
BREA
CANNUBI BOSCHIS
LAZZARITO
CANNUBI
Vergne
CUCCO
CANNUBI MUSCATEL
MARENCA - RIVETI
PUGNANE
Perno
SANTO STEFANO
FONTANILE
Serralunga d'Alba
VIGNA RIONDA
BUSSIA SOTTANA
Barolo
PIAN DELLA POLVERE
BUSSIA SOPRANA
Castelletto Monforte
ORNATO
ARIONE
COSTA DI ROSE
Novello
GRASSI
GINESTRE
Monforte d'Alba
MONFORTINO
S. STEFANO DI PERNO
Monchiero
ARNULFO
SARMAZZA
DARDI
CANNUBI
GRANBUSSIA

Carta del Barolo
a cura del Museo Ratti dei Vini di Alba
Abbazia dell'Annunziata - La Morra (Cuneo)
1984
Le indicazioni geografiche e storiche
sono state individuate seguendo le tradizioni locali.

Indications of historic sub-regions of vine growing.

Indications of sub-regions with special caractheristics.

23

Characteristics of the Vineyards

We spoke at length with Renato Ratti about the area, trying to gain an overall impression of how the wines vary from one village to another and to pinpoint the particular characteristics of the individual vineyards. In our interviews with the producers we also attempted to gather an overall image of the Barolos of each *commune* and each major vineyard. To this we added our own impressions from personal tastings. Many people were involved in the formulation of the overview, but the evaluations, which we have given where we had sufficient experience to render them, are our own.

The Crus Themselves

Albarella (Barolo). Marchesi di Barolo has a piece of this vineyard.

Altenazze or **Altenazzo** (Castiglione Falletto). Paolo Scavino owns land in this vineyard.

★★**Annunziata** (La Morra). Many growers own land in Annunziata, including Giovanni Ferrero, Angelo Germano, and Silvio Grasso. "Rocche" Costamagna owns 9.6 acres (3.9 hectares) of vines, including 7 (2.8) of nebbiolo; this includes the subcrus of Francesco and Riccardo (see below). Renato Ratti finds a hint of tobacco in the aroma of the wines from this district.

> Some subcrus of Annunziata (see individual entries):
> Arborina, Arburina, or Arburine
> Cascina Nuova
> Conca dell'Abbazia
> Francesco
> Gattera
> Marcenasco
> Monfalletto
> Plicotti or Plucotti
> Riccardo
> Rocche di La Morra
> Rocchette or Rochetta

★**Arborina, Arburina,** or **Arburine dell'Annunziata** (La Morra). Elio Altare has bottled 4000 to 5000 bottles of Barolo a year since 1978 from his holdings in this part of Annunziata. Gianfranco Bovio started bottling a cru from his 1.3-acre (0.5-hectare) subplot in 1985.

★★**Arionda** (Serralunga d'Alba). Another name for Vigna Rionda.

Arione[1] (Serralunga d'Alba). Gigi Rosso bottles an Arione Barolo from his 10 acres (4 hectares) of vines in this historic subregion.

★**Arnulfo**[1] (Monforte). Accademia Torregiorgi buys grapes from Arturo Barale to produce his Arnulfo Barolo. This cru is in the Bussia district.

Baiolo (La Morra).

Bartu. Mario Savigliano has vines in this vineyard.

Batasiolo (La Morra). Kiola, now F. lli Dogliani, has vines here.

★★**Baudana** (Serralunga d'Alba). Giuseppe Cappellano buys grapes from this vineyard district. Giacomo Conterno, Moscone, and Giuseppe Massolino of Az. Agr. "Vigna Rionda" cultivate vines here. Basilio Zunino bottles a Barolo cru from his vines in Baudana.

Bettolotti Para (La Morra).

Bianca (Serralunga d'Alba). Fontanafredda produces about 3500 bottles of a Bianca Barolo from their 1.26 acres (0.5 hectares) of nebbiolo vines. These vines are planted at an altitude of 820 feet (250 meters).

★★**Blange-Brunate** (La Morra and Barolo). The Cerettos used to label their part of the Brunate vineyard as Blange-Brunate. They no longer do so. Some two-thirds of this vineyard are in La Morra.

Bonfani (Monforte). A subcru within the Bussia vineyard district.

Borgato di Sorano (Serralunga d'Alba). This district of Serralunga (also called Sorano Borgato) includes the vineyards of Carpegna, Galarei, and Nirane.

Boscareto or **Boscaretti** (Serralunga d'Alba). Kiola, now F.lli Dogliani, owns a piece of this vineyard. Scarpa buys grapes and produces some 8000 bottles of I Boscaretti from this cru.

Boschetti (Barolo). Marchesi di Barolo owns a piece of this vineyard.

Boschis (Castiglione Falletto). The most noted part of this vineyard is the top, Bricco Boschis, owned by the Cavallotto brothers.

Brandini (Verduno).

★**Brea** (Serralunga d'Alba). A regarded vineyard district.

★★**Briacca** (Castiglione Falletto). Briacca is a small 1.2-acre (0.5-hectare) parcel of Rocche owned by

Basilo Zunino. It faces southeast and is planted 100 percent to nebbiolo rose. These grapes are vinified by Alfredo Currado of Vietti for his very fine Barolo Briacca.[2]

Bric del Fiasc (Castiglione Falletto). Paolo Scavino owns 8.4 acres (3.4 hectares) of vines in Bricco Fiasco. He bottles a Barolo from his 5.9 acres (2.4 hectares) of nebbiolo vines and labels it with the dialect name.

★★**Bric in Pugnane** (Castiglione Falletto). This vineyard is the highest part of the Pugnane vineyard district. Giuseppe Mascarello has bought grapes from here for a Barolo cru since 1971.

Bricco (Barolo). Kiola, now owned by F.lli Dogliani, has vines here.

Bricco Boschis (Castiglione Falletto). The top part of the Boschis vineyard. This 50-acre (20-hectare) vineyard is owned in its entirety by Fratelli Cavallotto. The Cavallotto brothers have 40 acres (16 hectares) of vines, including 13 (5.3) of nebbiolo. Vines are planted at a median altitude of 1150 feet (350 meters). All of their wines, including the Barolo, are from this vineyard and are labeled with this cru name. They also bottle Barolo from three subcrus.

Subcrus	Nebbiolo vines	
	Hectares	Acres
Colle Sud Ovest	1.1100	2.74
Punta Marcello	0.7900	1.95
San Giuseppe	3.4427	8.51

★★**Bricco Cicala** (Monforte). A subcru within the Bussia Soprana vineyard district.

★★**Bricco Colonello** (Monforte). A subcru within the Bussia Soprana vineyard district.

Bricco Fava (Verduno).

Bricco Fiasco (Castiglione Falletto). This vineyard is more commonly known by its dialect name. See Bric del Fiasc.

Bricco Plaustra (La Morra). F.lli Oddero has vines here.

★★**Bricco Rocche** (Castiglione Falletto). The Ceretto brothers own a 2.5-acre (1-hectare) vineyard on the top part of Rocche known as Bricco Rocche. This part of the vineyard, on the other side of the road from the main part of Rocche, was planted by the Cerettos. They produce this Barolo[2] at their Az. Agr. "Bricco Rocche."

Bricco San Biago (La Morra).

Bricco Violeo (Barolo). G. D. Vaira owns 1.4 acres (0.6 hectares) of vines here.

Briccolina (Serralunga d'Alba). The firm of Kiola, now F.lli Dogliani, has vines in this vineyard.

Bricotto Bussia e Ciabot (Monforte). Clerico has bottled a Barolo from his holdings in these two crus since 1978.

★★**Brunate** (mostly in La Morra, a small part in Barolo). Brunate with a southwestern exposure is about 985 feet (300 meters) in altitude. Among the subdivisions of the Brunate hillside are Blange, Fontanarossa, Fontanazza or Fontanassa as it is variously known, La Serra, and Zonchetta, now Zonchera (as it is called in Piemontese). Renato Ratti notes in the aroma of Brunate nuances of licorice, cherries, and tartufi. Luciano Rinaldi finds his Brunate less perfumed but bigger in body than the Cannubi. Elvio Cogno, who vinifies a Brunate and a La Serra, finds the Brunate softer, more velvety and complete, and in its youth more austere and closed.

> *Owner–producers:*
> Az. Agr. "Bricco Rocche" di Ceretto,[3] 12.4 acres (5 hectares).
> Giovanni Bogletti's grapes go to the Terre del Barolo co-op.
> Cogno-Marcarini[3] owns 20 acres (8 hectares), 13 (5.3) in nebbiolo. These vines are planted at an altitude of from 820 to 985 feet (250 to 300 meters). He has vinified a Barolo from here since 1958. Average output is 25,000 bottles.[2]
> Luigi Coppo.[3]
> Franco Fiorina buys grapes.
> Kiola (now F.lli Dogliani) owns a part in Barolo.
> Marchesi di Barolo,[3] 7.2 acres (2.9 hectares).
> F.lli Oderro.
> Az. Agr. "Ponte Rocca" di Francesco Pittatore.
> Francesco Rinaldi,[3] 5.4 acres (2.2 hectares).
> Giuseppe Rinaldi[3] owns 3.7 acres (1.5 hectares); he bottled a Brunate cru in 1971.
> Renzo Roggieri's grapes go to the Terre del Barolo co-op.
> Terre del Barolo.[3]
> Vietti[3] buys from a 2.5-acre (1-hectare) plot.

Brunella (Castiglione Falletto). Vignolo-Lutati owns vines here.

Bruni (Serralunga d'Alba). Vezza has a vineyard in Bruni.

★★**Bussia** (mostly in Monforte, a small part in Castiglione Falletto). Bussia is actually a series of hills; the highest part, at 1475 feet (450 meters), belongs to Aldo Conterno. Bussia is subdivided into the upper and lower sections: *Bussia Soprana* (or *Alta*) and *Bussia Sottana* (or *Bassa*). Soprana borders on Barolo and Castiglione Falletto. Within Soprana are the crus of Bricco Cicala and Bricco Colonnello. The Cicala vineyard is situated higher up and at a steeper grade. Aldo Conterno's 3.2 acres (1.3 hectares) of vines in Cicala are more than thirty years old. His plot in Colonnello covers 2.5 acres (1 hectare). Conterno bottles some 5000 bottles of very fine Barolo from each of these two subcrus as well as a Granbussia Barolo, also from his own grapes grown in other parts of Bussia Soprana. In all Aldo Conterno owns 53 acres (21 hectares), 35 (14.5) planted, in Bussia Soprana; 15 (6.5) are in nebbiolo for Barolo.[2] Paolo Fennochio owns a 7.5-acre (3-hectare) subplot in Bricco Colonnello. He sells the grapes to Alfredo Currado for Vietti's Bussia Barolo. Giuseppe Mascarello has bought grapes from Bussia Soprana, from which he makes a very good Barolo, since 1970. Arnulfo, vinified by Accademia Torregiorgi, is part of Bussia. Bonfani is another vineyard within the Bussia district. Kiola, now F.lli Dogliani, owns vines in Bonfani. Some say Pianpolvere is another subcru. Giuseppe Colla of Prunotto says that his Bussia cru has better structure and is longer-lived that his Cannubi. He buys from a 10-acre (4.1-hectare) plot.

Other owner–producers:
F.lli Barale own 10 acres (4 hectares) of barbera.
Clerico produces a Barolo Bricotto Bussia e Ciabot.
Bruno Giacosa.[3]
Giacomo Fennochio owns vines in Bussia Sottana.
F.lli Oddero owns vines in Bussia Soprana.
Armando Parusso.

Camia (Serralunga d'Alba).

★★★**Cannubi** or **Cannubbio**[3] (Barolo). If there is a single finest vineyard in Barolo, and the consensus is that there is, that vineyard is Cannubi, or Cannubbio as it is sometimes called. Being located sort of halfway between the two valleys, the soils of both are intermingled in the Cannubi vineyard, and the wine combines some characteristics from both—"the best of both worlds," as Ratti put it. Cannubi has a south to southeastern exposure. It ranges in altitude from 755 to 1015 feet (230 to 309 meters) and is very steep, many slopes inclining at a 25 percent grade. Luciano Rinaldi described his Cannubbio as a perfumed wine that ages very well; he noted that it has less body than the Brunate, which he also bottles as a cru. This approximately 75-acre (30-hectare) vineyard is divided into several subsections and among fifteen owners.

Owner–producers:
F.lli Barale, 2.5 acres (1 hectare).
Beni Parrocchiali.
F.lli Borgogno[3] owns 7 acres (2.8 hectares), 5.2 (2.1) of nebbiolo which
    they use to produce 1250 cases of Barolo. The 3.1 acres (1.3
    hectares) of lampia were planted in 1981, and the 2 (0.8) of michet
    in 1945 and 1955. They also have 1.4 acres (0.6 hectares) of barbera
    and 0.5 (0.2) of dolcetto.
Giacomo Borgogno, 3.7 acres (1.5 hectares).
Dott. Damilano.
Michele Fontana.
Lucchini.
Marchesi di Barolo[3] (Scarzello e Abbona), 1.3 acres (0.5 hectares).
Cantina Mascarello owns 1.7 acres (0.7 hectares). In 1971, Giulio Mascarello
    produced 2110 bottles of a Cannubi Barolo.
E. Pira, 1.3 acres (0.54 hectares), all in nebbiolo.
Prunotto,[3] buys from 3 acres (1.2 hectares).
Francesco Rinaldi,[3] 5.4 acres (2.2 hectares).[2]
Francesco Sandrone.[3]
Luciano Sandrone, 3 acres (1.2 hectares).
Tenuta Carretta,[3] 6.7 acres (2.71 hectares).[2]

★★**Cannubi-Boschis** and **Cannubi-Muscatel** (Barolo). These two vineyards are subplots within the Cannubi vineyard district. Boschis is the northernmost part of this district, and Muscatel, just north of Barolo itself, is the southernmost portion. Some producers also include La Valletta and Monghisolfo as vineyards within the highly esteemed Cannubi district. Francesco Rinaldi owns a piece of Boschis. Marchesi di Barolo owns 8.6 acres (3.5 hectares) of Muscatel and 5 (2.1) of La Valletta; the two are bottled separately. Kiola, now F.lli Dogliani, also owns a piece of Muscatel (Moscatello). Teobaldo Prandi and Luciano Sandrone each own a piece of Monghisolfo.

Cannubi-Monghisolfo (Barolo). See Monghisolfo.

Capalot (La Morra). Az. Agr. "Santa Maria" bottles a Capalot Barolo from their vines here.

Cappellotti (La Morra). Az. Agr. "Santa Maria" has vines in this vineyard.

Carpegna (Serralunga d'Alba). This vineyard is in Sorano Borgato. Accademia Torregiorgi buys from Stefano Veglio and produces a cru Barolo from here. Pasquale Veglio of Cascina Bruni cultivates 7.4 acres (3 hectares) of vines here.

Cascina Adelaide (Barolo). Terzane-Benvenuti owns this property and bottles his Barolos under its name.

Cascina Badarina. This *cascina* takes in the vineyard holdings of the Seagram's-owned Bersano.

Cascina Francia (Serralunga d'Alba). This *cascina* represents the 37 acres (15 hectares) of vineyards owned by Giacomo Conterno. These holdings are scattered in various vineyards in Serralunga. Conterno uses the *cascina* name on the labels of his wines. Monfortino is a selection of his best nebbiolo grapes in the best vintages.

Cascina Massara (Verduno). Andrea Burlotto bottles his Barolo under this label. We suspect at least part of those holdings are in the Massara vineyard.

Cascina Mosconi (Barolo). Giovanni Scarzello labels his Barolo under this *cascina* name. Cascina Mosconi represents his vineyard holdings in Barolo.

Cascina Nuova (La Morra). Elio Altare owns this *cascina* in the Annunziata district. Since 1978, Altare has bottled 5000 to 6000 bottles of Barolo a year under this label.

Cascina Secolo (La Morra). This *cascina* takes in Contratto's holdings in Cerequio.

Cascina Traversa (La Morra). This *cascina* is in the Santa Maria area of La Morra.

Case Giuli (Grinzane Cavour).

Casenere (La Morra).

Castellero (mostly in Barolo, a small part in Monforte). F.lli Barale does a cru bottling from their 25 acres (10 hectares) in this vineyard. Giacomo Brezza and Francesco Pittatore's Az. Agr. "Ponte Rocca" also have vines here. Marchesi di Barolo owns 1 acre (0.4 hectares) here; part is in Monforte.

Castelletto (Monforte). F.lli Enrico e Giacomo Saffirio and Stefano Manzone of Az. Agr. "Ciabot del Preive" owns vines in this district. Renzo Seghesio buys grapes for his Barolo from Castelletto.

Castello (Castiglione Falletto). Luigi Coppo bottles a Barolo Castello.

Castello (Grinzane Cavour). Terre del Barolo produces a cru-bottled Barolo from here.

Caudane (La Morra). Oliviero Monticelli's Az. Agr. "Le Corte" bottles a Caudane Barolo.

★★**Cerequio** (mostly in La Morra, a part in Barolo). Cerequio's exposition is south to southwest. Renato Ratti finds notes of tobacco and cherries in the aroma of the Cerequio Barolo.

> *Owner–producers:*
> Cogno-Marcarini,[3] has not produced a Cerequio cru since 1971.
> Contratto (Cascina Secolo).
> Kiola, now F.lli Dogliani.
> Marchesi di Barolo.
> F.lli Oddero owns land in Cerequio-Serra.
> Tenuta Cerequio,[3] 16 acres (6.47 hectares), 15 (6.12) of nebbiolo.

Cerretta (Serranlunga d'Alba). Basilio Zunino owns vines in this vineyard district.

Ciabot (Monforte). Fia Rocca's La Vecchia Cantina has a piece of this vineyard.

Ciabot Mentin Ginestra (Monforte). Since 1980, Clerico has produced a cru Barolo from his holdings here.

Ciabot del Preive (Monforte). Stefano Manzone grows vines here. He named his Azienda Agricola for the vineyard.

Ciocchini (La Morra).

Ciocchini (Novello). Francesco Marengo farms grapes in this vineyard.

Codana (Castiglione Falletto). Paolo Scavino owns a piece of this vineyard. In 1971, Vietti produced 2900 bottles of Barolo Codana from the grapes he bought from a 1.7-acre (0.7-hectare) plot in this cru. The vines were 100% michet.

Colle Sud Ovest (Castiglione Falletto). A subcru of Bricco Boschis.

★★★**Collina Cannubi** (Barolo). This highly esteemed vineyard district is generally referred to as Cannubi.

★★**Conca dell'Abbazia dell'Annunziata** (La Morra). This vineyard, named for its shape, which curves like a shell, catches the sun's rays from the southeast and southwest. Conca is in the Marcenasco district. Renato Ratti produces a Conca Barolo from the grapes on his own 1.2 acres (0.5 hectares) of vines plus grapes purchased from another 2.5 acres (1 hectare). Ratti finds a pronounced aroma of tobacco in these wines. Ratti's Conca Barolo is softer and lighter than the one he produces from Rocche.

Contessa (La Morra). Marchese di Fracassi owns 2.8 acres (1.15 hectares) of vines here.

Convento di Santa Maria in Plaustra (La Morra). The Oddero brothers own vines here, in the section they call Bricco Plaustra.

Costa di Rose, Costa de Rose, or **Coste della Rose**[1] (Barolo). F.lli Barale have 7.4 acres (3 hectares) of dolcetto in this vineyard. Marchesi di Barolo also has vines here.

Croera or **Croesa** (La Morra). F.lli Casetta and Voerzio cultivate vines here.

Crosia (Barolo).

Crovera (La Morra). Marchesi di Barolo has vines in this vineyard.

Cucco (Serralunga d'Alba). This vineyard district is just north of the town itself.

Dardi[1] (Monforte). Dardi is a historic subregion of vineyards.

'dla Roul (Monforte, loc. Manzoni Soprana). Podere Rocche dei Manzoni has done a cru bottling from 'dla Roul since 1978.

★★**Enrico VI** (Castiglione Falletto). Paolo Cordero di Montezemolo bottles a Barolo Enrico VI from his 5.4 acres (2.2 hectares) of nebbiolo vines in the Villero vineyard.

Falleto (Serralunga d'Alba).

Fontana di Croera or **Fontana di Croesa** (La Morra). This is probably a part of the vineyard known as Croera or Croesa.

Fontanafredda[1] (Serralunga, partly in Diano d'Alba). Fontanafredda owns 250 acres (100 hectares) here, 173 (70) in vines, 69 (28) planted to nebbiolo.

Fontanassa (Barolo). Part of the Brunate vineyard district.

Fontanazza (La Morra, partly in Barolo). Marchesi di Barolo owns a piece of this vineyard. It is within the Brunate district.

Fontanile (Monforte). A vineyard district adjoining Pugnane to the north.

Fontanin (Castiglione Falletto).

Formica (La Morra). Oreste Stroppiana has vines here.

Fossati (La Morra). F.lli Borgogno owns 2 acres (0.8 hectares) of dolcetto. G. D. Vaira bottles a Barolo Fossati from his 6.2-acre (0.25-hectare) plot.

★**Francesco dell'Annunziata** (La Morra). "Rocche" Costamagna bottles a cru from its 1.2 (0.5 hectares) in Francesco.

★★**Gabutti** (Serralunga d'Alba). Dott. Cappellano buys grapes from Gabutti and does a cru bottling. Grignore is a subsection of Gabutti, and at one time the Ceretto brothers bottled a Barolo from there, but not since 1974.

★★**Gabutti-Parafada** (Serralunga d'Alba). This vineyard district, which has a southwestern exposure, includes the adjoining vineyards of Gabutti and Parafada and all of their subsections. Giacomo Conterno has vines in this district.

Galarei or **Galleretto** (Serralunga, partly in Diano d'Alba). Galarei is in the *borgato* of Sorano in Serralunga. Giacomo Ascheri has vines in that plot. Fontanafredda produce some 11,400 bottles a year of Gallaretto Barolo from their 4.1 acres (1.6 hectares) of nebbiolo vines.

Gallinotto Barolo). Francesco Rinaldi grows vines here.

Garbelletto (Castiglione Falletto). Bartolomeo Borgogno and F.lli Brovia grow vines in this district.

Garil (Serralunga d'Alba). Fontanafredda produce 2500 bottles a year of Barolo Garil from their 0.9 acres (0.4 hectares) of nebbiolo vines grown here.

Garombo (Serralunga d'Alba). Giacomo Conterno has vines in this vineyard.

★**Gattera dell'Annunziata** (La Morra). Bovio owns 4 acres (1.6 hectares) and bottles a cru. Marchesi di Barolo also owns a small part of Gattera.

Gattinera (Serralunga d'Alba). Fontanafredda have 11.1 acres (4.5 hectares) of nebbiolo here from which they produce 31,000 bottles a year of Barolo Gattinera.

Gavarini (Monforte). Elio Grasso owns 8.8 acres (3.6 hectares) of vines, 4.1 (1.7) in nebbiolo. He bottles Barolos from his subcrus of Chiniera, 0.9 acres (0.4 hectares), and Runcot, 2.8 acres (1.2 hectares). He also has 0.4 acres (0.2 hectares) of vines in the Dei Grassi plot. Giuseppe Mascarello produces a Barbera from grapes grown here.

★★**Ginestra** or **Ginestre**[1] (Monforte). Giuseppe Colla of Prunotto, who makes wines from Ginestra, characterizes these Barolos as soft.

> *Owner–producers:*
> Clerico,[3] Ciabot Mentin Ginestra
> Grasso,[3] 6.8 acres (2.7 hectares). 6.1 (2.5) planted to nebbiolo in the Case
>   Matè subcru.
> Giuseppe Mascarello, barbera.
> Prunotto,[3] buys from 3.3 acres (1.4 hectares).
> Renzo Seghesio buys grapes.

Giuchera or **Giunchera.** Dialect for Zonchera or Zonchetta.

Granbussia[1] (Monforte). Name used by Aldo Conterno[2] for his excellent Barolos from his holding in Bussia Soprana.

Grassi (Monforte). Accademia Torregiorgi buys grapes from Pietro Iberti to produce his Barolo Grassi. (See Gavarini dei Grassi.)

Grignore (Serralunga d'Alba). A subsection of Gabutti.

La Cormaretta, La Cornaretta (Monforte, loc. Manzoni Soprana). Podere Rocche dei Manzoni has vines here. Giuseppe Mascarello produces a Barbera from this vineyard.

La Delizia (Serralunga d'Alba). Fontanafredda has 8.9 acres (3.6 hectares) of nebbiolo vines in this vineyard which they use for their Barolo La Delizia. They produce on average 24,000 bottles a year.

La Mandorla (Barolo). Michele Fontana has vines in La Mandorla.

La Rosa (Barolo). Marchesi di Barolo owns vines in La Rosa.

La Rosa (Serralunga d'Alba). Fontanafredda produce their Barolo Vigna La Rosa from their 23 acres (9.3 hectares) of nebbiolo vines in this cru, averaging 65,000 bottles per year.

★★**La Serra** (La Morra). This esteemed cru is part of Brunate. Cogno Marcarini owns 25 acres (10 hectares); 10.5 (4.3) planted to nebbiolo. The vines are planted at an altitude of 1150 to 1310 feet (350 to 400 meters). Since 1973, Cogno has bottled some 20,000 bottles a year of the very fine La Serra Barolo.[2] Paolo Colla owns 20.5 acres (8.3 hectares) in this cru. The vines, planted at 835 feet (254 meters), are in Santa Maria La Morra. Since 1967, he has produced about 6000 bottles a year from this cru. Voerzio also has vines here, from which he produces a very good Barolo La Serra.

La Valletta dei Cannubi (Barolo). Marchesi di Barolo produces a cru Barolo from its 5.1 acres (2.1 hectares) of nebbiolo vines here.

La Villa (Barolo). Fontanafredda has 7.9 acres (3.2 hectares) of nebbiolo vines here that are used for its Barolo La Villa. Production averages 22,000 bottles a year.

Larocca (Barolo). Francesco Rinaldi has vines in Larocca.

Lazairasco (Serralunga d'Alba). Guido, Giovanni, and Carlo Porro grow grapes in this vineyard. This might be another name for Lazzarito.

★★**Lazzarito** (Serralunga d'Alba). Lazzarito has a southwestern exposition. Fontanafredda owns 6.5 acres (2.63 hectares) of nebbiolo vines which are used for its Barolo Lazzarito. Emilio Noschese of Cantina Lazzarito cultivates grapes in this vineyard.

Le Corte (La Morra). Oliviero Monticelli of Az. Agr. "Le Corte" produces a Barolo from his nebbiolo vines in this cru.

Le Coste (Barolo). Marchesi di Barolo has 1.5 acres (0.6 hectares) of dolcetto grapes in this vineyard. Giuseppe Rinaldi also cultivates grapes here in his 5-acre (2-hectare) plot, and G. D. Vaira has 2.4 acres (1 hectare) of dolcetto.

Le Coste (Monforte). Scarpa buys grapes from this vineyard; to produce about 12,000 to 14,000 bottles a year of its La Coste Barolo.

Le Turnote (La Morra). This vineyard district is in the Monfalletto region.

Liste (Barolo). Giacomo Borgogno cultivates grapes here, in both the main vineyard area and the subcru of Pascolo.

Mantoetto (La Morra). Marchese di Fracassi owns 5.4 acres (2.2 hectares) of dolcetto vines in Mantoetto.

★**Marcenasco dell'Annunziata**[1] (La Morra). This vineyard takes its name from the village and castle built around the fifteenth-century Abbazia dell'Annunziata. Renato Ratti produces a cru from grapes grown on his 12.4 acres (5 hectares) of Marcenasco, as well as from the subvineyards of Conca and Rocche.

Marenca (Serralunga d'Alba). Secondo Pira has vines here. This vineyard is included within the Marenca e Rivetti district.

Marenca e Rivetti (Serralunga d'Alba). This vineyard district, just west of the town itself and facing southwest, includes the vineyards of Marenca and Rivetti.

Margaria or **Margheria** (Serralunga d'Alba). Duca d'Asti produces a cru Barolo from this vineyard which is sold under the Gran Duca label. Secondo Pira owns a piece of the vineyard. Giuseppe Massolino of Az. Agr. "Vigna Rionda" owns 6.2 acres (2.5 hectares); 5 (2) planted to nebbiolo.

Maria Luigia (Serralunga d'Alba). Pasquale Veglio of Cascina Bruni owns vines here.

Marzio (Verduno).

Massara or **Massera** (Verduno). Andrea Burlotto's Cascina Massera owns part of this vineyard. Castello Verduno also has vines here.

Mentin Ginestra (Monforte). See Ciabot Mentin Ginestra.

Merenda (Barolo). Part of Sarmassa.

Meriondino (Castiglione Falletto). Alfredo Currado of Vietti buys grapes from a 2-acre (0.8-hectare) plot in this vineyard; in 1976, he produced 3850 bottles of Barolo Meriondino.

Miralanga (Barolo). Gigi Rosso cultivates grapes here; it is part of his holding in Arione.

Molino (Barolo). Marchesi di Barolo has vines in Molino.

★★**Momprivato** or **Monprivato** (Castiglione Falletto). Momprivato, like most of the best vineyards of Barolo, faces southwest. This 10-acre (4-hectare) vineyard district, north and northwest of Castiglione Falletto itself, is divided among four owners. Giuseppe Mascarello, who owns more than half (6.4 acres, 2.6 hectares), bottles some 9000 bottles in an average year of a Monprivato cru. Sobrero owns (or owned) a small piece (We understand that he sold it early in 1985 to Giuseppe Mascarello.).

★★**Monfalletto dell'Annunziata**[1] (La Morra). This vineyard district also includes Le Turnote. These Barolos are noted for an aroma more of tobacco than of tartufi. Paolo Cordero di Montezemolo makes a Barolo from his 30 acres (12.2 hectares) of nebbiolo in Monfalletto. In total he owns 40 acres (16.2 hectares), which also includes dolcetto.

Monfortino[1] (Serralunga d'Alba). Giovanni Conterno of Giacomo Conterno selects the best grapes from his Cascina Francia holdings to produce this very fine Barolo.[2] It is, however, not a cru bottling.

Monghisolfo (Barolo). Teobaldo Prandi and Luciano Sandrone own plots in this vineyard. Sandrone cultivates 3 acres (1.2 hectares) of vines.

Monprivato (Castiglione Falletto). See Momprivato.

★**Montanello**[1] (Castiglione Falletto). This vineyard is owned in its entirety by Tenuta Montanello. About 25 acres (10.2 hectares) are planted to vines; some 10 acres (4 hectares) are in nebbiolo, mostly the michet subvariety, but there is also some lampia and rose. Fontana, Pianello, and Pini are subplots of Montanello. Pini is bottled as a cru.

Montetetto (Cherasco).

Monvigliero (Verduno). F.lli Alessandria produces a Barolo cru from their nebbiolo vines grown here.

Mosca Brevi (Verduno).

Muscatel Ruè (Barolo). Giacomo Brezza grows barbera here.

Moscatello di Cannubi (Barolo). This vineyard is more commonly known as Cannubi-Muscatel.

Nirane-Sorano Bricco (Serralunga d'Alba). Giacomo Ascheri grows grapes in this vineyard, which is in Sorano Borgato.

Ornata (La Morra).

Ornato[1] (Serralunga d'Alba). Pio Cesare owns 25 acres (10 hectares) of vines here. He produces a *barrique*-aged Ornato from a blend of nebbiolo and barbera.

Otinasso (Castiglione Falletto). F.lli Brovia, which owns 2.5 acres (1 hectare) of vines here, produces an Otinasso Barolo.

Paiagallo (Barolo). Marchesi di Barolo has barbera planted here. Giorgio Scarzello has 2.7 acres (1.1 hectares) of dolcetto in this vineyard.

Panitale (Novello).

★**Parafada** (Serralunga d'Alba). Parafada is in the Gabutti district. Dott. Cappellano buys grapes from this vineyard. Giacomo Conterno has vines in Parafada. Giuseppe Massolino of Az. Agr. "Vigna Rionda" has 5 acres (2 hectares), 2.5 (1) of nebbiolo. He produces, on average, 13,000 bottles a year of a Barolo cru from here.

Pascolo (Barolo). A subcru of Liste.

Perias (Barolo). Part of Sarmassa.

Perno (Monforte). Renzo Seghesio buys grapes from this vineyard for his Barolo.

★**Pian della Polvere** or **Pianpolvere** (Monforte). Some growers consider Pianpolvere a part of Bussia. Thirty-five of its 50 acres (15 out of 20 hectares) are in vines; 24.6 (10) are nebbiolo, mostly michet. Riccardo Fenocchio, who owns 8.8 acres (3.6 hectares), two-thirds of which is nebbiolo, bottles a Barolo Pianpolvere Soprana. Renzo Seghesio buys grapes from this vineyard.

Pilone (Serralunga d'Alba). Pasquale Veglio of Cascina Bruni owns vines here.

★**Plicotti** or **Plucotti dell'Annunziata** (La Morra, partly in Barolo). Gigi Rosso owns 5 acres (2 hectares) here. The Lorenzo Denegri of Ca' Bianca makes a Barolo from its vines in Plicotti though it is not labeled as a cru.

★**Prapò** (Serralunga d'Alba). Ceretto's Az. Agr. "Bricco Rocche" owns 7.5 acres (3 hectares) in Prapò. At one time the Cerettos bottled this cru as Riccardo I; that name has since been dropped. They produce from 13,000 to 15,000 bottles a year of this Barolo cru.

Prea (Barolo).

Preda (Barolo). F.lli Barale owns 5 acres (2 hectares) of vines here.

★★**Pugnane** (Castiglione Falletto). This vineyard adjoins Fontanile to the south. Since 1971, Giuseppe Mascarello has bottled a cru from grapes he buys from this vineyard.

Punta (Castiglione Falletto). Alfonso Scavino bottles a Barolo cru from the nebbiolo vines he grows here.

Punta Marcello (Castiglione Falletto). A subcru of Bricco Boschis.

Rabera or **Ravera** (Barolo). Marchesi di Barolo owns dolcetto vines in this vineyard. G. D. Vaira has 1 acre (0.4 hectares) of nebbiolo from which he makes a Barolo. He also owns 1.7 acres (0.7 hectares) of barbera. Giuseppe Rinaldi has 5 acres (2 hectares) of vines.

★**Riccardo dell'Annunziata** (La Morra). "Rocche" Costamagna bottles a cru from their 1.2-acre (0.55-hectare) plot in Riccardo.

Riccardo I in Prapò (Serralunga d'Alba). See Prapò.

Rimirasso (Monforte).

★★**Rionda** (Serralunga d'Alba). Another name for Vigna Rionda.

Rivassa (Serralunga d'Alba). Pasquale Veglio of Cascina Bruni has vines in this vineyard.

Rivassi-Boschetti (Barolo). Luciano Sandrone cultivates 3.7 acres (1.5 hectares) of dolcetto here.

★**Rivette** or **Rivetti** (Serralunga d'Alba). This is part of the Marenca e Rivetti vineyard district.

★★**Rocche di Castiglione Falletto** (Castiglione Falletto). About ten owners have pieces of this vineyard. It lies south and southeast of the town of Castiglione Falletto itself, adjoining Villero to the west. Its exposure is southeast. Briacca and Bricco Rocche are subcrus here.

> *Owner–producers:*
> F.lli Brovia,[3] 2.5 acres (1 hectare).
> Natalino Cavallotto sells grapes to Vietti.
> Bruno Giacosa[3] buys grapes.[2]
> Elio Icardi sells grapes to Vietti.
> Giuseppe Mascarello (at one time, no longer).
> F.lli Oddero.
> Paolo Ornato, 5.6 acres (2.3 hectares).
> Tenuta Montanello,[3] 2 acres (0.8 hectares).
> Arnaldo Rivera belongs to the Terre del Barolo co-op.
> Terre del Barolo,[3] 4.4 acres (1.8 hectares).
> Vietti [3] buys from about 1.6 acres (0.7 hectares).[2]

★★**Rocche di La Morra** (La Morra). This vineyard district, facing southwest, lies within the Marcenasco area of Annunziata. The wines frequently have a note of tartufi in their aroma. Some eight to nine growers own pieces of Rocche. Renato Ratti has 1.2 acres (0.5 hectares) and buys grapes from another 3.7 (1.5). Parroco di La Morra, Aurelio Settimo, and Fratelli Veglio also own pieces of this esteemed cru. Ratti's Barolo from Rocche is bigger and more tannic than his softer, more gentle Conca cru.

★**Rocchette** or **Rochetta dell'Annunziata** (La Morra). This vineyard district lies within the Marcenasco area of Annunziata. G. Accomasso and F.lli Oberto bottle crus from this subplot. Fratelli Oberto owns 3 acres (1.2 hectares) of vines here.

Rocchettevino (La Morra). F.lli Oddero grows grapes here. We believe this is their name for their part of the Rocchette district of Annunziata.

Roero (Barolo). Cantina Mascarello owns 0.7 acres (0.3 hectares) of vines here.

Roncaglia (La Morra). Marchesi di Barolo owns a piece of this vineyard. Scarpa has bottled about 3400 bottles a year since 1978 from grapes bought from here.

Rotonda (Serralunga d'Alba). Another name for Rionda.

Ruè (Barolo). Giacomo Borgogno and Cantina Mascarello grow grapes in this vineyard.

San Bernardo (Serralunga d'Alba). Cantina Palladino owns 7.4 acres (3 hectares) of vines in this vineyard. They produce 50,000 bottles of San Bernardo Barolo from 3 acres (1.2 hectares) of nebbiolo.

San Giacomo (La Morra). Oreste Stroppiana owns vines here.

San Giuseppe. A subcru of Bricco Boschis.

San Lorenzo (Barolo). Cantina Mascarello owns 1 acre (0.4 hectares) of vines in this vineyard, and E. Pira owns 2 acres (0.8 hectares). Michele Fontana owns a piece as well.

San Pietro (Barolo). Giacomo Borgogno grows vines in this vineyard.

San Pietro (Serralunga d'Alba). Fontanafredda owns 7.6 acres (3.1 hectares) of nebbiolo vines here, from which they produce 22,000 bottles of Barolo a year.

Santa Caterina (Serralunga d'Alba). Guido, Giovanni, and Carlo Porro cultivate vines in this vineyard.

Santa Maria (La Morra). Renato Ratti finds in the Barolos of Santa Maria notes of black cherries, prunes, camphor, and mint. Az. Agr. "Santa Maria" and F.lli Oddero have vines in this vineyard area.

Santo Stefano (Monforte). This vineyard has a southwesterly exposition. It is within the district of Santo Stefano di Perno.

★★**Santo Stefano di Perno**[1] (Monforte). This property, owned by the church, is no longer planted to vines. At least one fine producer put that vineyard on the same level as Cannubi.

★★**Sarmassa** or **Sarmazza**[1] (Barolo, partly in La Morra). There are two subcrus of this vineyard district: Merenda and Perias.

> *Owner–producers:*
> Giacomo Brezza.[3]
> Marchesi di Barolo,[3] 4.8 acres (1.9 hectares).
> Francesco Rinaldi

Giorgio[3] Scarzello owns 8.2 acres (3.3 hectares) of nebbiolo in Merenda;
he has bottled some 5000 bottles a year of a Barolo cru from here
since 1979. He owns 1.5 acres (0.6 hectares) of dolcetto in Perias.

Scarrone (Castiglione Falletto). This vineyard district is regarded for its barbera. Alfredo Currado of Vietti owns 2.3 acres (1.5 hectares) in the Fioretto vineyard, from which he produces a nebbiolo–barbera–dolcetto–neirano blend.

Sirionato (Serralunga d'Alba). Giacomo Conterno has vines here.

Sorano (Serralunga d'Alba). Also called Borgato di Sorano, this is a *borgato,* or section, of Serralunga. Vineyard areas within Sorano include Carpegna, Galarei, and Nirane.

Sori (Serralunga d'Alba). Pasquale Veglio of Cascina Bruni owns about 25 acres (10 hectares) of vines here, 17.3 (7) in nebbiolo, from which he does a cru bottling.

Specola (La Morra). F.lli Oddero have vines here.

Terlo (Barolo). Luigi Einaudi grows nebbiolo for his Barolo in this vineyard.

Terra Hera (Barolo). F.lli Casetta has vines here and does a cru bottling from them.

Tetti (La Morra). Scarpa bottles some 15,000 bottles a year from this cru.[2]

Torriglione (La Morra). Francesco Rinaldi and Cantina (Bartolo) Mascarello own vines in this vineyard. Mascarello has 3.7 acres (1.5 hectares).

Vergne (Novello).

Vezza (Barolo). Francesco Rinaldi owns vines here.

Via Nuova (Barolo). The firm of E. Pira owns 1.1 acres (0.4 hectares) of vines in Via Nuova. Teobaldo Prandi also has vines here.

★★**Vigna Rionda** (Serralunga d'Alba). This vineyard, south of Serralunga itself, covers about 30 acres (12 hectares). It is divided among five or six owners. It is also called Arionda, Rionda, and occasionally Rotunda.

> *Owner–producers:*
> Aldo Canale.[3]
> Dott. Giuseppe Cappellano buys grapes.
> Giacomo Conterno.
> Bruno Giacosa[3] buys grapes.[2]
> Az. Agr. "Vigna Rionda" di Giuseppe Massolino,[3] 6.2 acres (2.5 hectares);
> 5 (2) in nebbiolo.
> Giuseppe Mascarello[3] bought grapes and produced 7000 to 7500 bottles
> of Rionda; he no longer produces a Barolo from here.
> F.lli Oddero.
> Cantine Palladino[3] labeled Riunda.

Vignane or **Vignave** (Barolo). Marchesi di Barolo and Francesco Rinaldi have vines here. Rinaldi cultivates 6 acres (2.4 hectares).

★★**Villero** (Castiglione Falletto). This vineyard district, the largest in Castiglione Falletto, is just southwest of the town itself and adjoins Rocche to the east. It has a southwesterly exposure. Enrico VI is the name of the plot owned by Montezemolo, who bottles the wine as a cru under that name.

> *Owner–producers:*
> Ceretto[3] (no longer).
> Bruno Giacosa[3] buys grapes in certain vintages.[2]
> Giuseppe Mascarello[3] buys grapes and produces from 7000 to 15,000
> bottles; he has bottled this cru since 1978.
> Paolo Cordero di Montezemolo,[3] Enrico VI.
> Sobrero, reportedly sold his holdings to Giuseppe Mascarello.
> Vietti[3] buys grapes from vines that are more than thirty years old.

Zonchetta (Barolo). Kiola, now F.lli Dogliani, owns a piece of this vineyard.

★★**Zonchetta** or **Zonchera**[1] (La Morra). The Cerettos have a lease that expires in the year 2000 on 7.4 acres (3 hectares) in this part of the Brunate vineyard. Since 1968, they have bottled a Barolo cru from Zonchetta, now labeled Zonchera.[2] Their production averages 18,000 bottles a year.

Notes, definitions, and abbreviations:

1. Listed by Renato Ratti as a historic subregion for vine growing.

2. This combination of producer and cru is among our favorites in Barolo.

3. Labeled with the cru name.

Az. Agr.: Azienda Agricola, a winery that only uses its own grapes to produce wine.

Cascina: Literally holdings, it could refer to a single vineyard or a group of vineyards owned by a single proprietor or estate.

F.lli: Fratelli, brothers.

1 hectare = 2.4711 acres

1 hectoliter = 26.42 gallons = 11.11 cases

1 meter = 3.281 feet

The Barolo Producers Rated

★★★★

Cantina Mascarello di Bartolo Mascarello
Cogno-Marcarini di Elvio Cogno
Giacosa Bruno
Rinaldi Francesco di Luciano Rinaldi
Vietti di Alredo Currado
Ceretto, Az. Agr. "Bricco Rocche" and Casa Vinicola
Conterno Aldo
Rinaldi Giuseppe
"Monfortino" di Giacomo Conterno
E. Pira di Luigi Pira (E. Pira di Chiara Boschis, 0)

★★★

Barale F.lli
Bovio Gianfranco
Conterno Giacomo di Giovanni Conterno
Cordero di Montezemolo Paolo (prior to 1979; since 1979, ★★)
Einaudi Luigi (most recent vintage tasted was 1974)
Giacosa F.lli
Grasso Az. Agr. di Elio Grasso
Mascarello Giuseppe di Mauro Mascarello
Oddero F.lli
− Pio Cesare (since 1978; previously ★★ −)
Prunotto Alfredo di Colla and Filiberti
Ratti Renato
+ Scarpa Antica Casa Vinicola
Sobrero Filippo (sold vineyards in 1985)
+ Tenuta Carretta dei F.lli Veglia

★★

Accademia Torregiorgi
Borgogno F.lli Serio e Battista, Vigna Cannubi (for their regular Barolo, ★)
Borgogno Giacomo (prior to 1968; since 1968, ★)
− Cabutto Bartolomeo, Tenuta La Volta (prior to 1978; since 1978, ★)
Cavallotto F.lli
Clerico
+ Contratto Giuseppe di Dott. Alberto Contratto
Cordero Paolo di Montezemolo (since 1979; previously ★★★)
Fenocchio Riccardo, Az. Agr. Pianpolvere Soprano
+ Franco Fiorina
Fontanafredda crus (the regular, ★)
Marchese Maurizio Fracassi Ratti Mentone
− Palladino (since 1978; previously ★)
− Pio Cesare (prior to 1978; since 1978, ★★★ −)
Podere Rocche dei Manzoni di Migliorini Valentino
"Rocche" Costamagna
Sandrone Luciano
Scarzello Giovanni, Cascina Mosconi
Scavino Alfonso
Scavino Paolo
Tenuta Cerequio, Vinicola Piemontese
Tenuta Coluè di Massimo Oddero
− Tenuta Montanello di F.lli Monchiero
Terre del Barolo crus (the regular ★)
Vaira, G. D.
+ Voerzio Giacomo dei F.lli Voerzio (since 1982; previously 0)

★

Altare Elio
Ascheri Giacomo

Borgogno F.lli Serio e Battista regular (Vigna Cannubi, ★★)
Borgogno Giacomo (since 1968; previously ★★)
Brovia F.lli
Cabutto Bartolomeo "Tenuta La Volta" (since 1978; previously ★★ −)
Calissano Luigi (most recent vintage tasted was 1971)
Cascina Bruni di Pasqual Veglio
− Casetta F.lli
Castello Feudale
Coppo Luigi
Damilano Dott. Giacomo
Denegri di Ca' Bianca
Dosio
Fenocchio Giacomo (most recent vintage tasted was 1976)
Fontanafredda regular (for the crus, ★★)
Gemma
Giri Guido (most recent vintage tasted was 1971)
"Gran Duca," Cantine Duca d'Asti
Lodali Giovanni (most recent vintage tasted was 1961)
Manzone Stefano, Ciabot del Preive
Marchesi di Barolo crus (the regular, 0)
Marchesi Spinola (most recent vintage tasted was 1967)
Massolino Giuseppe, Az. Agr. "Vigna Rionda"
Mirafiore (haven't tasted it in some time)
Oreste Stefano
Ornato Paolo (doesn't bottle; at one time ★★)
Palladino (prior to 1978; since 1978, ★★ −)
Rolfo Gianfranco
Rosso Gigi
Sandrone Francesco
Scarzello Giorgio
Settimo Aurelio
Terre del Barolo regular (for the crus, ★★)
− Valfieri (most recent vintage tasted was 1971)
Veglio Angelo

0

Alessandria F.lli
Asteggiano Vincenzo
− Bel Colle
Bersano
− Bosca Luigi
Bosso (the most recent vintage tasted was 1971)
Brero Cav. Luigi
Brezza Giacomo
Bruzzone (the most recent vintage tasted was 1971)
− Castello Sperone (the most recent vintage tasted was 1970)
− Cauda Cav. Luigi
Cella
− Ceste Cav. (the most recent vintage tasted was 1971)
Chiadò Mario (the most recent vintage tasted was 1971)
− Colla Paolo
Colli Monfortesi di Conterno Fantino
− Cossetti Clemente
Dellavalle
Ferrero Virginia (the most recent vintage tasted was 1970)

Gherzi (the most recent vintage tasted was 1971)
Grazziola (the most recent vintage tasted was 1971)
Grimaldi Cav. Carlo e Mario, Az. Agr. Groppone
Il Vecchio Tralcio
– Kiola, now F.lli Dogliani
"La Brenta d'Oro", Cantina d'Invecchiamento (the most recent vintage tasted was 1974)
Marchesi di Barolo regular (the crus, ★)
Molino Guido (the most recent vintage tasted was 1975)
Morando Cav. A.
Nicolello
Oddero Luigi
Osola (the most recent vintage tasted was 1973)
– Osvaldo Mauro
Pavese Livio
Pippione (the most recent vintage tasted was 1971)
E. Pira di Boschis (bottled by Luigi Pira, ★★★★)
Porta Rossa di Berzia e Rizza, Cantina della (the

most recent vintage tasted was 1967)
"Roche" Azienda Vinicola (to watch since Carlo Brovia is their consultant)
Savigliano Mario
– Scanavino Giovanni
Seghesio Renzo
Stroppiana Oreste (the most recent vintage tasted was 1970)
Saffirio F.lli Enrico e Giacomo
Troglia Giovanni (they were better in the 1960s)
Vecchio Piemonte Soc. Coop.
Vignolo-Lutati (the most recent vintage tasted was 1971)
– Villadoria Marchese
Vinicola Piemontese (now Tenuta Cerequio, rated ★★ –)
Voerzio Giacomo (prior to 1982; since 1982, ★★ +)
Zunino Basilio (the most recent vintage tasted was 1974)

Tasting Notes
1984

The year began with a wet spring, and the rain continued until June 15, retarding the growth of the vines. The summer, however, was warm and fairly dry. Nevertheless, selection was required during the harvest to obtain good-quality fruit. Giovanni Conterno of Giacomo Conterno and the firm of Scarpa didn't produce any Barolo in '84, Giacomo Borgogno made only one 10,500-gallon (400-hectoliter) cask. Cavallotto, however, said that for them the vintage was a good one.

At this stage (Feb. '85) our tentative assessment of the vintage, based on the few wines (six) we've tasted, is that it is mixed. The best producers appear to have made good wines. We've found the wines tasted thus far to be light in body and high in acid. We were especially impressed with Vietti's Brunate, which displays some delicacy and elegance (★★); there is a lot of quality already evident in Vietti's Rocche also. Another good '84 is from Gianfranco Bovio; his Gattera dell'Annunziata has a surprising amount of fruit (★★).

1983 [★★ +]

This was a difficult vintage. Many experts rate it three stars; we give it a bit less. Scarpa didn't produce any Barolo. Cavallotto found it a so-so year. Renato Ratti said the wines ranged from OK to good. Alfredo Currado of Vietti considered it a difficult vintage.

We find the wines for the most part good, at their best surely worth three stars, but in other cases light and perhaps a bit deficient in fruit for their tannin, and there are those that are simple, light luncheon wines which will mature early and not last. Based on ten different wines we tasted from cask, some more than once, we find the wines fairly light-bodied and with a forward fruitiness. The best have elegance and balance. Overall we rate the vintage two stars plus.

The most impressive tasted thus far are the following:

Giacosa Bruno, Villero. At this point our single favorite, with a cherry, cassis aroma and a forward, sweet ripe fruitiness; elegant and stylish.★★★
Rinaldi Francesco, Cannubbio. Elegant and gentle with fragrant perfume; fairly forward.★★★
Vietti, Rocche. Already exhibits style and elegance, with suggestions of mushrooms, tobacco, and cherries on the nose; a lighter, softer style with some firmness.★★★

Also worth noting:
Bovio Gianfranco, Gattera dell'Annunziata. The aroma suggests cherries and gingerbread; forward, sweet fruit.★★
Cappellano Dott. Giuseppe. Raspberry and strawberry aroma and flavors ; fruit seems sweet and ripe.★★
Pio Cesare. One of the fullest of the '83s we've tasted.★★

1983

Voerzio Giacomo, La Serra. Has class and sweet ripe fruit, with an aroma of black cherries and spice; moderate tannin; some elegance.★★(+)

Others tasted:
Borgogno F.lli Serio e Battista. Moderate tannin; vaguely bitter.
Massolino Giuseppe, Margheria. Rather light and a bit simple.
Ornato Paolo. A bit light; has fruit.

1982 [★★★★]

Many producers told us that they've never seen such perfect fruit; Cavallotto said that "the grapes looked so perfect it seemed a shame to crush them." The weather was exceptional throughout the season, and the wines have perfect balance and ripeness. Giovanni Conterno says they have great perfume and will be feminine wines like the 1970s. Pio Boffa finds them very fruity, with a softness; he said they will mature sooner than 1978 or 1971. Ratti said they are complete wines that could be grand if allowed to mature. Alfredo Currado said they are better than 1978, with better structure; if they have any deficiency it is perhaps a touch too little acidity. He believes they will mature earlier than the higher-acid '78s.

As for our assessment, four stars pretty much says it. These are exceptionally fine Barolos, complete and finely balanced, with more elegance and fruit than either '78 or '71. While they might not measure up to the '71s for sheer weight, power, and concentration, there is no question that they make up for that with their elegance and finesse. While we feel they will mature fairly early, perhaps between five and eight years from the vintage, we also believe they will keep well.

Our assessment is based on nearly three dozen different wines tasted from cask from more than two dozen producers since 1983. Some of those wines were tasted two, three, and even four times. There is no doubt about it; this vintage is of a very high level, one of the best. For us, it is superior even to 1978, at least for now.

Our favorite wines had very few if any surprises, and all merited three stars with potential for four:

Ceretto Az. Agr. "Bricco Rocche", Prapò. Perfumed aroma; enormous fruit and style; so well balanced it is tempting to drink now but obviously needs four or five years to really show itself; impressive.
Cogno-Marcarini, Brunate. Expansive aroma; richly concentrated with firm tannin; at this point it shades out the La Serra.
Cogno-Marcarini, La Serra. Rich, ripe, sweet fruit; exceptional balance; fine quality.
Conterno Aldo, Bussia Soprana. Rich, ripe, concentrated fruit; has a tannic vein; impressive.
Giacosa Bruno, Arionda. More closed than Villero but with an intensity of sweet ripe fruit and strikingly well balanced.
Giacosa Bruno, Villero. Enormous concentration and weight, firm and full-bodied; will surely be one of the best of this exceptional vintage.
"Monfortino" di Giacomo Conterno. Incredible perfume; enormous richness and concentration, sweet ripe fruit underneath a mass of tannin. Would you believe Giovanni Conterno only made about 330 cases of this outstanding wine? He said the rest of the fruit didn't quite measure up to his standards for this special reserve. Surely one of the stars of the vintage.
Rinaldi Giuseppe. A core of ripe fruit under a tannic frame; tremendous potential.
Scarpa, Tetti di La Morra. Perfumed aroma; impressive balance; has a heap of sweet ripe fruit and soft tannins; full-bodied. A finely honed wine that suggests berries of all types—black, blue, and red—as well as pecans.
Vietti, Briacca. A heap of fruit and style; the aroma displays various nuances. This wine surely has a great future. The most forward of the Vietti crus.
Vietti, Rocche. Incredible ripeness and concentration. Will surely be one of the greatest of this outstanding vintage; the line forms after us.

Very close behind these wines and perhaps even on the same level are the following:

Rinaldi Francesco, Cannubbio. Perfumed and elegant, with a lot of quality evident; too cold to fully assess. ★★★ for now, perhaps merits ★★★(★)

Others tasted:

Borgogno F.lli Serio e Battista, Vigna Cannubi. Expansive aroma; rich and full with some elegance and a fair amount of tannin.★★
Bovio Gianfranco, Gattera dell'Annunziata. Intense cherrylike aroma; a mouthful of ripe fruit; moderate tannin; style evident.★★★ –

Cascina Bruni di Veglio Pasqual. A lot of fruit and a fair amount of tannin, but seems more forward and lighter than many others.★
Cavallotto F.lli, Vigna Bricco Boschis–San Giuseppe. Heaps of tannin, heaps of fruit, enormous richness; a real mouthful of wine. At this point backward, but a lot of quality.★★(★)

1982

Ceretto Az. Agr. "Bricco Rocche", Brunate. More restrained than Prapò, but also seems fuller and richer; should develop slower and perhaps last longer.★★(★★)

Conterno Giacomo, Cascina Francia *(11/84)*. Forward aroma of ripe fruit; vague note of tartufi; enormous concentration of fruit and tannin; flavor of ripe grapes.★★★

Fenocchio Riccardo, Pianpolvere Soprano *(4/85)*. Firm tannic frame over a core of fruit; needs time, but potential is evident.★★(★ −)

Grasso, Vigna Gavarini-Runcot. Rich and intense aroma, with cherry and floral notes; soft tannins; some firmness; a gentle, elegant style.★★(★)

Ornato Paolo, Rocche. Good fruit and structure; a bit light.★★

Pio Cesare. Sweet, ripe fruit and soft, round tannins; a full-bodied Barolo.★★(★)

E. Pira di Boschis. Nice nose. At this stage tannin seems a bit high for the fruit, but admittedly it is still young.(★)

Prunotto, Cannubi. Rich, ripe fruit underneath a lot of tannin; already a softness evident, but years from ready.★★(★ +)

"Rocche" Costamagna. Concentrated ripe fruit and a fair amount of tannin.★★(+)

Tenuta Cerequio (Vinicola Piemontese). Cherry, tobacco, vanilla aroma with berrylike notes; a lot of fruit.★★(★)

Tenuta Montanello, Rocche. Lacks the richness of the '78, but does have a lot of fruit.★

Vietti, Bussia. Sweet ripe fruit; soft tannin; well balanced.★★★

Vietti, Castiglione Falletto. Fruit evident but still closed and somewhat backward compared to the other three crus.★★

Voerzio Giacomo, La Serra. Aroma of tobacco and blackberry jam; richly concentrated with intensity and ripeness.★★(+)

We also tasted some wines that were rather difficult to assess for one reason or another, having been just racked, in need of racking, or just too darn cold (ex-cask in January and February 1985). These include Borgogno F.lli Serio e Battista, Cappellano Dott. Giuseppe, Massolino Giuseppe Margheria and Parafada crus, and the Montezemolo crus of Enrico VI and Monfalletto.

1981 ★

Surely a mixed bag of wines. Accademia Torregiori, Rocche dei Manzoni, Marchese Fracassi, Giacomo Conterno, Scarpa, and Voerzio, among others, produced no Barolo. Bovio doesn't know whether he'll bottle a Barolo. Bartolo Mascarello declassified all or most of it, selling the wine as Nebbiolo delle Langhe. Bruno Giacosa produced a very small quantity. "Rocche" Costamagna's quantity was less than 50 percent of normal. What happened?

The weather started out fine and went well until the middle of August; then very high humidity and rain created conditions where the grapes couldn't dry out or ripen. During September it rained on and off. Ratti told us he fermented his Barolo for only ten days on the skins, while in the best years he keeps them twice as long.

As for the wines, based on nineteen different wines from fifteen producers—many among the best in Barolo—we find the wines mixed, with the best meriting two stars and the least earning zero, on average, perhaps one star. Clearly, careful selection of grapes was in order.

Altare Elio, Vigneto Aborina dell'Annunziata *(4/85)*. Mushroomy aroma with a flavor to match; unbalanced, some tannin, a bit shallow; finish is all tannin.

Borgogno F.lli Serio e Battista, Vigna Cannubi *(ex-cask 11/84)*. Surprisingly deep color; aroma still reticent, but some fruit already evident; light–moderate tannin, good fruit, medium body, some elegance.★(★)

Cavallotto F.lli, Vigna Bricco Boschis *(ex-cask 6/82)*. Harsh and tannic, not a lot of fruit at this stage; seems unstructured.

Ceretto Az. Agr. "Bricco Rocche," Bricco Rocche *(ex-cask 11/84)*. Mushroomlike aroma; fairly forward on the palate, light-bodied, nice flavor. In all a nice wine that will be declassified; it doesn't meet the Ceretto brothers' standard for the vineyard.★

Ceretto Az. Agr. "Bricco Rocche," Brunate *(twice 1/85)*. Bottled ten days earlier, some bottle sickness evident, but shows quality and fruit; light to moderate tannin; will be ready early; somewhat less open than the Prapò.★★

Ceretto Az. Agr. "Bricco Rocche," Prapò *(twice 1/85)*. Spicy, vanilla, raspberry aroma shows more development than expected; moderate tannin, some astringency but nice fruit, a little light; will make a nice bottle in perhaps three years.★★

Clerico *(4/85)*. Nice characteristic aroma; fairly tannic, seems to have sufficient fruit beneath; should be ready soon.★(+)

Cogno-Marcarini, Brunate *(ex-cask 11/84)*. Light nose with a cherry, tobacco note; rather light-bodied for a Barolo, some tannin and a lot of flavor; should be ready early.★★(+)

Cogno-Marcarini, La Serra *(ex-cask 11/84)*. Tobacco, cherry aroma with a mushroomlike note, more open than the Brunate; fairly well balanced, has a lot of flavor and a fair amount of tannin.★★

Colli Monfortesi di Fantino Conterno *(4/85)*. Reticent aroma; light tannin, low fruit, light-bodied; tannic finish.

1981

Fenocchio Riccardo, Pianpolvere Soprano (*ex-vat 4/85*). Firm tannin up front, with the fruit to support it; not bad for the year. ★

Grasso, Vigna Gavarini-Chiniera (*ex-cask 2/85*). Open, forward fruity aroma; light tannin, fairly soft already, with a gentle nature; will mature early, but no doubt it was a success for the vintage. ★★

Mascarello Giuseppe, Monprivato (*ex-vat 6/82*). Has more body and fruit than one could reasonably expect from this vintage; some quality evident. ★(★)

Osvaldo Mauro (*4/85*). Unbalanced; high in tannin, low in fruit.

Ratti Renato (*ex-cask 5/82*). Somewhat astringent but nice flavor; should make a nice light luncheon wine. ★

"Rocche" Costamagna (*ex-cask 2/85*). Floral, fruity aroma; fairly open and forward, with a tobacco, cherry nuance; light-bodied, almost sweet; fairly good quality though simple. ★(★)

Sandrone Luciano (*1/85*). Lovely nose with notes of tobacco and fruit and a suggestion of tartufi; moderate tannin; still somewhat young but should be ready in two to three years. ★(★)

Settimo Aurelio (*5/85*). Cherrylike aroma; moderate tannin; somewhat astringent; fairly ready; doubtful future. ★ −

Vietti, Briacca (*ex-cask 6/82*). More color than the Rocche; delicate floral aroma has a vanillalike note; fairly full-flavored but has a softness; should make a nice bottle. ★(★)

Vietti, Rocche (*ex-cask 2/85*). In all developing as we predicted; tobacco, tea, and tarlike notes; shows more development than one might expect for its age; has a softness on the palate that suggests it will be ready early; some tannin at the end. ★★(+)

1980 ★★ −

Overall, 1980 is like 1979 in that it was a mixed vintage of fairly light-bodied, early-maturing wines. For us at least, the best wines equal the best of 1979, but the results are somewhat more mixed. Renato Ratti said the wines range from medium quality to good. The real problem was the snow that fell before the harvest. Scarpa didn't like the quality of the grapes and produced no Barolo in 1980; neither did Rocche dei Manzoni or Marchese Fracassi. Giovanni Conterno produced a Barolo but no "Monfortino." Alfredo Currado told us it was a difficult vintage; one had to select the grapes carefully to make a good wine. Giuseppe Rinaldi said that for him the vintage was a good one, and Pio Boffa found the quality satisfactory.

Many experts give 1980 three stars. Based on our tastings of more than sixty different wines, some of them multiple times from some fifty producers, we find that the best wines certainly merit three stars. But more than a few received no marks from us. In all, we rate the vintage two stars minus. These rather light-bodied wines will mature fairly soon and make pleasant drinking from 1986 or 1987. The best should last.

Allesandria F.lli, Monvigliero (*4/85*). Overly tannic; shy of fruit; harsh, tannic finish.

Altare Elio, Cascina Nuova, Vigneto Aborina dell'Annunziata (*3 times 4/85*). Medium dark garnet; some fruit evident on the nose which is still a bit closed; moderate tannin, nice fruit; lacks some style; hard finish; still needs another two or three years. ★

Ascheri Giacomo (*twice 4/85*). Small nose; has tannin but not a lot of fruit. ★ −

Asteggiano Vincenzo (*4/85*). Light and fruity; overly simple. +

Barale F.lli (*ex-cask 6/82*). Well balanced; fairly rich for the vintage; shows promise. ★(★)

Barale F.lli, Castellero (*3 times 4/85*). Fairly well balanced; fruit up front gives way to a tannic firmness; has a resinlike aspect; a real success. ★★(+)

Borgogno F.lli Serio e Battista (*ex-vat 11/84*). Fruity nose which suggests blackberries; light to moderate tannin; lots of flavor; good quality only marred by some alcohol at the end. ★

Borgogno F.lli Serio e Battista, Vigna Cannubi (*ex-vat 11/84*). Expansive aroma; good fruit; already shows some class. ★(★)

Bovio Gianfranco, Gattera dell'Annunziata (*twice 2/85*). Aroma shows some development; moderate tannin, lively acidity; fairly well structured; a lot of flavor, good quality; finishes on a tannic note. ★★(+)

Cappellano Dott. Giuseppe (*1/85*). Surprisingly dark color; rich nose suggesting gravel and tar; moderate tannin, some firmness, a lot of fruit, young yet; a success for the vintage. ★★ (Avoid those in the weird bottle sold with the G. Troglia label.)

Cavollotto F.lli, Vigna Bricco Boschis (*ex-cask 2/85*). Fairly rich with a lot of tannin and a lot of fruit; thins out a bit toward the finish. ★

Cavallotto F.lli, Vigna Bricco Boschis-Conte Vassallo (*ex-cask 6/82*). Seems overly tannic, but the sense of a lot of fruit is there; might make a nice bottle in time, especially considering the way the San Giuseppe has developed over the same period. ★

Cavallotto F.lli, Vigna Bricco Boschis-San Giuseppe (*ex-cask 1/85*). Rich nose of fairly ripe fruit suggestive of strawberries and blackberries; lots of tannin but with the fruit to support it; needs a lot of time but should be worth the wait. ★★(★)

Ceretto Az. Agr. "Bricco Rocche," Brunate (*twice 2/85; 24,812 bottles*). Rich, ripe fruit rises out of the glass, with hints of berries, mint, vanilla, and flowers, fabulous nose; medium body, light tannin, and a lot of fruit; moderate length, nearly ready. ★★(★)

Ceretto Az. Agr. "Bricco Rocche," Prapò (*3 times 2/85; 11,908 bottles*). Nose offers little interest at this point; well balanced, nice fruit; on the light side. ★(+)

Ceretto, Zonchera (*2/85*). Forward rush of fruit

up front; seems almost sweet, a bit light but has style and elegance; light tannin, well balanced, very nice; nearly ready.★★(+)

Clerico (1/85). Cherrylike aroma, vaguely floral; moderate tannin and a surprising amount of fruit for the vintage; needs a few years yet, but potential evident.★★

Cogno-Marcarini, Brunate (twice 11/84). Lovely cherry, tobacco, tarry aroma; well balanced, with some tannin to lose, but a lot of flavor; already displays style.★★(★)

Cogno-Marcarini, La Serra (twice 11/84). Nice nose dominated at this point by cherries; very well balanced, good quality, some firmness; seems more closed than the Brunate, but the style is evident.★★(+)

Colla Paolo (4/85). Hot and heavy-handed, not unlike a southern wine; low in acid.

Colli Monfortesi di Fantino Conterno (4/85). Small cherrylike aroma; light tannin, light body; a bit simple.★ −

Conterno Aldo, Bricco Bussia Vigna Colonnello (twice 4/85; 5120 bottles). Surprising richness; nuances of tobacco and flowers; fairly long; one of the real successes of the vintage.★★★ −

Conterno Giacomo, Cascina Francia (3 times 4/85). Opaque color; reticent aroma but rich fruit evident and a touch of camphor and mushrooms; moderate tannin; has a lot of fruit, though locked in by the tannin at this time; the finish is quite tannic; difficult to predict.★(★?)

Denegri Lorenzo di Ca'Bianca (3 times 5/85). Some fruit evident on the nose and a hint of flowers; moderate tannin, but seems to have sufficient fruit; alcohol intrudes at the end.★

Fenocchio Riccardo, Pianpolvere Soprano (twice 4/85). Aroma has a forward fruitiness with suggestions of vanilla, almonds, tobacco, cherries, flowers, and raspberries; light and fruity, with a hint of cherries; light tannin; in all a soft, light, easy style that should make a nice luncheon wine.★ +

Fontanafredda (1/85). Lovely nose, full and fairly rich with hints of tartufi, mint, and berries; well balanced, some tannin to shed but also a lot of fruit; young but displays potential.★

Franco Fiorina (twice 5/85). Raspberry aroma with notes of tea and tobacco; entry on palate somewhat astringent; moderate tannin, some fruit; fairly well balanced; drinkable; not for long aging.★★ −

Giacosa Bruno, Rocche (ex-cask 10/81). A surprising amount of fruit but also tannin to shed; surprisingly well balanced for the vintage.★★

Giacosa Bruno, Vigna Rionda (11/84). Shows a lot of fruit and well balanced with some style; the most forward of the three crus.★★(★)

Giacosa Bruno, Villero (ex-cask 11/84). Aroma recalls mushrooms and tartufi with a floral note; fairly full-bodied, moderate tannin, heaps of flavor; firm and very young, but impressive quality.★★(★)

Giacosa F.lli (twice 4/85). Aroma a bit reticent, but some fruit evident; light to moderate tannin; some firmness, flavorful, note of licorice; pleasant drinking in spite of the tannin.★★

Granduca (1/85). Tobacco and tea on aroma that is still rather closed; some tannin but a lot of fruit, fairly well balanced, still needs more time to soften;

good quality though a bit short; shows promise.★(★)

Grasso, Vigna Gavarini-Chiniera (twice 2/85; enormous production of 2650 bottles). Aroma yields hints of cherries and flowers; light tannin, light body, but well balanced and elegant, with a lot of flavor; an earlier bottling displayed notes of tobacco and camphor and seemed more closed on the palate.★★(★)

Il Vecchio Tralcio (1/85). Smallish nose; overly tannic though some fruit evident; a bit shallow; this producer does better with white wines.

Mascarello Cantina (3 times—all in 1/85). Considering the quality of this Barolo, three times isn't enough; an elegant wine with a bouquet of flowers, tartufi, and vanilla; a lot of interest; especially well balanced with a lot of style; still has tannin to shed, but approachable; an elegant wine that exudes style and balance.★★★

Mascarello Giuseppe, Monprivato (4 times 4/85; 10,422 bottles plus larger sizes). Lovely nose with notes of tobacco and mushrooms; moderate tannin, sufficient fruit to balance; has an easy nature typical of the vintage.★★(+)

Massolino Giuseppe, Vigna Rionda (3 times 2/85). In all a light, soft, simple wine with a Zinfandel-like raspberry aroma and some spice; light-bodied, soft, and easy; for current consumption.★

Montezemolo Paolo Cordero di, Enrico VI Villero (2/85). Forward fruitiness with suggestions of cherries and prunes; light tannin, sweet, ripe fruit; fairly well balanced but quite forward; drinks nice now.★(★)

Montezemolo Paolo Cordero di, Monfalletto (2/85). Aroma of moderate intensity; fairly fruity and simple; light–medium body; light–moderate tannin and a sweetness; seems nearly ready.★★

Nicolello (4/85). Hot nose; low in fruit; unbalanced.

Oddero F.lli (twice 5/85). Lovely bouquet with nuances of cherries, tobacco, mushrooms, and flowers; a rush of fruit on entry that carries across the palate, marred by a touch of astringency; for early drinking.★★

Osvaldo Mauro (4/85). In flavor and structure reminiscent of a southern wine.

Palladino (twice 5/85). Some alcohol intrudes on nose, a lot of fruit evident, camphor note; fruity, light–moderate tannin; young but has style and balance.★★ −

Pio Cesare (ex-cask 1/85). Soft and well balanced, forward; quality evident; needs time but bound to make a good bottle.★★

E. Pira di Boschis (ex-cask 1/85). Vague chemical stink; seems overly tannic for the fruit; shallow; short tannic finish.

Ratti Renato, Marcenasco (1/85). Tobaccolike aroma; light tannin, fairly nice fruit, a little light but well balanced, will be ready early.★★

Ratti Renato, Marcenasco Conca (1/85; 8720 bottles) Tobacco and cherries on aroma; has tannin and fruit; will be ready early.★★

Ratti Renato, Marcenasco Rocche (1/85; 8560 bottles) The fruitiest of the three Barolos, with nice fruit, fairly forward; quality quite evident.★★(+)

Rinaldi Francesco, Cannubio (1/85; 10,000 bottles). Delicate perfume; a lot of style and elegance; a wine of quality, perhaps the best wine of the vintage.★★★

Rinaldi Giuseppe (ex-cask 11/84). Delicate berrylike aroma; some tannin to shed but fairly forward with nice fruit; a bit light but shows some quality.★★

1980

"Rocche" Costamagna *(2/85)*. Interesting aroma, with a minerally aspect and a hint of almonds; some tannin, rather light and a bit shallow, vaguely bitter; not a success.

"Rocche" Az. Vin. *(1/85)*. Strange nose; a bit shy on fruit; astringent; not a success.

Rosso Gigi, Vigneti della Cascina Arione *(2/85)*. Nice nose characteristic of nebbiolo, with hints of raspberries and camphor; light tannin, quite approachable, still a bit young, some firmness; needs a few years yet.★

Sandrone Luciano *(1/85; 2940 bottles)*. A lot of ripe fruit on nose; well balanced and stylish, surprisingly soft, light tannin; nearly ready.★★

Scarzello Giorgio *(4/85)*. Characteristic aroma, more toward the fruity end of the spectrum fairly good fruit, some acid at the edges; short finish that hints of tobacco.★

Scavino Alfonso, della Punta *(ex-cask 10/81)*. Seems rather light and overly tannic for the fruit, but difficult to fully assess at this point.

Scavino Paolo, Bric del Fiasc *(3 times 4/85; 5385 bottles)*. Characteristic Barolo aroma, some oak; moderately rich, light tannin; easy; not really ready, still some firmness, but will be soon.★★ –

Settimo Aurelio *(5/85)*. Nice nose; some tannin; good fruit; should be ready soon.★

Tenuta Carretta, Podere Cannubi *(4/85; 12,533 bottles)*. Perfumed aroma with a mushroomy, earthy, woodsy aspect; from the first taste the wine says *class;* well balanced, full of style and flavor, tannin to lose; needs more time.★★★

Tenuta Coluè di Massimo Oddero *(1/85)*. Typical aroma of fruit and tar; a bit young yet, but forward and nearly ready; should keep.★(★)

Tenuta La Volta di Cabutto Bartolomeo *(1/85)*. Mint and berries, rather a nice nose; rather simple flavors and fairly forward; soft and nearly ready.(★)

Tenuta Montanello *(1/85)*. Some tobacco on nose; moderate tannin, fairly nice fruit, though a bit light and forward; some tannin at the end.★

Vaira G. D., Bricco Viole *(ex-cask 2/85)*. Complex aroma; a fair amount of tannin; a mouthful of fruit; well structured; needs age but forward.★★

Vecchio Piemonte *(1/85)*. Corked.

Vietti, Briacca *(ex-cask 6/82)*. Delicate aroma with hints of flowers; delicate and harmonious, surprisingly forward though has tannin.★★

Vietti, Rocche *(9 times 4/85; 10,500 bottles)*. Aroma suggests truffles, cherries, blackberries, and tobacco; a lot of fruit though a bit light; quality quite evident; finishes rather tannic; needs some time.★★(+)

Voerzio Giacomo *(2/85)*. Light cherrylike aroma, touch of vanilla; light but sweet ripe fruit; light and soft, even a bit simple; a soft, easy style.★

1979 ★★+

Because of rain during the harvest and snow toward the end of it, the results were somewhat mixed. Overall 1979 was a good vintage of rather light Barolos that will be ready for drinking early. In fact, a number of them are showing well now, but another year or two will soften them further. Wines made from grapes picked during the rain were somewhat diluted; those picked before the rain and afterward made more successful Barolo.

Aldo Conterno considers the vintage on the same level as 1970 and 1974, and says 1983 was also similar. Giovanni Conterno describes the wines, at this stage at least, as still very young and dense. Pio Boffa again found the quality satisfactory. Renato Ratti ranks the vintage as good to very good. Scarpa, however, didn't produce any Barolo; they were dissatisfied with the grapes, which had been snowed on. This vintage has been given three stars; for us, two stars plus seems more appropriate. While the best wines merited three stars, many of the more than five dozen we tasted from nearly fifty different producers received one and two. No doubt about it, many good and very good wines were made, but also too many were not so good. This was the last vintage in which grapes were crushed in the old-fashioned way, by feet. Luigi Pira was the last producer in the zone to carry on the old tradition; he died in 1980.

Accademia Torregiorgi, Carpegna *(2/85)*. Aroma of fairly ripe fruit, vaguely of cherries and a hint of tobacco; light–moderate tannin, somewhat light but with some style; well balanced, a lot of flavor; a light gentle style, some elegance; nearly ready.★★(★)

Allesandria F.lli *(twice 1/85)*. Tobacco, tealike aroma; tannic. Is there enough fruit? Only time will tell; at this point it's doubtful.

Ascheri Giacomo *(twice 4/85)*. Some nebbiolo character evident in aroma; quite tannic but fruit is apparent. Is it sufficient? Needs perhaps another four or so years to find out.

Barale F.lli, Castellero riserva *(3 times 2/85)*. Nice nose though a bit light, vaguely floral, some berries and vanilla notes; light–moderate tannin, fairly nice fruit; already nice though it needs a few more years to develop and round out.★★

Bersano *(5/84)*. A simple aroma; light, soft, and gentle; a nice little red wine but lacks structure and personality.

Borgogno F.lli Serio e Battista riserva *(twice 3/85)*. Fairly full, typical nose with a tartufi note; some tannin, but there seems to be sufficient fruit to support it; alcoholic toward the end.★(+)

Borgogno F.lli Serio e Battista, Vigna Cannubi riserva *(twice 4/85)*. Full, fairly intense aroma with a tartufi note; quite tannic; some elegance; good fruit; needs a few years yet to soften and be at its best.★(★)

1979

Borgogno Giacomo riserva (*twice 5/85*). Nose is undeveloped, notes of tobacco and tea; moderate tannin, a bit light, but soft-centered with nice fruit; finishes on a tannic note; should make a nice bottle in a few years.★(+)

Bovio Gianfranco, Gattera dell'Annunziata (*twice 2/85*). Floral perfume over various types of fruit; moderate tannin, medium body; some style and elegance; nice fruit; still somewhat closed; say about three years to really show itself.★★(+)

Cascina Bruni di Veglio Pasqual (*ex-cask 1/85*). Lovely aroma; ripe fruit flavor; soft, light tannin, some spice; seems ready.★+

Casetta F.lli (*twice 5/85*). Brick to orange; not much aroma; has some tannin and also a fair amount of fruit; very tannic at the end; dull but drinkable.★−

Cauda Luigi (*1/85*). Has tannin, low in acid, a bit shy in fruit; structurally like a southern wine.

Cavallotto F.lli, Vigna Bricco Boschis (*ex-cask 11/84*). Vaguely floral; has a fair amount of tannin but with the fruit to back it up; still needs a few years yet.★(★)

Cavallotto F.lli, Vigna Bricco Boschis-Punta Marcello riserva (*twice 3/85*). Loads of fruit on the nose, some cherries; moderate tannin; fruity; fairly forward for this house, though needs a couple of years yet.★★−

Cavallotto F.lli, Vigna Bricco Boschis-San Giuseppe (*1/85*). Fairly rich aroma, has a vaguely brambley character; heaps of tannin but with a lot of fruit beneath; needs perhaps three to four years to soften and show its real quality.★(★)

Ceretto Az. Agr. "Bricco Rocche," Brunate (*3 times 2/85; 21, 813 bottles*). A lot of fruit on the nose which has a hint of mint, tartufi, and cherries; soft tannin; still backward but fuller and richer than is normal for this vintage; has richness of ripe fruit and a lot of style.★★(★)

Ceretto Az. Agr. "Bricco Rocche," Prapò (*twice 1/85; 11,868 bottles*. Richly fruited aroma with suggestions of vanilla and raspberries as well as a somewhat floral note; moderate tannin, some elegance; fruit all across the palate, licorice note.★★★−

Ceretto, Zonchetta (*twice 2/85; 18,656 bottles*). Vaguely floral and richly fruited aroma, has a hint of cassis and tar; moderate tannin, sweet ripe fruit; seems nearly ready, perhaps in '86.★★(+)

Conterno Aldo, Bricco Bussia Cicala (*twice 10/83; 5768 bottles*). Lovely aroma with an open fruitiness; a mouthful of fruit, light tannin, firm, enjoyable now but with room for improvement.★★+

Conterno Giacomo, Cascina Francia riserva (*twice 1/85*). Aroma of cinnamon and spice; medium body, somewhat unbalanced with overly high tannin for the fruit and some alcohol. Could it develop? It seemed better (★★) when tasted 11/84 from cask, though that was a different batch; this one was bottled 8/83.

Contratto *5/85*). Fruity aroma with a touch of flowers; a bit light, soft, smooth, room to improve; drinkable now, but give it a year or two.★★−

"Monfortino" di Giacomo Conterno (*ex-cask 11/84*). Lovely bouquet suggesting chestnuts and vanilla; young and not surprisingly more forward than the '78, but with a richness and concentration uncommon for the vintage.★★(★)

Coppo Luigi, Vigneto Brunate (*1/85; 1310 bottles*). Vague berrylike fruit on the nose, medium-bodied, soft, light tannin, fairly forward, a lighter style; has a tannic finish.★+

Coppo Luigi, Vigneto Castello (*1/85*). Less color and more age in appearance than the Brunate; floral, berrylike aroma; somewhat more tannic than Brunate and a bit leaner and firmer in structure; a nice wine, though a bit young.★(★)

Dosio (*twice 5/85*). Expansive aroma, varietal character with cherrylike fruit and flowers; moderate tannin, has fruit; somewhat uncomplicated though authentic.★+

Fenocchio Riccardo, Pianpolvere Soprano (*twice 4/85*). Lightly fruited aroma, has nuances of tobacco and cherries; some tannin to lose; has the fruit to back it up; coming ready; tannic finish.★+

Franco Fiorina riserva speciale (*twice 5/85*). Raspberries up front on nose, woodsy scents; still fairly tannic but with the stuffing to support it; try again in three years.★★+

Gemma (*4/85*). Mushrooms and cherries on aroma; a bit light, flavorful; quite nice now.★

Giacosa Bruno, Rocche (*ex-cask 11/84*) Big, richly fruited aroma; has a surprising fullness and richness for the vintage, quite young and with a lot of potential.★★(★)

Giacosa F.lli (*3 times 4/85; 16,800 bottles*). Lovely nose with champignons and flowers; moderate tannin, fruity; has quality; needs age.★★(+)

Grasso, Vigna Ginestra Case Matè (*twice 2/85; 3300 bottles*). Lovely nose, has a suggestion of camphor; fairly soft, light tannin; ready though room for improvement yet; has a gentle, elegant nature.★★+

Manzone Stefano Az. Agr. Ciabot del Preive, Castelletto (*twice 4/85*). Noticeable fruit on nose and palate; light tannin, fairly forward, some harshness at the end; in all, an agreeable wine.★−

Marchese Maurizio Fracassi Ratti Mentone (*11/84*). Expansive aroma suggestive of tartufi and tobacco; a feminine-style Barolo, delicate and elegant; some tannin (Barola).★★

Mascarello Cantina (*3 times 2/85*) Aroma has a richness and intensity that's uncommon for the vintage, truffle, cherry, and tealike notes; finely made; light–moderate tannin, elegant and stylish; impressive quality, with a very long finish.★★★

Mascarello Giuseppe, Monprivato (*3 times 4/85; 8516 bottles plus larger sizes*). Tobacco, cherry, tartufi aroma; similar to 1980, but firmer and more tannic; firm vein of tannin; has the stuffing and balance to carry that tannin; say three years.★★(★)

Mascarello Giuseppe, Villero (*4 times 4/85*). Aroma of cherries, tobacco, and flowers; moderate tannin, less than Monprivato; heaps of flavor; needs two or three years.★★(+)

Massolino Giuseppe, Vigna Rionda (*1/85*). Berrylike fruit on nose; light tannin, light body, soft, fruity, a bit simple and easy; ready. +

Montezemolo Paolo Cordero di, Enrico VI–Villero (*2/85*). Vague off-note mars the aroma, which recalls cherries; light-bodied, softer than the Monfalletto with more body and structure; tannin builds up at the end.★(+)

1979

Montezemolo Paolo Cordero di, Monfalletto *(2/85).* Nice nose though rather simple, fairly open, fruity, and fresh; light body, light tannin, easy fruity style that can improve; finish is short and rather tannic. ★(+)

Oddero F.lli *(4 times 5/85).* Nose has notes of tobacco and fruit; light tannin, sweep ripe fruit, accessible and soft; an easy style but quite nice; will improve over the next two years. ★★(+)

Ornato Paolo, Rocche *(twice 2/85).* Aroma of tar and nebbiolo fruit; some tannin, good fruit, forward; some tannin at the end. ★ +

Pio Cesare riserva *(4 times 3/85).* Intense aroma with tobacco, cherries, and oak; a lot of fruit, round and fairly soft though still has tannin to lose; has a forward fruitiness. ★★

E. Pira di Boschis *(1/85).* The last Barolo crushed by feet, which unfortunately didn't turn out the way it would have had Luigi Pira been around to tend and finish it; the aroma suggestive of grape pips and tobacco, light-bodied, surprisingly shy of fruit vis-à-vis the tannin; shallow. Where will it go?

Prunotto, Bussia riserva *(1/85; 13,227 bottles).* Color is deeper and younger in appearance than the Cannubi; aroma more closed; has a richness of fruit and a surprising softness; long finish; still has tannin to shed and quite a lot. ★★(★)

Prunotto, Cannubi riserva *(1/85, 13,220 bottles).* Perfumed bouquet has a tartufi note; well balanced, a mouthful of fruit and a soft center; still with tannin to lose. ★★(★)

Ratti Renato, Marcenasco *(4 times 11/83).* Fresh, fruit aroma is open; light tannin, gives way to a rush of fruit; enjoyable now but has room for improvement; some elegance. ★★

Ratti Renato, Marcenasco Conca *(5/83).* Aroma of cherries and tar; a lot of flavor, more tannin than the Marcenasco; still needs two or three more years. ★★ +

Ratti Renato, Marcenasco Rocche *(4 times 11/83; 7074 bottles).* Aroma is full and rich with fruit, flowers, truffles and tea; a mouthful of fruit, has tannin but deceptively soft, very well balanced; the most impressive of the three. ★★★

"Rocche" Costamagna, Vigna Riccardo riserva *(twice 2/85; 1450 bottles).* Tobacco, cherry, camphor aroma; light-bodied, moderate tannin, should be ready early; a fair amount of fruit. ★(+)

Rocche dei Manzoni riserva *(11/84).* Aroma is restrained with some alcohol in background; astringent on entry gives way to a lot of fruit; fairly well balanced with a suppleness, but deficient in Barolo character; still needs some time. ★

Rolfo Gianfranco *(1/85).* Nice fruit on nose and palate; moderate tannin, a bit light; could use more character but drinkable enough. ★

Rosso Gigi, Vigneti della Cascina Arione *(twice 2/85).* Strawberries rise up out of the glass, touch of camphor; moderate richness, a bit light and forward; exhibits some style, astringent finish; in all a bit light but fairly good. ★(+)

Saffirio F.lli Enrico e Giacomo *(11/84).* Big-fruited aroma, some cassis and tar; high tannin, moderate fruit; something is missing, but it's not unpleasant.

Savigliano Mario *(1/85).* Old-style Barolo aroma, more tar than fruit, also a tobacco note; overly tannic. Has some fruit, but is it enough?

Scavino Paolo, Bric del Fiasc riserva *(4 times 4/85; 5330 bottles).* Nice nose with some depth, richness, nebbiolo character and hints of tobacco, berries, and a touch of oak; a bit light with some tannin and nice fruit, nearly ready; well balanced; give it another year or two to soften further. ★★

Seghesio Renzo *(4/85).* Some oxidation apparent; overly tannic; unstructured.

Settimo Aurelio *(5/85).* Light but nice aroma; some tannin; fruity, easy, some character. ★★

Tenuta Carretta, Podere Cannubi *(twice 4/85; 12,600 bottles).* Aroma is closed in; a mouthful of fruit beneath the gobs of tannin makes this a promising bet for long-term growth potential; its style and class are already evident. ★★(★?)

Tenuta Cerequio (Vinicola Piemontese) *(2/85).* Tobacco, cherry, caramel, floral aspects on aroma; a lot of nice fruit in a forward, easier style, well balanced; a touch of mint and camphor on the finish, which is still tannic. ★★

Tenuta Montanello riserva speciale *(1/85).* Reticent aroma; moderate tannin; a lot of nice fruit in a softer, more accessible style; some firmness at the end; nearly ready; won't be a keeper. ★(+)

Tenuta Montanello, Vigneto dei Montello-Pini *(ex-cask 1/85).* A bit light but fairly well balanced; some tannin; shows more character than the previous wine. ★★

Vaira G. D., Vigneto Fossati *(twice 2/85; 1760 bottles).* Woodsy aroma, suggestions of pine, resin, and peppermint; soft-centered and supple, still some tannin; peppermint flavor, also on the finish. ★★(+)

Vietti, Castiglione Falletto *(2/85).* Vaguely floral aroma, also hints of tobacco and tar; seems to be aging faster than expected but quite nice; has flavor and length; still rather tannic at the end. ★★ −

Vietti, Rocche *(10 times 11/84).* Tobacco and cherry aroma with notes of tartufi, leather, and flowers; well balanced and stylish, soft and nearly ready; a lot of flavor, very long finish, some tannin and firmness at the end. ★★★

1978 ★★★

This vintage produced highly regarded wines from a very small crop—about 50 percent of normal—of ripe, mature grapes. These richly concentrated, fairly high-acid wines should be long-lived. At one time many authorities regarded '78 as equal to or even better than '71. Today this is rarely the case. Very few producers put it on the same level as '71 or even '82. The Ceretto brothers are one exception; they consider their '78s even better than the '71s. Aldo Conterno considers it the equal or nearly the equal of '71 and similar in quality to '82. Bruno Giacosa said they are grand wines that might equal the '71s but will not be as long-lived. Bartolo Mascarello said that '71 is clearly the better vintage. Renato Ratti regards them as fabulous, grand wines on a par with '82, both wines to lay down. Pio Boffa described them as bigger then the '74s but with less intensity than the '71s. Giovanni Conterno said that in weight and depth of flavor they are between '71 and '82. According to Alfredo Currado, these high-acid wines will be long-lived; they are still closed and need at least five or six more years to really show their quality.

We disagree with those who rate 1978 at four stars. Based on more than six dozen different wines tasted from more than fifty producers since 1979, we rate this vintage at three stars. There is no question, though, that the best wines merit four, or they will when they reach maturity.

Accademia Torregiorgi, Arnulfo (2/85). Nose somewhat closed with a suggestion of tobacco; moderate tannin, fairly well balanced, more open on palate than on nose; a softer, gentler style with a firm tannic vein; not ready but beginning to open; finish is still tannic.★★

Ascheri Giacomo riserva (twice 4/85). Characteristic aroma, vague tartufi note; heaps of tannin, seems to have sufficient fruit to support it; time will tell.★

Barale F.lli (6/85). Minerally aroma has suggestions of tobacco and tea as well as a vague cherrylike note; still has considerable tannin, some astringency from the tannin and somewhat high acid; the fruit is there, however; quite young, although this bottle seemed to be off.★(★)

Barale F.lli, Castellero riserva (6/85). Moderately intense varietal aroma, notes of berries and cherries; fairly high acid; still young but the stuffing is there.★★(+)

Bel Colle (10/82). Pale color; atypical aroma; nothing to it.

Bersano riserva speciale (5/84). Fruity aroma has a sense of oak, lacks depth, rather simple; softer, gentler style; drinkable now; more like a Nebbiolo than a Barolo.

Borgogno F.lli Serio e Battista riserva speciale (11/84). Big nose, rich fruit suggestive of blackberries, some alcohol intrudes; rich fruit in mouth; less tannin than expected, balanced; needs a few years but almost drinkable now; finishes short with some alcohol.★(+)

Borgogno F.lli Serio e Battista, Vigna Cannubi riserva speciale (twice 4/85). Deeper color and richer bouquet than the above, with a suggestion of tartufi, blackberries, some alcohol intrudes; has tannin, fairly nice fruit and balance; still backward but shows promise.★(★)

Borgogno Giacomo riserva (twice 1/85). Characteristic aroma with a note of tartufi, marred by some volatile acidity; a nice wine that lacks the intensity of the vintage; moderate tannin, fairly nice fruit, still undeveloped; some potential, tannic finish.★(+)

Brero Cav. Luigi (1/85). Caramel candy aroma; low fruit, moderate tannin.

Brezza Giacomo (ex-cask 10/79). Very light and fruity; not a lot of tannin.

Brovia F.lli (ex-vat 6/82). Nice nose with hints of oak and mushroom; moderate intensity; some alcohol evident (14.7 percent); quite tannic, unstructured, seems to be losing its fruit; not a success.

Cascina Bruni di Veglio Pasqual, Vigneto di Sori (1/85; 5200 bottles). Nebbiolo character and fruit evident on nose which is still somewhat closed; moderate tannin, nice fruit, fairly forward and surprisingly soft.★

Casetta F.lli (twice 5/85). Tarlike aroma has cherry and floral notes; some tannin; nearly ready; a bit light and simple; somewhat common.★ −

Cauda Luigi (1/85). Very reminiscent of a southern wine on aroma, structure, and flavor.

Cavallotto F.lli, Vigna Bricco Boschis (ex-cask 1/81). Rich and concentrated, with a lot of tannin, but soft-centered.★(★)

Cavallotto F.lli, Vigna Bricco Boschis–Colle Sud Ovest (twice 1/85). Lovely aroma, fairly rich with suggestions of strawberries and blackberries; quite tannic but with the fruit to support it; will need some time to be ready but should make a good bottle.★(★)

Cavallotto F.lli, Vigna Bricco Boschis–S. Giuseppe (6/82). Fairly rich aroma still somewhat closed, has a hint of mushrooms; rich and full of flavor as well as tannin; young but with potential evident.★★(+)

Ceretto "Bricco Rocche," Brunate (6 times 1/85, 10,846 bottles). Aroma has an intensity of ripe fruit, deep and profound; enormous richness, exceptional balance; not ready but tempting.★★★(★)

Ceretto "Bricco Rocche," Prapò (3 times 1/85). Bouquet seems somewhat closed but has the richness of ripe fruit; fairly tannic, but the fruit is evident right across the palate; very long finish; young but tempting—resist.★★★(+)

Ceretto, Zonchetta (3 times 3/83). Lovely, deep, rich, intense aroma; full of flavor and style; an elegant wine that lacks some length at this point; try again in '86 or '87.★★(★)

Cogno-Marcarini, Brunate (ex-cask 10/81; the last cask, all the rest had been bottled). Expansive aroma recalling raspberries and mushrooms; well structured, has style, balance, flavor, and elegance; very well made, classic, impressive.★★★(★)

Colla Paolo, della Serra (4/85). Some oxidation; a lot of tannin; deficient in fruit.

Conterno Aldo, Bussia Soprana (3/83). Enormous richness on nose; richly concentrated with a lot of weight and extract; impressive quality; resist the temptation until '86 or '87 at least.★★★(★)

Conterno Giacomo, "Monfortino" (ex-cask 11/84). Very deep color; aroma of cherries and tar; sweet, rich, ripe fruit; a wine of classic dimensions that will need many years to shed its considerable tannin and evolve, but its quality is evident now.★★★(?★)

Contratto riserva (5/85). Aroma of berries with floral notes; moderate tannin, then loads of fruit; at the end, more tannin.★★(+)

Dosio riserva speciale (3 times 5/85). Barnyard aspect to aroma; better on palate; some tannin, lacks intensity of the vintage; drinkable enough if overly simple; vaguely bitter aftertaste.★ −

Fontanafredda (12/83). Richly intense aroma recalls tar, flowers, and fruit; has tannin to shed, well balanced, nice flavor; give it a few years.★★

Fontanafredda, Vigna Gattinera (1/85). Deeper color than the Lazzarito; nose more closed; firmer and

1978

more tannic; closed and backward as well but displays potential.★(★)

Fontanafredda, Vigna La Delizia *(12/83)*. Richly fruited aroma; fairly forward and soft, though tannin still there; quality evident.★★(+)

Fontanafredda, Vigna La Rosa *(twice 1/85)*. Color seems a shade lighter than the other crus; mushroom and truffles on the nose; seems softer and more open than Gattinera or Lazzarito but also the fullest and most accessible; a touch of almonds in the finish.★★(+)

Fontanafredda, Vigna Lazzarito *(twice 1/85)*. Richly fruited aroma with touches of camphor, mushrooms, and tartufi; quite tannic and firm, a lot of nice fruit, but needs time to soften and develop; quality evident.★★(+)

Franco Fiorina *(3 times 5/83)*. Aroma brings up cherries, tobacco, and grappa in a nice way; full of fruit and flavor; needs time to develop but approachable now.★★(★)

Gemma *(twice 4/85)*. Nice fruit on the nose; some tannin and firmness; flavorful; a bit light at the end.★(+)

Giacosa Bruno, Arionda *(ex-cask 11/84)*. Very deep in color; aroma is rich, deep, and intense, profound; on the palate enormous fruit and tannin, finely structured, a wine of classic dimensions; sure to be one of the stars of the vintage.★★★(★)

Giacosa F.lli *(3 times 4/85)*. Intense, penetrating aroma; heaps of tannin, with the stuffing to support it, rich in fruit; shows a lot of promise.★★(★)

Granduca riserva speciale *(1/85)*. Nose is quite closed with some fruit evident; tannic entry gives way to ripe fruit; needs perhaps two years to soften.★(★)

Grasso, Vigna Gavarini-Runcot *(twice 2/85; 3000 bottles)*. Fairly rich and intense aroma of ripe fruit with notes of camphor and tobacco; well balanced, light tannin, more elegant than powerful; tempting now but will certainly improve; well structured.★★(★)

Grimaldi Cav. Carlo e Mario, Az. Agr. Groppone *(4/85; 4500 bottles)*. A simple little wine with light tannin.

Marchesi di Barolo, Vigna Cannubi riserva *(10/82; 8450 bottles)*. Fairly rich but somewhat reticent aroma vaguely reminiscent of tea; has a sweetness to it; still needs further age but surprisingly forward; while it is very good, it doesn't live up to either the vintage or the vineyard.★★ −

Mascarello Cantina *(11/84)*. Beautiful robe, garnet with orange reflections; expansive bouquet rises from the glass and fills the room; enormous fruit and concentration; exudes style and elegance, exceptional quality; if this isn't *the* wine of the vintage, it certainly comes close; a wine of meditation, of contemplation.★★★★

Mascarello Giuseppe, Monprivato *(ex-cask 6/82)*. Fairly rich nose suggestive of mushrooms and tartufi; full-bodied, with richness and concentration; well balanced, has a lot of tannin but not apparent at first because of the enormous amount of fruit.★★(★)

Massolino Giuseppe, Vigna Rionda *(twice 2/85)*. Aroma still somewhat closed but hints of flowers, vanilla, and camphor; light tannin, light-bodied, fairly soft, easy style; lacks richness expected from the vintage but nice fruit; surprisingly forward; medium length.★

Montezemolo Paolo Cordero di *(ex-cask 10/80)*.

Fruity aroma; a forward rush of ripe fruit gives way to light tannin; well balanced; should be a fine bottle in three or four years.★★(★)

Oddero F.lli *(5 times 5/85)*. Nose somewhat ungiving though with a tobacco and tarry aspect; fairly tannic but with the fruit to support it, seems almost sweet, somewhat astringent at the end; has quality; give it four or five more years.★★(+)

Oddero Luigi *(4/85)*. Lacking in flavor, structure, and character.

Ornato Paolo, Rocche *(ex-cask 10/81)*. Very deep color; aroma is rich and concentrated; balanced with considerable flavor and tannin; medium length.★ +

Palladino, S. Bernardo riserva *(5/85)*. Some firmness; moderate tannin; needs some age but potential evident.★(★ −)

Palladino, Vigna Riunda *(1/85)*. Nose has a harshness; moderate tannin, fairly well balanced, a lot of nice but undeveloped youthful fruit.★(★)

Pavese Livio *(1/85)*. Ripe fruit aroma; some tannin; a lighter softer style of Barolo that is simple and quite accessible; forward and ready though it might improve somewhat.(★)

Pio Cesare *(4 times 3/85)*. Aroma somewhat reticent, oak, licorice, and a hint of chocolate; rich, ripe fruit, moderate tannin; needs a few years but already shows a roundness and smoothness of texture, probably from the *barrique*.★★(★)

E. Pira *(twice 1/85 and ex-cask 10/79)*. Minerally aroma, some fruit and tobacco; lacks some weight and definition, a bit shallow, seems overly tannic for the fruit though not a bad wine, nor a success either. The wine tasted ex-cask in Oct. '79 had a rich, expansive aroma and exceptional balance with raspberries on the aroma and palate; at the time we expected a lot, but...

Prunotto, Bussia *(3 times 1/85, 12,525 bottles)*. More truffles and mushrooms on aroma than fruit; on palate rich, ripe fruit under a mouthful of tannin; clearly needs a lot of age but should be worth the wait; try again in '88 or '89.★★(★)

Prunotto, Cannubi *(twice 1/85, 6,195 bottles)*. Lovely aroma still somewhat reticent; on the palate gives an initial impression of sweet, ripe fruit that gives way to a lot of tannin; might be ready before the Bussia, but give it also until '88 or '89.★★★(+)

Prunotto, Ginestra *(twice 10/83)*. Reticent aroma; balanced, firm, a bit rough but a lot of fruit as well as tannin; probably will mature the slowest of the three crus.★(★★)

Ratti Renato, Marcenasco *(1/85 magnum)*. Aroma still closed somewhat but has hints of cherries, tobacco, and grape pips; very well balanced with some tannin and a load of fruit; nearly ready but hold off until '88 or '89.★★(★)

Rinaldi Francesco *(1/85)*. Very dense color; aroma is deep and rich; a lot of tannin, richly fruited, very young, but its style and elegance are apparent; a gentler, more elegant style of Barolo; tempting now but, like many other fine wines of this vintage, best held until '88 or '89 at the least.★★★(★)

Rinaldi Giuseppe *(11/84 magnum)*. Richly intense and concentrated bouquet suggests cassis; enormous core of fruit beneath a tannic structure, seems more forward at first due to the rich, sweet, mouth-filling

1978

fruit; a classic Barolo that needs time and will surely be worth the wait.★★★(★)

"Rocche" Costamagna, Vigna Riccardo riserva *(2/85; 2000 bottles)*. Tobacco, cherry aroma, fairly intense; a lot of tannin, a bit astringent; good but not special; could use more style.★(★)

Rocche dei Manzoni riserva *(twice 11/84)*. Fairly full bouquet of tar and nebbiolo fruit; has some tannin and fruit but lacks the weight and concentration of the vintage, though admittedly has a nicely fruited middle palate; could use more style.★(★)

"Roche" Az. Vin. riserva speciale *(1/85)*. Fruity aroma has a touch of tar; fairly sweet fruit up front, then astringent and tannic; fairly firm; not a bad wine but not special either.

Rosso Gigi, Vigneti della Cascina Arione *(twice 2/85)*. Vaguely floral, ripe fruit aroma recalls blackberries and a hint of tar; medium body, light–moderate tannin, nice flavor; could improve but drinkable enough now.★ +

Scarpa, Le Coste *(2/85; 15,703 bottles)*. Complex bouquet suggestive of mint, green leaves, tar, resin, and cherries; a mouthful of soft tannin gives way to enormous fruit; strikingly well balanced; very tannic at the end.★★★ +

Scavino Alfonso, della Punta *(10/81)*. Reticent aroma offers some fruit and a touch of tar; medium body, a fair amount of tannin; the fruit is evident; should be ready early, about '84 or '85.★(★)

Scavino Paolo, Bric del Fiasc *(3 times 4/85; 2360 bottles)*. Some oak over a richly fruited aroma; a bit astringent; fruity; has an oak component; good.★★(+)

Seghesio Renzo *(4 times 4/85)*. Has tannin and some fruit but somewhat shallow and unbalanced; not a success, though not offensive either.

Sobrero Filippo *(5/84)*. Color is black; bouquet has a richness and intensity though still somewhat reticent; on the palate an incredible mouthful of refined fruit, exceptionally balanced; young and full-bodied but tempting now.★★★(★)

Tenuta Carretta, Podere Cannubi *(twice 4/85; 7260 bottles)*. Intense aroma, tobacco, vaguely floral with notes of cherries and berries; very well balanced; masses of fruit and gobs of tannin; years from ready, but everything is there to make a splendid bottle; class already evident.★★★(+)

Tenuta Cerequio (Vinicola Piemontese) *(2/85)*. A lot of fruit on nose but not particularly complex; a mouthful of nice fruit over moderate tannin; medium body; still young.★★(★)

Tenuta La Volta di Cabutto Bartolomeo *(1/85)*. Aroma of berrylike fruit; light tannin, forward fruit, fairly well balanced; light and surprisingly ready for the vintage; simple, might make a nice luncheon wine.(★)

Tenuta Montanello riserva speciale *(1/85)*. Aroma still somewhat closed and undeveloped; ripe fruit seems almost sweet, moderate tannin; finishes with a hint of licorice and a buildup of tannin; give it two or three more years.★(★★)

Terre del Barolo, Brunate *(ex-cask 12/80)*. Has character and flavor, fairly well balanced, less tannin and softer than the Rocche.★(★)

Terre del Barolo, Rocche *(ex-cask 12/80)*. Well structured, some firmness, more to it than the Brunate.★(★ +)

Vaira G. D. *(twice 2/85)*. Fairly deep color; intensely rich bouquet, vaguely floral; a lot of fruit but still firm; needs a few years yet but quality evident.★★(+)

Vietti, Briacca *(3 times 6/82; 2000 bottles)*. A shade deeper than the Rocche; delicate floral perfume; lively and richly flavored with superb balance and some elegance; at this point it seems a bit fuller than the Rocche.★★★(★)

Vietti, Rocche *(10 times between 4/80 and 2/85)*. Dense color; bouquet reveals enormous richness and fragrance with hints of licorice, flowers, tea, tobacco, and cherries; incredible concentration of rich, ripe fruit; so well balanced that the tannin hardly seems evident at first; very young but even now a wine of meditation.★★★(★)

Villadoria Marchese riserva speciale *(twice 6/85)*. Baked, hot nose, ditto the taste—ugh!

Voerzio Giacomo *(ex-cask 12/80)*. Light but nice aroma; medium body, good fruit, some tannin; a bit fleeting at the end.(★)

1977 0

Only 1972 was worse in the decade. There was a lot of rain throughout 1977. Numerous producers didn't bottle a Barolo. Bartolo Mascarello declassified his entire nebbiolo crop to Nebbiolo delle Langhe. Alfredo Currado also didn't produce a Barolo in '77, nor did "Rocche" Costamagna, Marchese Fracassi, or Aldo Conterno. Giovanni Conterno said the vintage was so bad that he didn't even pick his grapes. Luciano Rinaldi rates it as among the worst ever. The best wines were at one time, however, fairly good if not special. The Ceretto brothers selected carefully and managed to produce 6500 bottles of Prapò (instead of the usual 13,000 to 15,000). We found it quite nice, surprisingly good; without question, it was the Barolo of the vintage.

Overall we give the vintage a rating of zero today. If you have any left in your cellar, drink them up; there's no reason to hold them any longer.

Ascheri Giacomo *(10/82)*. Light to pale color; some va; light-bodied; some flavor.

Cavallotto F.lli, Vigna Bricco Boschis *(ex-cask 12/80)*. Fruity aroma; moderate tannin, fairly good fruit for the year; lacks some structure.(★)

Ceretto "Bricco Rocche," Prapò or Prapò–Riccardo I *(6 times 11/84 at the winery; 6376 bottles)*. Bouquet of leather, berrries, cherries, underbrush, and tobacco; still some tannin over a nicely fruited core; a bit light in body, very good indeed, no need to hold it any longer.★★

Ceretto, Zonchetta *(4 times 3/83; 14,587 bottles)*.

1977

Light to pale garnet; light nose with moderate fruit marred by some alcohol; light-bodied, fairly nice on palate although some roughness; not to keep; some signs of drying out on the finish.★ −

Franco Fiorina *(3/83)*. Pale brick color; aroma recalls wheat and toast; moderate to light fruit, some tannin, nice flavors; not to keep, but a nice drinkable luncheon wine.★ −

Granduca *(3/83)*. Pale garnet; some fruit evident on nose and palate, but has harsh edges. Drinkable, but so what?

Montezemolo Paolo Cordero di, Monfalletto *(3/83)*. Nice nose; has a surprising richness but then seems overly tannic; in all not a bad bottle and certainly a success.★ −

Ratti Renato *(twice 2/85)*. Light tawny toward onionskin; characteristic Barolo aroma of tar and flowers; a lot of flavor, some alcohol intrudes; fading fast; was better in early 1983 when it merited ★ − .

Sandrone Francesco, Zona Cannubi *(10/81)*. Aroma has hints of kirsch and tar; a little light, some tannin, fairly nice fruit; not bad for the year.★

1976 ★ −

The one strong point of the '76 vintage is perhaps its position between 1975 and 1977; it stands out as the best of this trio of mediocre vintages. Bartolo Mascarello describes the wines as rather similar to '73. Renato Ratti said the wines ranged from so-so to medium. Giuseppe Rinaldi and Marchese Fracassi produced very little Barolo; Giovanni Conterno produced none. Very few wines amounted to much. Cogno-Marcarini, Paolo Cordero di Montezemolo, Aldo Conterno, and Renato Ratti were quite interesting at one time.

The wines for the most part should already have been drunk up. The best can still be pleasant drinking. We give the vintage one star minus.

Ascheri Giacomo *(10/82)*. Pale garnet; va mars the bouquet; better on the palate, though lacks structure and flavor; drying out.

Brovia F.lli, Vigneti di Rocche *(twice 11/80)*. Perfumed bouquet; some tannin, but the fruit seems sufficient for it; very good for the vintage.★ −

Casetta F.lli *(10/82)*. Pale; light nose and palate; not much to it, though drinkable.

Cavollotto F.lli, Vigna Bricco Boschis *(5 times 6/82)*. A bit closed; seems overly tannic, not a lot of fruit; some dullness; it was better in cask; should've been bottled sooner.

Cogno-Marcarini, Brunate *(2/82)*. Bouquet of almonds and fruit, also a touch of tartufi, moderately intense; soft and fruity with kirschlike notes; some style; medium length.★★

Conterno Aldo, Bricco Bussia Vigna Colonnello *(4/81; 4970 bottles)*. Nice nose; some tannin, well balanced; a lot of flavor.★★ −

Contratto riserva *(twice 3/83 and 6/85)*. Bottle of 3/83: Brick rim; bouquet offers hints of fruit and flowers; has the flavor and the tannin but lacks the structure; still in all, not bad.★ −

Bottle of 6/85: Fragrant, perfumed bouquet, woodsy, tobacco nuances; shows age on the palate; still has flavor but beginning to dry out.★ +

Fenocchio Giacomo *(4/80)*. Some alcohol intrudes on aroma; rather light, a lot of fruit, some tannin, perhaps too much; harsh finish.★ −

Montezemolo Paolo Cordero di, Enrico VI *(12/80)*. Good color; aroma somewhat subdued; soft, nice fruit; fairly well balanced; some style. ★★

Montezemolo Paolo Cordero di, Monfalletto *(3 times 3/83)*. Medium garnet, orange rim; nose yields up hints of cherries, flowers, tar, and Barolo character; some refinement; a lot of flavor; well made; very nice now, not to keep.★★

Morando riserva *(twice 2/83 and 3/83)*. Very pale color; one bottle had some volatile acidity, the other noticeable oxidation. In all a dull wine with no future and little or no interest.

Osvaldo Mauro *(4/80)*. A big zero; atypical Barolo.

Prunotto, Bussia *(3/83)*. Pale; some oxidation and some fruit on aroma; overly tannic, lacks structure and weight, but not bad with food.

Ratti Renato *(7 times 6/85)*. Medium garnet, orange rim; complex aroma of tobacco and tea, fruit, and tar; camphor, wood, and camomile on palate; still some tannin; light; still good, though starting to fade.★

"Roche" Az. Vin. *(11/80)*. Odd aroma; high in tannin, moderate fruit, high acid; in short, unbalanced and light.

Veglio Angelo *(4/80)*. Aroma suggestive of corn; fairly soft, some tannin and fruit; ready.★ −

Voerzio Giacomo *(12/80)*. Aroma is somewhat alcoholic; rather light and somewhat unbalanced; perhaps too much tannin for the fruit, but drinkable enough.

1975 ★ −

Hail took its toll in some vineyards, reducing the crop by 50 percent or more. Renato Ratti said the vintage was better even than '76 or '77, as did Bartolo Mascarello, who also found it superior to '73. Alfredo Currado said the wines were not especially good, medium quality perhaps. Marchese Fracassi and Giovanni Conterno, once again, didn't produce a Barolo. Cavallotto, on the other hand, said for them the wines were good. Very few wines amounted to much. Pira and Ratti were two notable exceptions.

1975

We found the wines light and fairly forward, wines that at their best offered pleasant drinking, but not serious wines. For the most part they should have been drunk up a few years ago.

Brezza Giacomo (10/79). Color shows age; alcohol and va evident on aroma; nice entry but shallow; short alcoholic aftertaste.

Brovia F.lli (11/80). Some fruit on nose and palate; somewhat deficient in flavor; a surprising amount of tannin.

Cavallotto F.lli, Vigna Bricco Boschis riserva speciale (5 times 10/81). Medium brick red; fairly nice nose; fruit fairly soft; not at all bad; some bottles showed noticeable oxidation from overlong wood aging, but the best bottles deserve ★.

Ceretto, Zonchetta (10/79). Aroma has some oak and nice fruit; considerable tannin for the fruit, somewhat shallow; short, somewhat alcoholic aftertaste.

Colla Paolo (4/80). Lacks aroma, body, substance, and distinction; has tannin and moderate flavor.

Fontanafredda (twice 3/83 and 5/83). One bottle was soft and smooth, quite nice for the vintage★; the other suffered from some oxidation and was unbalanced with tannin.

Gemma (3 times 3/85). Characteristic tar and floral aroma, vague mushroomlike note; overly tannic on entry; fruit in the center; surprisingly still good.★ –

Granduca riserva (twice 12/81 and 2/83). One bottle was shot, the other surprisingly drinkable though with an odd nose; quite soft and lacked some character.

Molino Guido (4/80). Aroma has tarry notes on an alcoholic background; has tannin but insufficient fruit; some alcohol mars the finish.

E. Pira di Luigi Pira (4 times 2/85). Dark brickish robe; expansive perfumed bouquet; soft, round, and very smooth; has tannin which shows more on the finish; still very good but approaching the end of its useful life.★★ +

Ratti Renato, Marcenasco (twice 11/83). Lovely bouquet suggestive of tobacco, cherries, tartufi, and vaguely of cassis; soft and round, still some tannin; very ready.★★

Tenuta La Volta di Cabutto Bartolomeo (twice 4/80). Oxidized both times.

Tenuta Montanello (3/83). Some oxidation; lacking in fruit; harsh.

1974 ★★+

Many experts and producers rate this vintage highly. Alfredo Currado puts it in the second rank after '71, '82, and '78. Renato Ratti considers it very good to great. Bruno Giacosa places it in the top rank. Giovanni Conterno describes the wines as refined and masculine, while Pio Boffa said the '74s have less tannin and intensity than the '71s.

Today, of the more than five dozen different wines we've tasted, too many received no marks (or negative ones); very few earned three stars or more. Most wines seem to be ready now, and only the best will improve further. In all, we find the vintage has not lived up to expectations, though without question a few splendid wines were made. Our overall opinion today is summed up by two stars plus.

Ascheri Giacomo (twice 10/82). Chocolate note on the aroma; seems overly tannic for the fruit; finishes on a harsh note.

Barale F.lli (6/82). Deep, rich, complex bouquet; palate almost sweet with ripe fruit; still has tannin to shed but quality and style evident; very good indeed.★★★

Barale F.lli riserva (6/85). Warm nose, some seaweed in the background; high acid, a bit thin; past its best.

Borgogno F.lli Serio e Battista riserva speciale (3 times 3/85). Two bottles were compared in Nov. '84. One had been transferred and filtered to remove the sediment; the other still had some. Along with the sediment, flavor and character were also removed. The wine was shallow and short, offering very little interest. The other bottle, which contained some sediment, had a beautiful brick-orange robe and a fairly rich bouquet; it had tannin and fruit and some character though marred by an alcoholic finish.★ The bottle of 3/85 had a vaguely hot nose with a baked character in the background, some nebbiolo fruit evident; light tannin; fairly ready; not much character.★ –

Borgogno F.lli Serio e Battista, Vigna Cannubi riserva speciale (3/85). Characteristic nebbiolo aroma; flavorful; tails off toward the finish; ready now.★ +

Borgogno Giacomo riserva (twice 9/83). Brick with orange rim; light nose, some harshness; moderate tannin; nice flavor; still young but flavorful; offers more on the palate than on the nose; needs perhaps two or three more years.★

Bosca Luigi (2/80). Very poor; lacks body, flavor, structure, and character; mercifully it has no finish either.

Brezza Giacomo (3 times 4/80). Aroma rather closed though some fruit is evident along with tealike notes; somewhat light but has fruit and tannin; could use more weight but drinkable; slightly bitter finish.★ –

Burlotto riserva (4/80). Although the bottle we tasted was slightly corked, the wine showed some quality, especially in the structure. Unfortunately, we never had an opportunity to try another.★★(?)

Cavallotto F.lli, Vigna Bricco Boschis riserva speciale (8 times 12/83). Aroma recalls tar and varnish over cherrylike fruit; seems overly tannic and drying out though drinkable; the bottles from three years earlier were considerably better; in fact, they even seemed a bit too young.

Ceretto, Grignore (3/80). Expansive bouquet that's richly concentrated; lots of tannin and heaps of flavor; fine quality; still young but quality evident.★★(★)

Ceretto, La Morra (1/82; 17,700 bottles). Fairly

1974

rich, intense aroma; quite tannic but with sufficient fruit in reserve; give it perhaps three years.★★(★)

Ceretto, Zonchetta *(1/85; 16,548 bottles and 2100 magnums)*. Complex bouquet with lots of woodsy nuances; moderate tannin; fruit seems a bit shy but tasty enough, could even improve.★(★)

Cogno-Marcarini, Brunate *(4 times 1/84)*. Floral bouquet recalls tobacco and cherries; soft with a tannic vein; a shade astringent but still in all very good. An earlier bottle seemed to offer more depth of flavor without the astringency.★★ +

Colla Paolo *10/78)*. Lacks aroma; a lightweight little wine with some fruit and some tannin; overall undistinguished and without character.

Conterno Aldo, "Gran Bussia" Vigna Bricco Cicala *(3 times 5/82; 5382 bottles)*. Richly concentrated bouquet and palate; still has tannin to shed; a full-bodied Barolo that needs time, though its splendid quality is apparent now.★★★

Conterno Giacomo riserva *(9/83)*. Full, rich aroma, character of Barolo, with a cherrylike note; still tannic but with considerable substance; bitter, cherrylike finish.★★(★)

Conterno Giacomo, "Monfortino" *(ex-cask 11/84)*. Aroma is fairly expansive with suggestions of flowers and chestnuts; tannic and firm, with a lot of fruit beneath; seems surprisingly young, with hints of better things to come.★★(★)

Conterno Giacomo, "Monfortino" riserva speciale *(twice 1/85 and 4/85)*. Bottle of 1/85: Intense bouquet with a hint of tobacco and freshness of fruit; a mouthful of tannin gives way to immense fruit and a hint of licorice, enormous richness but quite tannic, robust; finish is quite long; give it at least four or five years; it should be long-lived.★★(★ +) Bottle of 4/85: Tarry aroma has a touch of oxidation; a mouthful of tannin. Is there enough fruit? Difficult to say. Hardly seems like the same wine tasted months earlier; perhaps an off bottle.

Contratto *(8/81)*. Richly intense bouquet suggestive of tar and flowers; full-bodied, a lot of flavor, still has tannin to shed.★★(+)

Contratto riserva *(6/85)*. Corked.

Damilano Dott. Giacomo *(3/84)*. Ripe fruit aroma with a minty note; has tannin and good fruit but not a lot of Barolo character; finish is quite tannic.★ −

Dellavalle F.lli *(11/80)*. Color rather light; not much aroma; some tannin and fruit but lacks distinction and character; finishes on a bitter note.

Dosio reserva speciale *(3 times 5/85)*. Characteristic Barolo aroma; moderate tannin; still has some fruit but beginning to dry out; overly tannic finish; drink up.★

Einaudi Luigi *(twice 10/83)*. Some va mars the aroma; fairly tannic and fairly fruity; in all a nice glass of Barolo.★(★)

Fenocchio Giacomo *(11/80)*. Overly tannic, though it does have some fruit; oxidized; it could have been a good bottle.

Fontanafredda *(1/82)*. Aroma of tar and flowers; fairly rich; has tannin but enjoyable now due to the amount of fruit; some harshness; tannin builds up at the end.★

Fontanafredda, Vigna La Rosa *(5 times 1/85)*.

Nose offers more fruit than Lazzarito, also a touch of camphor and tar; fairly soft entry; some tannin but nearly ready; medium length.★ +

Fontanafredda, Vigna Lazzarito *(1/85)*. Tarry aroma recalls camphor, cheese, and wood, vaguely seaweed; tannic entry, soft center over a tannic framework; has a lot of flavor but perhaps too tannic for the fruit.(★)

Franco Fiorina *(twice 4/82)*. Floral perfume with hints of tar and fruit; well balanced, moderate tannin, tasty, some style, well made.★★

Giacosa Bruno, Vigna Rionda *(twice 11/80)*. Dark color; nose somewhat backward but displays a richness of fruit; exceptional balance with a lot of extract and flavor; quite young but especially fine quality.★★★(+)

Granduca riserva speciale *(12/84)*. Aroma rather light though characteristic, with fruity overtones; light tannin, soft, round, and fruity; lacks some weight but a drinkable, small-scale Barolo.

"La Brenta d'Oro," Cantina d'Invecchiamento *(11/78)*. Smallish nose; rather light-bodied but nice flavor on entry; shallow; finishes short and alcoholic.

Marchesi di Barolo *(11/79)*. Hot, alcoholic nose; light-bodied and unstructured with high acidity; lacks substance and weight; high in tannin; short.

Mascarello Giuseppe, Vignola *(11/80)*. Some fruit on the nose; fairly tannic but with sufficient fruit in reserve to allow aging; aftertaste is long and tannic; give it four or five more years (should be ready now).★(★)

Massolino Giuseppe, Vigna Rionda *(10/81)*. Not well made; rather poor, in fact.

Oddero Luigi *(4/85)*. Old, dull, and dried out.

Oreste Stefano *(1/85)*. Medium brick; aroma has suggestions of fruit and tar; some tannin on entry, nice fruit flavors; it could improve, but there's not much reason to hold it much longer.★(+)

Osvaldo Mauro *(11/79)*. The nose brings up southern wine; uncharacteristic Barolo; some tannin, but lacks weight and structure.

Palladino *(11/79)*. Nose brings up aroma of burnt hair but not unpleasantly so; rather nice in the mouth; still has tannin to shed; the finish recalls the unusual aroma.★

Pio Cesare *(twice 1/85)*. Aroma marred by some va; on the palate a lot of tannin; appears to have sufficient fruit, though perhaps not; only real problem is the volatile acidity.

E. Pira di Boschis *(in Albeisa bottle; 4 times 9/84)*. Rubber tire, va, and tar on the aroma; low in fruit, high in tannin, unbalanced; drinkable, no more; questionable future.

E. Pira di Luigi Pira *(3 times 11/80)*. Rich and intense on the aroma and palate, heaps of flavor and concentration, very well balanced; a lot of glycerine adds a smoothness and a roundness to the wine; very long finish; young but tempting; resist, still needs time for the tannin to resolve itself; a lot of style and class.★★★(★)

Prunotto, S. Casciano riserva *(twice 1/83)*. Color showing age at rim; bouquet rather dull; astringent and quite tannic. Does it have sufficient fruit? Seems to.★(?)

Prunotto, Vigneto Bussia riserva *(1/85; 11,015 bottles)*. Alcohol all too evident on nose, along with a vague trufflelike note; still a lot of tannin; some va but

1974

also a lot of fruit. Where will it go??★

Ratti Renato, Marcenasco (*4 times 3/85*). Lovely bouquet suggestive of fruit, tobacco, flowers, and tartufi; very well balanced; still some tannin but soft and supple; near its peak; a lot of character.★★★

Rinaldi Giuseppe (*twice 5/82*). Bouquet of raspberries, cassis, and alfalfa; incredible concentration of ripe fruit; has balance, length, and style; still room for improvement but superb now.★★★(+)

Saffirio F.lli Enrico e Giacomo (*4/85*). Tar and rubber tire aroma, seaweedy; awful.

Scarzello Giovanni, Cascina Mosconi (*10/81*). Fairly deep color; richly intense bouquet; well balanced with a lot of fruit and a kirschlike note at the end, which is a bit short; still in all a good bottle.★(★)

Scavino Alfonso (*1/84*). Deep color; characteristic aroma; lots of fruit, light tannin, quite ready; medium length.★★

Seghesio Renzo (*10/81*). Aroma of fruit and tar; moderate fruit though somewhat shallow; faintly bitter, undistinguished.

Sobrero Filippo (*4/81*). Bouquet of tar and flowers with overtones of leather; has tannin but also heaps of flavor; fairly long finish that's overly drying; a very good Barolo overall.★★(★)

Stroppiana Oreste (*11/79*). Color is browning; alcoholic, oxidized aroma; surprisingly, there's still some flavor and tannin; rather short.

Tenuta Carretta, Vigna Cannubi (*twice 4/80*). Perfumed bouquet; well balanced, some elegance, a lot of flavor; nearly ready.★★★(+)

Tenuta Cerequio (Vinicola Piemontese) (*2/85*). Aroma suggests wheat and hay, plus nebbiolo fruit and tar that emerged with some time in the glass; also a touch of camphor, tobacco, and cherries; a lot of good fruit, still some tannin to shed if the fruit holds up; finish is very tannic.★★(?)

Tenuta La Volta di Cabutto Bartolomeo riserva (*twice 1/85*). The bottle of 1/85 was far superior to that of 4/80. An aroma of truffles, tobacco, tar, and fruit marred by a slight touch of oxidation; light–moderate tannin; good fruit, fairly well balanced; very drinkable though lacking some weight.★★−

Tenuta Montanello (*5/83*). Aroma recalls oats and wheat; still some tannin, nice fruit; more or less ready.★

Terre del Barolo riserva speciale (*7 times 4/80*). *Riserva (3 times)*: Cheesy aroma with a background of seaweed; softer and more ready than the riserva speciale, with good body and a moderately long finish marred by some alcohol.★ *Riserva speciale (4 times)*: Nose shows some development with considerable fruit and a note of vanilla; still has tannin to shed which is beginning to soften and a surprising amount of fruit; some length and some style.★★

Terre del Barolo, Vigna Brunate riserva and riserva speciale (*6 times 12/80*). Riserva: Tarlike aroma has a hint of seaweed; flavorful, considerable tannin; the best of the three riservas.★★+

Riserva speciale: Some alcohol lurks beneath the fruit on the nose; softer and more open than Rocche and more ready.★★

Terre del Barolo, Vigna Rocche riserva and riserva speciale (*6 times 12/80*). Riserva: The deepest color of the three riservas; tarry, seaweed aroma; still has tannin to lose; the most tannic of the three.★★ Riserva speciale: Fruity aroma over a tarlike background marred by intrusion of alcohol; a chewy wine with loads of flavor and considerable tannin; moderately short, tannic finish.★★(+)

Vietti, Castiglione Falletto (*12 times 11/84*). Nice nose which brings up tobacco, cherries, and a vague tartufi note; still has tannin but a lot of flavor too; fairly ready, could improve; good quality.★★+

Vietti, Rocche riserva speciale and riserva (*12 times 6/83*). Bouquet of ripe fruit with nuances of cherries, tobacco, tar, mushroom, and flowers, a classic Barolo bouquet; rich and flavorful, very well balanced, still some tannin but more or less ready now; the riserva speciale is perhaps somewhat more forward.★★★

Villadoria Marchese (*3/81*). A candylike aroma; light-bodied, some tannin, lacks weight and substance; short on the finish; recalls a southern wine.

Voerzio Giacomo (*4 times including normal, riserva, and riserva speciale; most recent, regular bottling 3/84*). Onionskin; atypical aroma but has interest; fruit, moderate tannin, a bit shallow though drinkable; some alcohol at the end.

Zunino Basilio, Zona Sorì di Baudana (*10/81*). Characteristic aroma, some oxidation, shows age badly. Perhaps only this bottle; we hope so.

1973 0

Ratti said the wines of '73 were of medium quality and holding. Luciano Rinaldi and Aldo Conterno rated them among the lesser vintages for quality. Conterno, who in fact didn't bottle '72 or '77, rated the '73s as the worst wines he has bottled. Bartolo Mascarello puts the vintage on a par with '76. Alfredo Currado said the year, like '75, wasn't very good, and he didn't bottle any of his crus. Cavallotto agreed that it wasn't a very good vintage.

Right from the start the wines lacked body and substance. At this point, with very few exceptions—possibly Sobrero—they are too old. They might have been better at one time, but for now they get a zero rating.

Cavallotto F.lli, Vigna Bricco Boschis (*twice 12/80*). Light color; fragrant perfume; a little light and soft, some tannin; weak finish, not to keep.★

Conterno Giacomo (*4/80*). Tarlike notes evident, but overall the aroma is closed and ungiving; light–medium body with insufficient fruit for the tannin.

Osola (*11/79*). Alcoholic aroma; overly tannic for the fruit which is lacking; unbalanced.

Sobrero Filippo (*twice 5/82*). Must be the wine of the vintage; classic Barolo nose suggestive of tar, alfalfa, and flowers; has a surprising intensity of flavor; well structured; has style.★★★

1972 0

Constant rain during the growing season didn't allow the grapes to ripen. There was insufficient alcohol to make the wine. No Barolo was produced. The entire nebbiolo crop was declassified. The worst.

1971 ★★★★

April, May, and June were marked by a lot of rain which reduced the crop drastically. Then the sun came out and shone warmly almost until Christmas. The weather was consistently good for the rest of the season.

The result was a very small crop of richly intense, highly concentrated wines, rich in extract and very well balanced—overall splendid wines. Alfredo Currado described the '71s as complete wines, more consistent than 1978, at a higher level. Giuseppe Rinaldi said it was the best vintage in memory. Bartolo Mascarello ranks it as the best of the decade. Renato Ratti said the best '71s are at a very high level, and although they will be very long-lived they can be enjoyed now. Pio Boffa said the wines were extremely big and tannic; his wine spent eight years in oak. Giovanni Conterno characterized them as masculine wines like the '74s.

Despite the obvious odds, there were many mediocre and even downright poor wines produced; for the most part these wines came from the likes of Marchese Villadoria, Kiola, Scanavino, and a few others who consistently fail to raise their quality to the level of mediocrity, frequently even drinkability. After exempting them, we find a preponderance of highly rated Barolos with many wines meriting two, three, and even four stars. There's no doubt about the high quality of the vintage. As for now, they are beginning to come ready, although the best ones will improve further; they are still young and have a lot more to give. Our overall rating is four stars.

Bersano riserva speciale *(5/84)*. Brick red with orange highlights; not much bouquet; has tannin and a fair amount of flavor; alcohol mars the finish, which is short and somewhat grating; unimpressive.

Borgogno Aldo riserva speciale *(3/85)*. Old-style nebbiolo aroma of tar and fruit, vague touch of oxidation; unbalanced, high acid, and volatile acidity; some berrylike fruit; drying out, still drinkable. ★

Borgogno F.lli Serio e Battista riserva speciale *(twice 11/84)*. One bottle had had its sediment removed; the other did not. The difference was all too apparent: the first lacked in character and was somewhat shallow; the latter bottle had more aroma, more flavor, and more character. Although some alcohol intruded, this wine still had a fair amount of tannin and flavor. It was, in short, a more interesting wine. ★(+)

Borgogno Giacomo riserva *(4 times 1/82)*. Light–medium brick, light orange rim; tar, fruit, and vaguely floral on aroma; has tannin but with sufficient fruit to support it, though out of balance with alcohol which is noticeable on the finish. ★

Brezza Giacomo *(twice 10/79)*. Perfumed aroma marred by the intrusion of alcohol; nice flavor on entry, then shallow; short alcoholic finish; not a success.

Bruzzone *(3/81)*. Some oxidation mars the aroma; unstructured, some tannin, lacks weight, flavor, and substance; happily there is no aftertaste.

Castello Feudale riserva speciale *(twice 4/85)*. Brick red color shows age; characteristic bouquet of tar and flowers with a chocolate note; beginning to dry out but still has flavor interest. ★

Cavallotto F.lli, Vigna Bricco Boschis riserva speciale *(13 times 3/85)*. Expansive old-style nebbiolo aroma, vaguely floral with a tarlike note; still quite tannic but a lot of flavor evident; soft-centered; a full-

bodied and robust Barolo that lacks some style; nearly ready. ★★(+)

Ceretto, Zonchetta *(11 times 3/85; 17,500 bottles)*. Bouquet is a bit light, raspberry woodsy nuances; superbly balanced; firm vein of tannin; full of flavor and style; a very fine wine that appears to be coming ready, though room to improve. ★★★(+)

Chiadò Mario riserva speciale *(4/80)*. Corked.

Cogno-Marcarini, Brunate *(3 times 10/81, 3/83 and 3/85; 29,600 bottles)*. Bottle of 10/81 tasted at the winery from a magnum that had been opened for 24 hours *('n fund 'd buta)*: Enormous bouquet of flowers, fruit, champignons, and raspberries; full and rich with the taste of sweet, ripe fruit; loads of style, coming ready. ★★★(★) Bottle of 3/83: A rich and intense woodsy aroma with a cherrylike nuance; full of flavor; well balanced but not quite as exciting as it should be. ★★(★) Bottle of 3/85: Brick, almost onionskin robe; richly perfumed bouquet, floral and tartufi notes; sweet and flavorful; elegant and stylish; nearly peak, but more to give; a real classic. ★★★(★)

Colla Paolo *(10/78)*. A big tarry aroma; light–medium body and soft; lacks guts, weight, and substance.

Conterno Aldo, Bussia Soprana *(11/84)*. Perfumed bouquet suggesting tartufi and leather with hints of chocolate and flowers; tannic entry, richly fruited center; still young but balance and quality evident; will make a splendid bottle in perhaps four or five years. ★★★(★)

Conterno Aldo, Cascina Masante della Bussia Soprana *(3/85)*. Smallish nose, vague harshness; quite tannic though sufficient fruit to balance; a real disappointment. ★★(+)

Conterno Giacomo riserva *(twice 3/85)*. Old-style Barolo aroma; considerable tannin remains; the struc-

1971

ture and fruit are sufficient to carry it; needs at least five more years, try again in 1990.★★(★)

Conterno Giacomo, "Monfortino" riserva speciale *(7 times 5/83).* Bouquet beginning to open up, revealing enormous richness and concentration; exceptionally well balanced, an immense concentration of fruit and still a heap of tannin; without question it needs years of age but should make an outstanding bottle; one of the stars of the vintage.★★★(★)

Contratto riserva *(4 times 3/85).* Floral bouquet with the characteristic tarlike note; a full-bodied and fairly rich wine that still has considerable tannin to shed; has the sweetness of ripe fruit; sure to be worth the wait; try in about three years.★★(★)

Cossetti Clemente *(3/81).* Hot, cooked nose reminiscent of a southern wine; low in acid, lacking character, flavor, and substance; poor balance; dull; mercifully short.

Dosio riserva speciale *(twice 5/85).* Typical floral and tarlike aroma; tannic entry gives way to fruit; could use more weight and definition; not to keep; troublesome tannic ending.★ +

Einaudi Luigi *(twice 3/85).* Expansive with some complexity, heaps of flavor, moderate tannin, good weight and concentration, well structured; long finish; has style; enjoyable now.★★★

Fontanafredda *(11/78).* Characteristic Barolo aroma; quite tannic and harsh, but seems to have sufficient fruit to allow it to age and develop; needs perhaps six to eight years.

Fontanafredda, Vigna La Rosa *(5 times 1/85).* Aroma is more open, with more fruit than the Lazzarito, has a note of camphor; round and soft; enjoyable now but has room for improvement.★★(★)

Fontanafredda, Vigna Lazzarito *(1/85).* Aroma offers notes of tar and fruit, with a vague note of seaweed; tannic entry gives way to sweet, ripe fruit; finish is very tannic; a full-bodied, robust Barolo that needs years yet.★★(+)

Giacosa Bruno, Rocche riserva speciale *(3/85; 4070 bottles).* Beautiful brick red robe shading to orange; toasty, berrylike nuances on the floral bouquet; finely honed, still has tannin but full of flavor and incredible concentration; a real classic.★★★★

Granduca riserva speciale *(3/81).* Alcohol intrudes on the tarlike aroma; too much tannin and insufficient flavor to carry it.

Kiola *(3/81).* A soft, light little wine that lacks structure and distinction; in fact, has nothing to recommend it.

Mascarello Giuseppe, Monprivato *(6/82; 6476 bottles and some larger sizes).* Richly intense aroma marred by some alcohol; full-bodied and thick, with heaps of flavor; will improve but very good even now.★★(★)

Oddero F.lli *(1/85).* Old-style Barolo bouquet with a lot of tar; still firm and hard and fairly full-bodied; quite young but has the stuffing to enable it to develop.★★(★)

Palladino *(11/78).* Expansive perfumed bouquet; soft and flavorful; still has some tannin, nearly ready; lacks a bit on length.★ +

Palladino, Vigneto S. Bernardo riserva speciale *(twice 3/85).* An almondlike aroma with a hint of Marsala; oxidation is more apparent on the palate;

both bottles, tasted two months apart, were the same.

Pio Cesare *(12/81 and 1/85).* The earlier bottle was unbalanced, harsh, tannic, and alcoholic. The latter bottle, tasted at the winery, had a fresh, well-developed bouquet, fairly rich and intense with suggestions of licorice, flowers, and berries; full-bodied and rich with a lot of concentration and tannin; hardly seems it could be the same wine.★★★

E. Pira di Boschis *(Albeisa bottle, 3/85).* It would have been better left unbottled; nothing of interest here.

E. Pira di Luigi Pira *(twice 11/80).* Perfumed bouquet with an incredible richness and concentration of rich, ripe fruit and flowers; exceptional balance, enormous flavor, so well balanced the wine at first seems quite accessible but then the rich tannin becomes evident; very young but incredible quality.★★★★

Prunotto, Bussia riserva di Count Riccardo Riccardi *(one year in wood; 1/85).* Enormous bouquet of ripe fruit and hints of tartufi; richly concentrated; a lot of class; sweet and velvety; still has a lot of tannin; a splendid wine.★★★(★)

Prunotto riserva *(3/85).* Light nose, some fruit; light tannin; has a sweetness to it; some alcohol mars the end; it can improve but ready now.★★ +

Ratti Renato, Marcenasco *(twice 11/83).* Full, rich floral bouquet with hints of cherries, kirsch, and tartufi; a complete wine; still has some tannin to shed but ready and enjoyable now with the flavor and sweetness of ripe fruit; very long.★★★(+)

Rinaldi Francesco *(11/78).* Fairly complex and characteristic Barolo bouquet of tar and flowers overlaid with a suggestion of tartufi; well balanced, still somewhat tannic but loads of flavor; young but tempting (by now, it's probably close to ready).★★★(+)

Rinaldi Giuseppe *(4 times 3/85).* From magnum 11/84: Complex bouquet of cassis, mushrooms, and tartufi; still has tannin but underneath is an enormous core of youthful fruit and a firm tannic vein; an elegant Barolo; a delight to drink now but will continue to improve for years.★★★(★) From bottle 3/85: Tartufi, berries, and flowers characterize the intense bouquet; still has tannin and a surprising harsh edge; astringent entry; a lot of flavor; not up to previous bottles.★★

Rinaldi Giuseppe, Brunate riserva *(3/85).* Deep color; mint and ripe fruit on aroma and more than a hint of almonds; exceptional balance; still has tannin, enormous richness; very long; a stylish Barolo.★★★(★)

Scanavino Giovanni *(too many times, 8/82).* Awful nose; light and insipid, no character, flavor, or interest; some oxidation on the finish.

Scavino Alfonso, Vigna della Punta *(10/81 and 6/83).* Earlier bottle: Closed in aroma with a suggestion of fruit and tar; considerable tannin but appears to have sufficient fruit in reserve; seems rather young.★(★) More recent bottle: Fairly nice nose marred by alcohol and va; could be an off bottle or else aging rapidly.

Scavino Paolo *(5 times 4/85).* Characteristic old-style Barolo aroma, some champignons; still has some tannin and a firmness remains, but beginning to soften and come ready; flavorful; a bit light at the end.★★ −

Tenuta Carretta, Vigna Cannubi *(11 times 3/85).* Bouquet still somewhat reticent and not fully developed, hints of flowers and tartufi; firm, still a lot of tannin, but with the fruit necessary to carry it; long finish; not

1971

ready. At a tasting of seventeen 1971 Barolos in March '85, this wine was the youngest and needed the most age; it was also one of the most impressive.★★(★ +)

Tenuta Carretta, Vigna Cannubi riserva speciale *(3 times 11/79)*. Bouquet is rich and deep, a faint mustiness in the background; more tannin than the regular bottling and more subdued in flavor; a very good bottle, but doesn't measure up to the regular.★★(?)

Tenuta Cerequio (Vinicola Piemontese) *(2/85)*. Well-developed bouquet recalls raspberries and tar, with a barnyard aspect in the background; still has a lot of tannin but seems to have sufficient fruit to support it; finish is somewhat astringent.★(★)

Tenuta La Volta di Cabutto Bartolomeo *(twice 1/85)*. Odd nose has a vaguely vegie and cereal aspect which carries through on the palate; good fruit, ready now, light tannin; lacks some richness and weight but a nice Barolo for current consumption,★

Tenuta Montanello riserva speciale *(4/83 from magnum)*. Intensely rich bouquet; has a lot of flavor and some tannin, but quite ripe and ready.★★ −

Terre del Barolo riserva speciale *(4/80)*. Moderately complex bouquet; nearly ready; soft and round with a lot of flavor, still some tannin.★★

Vietti, Briacca, regular, riserva, and riserva speciale *(13 times 6/83 and 3/85; 4500 bottles)*. Bottle of 6/83:

Complex bouquet has floral overtones, notes of cherries and kirsch; still has tannin but richly flavored, with elegance and style, velvety texture; very long finish; tempting now but has more to give; try again in 1986.★★★(★) Bottle of 3/85: Minerally aroma, some fruit; more fruit on the palate; still some tannin; seems to have closed up since the earlier bottle; has a sweetness to it.★★(★)

Vietti, Codana *(4/84)*. Moderate garnet, orange at rim; floral bouquet with a suggestion of tartufi; well balanced and firm, a lot of flavor, beginning to come ready.★★★(+)

Vietti, Rocche *(7 times 3/85; 4000 bottles)*. Refined bouquet offers suggestions of tobacco, tea, cherries, and flowers; like liquid velvet on the palate with an enormous richness and concentration of sweet, ripe fruit; this complete and stylish Barolo is near its peak.★★★★

Vignolo-Lutati *(11/78)*. Lacks aroma; light-bodied and unstructured, overly tannic; lacks substance and length.

Villadoria Marchese *(11/79)*. Hot nose; light-bodied and unstructured, low in fruit; short; alcohol and va and very little else on the nose; on the palate, the same, plus tannin.

1970 ★★★

The 1970 vintage was unfortunately overshadowed by the spectacular year that followed. Giovanni Conterno said that the '70s, like the '82s, are feminine wines. Bartolo Mascarello rates only '71 and '78 better in the decade. Overall, it was a good year. Based on the eleven '70s tasted since 1982, it seems the best wines from the best producers are still developing, but there are some clear disappointments as well. Based on those eleven wines, we rate the vintage at three stars, although admittedly many poor bottles were produced.

Borgogno Giacomo *(twice 11/78)*. One bottle was tasted in Italy, the other in New York; both were oxidized.

Castello Sperone riserva *(6/79)*. The awful stench on the nose carries through on the palate.

Ceretto, Zonchetta *(1/85)*. Nose shows a lot of age, with the characteristic seaweed aroma of an old Barolo; still good on palate; no need to keep any longer.★

Conterno Aldo, "Granbussia" Vigna Bricco Colonnello riserva speciale *(4/80)*. Expansive bouquet; well balanced with heaps of flavor and loads of tannin still to shed.★★(★)

Conterno Giacomo, "Monfortino" riserva speciale *(4 times 4/85)*. Ex-cask 11/84: Fragrant perfume; very tannic and closed but seems to be a lot of fruit underneath that tannin. Giovanni Conterno has been bottling this wine for three years.★★(?) Latest bottle, 4/85: Bouquet suggests mushrooms, tartufi, and hazelnuts; still has considerable tannin over a core of fruit which is just beginning to come out; firm and flavorful; still young but very good quality; try again in no less than two or three years.★★(★)

Contratto Giuseppe riserva *(twice 3/85)*. Orange rim; richly intense and fragrant bouquet with hints of flowers and tar; well balanced; soft and smooth; the tannin has resolved itself; lots of flavor; moderately long finish; the bottle of 9/80 needed more time; that of 3/85 is at its peak.★★★ −

Einaudi Luigi *(2/85)*. Floral bouquet with hints of tar and kirsch and a vague harshness; light tannin, good fruit, soft and round; very ready.★★★ −

Ferrero Virginia *(11/78)*. Light but fragrant bouquet; lots of tannin, perhaps too much; the wine lacks some stuffing and flavor; rather brief finish.

Fontanafredda *(6/79 and 2/82)*. Lacks fruit, drying out; more or less the same impression from both bottles.

Giri Guido *(9/80)*. Smallish nose with some fruit apparent; flavorful, some tannin to lose; rather short aftertaste. (Should be ready by now.)★

Mascarello Giuseppe *(twice 3/82)*. Fragrant bouquet with a hint of mint marred by an off note; some tannin to shed, a bit shy in fruit; harsh, tannic aftertaste. Will it ever develop?(★)

Mascarello Giuseppe, Bussia Soprana *(twice 3/85; 4702 bottles plus larger sizes)*. Floral, fruity aroma has some delicacy and a tartufi note; rich and full in the mouth with a lot of flavor; some tannin adds backbone; like velvet; has a gentleness about it.★★★

Mascarello Giuseppe, Monprivato *(10/80)*. Somewhat reticent aroma with traces of flowers and fruit; good flavor; the tannin is beginning to soften, but there are still some rough edges. (Should be ready by now—1985)★★(★)

Pio Cesare *(11/78)*. Backward on aroma; considerable tannin to lose but seems sufficiently well balanced to turn into a good bottle.★(★ +)

51

1970

Prunotto, Cascina S. Cassiano riserva *(3 times 2/85)*. Aroma somewhat closed, have to work for it, tartufi, smoky, tobacco, tar, and flowers; full-bodied, still some tannin and lots of fruit; velvet center; ready, could improve.★★★

Ratti Renato, Marcenasco *(11/83)*. Lovely, well-developed floral bouquet with the characteristic note of tar; fairly well balanced and flavorful, though still some tannin.★★(+)

Rinaldi Francesco *(1/85)*. Floral bouquet recalls berries and tartufi; still quite tannic but with loads of fruit in reserve, firm and well balanced, good quality; long finish; needs a lot of time yet; try in about 1990.★★(★)

Sobrero Filippo *(3 times 11/84)*. High in alcohol, unbalanced, drying out.

Stroppiana Oreste *(4/80)*. Alcoholic and oxidized aroma, also on palate, but still some flavor; perhaps a bad bottle.

Tenuta Carretta, Vigna Cannubi *(10/78)*. Aroma somewhat closed but some fruit peeking through; considerable tannin to shed but with a richness that bodes well; fine quality.★★(★)

Tenuta Cerequio (Vinicola Piemontese) riserva speciale *(6/79)*. Vegies dominate the nose; soft and dull on the palate with some tannin; finishes on a bitter note; undistinguished and uninteresting.

1969 0

This vintage was considered from the start to be of average quality. Today we doubt there are many wines of interest left. Most of the few we've tasted, mostly in 1982 and 83, would have been better a few years earlier. For today, then, we rate it at zero.

Barale F.lli, Vigneti Castellero *(twice 1/82)*. Bouquet of vanilla and fruit, some oak; still tannic though it seems to have sufficient fruit to develop.★(★)

Borgogno Giacomo *(1/82)*. Light–medium brick, orange at rim; moderately intense bouquet marred by the intrusion of some alcohol; fairly nice flavor, still some tannin; tails off at the end; ready now, no need to keep it any longer.★

Conterno Giacomo, "Monfortino" riserva speciale *(4/81)*. Tar and alcohol dominate the nose, some fruit comes up with a lot of swirling; unbalanced, high tannin, and alcohol dominate on the palate, some fruit; astringent aftertaste.

Contratto *(twice 3/83)*. Still some interest though drying out.

Terre del Barolo riserva *(twice 1/83)*. Chocolate and tar on aroma, marred by some oxidation; still some flavor, but drying out.

1968 0

This vintage was perhaps more highly regarded than 1969 at first. The few wines that we've tasted in the past few years, as with the '69s, would have been better a few years earlier.

Borgogno Giacomo riserva *(3 times 10/83)*. Alcohol and va and very little else on the nose; on the palate the same, plus tannin.

Ceretto, Zonchetta *(6/82; 12,000 bottles)*. Bouquet hints of filberts; has fruit and interest but is beginning to dry out.★

Conterno Aldo, Vigna Bussia *(4/80)*. Color shades to orange at rim; lovely fragrant bouquet; well structured and smooth in texture, with a soft, velvety feel, still some tannin, and a lot of flavor; stylish and pretty much at its peak.★★ +

Contratto *(twice 2/83)*. Showing age on the nose, va intrudes; overly tannic and fruit is fading.

Conterno Giacomo, "Monfortino" *(5/81)*. Not a pleasant wine; stinky and unimpressive; could be a bad bottle.

Sobrero Filippo *(5/84)*. Oxidized but still some flavor interest.

1967 ★★[+]

Renato Ratti said the year was considered very fine at first, but the wines have lost a lot and are generally disappointing today; he advised they be drunk up. Bruno Giacosa places them in the top rank. While there's no question they deserved three stars at one time, many of the wines are fading today. The best, however, will keep. For today, we give them two stars, perhaps two plus.

Borgogno F.lli Serio e Battista riserva *(11/84)*. Brick with orange reflections; nose shows some age with a vague oxidation and intrusion of alcohol; still some tannin but fairly nice fruit; ready now, might keep but alcohol on finish is troublesome.

Borgogno Giacomo riserva *(1/82)*. Moderately intense bouquet with noticeable alcohol; overly tannic and harsh; too old.

Cogno-Marcarini, Brunate *(3/85)*. Beautiful brick robe with orange reflections; expansive, perfumed bouquet; firm tannic vein; texture of liquid velvet; a complete wine, elegant and stylish; very ready, but there's no rush to drink it.★★★★

Contratto riserva *(4 times 3/85 and 6/85)*. Bottle of 3/85. Very little of interest left; sadly past its best; alcoholic, drying out; acid finish; considerably better when tasted two years earlier, even then it was drying out but still had some interest; a characteristic aroma of tar and flowers; some nice flavors, but we expected more.★ — Bottle of 6/85, came from the winery a few months earlier: Floral bouquet, woodsy nuance, hints of underbrush; still some tannin, soft-centered, flavorful; like the aroma, the flavor is somewhat woodsy; as ready as it will ever be; somewhat harsh finish.★★

Dosio riserva speciale *(4/85)*. Browning; a touch of oxidation on nose, also notes of tobacco and tar;

1967

light tannin; very drinkable, not to keep.★

Fontanafredda (*twice 1/83*). Aroma of tar and rubber; shows age but still has interest.★ —

Fontanafredda, Vigna La Rosa (*5/80*). Not much aroma; soft, some tannin, not much to it; short aftertaste.★ —

Giacosa Bruno, Collina Rionda di Serralunga riserva speciale (*3/85; 5500 bottles*). Complex bouquet, concentrated cherries, and a hint of tartufi; still has tannin, but the rich fruit makes it enjoyable now; still has more to give.★★★

Granduca riserva speciale (*3/81*). Color shows age; interesting bouquet but some oxidation apparent; seems overly tannic on entry, shallow and lacking substance, drying out; alcohol and tannin at the end.

Pio Cesare (*4/80*). Some oxidation on nose; dried out though some flavor remains.

Porta Rossa di Berzia & Rizzi, Cantina della (*10/81*). High alcohol, noticeable va; some flavor; too old.

Prunotto, Bussia (*7 times 2/85; 21,355 bottles*). Garnet, orange at rim; characteristic bouquet of flowers and tar, some alcohol; soft, round, and flavorful; quite ready; has a slight bite on the finish; a good example of an old-style Barolo at its peak.★★★

Ratti Renato (*11/83*). Lovely, rich floral bouquet shows some refinement; soft and round, near its peak, has some style.★★★

Rinaldi Francesco (*1/85*). Fairly deep color; expansive bouquet, vaguely floral, has some delicacy; still has tannin but a lot of flavor, velvety, nearly ready but with more to give; an elegant, gentle Barolo with a very long finish.★★★(+)

Vietti, Rocche (*11/84 magnum*). Medium deep, brick at rim; expansive bouquet, complex and perfumed, with nuances of flowers, kirsch, tartufi, mint, leather, licorice, cherries, and tobacco; a complete and well-balanced Barolo, velvety and tasty; perfect today, but as it sits in the glass it grows and expands indicating more life ahead; very long finish—five hours later it was even more impressive.★★★ +

1966 0

This vintage never amounted to much. Without question, only 1963 was as bad in the decade.

Borgogno Giacomo riserva (*1/82*). Alcoholic and unbalanced.

Franco riserva (*12/78*). Oxidation, bitter.

1965 0

Some pundits rated this vintage at three stars. We had a lot more exposure to it in the early and mid-1970s, but we haven't seen any bottles in some time. At their best we wouldn't have given them more than two stars, today zero.

Borgogno Giacomo riserva (*1/82*). Some oxidation, some flavor interest; ends on a bitter note.

Calissano riserva speciale (*2/82*). Seaweed and

oxidation; best forgotten.

Mascarello Giuseppe (*twice 3/82*). Va and alcohol, harsh edges, some flavor interest; going but not gone.

1964 ★★★

This was a very highly thought of vintage. Renato Ratti said it is still holding and should be good for another ten to fifteen years. Alfredo Currado puts it on the same level as '61 and '67.

The few we've tasted in the past few years seem to be holding; perhaps three stars.

Bersano riserva speciale (*5/84*). Some quality evident though beginning to dry out; drinkable but not to keep.

Borgogno F.lli Serio e Battista riserva (*11/84*). Brick red; vaguely resinlike aroma, but pleasant; almost seems sweet, light tannin, ready now; could use more character.★

Borgogno Giacomo riserva (*6 times 1/85*). Some va mars the nose, which has a vague hint of seaweed; still has considerable tannin but also a lot of flavor, smooth texture; fairly well balanced; nice now but can improve further; a wine that gave us immense pleasure when it was ten or twelve years old and continues to

offer a lot of drinking pleasure even today.★★(+)

Conterno Giacomo, "Monfortino" riserva speciale (*many times 3/81*). Nearly every bottle tasted was shot, either bad or too old. Most recent bottle: Tarry notes and a slight harshness (va) on the nose; still has tannin but a lot of flavor. Where will it go? The va is troublesome.★(?)

Dosio riserva speciale (*4/85*). Browning; oxidized; drying out.

Ratti Renato (*10/83*). Fairly intense bouquet; still fairly tannic on the palate, seems to have the fruit to develop. Will it?★★(?)

1963 0

This vintage never amounted to much.

1962 [★]

This vintage was considered average from the start, but we've had better experiences than that, especially through the 1970s. Except for the Calissano tasted in 1983 and 1981, we haven't tasted a '62 since 1978, so we put a tentative evaluation on the current state of the vintage.

1962

Borgogno Giacomo *(9/78)*. Has good Barolo character, soft though still some tannin; no need to keep any longer.★★+

Calissano riserva speciale *(4 times 1/83)*. At one time it was much better; this wine is typical of a Barolo beginning to break up, seaweed aroma and a mouthful of alcohol and tannin though some fruit remains; this Barolo was at its best through the end of the 1970s.

1961 ★★+

Renato Ratti said that although they were very rich wines, the '61s aged quickly and already taste too old. Alfredo Currado rates the vintage equal to '64 and after '71, '78, and '82. Some producers, notably Beppe Colla of Prunotto, place it ahead of 1958.

Most of the few we've tasted showed age, and although they're beginning to decline they are still good. Two stars plus would seem to reflect their current state based on the few wines we've had the opportunity to sample.

Borgogno F.lli Serio e Battista riserva *(11/84)*. Onionskin robe; some oxidation on the nose, also some tar; still some tannin but soft; some flavor; not to keep.★(?)

Borgogno Giacomo riserva *(twice 1/82)*. Light brick with an orange rim; characteristic bouquet of moderate intensity; nice entry, almost sweet, velvety; rather short finish but a nice bottle showing no signs of decay.★★

Bosca Luigi riserva speciale *(too many times 3/85; 27,000 bottles)*. Southern aroma, raisins beneath the oxidation; Bosca has a knack for producing poor wine even in the great years—no surprises here.

Conterno Giacomo *(4/80)*. Nose is marred by high alcohol and va; still has considerable tannin but with fruit beneath; questionable future.(?)

Contratto *(10/79)*. Color shows very little age; aromatic bouquet suggesting tartufi; smooth in texture, heaps of flavor, very well balanced; can improve, but near its peak.★★★

Contratto riserva *(5/85)*. Beautiful brick orange robe; a lot of nebbiolo character and complexity, berrylike, some volatile acidity; some harsh edges but soft and flavorful; fairly long finish, recalls blackberries, vaguely chalky; ready.★★+

Fontanafredda *(1/85, at winery)*. Beautiful brick red robe; lovely floral bouquet, with licorice and mint; still some tannin but fairly soft, round, and smooth-textured; still has holding power and should improve, but a nice glass right now.★★(★)

Lodali Giovanni *(3/85)*. Caramel candy and a baked character to the aroma; full-bodied, flavorful, lacking in style, coarse but drinkable.★

Prunotto, Bussia riserve *(4 times 2/85; 26,500 bottles)*. Beautiful, brick orange robe; rich, intense bouquet of flowers and goudron with a touch of seaweed; at its peak, one could hardly ask for more, smooth-textured and velvety; a complete wine and very fine quality.★★★+

Tenuta La Volta di Cabutto Bartolomeo *(twice 1/85)*. Onionskin; bouquet shows a lot of age, floral with hints of tea and coffee; has a hint of sweetness, also a fullness and yet seems delicate; has held up but is not to keep any longer.★★+

Vietti *(twice 6/82)*. Brick robe; some oxidation but not much; sweet, smooth-textured, velvety; past its best but still good.★★+

1960 0

The vintage was considered poor from the start. The only one we've personally tasted was the Gaja *(11/84)*. The color was onionskin; it showed some decay but still offered some interest.

1959 0

Like 1960, this vintage was considered a poor one. And like 1960, the only one from the vintage that we've had the opportunity to taste was from Gaja *(11/84)*. It was cloudy and alcoholic—in a word, gone.

1958 ★★★★

Many authorities rate this vintage as one of the all-time greats. In our limited experience with it, no vintage has impressed us more, and only '71 and '82 have impressed us as much. Suffice it to say that while we have tasted some very impressive '47s, our experience isn't sufficient to say which is better and, in fact, if '47 is or ever was as good. But make no mistake about it, this was a great vintage. The best wines have still more to give. While we tasted many more during the 1970s, the few we've had more recently are still impressive.

Borgogno Giacomo riserva *(numerous times 1/85)*. Medium brick in color; aroma brings up seaweed, beets, and cheese and also has a harsh backnote; still has tannin and some firmness, nice flavor and a lot to it; enjoyable now with room for improvement; the only flaw is in the bouquet.★★(?)

Fontanafredda *(12/83 and 1/85)*. Deep garnet robe, brick at rim, orange reflections; complex bouquet suggesting licorice, camphor, flowers, and toast; liquid velvet; seems ready, though still some tannin.★★★(+)

Prunotto *(1/85)*. Beautiful robe, brick to orange; some volatile acidity and alcohol intrude on the bouquet; considerably better on the palate, light tannin, velvety and round; an enormously long finish; the palate merits★★★★, overall★★★

1957 ★★ + ?

The vintage was always highly regarded but lived in the shadow of 1958. As for today, we've only tasted one and it was very good indeed.

Contratto riserva *(5/85)*. Tawny robe, orange reflections; leather, woodsy, tar, and berry notes characterize the bouquet; still some tannin, soft and smooth-textured; very ready; the only flaw is a slight harshness at the end.★★★ −

1956 [0]

At one time 1956 was considered an average year. Today they're probably too old.

1955 ★★★

We always rated this vintage higher than those who gave it two stars. The few bottles we've tasted were surely better; for those, at least, it rates three stars.

Borgogno Giacomo riserva *(many times 9/83)*. Orange robe, brick center; light bouquet though quite nice, characteristic; moderate tannin, tasty; more or less ready, with some room for further improvement.★★(+)

Contratto riserva *(6/85)*. Incredible richness and intensity on the nose, tobacco, berries, flowers, and woodsy nuances, marred by a touch of alcohol and a vague wet dog backnote; soft and velvety, tasty, at its peak and splendid; long, complex finish; has a barnyard character but in a pleasant way.★★★

Mascarello Cantina *(6/82)*. Beautiful robe; expansive, perfumed bouquet; has delicacy and elegance, like liquid velvet on the palate; incredible length; nearly perfect.★★★★

Villadoria Marchese riserva speciale *(many times 2/80)*. Beautiful orange robe; lovely perfumed bouquet; soft and velvety, seems almost sweet; heaps of flavor and very long finish; at its peak. How could Villadoria have produced such a wine?★★★

1954 [0]

At one time this was considered a two-star vintage. Unfortunately, we've not had the opportunity to taste any '54s. Today the wines are probably too old, although there might be some exceptions.

1953 [0]

This vintage was rated by authorities, along with 1959, as the worst of the decade. The only '53 we tasted was feeble and fading.

Pio Cesare *(11/79)*. Garnet color; oxidized, seaweed aroma that still offers some interest; surprisingly nice flavor; still has tannin; on the decline, but surprisingly drinkable for what it is.★

1952 ★★ +

Originally rated as a three-star vintage, the best wines merited four. As for their state today, based on the seven '52s we tasted between 1978 and 1985, we give two stars plus.

Borgogno Giacomo riserva *(many times 3/79)*. Beautiful orange robe; typical seaweed aroma of an old Barolo; round and smooth, at or near its peak; fairly long finish.★★

Conterno Aldo riserva speciale *(10/78)*. The bottle had been opened twenty hours earlier; tawny robe; delicately scented bouquet with a suggestion of fennel; soft, round, and velvety; fine quality; has style and distinction; nearing its peak.★★★ +

Conterno Giacomo *(4/81)*. Oxidized, but still has interest on the nose; none on the palate.

Conterno Giacomo, "Monfortino" *(10/79)*. Intense bouquet with suggestions of tartufi; delicate, nice structure, still some tannin; has length and style.★★★

Fontanafredda *(2/82)*. Brick red; seaweed and tar aroma so characteristic of an old Barolo; smooth-textured with a lot of flavor; some harshness at the end; on the way down.★

Franco Fiorina *(1/85)*. Medium brick red; some oxidation on the nose but also a lot of interesting woodsy nuances; very soft and smooth, with a touch of tannin which adds life and backbone; an old wine but firm; on the way down but still very good.★★ +

Mascarello Cantina *(10/79)*. Beautiful robe; floral bouquet is deep, rich, and intense with hints of fruit and leather; still has tannin and life; smooth-textured with heaps of flavor; enormously long finish; a classic Barolo.★★★★

1951 ?

This vintage was rated a three-star year. As for its status today, we couldn't say; we've never tasted a 1951 Barolo that we can recall.

1950 [★]

This year was given two stars by the authorities at the time. We've only personally tasted one bottle.

Franco Fiorina *(1/85; tasted at the winery)*. Medium brick red color; a bit of oxidation and a vague wheatlike note on the nose; has more interest on the palate, with a smooth texture and almost a sweetness to the flavor; still some tannin; past its prime, but still good.★★ −

1949 [0]

The vintage was never highly regarded. It's probably safe to say that the wines today are too old.

1948 [0]

Like the '49s, the '48s were never well thought of. Today the wines are probably gone.

1947 ★★★

The harvest produced a very small quantity of very ripe grapes. According to Giuseppe Fontana of Franco Fiorina, there might have been twenty producers who bottled Barolo at that time, while today there might be twenty times that number. For him, 1947 was the greatest vintage of the century. His wine, he said, was more than an expression of the vintage; it represented the family's dedication to the wine, the love they had for it. They put everything into it.

Borgogno Giacomo riserva *(many times over the past 12 years, 9/83)*. Brick robe with orange reflections; aspects of seaweed and rubber tire in the bouquet suggest the wine is on the decline though without question still interesting; fairly soft and enjoyable but not to keep; this wine was better in the late 1970s; for now ★★.

Franco Fiorina *(1/85; tasted at the winery)*. Medium garnet shading to orange; bouquet has delicacy; on the palate, liquid velvet, has a lot going for it, structure,

flavor, style, and length; has the sweetness of ripe fruit, still some tannin and a lot of life left though near its peak; only the bouquet doesn't measure up to the rest; still in all, a great bottle.★★★ +

Marchesi di Barolo *(many times over the past 12 years, 4/82)*. Medium orange; seaweed and tar on the nose; nice entry gives way to a harsh astringent edge; still has tannin and not much else; breaking up; it was considerably better in the mid to late 1970s.

1946 [0]

This vintage was originally given two stars. Today the wines are probably too old.

1945 [0]

The vintage was rated three stars. The only example we've tasted, in November of 1979 was, alas, too old.

Marchesi di Barolo *(11/79)*. Tawny robe; oxidized aroma recalls Marsala; still some flavor and interest, and even a touch of tannin; on the way downhill.

1931 [★★★★]

This vintage is considered to be *the* greatest of the century. Going by this one wine, it seems an evaluation well justified.

Conterno Giacomo *(4/85)*. This wine was transferred from a quarter *brenta* (12.5 liters) to a regular bottle sixteen or seventeen years ago. Aldo Conterno uncorked this bottle in the morning, some four hours before serving. Beautiful robe, onionskin; fragrant floral bouquet with a suggestion of clover; still has some tannin, seems sweet, impressive depth of flavor; velvety

texture, very much alive, showing no signs of fading, still has grip; very long finish, with a hint of licorice; sheer perfection.★★★★

This magnificent wine demonstrates the grandeur possible in a fine old Barolo. Thank you, Aldo Conterno, for your generosity in sharing it.

Barbaresco

The Barbaresco production zone is a small area of about 1265 acres (512 hectares) to the east and north of Alba. The name does not describe the character of the wine, which isn't in the least barbaric; in fact, it can be quite refined indeed. The wine takes its name from the town of Barbaresco, a village in the northwestern part of the zone dominated by an eleventh-century tower built as a lookout and signal point to warn of barbarian invaders.

Besides the *commune* of Barbaresco, there are two others and a part of a fourth making up the production zone: Neive in the northeast, Treiso in the south-central part, and, in the west, part of San Rocco Senodelvo d'Alba.

Village	Growers	Hectares	Maximum production (hectoliters)	Percentage of total production
Barbaresco	135	237.3799	13,293.27	46.39
Neive	238	154.3815	8,645.36	30.17
San Rocco Senodelvo	24	25.2600	1,414.56	4.93
Treiso	105	94,7290	5,304.83	18.51
Total	502	511.7504	28,658.02	100.00

Source: Regione Piemonte (1984).
Notes: 1 hectare = 2.4711 acres.
1 hectoliter = 26.42 gallons or 11.11 cases.

Barbaresco is a similar wine to Barolo, though generally lighter and earlier maturing, and often more stylish and elegant. Lighter in this context does not mean light; Barbaresco is a full-bodied wine with depth of fruit and character. It has a tannic spine, giving it a youthful hardness which softens with age to a velvety texture and underlying firmness.

Barbaresco has often been referred to as the little brother of Barolo, a description that is misleading as well as disparaging. These are not lesser wines; they can be truly great. The Santo Stefano of Bruno Giacosa or Castello di Neive, Camp Gros-Martinenga of Marchese di Gresy, Rabajà of Produttori del Barbaresco, Podere del Pajorè of Giovannini-Moresco, and Bricco Asili of Ceretto, among others, can achieve a grandeur to match the best from Barolo or, for that matter, from anywhere else.

Barbaresco is a fine wine to accompany roast red meat, game birds, or pigeon. In the medieval upper town of Neive, at Ristorante Contea de Neive, there is an excellent selection of Barbarescos available as well as menu of superb regional dishes typical of the Langhe. We can't think of a more enjoyable way to study the wines of Barbaresco than to accompany some fine bottles with a meal prepared by Claudia Verro, the fine chef at Contea.

Barbaresco is drinkable from five to eight years after the vintage and can be splendid from twelve to fifteen years, in better vintages perhaps even longer. Bruno Giacosa recommends drinking his after ten to twenty years.

It's not unusual for a producer's regular Barbaresco to have better fruit and balance than his riserva or riserva speciale, as these two are frequently given longer wood aging, which tends to diminish their fruit. There are exceptions, of course, particularly from the best producers and the best vintages, wines which have more intensity and concentration of fruit to begin with.

DOC/DOCG Requirements			
	Minimum Age *(years)*	Minimum alcohol	Maximum yield (gallons/acre)
	cask	total		
DOC Regular	1	2	12.5%	599
Riserva	1	3	12.5%	599
Riserva Speciale	1	4	12.5%	599
DOCG Regular	1	2	12.5%	599
Riserva	1	4	12.5%	599

Our discussion of the new legal category, DOCG, covered in the Barolo section, applies for Barbaresco also.

In buying Barbaresco, the producer is, as always, the most important factor to consider, followed by the vintage and the vineyard, but the general level of quality in Barbaresco is very good; in fact, Barbaresco represents the highest average quality of any Italian wine. And the wines are generally quite reliable; there is much more consistency than in Barolo, for example. This is not unrelated, of course, to the fact that Barolo is a much better known wine. Even a producer such as Villadoria, who makes miserable Barolo, turns out a drinkable Barbaresco. There is obviously not much of a market for a mediocre Barbaresco, while a poor Barolo can draw on the strength of the Barolo name. And since Barolo generally commands a higher price, there is also more of a temptation to play games. Rating★★★★

The Crus of Barbaresco

It has been said that the differences among the wines from the *communes* of Barbaresco are less evident than those in Barolo and, further, that the wines of a particular hillside evince less variation from one plot to another. ("Little brother" Barbaresco traditionally doesn't get the attention or appreciation of the more prestigious Barolo.)

The hills are not as steep in the Barbaresco zone as those in Barolo; they are rounder and gentler, ranging in altitude from an average of 655 to 985 feet (200 to 300 meters). The vineyards are planted on the slopes at altitudes of from 600 to 1200 feet. The best vineyards generally face southwest, receiving the benefit of the warmer afternoon sun. The soil here is limestone and clayey marl, compact and rich in potassium and other minerals, similar to that in Barolo and of the same marine origin.

Barbaresco is made from 100 percent nebbiolo grapes, which may be from three subvarieties: lampia, michet, and rosé. There is more of the lampia planted in the Barbaresco vineyards than the other two.

The Character of the *Communes*

The producers point out that the Barbarescos of Barbaresco itself are lighter in color and body; they are noted for their structure and perfume. Those of Treiso are regarded for their finesse. The wines of Neive, with a less pronounced perfume, are the fullest in body and the most tannic.

The best position in the zone is considered to be La Martinenga, regarded as Barbaresco's top cru. This 54-acre (21.8-hectare) vineyard is at the curve formed where the southeast slope of Asili and the southwest slope of Rabajà meet.

The Top Sites

The most frequently named as the top Barbaresco vineyards are as follows:

In the *commune* of Barbaresco
- ★★Asili
- ★★★Martinenga
- ★★Montestefano
- ★Montefico
- ★Pajè or Pagliari
- ★Pora or Porra
- ★★Rabajà or Rabajat
- ★Rio Sordo or Rivosordo
- ★Secondine

In the village of Neive
- ★★Albesani
- ★Basarin
- ★Chirra
- ★Cotta or Cotà
- ★★Gallina
- ★★Santo Stefano

In the Treiso district
- ★Casotto
- ★Giacosa
- ★Marcarini
- ★Pajorè

Carta del Barbaresco
Renato Ratti
LA MORRA (CUNEO) ITALIA

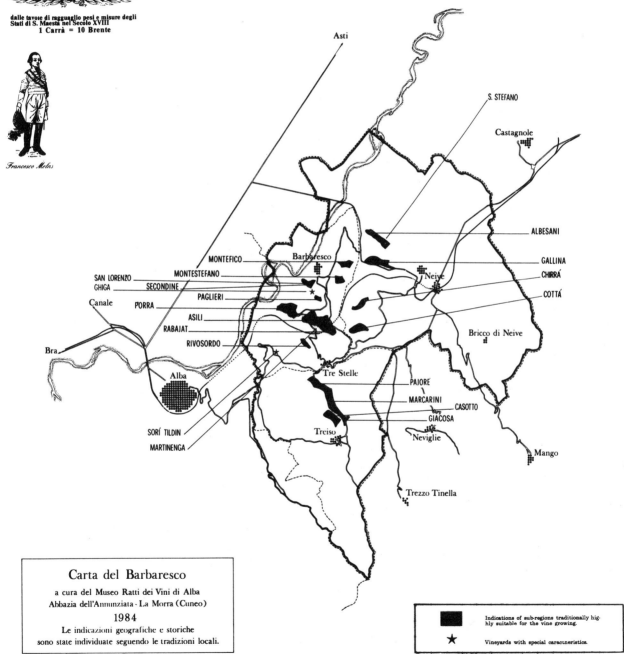

Alli Sindaci di Barbaresco.
Il 4 Novembre le truppe francesi comandate dal Generale Championet sono state sconfitte dai miei valorosi soldati nei pressi di Genola. - Per festeggiar degnamente la vittoria vi ordino di consegnare al mio quartiere in Bra 4 carrà del vostro più eccellente vino.
dato in Savigliano, il 5 Novembre 1799
Generale Francesco Melas

dalle tavole di ragguaglio pesi e misure degli Stati di S. Maestà nel Secolo XVIII
1 Carrà = 10 Brente

Francesco Melas

Asti

S. STEFANO

Castagnole

ALBESANI

Barbaresco

GALLINA

MONTEFICO
MONTESTEFANO
SAN LORENZO
GHIGA   SECONDINE
PAGLIERI
PORRA
ASILI
RABAJAT
RIVOSORDO

Neive

CHIRRÁ

COTTÁ

Canale

Bricco di Neive

Bra

Alba

Tre Stelle

PAJORE
MARCARINI   CASOTTO
GIACOSA

SORÍ TILDIN
MARTINENGA

Treiso

Neviglie

Mango

Trezzo Tinella

Carta del Barbaresco
a cura del Museo Ratti dei Vini di Alba
Abbazia dell'Annunziata - La Morra (Cuneo)
1984
Le indicazioni geografiche e storiche sono state individuate seguendo le tradizioni locali.

Indications of sub-regions traditionally highly suitable for the vine growing.

★ Vineyards with special caractneristics.

59

The Crus Themselves

★**Albesani** (*Neive*). Santo Stefano is within this vineyard district.

Albina (*Barbaresco*).

Ansario (*Treiso*).

★★**Asili** or **Asÿ** (*Barbaresco*). This highly esteemed cru adjoins Martinenga to the north. Bricco Asili, the top part of Asili, is bottled as a cru by the Cerettos.

> *Owner and/or producer*
> Ceretto[1] buys grapes from 6.2 acres (2.5 hectares).
> Fontanafredda buys grapes.
> Bruno Giacosa,[1] not made for some time.
> Donato Giacosa, 0.9 acres (0.35 hectares).
> Produttori del Barbaresco.[1,2]
> Roagna (we don't know if he still bottles an Asili cru).[1]

Augenta. Fontanafredda buys grapes from this vineyard. Luigi Pelissero owns 6.2 acres (2.5 hectares) of vines here.

Ausario (*Treiso*). F.lli Casetta grows grapes in this vineyard.

Balluri (*Neive*).

★**Basarin** (*Neive*). Castello di Neive owns 2.5 acres (1 hectare) of vines in Basarin. Az. Agr. "Moccagatta" has produced a Barbaresco cru from this vineyard since 1982. Parroco del Neive owns 5 acres (2 hectares) of nebbiolo from which they produce their Barbaresco cru Basarin.

Bernardotti (*Treiso*). Giuseppe Mascarello buys grapes from here for his Barbaresco cru. He produces 5300 bottles a year.

Bernino (*Barbaresco*).

Boito (*Treiso*).

Bongiovanni (*Treiso*).

Bordini (*Neive*).

Bordino (*Treiso*). Az. Agr. "Le Colline" has 12.4 acres (5 hectares) of nebbiolo vines in Bordino which they use for their Barbaresco. They don't indicate the cru name on the label.

Bricco (*Treiso*). Pio Cesare owns 20 acres (8 hectares) of vines here.

★★**Bricco Asili** (*Barbaresco*). The Az. Agr. "Bricco Asili" of Ceretto owns 3 acres (1.2 hectares) of nebbiolo vines on Bricco Asili, the ridge of Asili, from which they produce 7000 to 8000 bottles a year of their highly regarded Barbaresco cru.[2] They are the sole owners of this part of Asili, which is planted at an altitude ranging from 885 to 1300 feet (270 to 300 meters).

Bricco Codevilla (*Barbaresco*). The Az. Agr. "La Spinona" of Pietro Berutti owns vines here.

Bricco Faset (*Barbaresco*). Pietro Berutti of Az. Agr. "La Spinona" produces a Barbaresco cru from his 6.7 acres (2.7 hectares) of vines in the upper portion of the Faset hillside.

Brichet. A subcru within the Cotta vineyard.

Cabanet (*Barbaresco*). Mario Minuto has vines in this vineyard.

★★★**Camp Gros** (*Barbaresco*). This plot is in the part of Martinenga adjacent to Rabajà. Alberto di Gresy[2] bottles Camp Gros as a separate cru.

Canova (*Barbaresco*). Donato Giacosa owns 2.8 acres (1.15 hectares) of vines in this vineyard. Romualdo Giacosa bottles a cru from his grapes in Canova.

Cars (*Barbaresco*). Also known as Don' Cars.

Cascina Alberta (*Treiso*). This *cascina* represents Contratto's holdings in Barbaresco.

Cascina Boito (*Treiso*). See Boito.

Cascina Bordino (*Treiso*). See Bordino.

Cascina Bricco (*Treiso*). See Bricco.

Cascina Bruciato–Tre Stelle (*Treiso*). Balbo Marino bottles a Barbaresco under this name from his holdings in Treiso.

Cascina Congroia (*Neive*). F.lli Toso produce a Barbaresco from their Cascina Congroia holdings.

Cascina Ghiga (*Barbaresco*). Bersano occasionally bottle a Cascina Ghiga from their vines in Barbaresco.

Cascina Nuova (*Neive*).

Cascina Rocca (*Barbaresco*). Riccardo Cortese produces a Barbaresco from his Cascina Rocca holdings.

Cascina Rombone (*Treiso*). See Rombone.

Cascinotta (*Neive*). Parroco del Neive owns vines here.

Casot (*Barbaresco*). Luigi Pelissero owns 1.2 acres (0.5 hectares) of vines here. Vietti bought grapes from the Casot vineyard to produce a small quantity of a Barbaresco Casot in 1980 and 1981. Vilalotti and Vecchia Casot are subcrus within this vineyard.

★**Casotto** (*Treiso*). This vineyard district is close to the Giacosa and Marcarini vineyards. The Vignaioli

"Elvio Pertinace" co-op owns 12.4 acres (2.5 hectares) in this vineyard, 3.7 (1.5) planted to nebbiolo. They did a cru bottling in 1982. Vietti produced 100 bottles of a Barbaresco cru from Casotto from the 1980 and 1981 vintages.

Castellissano or **Castellizzano** *(Treiso)*. Vignaioli "Elvio Pertinance" owns 8.2 acres (3.3 hectares) in this cru, 3.2 (1.3) in nebbiolo, from which they produced a cru in 1982.

Cavalli *(Neive)*.

Cavanna *(Barbaresco)*. Giovanni Giordano has vines in Cavanna from which he bottles a Barbaresco cru.

Chirella *(Treiso)*.

★**Chirra** *(Neive)*.

Ciabot *(Barbaresco)*.

Cole *(Barbaresco)*. Donato Giacosa owns 0.9 acre (0.4 hectare) of vines in this vineyard. Mario Minuto of Az. Agr. "Moccagatta" produced their first Barbaresco Cole from vines here in 1982.

Costa Russi *(Barbaresco)*. Gaja is the sole owner of this 9.6-acre (3.9-hectare) vineyard. He has bottled a Barbaresco Costa Russi since 1978. Of his three crus, this one is planted at the lowest altitude. His average production of this cru is 14,000 bottles a year. Although it is a very good Barbaresco, we find it the least of Gaja's three crus as well as the earliest maturing.

★**Cotta, Cotà,** or **Cotto** *(Neive)*. Confratelli di San Michele produces a Barbaresco cru from holdings in this vineyard. Parroco del Neive also owns a piece. There are two subcrus: Brichet and Ca' Nova. Sottimano owns 1.6 acres (0.67 hectares) of Brichet and has bottled a Barbaresco cru from these vines since 1984. Dario Rocca and F.lli Rocca (Giulio and Franco) bottle a Barbaresco Ca' Nova from their holdings in that subcru. Sottimano owns 0.9 acre (0.4 hectare) of Ca' Nova.

Crichet Pajè *(Barbaresco)*. Roagna bottles their best Barbaresco under this name. We believe the grapes are from their vines in the Pajè vineyard.

Crocetta *(Neive)*. Accademia Torregiorgi buys grapes from Giovanni Antona for its Barbaresco Crocetta.

Cuba *(Neive)*. Cantina Glicine bottles a Barbaresco cru from Cuba.

Curà or **Curra** *(Neive)*. Adriana Marzi, winemaker of Cantina Glicine, produces some 8000 bottles a year of Barbaresco Curà from their 2.9 acres (1.2 hectares) of vines in this vineyard.

Darmagi *(Barbaresco)*. Gaja farms cabernet sauvignon in this vineyard.

Del Sorì *(Treiso)*. Ernesto Dellapiana of Az. Vit. "Rizzi" cultivates vines in this vineyard, which seems to be another name for his Sorì del Noce vineyard.

Don' Cars *(Barbaresco)*. The Az. Agr. "La Spinona" of Pietro Berutti owns 10.1 acres (4.1 hectares) of vines in this vineyard. They do a cru bottling from them.

Faset *(Barbaresco)*. Mario Minuto bottles a Barbaresco cru from this vineyard. F.lli Oddero has vines here, and Pietro Berutti owns the top section, Bricco Faset.

Fassetto *(Barbaresco)*.

Fondetta *(Treiso)*. The Az. Vit. "Rizzi" of Ernesto Dellapiana owns 4 acres (1.6 hectares) of vines, planted to nebbiolo michet, from which they bottle a Barbaresco cru.

Gaia or **Gaja** *(Neive)*. Maria Feyles and Cantina Glicine bottle Barbaresco crus from this vineyard. Glicine owns 0.9 acre (0.4 hectare) of vines and produces some 2000 bottles a year.

★★★**Gaiun** *(Barbaresco)*. Marchese Alberto di Gresy bottles a cru from this section of La Martinenga adjacent to Asili.

★★**Gallina** *(Neive)*. Castello di Neive and Confratelli di San Michele have vines here. Parroco del Neive owns 3.7 acres (1.5 hectares), 2.5 (1) planted to nebbiolo. They sell some of the grapes to Bruno Giacosa, and both Parroco and Giacosa produce a Gallina cru. Gemma also buys grapes to produce a Gallina cru. Cantina Glicine produces a Barbaresco Gallina as well. While these are all good Barbarescos, we find the one from Bruno Giacosa[2] superior to the rest.

Gallinetta *(Neive)*. Sottimano buys grapes from a 3-acre (1.2-hectare) plot here.

Giachello *(Treiso)*.

★**Giacosa** *(Treiso)*. This vineyard district adjoins Marcarini to the north. Gigi Rosso owns vines here. Cascina Carlo Viglino produces 9300 bottles of Barbaresco from this vineyard.

Gresy *(Treiso)*.

La Ghiga *(Barbaresco)*. Pietro Berutti of "La Spinona" bottles a very good Barbaresco cru from his 8.6 acres (3.5 hectares) in La Ghiga. A few years ago he bought this plot from Bersano. Berutti has produced a La Ghiga cru since 1983.

Loreto *(Barbaresco)*. Paolo de Forville owns vines in this vineyard. Anfosso de Forville has bottled a Barbaresco Loreto since 1974.

Manzola *(Treiso)*.

★**Marcarini** or **Marcarino** *(Treiso)*. Marcarini is in between the regarded crus of Pajorè to the north and Giacosa to the south. Castello di Neive owns a piece of this vineyard. Cantina Glicine and Vignaioli "Elvio Pertinace" bottle Barbaresco crus from here. Glicine produces about 2000 bottles a year. The Vignaioli own 5 acres (2 hectares) and have bottled a Barbaresco from this cru since 1982.

Maringota (*Bricco di Neive*). Giuseppe Traversa of Cascina Chiabotto bottles a Barbaresco Maringota from his vines here.

★★★**Martinenga** (*Barbaresco*). This 54-acre (21.8-hectare) vineyard, which many consider the finest in the zone, is at the curve formed where the southeast slope of Asili and the southwest slope of Rabajà meet. La Martinenga is owned by a single proprietor, Marchese di Gresy. Some 32 acres (13 hectares) are planted to nebbiolo. Di Gresy bottles three Barbarescos from this vineyard, La Martinenga and two subcrus: Camp Gros (since 1978) and Gaiun. Of the two, Camp Gros, from the plot near Rabajà, has more tannin, structure, acid, and firmness; it matures slower and should live longer. Gaiun, adjacent to Asili, is softer and rounder, with more perfume and elegance; it is gentle and feminine. The Barbarescos of Martinenga are among our favorites.

Masseria (*Neive*). Alfredo Currado of Vietti is the sole producer of Masseria Barbaresco. He buys the grapes from Eugenio Voghera, as he has since 1964. Currado produces some 6000 bottles a year of this cru. This 5-acre (2-hectare) vineyard, in the *località* Bruciati di Neive, is planted 100 percent to nebbiolo lampia. This Barbaresco, not unexpectedly, is full-bodied and robust, as far as Barbarescos go.

Messoirano (*Neive*). Accademia Torregiorgi buys grapes from the Messoirano vineyard from Castello di Neive; both bottle a Barbaresco cru from this vineyard.

★**Moccagatta** (*Barbaresco*). Il Vecchio Tralcio, Az. Agr. "Moccagatta," and Produttori del Barbaresco bottle Barbaresco crus from this vineyard. "Moccagatta" owns 25 acres (10 hectares), 15 (6) of which are planted to nebbiolo.

Monferrino (*Treiso*).

Monprandi (*Bricco del Neive*). Franco Bordino cultivates vines in Monprandi from which he produces a cru bottling.

Monta (*Treiso*).

Montarsino (*Treiso*). Another spelling of Montersino.

Montebertotto (*Neive*). Castello di Neive owns 6.7 acres (2.7 hectares) in this vineyard, planted to arneis.

★**Montefico** (*Barbaresco*). The Produttori del Barbaresco produced a Barbaresco cru from this vineyard. Ceretto and Bruno Giacosa used to bottle Barbaresco Montefico crus, but neither buys the grapes any longer. Ceretto hasn't produced a Barbaresco from here since 1974.

Montersino (*San Rocco Senodelvio d'Alba*). The Az. Agr. "Santa Maria" of Mario Viberti produces a Barbaresco cru from vines here.

Montersino (*Treiso*). Prunotto bought grapes from this vineyard at one time.

Montesomo (*Barbaresco*). Cantina Glicine bottles a Barbaresco Montesomo.

★★**Montestefano** (*Barbaresco*). The Barbarescos of this cru tend to be quite tannic and long-lived, especially those from Prunotto. Montestefano has been called the Barolo of Barbaresco; it is, in fact, more like a Neive Barbaresco than one from Barbaresco.

> *Owner and/or Producer*
> [Anfosso] de Forville,[1] since 1974.
> Paolo de Forville.[1]
> F.lli Oddero.
> Produttori del Barbaresco.[1]
> Prunotto,[1] buys grapes from 7.2 acres (2.9 hectares).

Moretti. Valfieri buys grapes from here to produce its Barbaresco Moretti.

Muret (*Treiso*).

Nervo (*Treiso*). The Vignaioli "Elvio Pertinace" co-op owns a total of 12.4 acres (5 hectares) in Nervo. They produced a Barbaresco cru from their 7.4 acres (3 hectares) of nebbiolo in 1982. Torino wine merchant Giovanni Troglia sells a Podere Nervo Barbaresco with his label.

Ovello (*Barbaresco*). Paolo de Forville and the Produttori del Barbaresco own vines here. The Produttori bottle an Ovello cru which is quite good indeed and in certain years can match any other Barbaresco for quality.

Pagliuzzi or **Pagliuzzo** (*Barbaresco*). F.lli Oddero cultivates vines in this vineyard.

★**Paje, Pagliari,** or **Paye** (*Barbaresco*). Produttori del Barbaresco and the Roagnas have vines in this vineyard. Both do a cru bottling. Crichet Pajè is Roagna's best Barbaresco.

★**Pajorè** (*Treiso*). Pajorè, just south of Tre Stelle, adjoins Marcarini on the north. The name is sometimes spelled Payorè. Giovannini-Moresco[2] owns 17.8 acres (7.2 hectares) of vines here, planted 100 percent to nebbiolo rosé. The 20,000 bottles of Barbaresco that Moresco produces comes from those vines. He has produced this outstanding Barbaresco since 1967.

Pas *(Treiso).* Luigi Pelissero owns 2.5 acres (1 hectare) of vines in this vineyard.

Pastura *(Neive).* Accademia Torregiorgi and Cantine Glicine produce good Barbarescos from this vineyard. Glicine produces on average 2000 bottles a year.

★**Payore-Barberis** *(Treiso).* Scarpa[2] buys grapes from Barberis to produce 4000 bottles a year of their fine Barbaresco cru. They label it Payore not to create confusion with Moresco's Pajorè. Both are parts of the same vineyard.

★**Pora** or **Porra** *(Barbaresco).* F.lli Oddero and the Produttori del Barbaresco own vines in this vineyard. The Produttori bottle a Pora cru. In 1980, Vietti bought grapes and produced a small quantity of a Barbaresco Pora.

Pozzo *(Barbaresco).* Anfosso de Forville has bottled a Barbaresco Pozzo since 1974. Giuseppe Rocca has vines here.

Qualin *(Barbaresco).* Pietro Berutti of Az. Agr. "La Spinona" owns 5.4 acres (2.2 hectares) in this vineyard from which he bottles a Barbaresco cru. Gaja also owns a section of Qualin; at one time he bottled a Freisa from his 2.9-acre (1.2-hectare) plot here.

★★**Rabajà** or **Rabajat** *(Barbaresco).* This fine cru, adjoining Martinenga to the south, is in the Pora zone.

> *Owner and/or Producer*
> F.11i Barale[1] has rented 2.5 acres (1 hectare) of fifty-five-year-old vines in
>   this vineyard since 1982.
> Cortese Giuseppe.[1]
> [Anfosso] de Forville,[1] since 1974.
> Cantina Glicine,[1] 0.47 acre (0.2 hectare); 1700 bottles a year.
> Produttori del Barbaresco.[1,2]
> Prunotto[1] buys grapes from 5 acres (2 hectares); they have produced a
>   Barbaresco cru from here since 1971.
> Giuseppe Rocca.
> Valfieri[1] buys grapes.
> Vietti[1] buys grapes from 2.5 acres (1 hectare); he has produced a Barbaresco
>   Rabajà since 1984.

Rigo *(Neive).* Parroco del Neive owns vines here.

★**Rio Sordo** or **Rivosordo** *(Barbaresco).* F.lli Brovia and Produttori del Barbaresco bottle crus from this vineyard. Fontanafredda buy grapes for their Barbaresco.

Rivetti *(Neive).*

Rizzi *(Treiso).* Ernesto Dellapiana of Az. Vit. "Rizzi" owns vines here.

Rombone *(Treiso).*

Roncagliette *(Barbaresco).*

Roncalini *(Barbaresco).* Fontanafredda buy grapes from this vineyard for their Barbaresco.

Ronchi *(Barbaresco).* Giuseppe Rocca owns vines in Ronchi.

San Cristoforo *(Neive).* This vineyard is part of the Basarin district. Confratelli di San Michele and Parroco del Neive each own a piece. The Confratelli bottle a San Cristoforo cru. Bruno Giacosa used to bottle a cru from here but hasn't done so in some time.

San Giuliano *(Neive).* Parroco del Neive has 2 acres (0.8 hectare) of nebbiolo vines in this vineyard.

San Stefanetto *(Treiso).*

★★**Santo Stefano** *(Neive).* Castello di Neive[2] owns 100 percent of this 20-acre (8-hectare) vineyard. They sell some of their grapes to Bruno Giacosa.[2] Their Santo Stefano Barbarescos are among the best produced.

★**Secondine** *(Barbaresco).* This vineyard is just south of Barbaresco itself. Gaja's Sorì San Lorenzo is from grapes grown in this vineyard district.

Serra Boella *(Bricco di Neive).* Cigliuti produces some 4650 bottles a year of a Barbaresco cru from his 7 acres (2.8 hectares) of vines in Serra Boella. Pasquero-Elia owns vines here as well.

Sorì del Noce *(Treiso).* The Az. Vit. "Rizzi" of Ernesto Dellapiana owns 17 acres (6.9 hectares) of vines in Sorì del Noce from which he bottles a Barbaresco cru.

Sorì d' Paytin *(Bricco di Neive).* Secondo Pasquero-Elia owns a total of 9 acres (3.6 hectares) of vines in this vineyard. He bottles a fine Barbaresco cru from his 7 acres (2.8 hectares) of nebbiolo vines.

★**Sorì San Lorenzo** *(Barbaresco).* Gaja is the sole owner of this 3-acre (1.2-hectare) vineyard. He has bottled it as a cru since 1967. In altitude it is between the other two Gaja crus and lies within the vineyard district of Secondine.

Sorì Tildin *(Barbaresco).* Gaja is the sole owner of this 4-acre (1.6-hectare) vineyard. He has bottled a Sorì Tildin Barbaresco since 1970. Of the three Gaja crus, the vines here are grown at the highest altitude.

Speranza *(Treiso).* Ernesto Dellapiana of Az. Vit. "Rizzi" owns grapes here.

Stella *(Treiso).*

Suri *(Barbaresco).* Donato Giacosa owns a 0.9-acre (0.4-hectare) section of this vineyard.

Suri *(Treiso).* The Az. Vit. "Rizzi" of Ernesto Dellapiana owns vines here. It might be still another name for Sorì del Noce.

Tamburnas *(Neive).* Sottimano buys grapes from a 1-acre (0.4-hectare) piece of this vineyard.

Tetti *(Neive).* Scarpa buys grapes from this vineyard to produce some 10,000 to 12,000 bottles a year of its very fine Barbaresco I Tetti.[2]

Trifolera *(Barbaresco).* Sottimano buys grapes from a 1-acre (0.4-hectare) piece of Triofolera.

Valeriano *(Treiso).*

Valgrande *(Treiso).* Paolo Colla produces a Barbaresco cru from his grapes in Valgrande.

Valtorta *(Neive).* Castello di Neive owns 7.4 acres (3 hectares) of dolcetto vines in this vineyard.

Vanotu *(Treiso).* Luigi Pelissero produces a Barbaresco cru from his 5 acres (2 hectares) of vines in Vanotu.

Varaldi *(Treiso).*

Vecchia Casot *(Barbaresco).* Carlo Boffa produces a Barbaresco cru from his holdings in this vineyard, which is part of the Casot vineyard district.

Vincenziana *(Barbaresco).*

Vitolotti *(Barbaresco).* Luigi Bianco and Carlo Boffa own vines here. Boffa produces a Vitolotti cru from his 22 acres (9 hectares) of vines here. This vineyard is part of the Casot district.

Notes, definitions, and abbreviations:

1. Labeled with the cru name.

2. This combination of producer and cru is among our favorites in Barbaresco.

Az. Agr.: Azienda Agricola, a winery that only uses its own grapes to produce wine.

Cascina: Farm, it could refer to a single vineyard or a group of vineyards owned by a single proprietor or estate.

F.lli: Fratelli, brothers.

1 hectare = 2.4711 acres.

1 hectoliter = 26.42 gallons = 11.11 cases.

1 meter = 3.281 feet.

The Barbaresco Producers Rated

★★★★

Giacosa Bruno
Giovannini-Moresco Enrico
"Bricco Asili" Az. Agr. and Casa Vinicola Ceretto
Castello di Neive
Gaja
Martinenga di Marchese di Gresy
Produttori del Barbaresco
Vietti di Alfredo Currado

★★★

Cantina Glicine
Cigliuti F. lli
Conterno Giacomo (not produced since 1971)
Giacosa F.lli
"La Spinona" Az. Agr. di Pietro Berutti
Pasquero-Elia Secondo
Prunotto Alfredo
Rinaldi Francesco (we haven't tasted it for some time)
+ Scarpa Antica Casa Vinicola

★★

+ Barale F.lli
+ Bordino Franco (most recent vintage tasted was 1974)
Borgogno Giacomo (before 1968; since 1968,★)
Contratto Giuseppe
De Forville Anfosso
Franco Fiorina
Giacosa Donato
Mascarello Giuseppe
Oddero F.lli
Parroco del Neive
Pelissero Luigi

"Punset" di R. Marcarino (before 1975; since 1974, 0)
Ratti Renato
"Rizzi" di Ernesto Dellapiana
Roagna "I Paglieri" di Alfredo e Giovanni
Rosso Gigi

★

+ Accademia Torregiorgi
Bianco Luigi
Boffa Carlo
Borgogno F.lli Serio & Battista
Borgogno Giacomo (since 1968; previously★★)
Calissano Luigi (most recent vintage tasted was 1971)
Castello Feudale
Coppo Luigi
De Forville Paolo
Feyles Maria (most recent vintage tasted was 1976)
Fontanafredda
Gemma
Giordano Giovanni
Giri Guido (we haven't tasted it for some time)
"Gran Duca" Cantine Duca d'Asti
Marchese Spinola (most recent vintage tasted was 1967)
Nicolello
Pio Cesare
Rocca Dario, Az. Agr. Ca' Nova
Traversa Giuseppe, Cascina Chiabotto
Vecchio Piemonte Cantine Produttori
Vezza Sergio
Vignaioli "Elvio Pertinace"

0

Ascheri Giacomo

Balbo Marino (most recent vintage tasted was 1974)
Bel Colle
Bersano
Bosca Luigi
Brero Cav. Luigi
Brovia F.lli
Bruzzone
Cabutto Bartolomeo (most recent vintage tasted was 1976)
Carra (most recent vintage tasted was 1973)
Casetta F.lli
– Cauda Cav. Luigi
– Cavaletto
Colla Paolo
Confratelli di San Michele (most recent vintage tasted was 1976)
"Conte de Cavour," Cantine Barbero (most recent vintage tasted was 1974)
Cossetti Clemente
Damilano Dott. Giacomo (most recent vintage tasted was 1975)
Gherzi (we haven't tasted it for some time)
Grazziola (we haven't tasted it for some time)
Il Vecchio Tralcio

– Kiola, now F.lli Dogliani
"La Brenta d'Oro" Cantina d'Invecchiamento (most recent vintage tasted was 1974)
Marchesi di Barolo
"Moccagatta" Az. Agr.
Osvaldo Mauro
Palladino
Pavese Livio
Pippione (we haven't tasted it in some time)
Podere Casot Nada
"Punset" di R. Marcarino (post-1974; pre-1975,★★)
"Roche" Azienda Vinicola (to watch since Carlo Brovia is their consultant)
– Scanavino
Serafino Enrico (most recent vintage tasted was 1974)
Tenuta Coluè di Massimo Oddero (most recent vintage tasted was 1974)
Troglia Giovanni (they were better in the 60s)
Valfieri
Villadoria Marchese
Voerzio Giacomo (most recent vintage tasted was 1976)

Tasting Notes
1984

The spring of 1984 was the wettest in memory; the rain never seemed to let up from the beginning of April through the first half of June. This, combined with low temperatures, slowed down the growth in the vineyards by at least twenty days and had a major impact on quantity. Rain during the flowering seriously hampered the cross-pollination. Quantity was down 30 to 60 percent from the previous vintage, with the nebbiolo crop being the most affected. Sugars at harvest were satisfactory, but acid levels were fairly high. Scarpa, for one, produced no Barbaresco.

As we have tasted only two '84 Barbarescos at this point, we can't really pass judgment on the vintage. But obviously it was a difficult year.

Vietti, Masseria (*ex-cask 2/85*). The high acid and aggressive tannins in the wine make it difficult to judge at this point.

Vietti, Rabajà (*ex-cask 2/85*). Perfumed aroma; firm, fairly tannic, has almost a sweetness to it; should become a nice wine.

1983 [★★★]

The 1983 harvest produced a fairly good-sized crop. The wines are well balanced and tend to be on the light side; they should be ready early.

Angelo Gaja compares them to the '79s, though he rates the year slightly higher in overall quality. Based on our tastings of ten wines from cask thus far, it appears that the vintage was more successful for Barbaresco than it was for Barolo. The wines are fairly well balanced and somewhat light-bodied, but can be elegant.

Borgogno F.lli Serio e Battista (*ex-cask 11/84*). Big, fairly rich aroma with hints of tartufi; a mouthful of fruit; a Barolo lover's Barbaresco.★★(+)

Cappellano Dott. Giuseppe (*ex-cask 1/85*). Berrylike aroma; taste of sweet, ripe fruit.★★(★)

Ceretto, Asÿ (*ex-cask 11/84*). A vague mushroomlike note on the aroma; a bit light but with some elegance; should be ready in two to three years.★★(+)

Ceretto, Bricco Asili (*ex-cask 11/84*). A lot of fruit on the nose and palate, more tannin and substance than the Asÿ; should make a nice bottle in about four to five years.★★(★)

Giacosa Bruno, Santo Stefano (*ex-cask 11/84*). Fairly full-bodied, sweet, rich, ripe fruit flavors; with time should make a splendid wine.★★(★)

"La Spinona" di Pietro Berutti, Bricco Faset (*ex-cask 11/84*). Nice flavor of ripe fruit, some elegance.★★(+)

"La Spinona" di Pietro Berutti, La Ghiga (*ex-cask 11/84*). Well balanced, some class, a lot of flavor.★★

Moccagatta Az. Agr. (*2/85*). This Barbaresco was aged for about ninety days in new barrique, which is quite obvious in the oak and fruit aroma and the oaky sweetness on the palate; has some tannin and not much nebbiolo character; a nice red wine, no more.★

Scarpa, Tetti di Neive (*ex-cask 2/85*). Fairly rich and full, with sweet berrylike fruit; very well balanced.★★(★)

Vietti, Masseria (*ex-cask 2/85*). A fairly full-bodied Barbaresco with some elegance and a lot of fruit.★★(★)

1982 [★★★★]

As in Barolo, the 1982 vintage in Barbaresco was nearly perfect. Cold weather in June slowed down the ripening process, and the harvest took place in the first part of October. The grape bunches were beautiful.

Angelo Gaja says his '82s have more elegance and class than the '78s. Alfredo Currado of Vietti feels the '82s might equal the '71s in quality, a point of view shared by many other producers. Giuseppe Colla of Prunotto said the vintage produced full-bodied wines of very high quality. Pio Boffa of Pio Cesare describes the wines as complex and fruity.

From our experience—if the uniform high quality of twenty-two wines is sufficient to go on—we put '82 ahead of '71 and think it might even surpass '78.

Ascheri Giacomo (4/85). Some oxidation on nose; has tannin and very little else; lacks character.

Borgogno F.lli Serio e Battista (ex-cask 11/84). Deep color; oak and blackberries on the nose; a lot of tannin but seems to have sufficient fruit; some alcohol at the end.★

Castello di Neive, Santo Stefano (2/85). A big, rich Barbaresco with heaps of fruit and a lot of tannin, a rich, fairly intense wine.★★★(+)

Ceretto, Asÿ (ex-cask 11/84). Floral aroma; moderate tannin over a core of rich, ripe fruit; well balanced.★★(★)

Ceretto, Bricco Asili (ex-cask 11/84). Floral aroma; moderate tannin, loads of fruit; shows a lot of potential but still somewhat closed.★★(★ +)

Cigliuti, Serra Boella (twice 1/85; 5580 bottles). Ripe fruit bouquet with nuances of berries, flowers, and tobacco; a lot of tannin and a lot of fruit; quality already evident.★★(★)

Gaja (4 times 4/85) Very dark color; oak obvious on nose; a nice mouthful of flavor once you get past the heavy oak which dominates; has a firm tannic vein; needs no less than three or four years; very fine quality.★★(+)

Gaja, Costa Russi (twice 4/85). Oak and ripe fruit on aroma; tannin is the dominant factor at this point, but a lot of fruit beneath; supple center, firm tannic vein; not really ready but tempting.★★(★)

Gaja, Sorì San Lorenzo (11/84). Aroma dominated by oak; firm and tannic; oak tannins and sweet ripe fruit as well as some spice, has balance and style; needs time for the oak and fruit to marry.★★★(+)

Gaja, Sorì Tildin (11/84). Deepest in color of the three Gaja Barbarescos tasted; oak is the most obvious component on the aroma, with some ripe fruit evident; a richly fleshed wine with the taste of sweet, ripe fruit and oak; should make a splendid bottle in time.★★★(★)

Giacosa Bruno, Gallina (ex-vat 11/84). Expansive floral aroma; enormous extract of sweet, ripe fruit; a wine of immense quality that is somewhat overshadowed by the Santo Stefano.★★★(+)

Giacosa Bruno, Santo Stefano (ex-vat 11/84). A mushroom, woodsy aroma; fuller and firmer than the Gallina; a profound wine that will need many years to attain its peak, but when it does it will surely be extraordinary.★★★(★)

Giacosa Donato (twice 2/85). Aroma reminiscent of a Rhône wine, rich fruit and spice, hints of raspberries, tobacco, and cherries; moderate tannin but with sufficient fruit to balance; acid a bit low; young yet, some character evident; could be longer on palate.★★

"La Spinona" di Pietro Berutti (twice 5/85). Lovely tobacco, berrylike aroma with hints of flowers and cherries; medium-bodied, some tannin and sweet, ripe fruit; stylish and elegant.★★(★)

"La Spinona" di Pietro Berutti, Bricco Faset (ex-cask 11/84). Tar and oak on aroma; firm and tannic with a rich core of ripe fruit.★★(★)

Martinenga, Marchese di Gresy (2/85). Tobacco and cherries on aroma; full of flavor; extremely well balanced; has elegance; long finish; the best Martinenga to date.★★★(★)

Nicolello (4/85). Light nose, some fruit, cherry notes; some tannin with the fruit to support it; tannic finish; quite young.★(+)

Oddero F.lli (5/85). Aroma suggestive of cherries, tartufi, and flowers; quite tannic, but the fruit is there to carry it.★★(+)

Pasquero Elia Secondo, Sorì d' Paytin (3 times 4/85). Aroma of concentrated blackberries; a full-flavored Barbaresco in a gentle, elegant style; some tannin; long tannic aftertaste; should be ready in about two years.★★(★)

Prunotto, Montestefano (ex-cask 1/85). Aroma is rich and intense, with hints of tartufi and oak; a lot of flavor; a rich, fairly full-bodied Barbaresco.★★(★)

Roagna, Vigna Pajè (ex-cask 1/85). Cherrylike aroma; rich fruit, some tannin; good quality.★(★)

Scarpa, Tetti di Neive (ex-cask 2/85). A big, fruity aroma with a touch of gingerbread and spice; still has a lot of tannin and firmness, but a mouthful of rich, ripe concentrated fruit; it should be splendid in perhaps five years.★★★(+)

Traversa Giuseppe, Cascina Chiabotto, Vigneto Maringota (4/85). Fruity aroma has peppery notes; some tannin; perhaps a touch too simple, but well made.★

Vietti, Masseria (ex-cask 4/85). Enormous richness on the nose; big, rich, deep, profound; the best Vietti Barbaresco to date and a superb wine by any standard. We have tasted this wine three times, all from cask, and each time has left us more impressed than the previous time.★★★(★)

1981 ★+

The vintage in 1981 was mixed. Overall it was not up to the level of 1980, another mixed year, though there were some notable exceptions.

Gaja produced all three of his crus in 1981; in 1980, he didn't bottle any. The Cerettos also

1981

made better wines in 1981 than in 1980. On the other hand, Bruno Giacosa said the '81s for him were very small wines; he didn't make any Barbaresco, nor did Castello di Neive. Giuseppe Colla described his '81s as medium-bodied wines of average quality.

The '81s will be ready early; the best have some elegance.

Ascheri Giacomo (4/85). Small nose; some tannin; shy in fruit.

Borgogno F.lli Serio e Battista (ex-cask 11/84). Aroma rather closed, with some alcohol and vague nebbiolo character evident; moderate fruit, moderate tannin; seems to lack a bit of structure.

Ceretto, Asy (twice 2/85). Mushrooms on the aroma; a lot of flavor, almost seems sweet, has character and style, some elegance; very good, especially for the vintage; moderately long on finish with tannin that indicates it still needs time, though it should be ready early. ★★

Colla Paolo, Valgrande (4/85). Color shows considerable age; light and fruity, soft, undistinguished, lacks structure and weight.

Fontanafredda (1/85). Floral aroma; moderate tannin, a lot of fruit; still young and somewhat astringent; some firmness at the end; shows promise. ★(★)

Gaja (twice 4/85). Light oak and a hint of mushrooms on the aroma; light- to medium-bodied, light tannin, good fruit; certainly a success for the vintage; ready early, perhaps in two years, though it can be enjoyed now; less fleshy and ripe than the crus. ★(★)

Gaja, Costa Russi (11/84; 6800 bottles). Notes of blackberries and oak on nose; light tannin; forward, berrylike fruit; can be enjoyed now though will certainly improve. ★★(+)

Gaja, Sorì San Lorenzo (twice 11/84; 5870 bottles). Perfumed, floral bouquet with notes of oak and mushrooms; sweet fruit and oak on palate, elegant and refined; has length; tannin at the end indicates further age needed though it's tempting now. ★★★ −

Gaja, Sorì Tildin (twice 11/84; 6615 bottles. Fairly intense floral aroma with notes of berries and oak; a mouthful of ripe fruit; well structured, some tannin; very, very good. ★★★

Glicine Cantina, Vigna dei Curà. (twice 1/85; 7450 bottles). Aroma somewhat reticent, a note of tartufi and nebbiolo fruit; fairly well balanced, gentle, and elegant, tasty; some length; won't be for keeping; should be ready relatively soon. ★★

"La Ca'Nova" Az. Agr., Dario Rocca (twice 1/85). Color shows a surprising amount of age; nice fruit on aroma, vaguely floral, tarry notes; tannin seems somewhat high for the fruit. Will it soften or dry out first? ★(?)

Martinenga, Marchese di Gresy (2/85; 14,800 bottles). The aroma is there, but you have to work for it, then vanilla, cherries, and flowers come out; has a fair amount of tannin but seems to have sufficient fruit; some style evident; short, tannic finish. ★(★)

Osvaldo Mauro (twice 4/85). Both were oxidized.

Pasquero Elia Secondo, Sorì d' Paytin (3 times 2/85; 14,500 bottles). Light, undeveloped aroma with hints of fruit and flowers; berryish fruit; soft, light tannin; forward but still needs another year or two; a soft, light style but a surprising richness and some elegance. ★★

Produttori del Barbaresco (1/85). Fairly nice aroma with a faint suggestion of tartufi; light tannin, medium-bodied, good fruit; could improve a bit but is nice drinking now. ★ +

"Punset" di R. Marcarino (1/85). Cherrylike fruit on nose; moderate tannin, seems to have sufficient fruit; somewhat on the light side; should be ready soon and won't be a keeper; tannic aftertaste. ★

Scarpa, Payore Barberis (2/85; 4002 bottles). Floral aroma; seems sweeter and softer than the Tetti di Neive and even rounder at first, but it does have more tannin and higher acid, also more fruit; finish is decidedly tannic. ★★(★)

Scarpa, Tetti di Neive (2/85; 10,575 bottles). Bouquet still somewhat reticent though fruit is evident; finely balanced; fruit seems almost sweet; some tannin but tempting now; give it two years or so. ★★ +

Traversa Giuseppe, Cascina Chiabotto, Vigneto Maringota (4/85). Light nose, a bit shy on fruit though some is there; not bad considering the year. ★ −

Vietti, Masseria (3 times 2/85; 4002 bottles). Perfumed bouquet with suggestions of cherries and tobacco; well balanced, a bit light in body; light tannin; quite a lot of flavor; nearly ready. ★★ +

1980 ★★ −

This was a mixed vintage, overall better than 1981. Angelo Gaja compares it to 1975, not a very impressive year. He bottled no crus. Alfredo Currado noted that the wines have style and perfume. He finds them about equal in quality to the '79s. Giuseppe Colla describes them as well balanced. Pio Boffa found the vintage satisfactory. Castello di Neive produced very little, choosing instead to sell most of their grapes to the large industrial producers.

The 80's will mature soon and not keep well, but overall they are fairly good wines.

Accademia Torregiorgi, Messoriano di Neive (2/85). Fairly intense aroma of dried fruit; moderate tannin; a lot of fruit; fairly well balanced; short, tannic aftertaste, nearly ready, needs another two years or so. ★(★)

Ascheri Giacomo (1/85). Light aroma, almost candylike; some fruit but atypical, bitter, not a lot of stuffing.

Barale F.lli, Rabajà riserva (twice 4/85). Up-front fruit on the nose, with suggestions of berries, tobacco, tartufi, and a vague floral note; firm, a soft center surrounded by tannin, a bit light; could be enjoyed now, but it really needs more time; for early drinking. ★★(+)

Bianco Luigi (twice 1/85). Aroma is closed in, though some nebbiolo fruit is evident; a bit light, some tannin, fairly well balanced; will be ready early. ★(★)

1980

Borgogno Giacomo riserva *(twice 5/85)*. Some volatile acidity and nebbiolo character on the nose; a fair amount of fruit but somewaht unbalanced and harsh; finish is short and somewhat acidic.★ –

Brero Cav. Luigi *(1/85)*. Nose has a southern character; same on palate, light tannin, low fruit.

Casetta F.lli *(twice 5/85)*. Cherrylike aroma; moderate tannin, decent fruit; a bit young and simple; should be ready soon.★

Castello di Neive, Santo Stefano *(1/85)*. Aroma reminiscent of cherries; more tannin than expected for the vintage, astringent, but the fruit is there, flavor already evident; give it about three years.★★(+)

Ceretto, Asili *(2/85; 25,554 bottles)*. Aroma reveals less than the '81; somewhat sweet on entry, fairly ripe fruit, some elegance.★★(+)

Ceretto, Bricco Asili *(twice 2/85; 8960 bottles)*. Expansive aroma with some spice, a lot of fruit, vaguely floral; already shows complexity; firm-textured, with a fair amount of fruit; moderate length; still needs time but very good quality.★★(★)

Contratto *(6/85)*. Pretty, raspberry aroma, fragrant; a nice mouthful of flavor, light tannin; nearly ready, drinkable now.★★

De Forville, Vigneto Loreto *(twice 4/85)*. Aroma of oak and tar; quite tannic with the fruit to back it up, some firmness; fairly nice though still young.★★

Franco Fiorina *(1/85)*. Light woodsy aroma; moderate tannin, fairly nice fruit, though not a lot of body; should be ready soon; short, tannic aftertaste.★

Gaja *(ex-cask 10/81)*. Open aroma of spice and fruit; seems fairly full at this stage, with more tannin than expected.★(+)

Giacosa Bruno, Gallina *(ex-cask 11/81)*. Raspberry aroma; a surprising amount of fruit and a fair amount of tannin as well.★★

Giacosa Bruno, Santo Stefano *(ex-cask 10/84)*. Rich aroma with suggestions of tobacco and strawberries; firm tannic vein, but fruit is quite evident; notes of chocolate and licorice.★★ +

Giacosa F.lli *(3 times 4/85)*. Nice fruit on the nose, vague tartufi note; some firmness, well balanced; young but potential evident, some class.★★

Giordano Giovanna, Vigneto Cavana *(twice 1/85)*. Ripe, berrylike fruit on aroma; light tannin, fairly soft, medium-bodied; a bit simple; nearly ready.★

Giovannini-Moresco Enrico, Podere del Pajorè *(ex-cask 10/81; grapes picked 11/11)*. Very deep color; surprisingly rich and concentrated aroma with hints of blackberries and other fruit; quite tannic but full of fruit; should become a very fine bottle.★★(★)

Glicine Cantina, Vigna dei Curà *(4 times 4/85; 12,525 bottles)*. Light floral aroma with hints of tartufi and mushrooms; a little light in body, gentle, some tannin, nice flavor; could use another year or two to round out the tannin at the end; not a wine for laying down.★★

Glicine Cantina, Vigna dei Gaja *(3/85; 2100 bottles)*. Nice nose, has fruit and floral aspects, some pine; acid on the high side, light tannin, flavorful, gentle; nearly ready.★★ –

Glicine Cantina, Vigna Rabajà. *(twice 3/85; 2190 bottles)*. Most characteristic varietal aroma of the three crus, cherry note; acid a tad high, overall well balanced, gentle, some elegance; nice now; has length.★★ +

Granduca *(1/85)*. Aroma displays some richness and vague notes of cherry and tar; tannin up front gives way to fairly decent fruit; fairly well balanced; finishes on a short, tannic note.★

I1 Vecchio Tralcio, Moccagatta *(twice 1/85; 10,000 bottles)*. Tobaccolike aroma; fairly tannic. Is there enough fruit? Short, tannic aftertaste.

"La Spinona" di Piero Berutti *(5/85)*. Aroma recalls resin and berries with a woodsy overtone; some elegance and a lot of style; enjoyable now, with room for improvement.★★★ –

"La Spinona" di Piero Berutti, Bricco Faset *(11/84)*. Interesting aroma with a suggestion of wheat or other grain; moderately intense aroma; soft and tasty, light tannin, some sweetness; already now.★★

Martinenga, Marchese di Gresy *(2/85; 16,420 bottles)*. Bouquet displays some complexity, tobacco and cherry notes; still some tannin, well balanced, some elegance, a little light; good quality; nearly ready.★★(★)

Moccagatta Az. Agr. *(2/85)*. Reticent aroma with a faint suggestion of tobacco; moderate tannin, fairly nice fruit; tannic aftertaste with a touch of bitterness; fairly good but lacks style.★

Oddero F.lli *(twice 1/85)*. Reticient aroma revealing some fruit; moderate tannin but should be ready fairly soon, well balanced, has some character.★(★)

Pasquero Elia Secondo, Sorì d' Paytin *(ex-cask 5/81)*. Fresh, cherrylike aroma; a bit light, some tannin, acid seems a bit high and out of balance, but it is too soon to say for sure.?

Pelissero Luigi *(twice 1/85)*. Lovely, fruity aroma with floral overtones; some tannin, tasty, has a gentleness; good potential.★★

Produttori del Barbaresco *(3 times 5/85)*. Moderately intense aroma has a woodsy slant and a note of mushrooms; a bit light, some tannin, fairly well balanced; tasty, nearly ready, or should be soon; finish recalls chocolate.★★

Produttori del Barbaresco, Pora *(ex-cask 11/82)*. Cherrylike fruit, not a lot of tannin; should be ready early.★★

Prunotto, Montestefano *(1/85; 10,400 bottles)*. Aroma has a harshness to it. Va? Alcohol? Or both? Some fruit, but overly tannic, unbalanced; not a success.

"Punset" di R. Marcarino *(1/85)*. Cherries on aroma; overly tannic, light-bodied, some fruit.

Ratti Renato *(twice 10/83)*. Perfumed bouquet, vague hint of tartufi; light tannin, well structured, smooth, and tasty, a bit light in body; quite ready.★★ –

Roagna, Vigna Pajè. *(twice 1/85)*. Light aroma; moderate tannin, some fruit, soft-centered, not a lot of character; nearly ready.★

"Roche" Az. Vit. *(1/85)*. Flat and dull, some fruit.

Traversa Giuseppe, Cascina Chiabotto, Vigneto Maringota *(4/85)*. Tobacco, mushroom aroma; some tannin, has the fruit to balance; should make a nice little luncheon wine soon.★

Vezza Sergio *(twice 1/85)*. Aroma suggests strawberries; some tannin, fairly nice fruit; nearly ready, perhaps in a year or two.★

Vietti, Masseria *(4 times 5/84; 4600 bottles)*. Light floral aroma; fairly well balanced; tasty, needs another year or two; has some elegance and style.★★(+)

Vignaiolo "Elvio Pertinace" riserva *(2/85)*. Smallish aroma; light-bodied, light tannin, fruit seems almost sweet, lacks some style but drinkable enough; short, tannic aftertaste.(★)

1979 ★★+

This was another uneven vintage; the quality of the wines depends on when the grapes were picked. There was some rain during the harvest.

Gaja found the wines more elegant than the '78s, and they will be ready sooner; they have less body and structure. He felt that Costa Russi was his best wine. For Alfredo Currado the vintage was very good indeed, producing more velvety wines with more glycerine than the '80s. Giuseppe Colla characterized the '79s as soft and mellow. Pio Boffa found the quality satisfactory. Bruno Ceretto considers them, while not equal to the '78s, certainly very good wines. Bruno Giacosa said that although they are easy wines that will be ready early, it was a very good vintage. He also said that the wines won't be long-lived.

For us, the wine of the vintage was Enrico Giovannini-Moresco's. It is truly an outstanding wine, even finer than his excellent '78.

Ascheri Giacomo (10/82). Lacks structure and weight, some tannin, very little else.

Barale F.lli (5/85). Tobacco and flowers on aroma; some fruit in back, light tannin, touch of acid, light-bodied, soft in center, lacks somewhat in depth; ready.★★−

Bel Colle (10/82). Pale color; some tannin; in all, an anemic wine.

Boffa Carlo, Vigna Vecchia Casot (ex-cask 4/80). Light to medium in color; some volatile acidity; has some tannin and some fruit, but already showing signs of age.

Boffa Carlo, Vigna Vitolotti (ex-cask, 4/80). Fruity aroma; a bit light but nice flavor, some tannin; a light weight, little wine.(★)

Brovia F.lli (ex-cask 6/82). This wine should have been bottled some time ago, volatile acidity is painfully obvious; still has nice fruit, but a bitter tannic edge; it seems to us it's downhill from here.

Casetta F.lli (twice 5/85). Small aroma, with a vague hint of tobacco and some nebbiolo fruit; somewhat unbalanced, a bit simple, nice fruit.★−

Castello di Neive, Santo Stefano (4 times 4/85). Lovely perfumed bouquet displays the richness of ripe fruit and nuances of mint, flowers, and tobacco; moderate tannin, a lot of fruit, some firmness, well balanced, a bit light toward the finish, which is somewhat tannic.★★(★)

Cauda Cav. Luigi (1/85). Wine has a southern character to it, on nose and palate; flat, low in acid.

Ceretto, Asili (twice 2/85; 26,500 bottles and 650 magnums). Big, rich bouquet of ripe fruit recalls cherries, flowers, and tartufi; firm tannin, still quite young, but a lot of fruit makes it tempting now; the tannin suggests that you resist, give it two or three years at least; has style and some elegance.★★(★)

Ceretto, Bricco Asili (5 times 1/85; 7985 bottles). A lot of fruit on bouquet, strawberries, raspberries, also mushrooms and a hint of tartufi; still somewhat tannic and firm; still young, but the quality is already evident; should make a splendid bottle in another three or four years.★★(★)

Cigliuti, Serra Boella (ex-cask 10/81; 7200 bottles). Fruity aroma with a cherrylike note; moderate tannin, well balanced, lots of flavor; should make a nice wine.★★

Contratto (5/85). Berrylike fruit and flowers; light tannin, tasty, soft-centered; fairly long finish; very ready.

De Forville (twice 4/85). Big, fruity aroma marred by an off odor vaguely like that of a wet dog; moderate tannin with sufficient fruit to carry it; needs two or three years.★(+)

Fontanafredda (12/83). Tartufi and cherries, some vanilla on nose; a surprising mouthful of nice fruit; ready now.★★

Franco Fiorina riserva and riserva speciale (twice 5/85). Lovely bouquet of mushrooms and raspberries seems more suggestive of pinot noir than nebbiolo; medium-bodied, light tannin, soft and round, nice flavor, very well balanced, and nearly ready; fairly long aftertaste.★★+

Gaja (8 times 11/84; 118,420 bottles). Bouquet exhibits a mellowness from age as well as complexity, a mushroom note, strawberries, tartufi, cherries, and nebbiolo fruit over background of oak; sweet taste of ripe fruit, light tannin; somewhat light in body but elegant; loads of flavor and a lot of quality evident; nearly ready.★★+

Gaja, Costa Russi (3 times 11/84; 14,487 bottles and larger sizes). Oak character most evident at this stage but also mint and cherries; has a firm tannic vein and a lot of fruit; still young but splendid quality.★★★

Gaja, Sorì San Lorenzo (4 times 11/84; 5281 bottles). Surprisingly rich Burgundian bouquet; a mouthful of flavor, finely balanced and elegant, heaps of style, splendid wine, still has room to improve.★★★(+)

Gaja, Sorì Tildin (5 times 11/84; 6150 bottles and larger sizes). Bouquet already offers some complexity, hints of strawberries, cherries, and tobacco over background of oak; lovely, round fruit flavors, some tannin, stylish and elegant; a bit light but well structured; lingers on palate.★★(★)

Giacosa Bruno, Gallina (ex-cask 10/81). Fruit rises out of the glass; for Giacosa perhaps a light Barbaresco, but overall it has a surprising richness and concentration; very well made; should make a lovely bottle when ready.★★(+)

Giacosa F.lli (twice 4/85; 12,400 bottles). Nice aroma with notes of tartufi, fruit, and vanilla; well balanced, still has tannin to shed, loads of flavor.★★+

Giovannini-Moresco Enrico, Podere del Pajorè (14 times 3/85; 20,765 bottles—not often enough). This is certainly the wine of the vintage, and more than that—an outstanding wine that might even surpass Moresco's legendary '71—a superstar. A bouquet of enormous richness with suggestions of ripe black cherries, tobacco, and tartufi; a fleshy wine that is a virtual explosion of sweet ripe fruit, complete and harmonious; though still young, it offers many nuances; fabulously rich; enormous concentration; very long finish. If we

1979

give it four stars now, what do we do when it reaches its peak?★★★ + (★★★★)

Glicine Cantina, Vigna dei Curà (*ex-cask 12/80*). A lot of fruit on both nose and palate, some elegance, well balanced, good quality though a bit light.★★ +

Glicine Cantina, Vigna Marcarino (*ex-cask 4/80*). Cherrylike aroma; well-knit, some tannin, considerable fruit; already shows style.★★(+)

"La Spinona" di Piero Berutti (*6/82; bottled 20 days earlier*). Still seems tight and ungiving, though fruit is evident if you work for it; some elegance, well structured, moderate tannin, a lot of flavor; seems a bit short at this stage; has potential.★(★)

"La Spinona" di Piero Berutti, Bricco Faset riserva speciale (*twice 5/84*). Still a bit closed on aroma; sweet ripe fruit flavors in spite of being somewhat light-bodied; has style, well made; firm tannic vein, needs time to soften.★★(★)

Marchesi di Barolo (*10/82*). Pale color; not a lot to the aroma; light tannin, fairly nice fruit on entry; light-bodied, lacks some weight and style; rather pedestrian, an industrial wine.

Martinenga–Camp Gros, Marchese di Gresy (*3 times 2/85; 6500 bottles*). Floral, woodsy bouquet has a cherrylike note; finely structured, has elegance and style; long finish recalls licorice; young but tempting; a wine of very high quality. (Crazy Gresy, we raise our glasses to you, and wouldn't mind a refill!)★★★(+)

Moccagatta Az. Agr. (*2/85*). Stinky odors; rather light-bodied, moderate tannin, has fruit; bitter on the finish; lacks quality and style.

Palladino (*twice 1/85*). Vaguely floral bouquet; light-bodied, light tannin, fairly nice fruit up front, but tails off as it goes back.(★)

Parroco del Neive (*ex-cask 10/81*). Considerable fruit evident on both aroma and flavor, seems rather light; some tannin and not much character.

Pasquero Elia Secondo, Sorì d' Paytin (*twice, ex-cask 4/80 and 11/80*). Seems overly astringent and rather thin, without much fruit or character; a big surprise from what is normally a very good producer.

Pavese Livio (*1/85*). Some fruit evident on the nose; moderate tannin, some astringency, fairly forward; marred by intrusion of alcohol at the end.

Pelissero Luigi (*ex-cask 4/80*). Grapey aroma; fruity, some style, on the light side, some tannin, fairly nice.★

Pio Cesare (*1/85*). Light nose, still somewhat reticent, with a suggestion of *barrique* and not much else at this stage; firm tannic vein, seems to be sufficiently well balanced to carry the tannin.★

Produttori del Barbaresco (*4 times 5/85*). Full, fruity, woodsy aroma, recalling cherries and berries; lovely now, with ripe fruit flavors.★★

Produttori del Barbaresco, Asili riserva (*3 times 5/85; 6790 bottles*). Floral bouquet has a suggestion of tartufi; ripe fruit on palate seems sweet and fairly forward; should be ready soon, but drinkable now; stylish.★★★

Produttori del Barbaresco, Moccagatta riserva (*twice 5/85; 13,560 bottles*). Quite tannic, fuller and harder than the Asili or Rabajà; quite young, could use more style.★(★)

Produttori del Barbaresco, Montefico (*ex-cask 4/80*). Fairly intense aroma; seems overly tannic; some quality evident.★(★)

Produttori del Barbaresco, Montestefano riserva (*3 times 11/84*). Richly fruited aroma, marred by some alcohol; seems overly tannic; a real disappointment.★

Produttori del Barbaresco, Ovello (*twice 1/85*). Aroma has suggestions of cigars, fruit, and tartufi; well balanced, loads of flavor; a fair amount of tannin, perhaps a bit too much; some length.★★(+)

Produttori del Barbaresco, Payè (*ex-cask 4/80*). Tartufi on the aroma; on the light side but well balanced and tasty; a wine of quality.★★(+)

Produttori del Barbaresco, Pora (*ex-cask 4/80*). Tartufi on aroma; considerable tannin but a lot of fruit; a Barbaresco with class.★★(★)

Produttori del Barbaresco, Rabajà riserva (*4 times 5/85; 27,180 bottles*). Tobacco, cherries, and strawberries under a woodsy aroma; fullest in body of all the crus and one of the most tannic, also along with Asili the most impressive, but has some delicacy.★★(★ +)

Produttori del Barbaresco, Rio Sordo (*ex-cask 4/80*). A bit light but loads of flavor; quality evident.★★

Prunotto, Montestefano (*1/85; 10,585 bottles*). Nose is marred by the intrusion of volatile acidity; some fruit evident but a questionable future.★(?★)

Rizzi Az. Agr. di Ernesto Dellapiana (*4/81*). Note of cherries on aroma; medium-bodied, well structured, moderate tannin, has some style.★(★)

Rizzi Az. Agr. di Ernesto Dellapiana, Vigna Surì (*ex-cask 4/80*). Aroma brings up peaches; has lots of fruit, not a lot of tannin, good quality.★(★)

Roagna, Crichet Pajè (*ex-cask 12/80*). Fruity nose; a little light but good fruit flavors, some tannin, well balanced.★(★)

Roagna, Vigna Pajè. (*ex-cask 11/80*). Aroma like a bowl of cherries and berries; moderate tannin, lots of fruit, soft undertone.★(★)

Rosso Gigi riserva. (*1/85*). Expansive bouquet recalls tartufi, fresh fruit, strawberries; some tannin, flavorful, almost sweet, very well balanced.★★(+)

Scarpa, Tetti di Neive (*twice 2/85; 14,745 bottles*). Deep, rich aroma with suggestions of mint and pine; fairly rich with sweet ripe fruit flavors, some tannin to lose, finely balanced; lingering finish leaves a memory of raspberries behind.★★★(+)

Vecchio Piemonte Cantine Produttori (*1/85*). Vague tobaccolike note and some fruit on nose; has a fair amount of fruit, somewhat astringent; rather simple.★ −

Vietti, Masseria (*4 times 2/85; 6070 bottles*). Floral bouquet with notes of cherries and tartufi; still some tannin but also nice fruit, perhaps a trifle light; can use another two years.★★(+)

Vignaioli "Elvio Pertinace" (*3 times 2/85*). Nice nose, ripe fruit and a note of mushrooms; light to moderate tannin; fairly well balanced, flavor of ripe, almost sweet fruit; a bit short and tannic at the end.★(★)

1978 ★★★★ −

Bruno Ceretto calls the '78s wines for the poets. Bruno Giacosa said they are grand wines and possibly better than the '71s. And judging by his Santo Stefano—the wine of the vintage for

1978

us—we have to concur. Giovannini-Moresco said that for him the vintage produced fat wines that perhaps lack some elegance. Angelo Gaja said the very best are better balanced than the '71s and that they should be long-lived wines. Giuseppe Colla considers them outstanding Barbarescos notable for their harmony and balance. Alfredo Currado also finds them exceptional.

For us, the '78s are simply superb wines, more impressive for their balance and elegance than the '71s. Although it is difficult at this point to predict the quality of the '82s compared to the '78s, we think that eventually the '82s will shade them out. The '78s are definitely Barbarescos to cellar.

Bel Colle (10/82). Pale in color; uncharacteristic aroma; light to moderate tannin; totally undistinctive.

Bersano (5/85). Surprisingly, this wine has more class and character, is rounder and smoother on the palate than the riserva speciale.★

Bersano riserva speciale (5/84). Straightforward, fruity aroma; light tannin, medium-bodied, fruity, grating at the edge; a simple little agreeable wine that's beneath its class.

Bianco Luigi (twice 2/82 and 11/82). First bottle: An acceptable red wine, but not up to either the vintage or the zone. Second bottle: Lacks weight and substance.

Boffa Carlo, Vigna Vitolotti (ex-cask 4/80). Simple grapey aroma; some tannin, a bit light in body, tasty, lacks intensity.(★)

Casetta F.lli (twice 1/85). Pale; tar and seaweed on aroma; overly tannic, insufficient fruit.

Castello di Neive, Messoriano (ex-cask 10/79). A richly concentrated wine with considerable tannin; its fine quality is evident.★★(★)

Castello di Neive, Santo Stefano riserva (3 times 2/85; 6150 bottles). Richly intense bouquet, expansive, has notes of hazelnuts and tartufi; enormous richness and concentration; superbly structured; has a tannic firmness; no doubt that this will make a very fine bottle in three or four more years.★★★(+)

Castello Feudale riserva speciale (twice 4/85). Characteristic bouquet, expansive and somewhat floral with a mushroomlike note; medium body, some tannin but soft open fruit; well made, lacks some style; tails off toward the end; more or less ready.★+

Ceretto, Asili (5 times 11/82; 21,425 bottles). Oaky notes over a background of rich fruit; well structured, supple texture, still some tannin to lose; very good quality.★★(★)

Ceretto, Bricco Asili (twice 1/85; 5960 bottles). Bouquet still somewhat undeveloped but displays woodsy nuances as well as notes of tartufi and raspberries; superbly crafted wine, well structured; tannin is there, but the enormous concentration almost makes it seem ready; resist.★★★(+)

Cigliuti, Bricco di Neive (4/81). Fresh fruit and notes of tar on aroma; has tannin but a lot of fruit; its style is already evident; needs perhaps another three years.★★(+)

Cigliuti, Serra Boella (twice 10/81). Somewhat reticent aroma has a cherrylike note; well balanced, tasty though still rather closed and undeveloped.★★(★)

Colla Paolo, Valgrande riserva speciale (4/85). Southern character; low acid, mineral notes; flat and dull.

Contratto riserva (6/85; 5600 bottles). Fairly rich and characteristic aroma, woodsy, floral, berryish nuances; some tannin remains but drinkable now; should improve; well balanced; moderately long finish.★★★−

Coppa Luigi (1/85). Tobacco and fruit on aroma; light tannin, fairly forward, soft-centered, nearly ready; aftertaste brings up hints of cherries.★(+)

De Forville Paolo (11/82). Light aroma reminiscent of apricots; light tannin, light body, shallow; fell apart in the glass!

De Forville, Vigneto Montestefano (twice 4/85). Oak, fruit, and tobacco aroma; moderate tannin, firm, chewy, richly flavored; could use more style.★★(+)

Fontanafredda (1/85). Richly fruited bouquet suggests cherries and berries; has a lot of flavor, light tannin, very well balanced, very nice for current drinking, though could improve.★★+

Franco Fiorina riserva (4 times 5/83). Aroma of nebbiolo fruit and grappa; flavorful, somewhat lean, still has tannin to shed; comes up a bit short.★

Franco Fiorina riserva speciale (11/83). Bouquet still somewhat reticent, has a note of methanol; fairly tannic. Is there enough fruit?

Gaja (9 times 11/84; 82,498 bottles). Bouquet of enormous richness, background of oak and a hint of mushrooms; sweet ripe fruit with a tannic vein; still needs time but tempting.★★(★)

Gaja, Costa Russi (3 times 11/84, 5804 bottles). Open, complex bouquet with suggestions of cherries, burnt sugar, mint, flowers, berries; rich and concentrated, a complete wine with style and class; seems ready now but has room for improvement★★★(+)

Gaja, Sorì San Lorenzo (twice 2/82). Richly scented bouquet of spice, fruit, and flowers; has tannin and richness, flavorful, supple, lots of style; outstanding pretty much says it all.★★★(★)

Gaja, Sorì Tildin (4 times 6/82). Bouquet is deep, rich, and intense, with a mushroom note and oak in back; rich and harmonious, supple core beneath the tannin; young, but fine quality evident; very long; exudes style.★★★(★)

Giacosa Bruno, Gallina (twice 11/82). Considerable fruit on aroma and a seeming off note that didn't last; well balanced, has richness and concentration, tannin and style; should make a splendid bottle in time.★★(★)

Giacosa Bruno, Santo Stefano (twice 11/84). This bottle was tasted seventeen days after it was opened. Expansive bouquet virtually leaps out of the glass, offering notes of raspberries, flowers, mushrooms, tartufi, leather, almonds, chestnuts, kirsch. The bouquet alone is ★★★★. An abundance of flavor, a superbly structured wine of impressive quality; enormously long on finish that leaves reminders of anise, cherries, flowers. This is for us, without question, the finest wine of a very fine vintage and one of the greatest wines we have ever tasted.★★★★

1978

Giacosa F.lli *(3 times 4/85; 4400 bottles)*. Intense aroma suggestive of cherries; a rush of fruit on entry gives way to a tannic firmness, well structured; loads of potential.★★(★)

Giovannini-Moresco Enrico, Podere del Pajorè *(es-cask 12/80)*. Cherries all over the nose; a big, rich, concentrated wine that, as good as it is, falls down somewhat; just not up to the level we expect from Moresco, though it is certainly a very good Barbaresco.★★★

Glicine Cantina, Vigna dei Cuba *(es-cask 11/80)*. Seems a little light on the nose and palate, but has elegance and style, seems almost sweet; difficult to fully assess as it needs to be racked, but some quality is evident.★★ +

Glicine Cantina, Vigna dei Curà *(4 times 11/82)*. Bottle of 10/81: Light, soft, and tasty, with a nice bouquet; some elegance and style evident. Those tasted 4/80 and 12/80 ex-cask were similar.★★(★) Bottle of 11/82: A light aroma with a vague off note, well balanced, nice flavor overall but somewhat weak on the middle palate.

Glicine Cantina, Vigna Marcarino *(ex-cask 12/80)*. Perfumed aroma; has tannin, fruit, and structure; some length; good quality.★★(+)

Glicine Cantina, Vigna Rabajà *(ex-cask 12/80)*. Has a lot of flavor and style, like the others somewhat light but well balanced and elegant; the best of the four crus.★★(★)

"La Spinona" di Piero Berutti *(6/82)*. Perfumed bouquet, though still somewhat reticent, suggests blackberries; seems almost sweet; well structured; gives an impression of being ready at first but it does need a few more years; has elegance.★★(+)

"La Spinona" di Piero Berutti, Bricco Faset riserva speciale *(10/82)*. A classic Barbaresco that's still somewhat closed, good balance and weight, comes up to the expectations of the vintage; young, but will surely be a splendid bottle in time.★★(★)

Martinenga, Marchese di Gresy *(8 times 10/81; 19,580 bottles)*. Still somewhat closed in, but style and elegance are apparent; a lot of potential, well balanced, has class.★★(★)

Martinenga-Camp Gros, Marchese di Gresy *(2/85; 6400 bottles)*. Intensely rich and concentrated bouquet of ripe fruit with a suggestion of tobacco; has a fair amount of tannin to shed, but also a heap of rich, ripe fruit; very fine balance.★★★(+)

Mascarello Giuseppe, Bernadotti *(twice 11/82)*. Fairly rich fruit on bouquet with suggestions of mushrooms and cherries; considerable tannin, but has sufficient fruit in reserve to enable it to develop.★(★)

Moccagatta Az. Agr. *(twice 2/85)*. Smallish nose; very little on the palate; has tannin and some firmness but not a lot of fruit. Where will it go?

Parroco del Neive *(twice 11/84)*. Not at all bad; characteristic Barbaresco but rather slight.★

Parroco del Neive, Vigneto Gallina *(4 times 3/83)*. Very little aroma; tannic but full of flavor; quite young but should make a good bottle in time.★(★ +)

Pasquero Elia Secondo, Sorì d' Paytin *(8 times 2/85; 3650 bottles)*. Vaguely tobaccolike aroma; richer and more intense than the '82 but with some elegance; has potential.★★(★)

Pelissero Luigi *(ex-cask 4/80)*. The aroma is still somewhat unyielding, but some fruit is beginning to emerge; full of flavor; tannin needs some time to soften; good quality.★★(+)

Pio Cesare riserva *(3/85)*. Lovely nose, some oak; light tannin, surprisingly approachable, well balanced, flavorful; has character.★★

Podere Casot Nada riserva speciale *(11/84; 4000 bottles)*. Some sulphur on nose; unbalanced, too much tannin for the fruit.

Produttori del Barbaresco, Moccagatta riserva *(3 times 11/82)*. A well-structured Barbaresco that already shows complexity and style; still young; needs time, but fine quality evident.★★(★)

Produttori del Barbaresco, Montefico riserva *(6 times 6/83; 14,810 bottles)*. Lovely nebbiolo bouquet, refined; a well-structured, classic Barbaresco that should make a splendid bottle in time.★★★(+)

Produttori del Barbaresco, Montestefano riserva *(5 times 11/82)*. Rich, cherrylike aroma, fairly intense; still has tannin to shed; rich and flavorful.★★(★)

Produttori del Barbaresco, Ovello riserva *(3 times 11/82)*. Richly fruity aroma; still has rough tannic edges but lots of fruit; shows promise.★★(+)

Produttori del Barbaresco, Pajè *(ex-cask 4/80)*. A cherrylike aroma; seems somewhat lighter than the others, but well balanced.★★

Produttori del Barbaresco, Pora riserva *(7 times 1/85)*. Big, full aroma of nebbiolo fruit; a mouthful of tannin and rich ripe fruit; seems more backward than a bottle tasted about a year ago; a young Barbaresco of quality; give it four more years, perhaps five.★★(★)

Produttori del Barbaresco, Rabajà riserva *(3 times 11/82)*. Richly fruited bouquet, not fully open yet; still tannic and rough but has the weight and stuffing to carry it; give it at least three, maybe four more years.★★(★)

Prunotto, Montestefano riserva *(3 times 1/85; 5754 bottles)*. Bouquet still a bit closed, but fruit is evident, alcohol intrudes; quite tannic, sensation of ripe fruit in the center indicates it can carry the tannin. If it does, this could be a great wine in time.★★(★?)

"Punset" di R. Marcarino *(twice 1/85)*. Oxidized.

Ratti Renato *(11/83)*. Lovely, fragrant bouquet with a faint suggestion of tartufi; balanced and stylish, elegant, tasty; enjoyable now, but has room for improvement.★★(★)

Rizzi Az. Agr. di Ernesto Dellapiana *(ex-cask 4/80)*. Richly intense aroma with a hint of licorice; forward, intense, and tannic; its potential is evident.★★(+)

Roagna, Crichet Pajè *(twice 1/85)*. Lovely bouquet with suggestions of tartufi; some tannin, a lot of flavor, not quite ready; finish marred by a touch of alcohol.★(★)

Roagna, Vigna Pajè *(4 times 2/82)*. Color showing age; faint off note on aroma and some alcohol; shallow, not a success—maybe it's the bottle. When we tasted from cask in 1980, the wine did show promise.

"Roche" Az. Vit. riserva speciale *(1/85)*. Light but typical nebbiolo aroma; rather light in body, some tannin, astringent finish; lacks character.

Vezza Sergio *(1/85)*. Vague off note on aroma (sulphur?); some tannin, seems to have enough fruit, rather light; an agreeable little wine.

Vietti, Masseria *(10 times 2/85; 6000 bottles)*. An

1978

expansive bouquet with woodsy nuances, flowers and berries, quite complex; a splendid wine with a lot of class and style; still has tannin, but so well balanced and full of flavor it seems hard to resist right now; be patient.★★★(+)

Villadoria Marchese *(6/85)*. Unbalanced, harsh, some fruit, overall dull and uncharacteristic.

1977 0

The 1977 vintage produced poor wines overall, though a few acceptable wines were made. Only 1972 was worse in the decade. Italo Stupino of Castello di Neive described the vintage as very poor, as did Angelo Gaja. Bruno Giacosa and Alfredo Currado didn't produce any Barbaresco in 1977. The Cerettos didn't bottle their top cru, Bricco Asili. Giuseppe Colla, on the other hand, rates the vintage as normal.

There's no need to hold them any longer; if they are not already too old, they soon will be.

Castello di Neive, Santo Stefano *(ex-vat 10/79)*. Perfumed aroma; fairly well balanced, some tannin, fruity, good for the vintage.★

Ceretto, Asili *(3 times 3/83; 24,835 bottles)*. Pale brick in color; lovely perfume, with suggestions of mushrooms and a vaguely Burgundian character; soft, tasty, some tannin, very nice; ready, not to keep; surprisingly good for the vintage.★★

Gemma *(3/85)*. Tawny; a surprising amount of fruit on the nose, berries and cassis; drying out, still has flavor.★ —

Glicine Cantina, Vigna Montesomo *(4/80)*. Light aroma with suggestions of cherries; light-bodied, some tannin, unbalanced by high acid.

Roagna, Vigna Pajè *(3 times 12/80)*. Some alcohol on nose; has fruit on entry, but shallow; ends abruptly with some tannin; was better in cask.

1976 ★ —

Bruno Ceretto said that for them the vintage was quite good; the wines are fine and elegant. Alfredo Currado bottled 20 percent of his Barbaresco as a cru, the remainder as straight Barbaresco. Giuseppe Colla said it was a normal year. Angelo Gaja feels the '76s are beginning to decline now and should be drunk up.

Overall, we found the wines ranged from poor to average, more often poor. They are for current drinking and won't last much longer.

Cabutto Bartolomeo *(4/80)*. Pale color; light floral bouquet has a tarlike note; light-bodied; some fruit; not bad for the vintage.

Castello di Neive, Santo Stefano *(twice 12/81)*. Nice nose; some tannin, light, fairly well balanced for the vintage.★

Ceretto, Asili *(1/82; 17,302 bottles)*. Garnet, orange at rim; some oak on the aroma overlaid with fruit and an almondlike nuance; light-bodied, soft, somewhat unbalanced but not at all bad for the year; not to keep.★ —

Ceretto, Bricco Asili *(1/85)*. Complex floral bouquet with suggestions of mushrooms, raspberries, mint, tobacco, and chocolate; has delicacy and elegance, a touch of tannin but velvety; very ready and very good—impressive.★★★

Confratelli di San Michele, Vigneto Cotto *(10/81)*. Aroma has some fruit and a faint peppery note; light-bodied and rather shallow.

Contratto riserva *(1/82)*. Garnet, tending to orange; moderate varietal aroma; thin and unbalanced; biting aftertaste.

Feyles Maria, Vigna dei Gaia in Neive *(4/80)*. Some alcohol on aroma and not much fruit; has tannin,

rather closed, seems to have sufficient fruit in reserve to develop; shows some promise. (★)

Gaja *(2/82)*. Pale garnet, showing age; pretty bouquet of moderate intensity, with hints of cherries and flowers; light-bodied, some tannin, nice flavors; ready.★

Gemma *(11/80)*. Sweet, almost candylike aroma; not much fruit, not enough for the tannin.

Glicine Cantina, Vigna Marcarino *(5 times 4/80)*. Nice nose; light-bodied, light tannin, has fruit and some length; ready.★

"La Spinona" di Piero Berutti *(3/83)*. Drying out and showing its age.

Martinenga, Marchese di Gresy *(13 times 2/84)*. This wine was at its best from late 1979 into 1981; the last bottle tasted was beginning to go, showing some volatile acidity and signs of drying out; it still has nice flavor, though, and some class.★

Produttori del Barbaresco *(10/81)*. Some oxidation on the nose; lacks depth and richness, light and soft, tasty; not to keep.

Roagna, Vigna Pajè *(twice 4/80)*. Insufficient fruit for the tannin.

Voerzio Giacomo *(twice 12/80)*. Weird aroma; unbalanced, thin, and harsh.

1975 0

This vintage produced poor to average Barbarescos, mostly poor. The Cerettos didn't bottle their Bricco Asili cru in 1975. Gaja says the '75s are now on the decline.

The wines should be drunk up; they are fading, if they haven't already.

1975

Castello di Neive, Santo Stefano (*6 times 2/85*). Floral bouquet shows development and complexity from bottle age; still some tannin but tasty and very ready, a lot of flavor, smooth textured; not to keep. (This wine was tasted at the winery; in the U.S. it seemed to peak about three years ago, perhaps even four.)★★ +

Ceretto, Asili (*1/85*). Lovely bouquet with notes of tobacco and raspberry; light-bodied, light tannin, smooth, some style and elegance; very ready.★★★

Damilano, Dott. Giacomo (*3/84*). Ripe fruit on aroma; a bit shallow; very short. Is this a Barbaresco?

De Forville Paolo (*11/78*). Characteristic aroma; tannic, but seems to have sufficient fruit; young yet and closed; has potential.★★

Fontanafredda (*3/83*). Toasty, caramel aroma with some oxidation; on palate not bad, but not good either.

Glicine Cantina, Vigna Marcarino riserva speciale (*twice 10/81; 1866 bottles*). Some fruit on the nose as well as nebbiolo character; soft, light, and tasty; very ready; lacks some length, but good.★

"La Spinona" di Piero Berutti (*3/83*). Pale brick color; stinky nose; a disappointment from this normally reliable producer.

Martinenga, Marchese di Gresy (*3 times 12/82*). Light but nice aroma, fragrant; soft and tasty, still a bit of tannin; at its peak or just past, perhaps better a year and a half ago.★

Moccagatta Az. Agr. di Mario Minuto (*11/78*). A small-scale, somewhat unbalanced wine; has an alcoholic aftertaste.

Produttori del Barbaresco (*6 times 11/80*). Soft, fairly well balanced, has character, light; no need to hold it longer.★

Roagna, Vigna Pajè (*3 times 12/80*). Too old, was at its best in 10/78, when it had some flavor and character, but even then not really impressive.

1974 ★★ −

At one time 1974 was a highly regarded vintage. And there are many producers who still rate it highly. Others now feel that it was overrated. Angelo Gaja feels the wines were overrated; he ranks the year fourth after 1971, 1978, and 1979. Bruno Ceretto puts it fifth in the decade after 1978, 1971, 1979, and 1970. Giuseppe Colla described it as excellent. Bruno Giacosa said only 1971 and 1978 were better for him in the decade. Alfredo Currado considers it a very good vintage. Pio Boffa said his wines had less tannin and less intensity than in 1971.

We also believe the vintage was originally overrated. Too many wines aren't living up to expectations, ours as well as those of many others. While the best of the '74s will hold and possibly improve further, most are ready now, and some are even beginning to decline. Very few will benefit by further aging.

Accademia Torregiorgi, Pastura di Neive (*2/85*). Bouquet shows a complexity and mellowness from bottle age; tannin remains, some fruit but beginning to dry out a bit; a drinkable wine though showing some age.★

Balbo Marino, Cascina Bruciato (*4/80*). Although it was a corked bottle, the quality, due to the structure, was quite evident.

Bordino Franco (*4/81*). Cherrylike notes in the bouquet; moderate tannin, has the fruit to match it; needs perhaps another year or two.★★

Casetta F.lli (*4/80*). Very light color, browning; alcohol, volatile acidity, and some oxidation—gone.

Castello di Neive, Santo Stefano (*4 times 2/85*). Brick red; vaguely floral bouquet displaying development and complexity of bottle age; still has a fair amount of tannin but with sufficient stuffing to enable it to smooth out; nearly ready.★★ −

Ceretto, Bricco Asili (*twice 1/85*). Floral bouquet with woodsy, mushroom notes; texture like velvet, ripe fruit and chocolate flavors, near its peak, elegant; still room for improvement.★★★(+)

Cigliuti F.lli (*twice 10/78*). Soft and flavorful, some tannin, balanced, has style.★★ +

"Conte de Cavour" Cantine Barbero (*10/78*). Alcohol and candylike notes define the aroma; light-bodied, out of balance with high alcohol, low fruit and high tannin.

Contratto riserva (*12/81*). Color shows some age; characteristic nebbiolo aroma with tar and fruit; some tannin but fairly soft; vaguely bitter aftertaste.★ +

Fontanafredda (*1/85*). Bouquet shows some development, but marred by a harshness; very soft and ready, tasty on entry but tails off toward the end; no need to hold it any longer.★

Franco Fiorina riserva speciale (*twice 4/82*). Reticent aroma with hints of nebbiolo fruit, tar, and flowers; well structured, moderate tannin, tasty, shows some quality.★★

Gaja (*10/82*). Moderately rich bouquet; some tannin, flavorful; if it only had more length on the palate.★

Gemma riserva speciale (*4/85*). Aroma of champignons and berries; some tannin, berrylike fruit, soft and ready.★★

Giacosa Bruno, Gallina (*10/79*). Perfumed bouquet; well balanced, tannin to shed but with the fruit in reserve.★★(+)

Giacosa Bruno, Santo Stefano (*twice 9/81; 7200 bottles*). Bouquet is fairly intense and concentrated; has structure, style, and loads of flavor; still some tannin to lose but smooth-textured and drinkable now.★★(★)

Giovannini-Moresco Enrico, Podere del Pajorè (*7 times 5/81*). Expansive, perfumed bouquet recalls cherries and rich ripe fruit, also a touch of alcohol; considerable tannin remaining; enormous weight and extract; young, has potential.★★(★)

"La Brenta d'Oro," Cantina d' Invecchiamento riserva speciale (*11/78*). Ho hum.

Martinenga, Marchese di Gresy (*3 times 2/85*). Not a lot of aroma; some tannin and a lot of flavor; sweet and smooth; at or near its peak.★★ −

1974

Palladino (11/78). Aroma of burnt hair; thin, tannic backbone; short, unpleasant aftertaste.

Parroco del Neive, Vigneto Basarin (11/80). Beautiful robe; penetrating aroma; heaps of flavor upon entry that tails off; shallow and short.

Parroco del Neive, Vigneto Gallina (10/78). Bouquet of richness and depth; has style and balance, still with tannin to shed; fine quality.★★★

Pasquero Elia Secondo, Sorì d' Paytin (twice 11/80). Reticent aroma reveals some fruit; has tannin to lose but a lot of flavor; holds out some promise; good quality.★(★ +)

Pelissero Luigi riserva (4/80). Nice nose with still more to give; has tannin, flavor, and length on the palate.★(★)

Pio Cesare (twice 5/83). Browning; some oxidation and some nebbiolo character on aroma; dried out, too old; the bottle was better a year ago but seemed perhaps too tannic at the time.

Produttori del Barbaresco, Montestefano riserva (3 times 11/84). Lovely, fragrant perfume with touches of cherries and tobacco; light tannin, soft, well balanced; at or near its peak.★★ +

Produttori del Barbaresco, Pora riserva (8 times 12/83; 14,000 bottles). Characteristic bouquet with tarlike notes and a touch of volatile acidity; a mouthful of flavor, light tannin; some alcohol at the end; was better in 1981.★★

Produttori del Barbaresco, Rabajà (4/80; 14,118 bottles). Perfumed bouquet; still has tannin but very nice now; a mouthful of nice fruit flavors.★★ +

Prunotto, Montestefano (1/82). Floral, fruity bouquet with a characteristic hint of tartufi in the background; considerable tannin, but seems to have the fruit to back it up; needs a few years yet.★★(+)

"Punset" di R. Marcarino (3 times 11/80). Incredible perfume, has a note of apricots; nice entry, good flavor, but falls down on the finish—short and alcoholic; was better six months to a year ago; perhaps an off bottle.★★ −

Rizzi Az. Agr. di Ernesto Dellapiana (ex-cask 4/80). Nice nose; tannic but with sufficient fruit to develop.★(★)

Rizzi Az. Agr. di Ernesto Dellapiana, Vigna Fondetta (ex-vat 4/80). Aroma of fresh cherries; fairly rich, has tannin and some elegance.★★

Roagna, Vigna Pajè riserva (8 times 1/84). Characteristic bouquet, has a suggestion of cherries; nice flavor, some richness, still some tannin and some elegance; could improve but ready now, as good as it's ever been.★★

Roagna, Vigneto Asili riserva (12/84). Shy aroma, some character and varietal nuances; has fruit up front but without any follow-through; still tannic but losing its fruit.

Scarpa (10/81). Bouquet seems subdued; some tannin and a lot of flavor; very good, with room for improvement.★★(+)

Serafino Enrico (4/80). Aroma of fruit, tar, and raisins; has tannin and some fruit, shallow; alcoholic aftertaste.

Tenute Coluè di Massimo Oddero (2/80). Characteristic aroma of tar and flowers; a little light, some tannin, hollow.

Vietti, Masseria (20 times 12/84; 7000 bottles). Nearly every bottle showed the same high level of quality, complex bouquet with hints of ripe fruit, tea, tobacco, chocolate, spice, cinnamon, flowers; a well-crafted wine, soft, round, and full of flavor; a complete wine that is at its peak now; has a long, lingering finish with a suggestion of blackberries; elegant.★★★

Vignaioli "Elvio Pertinace" (10/78). Oxidized.

1973 0

Overproduction in 1973 resulted in thin wines that were nevertheless, on balance, better than the '75s, '76s, and '77s.

Alfredo Currado bottled very little Barbaresco in 1973; Bruno Giacosa bottled none. Giuseppe Colla rated it as a normal vintage. Gaja describes 1973 as a small vintage of medium quality. He bottled a small quantity of Sorì Tildin and no Sorì San Lorenzo.

Most of the '73s are already too old, and there's no reason to keep the rest.

Carra (11/79). Awful odor; some tannin and then...

Castello Feudale riserva speciale (1/85). Bouquet, though small, shows varietal character; still has tannin and a surprising amount of fruit; not to keep, beginning to dry out, though still good.★

Ceretto, Asili (1/85). Flowers, raspberries, vanilla, and spice suggestive of a Rhône wine; the softest and most ready at this vertical tasting from '80 to '73 (at the winery); a soft center and a taste of ripe raspberries.★★★ −

Colla Paolo (10/78). Nice entry, has tannin, lacks middle body.

Gaja (13 times 11/84). There has been variation; some bottles were too old, others very nice indeed; the most recent bottle, tasted at the winery, had strawberries and mushrooms on the bouquet, quite Burgundian, some alcohol intrudes; a bit light but well balanced, loads of flavor; beginning to dry out a bit but still very good.★★

Gaja, Sorì Tildin (9/83). Bouquet has some interesting nuances though somewhat fleeting; soft, almost sweet, light tannin; might hold for a while but certainly no need to keep it longer.★★ −

Glicine Cantina, Vigna Marcorino riserva speciale (twice 10/78). Tar and tartufi on aroma; has tannin, also good flavor; a nice bottle.★★

1972 0

The weather in 1972 was dismal; the grapes did not ripen. As in Barolo, no Barbaresco was produced in 1972. The entire crop was declassified.

1971 ★★★

There was rain during the flowering in 1971, which reduced the size of the crop. Toward the end of June the sun came out and the weather took a turn for the better. The remainder of the summer was very hot. The harvest took place under ideal conditions and was over by the end of September.

Giuseppe Colla says the vintage was exceptional. Alfredo Currado agrees, describing it as a first-rate year. For Bruno Giacosa the '71s are the best of all. Angelo Gaja feels that perhaps they're too much of a good thing; they are Barbarescos to cut with a knife, very rich wines that seem more like Barolo than Barbaresco.

He pretty much sums up our view, too. They are excellent wines, to be sure, but our one criticism is that they are uncharacteristic. They lack the Barbaresco style, the finesse. If we want a Barolo, we drink Barolo; when we want a more elegant wine, we drink a Barbaresco. Too many of these wines seem to be Barolos in the guise of Barbaresco. They have enormous richness and concentration and very high alcohol. The best need more age and will be very long-lived. Rating the wines as Barbarescos, we could only give them three stars; as Barolos, we would be tempted to give them four. Overall, we would have to call it a three-star vintage because we are in fact rating them as Barbarescos.

Bersano riserva speciale (5/84). Fair aroma, lacks richness and depth expected from this vintage; well balanced, moderate tannin and the fruit to match; drink it now, it's not going anywhere.★

Boffa Carlo (4/80). Some complexity of bottle age; soft though still has tannin, tasty, ready; moderately long.★ +

Castello di Neive, Santo Stefano riserva (2/85; 4250 bottles). Complex floral bouquet; enormous richness and concentration; a Barbaresco for Barolo lovers; liquid velvet on palate, sweet, rich, ripe fruit; enormous length.★★★ +

Ceretto, Montefico (5/85; 15,100 bottles). Old-style nebbiolo aroma, tar and rubber tires, alcohol intrudes; dried out, very little of interest remains.

Conterno Giacomo (5/81). Aroma of tar, fruit, and alcohol; rich, thick, and tannic; a big, big wine, more like a Barolo than a Barbaresco.★★★

Gaja (4 times 9/83). Bouquet has various nuances though somewhat closed; heaps of flavor, well balanced, still has tannin; a big, rich, concentrated wine that is still quite young; should be splendid in time.★★★

Gaja, Sorì San Lorenzo (10/78). Incredible depth of flavor and richness; needs a lot of age yet, but splendid.★★★(+)

Gaja, Sorì Tildin (3 times 9/83). Age beginning to show in brick color and bouquet with signs of oxidation and seaweed; still has some tannin and fruit, somewhat astringent; was better in 1982; most likely this bottle was not up to par.★★ +

Giacosa Bruno, Santo Stefano (twice 10/81). Dark brick red; intense and complex bouquet with a note of tartufi; still young, a lot of tannin, enormous richness and concentration; exceptional quality.★★★★

Giacosa F.lli (11/78). Expansive bouquet with a note of tartufi; well balanced, tasty, still some tannin to shed.★★★

Giovannini-Moresco Enrico, Podere del Pajorè (19 times 3/85; 12,555 bottles). Brick robe has an orange cast; floral bouquet is incredibly rich and intense, with suggestions of cherries, tar, tobacco, and loads of fruit; a big, rich mouthful of wine, with enormous richness and concentration, velvety almost like an unfortified Port; extremely well structured; a Barbaresco of immense proportions and depth. Right from the first time we tasted it in 1978, this wine has impressed us and thus far shows no signs of age. Lucky us, we still have a case.★★★★

"La Spinona" di Piero Berutti (6/82). Vague hint of volatile acidity, also cheese and chocolate; fairly intense and rich, moderate tannin, richly flavored; needs time, has potential.★★(+)

Produttori del Barbaresco, Ovello riserva (10 times 2/84; 13,260 bottles). Cigar box and cherries on bouquet, also a note of tartufi; still has tannin, full of flavor, quality; long finish; a complete wine that can still improve.★★★(★)

Produttori del Barbaresco, Pora riserva (twice 10/79). Cherrylike aroma; well balanced, flavorful, some style; nearly ready.★★(+)

Prunotto, Montestefano (1/85). Expansive bouquet of ripe blackberries and tartufi; soft, round, and velvety; still some tannin but hardly seems noticeable; full-bodied and richly concentrated; still has more to give, but the quality is already evident.★★★(+)

1970 ★★ +

The 1970 vintage produced very good wines that, on balance, were and still are better than the '74s. Some producers equate them with the '62s. The '70s are enjoyable now, but the best could improve further.

Borgogno Giacomo riserva (3/80). Well-developed bouquet with some complexity; soft and smooth-textured, some tannin; quite ready; short.★★ −

Contratto (twice 2/80). Floral bouquet, character-istic, some depth and complexity; a lot of flavor, still some tannin; very ready; only problem is a touch of alcohol at the end.★★ +

Gaja, Sorì Tildin (11/84). Toasty notes, hint of

1970

mushrooms on characteristic nebbiolo bouquet, marred by some alcohol and a touch of volatile acidity; a fair amount of tannin but a lot of fruit in the center; typical old-style Barbaresco. Will it develop and soften, or will it dry out first? We think that in spite of the va, it'll improve.★★(+)

Produttori del Barbaresco, Moccagatta riserva

(4/80). Floral perfume with a tarry note; quite full in the mouth; still has tannin, but flavorful and ready.★★+

Produttori del Barbaresco, Rabajà riserva *(4/80)*. Rich bouquet, intense and full of fruit, has a nutlike aspect; velvety, elegant, heaps of flavor, very nice indeed and quite ready; some tannin and a lot of fruit; should last.★★★

1969 0

The wines of 1969 were average at best. Too many never amounted to anything. Italo Stupino of Castello di Neive described it as a very bad year.

Overall, they're too old now; they should have been drunk up long ago.

Contratto *(12/81)*. In all, a nice glass of wine though past its prime; has flavor, but the harsh edges and alcoholic aftertaste suggest it's on its last legs.★

1968 0

Perhaps average in the beginning, the '68s are fading now, and there's no point in holding them any longer.

Contratto *(twice 12/81)*. Still has fruit, but harshness and signs of drying out indicate there's no reason to hold it any longer.

1967 ★★

Gaja considers 1967 overall a medium-quality vintage; the wines, he feels, are probably at their peak now. For Bruno Giacosa, on the other hand, it was a very good year, among the best.

We found the '67s to be very good wines. The best are drinking well now. A few will improve further. Others are showing signs of decline. For the most part, there's no reason to hold them any longer.

Contratto *(6/85)*. Corked.

Gaja *(3/83)*. Garnet tending to orange; expansive bouquet with richness and concentration; very tannic but seems to have sufficient fruit given enough time to soften.★★(?)

Gaja, Sorì San Lorenzo *(twice 11/84)*. Brick red, orange reflections; old-style Barbaresco bouquet; loaded with flavor, a firm tannic vein; starting to show age, might hold but future doubtful.★+

Giovannini-Moresco Enrico, Podere del Pajorè *(10/79)*. Bouquet has a lot to it, notes of mushrooms and fruit; falls down on the palate; drying out, too old. (We tasted this wine at the winery. Moresco poured it as a curiosity; it was his first and least successful wine.)

Produttori del Barbaresco *(6 times 3/81)*. Bouquet of vanilla and nebbiolo fruit, beginning to show some age; soft with a vague harshness which wasn't there a year ago (or the bottle is showing age), tasty, has style; some length on finish, but some alcohol intrudes; still a very good bottle.★★

1966 0

This vintage produced poor wines that never amounted to much.

1965 0

It was an average year. Some rated it as good. The wines today are too old.

1964 ★★★

This was an exceptional vintage, perhaps the best of the decade. Angelo Gaja thinks 1964 was overrated. The wines received a lot of very good press. For Bruno Giacosa it was a top-flight year, on a level with 1971.

The best Barbarescos, if well stored, should still be splendid. Although they can still age, they are certainly ready now.

Bersano riserva speciale *(5/84)*. Beginning to dry out, though still has flavor interest.★−

Castello di Neive, Santo Stefano *(2/85; from a private bottling of 2/70, never in commerce)*. Lovely, well-developed perfume; rich, round, and velvety; at its peak, a superb wine with enormous length.★★★+

Gaja *(3 times 11/84)*. Brick red, orange at rim; lovely bouquet, vaguely floral; finely balanced, round and soft, sweet, ripe, elegant; a well-knit Barbaresco of quality.★★★

Giacosa Bruno, Santo Stefano *(11/84)*. Expansive bouquet with notes of flowers and tartufi; still has

1964

tannin but also heaps of fruit; seems sweet; unbelievable that it has 15 percent alcohol—it doesn't show; very well structured, enormously long finish. Bruno Giacosa said this wine is medicine; for us it is a wine for meditation.★★★★ —

Mascarello Giuseppe (*4 times 11/82*). Some oxidation and signs of drying out, but still shows quality; mellow and smooth on palate.★

1963 0

These wines were, for the most part, born too old. They're best forgotten now.

1962 0

This was a mixed vintage. The wines ranged in quality from fair to good. With few, if any, exceptions, they should have been drunk up years ago.

1961 ★★+

Hail at the end of June during the flowering reduced the crop size. July turned very hot, and the heat of summer continued into October. The grapes, all picked by the end of September, had very high sugar levels. The grapes themselves were quite warm when brought into the wineries; consequently, fermentation started immediately and at very high temperatures.

At Gaja the fermentation got stuck and stayed that way for three and a half months. When it restarted, the must fermented very slowly. In fact, there was still some sugar remaining in the wine for a number of years. They held the wine in the cellar for a long time before they offered it for sale. Angelo Gaja rates this as the best vintage of the decade. Bruno Giacosa considered it, though not quite the equal of 1964, an exceptional vintage.

For the most part, the '61s are beginning to show their age. If you have any, drink them up while they're still good.

Gaja (*10 times 11/84 and 3/85; the variations among bottles have been tremendous, with some wines meriting ★+, others ★★★+*). Bottle of 11/84: Medium brick, orange at rim; bouquet of fruit and tar with some alcohol; has a lot to it; sweet and tasty, still some tannin; a lot of wine here, has character, but for us it's not quite up to the '64, though showing some indication that there's still more to come with further age; a wine of quality.★★★

Bottle of 3/85: Floral bouquet, hints of cassis, vanilla, and wheat; harsh acid edge, soft-centered and velvety.★★★ —

Giacosa Bruno (*twice 4/85*). Beautiful brick robe; classic bouquet of flowers, tar, and tartufi, intense and rich; still has grip and firmness, liquid velvet, incredible length. The first bottle of 3/85 was tasted alongside the Gaja; it was, not surprisingly, better. The second and more recent bottle was tasted after chocolate, and it had the richness to follow it. Both bottles ★★★★ —

Mascarello Giuseppe (*4 times 4/84*). Orange robe; floral bouquet, characteristic; soft, round, and smooth; somewhat past its peak but still very good.★★ +

1960 and 1959 0

Neither vintage amounted to much, and both are long gone.

1958 ★★★

Originally this was a four-star vintage, producing splendid wines overall, full-bodied, rich, and harmonious. Very few remain today, and those few could be very good, but fewer still will deserve full marks. There's no need to hold them.

Gaja (*5 times 11/84*). Medium brick shading to orange at rim; complex bouquet; velvety, sweet, lots of style, still has loads of flavor; a complete wine that is still approaching its peak.★★★

1957 [★★−]

At the time rated as a three-star vintage; for today two stars minus is the most one could expect from the '57s. They're undoubtedly showing their age.

1956 0

Most likely the '56s are long gone now.

1955 ★★−

The 1955 vintage was never highly regarded by authorities. We have nevertheless tasted some very good bottles. By now, with few exceptions, they would be too old.

1955

Gaja *(2/82)*. Light to medium brick; a musty aspect to the aroma which blows away to reveal a lovely, fragrant perfume; some age evident on palate, but smooth and sweet, with some style; very good quality; not to keep.★★+

1954 0

This was not much of a vintage, but better than 1953. The wines are all too old today.

1953 0

This was a very poor vintage. The wines today are best forgotten.

1952 and 1951 [★]

Both vintages were originally rated three stars; today we suspect they're probably on their last legs.

1950, 1949, 1948, 1947, 1946, and 1945 0

Most likely, all of these wines are long past their prime. The 1945 vintage was the most highly rated, at three stars, and just possibly if you find a bottle that has been well stored, it could be good. We doubt if any of the other vintages could offer anything more than academic interest.

Other Nebbiolo Wines of the Langhe and Monferrato Hills

BARILIN *(Cuneo)*. Ferrucio Nicolello produces this wine from nebbiolo grapes grown in Borgato Sorano in Serralunga d'Alba. We have heard that some barbera may also be blended in. Barilin is a full-bodied dry red of about 12.5 to 13 percent alcohol.

BAROLINO *(Cuneo)*. This "little Barolo" is a wine made in the Langhe from dolcetto grapes fermented on the lees of the Barolo. The only one we can recall tasting was that made by Marchese Fracassi, at her winery in Cherasco. It is a medium-bodied, dry wine with about 12 percent alcohol, best drunk within a year or two of the vintage.★★

BRICCO DEL DRAGO *(Cuneo)*. Luciano di Giacomini produces about 15,000 to 20,000 bottles a year of this proprietary blend. It is made from dolcetto (85 percent) and nebbiolo (15 percent) grapes grown in San Rocco Senodelvio d'Alba at the top of the "Dragon Hillside," from which it takes its name. The wine is aged for about one year in cask. In 1982, di Giacomini produced 6,238 bottles of a riserva from Vigna 'd le Mace. Bricco del Drago is at its best within two to five, perhaps six years of the vintage, when it has a fresh, cherrylike aroma, is soft and fruity, with a zesty nature and some charm.★★

Tasting Notes

1979 *(5/84; 14,124 bottles)*. Fresh, cherrylike aroma; soft and fruity with a taste of sweet, ripe fruit, some charm.★★

1978 *(twice 12/84)*. Nebbiolo character and cherrylike notes on the nose; well balanced, zesty, full of flavor.★★+

1974 *(6/79)*. Fragrant, berrylike scent; light to medium body; soft and fruity with a berryish flavor.★★

BRICCO MANZONI *(Cuneo)*. Valentino Migliorini produces about 25,000 bottles a year of this 80-20 nebbiolo–barbera blend from grapes grown on his Rocche dei Manzoni estate in Monforte. The wine is aged in small barrels for eight to twelve months. We have tasted some from a different mix of the same two grapes. The wines we have tasted—from the 1978, 1979, and 1980 vintages— were medium- to full-bodied, with tart acidity and a cherrylike character.★★

Tasting Notes

1980 *(11/84; 24,811 bottles)*. This 60-40 nebbiolo–barbera blend was the first Bricco Manzoni aged in *barrique*. Barbera cherries and oak on the nose give way to nebbiolo fruit; some tannin, a bit light on middle palate; finishes on a licorice note★★

1979 *(twice 3/83)*. Barbera character evident on nose; fruity, lively, tart edge, some tannin; might improve a bit but very nice now.★★

1978 *(2/82)*. Straightforward, grapey aroma; tart and lively, fruity and agreeable; enjoyable now.★

CASTELLO DI CAMINO *(Alessandria)*. This wine is made from barbera, grignolino, and nebbiolo grapes. It is a medium-bodied dry red of about 12 percent alcohol, best drunk within two to three years of the vintage.

CASTELLO DI CURTEIS *(Cuneo)*. This is a nebbiolo–dolcetto–pinot blend produced in the Langhe. It is a medium-bodied dry wine of about 12% alcohol that is best drunk young.

COLLE SAMPIETRO *(Cuneo)*. Fontanafredda produced this medium-bodied dry red from nebbiolo grapes; we don't know if they still make it. It is meant for early consumption.

CONCERTO *(Cuneo)*. Paolo Colla produces this wine from a 50–50 blend of barbera and nebbiolo. It is a wine meant to be drunk young. We found it simple and one-dimensional, with a raisiny, overripe character. 0

ELIORO *(Cuneo)*. Montezemolo produces this totally unimpressive blend of nebbiolo (80 percent) and dolcetto (20 percent)grapes. Their first, from the 1984 vintage, was unbalanced and reeked of mercaptans when we tasted it in January 1985 at their Az. Agr. Monfalletto winery. 0

FIORETTO *(Cuneo)*. Alfredo Currado produces this wine at the Vietti winery from a blend of nebbiolo, barbera, dolcetto, and neirano grapes grown in his Fioretto vineyard in the Scarrone district of Castiglione Falletto. The wine is made specifically for the U.S. market. In the first vintage, 1982, some 4000 bottles were produced. There was no Fioretto in 1983, as Currado wasn't satisfied with the quality of the grapes. The '84 will be given some time in *barriques* of Alliers oak. Fioretto is a richly colored wine (the local neirano variety adds good color) with a cherrylike aroma underlaid with notes of tobacco; it is soft, fruity, and balanced, with a lively tartness from the barbera.★★

Tasting Note

1982 *(6 times 1/85).*Deep purplish color; cherrylike notes characteristic of barbera up front give way to a tobaccolike nuance from the nebbiolo; soft and lively; full of flavor; enjoyable now, but can improve.★★★

NEBBIOLATO *(Cuneo)*. This is a nebbiolo wine produced in the early-drinking style.

NEBBIOLO D'ALBA *(Cuneo)*. The growing zone for Nebbiolo d'Alba lies between those of Barolo and Barbaresco, mostly northwest of the city of Alba, with a small part extending to the south. The zone encompasses twenty-four *communes* and three main districts: Roero, the Alba area itself, and Castellinaldo. Roero, a new DOC (effective from 1984), is on the left bank of the Tanaro River in the northern part of the Nebbiolo d'Alba area. The soil here is sandy and cultivation difficult. The villages in Roero include Canale, Monteu Roero, Piobesi, Santa Vittoria, and Vezza d'Alba. The nebbiolo wines of Roero are noted for their bouquet. They are best from two to four years but can last five or six. The nebbiolo wines of the Alba area, on the right bank of the Tanaro, are the fullest in body in the zone; those of Castellinaldo are the lightest. Besides the dry red nebbiolo wines, there are also sweet reds and semisweet sparkling nebbiolos produced in this area.★★/★★★

Recommended Producers

★★(★)	Baracco F.lli, San Vincenzo di Monteu Roero
★★★	Ceretto, Vigneto Bernardine
★★	Franco Fiorina
★★★	Gaja, Vignaveja
★★★	Giacosa Bruno, Valmaggiore di Vezza
★★	Malvira, del Roero
★★	Mascarello Giuseppe, San Rocco
★★	Negro Angelo
★★	Pasquero Giuseppe, Vignadogna
★★★	Pezzuto F.lli, Vigneto in Vadraman del Roero
★★	Prunotto, Bric Rossino di Monteu Roero
★★★	Occhetti di Monteu Roero
★(★)	Rabezzana Renato
★★★	Ratti Renato, Occhetti di Monteu Roero
★★★	Scarpa, San Carlo di Castellinaldo
★★★	Tenuta Carretta, Bric' Paradiso
★★★	Bric' Tavoletto
★★	Tenuta Coluè di Massimo Oddero
★(★)	Terro del Barolo

★★ Verro Tonino, Vigneto Bricchet del Roero
★★★ Vietti, San Giacomo di Santo Stefano Roero
★★★ San Michele di Santo Stefano Roero

Tasting Notes

1984

Vietti, S. Michele *(ex-vat 2/85)*. Aroma of fresh fruit, vaguely tobacco; a nice mouthful of fruit, lively and zesty.★★★

1983

Il Vecchio Tralcio, del Roero *(1/85)* Fresh and fruity, light and easy.★ +

Malvira, del Roero *(1/85; 9600 bottles)*. Lovely nose, cherries and flowers; fruity, tempting, but could improve.★★

Negro Angelo, Roero *(1/85)*. Aroma closed, some fruit evident; has tannin, needs a year, perhaps two; a lot of fruit; short; quite a nice wine.★★

Pezzuto F.lli, del Roero, Vigneto in Vadraman *(1/85)*. Big, rich, spicy nose, berrylike notes, fresh; a nice mouthful of fruit, very well balanced.★★★

Savigliano Mario *(1/85; bottled 3 days ago)*. Cherrylike fruit on aroma and palate.(★)

Vietti, S. Michelle *(ex-vat 2/85)* Aroma of cherries, flowers, and vanilla; light tannin, fruity, well balanced.★★★ −

1982

Cabutto Bartolomeo *(1/85)*. Not a lot of varietal character on the nose, though nice fruit; a bit simple and straightforward but quite pleasant and drinkable.★

Casetta F.lli, Vigna Pioiero *(1/85)*. Aroma of gingerbread and fruit; some tannin and firmness, fairly nice fruit. Is there enough?★ −

Cerretto, Fantasco *(2/85)*. Cherrylike fruit on the nose and palate; could improve, nice now.★★ +

Dosio *(2/85)*. Fresh fruit aroma, some charm, dolcetto-like; a lot of flavor, fruity.★★ −

Giacosa Bruno, Valmaggiore *(twice 11/84; 12,000 bottles; 1 month in bottle)*. Big, rich aroma; exceptional balance, heaps of flavor and extract, has a tannic vein;

1982

very long finish; impressive indeed.★★★ +

Pasquero Giuseppe, Vignadogna *(2/85)*. Light nose of ripe fruit; full of flavor, almost sweet, some firmness.★★ +

Prunotto, Occhetti di Monteu Roero riserva *(1/85; 26,315 bottles)*. Closed nose, noticeable alcohol (13 percent); a mouthful of fruit, some tannin, needs time for the bouquet to develop, but the potential is there.★★(★)

"Punset" di R. Marcarino *(1/85)*. Odd nose; some fruit but, like the nose, odd.

Rabezzana *(1/85)*. A big wine with heaps of fruit and a lot of tannin.★(★)

Ratti, Occhetti di Monteu Roero *(1/85)*. Nose has a lot of fruit, vague tarlike note; soft, round, and fruity; quite ready now.★★ +

Scarpa, San Carlo di Castellinaldo *(2/85; 18,100 bottles)*. Richly concentrated aroma, tar and tealike notes; loads of sweet, ripe fruit, light tannin, soft-centered, well balanced; loads of style, impressive.★★★

Tenuta Carretta, Bric' Tavoleto *(4/25)*. Nebbiolo character evident on the nose, tar and flowers; tannic, loads of fruit beneath; needs a lot of age, but the quality is evident.★★(★).

Tenuta Coluè di Massimo Oddero *(1/85)*. A lot of nice fruit on the nose, moderately intense; some tannin to lose, but loads of flavor make it tempting now; has a firm tannic vein.★★ +

Vietti, San Giacomo di Santo Stefano Roero *(11/84; 3200 bottles)*. Lovely perfumed bouquet suggestive of flowers, cherries, and strawberries; light tannin, low acid, forward fruitiness, very well balanced; long finish recalls almonds; has class and style.★★★

Vietti, S. Michelle *(twice 2/85)*. Cherries and ripe fruit, soft and tasty.★★★

Older Vintages

For the most part, these wines should be drunk up. We are including a few notes from those wines that might offer further interest or have a point to make. Some '78s are still good, but there is no need to hold them any longer.

1980 Tenuta Carretta, Bric' Paradiso *(4/85)*. Lovely berrylike fruit aroma; some tannin still, heaps of flavor, well balanced; fairly long finish; still needs some time; without question the best 1980 nebbiolo we tasted.★★★ −

1971 Tenuta Carretta, Bric' Paradiso *(5/84; gallon)*. Richly fruited aromy and flavor, soft, round, and smooth; at its peak, quite impressive.★★★

NEBBIOLO DELLE LANGHE *(Cuneo)*. These wines are similar to the Nebbiolo d'Alba wines, but with more body and flavor. Not infrequently those from the better producers are declassifed Barolo or Barbaresco. In 1977, some producers like Bartolo Mascarello declassified all of their Barolo, feeling that it lacked the weight and structure a Barolo should have.★★/★★★

Recommended Producers
★★Cascina Rombone di Nada Fiorenzo
★★Clerico
★★★Cogno Elvio
★★★Conterno Aldo, delle Bussia Conca Tre Pile
★Denegri Lorenzo

★★Grasso, di Monforte
★★Marchese di Gresy, della Martinenga
★★★Mascarello Bartolo
★★Produttori del Barbaresco
★★Rinaldi Giuseppe
★★Vaira, Bricco delle Violeo

Tasting Notes

1984

Scarzello Giorgio *(4/85)*. Fresh, fruity, and soft; a good quaff.★

1983

Clerico *(1/85)*. Fresh aroma suggestive of berries and cherries; fruity, easy, very drinkable.★★

Denegri Lorenzo *(1/85)*. Fruity nose; forward, open style, simple and easy.★ +

Grasso, di Monforte *(2/85)*. Cherry aroma, vaguely tobaccolike note; a lot of fruit, acid a bit low; very good.★★

Marchese di Gresy, della Martinenga *(2/85; 18,200*

1983

bottles). Expansive aroma rises from the glass, suggestions of cherries and gingerbread; a lot of fruit upon entry and a lot of fruit at the end, it seems to miss some fruit in the middle.★★ –

Nada Fiorenzo, Cascina Rombone *(1/85)*. Fresh, berrylike aroma, cherry notes; light, fruity and quaffable.★★

1982

Conterno Aldo, della Bussia *(4/85)*. Big, richly fruited aroma; full-flavored, some tannin adds backbone; very ready and very good.★★★

NEBBIOLO DEL PIEMONTE. These wines are made from nebbiolo grapes grown anywhere in Piemonte. They range in style from light to full, dry to sweet, fresh, fruity, and charming to dull, flat, and uninteresting. Your only guide, as always, is the producer.★/★★

Tasting Note

1983 Pio Cesare, del Piemonte *(11/84)*. Fresh, strawberrylike aroma and taste, some charm.★★

NEBBIOLO DI TORTONA *(Alessandria)*. This wine is produced by Spinetto, Padeira, and Carbonara from nebbiolo grapes grown in the Tortona area.

NEBBIOLO PASSITO *(Cuneo)*. This is a semisweet red wine made from late-harvested nebbiolo grapes dried on mats for about three weeks. The wine is a throwback to the old days in Piemonte before the change was made to dry wines. It is rarely seen today. We tasted one made by Pasquero Elia Secondo of Neive from the 1976 vintage and another from Vietti of Castiglione Falletto from the 1980 harvest. The Vietti was from a production of only 300 bottles.★★

ORNATO *(Cuneo)*. Pio Cesare produce this full-bodied wine from a blend of 60 to 80 percent nebbiolo and 20 to 40 percent barbera grapes grown in their Ornato vineyard in Serralunga d'Alba. In the first year of production, 1982, they made 200 cases. The wine was given eight months of *barrique* aging.★★

Tasting Note

1982 *(Twice 6/84)*. Barbera fruit up front, nebbiolo in the back, some oak evident; good structure, light tannin, flavorful.★★

PAIS *(Cuneo)*. This wine is made from nebbiolo grapes grown in the Pais area.

PERTINACE ANTICO *(Cuneo)*. This wine is produced from nebbiolo grapes grown in the Barbaresco zone. It is a full-bodied dry red of about 13 percent alcohol, with an austere nature and a moderate capacity to age.

ROSALBA *(Cuneo)*. This wine is a nebbiolo–dolcetto blend.

RUBELLO DI SALABUE *(Alessandria)*. Carlo Nob. Cassinis produces this light-bodied wine at Castello di Salabue from a blend of barbera and nebbiolo grapes. The '82 we tasted was high in acid and low in fruit.0

SAN MARZANO *(Asti)*. This is one of the many barbera–nebbiolo blends produced in the Asti area.

ZANE *(Asti)*. This light-bodied dry red is made in San Desiderlo from a subvariety of the nebbiolo known as zane. It is a soft, fruity wine of about 11 percent alcohol, best drunk young while it is still fresh.

ZIO GIOVANNI *(Cuneo)*. Az. Agr. "Roche" produces this light-bodied wine from a blend of 60 to 65 percent nebbiolo and 35 to 40 percent freisa grapes. It has a fresh, berrylike character and is best drunk young and cool.★

Barolo and Barbaresco Producers

Accademia Torregiorgi *(Neive) 1976*. This producer owns no vineyards. They buy all of their grapes, selecting at the time of the harvest to get the best fruit and consequently paying a premium. Torregiorgi produces a number of wines, including about 10,000 bottles each of Barolo and Barbaresco. Both of these wines are made in the gentler, more elegant style.

Crus	**Barolo**	Arnulfo di Monforte
		Carpegna di Serralunga d'Alba
		Grassi di Monforte
	Barbaresco	Crocetta di Neive
		Messoriano di Neive
		Pastura di Neive

Not all of these crus are bottled every year. Barolo★★; Barbaresco★ +

Accomasso Giovanni *(Pozzo, fraz. Annunziata, La Morra)*. This highly regarded producer (Veronelli gives him three stars) bottles a Barolo from the vineyard of Rocchette dell'Annunziata. Unfortunately, we've never tasted it.

Alessandria F.lli di G.B. Alessandria *(Verduno)*. Alessandria bottles a Barolo from Monvigliero. Thus far, we've been unimpressed with this producer's Barolo, cru or no. Barolo 0

Altare Elio *(Annunziata, La Morra) 1978*. Altare produces, from his 12.4-acre (5-hectare) Cascina Nuova holdings, 26,500 to 33,000 bottles of wine a year. This includes 9500 to 11,000 bottles of Barolo plus Dolcetto and Barbera. We can't say that we've been impressed with them, but they are honest wines.

| *Crus* | Arborina |
| | Cascina Nuova |

Barolo★

Anforio Vini Del Piemonte This brand is owned by the Folonari brothers, of Ruffino fame. We suspect their Barolo is made by the reliable cooperative cellars of Terre del Barolo.

Ascheri Giacomo *(Bra) 1918*. Ascheri owns 106 acres (43 hectares) of vineyards and produces a wide range of Piemontese wines, including Barolo and Barbaresco. The wines are honest but could have more style. The Barolo is made from grapes grown in La Morra and Serralunga, about half and half. Ascheri owns vines in Nirane-Sorano Bricco and Galarei in Serralunga. Barolo★; Barbaresco0

Asteggiano Vincenzo *(Castiglione Falletto)*. In our limited experience we've found the Asteggiano Barolo to be rather simple. Barolo 0

Balbo Marino *(Treiso)*. We haven't tasted their Barbaresco since the 1974 vintage, and we found that wanting. Perhaps they have improved. Balbo owns Cascina Bruciato in Tre Stelle. Barbaresco 0

Barale F.lli, Az. Agr. "Castellero" *(Barolo) 1870*. Barale owns 52 acres (21 hectares) of vineyards from which they produce 100,000 bottles a year, including 40,000 bottles of Barolo and 10,000 of Barbaresco. Overall, we have found their wines to be very good and generally reliable.

Vineyards	**Barolo**	Bussia (Barbera d'Alba)
		Cannubi
		Costa di Rose (Dolcetto d'Alba)
		Preda

Carlo Barale of Fratelli Barale

Crus	**Barolo**	Castellero
	Barbaresco	Rabajà

Barolo★★★; Barbaresco★★ +

Barbero Cantine *(Fraz. Valpone, Canale)*. This firm sells a mediocre Barbaresco under the brand name of "Conte de Cavour." Barbaresco 0

Bava Cantine *(Cocconato Asti)*. Bava produces a wide range of wines of varying quality, including Barolo and Barbaresco which we've not yet tasted.

Bel Colle Az. Vitivin. di Pontiglione Palmino Franco, Carlo & Priola Giuseppe *(Verduno)*. We have found these wines at best unimpressive, at worst undrinkable. Barolo 0; Barbaresco 0

Bersano, Antico Podere Conti della Cremosina *(Nizza Monferatto) 1896*. Probably the most interesting thing about this Seagram's-owned company is their wine museum. They have 143 acres (58 hectares) of vineyards which provide about 40 percent of their grapes; they buy the balance. Their Barbaresco is produced from grapes grown in their own vineyards in Treiso and Neive. A few years ago they sold their holdings in the La Ghiga vineyard to Pietro Berutti of Az. Agr. "La Spinona." Bersano produces some 355,000 cases of wine a year, in a wide range of types. Their Barolo and Barbaresco are made in the softer, fruitier more approachable style. For the most part, although lacking in structure and personality, they are drinkable enough.

Vineyards	**Barolo**	Cascina Badarina
	Barbaresco	Cascina Ghiga
	Nebbiolo d'Alba	Cascina Cortine

Barolo and Barbaresco 0; Nebbiolo★.

Bertolo Lorenzo *(Torino)*. This merchant sells a wide range of Piemontese wines, including Barolo and Barbaresco, as well as those of the Novara–Vercelli hills.

Bianco Luigi & Figlio *(Barbaresco)*. Although we have found their Barbaresco somewhat variable in quality, it can be good. Bianco owns vines in Vitalotti, a part of the Casot vineyard district. Barbaresco★

84

Boffa Carlo & Figli *(Barbaresco).* Their Barbaresco can be fairly good; it could use more style. Both of the crus—Vecchia Casot and Vitalotti—are in the Casot vineyard district. Barbaresco★

Bordino Franco *(Neive).* We have found their Barbaresco to be quite good. We haven't tasted it in some time, since the '74 vintage to be exact. Bordino bottles the Barbaresco cru of Monprandi in Bricco de Neive. Barbaresco★★ +

Borgogno Aldo *(La Morra).* The only bottle of Barolo from this producer we've tasted, a '71, was oxidized. There was some quality still evident, however.

Borgogno F.lli Serio & Battista di Serio Borgogno *(Barolo) 1897.* This firm owns 7 acres (2.8 hectares) of Cannubi, a vineyard considered the top cru in Barolo. They have 2.7 acres (1.1 hectares) planted to nebbiolo. From their nebbiolo—lampia and michet—they produce some 1250 cases a year of Cannubi Barolo. The balance of their acreage on Cannubi is mostly in barbera, with some dolcetto. They also buy grapes from Barolo, La Morra, Diano d'Alba, and Castiglione Falletto for their other Barolo and from Treiso for their Barbaresco.

They told us that their older vintages of Barolo are aged until they're ready to be shipped; then the wine is *traversato,* drawn out of the bottles through a rubber tube into a barrel, where it is left for the sediment to settle, then filtered and rebottled. Besides losing their sediment, these wines, not surprisingly, also lose their personality. They are still drinkable, but not much more. Aside from this aberration, the firm is fairly traditional in its methods. Their wines overall are correct for their type and display the character of the grapes they're made from, but we find them unexciting. There is no question that their cru bottling from Cannubi is a superior wine to the regular Barolo.

Barolo, Cannubi★★; Barolo and Barbaresco★

Borgogno Giacomo e Figli *(Barolo) 1848.* Borgogno, owned by the Boschis family since 1968, produces 300,000 bottles a year, somewhat less than half of which is Barolo. Their own grapes furnish about 35 to 40 percent of their requirements; for the rest they buy grapes, though never must or wine, they point out.

They own 50 acres (20 hectares) of vineyards, 37 (15) of which are in Barolo; they also purchase grapes from Barolo, Annunziata di La Morra, Novello, and Verduno. Since the grapes arrive at the winery at different times, they are fermented separately but blended and aged together.

At Borgogno they have not considered bottling a separate cru because they want their Barolo to represent the area in general and the house style in particular.

At one time we found their wines to be on a higher level. That was up until and including the 1967 vintage. In 1968, Cesare Borgogno died. Since then the firm has been run by his nephew, Franco Boschis. It's not that the wines today are bad—they're not—but they're not what they used to be. The house style is for traditional wines, relatively slow-maturing and quite robust and tannic in their youth. They are sometimes overly tannic and deficient in fruit, but honest wines that can be good though rarely more.

They produce 18,000 to 20,000 bottles of Barbaresco a year. This wine is made entirely from grapes purchased from the *commune* of Barbaresco. They also produce a Barolo Chinato as well as the standard Albeisa wines.

Vineyards	**Barolo**	Cannubi
		Liste
		Pascolo
		Ruè
		San Pietro

Barolo and Barbaresco★ since 1968; previously★★

Bosca Luigi e Figli *(Canelli) 1831.* Bosca's best wines, while they can be drinkable, lack character, structure, and interest—and in this regard they are consistent. Barolo 0 − ; Barbaresco 0 −

Gianfranco Bovio

Bosso. There is little we can say about this producer since we don't know anything about him except for his Barolo which we haven't tasted since the 1971 vintage. Barolo 0

Bovio Gianfranco *(La Morra)*. Bovio is the proprietor of Ristorante Belvedere, which offers a beautiful panorama of the La Morra vineyards. He has 9.4 acres (3.8 hectares) of vines in Annunziata di La Morra from which he produces 15,000 to 20,000 bottles of wine a year. Some 8000 bottles of this are Barolo; the balance is Dolcetto. Bovio's Barolo is a good example of the La Morra style, tending more toward elegance than bigness. Overall, these are very good wines, with character and balance.

Crus	Arburina
	Dabbene (Dolcetto d'Alba)
	Gattera

Barolo★★★

Brero Cav. Luigi *(Verduno)*. There is little we can say about Brero's wines that our zero rating doesn't already say. Barolo and Barbaresco 0

Brezza Giacomo *(Barolo)*. We have found these wines uneven and at best rather ordinary.

Vineyards	Arbarella (dolcetto)
	Castellero
	Muscatel Ruè (barbera)
Cru	Sarmassa

Barolo 0

"Bricco Asili" Az. Agr. *(Barbaresco) 1973*. See Ceretto.

"Bricco Rocche" Az. Agr. *(Castiglione Falletto) 1978*. See Ceretto.

Brovia F.lli *(Castiglione Falletto)*. Brovia owns 5 acres (2 hectares) of vineyards in Castiglione Falletto, half in Rocche, and the other half in Otinasso, from which they produce some 12,000 to 14,000 bottles a year divided about evenly between the two crus. They also make 5000 to 10,000 bottles of Barbaresco, including a cru bottling from Rio Sordo. Thus far, we've not been overly impressed with their wines. Their Barolo is fairly consistent in quality but a bit pedestrian. Barolo ★; Barbaresco 0

Bruzzone *(Strevi)*. These wines, from our experience, lack character and structure. We haven't tasted them in some time now and don't know, in fact, if they are still being produced. A few years ago the majority interest of this winery was acquired by the large American importer Villa Banfi. Barolo 0; Barbaresco 0

Ca' Bianca *(Alice Bel Colle) 1952*. Ca' Bianca produces 300,000 bottles of wine a year, in a wide range of types, as well as 100,000 bottles of grappa (a good one). They own 60.5 acres (24.5 hectares) of vines in Alice Bel Colle and La Morra, from which they get 60 percent of their grapes. In August 1984, they purchased the vineyard and winery of Denegri.

Cabutto Bartolomeo *(Barolo) 1920*. This producer owns about 17.3 acres (7 hectares) of vines, which supply 70 to 75 percent of their grapes. Besides Barolo and Barbaresco (if the Barbaresco is still made), they also produce the other typical Albeisa wines. Through the years we have found their wines to be somewhat variable. Their Barolo is reasonably good, meriting one star, though prior to the 1978 vintage, when their wines displayed more character, two stars minus would have been justified. They sell their Barolo as Tenuta La Volta. Barolo★; Barbaresco 0

Calissano Luigi & Figlio *(Alba) 1872.* This Winefood-owned company produces some 500,000 cases a year of a wide range of Piemontese wines, including spumante, and vermouth. Their wines are of decent quality and can offer good value if not much else. Barolo★; Barbaresco★.

Canale Aldo *(Serralunga d'Alba).* Canale owns part of the regarded vineyard of Vigna Rionda. He does a cru bottling from those vines.

Cappellano, Dott. Giuseppe di Teobaldo e Roberto Cappellano *(Serralunga d'Alba) 1870.* Cappellano buys all the grapes for their wines. They produce some 25,000 to 30,000 bottles a year, including 7000 each of Dolcetto, Barbera, and Barolo. The balance consists of very small quantities of Arneis, Favorita, and other wines including a Barbaresco. The grapes for their Barolo come from three of the top vineyards in Serralunga d'Alba: Baudana, Gabutti, and Parafada. Cappellano does a limited cru bottling from Gabutti.

While we have enjoyed his wines and can, in fact, recommend them, we are complying with Dott. Cappellano's request not to be rated. He states quite definitely that he makes the best wine for his own taste and doesn't want to be compared to others. Fair enough.

Cappellano's Barolo Chinato is simply the finest we have tasted. Admittedly, they have had time to perfect their product; they were the first producers to offer a Barolo Chinato in the last century and have been selling it commercially ever since.

Carnevale Giorgio *(Rocchetta Tanaro Cerro) 1880.* Carnevale produces about 30,000 bottles of wine a year, including Barolo and Barbaresco. They have a very good reputation.

Carra. The last time we tasted Carra's Barbaresco was some time ago. Barbaresco 0

Carretta. See Tenuta Carretta.

Cascina Bruni di Pasquale Veglio *(Serralunga d'Alba).* Veglio owns between 27 and 30 acres (11 and 12 hectares) of vines. He owns 17 (7) of nebbiolo vines in Vigneto Sorì, which he bottles as a Barolo cru. Cascina Bruni also owns 7.4 acres (3 hectares) of Carpegna plus parts of Maria Luigia, Pilone, and Rivassa, all in Serralunga. Their average production of nebbiolo, mostly for Barolo, is 22 tons (200 quintali) of grapes a year. This Barolo is in the lighter, earlier-maturing style. Barolo★

Casetta F.lli di Ernesto Casetta *(Vezza d'Alba, fraz. Barbore) 1956.* Casetta produces an average of 33,300 cases annually of the characteristic Albeisa wines, including both Barolo and Barbaresco. The grapes for their Barolo come from Serralunga d'Alba, La Morra, and Castiglione Falletto; those for their Barbaresco are from Treiso and S. Rocco Senadelvio d'Alba. We've found their wines overall to be ordinary, though drinkable, regardless of type. Casetta bottles a Barolo cru from his holdings in the Terra Hera vineyard. Barolo★−; Barbaresco 0

Castello di Neive di Italo Stupino *(Neive)* 1957. Castello di Neive produces 14,650 cases of wine a year; 5550 are Barbaresco. The balance is made up of the typical wines of this area: Dolcetto, Barbera d'Alba, Grignolino, Arneis, and Moscato d'Asti. All of their wines are produced from their 62 acres (25 hectares) of vines. They also sell grapes to producers such as Bruno Giacosa and Accademia Torregiorgi. Since Stupino lives and works in Torino, his cellarman, Talin Brunettini, is in charge of following the wines on a day-to-day basis. At our tasting last winter in the beautiful but chilly *castello,* as the old wines sat in decanters near the heat to warm and open up a bit, Stupino also warmed with enthusiasm talking about the wines of Castello di Neive. He is obviously very involved with them, and his care and concern is evident in their quality. The Barbarescos of Castello di Neive are among the most consistent and reliable in the zone. They are full-bodied and concentrated, reflecting the characteristic of the district but with particular class and distinction; they are harmonious, complex, with that extra dimension called style that sets them apart.

Vineyards	Basarin (Dolcetto d'Alba)
	Montebertotto (Arneis)
	Valtorta (Dolcetto d'Alba)
Crus	Messoirano
	Santo Stefano

Barbaresco★★★★

Castello Feudale di Motta Renzo, Cantina del (*Montegrosso d'Asti*). The *castello* itself dates from 1134, but we expect that the winemaking is of a somewhat more recent vintage. The wines are produced in the lighter style. Barolo★; Barbaresco★

Castello Sperone. Our experience with these wines, we don't regret to say, has been limited. Barolo 0

Castello Verduno [di Castello Re Carlo Alberto] di Burlotto Dr. Lisetta & Sorelle (*Verduno*). This producer owns at least a part of the vineyard of Massera in Verduno.

Cauda Cav. Luigi (*Loc. Montebello di Vezza d'Alba*), *1946*. Cauda owns 25 acres (10 hectares) of vineyards planted to nebbiolo and barbera, which supply 30 percent of their grapes. Their annual production, which includes the typical wines of the area plus spumante, is 66,600 bottles. We have rarely tasted such mediocre—make that poor—wines from the Langhe. Barolo 0−; Barbaresco 0−.

Cavaletto. These wines are as inferior as they are uncharacteristic, the Barbaresco in particular. We would expect their Barolo, if anything, to be worse. Barbaresco 0−

Cavallotto, F.lli Olivio & Gildo, Az. Agr. "Bricco Boschis" (*Castiglione Falletto*). This very traditional firm produces Barolo, Dolcetto, Barbera, Grignolino, and Favorita from grapes grown in their own vineyards on Bricco Boschis, where some 40 of the 50 acres (16 of the 20 hectares) are planted to vines. From the 13.2 acres (5.3 hectares) of nebbiolo, they produce an average of 3155 cases of Barolo. Their total annual production is 11,000 cases. They have three Barolo crus:

Cru	Hectares	Acres	Cases	Year planted
Colle Sud Ovest	1.1100	2.7	655	1951
Punta Marcello	0.7900	2.0	465	1967
San Guiseppe	3.4427	8.5	2035	1947

We tasted what we thought was a fourth cru from the 1980 vintage, a Conte Vassallo. We haven't heard a thing about it since.

Since the 1978 vintage, they have bottled the wines from each of the vineyards separately, indicating the cru on the label. Punta Marcello, with sandier soil, is in their opinion the best of the three; this is due in part to its smaller yields. This wine is the more perfumed. The other two, from more calcerous soil, are bigger in body. We find their wines overall to be full-bodied and robust, often high in alcohol, and very tannic when young, but in the best vintages they develop well. Cavalotto tend to keep their Barolos very long in cask, sometimes too long, especially in some of the lighter vintages. The oldest Barolo from Cavalotto we've tasted, the '71, is still holding well. Overall, their wines are good and reliable, if somewhat lacking in style and perhaps even a bit coarse. Barolo★★

Cella. These wines, while drinkable enough, lack character and structure. Barolo 0

Ceretto (*Alba*), *1968*. The Ceretto brothers, Bruno and Marcello, administrator and winemaker respectively, are the proprietors of Casa Vinicola Ceretto in Alba. In the early years they bought the grapes for their wines. Later, in order to control more closely the quality of the grapes as well as the wine, they set about acquiring prime vineyard land in Barolo and Barbaresco. In the 1970s, they added Bricco Asili in Barbaresco and Bricco Rocche in Castiglione Falletto to their holdings. They also own a small distillery in Treiso where they make grappa.

Marcello Ceretto was among the first to adopt and is a leading proponent of the modern style for Barolo and Barbaresco. He began experimenting in 1972 with modern techniques, seeking to produce a finer, more drinkable wine. He shortened the period of skin contact during fermentation and of wood aging for his wines, feeling that Barolo and Barbaresco made in the old style had too much tannin and not enough fruit. In 1973, he began fermenting his red wines in stainless steel tanks, being one of the first in the area to do so. We think few would dispute that the Ceretto wines are among the best in the Langhe.

The Cerettos produce Barolo, Barbaresco, Nebbiolo d'Alba, Dolcetto d'Alba, and Barbera d'Alba. The very good Moscato d'Asti and Asti Spumante of the Vignaioli di Santo Stefano Belbo, produced from the grapes of seven different vineyard owners, is made at the co-op under their direction.

In February 1985, we had the excellent, and we believe quite rare, opportunity to taste a range of Barbarescos from their Asili and Bricco Asili crus, as well as a number of vintages of two of their Barolo crus, Prapò and Brunate. We were struck by the depth, the balance, and the style of the wines as well as the consistency maintained even in some of the lesser years.

The Cerettos are opposed to *barrique* aging, which they feel takes away personality from the wine while giving nothing in return except unnecessary tannin. Marcello demonstrated his point, offering us a couple of samples of his wine which had been put into *barrique*. The wine was harsh, tannic, and lacking in fruit, quite unlike the other wines proudly lined up for us in rows of fine stemware on the long table at the *cantina*.

The Ceretto brothers own a highly regarded piece of the Asili vineyard in Barbaresco called Bricco Asili, which they bought in 1969, planting the vineyard in 1970 and building a winery there shortly afterward. They also vinify grapes that they purchase from another part of Asili. Whatever can be said about Asili—perfumed, delicate, elegant—can also be said about Bricco Asili, only more so. This wine has a fine structure and is rich in extract and flavor.

In total, Ceretto produces some 27,000 to 33,000 bottles of Barbaresco a year; 7000 to 8000 are Bricco Asili or, as they now label it: Asÿ (the name in Piemontese dialect). Up until 1974, they also produced a Barbaresco from the Montefico vineyard.

They also produce 59,000 to 68,000 bottles of Barolo a year, divided among four crus: Bricco Rocche, Brunate and Prapò, which they own, and Zonchetta, now Zonchera (the dialect name), from the part of Brunate that they lease. Since the 1979 vintage, their Barolos have been produced at new facilities in Castiglione Falletto, Az. Agr. "Bricco Rocche."

The Barolo of Brunate has more perfume and complexity than the Prapò. We noted a suggestion of mint in the bouquet. Marcello, who was not commenting on his wines, compared it to a wild herb similar to mint, which grows wild in the Langhe. Reflecting the character ascribed to the wines from the two valleys, the Brunate is more accessible in its youth, softer and more open; the Prapò is firmer in structure, somewhat more tannic, and slower maturing.

Ceretto has also produced Barolos from Villero and Grignore, a part of Baudana.

Marcello and Bruno Ceretto

The Crus

	Hectares	Altitude (meters)	Exposure	Average production (bottles)	First produced
Barbaresco					
Asÿ[1]	2.5	220–270	sw	20,000–25,000	1966
Bricco Asili	1.2	270–300	sw	7,000–8,000	1973
Barolo					
Bricco Rocche	1.0	380–420	ssw	3,000–5,000	1982
Brunate[2]	5.0	280–350	sw	25,000–30,000	1978
Prapo[3]	3.0	300–370	s	13,000–15,000	1976
Zonchera[4]	3.0	250–300	sw	18,000	1971

Other crus	Wine	Average production (bottles)	First produced
Bernardina	Nebbiolo d'Alba	20,000–22,000	1975
Piana	Barbera d'Alba	8,000–10,000	1962
Rossana di Madonna Como	Dolcetto d'Alba	18,000–20,000	1967
Vigna	Dolcetto d'Alba	20,000	1967

Notes
[1] At one time bottled as Asili.
[2] At one time bottled as Blange-Brunate.
[3] At one time bottled as Riccardo I in Prapò.
[4] At one time bottled as Zonchetta.

Barolo★★★; Barbaresco★★★; Nebbiolo d'Alba★★★

Ceste Cav. G. These are wretched wines, among the worst in the zone. Barolo 0 −

Chiadò Mario. The most recent Barolo we tasted from Chiadò was his 1971, and it left us cold. Barolo 0

Cigliuti F.lli di Renato Cigliuti (*Loc. Serra Boella, Bricco di Neive*), *1962.* Cigliuti owns 7.5 acres (3 hectares) of vines. His annual production is 16,000 bottles, which includes 4650 bottles of Barbaresco; the balance is almost evenly divided between Dolcetto and Barbera. The Barbaresco is somewhat gentler in nature and more elegant than the Barbarescos of Neive in general, being in that respect like others from Bricco di Neive that we are familiar with. He bottles his best Barbaresco with the cru name, Serra Boella. Barbaresco★★★

Clerico Domenico (*Loc. Manzoni Cucchi, Monforte*), *1976.* Clerico owns 21 acres (8.5 hectares) of vines, which supply all of their grapes. Like many other Piemontese producers, Clerico is experimenting with *barriques*. Clerico bottles two Barolo crus: Bricotto Bussia since 1978, and Ciabot Mentin Ginestra since 1980. Barolo★★

Cogno Elvio. See Marcarini Poderi di Anna Marcarini & Elvio Cogno.

Colli Monfortesi di Conterno Fantino (*Monforte*). These Barolos are overly simple and rather unimpressive. Barolo 0

Confratelli di San Michele (*Neive*), *1972.* This is a cooperative of five members with vineyards in Neive. They have an annual production of 40,000 bottles, which includes Barbaresco, Dolcetto d'Alba, and Barbera d'Alba.

    Crus   Cotta
                   Gallina
                   S. Cristoforo

Barbaresco ★ −

"Conte di Cavour". See Barbero Cantine.

Conterno Aldo (*Loc. Bussia, Monforte*), *1968.* Aldo Conterno owns 52 acres (21 hectares), 36 (14.5) of which are in vines. From his 16 acres (6.5 hectares) of nebbiolo vines, he gets a yield of almost 50,000 bottles of wine. He selects only the best for his Barolo; the remainder becomes Nebbiolo. Conterno's annual production is about 90,000 to 100,000 bottles; of this, about 21,000 to 25,000 bottles are Barolo. When the year justifies it, Conterno produces about 5000 bottles

Aldo Conterno

each of his two special subcrus in Bussia Soprana: Bricco Cicala and Bricco Colonnello. The balance is Barbera, Dolcetto, Freisa, and Nebbiolo. Conterno said that the vines for his Barolo must be at least six years old, fifteen to be used in his cru bottlings. Conterno considers michet his best subvariety; he also has some lampia.

Conterno's Barolos are without question among the finest in the zone. These are finely balanced, stylish wines, rich in fruit, displaying depth and class. We find that while they are enjoyable from their sixth year, they approach their peak in their eighth to tenth, depending on the vintage.

On our most recent visit to Piemonte, Aldo Conterno shared a Barolo with us from his birth year, 1931. The '31 vintage is considered to be the finest this century, and if this outstanding wine is proof enough, then it certainly was a special year. This wine was produced by Aldo's father, Giacomo Conterno. The wine had a firmness about it under its more gentle nature (for our tasting note, see page 56).

Giovanni Conterno of Giacomo Conterno

Crus   Bussia Soprana
            Bussia Soprana-Cicala (2.5 acres)
            Bussia Soprana-Colonnello (3.2 acres)

Barolo★★★★; Nebbiolo★★★

Conterno Giacomo di Giovanni Conterno *(Monforte).* Unlike his brother, Aldo, Giovanni Conterno is a staunch traditionalist. He speaks somewhat sadly of the push in Italy today toward producing a younger, earlier-maturing wine, affirming that even if the market for the traditional wines should someday no longer exist, his wines will never be made other than by the traditional methods he believes in. His wife nods her head in agreement and support. Conterno realizes that he has chosen the more difficult path, but he believes in his wine.

He wants a full-bodied, ample, and long-lived wine, an old-style Barolo at its best. To achieve this he restricts his production severely, using only the finest fruit from the more favored vintages to produce a dense, robust wine that can stand up to the long wood aging that will smooth it out, rounding off its youthful rough edges.

When the grapes don't measure up to his demanding standards, which happens unfortunately rather frequently, he doesn't produce the wine. For example, in 1984, he sold all of his grapes; in 1983, he made very little wine and that only Freisa; in 1977, he didn't pick any grapes.

Conterno produced no Barolo in 1975 or 1976, and although he has some '81 in cask, he has decided not to bottle it; he will sell it *sfuso*.

His Cascina Francia holdings include 37 acres (15 hectares) in Serralunga d'Alba, from which he produces some 86,000 bottles of wine—30,000 of Barolo, the balance Dolcetto, Barbera, and Freisa. Up until 1971, he also produced a Barbaresco.

Conterno produces two Barolos: a regular and a special selection, "Monfortino." He ages the former no less than six years in cask and the latter for at least eight, and ten isn't uncommon. He began bottling his regular '74 Barolo in 1980, and the Monfortino in 1984. When we visited the *cantina* in November of 1984, we tasted a '70 Monfortino still in cask. The Monfortino is not named for a single vineyard; it is from selected grapes from his Cascina Francia holdings.

Dott. Alberto Contratto of Giuseppe Contratto

Like some of the other Barolos that are given long cask aging, Conterno's wines seem to be more susceptible to damage by improper handling or storage. While we've had many magnificent Barolos from Giovanni Conterno, we've had some that didn't measure up, which were in fact disappointments. We are convinced, however, that the problems occurred after the the wines left the winery.

Barolo "Monfortino"★★★★; Barolo★★★; Barbaresco [not made since 1971]★★★

Contratto Giuseppe di Dott. Alberto Contratto *(Canelli), 1867.* Contratto owns 116 acres (47 hectares) of vineyards including Cascina Alberta in Treiso and Cascina Secolo in La Morra. They also buy grapes. They produce a wide range of wines of fairly consistent quality. This serious-minded, traditional firm also produces some of Italy's finest champagne-method sparkling wines. Barolo★★ + ; Barbaresco★★

Coppo Luigi e Figli *(Canelli), 1892.* The Coppo Barolo and Barbaresco are a bit simple, but they can be good. They tend to mature fairly early. Coppo bottles two Barolo crus: Brunate and Castello. Barolo and Barbaresco★

Cortese Giuseppe *(Barbaresco, loc. Rabajà).* Cortese produces a Barbaresco from the fine Rabajà vineyard and a Nebbiolo delle Langhe.

Cortese Riccardo *(Canelli).* This producer owns vineyards in Cascina Rocca in Barbaresco.

Cossetti Clemente & Figli *(Castelnuovo Belbo).* Cossetti produces or sells under their own label a wide range of wines varying in quality from nondescript to downright poor. Barolo 0 – ; Barbaresco 0

Damilano Dott. Giacomo & Figli *(Barolo).* Damilano owns part of the highly prized Cannubi vineyard. We find this producer's Barolo superior to his Barbaresco. Barolo ★; Barbaresco 0

De Forville Anfosso *(Barbaresco), 1860.* De Forville owns 25 acres (10 hectares) of vineyards, which supply about 40 percent of his grapes. His annual production of 15,500 to 20,000 cases of wine includes a good Barbaresco. He has been bottling individual crus, when the vintage justified it, since 1974.

Crus   Loreto
         Montestefano
         Pozzo
         Rabajà

Barbaresco★★

De Forville Paolo *(Barbaresco).* At one time these wines had a good reputation; perhaps they still do. Our limited experience hasn't been favorable. There might be a connection between Anfosso and Paolo de Forville, but we don't know.

Vineyards	Loreto
Crus	Ovello
	Montestefano

Barbaresco 0

Dellevalle F.lli *(Gattinara).* We have found these wines lacking in personality and structure, though they can be drinkable enough. Dellevalle is primarily a producer of Novara–Vercelli wines. Barolo 0

Denegri Lorenzo *(fraz. Annunziata, La Morra), 1953.* We have heard favorable reports of this Barolo, but our limited experience doesn't concur. We have also heard that Sig. Denegri has been quite ill, which could account for the disappointing bottles we've had. He only made two wines: a Barolo and a Nebbiolo. In August 1984, Ca' Bianca of Alice Bel Colle bought out Denegri. We look for an improvement in the wines. Denegri's Barolo is from their holding in Plucotti dell'Annunziata, though the label doesn't indicate that. Barolo★

Dogliani F.lli *(loc. Batasiolo, La Morra).* In 1979, Dogliani bought the Kiola brand along with their *cantine* and vineyards from I.D.V., who had owned the brand since 1974. Dogliani 7 Cascina owns 284 acres (115 hectares) of vineyards, including holdings in Barolo, Castiglione Falletto, La Morra, and Serralunga d'Alba. They purchase grapes as well. Their annual production totals some 3 million bottles of mediocre wine, including 500,000 of Barolo.

Vineyards	**Barolo**	Batasiolo
		Boscaretto
		Bricco
		Briccolina
		Brunate in Barolo
		Bonfani-Bussia
		Cannubi-Moscatello
		Cerequio
		Zonchetta in Barolo

The ratings are for Kiola since we've yet to taste the wines of the new owners. Barolo 0 − ; Barbaresco 0 −

Dogliotti Amelio Vincenzo e Figli *(Castagnole Lanze).* This firm produces some 166,650 cases of all of the typical wines of this area, including Barolo and Barbaresco.

Dosio Giuseppe *(La Morra, loc. Serradenare), 1971.* Dosio produces 65,000 to 70,000 bottles of wine a year; 10,000 to 16,000 bottles are Barolo. These are light, early-maturing wines that are overly simple. Their riserva speciale is aged for five years in oak. Barolo★

Duca d'Asti Cantine *(Calamandrana).* This firm produces a wide range of fairly reliable and correct, though unexciting, wines, including Barolo and Barbaresco. They buy the grapes for their Barolo from Barolo, Serralunga d'Alba, Castiglione Falletto, and the borderlands. Their Barbaresco is from grapes grown in Barbaresco, Treiso, and Neive. Since 1974, they have produced a single-vineyard Barolo, from the lampia and michet subvarieties, grown in Vigneto Margaria in Serralunga d'Alba. Barolo★; Barbaresco★

Einaudi Luigi Podere *(Dogliani), 1907.* This producer is quite traditional. Einaudi has 247 acres (100 hectares), 62 (25) in vines, including 10 acres (4 hectares) of nebbiolo. From 6.2 (2.5) of these in the Terlo di Barolo vineyard, he produces a full-bodied, richly fruited Barolo. Besides this, he also makes 80,000 to 180,000 bottles a year of Barbera, Dolcetto, and Nebbiolo delle Langhe. We have found the Einaudi Barolo consistent and very good. Barolo★★★

Fenocchio Giacomo *(loc. Bussia Sottana, Monforte).* Our limited experience has left us with a somewhat favorable impression of Fenocchio's Barolo. Barolo★

Fenocchio Riccardo, Az. Agr. Pianpolvere Soprano *(Monforte), 1918.* Fenocchio owns 8.8 acres (3.6 hectares) on Pianpolvere Soprano, from which he produces 30,650 bottles of wine. Less than 6650 bottles are Barolo. In 1983, Fenocchio vinified all of his grapes for the first time. Previously he had sold his barbera to the Cerettos. His wineyard is planted approximately two-thirds to nebbiolo and one-third to barbera; there are also twelve rows of grignolino vines, rather unusual in this area. Fenocchio's Pianpolvere vineyard is, he told us, actually a part of Bussia. We've found his wines to be quite good. Barolo★★

Ferrero Virginia (*Serralunga d'Alba*). We haven't tasted Ferrero's Barolo since the 1970 vintage. Barolo 0

Feyles Maria & Figli (*Alba*). Feyles produces a Barbaresco cru from Gaia di Neive. The most recent one we tasted, from the rather mediocre 1976 vintage, was fairly good. Barbaresco★

Fontana Michele (*Barolo*). This producer owns part of the very fine Cannubi vineyard as well as part of the La Mandorla and San Lorenzo vineyards.

Fontanafredda, Tenimenti di Barolo e di (*Serralunga d'Alba*), *1878*. The Fontanafredda wine estate was founded by Count Emanuele Guerrieri, son of Vittorio Emanuele II of Italy and his mistress, "La Bela Rosin." The winery and its 250 acres (100 hectares) of vineyards were taken over in 1931 by Monte dei Paschi of Siena, the world's oldest bank. The vineyards on the estate today provide Fontanafredda with only 13 percent of the grapes they need for their annual production of 4.5 million bottles. Some 2.5 million of this is sparkling wine, including some very good Asti and fine champagne-method spumante. Of the remaining 2 million bottles, Barolo and Barbaresco make up 850,000 and 100,000 bottles, respectively; the remainder consists of a wide range of wines, generally reliable and characteristic of their type. Most of their grapes are purchased from growers with whom Fontanafredda has long-term contracts. The grapes for the Barbaresco come from Treiso and Barbaresco. While it is generally a good wine, this Barbaresco often reminds us more of a Barolo in style.

Fontanafredda bottles Barolos from 9 crus. Vigna Bianca has an austere nature and is regarded for its bouquet. Gallaretto is noted for its body and structure. Gattinera is austere in its youth, requiring age to bring it around. This last cru is also a source of pinot grapes for their especially fine *metodo champenoise* spumante, Gattinera brut. La Rosa is perhaps their most noted cru, not necessarily because it's the best, but because it has been the most widely distributed. Barolo La Rosa is perhaps the most robust of the wines and consequently requires aging to show its quality. The Barolos of La Delizia and La Villa are ready the soonest and San Pietro shortly afterward. The San Pietro also ages well and is regarded for its bouquet. The Lazzarito Barolo is the slowest to mature and, not surprisingly, ages very well.

Barolo cru	Acres	Hectares	Bottles	Meters	Exposure	sub-variety	First made
Bianca	1.26	0.5080	3500	250	south	100% michet	1971
replanted after the 1978 harvest							
Gallaretto	4.05	1.6400	11300	280	south	lampia michet	1974
part in Serralunga, part in Diano d'Alba							
Garil	0.94	0.3800	2500	250	south		1971
Gattinera	11.12	4.5000	31000	280	—	50/50 michet lampia	1970
planted in 1970							
La Delizia	8.87	3.5900	24000	350	south	100% michet	1967
La Rosa	23.10	9.3500	65000	mid-hill to 310	south/ southwest	michet lampia	1958
La Villa	7.89	3.1910	22000	300- 350	east	—	1958
in the Cannubi area of Barolo							
Lazzarito	6.50	2.6300	18000	350	southwest	mostly lampia some michet	1971
San Pietro	7.64	3.0900	22000	—	southwest	—	1974

Barolo crus★★, regular★; Barbaresco★

Fracchia Provino & Figlio (*Grazzano Badoglio*). Fracchia produces a Barolo and a Gattinara. We've never tasted either one.

Franco Fiorina (*Alba*), *1925*. Franco Fiorina, owned by Elsa Franco and Giuseppe Fontana, produces some 350,000 to 400,000 bottles a year of a fairly wide range of consistently good wines, wines that sometimes attain great heights. Of this, 40,000 to 50,000 bottles are Barolo and 30,000 to 40,000 are Barbaresco. They own no vineyards, but buy all their grapes from growers with whom they have long-standing agreements.

At Franco Fiorina they don't believe in the cru concept for Barolo or Barbaresco. They feel they can produce a more balanced wine by blending the grapes from the different *communes*. Their Barbaresco is made with grapes from Barbaresco itself, which gives structure, and from Treiso for finesse. In their Barolo, they use grapes from four *communes*. Those from Barolo, they point out, give structure to the wine; those from Castiglione Falletto provide body and strength; the grapes of Serralunga d'Alba provide less alcohol but add perfume; while those from La Morra, which give less color, add delicacy to the blend.

Franco Fiorina aims to produce a gentle wine—both Barolo and Barbaresco—but also one that can age.

Armando Cordero, the firm's enologist, recognizes the advantages of both the old methods and modern technology, and the disadvantages of both as well. While employing some modern techniques, he produces wines that are basically traditional. Franco Fiorina declassified part of the 1977 and 1976 crops and all of the 1975 harvest, preferring to sell the wine *sfuso* without their label rather than bottling a wine that didn't come up to their standards. Barolo★★+; Barbaresco★★

Gaja di Angelo Gaja *(Barbaresco), 1859.* This firm has been bottling wines since the early 1900s. Up until and including the 1961 vintage, they included a Barolo among their production. Since 1964, they have been an Azienda Agricola, making wines from only their own grapes.

Gaja is the largest private owner of vineyards in the Barbaresco zone, with 153 acres (62 hectares) of vines, including nearly 75 acres (30 hectares) in Barbaresco itself. Besides the local grape varieties, they have 10 acres (4 hectares) of chardonnay and 7.5 (3) of cabernet sauvignon.

Of their annual production, which averages about 220,000 bottles, 120,000 are Barbaresco. Gaja also produces Nebbiolo d'Alba, Dolcetto d'Alba, Barbera d'Alba, Cabernet Sauvignon, and Chardonnay, as well as a nouveau-style Nebbiolo, Vinot.

Angelo Gaja, present director of this family firm, has, like many of the winemakers of the Langhe, a degree in enology from Alba. He also attended schools in Germany and France. In 1974, he went to California, where he presumably fell under the spell of the *barrique*.

Angelo Gaja —Al Fisher, 1982

Gaja has, in fact, achieved a signal success aging his Barbaresco in small, new oak barrels, where the wine takes on a certain subtlety and suppleness without losing the personality of the nebbiolo grape. While we are not advocates of *barrique* aging for nebbiolo wines, we must give him credit for his accomplishment. There is no question that he is an exceptional winemaker and obviously proud of his achievement and his skill.

Gaja gives the impression of almost a naive conceitedness when speaking about his wines.

He describes himself as "vain," which may sound like a slightly mistaken translation from the Italian; but no, his English is quite good, and vanity is what he is speaking of. When we asked him why he had chosen to plant cabernet sauvignon and chardonnay vines, he replied that they are noble grape varieties that produce excellent wines, and as he is a vain man he wants to work with grape varieties of that proven caliber which make it possible for him to produce outstanding wines.

Gaja is an admirer of the fine French wines and the distributor in Italy for the burgundies of the Domaine de la Romanée-Conti, the champagnes of Gosset, and the Alsatian wines of Leon Beyer. He is quick to point out, however, that he isn't trying to make French wines himself.

Despite the oak, he wants to make an Italian Barbaresco. But not a typical Barbaresco. Gaja is obviously not interested in making typical wine. Yes, he wants his wine to let the drinker know that it is a Barbaresco, but he wants it to announce that it is a Gaja.

He aims for a harmonious wine with more aroma and flavor and less tannin. To this end he picks his grapes late, when they are fully mature and richer in extract and color, feeling that it is worth the greater risk for the potentially higher quality to be gained. Of his crus, the Sorì San Lorenzo is picked first, Sorì Tildin last.

Angelo has been in charge of winemaking at the *cantina* since the 1973 vintage. In 1976, he began employing some of the new techniques he had experimented with previously. These included a shorter fermentation time, at most two weeks on the skins, and the addition of 40 to 70 percent whole berries to the fermenting must (this is not carbonic maceration, which is whole-berry fermentation in a closed vat) to give a more evident fruitiness to the wine, to balance the tannin and oakiness imparted by the small barrels the wine is aged in.

Angelo started making tests with new *barriques* for aging the wine in 1969. He prefers barrels made from Yugoslavian oak; he finds the wine picks up less tannin from it than from the French oak. He replaces one-third of his *barriques* with new barrels each year.

The '79s were his first wines made entirely in the new style. While he notes that the wines aren't as rich as the '78s, he finds them more elegant.

Gaja's Barbarescos have a deceptive suppleness in their youth, picked up from the *barriques*, but they seem to have the underlying strength to age quite well, judging from the ones we've tasted thus far, and there have been quite a few.

Besides his regular Barbaresco, Gaja bottles three individual crus. These wines are not made every year, only when he feels the vintage justifies it. He didn't vinify any of the crus, for example, in 1980. In 1973, he made some Tildin but bottled no San Lorenzo.

Of the three single vineyard wines, Costa Russi matures the soonest. It is the most open, with a sweeter taste and more intense aroma. Tildin is more closed and concentrated; it is firm in texture and holds more in reserve. San Lorenzo is the hardest of all in its youth, requiring age to show its real quality. It is the slowest-maturing of the crus and should be the longest-lived.

Barbaresco cru	Hectares	Average production (bottles)	First bottled	Altitude (meters)
Costa Russi	4.00	14,000	1978	n/a
Sorì San Lorenzo	1.20	9,000	1967	170
Sorì Tildin	1.58	9,000	1970	240

Other crus
Darmagi (Cabernet Sauvignon)
Vignabajla (Dolcetto d'Alba)
Vignarey (Barbera d'Alba)
Vignaveja (Nebbiolo d'Alba)

Barbaresco★★★★; Nebbiolo★★★

Gemma *(Barbaresco).* At one time Alfredo Roagna was involved with this winery. Today it is owned jointly by Piemonte's Grand Ambassador of Wine, Giacomo Bologna, and Silvano Piacentini of the Istituto Enologica Italiano of Verona. While these wines thus far have been good, they haven't come up to our expectations. Considering the source, however, we look forward to better wines in the future. Gemma sometimes bottles the Barbaresco cru Gallina. Barolo★; Barbaresco★—for now.

Gherzi. We haven't tasted these wines in some time, but those we have were lacking in structure and character. Barolo 0; Barbaresco 0

Giacosa Bruno *(Neive), 1900.* Bruno Giacosa is without question one of Italy's—make that the world's—finest winemakers. A man of few words but eloquent talent, Giacosa has the ability to bring out a richness of flavor and an intensity of character in his wines, producing wines of meditation. The man is an artist. Besides a profound Barolo and a sublime Barbaresco, he produces superb Barbera, Dolcetto, and Nebbiolo d'Alba, also impressive Arneis and Grignolino d'Asti. There are few winemakers able to produce wines as finely honed or as consistent.

Bruno Giacosa

His annual production is 150,000 to 200,000 bottles, which includes 30,000 to 40,000 each of Barolo and Barbaresco. *Poco ma buono* (little but good) could be his motto. Giacosa has used the phrase frequently in speaking of his wines with us; it's typical of his tendency toward understatement.

Giacosa owns no vineyards; he buys grapes, selecting from some of the best sites in the area, and produces wines that epitomize the vineyards. He believes in the value of single-vineyard bottlings, noting that each vineyard has something to say. Although he's only been labeling the crus separately for about fifteen years, he vinified and aged the wines separately previously. He told us that his grandfather, Carlo, also kept the vineyards separate in the cellar. Giacosa bottles the crus only in the better vintages. These wines are bottled with a special label, maroon for the Riserva Speciale and white for the Riserva. On his regular Barolo and Barbaresco, with a tan label, he doesn't specify the vineyard name.

If the wine doesn't attain a certain very high standard, he doesn't bottle it as a Barbaresco or Barolo; he either declassifies it, selling the wine as a simple Nebbiolo, or he doesn't bottle it at all but sells it *sfuso*. For example, for Bruno Giacosa there was no 1981, 1977, or 1973 Barolo or Barbaresco; all were sold *sfuso*.

Sig. Giacosa practices the custom of "'*n fund 'd buta*," pouring for important guests the end from a previously opened bottle. He feels that his Barbaresco needs at least a few hours of air to open up and show itself. When we had lunch with him in November of 1984 and he served us from the half-down bottle of '78 Santo Stefano opened more than two weeks earlier (seventeen days, to be exact), we were both honored and pleased. This Barbaresco was a knock-out; in fact, for us it was the single finest wine produced in that very fine vintage. We told him so. Characteristically, he did not smile at the compliment. He did acknowledge it, however, in his way; he poured us a generous refill.

Crus	**Barolo**	Bussia
		Le Rocche
		Vigna Rionda
		Villero
	Barbaresco	Santo Stefano
		Gallina
	Nebbiolo d'Alba	Valmaggiore di Vezza d'Alba

Besides these crus, he has from time to time bottled a few others. Until recently he also produced a Barbaresco San Cristoforo di Neive, and a few years ago he made a Barbaresco Asili and a Montefico. Barolo★★★★; Barbaresco★★★★; Nebbiolo★★★

Giacosa Donato di Carlo Giacosa *(Barbaresco), 1967.* Giacosa owns 9.6 acres (3.9 hectares) of vines, including 5.3 acres (2.2 hectares) of nebbiolo in the hills of Barbaresco. He produces some 24,000 bottles of wine a year. Nebbiolo wines, including Barbaresco, account for 15,000 bottles. Barbaresco★★

Giacosa F.lli di Leone, Valerio & Renzo *(Neive), 1900.* The Giacosa brothers own no vineyards; they buy all the grapes they require to produce some 150,000 bottles of wine a year. We have found their wines reliable and very good. They are in the fuller, more tannic style, requiring age to round out and soften. Barolo★★★; Barbaresco★★★

Giacosa Romualdo. This Giacosa bottles a Barbaresco cru from his part of the Canova vineyard.

Giordano Giovanni *(Barbaresco).* Giordano owns vines in the Cavanna vineyard in Barbaresco; he does a cru bottling of Barbaresco from there. Barbaresco★

Giovannini-Moresco Enrico *(Treiso), 1967.* Moresco's Podere del Pajorè is without question one of the most outstanding wines of Barbaresco, and consistently so. It is a full-bodied, richly flavored wine of immense proportions, a fuller, more assertive style of Barbaresco. One of the major reasons for its bigness and intensity is the fact that Moresco believes in harvesting late, waiting until the grapes are totally ripe, despite the obvious hazards, and also in limiting the size of his yields by severe pruning.

His 28.5-acre (11.5-hectare) vineyard produces an average of only 20,000 bottles. The Podere del Pajorè vineyard is planted entirely to nebbiolo, the rose subvariety. That's the one that by reputation produces the lighter nebbiolo wines, if you can believe it.

Moresco produced his first Barbaresco in 1967; his second was from the 1971 vintage (12,500 bottles); these were followed by the 1974 (25,000 bottles), 1978 (3,500 bottles), 1979 (20,765), and 1980 (20,000). His '71 was, for us, the single finest wine of the vintage, and his '79 might be even better. Only the '78, while a very good Barbaresco, did not achieve the heights we expected from it.

Since 1979, Moresco's wine has been made, according to his instructions, by Angelo Gaja at Gaja's *cantina*; and since 1980, Gaja has been tending Moresco's Pajorè vineyard. As of this writing we are not sure whether Moresco will sell his holdings or take a more active part in the production of his outstanding Barbaresco. We hope it will be the latter. Barbaresco★★★★

Giri Guido, Contea di Castiglione *(Alba), 1969.* Giri owns no vineyards; he buys all the grapes he requires. We have found his wines reliable if unexciting, though admittedly we haven't tasted them in some time. Barolo★; Barbaresco★

Glicine Cantina del, di Adriana Marzi & Roberto Bruno *(Neive), 1974.* Glicine produces a number of single-vineyard Barbarescos, two from their own vineyards of Curà and Marcorino. They have an annual production of 45,000 to 50,000 bottles, 15,000 to 20,000 of which are Barbaresco. The balance includes a charming rose called Glicinello made from the free-run juice of freisa and nebbiolo grapes, a Dolcetto d'Alba, and a Barbera Nebbiolata, Barbera made with some 10 to 15 percent nebbiolo refermented on the nebbiolo lees. The Glicine Barbarescos, made by Adriana Marzi, are in a gentle, elegant style. They are consistent and reliable, even in the lesser vintages.

Adriana Marzi of Cantina del Glicine

Crus	Cubà
	Curà
	Gaia
	Gallina
	Marcorino
	Montesomo
	Pastura
	Rabajà

Not every cru is bottled every year. Barbaresco★★★

Granduca. See Duca d'Asti, Cantine.

Grasso Az. Agr. di Elio Grasso *(Monforte d'Alba), 1919.* The estate and the original Grasso winery date from 1919, but Elio Grasso, the present proprietor, has been bottling the wines only since 1978. His father sold the wines *sfuso*. All of Grasso's wines—Dolcetto, Barbera, and Nebbiolo—are made from his own grapes. He has 15.6 acres (6.3 hectares) of vines, 10.2 (4.1) in nebbiolo. More than 50 percent of his annual production of 4210 cases is Barolo (2600).

To ensure top quality, Grasso selects the bunches carefully; any that do not meet his standards are made into ordinary wine to be sold *sfuso*. We find his wines, especially the Barolos, to be of consistently high quality, elegant wines in a lighter, softer, more gentle style.

Crus	Gavarini
	Gavarini-Chiniera
	Gavarini dei Grassi
	Gavarini-Runcot
	Ginestra-Case Matè

Barolo★★★

Grazziola *(Canelli), 1887.* This firm produces the full gamut of Piemontese wines, including spumante, vermouth, and, of course, Barolo and Barbaresco. Those we've tasted have been rather unimpressive, though we must admit that it's been a while. Barolo 0; Barbaresco 0

Elio and Marina Grasso of Az. Agr. Grasso

Grimaldi Cav. Carlo & Mario Az. Agr. Groppone *(Diano d'Alba).* In 1978, Grimaldi produced 4500 bottles of Barolo. We found it, the only one we've tasted, overly simple, lacking in character and interest. He also produces Barbaresco, which we haven't tasted. Barolo 0

"Il Vecchio Tralcio" di Carlo Deltetto *(Canale), 1970.* This producer makes Barolo and Barbaresco as well as Arneis, Gavi, Favorita, and some interesting spumante. In our opinion, the spumante and the white wines are much more interesting than the Barolo and Barbaresco. They own 2.5 acres (1 hectare) in Roero, which provides them with 10 percent of their grapes. Deltetto does a Barbaresco cru from Moccagatta. Barolo 0; Barbaresco 0

Kiola. See Dogliani F.lli.

"La Brenta d'Oro" Cantine d'Invecchiamento. The few times we tasted these wines we've been totally unimpressed. Barolo 0; Barbaresco 0.

"La Martinenga," Tenute Cisa Asinari dei Marchesi di Gresy *(Barbaresco), 1973.* Marchesi di Gresy has four vineyards comprising some 66.5 acres (27 hectares) of vines. Only two at most concern us here: La Martinenga and Monte Aribaldo.

La Martinenga is considered the number one vineyard in the Barbaresco zone by many authorities and producers. It is entirely owned by Marchese Alberto di Gresy. All 30 acres (12 hectares) are planted to nebbiolo. These grapes are used to produce Barbaresco and Nebbiolo delle Langhe, the latter wine for early drinking. The La Martinenga is a Barbaresco of elegance and finesse rather than power and authority. Its class is evident from the first swallow.

The last time we saw La Martinenga we were not entirely sure we'd recognize it in the daylight, having only seen it at midnight illuminated by the headlights of di Gresy's car—both times before. But perhaps the charmingly unconventional proprietor did have his priorities in order; tasting the wine came first.

In the best vintages two parcels of La Martinenga are kept separate and bottled individually: Camp Gros and Gauin. Camp Gros, from the end of the vineyard near Rabajà, has more tannin, structure, acid, and firmness; it matures more slowly and will probably live longer. Gauin, from the opposite end of La Martinenga near Asili, is softer, richer in glycerine and in perfume. It is, in fact, the essence of La Martinenga Barbaresco—a gentle, feminine wine of elegance and breed.

The Monte Aribaldo vineyard includes a small plot of nebbiolo which can be used to produce Barbaresco. To our knowledge, however, those grapes are sold.

In all, di Gresy produces only 150,000 bottles of wine a year from the two vineyards. The rest of the grapes—some 50 percent or more—are sold. He also makes a Novello, a Dolcetto, and a Moscato and in a couple of years will be producing a Chardonnay.

For us, the '74 Martinenga didn't measure up to the vintage. The first to really impress us was the '76, which, although too old today, was at the time possibly the best wine of the vintage. With the '78 vintage and perhaps even more so with the '79, di Gresy has produced a Barbaresco that lives up to the lofty reputation of the vineyard. Since 1983, Piero Ballario has been the enologist at La Martinenga. We look forward to further improvements in quality.

In the *cantina*, as we tasted the full range of his wines, Alberto's normal cheerful nonchalance and infectious wit seemed suspended momentarily as we critically evaluated the wines, but they returned with a smile of obvious pleasure as we offered our compliments, words he gallantly deflected to his winemaker. Alberto remarks that he's considering taking a few names out of his aristocratic title on the label when the wine becomes a little better known, simplifying it for the consumer by making it simply "Crazy Gresy," a nickname that we (or to be more exact, Sheldon) have tagged him with for his original approach to life.

Crus	Martinenga
	Camp Gros-Martinenga
	Gauin-Martinenga
	Monte Aribaldo (Dolcetto)

Barbaresco★★★★; Nebbiolo della Martinenga★★

"La Spinona" Az. Agr. di Pietro Berutti & Figlio *(Loc. Fassetto, Barbaresco), 1963.* The Beruttis own 31 acres (12.5 hectares) of vines from which they produce about 88,400 bottles of wine a year, including 32,650 of Barbaresco. Their other wines are Dolcetto, Barbera, Freisa, and Nebbiolo delle Langhe, and they recently planted some Chardonnay.

Although he says he personally prefers the older style, like many others in the Langhe, Berutti is following the dictates of the market in producing a faster-maturing, more accessible style of Barbaresco. It is, however, a well-balanced wine with good fruit and some elegance.

Crus	Bricco Faset
	Cars
	La Ghiga
	Qualin

Barbaresco★★★

"Le Colline" Az. Agr. *(Neviglie), 1951.* This traditional firm, producers also of "Monsecco" Gattinara, owns Cascina Bordino, a 12.4-acre (5-hectare) vineyard in Treiso. They produce a Barbaresco from their own grapes, which we have not as yet tasted.

"Le Corte" Az. Agr. di Oliviero Monticelli *(fraz. Rivalta, La Morra).* Le Corte produces a Barolo Le Caudane di La Morra.

Lodali Giovanni & Figlio *(Treiso).* The only wine we've tasted from this producer was his 1961 Barolo. It wasn't really a bad wine, but it was quite atypical. It reminded us of a southern wine in both aroma and character. Barolo★

Manzone Stefano, Az. Agr. Ciabot del Preive *(Monforte).* Manzone has vines in the Castelletto vineyard district. He produces a decent Barolo from the vines he owns in the part called Ciabot del Preive. Admittedly our experience is limited. Barolo★

Marcarini di Anna Marcarini & Elvio Cogno *(La Morra), 1958.* Elvio Cogno produces 55,000 bottles of wine a year from Podere Marcarini's 23.6 acres (9.6 hectares) of vineyards. About 21 acres (8.5 hectares) are planted to nebbiolo for Barolo, which yields about 45,000 bottles; the balance is dolcetto. Cogno also produces Barbera, Freisa, and Tinello, a proprietary blend made from 80 percent barbera and 20 percent nebbiolo and dolcetto. Under the Elvio Cogno label he bottles Grignolino del Piemonte, Nebbiolo d'Alba, Freisa, and Barbera.

Cogno, one of the region's truly fine winemakers, produces outstanding wines. His Barolos epitomize balance, elegance, and finesse; they are consistently among the best produced.

Elvio Cogno of Podere Marcarini

In the old and dimly lit but clean and tidy aging cellar on our latest visit, Cogno cheerfully drew samples from various oaken casks of La Serra and Brunate for us to taste and to note the differences between the two crus. They are from different parts of the same vineyard in La Morra, but each has its own character. Cogno finds that the La Serra starts off fruitier, showing more of the La Morra perfume then the Brunate, which is more austere and closed when young; but as they develop, their personalities change, and the Brunate, which comes into its own later, smooths out to a softer, rounder, and more velvety wine. Would we like to see for ourselves without any influence? he asks with a twinkle in his eye. He offers the first glass blind—more closed, must be the Brunate. The second glass is more open, La Serra surely. Wrong, it's just the opposite! We taste again—same. He laughs and shrugs. Wines go through phases, but could it be he mixed them up? Shall we try again? We could spend the whole morning. Barolo★★★★

Marchesi di Barolo Gia' Opera Pia Barolo, Antichi Poderi dei (*Barolo*), *1861.* Marchesi di Barolo owns 100 acres (40 hectares) of vineyards, including some of the best sites in Barolo, a fact unfortunately not evident in their wines. These vineyards provide less than 20 percent of their grapes; the rest are purchased. At one time the name of Marchesi di Barolo was highly respected; it was in their cellars that the first Barolo as we know it today was produced. Though the label still carries their name, the present winery is turning out a wide range of wines that for the most part lack personality. Their single-vineyard Barolos can provide an interesting glass but are overpriced for their quality. As for their standard Barolo and Barbaresco, there are better Nebbiolo d'Alba wines around for a fraction of the price. The wines do offer one thing: consistency. They are, however, consistently ordinary.

Barolo cru/vineyard	Hectares	1979 quantity (*bottles*)
Brunate	2.9000	17,640
Cannubi	0.5312	3,370
Cannubi-Muscatel	3,4990	13,370
Castellero	0.4200	—
Costa de Rose	—	—
La Valletta	2.0794	13,840
Le Coste	0.6000	—
Sarmassa	1.9397	14,910

Barolo Crus★; Barolo 0; Barbaresco 0

Marchese Maurizio Fracassi Ratti Mentone (*Cherasco*), *1880.* Fracassi owns 15 acres (6 hectares) of vineyards, including 2.8 acres (1.2 hectares) of nebbiolo vines in La Morra. They produce 60,000 bottles of wine annually, all from their own grapes. Of this, a mere 7000 bottles is Barolo. This Barolo, perhaps Barol*a*, is in a gentle, elegant style, one might even call it a feminine style, which evidently reflects the taste of the winemaker, the Marchesa. Barolo★★

Marchesi Spinola (*Acqui Terme*), *1782.* These merchants at one time offered a decent Barolo and Barbaresco under their own label. We don't know if they still do; we haven't seen any in some time. Barolo★; Barbaresco★

Mascarello Cantina di Bartolo Mascarello *(Barolo), 1918.* Bartolo Mascarello owns 12.5 acres of vines from which he produces some 15,000 to 20,000 bottles a year of what is, in our opinion, *the* finest Barolo made. He also produces 5000 to 6000 bottles of Dolcetto, which is probably also top notch, but as we write these lines we realize we've never tasted it! In certain vintages Mascarello declassifies all or part of his Barolo, selling it as Nebbiolo delle Langhe; 1972 and 1977 were two such vintages.

Bartolo Mascarello of Cantina Mascarello

When we asked Bartolo about vinifying his vineyards separately and doing a cru bottling, he replied with a broad smile that he has one cru: "Bartolo Mascarello!" We doubt if anyone would disagree that Bartolo Mascarello is a *premier grand cru.*

In fact, Bartolo's name does not appear on his label, a situation that concerned us, as it might lead to some confusion with the other Mascarello wines, one of which in particular does not begin to approach his in quality. When we asked him about this, he seemed unconcerned. He uses the same label his father did. The label bears his crest. His customers would remember it. He has a point; these are memorable wines. There are no doubt winelovers searching for that Mascarello label with that crest, perhaps not knowing the producer's name but recognizing his style.

Bartolo's wines are the epitome of balance, harmony, style, elegance, distinction, and character. Like his father's wines before them, every bottle is a wine of meditation, best drunk with good friends who appreciate great wines; no food is necessary as an accompaniment—the wines are food for thought in themselves. The last time we enjoyed his splendid '55, it was served with a plate of fine local cheeses, offered by the mutual friends in whose house we were guests, but nobody paid any attention to the cheese once Bartolo had filled the glasses. The wine was fittingly drunk in an elegantly simple manner, accompanied by the warmth of his smile and our murmured comments of pleasure and appreciation.

Bartolo Mascarello's winemaking philosophy begins with the rule that the first thing is to make a wine without defects. Volatile acidity, a not uncommon problem in this area, is for Bartolo "public enemy number 1," and, as he said, it is the winemaker's job "to kill him." This is a simplification of a profound winemaking technique. But Mascarello is a simple man—uncomplicated, open. He does his work to the best of his considerable ability, laughs easily, and enjoys the simple pleasures, such as the company of friends around a simply marvelous bottle of wine.

Vineyards	Cannubi
	Roero
	San Lorenzo
	Torriglione

Barolo★★★★

Mascarello Giuseppe di Mauro Mascarello *(Monchiero), 1881.* Mauro Mascarello produces 75,000 bottles of wine a year. This includes 30,000 bottles of Barolo, 5300 of Barbaresco, and 6600 of Nebbiolo d'Alba. He owns about 6.4 acres (2.6 hectares) of the Monprivato vineyard in Castiglione Falletto and buys from some of the other top crus in the Barolo and Barbaresco zones. Mascarello prefers to bottle the crus separately, but in years when he feels the quality doesn't justify it, he bottles the wine simply as Barolo; in lesser years he declassifies it to Nebbiolo delle Langhe. And, like many fine producers in the Langhe, he has been operating this way since long before the DOCG. Mauro's wines, especially his Barolos, are well made and have a lot of character; they age quite well. He is traditional in his approach to winemaking.

*Mauro
Mascarello of
Giuseppe
Mascarello*

Crus	**Barolo**	Bussia Soprana
		Monprivato
		Pugnane
		Villero
	Barbaresco	Bernardotti

Barolo★★★; Barbaresco★★

Massolino Giuseppe & Figli Giovanni e Renato, Az. Agr. "Vigna Rionda" *(Serralunga d'Alba), 1910.* Massolino own 37 acres (15 hectares) of vines from which they produce 8800 cases of wine a year; 5500 cases are Barolo from the crus of Parafada, Margheria, and Vigna Rionda. These are Barolos with a forward fruitiness, produced in a soft, easy, uncomplicated style. Barolo★

Minuto Mario *(Barbaresco).* There is more than one Mario Minuto in Barbaresco. This one owns vines in Cabanet and Faset. He does a cru bottling from the latter vineyard.

Mirafiore. At one time Fontanafredda produced the Barolo sold under this label. It was a decent wine, rarely more than that. Barolo★

"Moccagatta" Az. Agr. di Mario Minuto *(Barbaresco).* Minuto, like many of the other producers in this area, has jumped aboard the *barrique* bandwagon. He aged a portion of his '82 Barbaresco in small barrels. Judging from the bottle we tasted in January 1985, he would have done better to have treated it the same as the rest. Besides the cru bottling from the vineyard which gave Minuto's *azienda* its name, he also bottles Barbarescos from Basarin and Cole. Barbaresco 0

Molino Guido *(Grinzane Cavour).* It's been some time since we tasted Molino's Barolo; perhaps they've improved. Barolo 0

"Monfalletto" Az. Agr. See Montezemolo, Paolo Cordero di.

Montezemolo, Paolo Cordero di *(La Morra), 1941.* Marchese di Montezemolo produced his first Barolo in 1945. Long an advocate of the modern style of winemaking, he aimed for a Barolo rich in flavor and fruit, and he succeeded. That forward rush of fruit on the palate was his trademark.

Montezemolo retired on January 1, 1982. Since his sons, Giovanni and Enrico, have taken over the winery, production has more than doubled. Montezemolo produced an average of 30,000 bottles of Barolo and 10,000 of Dolcetto a year. He sold more than 50 percent of the grapes from his 45.4 acres (18.4 hectares) of vineyards; his sons vinify them all. It shows. The '79 and '80 Barolos were made by Montezemolo, but something happened to the wine somewhere along the line. They are good wines, but they don't measure up to what we had come to expect from this very serious, dedicated winemaker. Perhaps one of the problems lies in the fact that the young men chose to vinify the entire crop in 1979, instead of selecting only the better grapes as their father had done. Since the increase in production, they have outgrown the old *cantina* in La Morra. In 1981, they moved to a vastly larger winery in Monfalletto. They currently produce 7500 cases of Barolo and 2500 of Dolcetto. There are two Barolos, one from the cru of Monfalletto in La Morra and the other from the part of Villero known as Enrico VI in Castiglione Falletto. The former wine matures somewhat sooner.

In 1984, they produced a blend of nebbiolo (80 percent) and dolcetto (20 percent) which they label Elioro. We tasted it in January 1985 along with the '84 Dolcetto, both of which were already bottled. Both wines reeked of hydrogen sulfide and mercaptans—signs of bad winemaking. Something is surely amiss.

Montezemolo felt that his Barolos showed their best from six years after the vintage and could last quite a long time. Unfortunately, we've never tasted one old enough to say whether we agree with this assessment. Barolo since 1979★★; pre-1979★★★

Morando *(Boglietto di Costiglione).* Morando produces a Barolo that is light in style with a forward fruitiness; it could use more personality, though it is certainly drinkable. He also produces a Barbaresco which we haven't tasted. Barolo 0

Nicolello Casa Vinicola *(Alba).* Our limited experience with Nicolello's Barolo has left us unimpressed. Their Barbaresco, on the other hand, can be a decent glass of wine. Barolo 0; Barbaresco★

Oberto F.lli *(Annunziata, La Morra), 1968.* Oberto makes one wine, a Barolo, from his 3-acre (1.2-hectare) vineyard in Rocchette dell'Annunziata.

Oddero F.lli Giacomo & Luigi *(Loc. Santa Maria in Plaustra, La Morra), 1878.* Oddero owns 111 acres (45 hectares), half of which is in vines. Their average annual production of 200,000 bottles includes 100,000 bottles of Barolo and 20,000 of Barbaresco. They enjoy a good reputation, and those bottles we've tasted indicate it is deserved.

Vineyards	**Barolo**	Brunate
		Bussia Soprana
		Convento di La Morra
		Rocche di Castiglione Falletto
		Rocchettevino
		Vigna Rionda
	Barbaresco	Faset
		Montestefano
		Pagliuzzo
		Pora

Barolo★★★; Barbaresco★★

Oddero Luigi & Figli *(Monforte).* The few Barolos from this producer that we've tasted we found wanting. Barolo 0

Oreste Stefano *(La Morra).* Oreste owns vines in the Formica vineyard in La Morra. Barolo★

Ornato Paolo *(Castiglione Falletto).* We are including Ornato in our survey of producers although he doesn't sell his wine in bottle. Like numerous other small growers in the area, he produces a Barolo that could be a very good bottle indeed, but because of his small production or lack of interest in the extra work involved in bottling, he prefers to sell his wine *sfuso.* The quality of his wine, however, is indicative of the greatness of this zone. Ornato owns 5.6 acres (2.3 hectares) planted mostly to nebbiolo, in the Rocche vineyard, from which he produces the equivalent of 16,650 to 20,000 bottles. Of this, 70 percent is Barolo.

A few years ago we rated his wines two stars; today, probably because of his advanced age, the quality has slipped somewhat although it is still pretty good. Barolo★

Osola. Barolo 0

Osvaldo Mauro *(Castiglione Falletto)* We've found these wines overall rather poor, lacking in structure and character. Barolo 0 − ; Barbaresco 0

Palladino Az. Vitivin. di Maurilio Palladino *(Serralunga d'Alba), 1974.* Palladino owns 7.4 acres (3 hectares) in the San Bernardo vineyard, which supplies them with 26 percent of their Barolo grapes and 67 percent for their Dolcetto. They have an annual production of 84,000 bottles; 45 percent of this is Barolo plus a small amount of Barbaresco. All of the grapes for the Barbaresco are purchased. Palladino produce three different Barolos, a regular and two crus: San Bernardo and Vigna Riunda (his own spelling). In all, the wines are decent enough though they could use more character, more personality. Barolo pre-1978★; from 1978★★ − ; Barbaresco 0

Paolo Colla di Gianni Gagliardo *(fraz. S. Maria, La Morra), 1922.* Colla produces more than 200,000 bottles a year of a wide range of mostly mediocre wines, including 27,000 bottles of Barolo and 3500 of Barbaresco. Some 65 percent of the grapes come from their own vineyards. Colla owns 47.7 acres (19.7 hectares), 20.5 (8.3) of the La Serra vineyard in La Morra from which they produce 6000 bottles a year. They make another 7000 bottles from their Valgrande vineyard in Treiso. In 1974, Colla bottled a small quantity of Barolo Treccani. Barolo 0 − ; Barbaresco 0

Parroco di Neive di Benefico Parrocchiale di Neive *(Neive).* The Parrocchiale was founded in about 1500; we have no idea how long they've been producing wine. They own 37 acres (15 hectares) of vineyards in Neive. All of their wine is from their own grapes. They also sell a part of their harvest. They produce a total of about 100,000 bottles of wine a year; 46,650 of these are marketed under their label; the balance is sold *sfuso* or in bulk. Overall, we have found their wines uneven, though the best can be very good.

Vineyards	Cottà
	S. Cristoforo
	S. Giuliano
Crus	Basarin
	Gallina

Barbaresco★★

Parusso Armando *(Loc. Bussia, Monforte)*. Parusso produced nearly 100,000 bottles of Barolo from the 1980 vintage.

Secondo Pasquero-I

Pasquero-Elia Secondo Az. Agr. *(Bricco di Neive)*, 1893. Secondo Pasquero-Elia produces 3750 cases of wine a year. He has 15.7 acres (6.4 hectares) or vines, including 6.9 (2.8) of nebbiolo, from which he makes about 1750 cases of wine, mostly Barbaresco. In lesser vintages, some of the nebbiolo is declassified to Nebbiolo delle Langhe. His other wines include Dolcetto, Barbera, Moscato, and a tiny amount of chardonnay.

On our recent visit to Piemonte, this genial producer provided us with the answer to the oft-asked question, where is Primo? There is no Primo; she is La Prima, Secondo's better half.

We have found Pasquero's Barbarescos, tasted over the years, to be well made, light, and well balanced, in the gentler style.

Cru	Sorì d'Paytin
Vineyards	Serra Boella
	Elisa

Barbaresco★★★

Pavese Livio *(Treville Monferrato)*. Pavese owns two wineries: Az. Agr. "Podere Sant' Antonio" and Az. Comm. "Pavese Livio & C." They have 30 acres (12 hectares) of vineyards, which supply 20 percent of their grapes. They produce a wide range of reliable, rather simple wines that, while unexciting, are certainly drinkable. Total annual production between the two wineries ranges from 77,700 to 93,300 cases, which includes both Barolo and Barbaresco. Barolo 0; Barbaresco 0

Pelissero Luigi & Figlio *(fraz. Ferrere, Treiso), 1970.* Pelissero has 15 acres (6 hectares) of vineyards, which supply all their grapes. They have an annual production of 34,650 bottles, 90 percent of which is Barbaresco. Pelissero bottles a Barbaresco cru from his Vanotu vineyard. Barbaresco ★★

Pio Boffa of Pio Cesare

Pio Cesare *(Alba) 1881).* This firm owns 44.5 acres (18 hectares) of vines, including 19.8 acres (8 hectares) in Cascina Bricco in Treiso and 24.7 acres (10 hectares) in the Ornato vineyard in Serralunga d'Alba. They also buy grapes from Castiglione Falletto, Monforte, and La Morra. Of the approximately 6000 cases of Barolo they produce a year, 60 percent is from their Ornato grapes. They recently acquired another vineyard and told us that in the near future they might be producing as much as 75 percent of their Barolo from their own grapes.

At Pio Cesare they don't believe in making a single-vineyard Barolo. They feel that such a wine would lack what they consider the traditional character of Barolo. They believe that the differences among the subvarieties of nebbiolo are not significant, but that it is the exposure and the soil that are the determining factors in the character of the wine, particularly the soil. Pio Boffa, who produces the Pio Cesare wines along with his father, Giuseppe Boffa, and winemaker Paolo Fenocchio, points out that the grapes from Serralunga d'Alba give their Barolo body, structure, and complexity; the nebbiolo of this area produces wines big in body and rich in tannin. The wines of Castiglione Falletto, he notes, are soft and fruity; they add perfume and finesse to the blend. The Barolos of Monforte are in the middle, with more body than the wines of Castiglione Falletto and more finesse than those of Serralunga d'Alba; and the wine of La Morra provides delicacy. They combine the grapes from the various areas in the fermentation vats to produce a house-style Barolo.

Their Barbaresco, on the other hand, is made 100 percent from grapes grown in their own vineyards, most coming from Treiso and a small part from San Rocco Senodelvio d'Alba. They produce on average 2000 cases a year. They apparently don't discern similar variations among the wines from Barbaresco, Neive, Treiso, and San Rocco, as they don't produce a Barbaresco representing a blend of the different districts. Or perhaps they consider single-vineyard Barbarescos to be traditional.

At one time, no house was more dedicated to the traditional methods of winemaking than Pio Cesare, and although Boffa says that they still consider themselves a traditional firm, changes have been made in the last few years that have, it seems to us, moved them decidedly closer to the modern camp.

Their Barolo and Barbaresco used to be fermented in wooden vats, where the wine was in contact with the grapeskins two and a half months. Today the fermentation lasts for twenty to twenty-five days, at controlled temperatures, in stainless steel tanks. Whereas previously the malolactic fermentation occurred when it happened to develop, generally within a year or two, under today's more controlled conditions it has always taken place by year's end for all their wines.

After the wine spends some time in 3965-gallon (150-hectoliter) holding tanks, it is moved to the aging cellar. Previously the wines were kept outside during the winter to precipitate the tartrates, then moved back indoors when the weather warmed. Today the wine is kept indoors and the temperature lowered to effect this cold stabilization. The Barolo and Barbaresco used to be aged in large, old Yugoslavian oak casks for six to nine years. These days they keep the Barolo and Barbaresco up to three or at most four years in a few different kinds and sizes of oak, including small barrels, or *barriques*, for some of the wine. They have used these techniques, including small-barrel aging, since 1978. Currently they use half French and half Yugoslavian *barriques*. The *barrique*-aged wine is blended with the rest of the wine before bottling. Part of the '78 Barolo spent six months in *barrique*. Bottling of the '78 Barolo and Barbaresco began in January 1983.

Have these changes affected the wines of Pio Cesare? The answer is clearly yes, and for the better. The wines are more accessible at an earlier age and better balanced. The older Barolos and Barbarescos of Pio Cesare were sometimes—in fact, too often—hurt by overlong cask aging, becoming dried out and high in volatile acidity, though this was less of a problem in great vintages, of course. The Barolos made at Pio Cesare today, while they might not equal those of the greatest producers in the zone, are just one step below. Barolo pre-1978★★ −; since 1978★★★ −; Barbaresco★

Pippione. It's been some time since we tasted these wines. Barolo 0; Barbaresco 0

Pira Enrico & Figli Az. Agr., di Chiara Boschis *(Barolo).* When he was still making wine, Luigi Pira was, for us, the single finest producer of Barolo. Pira died in July 1980. Some six months after his death, the *cantina* E. Pira & Figli was purchased by the Boschis family, owners of the Giacomo Borgogno winery.

Luigi Pira, up to and including his last vintage in 1979, maintained the old ways in making his wine, including the crushing of the grapes by feet. As Bartolo Mascarello and others have said, the tradition of *pigiatura a piedi* died with Luigi Pira. The grapes were brought into his cellar, where the bunches were put into the *tini*, large upright oak vats; men trod on them with bare feet and the wine fermented. Today at Pira small basket presses are used.

When the Boschis family took over the Pira *cantina*, they found some casks of '74 that Pira had not bottled. Pira didn't give his wines a lot of oak age; in fact, when we visited him in October 1979, he told us that most of the '74 had already been bottled; only a few casks remained. Unfortunately, he never finished the bottling. We were told that a relative helped to maintain the wine in the cellar after Pira's death, but at least one cask of wine had to be discarded. Pira's sister saw to the harvesting of the 1980 crop, and the wine was made with the assistance of the Boschis family.

E. Pira is now under the management of Chiara Boschis, a young woman in her twenties who was still in school when the *cantina* was purchased. The two properties, Borgogno and Pira, are kept separate, however. The firm of E. Pira is still an *azienda agricola*; the entire production of 10,000 bottles comes from their own 4.3 acres (1.8 hectares) of vines. Some 90 percent of the production of E. Pira today is Barolo; the remainder is Barbera.

To her credit, Chiara Boschis decided not to use the Pira coat of arms on the labels of their Pira wine; the present crest is a different one. And the words *"pigiate a piedi"* will be removed from the label, she said, starting with the 1980 vintage. Another difference consumers can note in the Pira and post-Pira bottlings is that Luigi Pira's bottles had a longer neck; Boschis uses the Albeisa bottle (stamped "Albeisa" into the glass at the shoulder).

Pira had vines in five vineyards, but shortly before his death he sold his holdings in Prea and Vignane. They still have holdings in Cannubi, S. Lorenzo, and Via Nuova.

How are the Pira wines today? Those bottled by Pira are still magnificent; even the '75, from a rather mediocre vintage, is still good. The '74 bottled by Boschis is dried out and lacking in fruit, undoubtedly from not being cared for as well as having spent too long in wood. The '78 and '79 we tasted were also disappointing. We hope that with the later vintages, which Chiara Boschis will be fully responsible for, there will be an improvement in quality, although we obviously can't hope for a return to their previous glory. Luigi Pira's wines were rich in extract and concentration, with so much fruit that you were tempted to drink them early, but given sufficient age they became truly magnificent, the best Barolo had to offer.

Chiara Boschis seems determined to produce fine wines; perhaps with more experience she will achieve that aim. Barolo for now 0; for the memory★★★★

Pira Secondo & Figli *(Serralunga d'Alba)*. Pira owns vines in the Marenca and Margaria vineyards.

Podere Casot Nada. Our limited experience with this Barbaresco has left us unimpressed. Even the '78 was found wanting. Barbaresco 0

Podere del Pajorè. See Giovannini-Moresco Enrico.

Podere "Rocche dei Manzoni" di Migliorini Valentino & Salomoni Iolanda *(Loc. Manzoni Soprano, Monforte), 1971*. This firm owns 45 acres (18 hectares) of vineyards. They produce nearly 115,000 bottles of wine a year—42,000 bottles of Barolo, 15,000 of spumante, and 55,000 of other wines. Their Barolos are fairly good, reliable enough, but lack intensity and even some character. We find their estate-bottled nebbiolo–barbera blend, Bricco Manzoni, more interesting; it has more personality.

In 1978, they bottled a Barolo cru from their 'Dla Roul vineyard. In 1980 and 1981, all of their nebbiolo was vinified for Bricco Manzoni. Barolo★★

Ponte Rocca Az. Agr. di Francesco Pittatore & Figlio *(Barolo)*. Pittatore owns a part of Brunate and Castellero.

Porro Guido, Giovanni e Carlo *(Serralunga d'Alba)*. This firm owns vines in the vineyards of Lazairasco and Santa Caterina.

Porta Rossa di Berizia e Rizzi *(Diano d'Alba), 1973*. We haven't tasted their Barolo or Barbaresco in some time and want to point out that our rating could be out of date. They do have a fairly decent reputation. Barolo 0; Barbaresco 0

Prandi Teobaldi *(Barolo)*. Prandi owns vines in Monghisolfo and Via Nuova.

Produttori del Barbaresco *(Barbaresco), 1958*. In 1894, Domizio Cavazza founded a cooperative winery in Barbaresco; it continued in operation until 1930. In 1958, a new co-op, Produttori del Barbaresco, was organized. Under the able hand of Celestino Vacca, Produttori del Barbaresco became not only the paragon for every other *cantina sociale* in Italy but also the rival of every producer in Barbaresco. There are a few producers making Barbaresco in the same class as the wines of the Produttori, but none who surpasses them.

Initially there were nineteen members in the co-op; today there are sixty-six. Among them they own about 300 acres (120 hectares) of vines—nearly one-quarter of the plantings in the Barbaresco zone—in some of the most highly regarded vineyards in the area.

They have an annual production of 333,000 to 600,000 bottles of wine, all of it nebbiolo, but at most 200,000 to 300,000 bottles are Barbaresco. The grapes from their single vineyards are vinified separately, and when they feel the quality justifies it they are bottled under the cru name. When it doesn't, these wines become part of their regular Barbaresco. If the wine doesn't come up to the standards set for the Barbaresco, it is de-classified to Nebbiolo delle Langhe. Lesser wine is sold off in bulk, *sfuso*.

Giancarlo Montaldo of Produttori del Barbaresco

Through the years we've found the wines of the Produttori on a consistently high level. They are stylish Barbarescos, elegant and rich and very well balanced. In fact, with wines this good, each time we pour one for friends and tell them that the producer is a *cantina sociale*, we almost expect an exclamation of "Holy cow!" (which would be particularly fitting, as the name of their founding director, Celestino Vacca, could be loosely translated thus).

Crus   Asili
Moccagata
Montefico
Montestefano
Ovello
Pajè
Pora
Rabajà
Rio Sordo

The Asili and the Rabajà tend to be the most highly regarded of their crus, but we have found their Ovello in some vintages, '71 for example, to be as good or even better. The cru bottlings of the Produttori offer the winelover an interesting opportunity to compare the individual characteristics of the nine different vineyards. As each wine is made by the same hand, the differences to be noted reflect the attributes contributed by the crus themselves. Barbaresco★★★★; Nebbiolo delle Langhe★★

Prunotto Alfredo di Colla & Filiberti (*Loc. San Cassiano, Alba*), *1904*. Prunotto doesn't own any vineyards; they buy all of their grapes. They have an annual production of some 16,650 to 19,000 cases of wine, all red. Besides Barolo and Barbaresco, they also make Dolcetto, Barbera, and Nebbiolo d'Alba. When they feel the vintage justifies it, they vinify each vineyard separately and designate the name of the cru on the label. In 1973, 1975, 1977, 1981, and 1984, they blended the crus into their regular Barolo.

Prunotto is considered one of the more traditional of the Barolo and Barbaresco producers. They have experimented with some of the new methods but have generally rejected them. They still age their wines in cask, of chestnut or Slavonian oak, for many years.

Giuseppe Colla of Alfredo Prunotto   —Al Fisher, 1982

Giuseppe Colla, a partner in the firm, is a serious and dedicated winemaker who has produced some truly magnificent wines. We sometimes find the wines, though, to have the typical problems of the old-style Barolos, being high in volatile acidity, dried out, and lacking in fruit. This can be the result of too long wood aging or bad storage or handling somewhere en route to the consumer. In our experience, this is a much more common problem with the more traditional style, wines which tend to have less fruit to begin with. These wines were not made for international shipment; they were styled for the local market and were perfectly suited to local conditions of serving and consumption. The rigors of international transport under conditions, shall we say, less than ideal, sometimes prove too much for them. It's worth noting here that we have been disappointed with these wines much more frequently in the U.S. than in Italy.

The Prunotto Barolo and Barbaresco are wines that require long age in bottle, but the best vintages, at least, will reward those who are willing to wait.

Crus:	**Barbaresco**	Montestefano
		Rabajà
	Barolo	Bussia
		Cannubi
		Ginestra
	Nebbiolo d'Alba	Rossino di Monteu Roero

From time to time, Prunotto also produces other crus of Barolo and Barbaresco. Barolo★★★; Barbaresco★★★; Nebbiolo★★

111

"Punset" di R. Marcarino *(Neive), 1962.* Punset produces an average of 10,550 cases of wine a year. They own 40 acres (16 hectares) of vines, including 15 acres (6 hectares) planted to nebbiolo, from which they produce 4450 cases of Barbaresco. We found their wine better and more reliable in the mid-1970s. Barbaresco pre-1975★★; post-1974 0

Ratti Renato, Antiche Cantine dell'Abbazia dell'Annunziata *(La Morra, Fraz. Annunziata), 1965.* The Ratti winery is in the cellars of the fifteenth-century desanctified Abbey of the Annunciation in La Morra.

Ratti owns 40 acres (16 hectares) of vines, which supply about 25 percent of the grapes for his annual production of 100,000 to 120,000 bottles. Of these, 40,000 to 45,000 are Barolo, 4000 are Barbaresco, and 10,000 to 12,000 are Nebbiolo. His Barolo vineyard, Marcenasco, is in the environs of the village of that name that grew up around the tenth-century Benedictine priory of San Martino. These vineyards are referred to in a deed dated 1162, the earliest documented evidence of vines in this area.

Renato Ratti of Abbazia dell' Annunziata

Renato Ratti is a scholar and an innovator. He has made a thoroughly researched study of the wines of Piemonte and generously shares his findings, unconcerned about being given personal credit for his work but appreciative of the opportunity to see it used to spread knowledge of the wines of his region. Renato notes that his map of the Barolo crus caused some disgruntled comments among growers whose vineyards were not included—"My second scandal," he quips, wide-eyed with a look of mock astonishment at his audacity.

His first: introducing new viticultural techniques to the Langhe, an "outsider" with the temerity to show the Langaroli how to make their own wine! He chuckles at the incongruity of the situation. But, in fact, he is responsible for introducing a number of innovative techniques to the winemaking of the Langhe in the 1960s.

Ratti has a degree in enology from Alba, as does his nephew Massimo Martinelli, who is responsible for the day-to-day operation of the *cantina* while Renato tours the world as the leading and charismatic spokesman for the wines of Piemonte.

Ratti is not really a newcomer to the Langhe. He was born and grew up there, but as none in his family had made wine previously (although they did own vineyards) and as he worked in the early years of his career in Brazil, he returned to the Langhe with a novel, perhaps even a foreign point of view, including the notion that these wines should be made in a more drinkable style. Renato credits his ability to take a fresh approach to winemaking to the fact that he is in one sense an outsider. He came back to the region with a new appreciation of the wines, which he, like many others, had previously tended to take for granted. This also, he feels, gave him a particular appreciation of the local history and winemaking traditions in the region. Frequently dragging home discarded items no longer considered of value by their owners but which he recognized as irreplaceable, Ratti began to put together what was to become an excellent wine museum. He assiduously and enthusiastically collected old winepresses, and other equipment used in the vineyards and the cellars, old photographs and documents, and ancient artifacts— valuable testimony tracing the winemaking tradition in the Langhe since the time of the Romans.

In the 1960s, Ratti came to the conclusion—which we feel is quite valid—that too many of the Barolos being produced were overly tannic, low in fruit, and high in volatile acidity. He was convinced that the vineyards of the region produced excellent base material; the problem was in the cellars.

He began producing a Barolo utilizing modern techniques, eventually employing temperature-controlled fermentation in stainless steel. He reduced the period of skin contact, encouraged the malolactic to follow directly after the alcoholic fermentation, and gave the wines shorter cask aging. The result was a more drinkable Barolo which has gained wider acceptance in the world marketplace.

But these are not light, early-maturing wines to be drunk fresh. Ratti's Barolos age quite well, as can be noted in our tasting notes of his '67, for example. The Abbazia wines consistently display a richness of flavor and an intensity of character that puts them in the forefront of the wines of the area. Ratti produced good Barolos even in 1975, 1976, and 1977—three rather dismal vintages. He also produces some of the best Dolcetto in the Langhe. His Colombè is a wine of immense fruit and charm. His production also includes 12,000 bottles a year of a *barrique*-aged barbera–nebbiolo blend, Villa Pattono, which we unfortunately have not yet tasted.

Noting the obvious as well as the subtle differences among the various growing zones in Barolo, Ratti was one of the first, if not the first, to advocate bottling the Barolos as single-vineyard wines. He is, in fact, in the process of classifying the Barolo crus but has hesitated to put it into print as yet, anticipating perhaps a third scandal on his record. The eyebrows over his expressive dark eyes quake at the thought.

Renato's puckish wit is evident in his marvelous sketches. Dashed off during a boring speech or a dull roundtable, they succinctly satirize the improbability of the obtuse statement, the nonsense of the pompous pronouncement. And provide amusement for friends, but, to their dismay, the artwork is casually, and perhaps diplomatically, discarded.

Cru	First vintage	Vinifies from (hectares)	Exposure	Average production (bottles)
Barolo Marcenasco	1965	5.0	s	30,000
Marcenaso-Conca	1978	1.5 (owns 0.5)	esw	5,000
Marcenasco-Rocche	1978	2.0 (owns 0.5)	sw	8,000
Dolcetto d'Alba Colombè	1969	3.0	s	25,000-30,000
Nebbiolo d'Alba Ochetti di Monteu Roero	1969	3.0		10,000-12,000

Rating—Barolo★★★; Barbaresco★★; Nebbiolo★★★

Rinaldi Francesco & Figli (*Alba and Barolo), 1906.* Luciano Rinaldi owns 25 acres (10 hectares) of vines which supply the grapes for 90 percent of his annual production of 60,000 bottles. Rinaldi buys the grapes for his Barbaresco.

At his *cantina* in Barolo he holds a small quantity of older riservas in demijohn, as was done commonly in the old days. He keeps some of his Barolo in these 9- and 14-gallon (34- and 54-liter) jugs for ten years or more. The wine is decanted off its sediment into bottles or magnums before being put on sale. Rinaldi still has some '70 and '67 in demijohn and one demijohn of '61; this last, though, will not be sold. It is the private reserve of the family (lucky family!).

At one time it was fairly common for Barolo producers to store their wine this way for aging. But it has become too expensive and is rarely done today. In the winter of 1929, temperatures dropped so low that half the *brente* and demijohns broke—a tragic loss indeed.

Luciano Rinaldi's wines are rich in color and extract, yet gentle and elegant—superb wines. Their quality was eloquently demonstrated to us on our recent visit to his place in Alba. We had just come from Franco Fiorina, where we had an impressive tasting culminating with a superb '47 Barolo. Despite the fact that this was our first appointment of the day and we knew full well there would be many wines to come, the '47 was just too good not to indulge in a second glass and to savor every drop. Then it was immediately back to work and off to the next winery, F. Rinaldi. The first wine Rinaldi poured for us was from one of the younger vintages, his '80 Cannubio. The wine was totally impressive in style, balance, and elegance, even after the splendid '47—a tough act to follow even for an older vintage. Rinaldi is a man with a quiet sense of humor and a gentleness of manner. This gentleness is reflected in his wines, which are first class in their elegance, balance, and style.

Vineyards	**Barolo**	Gallinotto
		Sarmassa
		Vezza
		Vignane
Crus	**Barolo**	Brunate
		Cannubio

Barolo★★★★; Barbaresco★★★

Luciano Rinaldi of Francesco Rinaldi   *Giuseppe Rinaldi*

Rinaldi Giuseppe *(Barolo), 1890.* Giuseppe Rinaldi owns 20 acres (8 hectares) of vines from which he produces 32,000 bottles of Barolo and another 20,000 bottles divided nearly evenly among Barbera d'Alba, Dolcetto d'Alba, and Freisa.

His Barolos are well-balanced wines with a lot of style and character. They are among our favorites, wines worth lingering over, and it has been our pleasure on a couple of occasions to savor some fine '71 Barolo from *bottiglione* at the house with Rinaldi, who judiciously paired it with some superb parmigiano.

The wine is bottled in standard-size bottles to be sold straightaway and in 2-liter *bottiglioni* which are stored standing up at the *cantina* for anywhere between six and ten years. When the time comes to market the wine, the *bottiglioni* are decanted into regular bottles. Sometimes the bottles are kept standing up, as is the custom in many of the old *cantine* in Barolo, for as long as thirty years with no apparent problem with corks drying out.

There is no doubt about it, Giuseppe Rinaldi's fine Barolos are among the best produced. It's Barolos like these that can convince skeptics that the Langhe does indeed produce world-class wines.

Vineyards	Le Coste
	Ravera
Cru	Brunate

Barolo★★★★

"Rizzi" Az. Vitivin. di Ernesto Dellapiana *(Treiso)*. Dellapiana has 53.5 acres (21.7 hectares) of vines in the vineyard district of Rizzi, from which they produce Barbaresco, Dolcetto, and a tiny amount of Chardonnay. While their wines are fairly consistent, and pretty good to boot, they could use more style.

Vineyard	Speranza
Crus	Fondetta
	Sorì del Noce

Barbaresco★★

Roagna, Az. Agr. "I Paglieri" di Alfredo e Giovanni *(Barbaresco), 1960.* The Roagnas own 12.8 acres (5.2 hectares) of vines from which they produce 5000 to 6000 bottles of Dolcetto and 10,000 to 20,000 of Barbaresco. In the mid-1970s, they labeled their Barbarescos either Pajè or Asili. Today they use the name Crichet Pajè. This wine either includes grapes from both vineyards or it is a more familiar name for their Pajè holdings. Besides a Crichet Pajè Barbaresco, they also produce a light, fruity table wine with the same name. We tasted the '82, which was made entirely from nebbiolo grapes, and found it easy and very drinkable, in short a nice little wine. Like many other producers in Piemonte, the Roagnas are experimenting with *barriques*.

The Roagna Barbarescos can be very good, but they lack consistency and some style. Barbaresco★★

Rocca Dario Az. Agr. "La Ca' Nova" *(Neive)*. This producer owns vines in the Ca' Nova part of the Cotto vineyard district in Neive. Barbaresco★

Rocca Giuseppe *(Barbaresco)*. Giuseppe Rocca owns vines in the vineyards of Pozzo, Rabajà, and Ronchi.

"Rocche" Costamagna di Ferraresi Claudia *(La Morra), 1841.* The Rocche *azienda* has 9.6 acres (3.9 hectares) of vineyards—7 (2.8) in nebbiolo—from which they produce 30,000 to 32,000 bottles a year. Barolo makes up the major part, with an annual production of more than 21,000 bottles. The balance is Barbera and Dolcetto. The wines are good, and we can recommend them. In special vintages their cru bottling of Barolo, or a part of it at least, carries specially designed labels. They bottle two Barolo crus, Riccardo and Francesco, both in the Annunziata section of La Morra. Barolo★★

"Roche," Az. Vin. di Ferrero Andrea *(Loc. Santa Rosalia, Alba), 1886.* This winery owns 35 acres (14 hectares) from which they produce 11,000 cases of wine a year. These are the typical Albeisa wines. Their Zio Giovanni is an interesting blend of Freisa and Nebbiolo. To date we must admit that their Barolo and Barbaresco have failed to impress us. The fine enologist

Claudia Ferraresi of "Rocche" Costamagna

Carlo Brovia is now consulting for them, however, and is sure to make a significant contribution to quality. Barolo 0; Barbaresco (for now) 0

Rosso, Gigi *(Castiglione Falletto), 1979.* Rosso owns 100 acres (40 hectares) of vines, which supplies 95 percent of their grapes. This includes 15 acres (6.1 hectares) planted to nebbiolo in Barolo. They produce the standard range of Albeisa wines, including 23,300 bottles of Barolo, 112,000 of Dolcetto, 75,000 of Barbera, and 3700 of Nebbiolo d'Alba. This is another highly regarded estate that has thus far failed to live up our expectations, although our experience has been admittedly somewhat limited. Surprisingly, we have found their Barbaresco better than their Barolo. They bottle a Barolo cru from their holdings in Arione. Barolo★; Barbaresco★★

Saffirio F.lli Enrico & Giacomo *(Loc. Castelletto, Monforte).* Our experience with this Barolo is limited, but we found the '79 and '74 wanting. Barolo 0

Sandrone Francesco *(Barolo).* Sandrone owns a piece of the prized Cannubi vineyard. The only Barolo we tasted of his was from the poor 1977 vintage, and that wine was pretty decent. Barolo★

Sandrone Luciano *(Barolo), 1978.* Sandrone has 6.7 acres (2.7 hectares) of vines, which supplies him with all of the grapes he requires to produce 10,000 to 12,000 bottles a year of Dolcetto and Barolo. His holdings are in the vineyards of Cannubi-Monghisolfo and Rivassi-Boschetti. Barolo★★

Santa Maria Az. Agr., Cantine di Mario Viberti Figlio *(Fraz. S. Maria, La Morra).* This *cantina* has 30 acres (12 hectares), half of which are planted to vines. Their Barolo vineyards are in La Morra; those for Barbaresco are in San Rocco Senodelvio d'Alba. All the wine they produce is from their own grapes.

Vineyards	**Barolo**	Cappellotti di La Morra
		S. Maria di La Morra
Crus	**Barolo**	Capalot
	Barbaresco	Montersino

Savigliano Mario *(Diano d'Alba), 1952.* Savigliano owns 27 acres (11 hectares) of vineyards, including some of the Barolo zone, from which they produce 6650 bottles of Barolo a year. The balance, 60,000 to 66,650 bottles, is made up of other wines typical of the Langhe. In all, their wines are decent enough though lacking in personality. Barolo 0

Scanavino Comm. Giovanni *(Priocca).* We have always found these wines at best mediocre. They are in style, aroma, and structure more like wines from the south than from Piemonte. Needless to say, we cannot recommend them, except as wines to avoid. Barolo 0 −; Barbaresco 0 −

Scarpa, Anticha Casa Vinicola *(Nizza Monferrato), 1870.* This firm owns some 124 acres (50 hectares) of vineyards, none of which is in Barolo or Barbaresco. They buy all of their nebbiolo grapes.

They produce some 155,000 bottles of wine a year, which includes 35,000 to 37,000 of Barolo and 14,000 to 16,000 of Barabesco, as well as Freisa Secco Moirano, Brachetto Secco Moirano, and Ronchet, a rare wine from the homonymous grape variety.

Scarpa is a very serious producer, dedicated to quality. They produced no Barolo in 1981, 1983, or 1984, as they were not satisfied with the quality of the grapes in any of those years. This was after 1980 and 1979, when, as the vines had been snowed on before harvest, they didn't vinify a Barolo either year.

The Scarpa wines that we have tasted were strikingly well balanced and finely honed, with a richness of flavor and a refined nebbiolo character. Unfortunately, we have insufficient experience with these wines to award our full marks, but we hope to correct that deficiency in the near future.

*Mario Pesce of
Antica Casa
Vinicola Scarpa*

	Cru	Bottles
Barbaresco	I Tetti di Neive	10,000-12,000
	Payore Barberis di Treiso	4,000
Barolo	Boscaretti di Serralunga d'Alba	8,000
	I Tetti della Morra	15,000
	Le Coste di Monforte	12,000-14,000
	Roncaglia di La Morra	3,400 (1978)

Barolo★★★+; Barbaresco★★★+; Nebbiolo★★★

Scarzello Giorgio & Figli *(Barolo), 1903.* Scarzello owns 12.4 acres (5 hectares) of vines from which they produce some 26,500 bottles of wine a year; 45 percent of this is Nebbiolo, mostly Barolo. They bottle a Barolo cru from Merenda. Their Barolo is a pretty decent wine. Barolo★

Scarzello Giovanni, Cascina Mosconi *(Barolo).* Scarzello produced quite a good '74 Barolo; that was the most recent vintage we had the opportunity to taste. Barolo★★

Scavino Alfonso *(Castiglione Falletto.)* Scavino has 11.1 acres (4.5 hectares), one-third planted to nebbiolo. From this he produces 35,000 bottles a year, 10,000 of which are Barolo, part of it bottled as a cru from Della Punta. Barolo★★

Scavino Paolo *(fraz. Garbelletto, Castiglione Falletto), 1921.* Scavino has 11.6 acres (4.7 hectares) of vines from which he produces 37,500 bottles of wine a year; nearly 15,000 are Barolo. Some 3.4 acres (1.4 hectares) of his 6-acre (2.4-hectare) Bric del Fiasc vineyard are planted to nebbiolo. From that plot he produces 9300 bottles of a Barolo Bric del Fiasc; it is quite a good wine. Barolo★★

Seghesio Renzo *(Monforte), 1967.* Seghesio doesn't own any vineyards. He buys either grapes or wine and produces some 60,000 to 70,000 bottles a year of some rather ordinary wines. About 20 percent is Barolo, mostly from vineyards in Monforte; the balance is the typical Langhe wines. Among the vineyards he buys from are Pianpolvere di Bussia, Perno, Castelletto, and Ginestre. Barolo 0

Serafino Enrico *(Canale d'Asti).* We haven't tasted Serafino's Barbaresco in some time, but it left us unimpressed. It could be better. We've never tasted his Barolo. Barbaresco 0

Settimo Aurelio *(fraz. Annunziata, La Morra).* Judging from the three vintages we've tasted, the Settimo Barolo is reliable and fairly good. Settimo owns vines in the fine vineyard of Rocche di La Morra. Barolo★

Sobrero Filippo & Figli *(Castiglione Falletto).* Sobrero's wines—12,000 to 13,000 bottles of Barolo plus some Dolcetto and Barbera—were produced from grapes grown on his 7.4 acres (3 hectares) of vines in Monprivato and Villero in Castiglione Falletto. When we visited him in 1982, he opened wine for us to taste, but told us that as he was getting old and had no children and since his only nephew wasn't interested in the *cantina*, his wines would not continue to be produced. In 1985, we were told that he was no longer making wine or receiving wine writers. It seems he has lost interest even in the vineyard, which was reportedly overrun with weeds.

Sobrero told us that he felt his wines needed at least eight to ten years to show their quality and that they age well for twenty or more. He is, or was, a very traditional producer. While we've enjoyed a number of his wines, we have also been quite disappointed with many others. The problem is rather typical and unfortunately quite common with the more traditional Barolos: overlong wood aging, which causes the wines to dry out and develop volatile acidity. When they were good, however, they were magnificent.

We recently heard that Sobrero sold his vineyards to Mauro Mascarello of Guiseppe Mascarello. At least the vineyards will remain in good hands. Barolo★★★

Sottimano, Az. Vinicola, di Sottimano Maggiore *(Loc. Cottà, Neive), 1973.* Sottimano owns 3.7 acres (1.5 hectares) of vines which provides 20 percent of the grapes they require to produce an annual average of 66,600 bottles; they buy from another 5 acres (2 hectares). They own part of two subcrus in Cottà Ca' Nova and Brichet. They do a cru bottling from Brichet. As we've never tasted it or any other of the Sottimano wines, we obviously cannot rate them. We understand that he also produces a Barolo.

Stroppiana Oreste. Stroppiana owns vines in the San Giacomo vineyard of La Morra. His Barolo has not impressed us. We haven't tasted it in some time, not since the 1974 vintage to be exact. Barolo 0

Tenuta Carretta di F.lli Veglia *(Piobesi d'Alba), 1939.* Carretta has 84.4 acres (34.2 hectares) of vines, including 2.71 in the Cannubi vineyard. Their annual production is about 295,000 bottles of wine a year. Barolo makes up some 21,000 bottles, and another 150,000 are Nebbiolo d'Alba. Their Bianco del Roero is an interesting white wine made from a blend of nebbiolo vinified in white and arneis. Besides these they produce a range of the typical wines of the area. The Carretta wines are consistent and very good.

Their Barolo is quite hard and tannic when young but matures very well. We have generally found their regular bottling superior to their riserva and riserva speciale. At a recent tasting of '71 Barolos (March 1985), their Cannubi, one of the seventeen wines tasted, needed the most further aging. It is a very fine wine but surely not typical of the cru. Their Nebbiolo d'Alba Bric Paradiso is one of the best Nebbiolos we've tasted, as well as one of the longest-lived. In 1984, we tasted a '71 from gallon; it was superb.

	cru/vineyard	commune	hectares	bottles	First bottled
Crus: Barolo	Cannubi	Barolo	2.71	21,000	1961
Nebbiolo d'Alba	Bric' Paradiso	Alba	2.00	17,000	1967
	Bric' Tavoleto	Piobesi	2.44	21,000	1982
Vineyard	Podere Podero e Carretta	Piobesi	12.68	—	—

Barolo★★★ + ; Nebbiolo d'Alba Bric' Paradiso★★★

Tenuta Cerequio *(La Morra), 1962.* This firm, formerly known as Vinicola Piemontese, changed their name in 1985. Whereas previously they bought grapes and made a range of wines, they will now produce wines only from their Cerequio vineyard: Barolo, Barbera d'Alba, and Dolcetto d'Alba. They are the largest owners of the Cerequio vineyard, with total plantings of 16 acres (6.5 hectares). They have a total of 30 acres (12 hectares) of vines, which provide them with the grapes to produce 4850 cases of wine a year; 3900 are Barolo.

Cerequio is considered one of the top vineyards in the zone. We recently tasted their '71, '74, '78, and '79 Barolo cru Cerequio. All were fairly tannic and firm, and all had a similar recognizable character. Barolo★★

Tenuta Cisa Asinari dei Marchesi di Gresy. See La Martinenga.

Tenuta Coluè di Massimo Oddero *(Diano d'Alba), 1967.* Coluè owns 30 acres (12 hectares) of vines which provide 70 percent of their grapes. They have an annual production of 80,000 bottles, which includes Barolo and Barbaresco as well as the other wines typical of the area. It's been some time since we tasted their Barbaresco and perhaps it's better than our rating suggests; their Barolo is quite good. They also produce a very good fizzy Moscato. Barolo★★; Barbaresco 0

Tenuta La Volta. See Cabutto Bartolomeo.

Tenuta Montanello *(Castiglione Falletto), 1954.* This winery has 25 acres (10.2 hectares) of vines in the Montanello vineyard, plus 2 acres (0.8 hectare) in Rocche; 11.4 (4.6) are in nebbiolo. Tenuta Montanello produces 33,000 bottles of Barolo a year and 41,000 of other wines. Like many others in Piemonte, they are separating their vineyards into subcrus. Montanello is divided into Pianella, Pini, and Fontana. Although the wines of each plot are kept separate throughout the production and bottled individually, they are not named on the label. Their Barolo is made in a less aggressive, somewhat lighter style. Barolo★★ −

Terre del Barolo *(Castiglione Falletto), 1958.* This *cantina sociale* is the largest producer in the Barolo zone. They crush more than 6000 tons (55,000 quintali) of grapes a year to produce nearly 400,000 cases of wine. This includes 1545 tons (14,000 quintali) of nebbiolo for nearly 100,000 cases of Barolo and Nebbiolo d'Alba. This co-op, with a production of approximately 1 million bottles of Barolo a year, represents a sizable portion of the zone's annual 5.7 million.

When the co-op was founded, there were 40 members; today there are 535, working 1780 acres (720 hectares) of vineyards. Terre del Barolo provides an important function in the zone in helping to ensure a decent income for the grape farmers. By offering their members a reasonable price for their grapes, they furnish a favorable alternative to their selling to the mediocre vinifiers in the district and consequently help raise the average quality of the Barolo produced.

It is somewhat remarkable under the circumstances and at these quantities, but they are able to produce quite a good Barolo. Their crus are very good. It is a tribute to their enologists.

> *Crus* Brunate [Giovanni Bogletti and Renzo Roggiero]
> Castello di Grinzane Cavour
> Rocche di Castiglione Falletto [Arnaldo Rivera]

Barolo★; Barolo crus★★

Traversa Giuseppe Cascina Chiabotto *(Neive), 1880.* Traversa owns 37 acres (15 hectares) of vines from which he produces some 80,000 bottles of wine a year, including an agreeable Barbaresco. Traversa does a cru bottling from his holdings in the Maringotá vineyard of Bricco di Neive. Barbaresco★

Troglia Giovanni *(Torino).* Giovanni Troglia, a wine merchant in Torino, sells under its label Barolo and Barbaresco and a number of other Piemontese wines, packaged in bizarre-shaped bottles. The wines are often just as bizarre. Oxidized wines, in fact, are quite common from them. We did find their wines from the 1960s better than those from the more recent vintages. They sell a Barbaresco from Podere Nervo; we haven't tasted it. Barolo 0; Barbaresco 0

Vajra G.D. Cascina San Ponzio *(Loc. Vergne, Barolo), 1972.* Milena and Aldo Vajra own 31 acres (12.5 hectares), 14.7 (6.0) of which are in vines; this includes 3 acres (1.2 hectares) of nebbiolo for Barolo. Their annual production is 33,000 bottles, all from their own grapes. They bottle two Barolo crus, one from their holdings in the Fossati vineyard and the other from their vines in Bricco Violeo. Overall, their Barolos are quite good and reliable besides. Barolo★★

Valfieri di Marengo e Cugnasco *(Alba).* This firm is part of the Riccadonna group. They have *cantine* in Costigliole d'Asti and Villa Montesino. Since they own no vineyards, they buy all their grapes. We haven't tasted their wines in some time, but when we did we found their Barolo and Barbaresco both mediocre. They produce two Barbaresco crus: Rabajà and Moretti. Barolo 0; Barbaresco 0

Vecchio Piemonte, Consorzio Cooperativo Soc. Coop. Cantine Produttori *(Grinzane Cavour).* This syndicate is made up of seven cooperative cellars with 2400 member–growers. They produce 1.4 million cases of wine a year. Their range is wide, as is their quality. The Cantina di Treiso produces Barolo and Barbaresco; the Cantina di Fara Novarese produces Fara and Spanna del Piemonte; and the Cantina di Castiglione Falletto makes Nebbiolo d'Alba. Barolo 0; Barbaresco★

Veglio Angelo. The only Barolo we can recall tasting from Veglio was from the mediocre 1976 vintage, and it was pretty decent. Barolo★

Veglio Pasquale. See Cascina Bruni di Pasquale Veglio.

Vezza Sergio *(Borgata Ferrere, Treiso), 1967.* Vezza owns 18.5 acres (7.5 hectares) in Treiso, from which he produces two wines: Barbera d'Alba and Barbaresco. We found his '78 Barbaresco rather ordinary and his '80 fairly decent! Barbaresco★ –

Vietti Cantina di Alfredo Currado *(Castiglione Falletto), 1960.* Alfredo Currado owns 7.5 acres (3 hectares) of vines, which supply 25 to 30 percent of his grapes. He buys the rest from growers with whom he has contracts giving him some control over the cultivation of the vines, the pruning in particular. He is looking for a small quantity of high-quality fruit. Currado produces some 120,000 bottles of wine a year, 80,000 of which are red wines; the balance is mostly Moscato, plus a tiny amount of Arneis.

Although he employs modern technology, Currado considers himself a traditional producer. The changes he has made, he points out, were only to give him a closer control over quality, not to change the character of the wine. He aims for a style of Barolo and Barbaresco that fits into the general concept of traditional wines—big, concentrated wines that improve with age.

Alfredo states with some modesty that his first aim is to produce a wine free of defects, and secondly a wine with style. He succeeds on both counts. Not only are his Barolo and Barbaresco

Alfredo Currado of Vietti   —Al Fisher, 1982

among the zone's finest, but his Dolcetto, Freisa, Barbera, Grignolino, Moscato, and Arneis are as well. Alfredo is a perfectionist who demands the best from himself and elicits the same from his grapes.

Currado graduated from the enological school at Alba in 1952 and went to work first for a *spumante* house. In 1957, he married Luciana Vietti, and three years later he began making the Vietti wine. Today he is assisted in the *cantina* by his daughter Elisabetta, also an enologist with a degree from Alba. The Vietti winery is a family operation. Luciana runs the office with the able assistance of son-in-law Mario Cordero (husband of daughter Emanuela, a veterinarian).

Currado is an art lover who has commissioned some fine artists to do his labels. At one time, Luciana, a talented artist in her own right, did some of the label designs, but she is too busy today managing the commercial end of the winery and providing superb hospitality to the frequent guests at the *cantina*. Most of the labels, including all of those for the nebbiolo wines, are done by Gianni Gallo, who is also much in demand by other wineries. But the Vietti wines were the first. As Alfredo tells the story, the idea took shape around a bottle, a dusty bottle of Barolo '64 from his *cantina*. It was a cold winter's evening in 1974, and he and some artist friends had been enjoying each other's company over a few bottles of good wine, when one of them remarked that such a beautiful wine as the '64 merited a beautiful label; it should be the work of an artist. Alfredo recalls with an easy laugh that he, as a good Piemontese, was alert enough not to let such an opportunity slip by; he promptly reached for a piece of paper to get it down in writing. In the euphoria of the moment, he relates, he soon had a list of artists willing to do the job. At first only the crus were bottled with the special labels, but in 1978 he adopted this style for all of his wines.

Alfredo Currado is a man firmly rooted in the Langhe, with a love for his region and its wines. But he is also interested in understanding the wines of other fine wine-producing regions. He has visited wineries in France and the U.S., where he and Luciana have become good friends of some fine California winemakers since their first visit in 1981. Alfredo has arranged for Elisabetta to work in wineries in California and Oregon, and in Bordeaux. There is a close bond between the two. Beneath Elisabetta's ebullient, outgoing personality and Alfredo's gentle, easy-going sincerity beat the hearts of a couple of hard workers with a dedication to quality and a desire for perfection.

Vietti's 1984 production included some 22,000 bottles of Barolo and 7200 of Barbaresco. There were Barolos from five crus—Briacca, Brunate, Bussia, Rocche, and Villero—and Barbaresco from two—Masseria and Rabajà. Currado points out that the differences in the subvarieties of the nebbiolo can be clearly noted in the crus that he makes, particularly between his Barolo Rocche (planted 75 percent to michet, 20 percent lampia, and 5 percent rosé), and his Briacca cru (actually a part of the Rocche vineyard, but planted 100 percent to rosé). Both have the same soil and exposure, and as they are vinified the same the only reasonable explanation for the differences between them is in the vines themselves.

Briacca produces a softer, more velvety wine with less body than Rocche. The Rocche Barolo is full-bodied and robust, with more alcohol and tannin, harder and more closed while young, and slower to mature. It ages the best of the Vietti Barolos. Of all the wines Alfredo makes, Barolo is his personal favorite, and of his Barolos he prefers the Rocche, it being the deepest, richest, and most intense.

But it is not only bigness or power that he is aiming for. His Brunate Barolo is elegant and perfumed. And the Bussia is more elegant still, with a fine perfume, moderate alcohol, and a lot of style. The '82 Bussia Barolo was made from a 20–75–5 blend of nebbiolo michet, lampia, and rosé. His Villero is high in alcohol and very robust.

From time to time, Currado vinifies other crus. He produced a Barolo from Codana (100 percent michet) in 1971 and 1982, and from Merriondino (mostly michet) on the other side of the road from Rocche in 1976.

Alfredo, who describes himself as a *barolista*, produces two excellent Barbarescos as well—Masseria and Rabajà. The Masseria, made from 100 percent lampia, reflects the character of the Neive Barbarescos and is in some respects more like a Barolo than a Barbaresco—fairly full-bodied and rich, requiring more time to come around than many other Barbarescos.

Crus	1984 Production (bottles)	First produced	Hectares	Nebbiolo subvariety
Barbaresco				
Masseria	4850	1964	2.0	100% lampia
Rabajà	2350	1984	1.0	100% lampia
Barolo				
Briacca	4300	1961	0.4	100% rosé
Brunate	5500	1984	1.0	mostly lampia
Bussia	2700	1982	3.0	70% lampia
Codana	none	1971	0.7	100% michet
Meriondino	none	1976	0.8	mostly michet
Rocche	7800	1961	0.67	70% michet
Villero	2000	1982	0.4	100% michet
Nebbiolo d'Alba	(At one time there were others, now only these two.)			
S. Giacomo	1400	1982		
S. Michele	6000	1974		

The Rabajà, from Barbaresco itself, is typically more elegant and more refined. It too is made from 100 percent lampia. He has also made small amounts of Barbaresco from other crus, including Casotto and Pora, in his search for the best grapes to produce his wines.

Currado makes two Nebbiolo d'Alba wines, both among the best we have tasted. He also makes a proprietary blend—Fioretto—from his Fioretto vineyard in the Scarrone district.

When we first tasted the Vietti wines in 1978 or 1979, we were struck by their style. These are far from just well-made wines, free of defects; they are wines that exemplify the best style and the character of the grape variety they are made from.

Barolo★★★★; Barbaresco★★★★; Nebbiolo★★★; Fioretto★★

"Vigna Rionda" Az. Agr. See Massolino Giuseppe.

Vignaioli "Elvio Pertinace" Cantina *(Treiso), 1973.*

The thirteen members of this co-op—named for the second-century Roman emperor born at Alba—own 110 acres (45 hectares) of vines, all in Treiso. From an average harvest they produce 225,000 bottles of wine. Besides Barbaresco and Nebbiolo delle Langhe, they also produce Dolcetto, Barbera, Moscato, and Chardonnay. They could produce considerably more Barbaresco but currently make only 50,000 to 60,000 bottles a year. Part of their production is sold *sfuso*. They recently started bottling individual crus, which are Casotto, Castellizzano, Marcarini, and Nervo. Their Barbaresco is a fairly good wine. Barbaresco★

Vignaioli Piemontese, Soc. Coop. *(Asti), 1976.* This *cantina sociale* is actually an association of twelve cooperatives made up of 3500 growers who have 11,100 acres (4500 hectares) of vines. Their annual production of 2.8 million cases (250,000 hectoliters) makes them a force in the marketplace. Barolo is one of the many different wines they produce.

Vignolo-Lutati *(Castiglione Falletto).* This producer owns 25 acres (10 hectares), 20 (8) in vines. Cascina Pilone belongs to him. These wines have a good reputation, but unfortunately those we tasted didn't come up to it. They bottle a Barolo cru from their Brunella di Castiglione Falletto vineyard. Barolo 0

Villadoria Marchese *(Rivoli).* Villadoria is not a marchese but a trademark of CE.DI.VI. They sell their wines in some rather eye-arresting bottles, including a misshapen one with a candle stuck onto it and another bagged in burlap. Perhaps these curiosities are meant to offer some interest for the consumer that the wines are unable to provide. (They certainly do nothing for the image of Italian taste.) The company would do better, we think, to give more thought to what they put into the bottle. Their Barolo might not be the worst in the zone, but it is not far from it. The Barbaresco is not as bad. At one time they sold some Barolo under their label from the 1952, 1955 and 1961 vintages which certainly rose above their current crop of wines; in fact, these wines were very good. Barolo 0 − ; Barbaresco 0

Vinicola Piemontese *(La Morra).* This firm is now, since 1985, Tenuta Cerequio. As Vinicola Piemontese, they were a less specialized winery, buying grapes and making a number of Albeisa wines, including a Barbaresco and a Barolo. Barolo 0

Voerzio Giacomo dei F.lli Voerzio *(La Morra), 1973.* This firm has been bottling wines since 1973, with mixed results. They have an average annual production of 12,000 bottles a year of Barolo and 70,000 to 85,000 bottles of other Albeisa wines. They own 21.5 acres (8.7 hectares) of vineyards and buy grapes for some of their wines, but they use only their own grapes from La Serra in their Barolo. Their first cru bottling of La Serra was the 1982. It is now the only Barolo they make. Their last regular bottling was from the 1980 vintage. They didn't make any Barolo in 1981. The '82 La Serra was very good indeed, but they feel the '83 might be superior.

Roberto Voerzio of Giacomo Voerzio

Vineyards	**Barolo**	Boiolo
		Ciabot della Luna
		Croera
		Roscaleto
Cru	**Barolo**	La Serra

Barolo since 1982★★ + ; pre-1982 0; Barbaresco 0

Zonino Basilo *(Serralunga d'Alba), 1974.* Zonino, owner of Trattoria del Castello in Serralunga d'Alba, produces a highly acclaimed Barolo from his holdings in Baudana. We haven't tasted his Barolo in some time, since the 1974 vintage to be exact, and that we found mediocre. He also owns vines in Cerretta. Barolo 0

Chapter 3

The Nebbiolo Wines of Torino and Aosta

In the province of Torino and the neighboring region of Valle d'Aosta, nebbiolo wines are produced from three local subvarieties: nebbiolo spanna, picotener, and pugnet. The name *picotener* is from picciolo tenero, "tender stem." *Pugnet* is a descriptive term referring to the small, compact, "fistlike" shape of the bunches, similar to the michet of the Langhe.

The two major wines from this area, both recognized under DOC, are Carema and Donnaz. Carema is made 100 percent from nebbiolo, or, as it is known locally, picotener. Donnaz is from at least 85 percent nebbiolo, and other local varieties may be blended in.

The vines planted in the morainic terrain of the steep mountainsides rising above the Dora Baltea River are trained on pergolas, the vine leaves spread out over the wooden framework to gain the maximum benefit from the sun to ripen the late-maturing nebbiolo. The sturdy supporting pillars of stone and concrete and the pale stones of the dry wall terraces reflect the sun's rays onto the vines and absorb the heat of the day to add an important extra measure of warmth to the vines after the sun has set.

The climate here is rather cold and windy. The picotener wines tend to be lighter in body, less tannic, and higher in acidity than the wines of the other major nebbiolo zones. And, not surprisingly, the vintages are more variable.

The Wines

AGLIE *(Torino)*. This wine is produced in two styles: semisweet and dry. We are concerned only with the dry Aglie, which is made from 100 percent nebbiolo. It is a medium-bodied wine at about 12 percent alcohol, at its best within four years of the vintage. Rating★

ARNAD *(Aosta)*. Arnad is made from nebbiolo plus neyret, freisa, vien de nus, and pinot grapes. A few producers in some years add very small quantities of other local varieties. Arnad is a light-bodied wine, of about 11 percent alcohol. It is best when drunk fairly young within about two to three years of the harvest. Rating★

CAMPIGLIONE *(Torino)*. The Marchesi di San Germano produces this wine in Campiglione Fenile from 100 percent nebbiolo grapes. The vineyards are in the Pelice valley at altitudes of from 2300 to 3280 feet (700 to 1,000 meters). It has been reported that a number of other grape varieties are used as well, but we were told that Campiglione is made only from the nebbiolo. The wine is light-bodied and rather low in alcohol at 11 percent. As Campiglione is meant to be drunk young, it is not vintage dated. Rating★

Tasting Note

nv Rosso di Campiglione, Marchesi di San Germano *(11/84)*. Light, fruity aroma; some tannin, nice flavor, agreeable if a bit simple; some alcohol at the end.★

CAREMA *(Torino)*. Carema has been known since at least the sixteenth century. It is today without a doubt the best-known wine of the Torino–Aosta production zone, and deservedly so. It is the best. This wine is made 100 percent from picotener grapes grown in the terraced mountain vineyards of Carema at altitudes ranging from 1150 to 2300 feet (350 to 700 meters).

The production zone, on the left bank of the Dora Baltea River east of Ivrea, extends to the Aosta border. In fact, although all the vines are in Piemonte, at least one producer has a cantina in a *frazione* of Pont-Saint-Martin called Ivery, which is in Aosta. There are more than 100 growers in Carema, who work about 100 acres (40 hectares) of vineyards. Very few own more than 2.5 acres (one hectare); most have only about 1.25 acres (0.5 hectare).

The climate here is cold and windy, and the picotener is a shy-bearing variety. The average production of Carema is about 11,100 cases (1000 hectoliters) a year. DOC sets a limit of 599 gallons per acre (56 hectoliters per hectare) and a minimum of 12 percent alcohol.

Production of Carema

Year	Hectoliters	Year	Hectoliters
1971	1302	1978	693
1972	579	1979	1025
1973	1385	1980	1030
1974	1406	1981	1056
1975	982	1982	895
1976	1006	1983	1194
1977	549		

Note: 1 hectoliter = 26.4 gallons, 11.11 cases, or 133 bottles.
Source: Regione Piemonte, 1984.

Up until a few years ago at least, some of the small producers of Carema were still crushing their grapes in the time-honored tradition. But it's difficult today to find men willing to do the work. Usually the grapes are destemmed and crushed by machine. When the grapes are to be crushed by feet, the bunches are put into the upright wooden *tini* and left for three or four days to warm up a bit before the men go in, up to their waists in the chilly mass, to do the laborious work of crushing the grapes manually—or, to be more precise, pedally. The fermentation lasts for three weeks to a month.

Generally, the grapes for Carema, crushed by machine, are fermented on the skins for seven to ten days, depending on the temperature and how much color is desired. The nebbiolo grape here doesn't attain a very deep color.

In the spring, when the weather warms, the wine undergoes malolactic fermentation—very important as the wines tend to be quite high in acid. In fact, they are sometimes deacidified so that the malolactic won't be inhibited.

Carema is aged for a minimum of four years, at least two of which are in oak or chestnut casks with a capacity of not more than 1056 gallons (40 hectoliters).

The wine is light garnet in color, with a fragrant, often floral perfume which for some recalls roses. It is light in body, with moderate tannin and a firmer acidity than its nebbiolo counterparts to the east in the Novara–Vercelli hills. Carema is a wine esteemed for its delicacy. It is best drunk five to eight years after the vintage, but in exceptional vintages it can live for twenty years, perhaps more.

Carema is a good choice to drink with roast pork or veal or the local fontina or toma cheeses.

Regarded crus:	*Owner–Producer*
Cassetto	—
Con	—
Costa	—
Lavrey	Ferrando
Nusy	Clerino
Paris	—
Piole	Ferrando, Morbelli
Rovarey	—
Siei	Ferrando, Clerino
Silanc	Ferrando
Villanova	—

Rating★★

Carema Vintages

The producers we've spoken with rated the best years for Carema as 1961, 1964, 1967, 1971, 1974, 1978, 1982, and 1983, 1961 being the best of all. One producer also includes 1968, 1975, 1979, and 1980 on his list. There is general agreement that 1963, 1972, and 1977 were the worst vintages in the zone; 1973 and 1976 were also nominated for this category by at least one producer.

The Niederbacher chart (adjusted for our four-star rating system) gives the following ratings:

1983	★★	1976	★
1982	★★★	1975	★★
1981	★	1974	★★★
1980	★★	1973	★★
1979	★★★	1972	★
1978	★★★	1971	★★★
1977	0	1970	★★★

Our limited experience suggests the following:

1980★(★) Fairly forward now but should get better.
1979★★ Could still improve.
1978★★★Very fine wines but still young; they should continue to improve for a few years yet.
1977 0 A poor year from the outset.
1976★ The best bottles are still quite good, but are not for keeping.
1975★ No need to hold any longer.
1974★★★ Very fine wines with still more to give.
1973 0 Never amounted to much.
1972 0 Ditto.
1971 0 Not up to the reputation of the vintage.
1970★ Not to keep any longer.
1968 0 Too old now.
1967★ Wines are starting to fade.
1964★★Very good, ready now, perhaps even fading a bit.

Tasting Notes

1980

Produttori "Nebbiolo di Carema" (*4 times 5/84*). A floral, fruity aroma; fairly well balanced though rather light; soft and quite forward.★+

1979

Ferrando (*3 times 4/85*). Perfumed bouquet with suggestions of flowers; somewhat light in body, moderate tannin, good fruit; needs a few years to really soften though can be drunk now; will improve.★(+)
Morbelli (*twice 1/85*). A bouquet of flowers and berries; a little light but fairly well balanced, somewhat soft but has tannin yet; some acid on the finish.★+
Produttori "Nebbiolo di Carema" (*8 times 1/85*). Light-bodied, light tannin, light fruit, rather short and simple; a disappointment.

1978

Ferrando, black label (*4/85*). Firm, flavorful, light tannin, a bit young; good quality★★(★)
Morbelli (*twice 1/85*). Medium garnet, brick at rim; lovely floral bouquet; still somewhat hard but has good fruit in center; quality already evident, needs perhaps three more years.★★

1978

Produttori "Nebbiolo di Carema," Carema dei Carema (*1/85*). A mineral note on aroma, which is somewhat closed; firm, still has tannin, some acid, medium-bodied, flavorful; still young but quite nice now.★★

1976

Ferrando (*1/85*). Deepest in color of the '79,'76, '74, and '71; fruity floral aroma but somewhat simple; a fair amount of tannin and acid, insufficient fruit, but with food it should be quite drinkable.★
Produttori "Nebbiolo di Carema" (*6 times 2/85*). Light color; small but nice floral aroma, somewhat fruity; light-bodied, some tannin, nice flavor; fairly ready.

1975

Produttori "Nebbiolo di Carema," Carema dei Carema (*6 times 2/85; 40,000 bottles*). Aroma vaguely like a rubber tire; a lot better on palate, light-bodied, nice entry, then a bit shallow; overall quite drinkable.★

Luigi Ferrando

1974

Ferrando, black label *(twice 1/85)*. Bouquet showing development, lightly floral notes, well balanced, still young, firm tannic vein, needs time to soften; some alcohol mars the aftertaste.★★

Produttori "Nebbiolo di Carema" *(at least 14 times, 11/79 to 12/83)*. Floral aroma with berrylike fruit; soft and smooth, round and fruity; at or very close to its peak.★★ +

Produttori "Nebbiolo di Carema." Carema dei Carema *(4/81; 40,000 bottles)*. Expansive bouquet of cherries and flowers; some tannin but soft, almost velvety; has some elegance and style★★★

1973

Produttori "Nebbiolo di Carema" *(3 times 3/80)*. Color shows age; some oxidation apparent on aroma; light-bodied, still some tannin, lacks body and fruit. Where will it go?

1971

Ferrando, black label *(1/85)*. Lovely bouquet with floral notes; well balanced, nice fruit; some alcohol mars the finish.★ +

1970

Ferrando *(9/80)*. Firm acidity, medium-bodied, still some tannin but very ready now; rather brief on the finish.★

1968

Morbelli *(1/85)*. Fruity, floral aroma; has tannin, good flavor, but beginning to dry out.

1967

Morbelli *(1/85)*. Browning at the rim; showing age, but there's still some interest left.★

1964

Ferrando, black label *(twice 3/82)*. Fragrant floral bouquet; fruity, still some tannin, but fairly soft and ready; nice now and near its peak, no need to hold any longer.★★

Carema Producers

Bertolo Lorenzo *(Torino)*. Bertolo is a negociant who deals in a wide range of wines including a Carema, which we cannot comment on, never having tasted it.

Calligaris Rino. Calligaris produces a very limited amount of Carema. Unfortunately, we've never tasted his wines.

Ferrando Luigi *(Ivrea), 1911.* Ferrando is a respected negociant of Carema and other wines, including Fara and Gattinara. He is also a grower, with 5 acres (2 hectares) of vines in some of the better Carema crus: Lavrey, Piole, Siei, and Silanc. His production of Carema is about 15,000 bottles a year. This includes, in some vintages, single-vineyard bottlings as well as a special reserve, which he distinguishes with a black label, as the term *riserva speciale* is not allowed by DOC regulations for Carema. His black-label Carema competes with the Carema dei Carema of the Produttori for the best wine of the area.

We are not sure if he is still making the cru bottlings, but in 1967 he bottled a Vigneto Nusy from Giuseppe Clerino and a Vigneto Lavrey from his own vines. In 1969 he made a Vigneto Siei, also from Clerino. Carema black label★★★ Carema★★

Morbelli *(Carema), 1891.* Morbelli owns 5 acres (2 hectares) of vines, including a piece of the regarded cru of Piole. Some 10 percent of his annual production of Carema (15,000 bottles) is from this vineyard. He also produces 20,000 bottles of the white Erbaluce.

We have heard that Morbelli also bottles Arnaz, Donnaz, and Montjovet, three other nebbiolo-based wines. Carema★ +

Produttori "Nebbiolo di Carema" *(Carema), 1960.* This cooperative has forty-three members who own 50 acres (20 hectares) of vines. Their annual production is 150,000 bottles (1120 hectoliters). Of this, about 57,000 bottles is their regular Carema; another 13,000 bottles is a special selection of their best wine. Up until 1978 this wine was sold as Carema dei Carema. Bureaucratic decree has since disallowed this name; they are now required to label their crème de la crème simply as Carema. To set it apart from the regular Carema, it is bottled with a dove-gray artist's label. This wine, which is not produced every year, was made from the 1974, 1975, and 1978 vintages. Carema★★ Carema dei Carema★★★

CESNOLA *(Torino).* Cesnola is produced, in a *frazione* of Settimo Vittone, from nebbiolo grapes. The wine reputedly often attains 13 percent alcohol. It is not a wine to age but is at its best within four years of the vintage. Rating★

Arturo Perono of Produttori "Nebbiolo di Carema"

DONNAZ *(Aosta).* Donnaz is produced in the Valle d'Aosta region from at least 85 percent nebbiolo (locally pugnet) grapes; the balance may include freisa, neyret, and/or vien de nus. The Donnaz vineyards, covering 371 acres (150 hectares), some at altitudes of up to 2000 feet (610 meters), are among the highest in Italy. The vines are grown on the sides of the mountains that rise above the valley of the Dora Baltea River in the *communes* of Donnas, Bard, Perloz, and Pont-Saint-Martin at the border of Carema.

There are some 111 growers cultivating the 60 acres (24 hectares) of vines in the Donnaz production zone. Production, which has ranged from as little as 810 cases (73 hectoliters) in 1977 to as much as 6950 cases (626 hectoliters) in 1979, generally averages about 4500 cases (406 hectoliters) as year.

Donnaz has a minimum alcohol of 11.5 percent. It is aged for at least three years, two in oak or chestnut casks no larger than 790 gallons (30 hectoliters). The wines are light-bodied and for early drinking, between three and six years of the harvest. They tend to be somewhat similar to those of Carema, but lighter.

Donnaz is a good choice to accompany white meats such as veal roast or chops, guinea hen, or turkey.

The best Donnaz vintages were 1983, 1982, 1979, 1978, and 1974.

Rating★★

Tasting Note

1974 Ferrando *(twice 7/83).* Still tasty, but beginning to break up; volatile acidity is apparent on nose and palate.

Donnaz Producers

Soc. Coop. Caves Cooperatives de Donnaz. Founded in 1971, this co-op has seventy members. It is by far the largest producer in the zone, with an annual output of some 36,000 to 50,000 bottles. In 1979, they produced 48,000 bottles; in 1980, 36,000.

Ferrando. Ferrando also sells a Donnaz, though we haven't seen any younger than the 1974 vintage.

F.lli Ghiglieri. This is another Donnaz producer we've heard about though we've never seen his wine.

ISSOGNE *(Aosta).* Issogne is the product of nebbiolo, gros vien, dolcetto, and vien de nus grapes. It is a light-bodied wine, with about 10.5 percent alcohol, and not a wine for aging.

MONTJOVET *(Aosta)*. This light to medium-bodied red wine is made from nebbiolo, neyret, vien de nus, gamay, pinot, and some other local varieties grown in Montjovet and Saint-Vincent.

NEBBIOLO DEL CANAVESE *(Torino)*. The Produttori "Nebbiolo di Carema" produces this wine from grapes grown in vineyards near Carema. It is a wine for early consumption.

RISERVA DEL GENERALE *(Torino)*. This is a medium-bodied red wine produced from a blend of nebbiolo, barbera, bonarda, dolcetto, and freisa grapes.

ROSSO DELLA SERRA *(Torino)*. This wine is produced by the Cantina Sociale della Serra from a blend of nebbiolo and barbera grapes in about equal proportions. The vineyards are near Ivrea, in the *communes* of Moncrivello, Roppolo, Viverone, and Zimone. It is a medium-bodied wine, ready to drink shortly after it is released for sale in its third year.

ROSSO DI BRICHERASIO *(Torino)*. This medium-bodied red wine is made from a blend of nebbiolo, barbera, freisa and other varieties grown at Bricherasio.

ROSSO DI FROSSASCO *(Torino)*. Frossasco is produced from nebbiolo with the addition of other local varieties. It is typical of the medium-bodied reds produced in this area.

ROSSO DI VALPERGA *(Torino)*. This wine, made from nebbiolo and other local grape varieties grown at Valperga, is similar in character to the Frossasco red.

TORRE DANIELE *(Torino)*. Torre Daniele, named for the hamlet in Settimo Vittone where it is produced, is made from nebbiolo grapes.

TORRE SAINT-PIERRE *(Aosta)*. Doret Esterina produces this wine from a blend of petit rouge (60 percent) and nebbiolo (40 percent). It is a medium-bodied red that should be drunk young.

VINO DELLA SERRA *(Torino)*. This light-bodied red wine is produced at the Cantina Sociale della Serra from a blend of barbera, freisa, and nebbiolo grapes.

Chapter 4

The Wines of the Novara–Vercelli Hills

The various nebbiolo-based wines of the Novara–Vercelli hills have certain characteristics in common. They are generally medium-bodied dry red wines with a floral bouquet often reminiscent of violets, occasionally roses, sometimes with notes of strawberries or raspberries. They tend to have a firm tannic vein and a slight bitterness on the aftertaste. These wines range in alcohol from 11.5 to 12.5 percent, and have a moderate capacity to age. Few are ready before their fourth year or are worth keeping past their eighth to tenth, although there are exceptions, particularly in the better vintages.

These wines make a fine accompaniment to roast red meat and game birds. Gattinara and Lessona, being bigger wines, also go well with pigeon and duck.

Most of the DOC wines are aged for three years, two or so in large, old casks of chestnut or Slavonian oak.

While nebbiolo, known here as spanna, is the most important grape in these wines, other varieties, especially bonarda, vespolina, and/or croatina, are often blended in. In general, the better the wine, the higher the percentage of spanna; and the lesser, the less.

It has frequently been reported that the name *spanna* and the grape variety itself come from Spagna (Spain). Cardinal Mercurino Arborio di Gattinara, who served as chancellor to Carlo V of Spain in the early fifteenth century, is credited with bringing the spanna grape from Spain to Gattinara. Authorities in Gattinara disagree, however, stating that it was just the reverse. They do point out that Cardinal Arborio deserves much credit for promulgating the name of the wine of Gattinara outside the region.

They trace the origins of the grape back to the second century, when the Vercellese were conquered by the Romans, who subsequently restructured the system of agriculture in the area, planting vines on the hillsides and other crops in the plains. Pliny reports that the Romans were responsible for the introduction of the spionia grape—a variety that he noted thrives in foggy climates—which was cultivated on the plains of Ravenna and in the prealpine hills of Lombardia and Piemonte.

Another theory behind the name links spanna to its method of cultivation, trained *"a spanna"*—at a short distance from the ground—as opposed to the Roman practice of training the vines high on trees or tall poles.

Novara

The main growing region of Novara is on the left bank of the Sesia River. The soil here is morainic, of glacial origin, rich in important micro-elements, and with a bit more limestone than the districts on the opposite bank. The Novara vineyards spread over 6700 acres (2711 hectares), cultivated by 4000 growers and three cooperative cellars. The average annual production of the Novara wines is about 1.1 million cases (100,000 hectoliters); of this, DOC wine amounts to a paltry 61,100 (5500). There are four wines recognized under DOC here, all made basically from spanna: Boca, Fara, Ghemme, and Sizzano.

131

The Wines of the Novara/Vercelli Hills — Production Statistics

Wine	Prov	Number of Growers	Extent of Vyds (ha)	Maximum Yield per hectare qli	Maximum Yield per hectare hl	Average Yield per year hls	Average Yield per year cases	Potential Production hl	Potential Production cases
Boca	No	20	12.00	90	63.0	327	3833	756	8392
Bramaterra	Vc	37	21.00	75	52.5	575	6388	1103	12238
Fara	No	25	15.56	110	77.0	664	7377	1309	14530
Gattinara	Vc	145	92.00	90	63.0	3584	39818	5040	55944
Ghemme	No	54	56.97	100	70.0	1539	17098	5250	58275
Lessona	Vc	3	4.87	80	56.0	223	2478	280	3108
Sizzano	No	69	35.47	100	70.0	1197	13299	2450	27195

Source: Regione Piemonte
Notes: Average production based on statistics for 1971-1983.
Exceptions are based on statistics from 1979-1983 for Bramattera
and 1978-1983 for Lessona.
All statistics include vintages when the entire crop was declassified.

Vercelli

Gattinara, Lessona, and Bramaterra are in the province of Vercelli. The major wine-producing area here encompasses 4940 acres (2000 hectares). Total annual production is 11,025 tons (100,000 quintali) of grapes. The five DOCs of Vercelli—Erbaluce di Caluso, Caluso Passito, Lessona, Bramaterra, and Gattinara—together account for some 77,700 cases (7,000 hectoliters) a year. These first two DOC zones, extending into the province of Torino not far from Carema, produce white wines. The last three produce spanna-based reds. The Gattinara zone is on the right bank of the Sesia; Lessona is off to the west; between the two is the relatively new DOC of Bramaterra.

The Wines of the Novara/Vercelli Hills — DOC Requirements

Wine	Prov	Spanna %	Bonarda %	Vespolina %	Others %	Alcohol %	Minimum Age Cask years	Minimum Age Total years	Best From	Best To
Boca	No	45- 75	0-20	20-40	0	12	2	3	4	- 12
Bramaterra[1]	Vc	50- 70	20-30	10-20	20-30	12	1½	2	6	- 10
Fara	No	30- 50	0-40	10-30	0	12	2	3	4	- 9
Gattinara	Vc	90-100	0-10	0	0	12	2	4	6	- 15
Ghemme	No	60- 85	0-15	10-30	0	12	3	4	6	- 12
Lessona	Vc	75-100	0-25	0-25	0	12	2	3	4	- 10
Sizzana	No	40- 60	0-25	15-40	0	12	2	3	4	- 10
Caramino[2]	No	30- 50	20-40	10-30	0	12	2	3	4	- 8
Spanna[3]	No/Vc	85-100	—	—	0-15	—	—	—	-	—

Notes: [1] Bramaterra: 20/30% Croatina and 10/20%. Bonarada and/or Vespolina.
[2] Non DOC: percentages of grape varities given are estimates only, not requirements
[3] The European Common Market requires that a varietally labelled wine contain at least 85% of that grape.

The Wines

AGAMIUM *(Novara)*. Antichi Vigneti di Cantalupo produces Agamium (labeled with the Roman name for the village of Ghemme) from an 80–15–5 blend of spanna, vespolina, and bonarda, after their best grapes have been selected to make their Ghemme. It is aged from twelve to eighteen months in cask. Rating 0

Tasting Note

1981 Antichi Vigneti di Cantalupo *(1/85)*. Smallish nose and rather stinky; shy of fruit though some flavor on middle palate, has a tart edge.

ARA *(Novara)*. This light-bodied, fresh, fruity wine, made predominantly from spanna grapes, is produced in the same area as Grignasco. Rating★★

BARENGO ROSSO *(Novara)*. This wine is produced by the Cantina Sociale dei "Colli Novaresi" from a blend of 50 percent spanna, 30 percent bonarda, and 20 percent vespolina grapes grown in Barengo. Rating★

BOCA *(Novara)*. Boca is made from 45 to 70 percent spanna with the addition of 20 percent uva rara, or bonarda novarese, and 20 to 40 percent vespolina grapes. The vineyards of Boca cover 30 acres (12 hectares) in the *communes* of Boca, Cavillirio, Grignasco, Maggiora, and Prato Sesia. There are twenty growers who produce a combined annual average of 3833 cases of wine.

This light-bodied, dry red wine is similar to Fara and Sizzano. It is noted for having an aroma of violets, and some find an aftertaste of pomegranates. Boca is best consumed from four to twelve years of the vintage.

Antonio Vallana's Boca is made from the grapes that used to go into his Montalbano and Traversagna Spannas, which are no longer produced.

DOC Requirements

Minimum age *(years)*		Minimum alcohol	Maximum yield *(gallons/acre)*
cask	*total*		
2	3	12%	673.5

Producers
Bertolo Lorenzo
Cantina Ronchetto dei Fornara
Conti Cav. Ermanno
Conti Gian Piero
Fornara Benedetta
Poderi ai Valloni
Ponti
Vallana Antonio
Valsesia A.

Vintages

★★★★	*1961, 1950, 1947*
★★★	*1983, 1982, 1981, 1980, 1978, 1974, 1971, 1970, 1969, 1964, 1962, 1959, 1956, 1945*
★★	*1979, 1976, 1975, 1973, 1958, 1955, 1954, 1949, 1948*
★	*1972, 1953, 1946*
0	*1977, 1968, 1967, 1966, 1965, 1963, 1960, 1957, 1952, 1951*

Based on our somewhat limited experience, we would suspect that all vintages earlier than 1970, with the possible exceptions of 1961, 1950, and 1947, are by now too old. Of the more recent years, 1974, 1978, 1980, 1981, 1982, and 1983 are probably the vintages for present drinking, although 1970 and 1971 could still be good.

Rating★★

Tasting Notes

1980 Vallana *(4/85)*. Floral bouquet with a tarlike component, a slight off note intrudes; some tannin and a lot of fruit; nearly ready.★★ −

1979 Vallana *(4/85)*. Stinky; a bit light in body, light tannin, flavorful; short; ready.★

1976 Conti Cav. Ermanno nel suo Castello di Maggiora *(4/80)*. Floral aroma gives way to a slight off odor; considerable tannin but seems to have the fruit to support it; needs a few years yet.(★)

1976 Vallana *(4/85)*. Browning; aroma has tarlike notes and a vague floral note over a vegetal background; acid too high, has tannin and fruit; doubtful future.(?)

1973 Cantine Ronchetto *(4/80)*. Floral, fruity aroma; soft and flavorful, though slightly alcoholic; short.

1969 Conti Gian Piero *(4/80)*. Floral aroma; fairly soft and flavorful, still some tannin to lose.★

BRAMATERRA *(Vercelli)*. The Bramaterra zone begins at the western edge of the Gattinara district and extends for 12 miles (20 kilometers) to the border of Lessona, with vineyards in the *communes* of Bramaterra, Brusnengo, Curino, Lozzolo, Masserano, Roasio, Sostegno, and Villa del Bosco. This district, being more protected from the north winds than the neighboring areas, has its own microclimate, which has been officially recognized and the zone given its own DOC.

Bramaterra is made from 50 to 70 percent spanna, 20 to 30 percent croatina, and 10 to 20 percent bonarda novarese (uva rara) and/or vespolina grapes.

DOC Requirements

	Minimum age *(years)*		Minimum alcohol	Maximum yield *(gallons/acre)*
	cask	total		
regular	1½	2	12%	561
riserva	2	3	12%	561

Average annual production of Bramaterra is about 6400 cases. Tenuta Agricola Sella has 14 acres (5.7 hectares) of vines, from which they produce an average of 3500 cases of Bramaterra a year, making them the larger of Bramaterra's two producers. The other producer, Luigi Perazzi, has 12.4 acres (5 hectares)

Bramaterra is a medium bodied wine with a firm tannic backbone. It is at its best from its sixth to tenth year.

Producers
Perazzi Luigi
Sella Tenuta Agricola

Vintages
★★★   1983, 1978, 1974, 1971
★★   1982, 1980, 1979, 1976, 1975, 1970
★   1973
0   1981, 1977, 1972

We can't disagree with the vintage ratings, but our experience does indicate that 1971, 1973, 1974, and 1976 *might* at this point be too old to offer further interest.

Rating★★

Tasting Notes

1980 Sella Tenuta Agr. *(1/85).* Light nose with nebbiolo character; firm structure, moderate tannin, well balanced; needs perhaps two to three years to round out and soften.★(★)

1979 Perazzi Luigi *(1/85).* Floral, fruity aroma with a touch of tar; a bit rough and tannic, but the fruit is there; needs perhaps three to four years.★(★)

1976 Perazzi Luigi *(11/80).* Color is showing age; vinous aroma with some varietal character; some tannin, moderate fruit; drinkable.

1976 Sella Tenuta Agr. *(twice 4/81).* Nice aroma, still somewhat reticent; some tannin to lose, but the fruit is there.★

1974 Sella Tenuta Agr. *(twice 11/78).* Tarlike aroma with floral notes; unbalanced with too much tannin, alcohol, and acid, some fruit; unpleasant aftertaste; not a success.

1973 Sella Tenua Agr. *(11/78).* Fruity aroma; light and soft, flavorful; moderate length; good quality.★

1971 Sella Tenuta Agr. *(11/78).* Fruity aroma; flavorful, but acid is somewhat on the high side.★ —

BRIONA *(Novara).* Briona is made from a blend of spanna, vespolina, and bonarda grapes grown in the *commune* of Briona. It is a medium-bodied wine that frequently attains 12.5 percent alcohol.

BRUSCHETT *(Novara).* Bruschett is produced from nebbiolo grapes, known here as prunent, and other local varieties grown in and around Domodossola near the Swiss border. It is a light-bodied red of about 11 percent alcohol, best drunk young and cool.

BRUSNENGO *(Vercelli).* This wine is produced from spanna, bonarda, and vespolina grapes grown in Brusnengo and Curino. Brusnengo is a medium-bodied wine, generally about 12.5 percent alcohol, that ages moderately well.

CARAMINO *(Novara).* The Caramino vineyards are located on a hillside north of Briona, bordering Fara Novarese. Many producers of Caramino use the typical spanna, bonarda, and vespolina blend. Dessilani claims to use 100 percent spanna, although we have heard that they include a small amount of the white erbaluce grape. Caramino is usually aged for three years, two in cask. Dessilani departs from the norm, aging his Caramino for four years in cask. Like the other wines of this area, Caramino generally attains 12 percent alcohol, although 12.5 percent isn't uncommon. This wine is drinkable from three to five years of age and can last longer.

Producers
Cantina Sociale dei "Colli Novaresi"
Dessilani
Ferrando Luigi

Rating★★

Tasting Notes

1978 Dessilani *(twice 10/83)*. Stinky nose has some nebbiolo character; moderate tannin, firm, fairly well balanced, tasty, better in mouth than on nose; room for improvement, give it two or three years.★

1976 "Colli Novaresi" Cantina Sociale *(4/81)*. Alcoholic nose; shy of fruit, tannic, drying out.

1974 "Colli Novaresi" Cantina Sociale *(10/78)*. Smallish nose; very light-bodied, thin in fact, lacks middle body; very short.

1974 Ferrando Luigi *(twice 5/82)*. Stinky odors that unfortunately carry through on the palate.

CASTEL D'ANTRINO *(Novara)*. This wine is the product of basically spanna grapes, plus some vespolina, grown in Oleggio. It has an alcohol content of 13 percent.

FARA *(Novara)*. Fara, which takes its name from an ancient village settled by Longobard warriors, is produced from 30 to 50 percent spanna, up to 40 percent bonarda novarese (uva rara), and 10 to 30 percent vespolina grapes. The Fara vineyards are located in the *communes* of Fara Novarese and Briona. Some twenty-five growers cultivate the 38.5 acres (15.6 hectares) of vines in this zone, producing on average 7375 cases of wine annually.

DOC Requirements

Minimum age *(years)*		Minimum alcohol	Maximum yield *(gallons/acre)*
cask	total		
2	3	12%	823

Fara has an aroma reminiscent of sweet violets. It is at its best between its fourth and ninth years.

Producers
Bianchi Giuseppe
Caldi Luigi
Cantina Sociale dei "Colli Novaresi"
Castaldi Giuseppe
Dessilani Luigi
Ferrando Luigi
Prolo Giovanni
Prolo Luigi
Rusca Attillio
Rusca F.lli

Vintages
★★★★	*1983, 1974, 1967, 1957, 1945*
★★★	*1979, 1978, 1971, 1970, 1964, 1962, 1961, 1958, 1953, 1947*
★★	*1982, 1976, 1969, 1965, 1960, 1955, 1954, 1951, 1949, 1946*
★	*1980, 1975, 1973, 1968, 1966, 1963, 1956, 1950, 1948*
0	*1981, 1977, 1972, 1959*
not rated:	*1952*

Our very limited tasting experience with Fara suggests that vintages before 1974, except possibly 1945, 1957, and 1967, and perhaps even 1964, 1970, and 1971, are probably too old by now, though there could be some other exceptions.

Rating★★

Tasting Notes

1980

Bianchi Giuseppe *(1/85)*. Floral bouquet with ripe fruit on a tarlike background; a nice mouthful of fruit under the tannin; give it perhaps three years.★(★)

"Colli Novaresi" Cantina Sociale *(1/85)*. Has a hot aroma very reminiscent of a southern wine though with some nebbiolo character; moderate fruit, perhaps too much tannin; needs age, but will it develop? (?)

1976

"Colli Noveresi" Cantina Sociale *(4/81)*. Somewhat fragrant aroma; has tannin but not a lot of fruit, seems rather shallow and somewhat out of balance.

1974

Castaldi Giuseppe *(twice 10/78)*. Bouquet has suggestions of berries and pine; nice flavor, still has tannin to shed; somewhat bitter aftertaste.★(★)

"Colli Novaresi" Cantina Sociale *(4/80)*. Aroma is a bit closed but nebbiolo fruit and tar evident; balanced, has fruit, tannin to lose; finish is somewhat bitter.(★)

Dessilani *(4/80)*. Reticent aroma with a touch of alcohol; undeveloped and backward, but fruit and tannin are evident.(★?)

Rusca Attilio *(4/80)*. Unbalanced and harsh, some fruit, and some tannin; unimpressive.

Tasting Notes

1972	1970

Ferrando Luigi *(11/78, from half-bottle)*. Light berryish aroma; nice flavor but unbalanced with high acidity; decent quality.

Prolo Giovanni *(4/80)*. Tar and alcohol on aroma; fruit insufficient for the tannin; bitter aftertaste.

Dessilani *(12/79)*. Nice bouquet with complexity of bottle age; soft and flavorful, a touch of tannin, ready; finishes very short.★

FOGARIN *(Novara)*. This straightforward fruity red is best within one to three years of the vintage. It is produced by the Ghemme producer Giuseppe Bianchi. Rating★

Tasting Note

1982 Bianchi Giuseppe *(1/85)*. Fresh, fruity aroma, vaguely floral; light tannin, fruity; very pleasant for current drinking.★ +

GATTERA *(Vercelli)*. This wine is made from spanna, barbera, spampigno, and bonarda grapes grown in the Gattera area of Serravalle Sesia.

GATTINARA *(Vercelli)*. Much archeological evidence has been unearthed in the Gattinara area tracing the history of winemaking here to the Roman era. By the time the town of Gattinara was founded in the thirteenth century, the vine was already established as an important part of the agriculture of the region. In an official document dated 1213, reference is made to the vineyards of Guardia, Ronco, and San Lorenzo. Letters in the archives of Milan from the fifteenth century record that requests were received at Romagnano, then part of the duchy of Milan, to supply wine from Gattinara to the dukes of Sforza for service at court dinners.

With the advent of the DOC for Gattinara in 1967, a number of wine houses bought large parcels of vineyard land to insure their supply of grapes as production was diminishing. New plantings were made where mechanical methods of cultivation are used, but there remain some small growers in the hills who continue to produce their wines by the old methods.

The Gattinara zone, on the right bank of the Sesia, is protected from the alpine winds sweeping down from Monte Rosa by a sheltering mountain spur.

The Gattinara vineyards range in altitude from 655 to 985 feet (200 to 300 meters) above sea level, averaging about 865 (263). The vines are mostly spanna. Gattinara is made from at least 90 percent spanna and no more than 10 percent of bonarda di Gattinara.

DOC Requirements

Minimum age *(years)*		Minimum alcohol	Maximum yield *(gallons/acre)*
cask	total		
2	4	12%	673

This wine, which has a relatively long aging period for a spanna-based wine, drinks well from its fifth or sixth year up to its twelfth to fifteenth. In the best vintages, twenty isn't too old. Gattinara has an aroma of violets that takes on hints of spice with age and a characteristic touch of bitterness on the aftertaste.

There are some 145 growers in Gattinara, cultivating 227 acres (92 hectares) of vineyards. Production averages 39,800 cases a year. Seven firms own 65 percent of the area under vines producing DOC wine. The largest producer is the Cantina Sociale, which vinifies 40 percent of all the grapes in Gattinara; not all of this is sold in bottle, however. Luigi e Italo Nervi, with an annual production of some 140,000 bottles, is the largest private winery. They are also, with 54 acres (22 hectares), the largest vineyard owners. Others are Antoniolo with 37 acres (15 hectares) and Travaglini with 27 (11).

The Gattinara consorzio, founded in 1962, represents 60 percent of the Gattinara sold in bottle. There are nineteen members:

Albertinetti Pasquale	—	Dellavalle F.lli	0
Antoniolo Mario	★★★	Delsignore Attilio	—
Barra Guido & Figlio	★★ –	Ferretti Carlo	—
Bertolazzi Luigi	—	Franchino Marco	0
Bertole Ing. Salvatore	★	Nervi Livio	—

Bertolo Armando	—	Nervi Luigi & Italo	★★
Caligaris Guido	★ −	Patriarca Bruno	—
Caligaris Ing. Vittorio	—	Patriarca Mario	★ +
Cametti Felice	—	Travaglini Giancarlo	★
Cantina Sociale Cooperativa	0		

Other Gattinara producers

Avondo	0	Fracchia Provino	—
Balbiano	★★	Francoli	—
Bertolo Lorenzo	—	Kiola	0
Borgo Cav. Ercole	0	"Le Colline" Az. Agr., Monsecco	★★★
Brugo Agostino	★	Orsolani Casa Vinicola	★★ −
Caldi Luigi	—	Troglia G.	★
Dessilani Luigi	★	Vallana Antonio	★★ +
Ferrando Luigi	★	Villa Antonio	0
Florè Umberto	0		

The crus of Gattinara

Vineyard	Owner–producer
Alice	Barra
Casaccia	
Castelle	Antoniolo
Guardie	
Lurghe	Franchino Marco
Molsino	Nervi
Osso San Gratò	Antoniolo
Permolone	Barra
Podere dei Ginepri	Nervi
San Francesco	Antoniolo
Valferane	Barra; Nervi
Valferrana	Le Colline "Monsecco"
Vivone	

Rating ★★★

Gattinara Vintages

These ratings, except where we have had sufficient experience to give a personal opinion, are based on the evaluations of the authorities.

1984 ? As in the rest of Piemonte it was a very difficult vintage. Very little, if any, wine of quality was produced.

1983 ★★

1982 ★★★

1981 ★★ We were unimpressed with the '81 we tasted, finding it unbalanced with high acid.

1980 ★★★ We haven't tasted any '80s yet.

1979 ★★★ This vintage was rated above '78. We agree with the ★★★, but better than '78?—no. The wines are lighter in body and lack the richness and balance of the '78s. They are still on the young side but will also develop sooner than the '78s.

1978 ★★ We strongly disagree. This was, from our experience, a splendid vintage. We've found the wines richly flavored and well balanced with a fair amount of tannin. The '78s are still too young and will improve to perhaps ★★★ + given the time they need.

1977 ★ We suspect the wines offer little or no interest today, 0.

1976 ★★★ The pundits rated this vintage higher than we did. We've found the '76s to be off-balance with high acid and felt that ★, perhaps ★ +, was a more accurate rating.

1975 ★★ The wines now seem too old, 0.

1974 ★★★★ A very highly touted vintage; for us, though, they rarely come up to that level. The best are still holding, at ★★★.

1973, 1972, and 1971 0 The '71 and '73 vintages were once rated ★; '72, 0. We find that all are too old now, 0. At Le Colline they consider their '71 Monsecco on a par with the '64, so it should still be very good.

1970 ★★★ We agreed with the original rating; these wines have given us a lot of pleasure; for today, though, ★★★ −.

1969 and 1968 ★★★ We dissent. Those bottles we've tasted through the late 1970s, and there were a fair number, never merited more than ★, and many weren't that good. For us, 0 would define their status today.

1967 ★★ We have consistently been amazed at the high level of quality in the bottles we've been fortunate enough to drink. We have personally found '67 to be an especially fine vintage and think ★★★ would have been a fairer rating. The wines are admittedly getting on a bit in age now, perhaps rating ★★ + today.

1966 ★ Today they are most likely too old.

1965 ★★ Today probably 0.

1964 ★★★★ Outstanding; our experiences indicate the wines can still merit ★★★★, but caution is advised as they are twenty years old now. Perhaps ★★★ is more realistic.

1963 0 Very bad.

1962 ★★ It's been some time since we tasted any '62s. We suspect that any bottles remaining today are long past their prime.

1961 ★★★ For now ★★. The few bottles we've tasted suggest that it's a vintage to drink now and not to keep any longer; they're beginning to fade.

1960 ★

1959 ★ While it's been six or seven years since we tasted any '59s, we remember fondly the '59 Antoniolo Gattinaras that we tasted from both bottle and half bottle; all were very fine wines, so for us ★ for 1959 seems severe.

1958 ★★★ The Spannas of Vallana rise above this rating.

1957 ★★★

1956 ★

1955 ★★★ Though we've never tasted any 1955 Gattinara, we've tasted some '55 Spannas from Antonio Vallana that were very good indeed and are holding very well.

1954 ★★ The Vallana Spannas that we've tasted, reputedly from the area around Gattinara, have been very find indeed. Perhaps the vintage was better than the ratings. Those wines are still good today.

1953 ★

1952 ★★★★ Outstanding; the wines could very well still be good if they have been properly stored.

1951 0 Very bad.

1950 ★★★

1949 ★★

1948 ★

1947 ★★

1946 & 1945 ★★★

Tasting Notes

1981

Nervi Luigi & Italo (*ex-cask 5/82*). Fresh cherrylike aroma; high acidity throws off the balance, light-bodied, somewhat unstructured and deficient in fruit.

1979

Antoniolo (*1/85*). Floral, fruity aroma; light-bodied, soft, agreeable enough but seems overly simple and a bit one-dimensional.★

Antoniolo, Osso San Gratò (*twice 1/85*). Floral bouquet with vague hints of almonds and cherries, somewhat more restrained than the San Francesco; firmer and more tannic, has more character, more stuffing, and more interest; tannic vein; quality evident.★★(★)

Antoniolo, San Francesco (*twice 4/85*). Floral perfume; not as full or as firm and tannic as the Osso San Gratò, but has more elegance.★★(★)

Balbiano (*1/85*). Floral bouquet with a touch of *goudron*; a bit light but well balanced; light tannin; ready now though could improve.★★

Barra Guido (*ex-cask 7/80*). Lovely nose with a suggestion of kirsch; has a fair amount of tannin but also the fruit to support it; should make a nice bottle.★★

Barra Guido, Preludono alla Val Sesia (*twice 1/85*). Floral bouquet with a touch of tar; tannin up front gives way to a lot of fruit, fairly soft in the center; ends on a tannic note; overall somewhat simple.★(★)

Barra Guido, Vigna Permolone (*3/85*). Old-style spanna aroma, has a southern accent; acid a bit out of kilter, has fruit; a bit dull.★

Bertole Ing. Salvatore (*twice 1/85*). Typical bouquet, fruit and flowers over a tarry background; fairly soft but a bit out of balance with acid.★

Bertolo F.lli (*twice 1/85*). Characteristic bouquet of flowers and tar; still has a firm tannic vein but the

Tasting Notes

1979

fruit is evident; needs two, perhaps three years. ★★

Brugo Agostino *(1/85)*. Some oxidation on aroma, recalls Marsala; moderate tannin, moderate fruit, not much character or style. (★)

Caligaris Guido *(twice 1/85)*. Aroma still closed; fairly well balanced but with noticeable acid and tannin, fruit is also evident; needs a few years to come together. (★)

Dellavalle F.lli, Vigneto Molsino *(twice 1/85)*. Aroma reminiscent of a southern wine; rather soft and forward, light tannin, ready; lacks personality.

Franchino Mario & Figlio *(twice 1/85)*. Rubber tire aroma with a hint of flowers beneath; low fruit, overly tannic; not a success.

Nervi Luigi & Italo *(3 times 6/85)*. Floral bouquet, with notes of berries and spice; firm, tannic vein, a lot of flavor; potential is evident. ★★(+)

Patriarca Mario fu Cesare *(1/85)*. A nice aroma with some richness; a fair amount of tannin but has the stuffing to carry it, firm; tannic finish; try in about three more years. ★(★)

Vallana *(4/85)*. Lovely floral bouquet with a hint of licorice; rich fruit, almost sweet; has style. ★★★

1978

Antoniolo, Osso San Gratò *(1/85)*. A shade deeper in color than the San Francesco; a vague chocolaty note on aroma; a big wine, more forward than the San Francesco; firm tannic vein, well structured, has weight and concentration; needs time but has so much flavor you might find it enjoyable now in a pinch. ★★★(+)

Antoniolo, San Francesco *(1/85)*. Perfumed aroma with some fruit; firmly structured with a tannic vein, full of fruit and flavor, but somewhat more backward than the Osso San Gratò. ★★(★)

Brugo *(5/85)*. Perfumed floral aroma; fairly soft, a bit light in body, could use more weight; a touch of harshness at the end. ★

Fiore Umberto *(10/84)*. Bouquet shows some development and complexity; somewhat unbalanced, lacks concentration and weight.

1976

Antoniolo *(5/82)*. Some varietal fruit on aroma and a suggestion of berries; acidity a bit high but not jarringly so; nice flavor, lacks depth; dry, tannic finish; should improve with another year or two. ★+

Fiore Umberto *(5/84)*. Thin, dull, unbalanced.

Franchino Mario, Vigna Lurghe (selected by Umberto Fiore) *(3/85; 4950 bottles)*. Orange at rim; rubber tires on aroma; some fruit, light tannin, soft, a bit shallow; very ready. ★−

Nervi Luigi & Italo *(5/82)*. Berries on aroma; acid a bit on the high side but reasonably well balanced; tasty, a bit lacking in middle body; moderate length with a tannic bite. ★

Nervi Luigi & Italo, Podere dei Ginepri *(7 times 6/85)*. Fragrant, floral perfume; a bit out of balance with high acid; firm structure, a lot of flavor; vague acid bite at the end, long finish. ★★−

Vallana *(4/85)*. Aroma has notes of tar and a mineral aspect, also a vague dankness; light tannin, light body, lacks some weight and character; drinkable. ★

1975

Antoniolo *(5/82)*. Nose displays considerable complexity, and a slight touch of oxidation only adds at this point though makes its future doubtful; soft and flavorful with some underlying tannin; enjoyable now, not to keep. ★+

Barra Guido *(3 times 5/82)*. Garnet color showing age; sweet aroma with a candylike note; gives an impression of sweetness upon entry, soft, some tannin, moderate fruit; ends on a somewhat bitter note; more or less ready now. ★

Borgo Cav. Ercolo *(5/82)*. Fresh berrylike aroma thrown off by a slight dankness; light-bodied, a soft and straightforward wine, agreeable enough though not characteristic, not up to its pedigree.

Brugo Agostino *(twice 5/82)*. Bouquet displays some complexity; fairly well balanced, acid a bit on the high side, moderate tannin; ready now. ★

Dellavalle *(11/80)*. Nice rose; some fruit, but dull and unbalanced.

Nervi Luigi & Italo *(10/80)*. Almond notes on aroma and some oxidation; light, unbalanced; harsh, bitter aftertaste.

Travaglini *(5/82)*. Volatile acidity and anchovies on the nose and palate.

Villa Antonio *(5/82)*. Rubbery aroma with the intrusion of alcohol; unbalanced with high acidity and high tannin, low in fruit, shallow; not ready, and probably never will be.

1974

Antoniolo *(1/85)*. Lovely bouquet with complexity and richness, floral and fruity; wine doesn't deliver what the nose promises; some tannin; short, tannic aftertaste; still rather young. ★(★)

Antoniolo, San Francesco *(5/82; 7426 bottles)*. Straightforward nebbiolo aroma marred by the intrusion of alcohol; perhaps too much tannin for the fruit, but some potential evident; needs at least three to four more years. ★(+)

Barra Guido *(4/82)*. Perfumed bouquet; firm vein of tannin, lots of fruit; very good indeed. ★★(★)

Borgo Cav. Ercolo *(11/79)*. Lightly scented aroma; rather light-bodied, some tannin, lacks substance.

Brugo Agostino *(3 times 5/82)*. Closed in aroma with some fruit beginning to emerge; still has tannin to lose, but also a lot of nice fruit, soft-centered; can be enjoyed now but it will improve. ★★−

Dessilani riserva *(1/83)*. Weird, off-putting aroma; much nicer on the palate, some tannin; has flavor but could use more length and style.

Nervi Luigi & Italo *(5 times 12/84)*. Light aroma showing some fruit but still closed and surprisingly backward; medium- to full-bodied, still quite tannic but with a richly fruited center; good length; give it perhaps two more years. ★★(★)

Nervi Luigi & Italo violet label *(10/80)*. Intense floral bouquet; fairly rich in flavor but without the elegance of the regular. ★★(+)

Orsolani *(5/82)*. Complex bouquet with suggestions of fruit and spice, black cherries, tar, and flowers; good fruit, still some tannin; enjoyable now but could improve. ★★

Travaglini *(5/80)*. Simple, fruity aroma; soft and tasty; a bitter finish. ★

Tasting Notes

1973

Barra Guido *(11/79)*. Perfumed bouquet; soft and smooth, some tannin, nice flavor, a little light, but has some style.★ +

Fiore Umberto *(2/85)*. Too old; alcohol, volatile acidity and tannin are all that remain.

1972

Barra Guido *(6 times 12/83)*. Floral, berrylike aroma with a pungent, tarlike aspect; some oxidation and volatile acidity on the palate but still offers interest (other bottles were barely drinkable).

Brugo Agostino *(9/82)*. Some complexity on aroma, marred by a vague off note; thin, shallow, unbalanced.

Fiore Umberto *(2/85)*. High acid, low fruit, vile.

1971

Antoniolo *(11/78)*. Light nose; acid on the high side, has nice flavor; ready; short.

Brugo Agostino *(9 times 11/82)*. Lovely floral bouquet; somewhat acidic but has good flavor; was better in 1979.★

Nervi Luigi & Italo riserva *(twice 9/82)*. Very small aroma; overly tannic for the fruit, shallow; short, dull aftertaste; was better in 9/79, when it merited ★. This bottle 0.

1970

Barra Guido *(10 times 2/85)*. Garnet with orange reflections; floral bouquet; tannic backbone, round and flavorful; finish is short and tannic; beginning to fade, though it's still good.★★

"Monsecco" Conte Ravizza Az. Agr. "Le Colline" riserva speciale *(4/81; 7935 bottles)*. Rich bouquet with suggestions of flowers and tar; well balanced; has tannin, a lot of flavor, and some style.★★(★)

1969

"Monsecco" Conte Ravizza Az. Agr. "Le Colline" riserva speciale *(twice 3/83)*. Color showing age; old-style nebbiolo nose with some oxidation; nice flavor, some tannin, not to keep (a bottle tasted a year earlier was similar but perhaps a bit better).★

1968

Antoniolo *(9/82)*. Bouquet has floral and fruity notes; acid a touch high, soft-centered and smooth; quite agreeable; ready.★

Brugo Agostino *(3 times 9/82)*. Aroma has vegie overtones and a barnyard back note; shallow, short, and offensive; was better in 11/78, though not a lot.

"Monsecco" Conte Ravizza Az. Agr. "Le Colline" riserva speciale *(6 times 5/83; 10,993 bottles)*. Aroma of cherries but with a rubbery, somewhat oxidized aspect; still has loads of tannin but seems to have the stuffing to support it; the only problem is the oxidation (nearly every bottle tasted was similar).★★(?)

1967

Antoniolo *(5 times 1/85)*. Orange cast; expansive floral bouquet with incredible richness; some tannin adds life; sweet, ripe fruit; has the structure to last and probably even improve, but ready now. This bottle, tasted in Torino, was brought directly from the winery; it was very similar to a bottle tasted a month earlier in the U.S., but had more life left in it.★★★

1964

Antoniolo *(4 times 1/85)*. The wine is like a bouquet of flowers from the lovely, fragrant aroma through the mouth-filling flavors and the incredibly long finish; a wine of elegance and style, superb now and shows no signs of age. This bottle, tasted in Torino, was brought directly from the cellars; a bottle tasted 10/84 in the U.S. was quite similar and very good indeed, but not up to the same level and showed some signs of age, meriting ★★ +. This bottle − ★★★★

Brugo Agostino *(12/80)*. Lovely bouquet; well balanced, soft, and tasty; some style and elegance; very good indeed.★★★

"Monsecco" Conte Ravizza Az. Agr. "Le Colline" *(11/78)*. Deep color; some harsh edges on aroma; soft and velvety; good length on palate, but marred by a touch of volatile acidity.★★

1961

Antoniolo *(twice 1/85)*. Garnet, brick at rim; floral bouquet has a vague Marsala-like note; a bit unbalanced with alcohol, but overall soft, round, and smooth-textured; age is beginning to show, but very good still.★★

GHEMME *(Novara)*. The wines of Ghemme have long been noted. In the medieval manuscript of St. Julius of Orta dating from the eleventh to the thirteenth century, mention is found of the wine of the Counts of Biandrate, feudal lords of Ghemme.

The Ghemme vineyards are cultivated high on the slopes that rise above the Sesia river, at an average altitude of 790 feet (241 meters). Some fifty-four growers cultivate the 141 acres (57 hectares) of vines here in the *commune* of Ghemme and the part of Romagnano Sesia known as Mauletto. The average annual production of Ghemme is 17,100 cases.

Ghemme is made from a blend of 60 to 85 percent spanna; 10 to 30 percent vespolina, or ughetta di Ghemme, and up to 15 percent bonarda novarese, also known as uva rara.

DOC Requirements

Minimum age (years)		Minimum alcohol	Maximum yield (gallons/acre)
cask	*total*		
3	4	12%	748

This medium-bodied wine is typically described as having an aroma of violets; some tasters also find notes of roses and resin; nebbiolo tar, or *goudron*, is also evident. Ghemme frequently has a vaguely bitter aftertaste. It is best drunk from its fifth or sixth year until its tenth or twelfth, but can last longer in the best vintages.

Ponti, with an annual production of 100,000 bottles, nearly half the total, is the largest producer of Ghemme.

Producers

Antichi Vigneti di Cantalupo	★	Ioppa F.lli	—
Collis Brecelmae	★★	"Le Colline" Az. Agr.	—
Bertinetti, Uglioni dei	—	Nervi Luigi & Italo	0
Bertolo Lorenzo	—	Paganotti Alberto e Giuseppe	—
Bianchi Giuseppe	★	Patti Angela	—
Borgo Cav. Ercole	0	Ponti	★★
Brugo Agostino	★	Rovellotti, A. F.	★★
Dellavalle F.lli	0	Sebastiani Antonio	—
Ferrari F.lli Romano & Guido	—	Sebastiani Giovanni Giuseppe	★★
Fiore Umberto	0	Sizzano e Ghemme Cantina Sociale	★
Fontana Allesandria	—	Troglia G.	★
Francoli Cantine	—	Tenuta San Vi' di Ferrante Dante	—

Vintages

★★★★	1978, 1974, 1947
★★★	1983, 1982, 1980, 1979, 1973, 1971, 1970, 1964, 1962, 1957, 1956, 1952
★★	1976, 1975, 1972, 1969, 1967, 1961
★	1981, 1968, 1958,1955,1951,1948,1945
0	1977, 1966, 1965, 1963, 1960, 1959, 1954, 1953, 1950, 1949, 1946

Of the vintages tasted in recent years, we've found that, except for 1964 and 1967, anything earlier than 1974 has been too old or was not very good from the start. Even the '74s failed to impress.

Judging by the number of vintages which have gotten ratings of zero or one star, one has to wonder if it is really worth the effort to make these wines.

Rating ★★

[handwritten: 1/88: Blah— what a dumb statement to anyone who has enjoyed the '67 or '69 Cantina Sociale Ghemme]

Tasting Notes

1979

Antichi Vigneti di Cantalupo *(twice 3/85)*. Fragrant aroma with a raisiny aspect; nice fruit, almost sweet, seems overripe; acid on the high side, some tannin; overall a fairly nice bottle.★

Antichi Vigneti di Cantalupo Collis Breclemae *(1/85; 14,271 bottles)*. Small nose with some fruit; soft-centered, still has some tannin and potential to improve.★(★)

Bianchi Giuseppe *(1/85)*. Stinky nose though varietal character is evident; has tannin and some fruit, but a doubtful future; a disappointment from a generally good producer.

Brugo Agostino *(1/85)*. Aroma has notes of chocolate and fruit; some tannin, lacks style and character; not up to the vintage.

Cantina Sociale di Sizzano e Ghemme *(1/85)*. Characteristic nebbiolo bouquet with floral notes; firm tannic vein, has fruit; give it two to three more years.★(★)

Rovellotti, A. F. *(twice 1/85)*. Floral bouquet with notes of tar; light tannin, firm, nice fruit; needs a few years.★(★)

1978

Cantina Sociale di Sizzano e Ghemme *(4/85)*. Reticent aroma offers hints of things to come; a lot of flavor; well structured, firm; needs time to soften, should make a nice glass in a few years.★★(+)

1976

Brugo Agostino *(6/85)*. Corked.

1975

Brugo Agostino *(5/82)*. Complex floral bouquet with notes of spice and tar, marred by a faint off note in back; light-bodied and agreeable; drying on finish, seems to be beginning to go.★

Ponti *(5/82)*. Bouquet marred by a slight dankness that blows off with airing; not much going for it, but not really flawed; no reason to keep it any longer.

1974

Brugo Agostino *(twice 5/82 and 6/85)*. Bottle of 5/82: Berrylike aroma; acid on the high side, lots of flavor; nearly ready.★

Bottle of 6/85: Dull nose, a bit stale; cooked, jammy taste.

Dellavalle *(11/80)*. Floral bouquet; some tannin to lose but structure and fruit indicate it should improve.★(+)

Sebastiani G. *(4/80)*. Oxidized; too bad, the quality was evident in the structure.

1973

Brugo Agostino *(twice 11/84)*. Floral bouquet, characteristic nebbiolo; somewhat light, soft; falls off abruptly at the end.

Tasting Notes

1972

Cantina Sociale di Sizzano e Ghemme *(10/79)*. Fragrant nebbiolo aroma; a bit light in body, has tannin; needs some time to soften (will it?).★

1971

Brugo Agostino *(11/81)*. Light, floral, fruity aroma; some tannin, some harshness, lacks structure, weight, and flavor; alcoholic aftertaste.

1970

Nervi Luigi & Italo *(10/79)*. Pale color; volatile acidity and alcohol on aroma; unbalanced with tannin; alcoholic aftertaste.

1967

Cantina Sociale di Sizzano e Ghemme *(3 times 4/85)*. Bottle of 5/82: Characteristic bouquet of flowers, tar, and fruit; smooth-textured; tannic backbone; ready, but should hold.★★ +

Bottle of 4/85: Browning; some oxidation sadly apparent, past its peak.

1964

Brugo Agostino *(10/80)*. Orange hue; tarlike notes on aroma; some tannin, considerable fruit; very ready; moderate length.★★

GRIGNASCO *(Novara)*. This wine is produced from a blend of spanna, vespolina, and bonarda grapes. Grignasco is a soft, light-bodied wine of about 12 percent alcohol. It ages moderately well.

LANGHERINO *(Novara)*. Langherino is the product of croatina, spanna, and vespolina grapes. It is a medium-bodied red wine of 12 percent alcohol, at its best drunk young and fresh.

LESSONA *(Vercelli)*. There are some 12 acres (4.9 hectares) of vineyards in Lessona, grown on hills facing southwest. In the last century the most respected name in this area was that of Villa Sperino. This property is owned by the di Marchi family, proprietors of the noted Chianti Classico estate of Isole e Olena. Villa Sperino was sold in bottle since the last century up until 1970. The vines continued to be cultivated by Sella up until a few years ago when they were uprooted. For Villa Sperino the great vintages were 1865, 1870, 1879, 1892, 1894, and 1900. Paolo di Marchi, the very able winemaker at Isole e Olena, hopes to produce the Villa Sperino wine again. We look forward to it.

The three growers in Lessona today produce an average of less than 2500 cases a year. Lessona must be made from at least 75 percent spanna. Vespolina, and/or bonarda may also be blended in. The Lessona of Maurizo Ormezzano is made from 100 percent spanna. Sella uses 75 to 80 percent spanna plus vespolina and bonarda.

DOC Requirements

Minimum age (years)		Minimum alcohol	Maximum yield (gallons/acre)
cask	total		
1	2	12%	598.5

Vintages

★★★	1983, 1980, 1978, 1974, 1971, 1970
★★	1982, 1981, 1979, 1976, 1975, 1973
★	1972
0	1977

Our experience is too limited to comment on many vintages, but we've found that anything from earlier than 1974 was too old or was not good to begin with.

Rating ★★

Tasting Notes

1980 Sella Tenuta Agr. *(twice 1/85)*. Lovely floral bouquet with a note of cherries, varietal character evident; very well balanced, some tannin to shed but overall fairly soft; nearly ready, could improve a bit.★★(+)

1975 Ormezzano Tenuta Eredi di Mario *(ex-cask 11/78)*. Fragrant bouquet; light bodied; fairly well balanced; nice flavor; forward, for early drinking.★★

1975 Sella Tenuta Agr. *(4 times 1/83)*. Light color, showing some age; fruit on nose marred by some oxidation; oxidation carries through on palate though still flavorful, acid on the high side; drinkable but showing its age.

1974 Sella Tenuta Agr. *(4 times 4/80)*. Fruity bouquet with hints of cassis and flowers has still more to give; tannin to lose, well balanced, a lot of flavor, some class.★★★

1971 Sella Tenuta Agr. *(11/78)*. Bouquet brings up tartufi; off-balance with high acidity, low fruit.

1970 Sella Tenuta Agr. *11/78)*. Similar nose to the '71; also unbalanced with high acid and low fruit; not a success.

LOZZOLO *(Vercelli)*. Lozzolo is the product of 50 to 70 percent spanna, 20 to 30 percent croatina (vespolina), and 10 to 20 percent bonarda grapes. It is a dry, tannic wine of 12.5 percent alcohol that reputedly ages well.

MAGGIORA *(Novara)*. Cav. Ermanno Conti produces this medium-bodied wine from a blend of spanna, vespolina, and bonarda grapes. We haven't tasted it in over a decade. Rating★

MASSERANO *(Vercelli)*. This wine is made from mostly spanna grapes with a small amount of bonarda blended in. Masserano is a soft, medium-bodied wine of about 12 percent alcohol. It can take moderate age.

MESOLONE *(Vercelli)*. Mesolone is produced from an *uvaggio,* or blend, of 50 percent spanna, 30 percent bonarda, and 20 percent vespolina grapes grown on the Colline della Measola in Barengo. It is a medium- to full-bodied wine with about 13 percent alcohol that is reputedly at its best between its fifth and eighth year.

It is produced by Avv. Armando Beccaro e Figlio

MOT ZIFLON *(Novara)*. Luciano Brigatti, the sole producer of this wine, makes about 15,000 bottles a year. It is the product of 70 percent spanna, 20 percent bonarda, and 10 percent vespolina grapes, grown in the Mot Ziflon district of Suno. The wine is fairly full-bodied, with 13 percent alcohol, and at its best within three to four years of the vintage, perhaps up to six in the better years.

Best vintages: 1983, 1974, 1964
Least vintages: 1973, 1966, 1965
Rating★★

Tasting Note

1980 Brigatti Luciano *(twice 1/85)*. Generous, warm, fruity aroma, vaguely floral; still has tannin but also a lot of flavor, drinkable now but really needs two or three years to soften and round out and develop more complexity.★★

MOTTALCIATA *(Vercelli)*. This wine is produced from spanna grapes grown in the *communes* of Mottalciata and Castellengo. It is a medium-bodied wine of about 12 percent alcohol.

NEBBIOLO DELLA SERRA *(Vercelli)*. This wine is produced from grapes grown in the *communes* of Moncrivello, Roppolo, Viverone, and Zimone. It is light to medium in body and best drunk young. Rating★

ORBELLO *(Vercelli)*. There are two producers of Orbello. Each uses a different formula, but both versions are based on the spanna grape. Sella blends in 20 to 30 percent cabernet sauvignon and franc, plus freisa, bonarda, and other local varieties. Luigi Perazzi adds 10 percent each of vespolina, bonarda, and croatina. Orbello is at its best drunk between two and five years of the vintage. Rating★

Tasting Notes

1983 Sella Tenuta Agr. *(1/85)*. Cabernet fruit evident on aroma; light tannin, well balanced, good fruit, has some character; to drink young.★★

1978 Perazzi Luigi *(11/80)*. Nice nose; some tannin, a bit light, tasty; should be ready soon.★(+)

PICCONE *(Vercelli)*. Sella produces this wine basically from spanna, with the addition of merlot, freisa, neretto di Bairo, and barbera grapes. Piccone is a wine to be consumed young. Rating★

PRUNENT *(Novara)*. This wine is produced from spanna grapes, known in Domodossola as prunent. It is light and soft, with about 11 percent alcohol, and at its best within four years, perhaps five, of the vintage.

ROASIO *(Vercelli)*. This wine is rather similar to many of the other spanna-based wines of this area.

ROMAGNANO SESIA *(Novara)*. Brugo produces this wine from bonarda, croatina, spanna, and vespolina grapes grown in the Ghemme region. It is a medium-bodied wine of 11.5 to 12.5 percent alcohol, with a floral aroma and a lightly bitter almond finish. It ages moderately well. Rating★

RONCO DEL FRATE *(Novara)*. This wine is produced in the Ghemme zone from bonarda, spanna, and vespolina grapes. It is a medium-bodied red of about 12.5 percent alcohol that can take moderate age.

ROSSO DELLA SERRA *(Vercelli)*. Another name for the Nebbiolo della Serra.

ROSSO DI COSSATO *(Vercelli)*. This wine is the product of spanna and other local grape varieties.

ROSSO DI GRIGNASCO *(Novara)*. This wine is produced from a blend of nebbiolo, bonarda, and other local grapes.

SIZZANO *(Novara)*. The vineyards of Sizzano are on the left bank of the Sesia between Ghemme and Fara. This district covers 87.6 acres (35.5 hectares). It is cultivated by sixty-nine growers who produce an average of 13,300 cases of Sizzano a year. Sizzano is made from a blend of 40 to 60 percent spanna, 15 to 40 percent vespoliina, and up to 25 percent bonarda novarese, or uva rara. The vineyards are planted at an average altitude of 740 feet (225 meters).

DOC Requirements

Minimum age (years)		Minimum	Maximum yield
cask	total	alcohol	(gallons/acre)
2	3	12%	748

Sizzano is at its best with from four to ten years of age. Like many of the spanna-based wines of this area, it is medium in body and has a floral aroma frequently described as reminiscent of violets.

Producers
Bianchi Giuseppe	★★
Dellavalle F.lli	0
Fontana Francesco	—
Ponti	★★
Sizzano e Ghemme Cantina Sociale	★★
Zanetta Ercolina	★★

Vintages
★★★★	1957, 1947
★★★	1980, 1978, 1974, 1970, 1964, 1945
★★	1983, 1981, 1979, 1976, 1975, 1973, 1971, 1969, 1967, 1961, 1953, 1950
★	1982, 1972, 1962, 1960, 1958, 1956, 1948
0	1977, 1968, 1966, 1965, 1963, 1959, 1955, 1954, 1952, 1951, 1949, 1946

The only vintages we can recommend first-hand are 1974 and 1978. We have no recent experience with vintages before 1971 but suspect very few are still good now. Since we haven't tasted the vintages younger than 1980, we can't comment on them except to point out that they are rated highly in the zone.

Rating★★

Tasting Notes

1980 Bianchi Giuseppe *(1/85)*. Aroma suggests Marsala; forward fruit, light to moderate tannin, flavor somewhat floral; drinkable though a bit pedestrian.

1978 Cantina Sociale di Sizzano e Ghemme *(3 times 4/85)*. Vaguely floral aroma; moderate tannin, has a tart edge, some firmness, nice fruit; should improve over the next year or two.★★(+)

1975 Cantina Sociale di Sizzano e Ghemme *(4/80)*. Fruity aroma marred by the intrusion of alcohol; still some tannin to lose, rather shallow, lacks the fruit ever to amount to much.

1974 Ponti *(4/80)*. Fragrant, fruity aroma; well structured, some tannin to lose but has sufficient fruit; very good.★★(+)

1974 Zanetta Ercolina *(4/80)*. Richly fruited aroma still somewhat backward; well balanced, tannin to lose, has a lot of flavor and some style.★★(★)

1973 Ponti *(10/78)*. Fruity nose; high acid, too much tannin for the fruit.

1971 Cantina Sociale di Sizzano e Ghemme *(11/82)*. Characteristic fruit and flowers on aroma; some acid throws the balance off, moderate tannin, nice flavor; more or less ready.★ —

SPANNA *(Novara & Vercelli)*. Spanna, the local name from the nebbiolo grape in the Novara–Vercelli production zone, is also the name of a wine—in fact, many wines—of varying styles and quality. Most today are labeled Spanna del Piemonte, and most are not very impressive. Generally they are medium-bodied red wines with the characteristic tannic vein typical of the nebbiolo-based wines of this area. Many Spannas carry a more specific denomination of origin. Among the more regarded Spannas of Vercelli are the Spanna di Bosca, di Casa del Bosco and di Sant'Emiliano from Sostengo, di Vigliano from Vigliano Biellese, and di Villa del Bosco from Villa del Bosco; from Novara, Spanna di Maggiora from Maggiora.

The regulations promulgated by the Common Market bureaucrats in Bruxelles who don't make wine, only wine laws, decree that a wine labeled with the name of a grape variety must be made from no less than 85 percent of that variety. Many producers use that prescribed minimum in their Spanna and blend in bonarda, vespolina, croatina, or anything they have handy, including wines and/or grapes trucked in from southern parts of the peninsula. This is not a new practice; it is something of a tradition here, where the name Spanna on a wine came to mean pretty much whatever the producer wanted it to. Many of the best wines labeled Spanna in days gone by were, in fact, made with a high proportion of fine southern varieties, like aglianico, which contributed body and richness to the wines. The local Spannas are very often thin and flavorless, especially in the lesser vintages, which are unfortunately, all too common in this region. While the best Spannas can be very long-lived, most should be consumed with not more than two to four years of age.

Producers

Vallana Antonio (older vintages)		Cosseti Clemente	0
Campi Raudii	★★★★	Curti	—
Cinque Castelli	★★	Dellavalle F.lli	0
del Camino	★★	Dessilani Luigi	★
Montalbano	★★★	Ferrando Luigi	★
San Lorenzo	★★★	Fiore Umberto	0
Traversagna	★★★★	Sogno del Bacco	0
Vallana Antonio (since 1968)	★★	Francoli Cantine	★
Antoniolo Santa Chiara	★★ –	Nervi Livio	—
Avondo	0	Nervi Luigi & Italo	★
Barra Guido	★	Ponti	★
Bertolo Lorenzo	—	Rivetti Ermanno, Villa Era	—
Borgo Cav. Ercole	0	Sizzano e Ghemme Cantina Sociale	★
Brugo Agostino	★	Travaglini	★
Riserva Cantina dei Santi	★	Troglia G.	★
Cantina Sociale dei		Villa Antonio	0
"Colli Novaresi"	★	Villadoria Marchese	0
Conti Cav. Ermanno	—		

Rating★ (The best can equal any wine of the Novara/Vercelli hills.)

Tasting Notes

All of these wines are Spanna del Piemonte, unless otherwise noted.

1981

Fiore Umberto "Sogno di Bacco" *(6/83)*. Light, fruity, rather simple aroma; light-bodied, light tannin, fairly fruity and straightforward.

1980

Nervi *(6/85)*. Expansive floral aroma, vaguely peppery; high acid, fruity, light tannin; good with a light chill.★

1979

"Colli Novaresi" Cantina Sociale *(4/81)*. A tarlike aroma with an alcoholic backnote; light to medium body; some tannin, moderate fruit; tannic aftertaste.
Dessilani *(1/83)*. Pale; Marsala-like notes on nose and palate; oxidized; lacks structure, flavor, and style.
Ferrando Luigi *(5/82)*. Musty, stinky odors in background; somewhat unbalanced with high acidity; rather shallow; short, bitter aftertaste.
Travaglini *(5/82)*. Straightforward, fresh, fruity aroma with a floral note; moderate fruit; agreeable now but with potential to improve.★(+)

1978

Barra Guido *(12/80)*. Nice aroma though small; light-bodied, soft, fruity, and simple; marred by a slight harshness at the end.★
Brugo *(6/85)*. Fruity, harsh edges, clumsy, a bit tired, has seen better days.

1977

Vallana "Traversagna" *(4/85)*. Floral aroma, with fruity notes; some tannin, heaps of flavor, drinkable now but should improve; a surprise for the year.★★(+)

1976

Antoniolo "Santa Chiara" *(5/82)*. Fresh berrylike aroma with a peppery note; lots of flavor, some tannin; enjoyable now.★ +
Borgo Cav. Ercolo *(5/82)*. Berrylike aroma; moderate fruit; a simple little wine in a straightforward, fruity style.★
Brugo Agostino *(5/82)*. Moderately intense aroma; some tannin to shed, has fruit; enjoyable now but can improve.★ +

Tasting Notes

1976

Dessilani *(5/82)*. Complex bouquet offers suggestions of blueberries, black pepper, and more; blueberries carry through on flavor; a nice bottle.★★

Nervi *(3 times 5/82)*. Characteristic aroma marred by a faint dankness in the back; acid and tannin on the high side, sufficient fruit to make it drinkable, even enjoyable, but drink it now.★

Vallana *(4/85)*. Floral bouquet with fruity notes; soft, round, and tasty, some tannin; very nice.★★ +

Villa Antonio *(5/82)*. A rubbery aroma that carries through on the palate; an awful wine.

1975

Brugo Agostino *(5/82)*. Straightforward, fruity aroma; some tannin, a bit shallow; as ready as it will ever be.

Brugo Agostino, Cantina dei Santi *(1/85)*. Characteristic old-style spanna aroma with a lot of tar; tannin up front, but has the fruit; could get better in a year or two.★

Nervi Luigi & Italo *(11/79)*. Fragrant, fruity aroma; some tannin, soft and flavorful; ready.★

1974

Brugo Agostino *(twice 3/83)*. Garnet, orange at rim; nice fruit on aroma; carries through on palate, unbalanced and showing age; drinkable but not to keep.

Brugo Agostino, Cantina dei Santi riserva *(5/82)*. Floral bouquet with berrylike notes; acid on high side; a quaffable wine that's quite ready.★

Francoli *(5/82)*. Fairly rich bouquet with some complexity; firm tannin, lots of flavor; ready now.★ +

Villadoria Marchese *(5/82)*. Moderately intense aroma with berries and spice, though an offnote intrudes; has fruit, acid somewhat on the high side; enjoyable now, not to keep.★ −

1973

Brugo Agostino, Cantina dei Santi *(twice 11/82)*. Tar and flowers on aroma; unbalanced, a bit shallow, some volatile acidity. The bottle tasted 3/80 was better and merited ★.

Fiore Umberto "Sogno di Bacco" *(5/82)*. Characteristic aroma, floral with some complexity; full of flavor, some tannin; ready now.★ +

Vallana, Castello di Montalbano *(11/78)*. High va; in fact, undrinkable; a wine for the salad.

1972

Vallana, Podere Due Torri di Traversagna *(11/78)*. A ghastly taste of sour seaweed; oxidized.

1971

Brugo Agostino *(10/81)*. Characteristic aroma; flavorful, but acidity throws the balance off, shows signs of drying out; tails off to a bitter ending.

Brugo Agostino, Cantina dei Santi *(6/79)*. Fragrant aroma; soft and mellow with some tannin, acid on the high side; enjoyable now but not to keep.

Vallana, Castello di Montalbano *(3/80)*. Characteristic spanna nose, with flowers and tar; considerable tannin but with the fruit to back it up; needs three or four years.★(★)

1970

Nervi Luigi & Italo *(10/79)*. Fruity aroma marred by some oxidation; fairly nice flavor.★ −

Vallana, Campi Raudii *(11/78)*. Awful flavor; must be an off bottle.

1969

Vallana, Spanna di Montalbano *(twice 9/83)*. Light, fruity, floral aroma; still has a fair amount of tannin, medium-bodied, tasty; should improve; short.★

1968

Vallana *(twice 9/83)*. More recent bottle: An off note, like bad fruit, mars the aroma; tannic, shy of fruit. A bad bottle?

Earlier bottle: Complex bouquet with suggestions of cherries and tobacco; firm and flavorful, still some tannin but with the fruit in reserve.★★

1967

Brugo Agostino *(twice 11/82)*. From gallon: Deep color; richer, more intense bouquet; soft and smooth and most agreeable; has potential for improvement perhaps; it will certainly hold.★★

From bottle: Soft and smooth but has nowhere to go, as ready as it will ever be.★ +

Vallana, Podere Due Torri di Traversagna *(4 times 5/85)*. Bottle of 9/84: Nice bouquet, well developed and complex; soft entry, a lot of flavor, indications of drying out at the end; it was better a year earlier; could be the bottle.★★

Bottle of 5/85: Barnyard aroma carries through on the palate, not offensive, just different; light tannin, soft, no sign of age, ready.★ +

1966

Vallana, Castello di Montalbano *(twice 9/83)*. Floral, fruity bouquet, fairly rich and intense; full-bodied; well balanced; full of flavor; ready.★★

1964

Vallana, Castello di Montalbano *(3 times 12/84)*. Deep red, garnet rim; deep, rich, intense bouquet with hints of vanilla and cherries, somewhat reminiscent of a late-harvest California wine; full-bodied, full of flavor, light tannin, lacks some delicacy but makes up for it in richness; as it sits in the glass it begins to resemble a late-harvest Zinfandel with a brambly, raspberry character.★★★

Vallana, Castello San Lorenzo *(3/82)*. Medium dark red shading to orange; big, rich, expansive bouquet; full of flavor, still some tannin to shed; give it two to three more years.★★(★)

1962

Borgo Cav. Ercolo *(11/78)*. Characteristic spanna nose; then nothing left but tannin; dried out.

1961

Vallana, Campi Raudii *(9/80)*. Intense, floral bouquet; soft and velvety; full of flavor; elegant; long on the finish; can still improve.★★★(★)

Vallana, Castello San Lorenzo *(5/79)*. Expansive bouquet; rich concentration of fruit, loads of flavor and loads of tannin; needs age, but the potential is quite evident.★★★(+)

146

Tasting Notes

1958

Vallana, Campi Raudii *(3/83)*. Deep brick robe; complex bouquet with a touch of oxidation; rich and flavorful; probably best drunk up now.★★★

Vallana, Castello San Lorenzo *(1/84)*. Richly intense bouquet; mouth-filling flavors, enormous richness and concentration, Portlike but without the alcohol and sweetness, perfectly balanced; a complete wine.★★★★

1955

Vallana, Campi Raudii *(4 times 5/85; 6250 bottles)*. Bottle of 1/82: Medium deep red, garnet rim; rich bouquet with suggestions of cassis; very rich, very full, and still young, firm tannic vein, not yet peak but very good drinking now.★★★(★)

Bottle of 5/85: Tawny, orange robe; floral, toasty bouquet, grainlike notes; full-bodied, some tannin sweet berrylike flavors; finishes with a hint of raisins.★★★

Vallana, Podere due Torri di Traversagna *(11/82)*. Richly fruited bouquet with a hint of mint and floral overtones; a rich concentration of ripe fruit flavors, velvety and elegant; enormous length.★★★ +

1954

Vallana, Campi Raudii *(twice 5/85)*. Bottle of 9/78: Fragrant bouquet with floral notes; soft and smooth, heaps of flavor; quite ready; impressive quality.★★★ +

Bottle of 5/85: Delicate, refined, floral bouquet, berrylike nuance; full-flavored and velvety, rich and intense, still some tannin; very long finish has a vague raisinlike note; no signs of age.★★★ +

VALDENGO, ROSSO DI *(Vercelli)*. Valdengo is the product of spanna, bonarda, and vespolina grapes. It is a soft, medium-bodied wine of about 12 percent alcohol that can take moderate age.

VECCHIA COLLINA *(Novara)*. The Cantina Sociale Coop. di Oleggio produces this wine from a blend of spanna, vespolina, and croatina grapes grown in Oleggio, Mezzomerico, and Barengo. It is a medium- to full-bodied wine of about 13 percent alcohol. At its best with at least four years of age, it drinks well until about its eighth.

VERCELLI, ROSSO DI *(Vercelli)*. This wine is the product of spanna, vespolina, and bonarda grapes.

VIGLIANO *(Vercelli)*. Vigliano is made from spanna, bonarda, and vespolina grapes grown in Vigliano Biellese. It is a firm-textured wine that sometimes attains 13 percent alcohol. It ages moderately well.

VILLA DEL BOSCO *(Vercelli)*. Villa del Bosco is the product of spanna, bonarda, and vespolina grapes grown in the villages of Bosco and Lozzolo. It is a light- to medium-bodied wine of about 12 percent alcohol, best drunk within four or five years of the vintage.

Novara–Vercelli Producers

Antoniolo Az. Vitivin. di Mario Antoniolo *(Gattinara), 1955*. Antoniolo owns 37 acres (15 hectares) of vineyards, which include the two crus of Osso San Gratò and San Francesco. Since 1974 they have kept aside a small part of the crop for these single-vineyard bottlings. The wine from San Francesco is generally softer and rounder than the bigger, more tannic Osso San Gratò.

Cru	Nebbiolo grapes		Avg yield (bottles)
	Hectares	Acres	
Osso San Gratò	4	9.9	3,000–6,000
San Francesco	3	7.4	3,000–4,000
(total)	7	17.3	6,000–10,000

In the future they also plan to do a cru bottling from their Castello vineyard.

Antoniolo produces an average of 60,000 bottles a year of Gattinara plus "Santa Chiara" Spanna del Piemonte. This wine is named for the fifteenth-century monastery where they have an aging cellar. Approximately 90 percent of their production comes from their own grapes.

We had been quite impressed with the Antoniolo Gattinaras up until the '68; from that vintage the wines seemed to have slipped. We are glad to report now that since 1978 they seem to be back in form. When we spoke with Rosanna Antoniolo about the changes, she noted that beginning in 1968 the fermentation time was shortened and stems omitted. With the 1978 vintage, they started adding back up to 50 percent of the stems and lengthened the fermentation again to 15 days.

Rosanna Antoniolo names as the best vintages 1961, 1964, 1967, 1974, 1978, and 1982. We are fortunate to have tasting notes on all but the '82. Gattinara★★★ Spanna★★ −

Avondo. It's been a number of years since we've tasted these wines, but when we did we found them mediocre at best. Gattinara 0 Spanna 0

Balbiano Az. Vitivin. *(Andezeno), 1935.* Balbiano produces 135,000 bottles of wine a year, 40 percent from their own grapes. They have long been regarded for their Freisa di Chieri and Malvasia Castelnuovo Don Bosco, both still and sparkling. They own 7.4 acres (3 hectares) of vines, none in Gattinara. In 1979, though, they did a limited bottling of Gattinara. We found the wine quite good. Gattinara★★

—photo by Tom Abruzzini

Barra Guido & Figlio Az. Vin. *(Gattinara).* Barra owns 28 acres (11.3 hectares); 11 (4.5) are planted to vines, (95) percent nebbiolo with (5 percent) bonarda. They have an annual production of more than 36,000 bottles of Gattinara. They also produce 72,000 bottles of Spanna del Piemonte made from purchased grapes, in a blend of 85 percent spanna and 15 percent bonarda.

In their own vineyards they have three crus.

In 1979, Barra bottled their first cru, 4500 bottles of Permolone. In 1980, this was increased to 6000 bottles. In 1980, they bottled two additional crus: Permolone Valferane (4500 bottles) and Alice (7500). The remainder of the grapes went into their regular Gattinara. The Barra wines, on occasion, like many in the region, have a taste that is suggestive of southern grapes. Gattinara★★ — Spanna★

Enzo Barra of Guido Barra

Cru	Hectares	Acres	Altitude (feet)	Year planted	Avg production (bottles)
Alice	1.6338	4.04	1380–1475	1970	13,000
Permolone	1.6780	4.14	1180–1310	1968	14,000
Permolone Valferane	1.1510	2.84	1180–1280	1971	9,500
(Total)	4.4628	11.02			36,000

Beccaro Armando Az. Vitivin. Beccaro is the only producer, as far as we know, who bottles Mesolone.

Bertole Ing. Salvatore *(Gattinara).* Our experience is limited, but the wine seems decent enough. Gattinara★

Bertolo Lorenzo *(Torino).* This producer–merchant bottles Boca, Gattinara, Ghemme, and Spanna. We've never had the opportunity to taste any of them.

Bianchi Giuseppe Az. Agr. *(Sizzano), 1785.* Bianchi owns 30 acres (12 hectares) of vines from which he produces the spanna-based Fara, Ghemme, and Sizzano. He also makes a small quantity of Fogarin del Piemonte from the rare Fogarina grape grown on the hilltops of Sizzano. Besides these, he produces a varietal Bonarda and a white Greco. Fara★★; Ghemme★; Sizzano★★; Fogarin★

Borgo Cav. Ercole. While we haven't tasted many of the Borgo wines, we can't say that we've been impressed with those we have. Gattinara 0; Ghemme 0; Spanna 0

Luciano Brigatti of Mot Ziflon

Brigatti Luciano *(Suno), 1938.* Brigatti owns 12.4 acres (5 hectares) of vines from which he produces about 3000 bottles of the white Costabella and 15,000 bottles of the spanna-based Mot Ziflon. Mot Ziflon★★

Brugo Agostino Antica Casa Vinicola *(Romagnano Sesia), 1894.* Brugo owns 50 acres (20 hectares) of vineyards including the cru Cantina dei Santi. From this 5-acre (2-hectare) plot in Ronchi and Panagallo, they produce 30,000 to 40,000 bottles of Spanna del Piemonte. Their annual production is 600,000 to 800,000 bottles, which includes the standard Piemontese varietals—standard both in type and in quality. Besides their Spanna cru, they also make Spanna del Piemonte from spanna plus bonarda and vespolina grapes, Romagnano Sesia, Gattinara, and

Ghemme. Their wines are aged in oak and chestnut casks. Gattinara★; Ghemme★; Romagnano Sesia★; Spanna (both)★

Caldi Luigi. Caldi produces a Fara and a Gattinara, neither of which we've tasted.

Caligaris Guido *(Gattinara)*. Our experience with their Gattinara has been limited. The wine was certainly drinkable if not much else. Gattinara★

Cantalupo di Alberto e Maurizio Arlunno, Antichi Vigneti *(Ghemme), 1977*. Antichi Vigneti Cantalupo owns 50 acres (20 hectares) of vines; 30 (12) are currently in production, and the remainder should be by 1985 or 1986. Their main vineyard, at an altitude of about 985 feet (300 meters), overlooks Breclema, the site of a once important castle and village. On the sunniest slopes of the vineyard is their 7.4-acre (3-hectare) cru, Collis Breclemae. Since 1979, they have bottled about 13,300 bottles (100 hectoliters) annually of this Ghemme cru. Their other vineyards are Baraggiola, Carelle, Rossini, and Valera.

They produce all of their wines from their own grapes. Their Ghemme is made from 75 to 80 percent spanna, 15 percent vespolina (also known as ughetta di Ghemme) which they say adds mildness and delicacy, and 5 to 10 percent uva rara (more commonly known as bonarda novarese). They also make a specialty wine called Agamium. They bottle their wines in the champagnotta bottle seen fairly frequently in Ghemme.

Their best vintages were 1974, 1978, 1982, and 1983. Ghemme★; Ghemme cru★★; Agamium★ −

Castaldi Giuseppe. Our experience with Castaldi's Fara has left us with a good impression. Fara★★

Colli Novaresi Cantina Sociale dei *(Fara Novarese), 1954*. This cooperative of 854 members produces a fairly wide range of wines, including the spanna-based Barengo, Caramino, Fara, and Spanna del Piemonte. Sixty percent of their production is sold in bottle. In 1983, they harvested 8.8 million tons (40,000 quintali) of grapes. Their vineyards are in the *communes* of Barengo, Briona, Cavaglietto, Cavaglio d'Agogna, Fara Novarese, Romagnano Sesia, and Suno. Barengo★; Caramino★; Fara★; Spanna★

Conti Cav. Ermano nel suo Castello di Maggiore *(Maggiora)*. Our experience with these wines is somewhat limited and unfortunately not recent. As far as we know, they are the only producer of Maggiora. Boca★; Maggiora★

Conti Gian Piero *(Maggiora)*. Their reputation is higher than our rating suggests. Boca★

Cooperativa di Gattinara Cantina Sociale *(Gattinara), 1908*. This co-op has nearly 200 members in Casa del Bosco, Lozzolo, Roasio, and Sostengo. They produce some 466,000 bottles (3500 hectoliters) of wine a year, which includes about 40 percent of the total of DOC Gattinara. Much of this wine, Gattinara and otherwise, is not bottled but is sold *sfuso,* or in bulk. Gattinara 0

Cooperativa Intercomunale Oleggio Cantina Sociale *(Ollegio), 1981*. This is the oldest cooperative in the region. Among their spanna-based wines are Vecchia Collina and Spanna del Piemonte. We have never tasted them.

Cosseti Clemente. Cosseti is primarily a producer of mediocre Langhe wines such as Barolo. In our experience, these wines to date have sometimes risen to the level of drinkability, though barely. Spanna 0

Dellavalle F.lli di Osvaldo & Adriano *(Gattinara)*. Dellavalle owns 6.3 acres (2.5 hectares) of the Gattinara cru Molsino, planted to spanna. They also buy grapes; in fact, most of the grapes they use are purchased. They produce a wide range of fairly ordinary wines, including Gattinara, Ghemme, Spanna del Piemonte, Sizzano, and Barolo. Gattinara 0; Ghemme 0; Spanna del Piemonte 0; Sizzano 0

Dessilani Luigi & Figlio *(Fara Novarese)*. Dessilani owns 50 acres (20 hectares) of vines and buys grapes under long-term contracts from another 150 (60). Their average annual production of 600,000 bottles (4500 hectoliters) includes four nebbiolo-based wines, three from 100 percent nebbiolo—Caramino (14,400 bottles), Gattinara (21,600), and Spanna del Piemonte (14,400)—as well as Fara, made from a 60–30–10 nebbiolo, bonarda, and vespolina blend (14,400).

Despite their reputation, we have been unimpressed with the Dessilani wines we've tasted. Discounting the bad bottles, we find the wines coarse and lacking in style and distinction. Caramino★; Fara★; Gattinara★; Spanna★

149

Ferrando Luigi *(Ivrea)*. Ferrando is a producer and merchant of the wines of Aosta–Torino and Novara–Vercelli. Besides Carema and Donnaz, he sells Caramino, Fara, and Spanna del Piemonte. Overall, his wines are reliable. Caramino★; Gattinara★; Spanna del Piemonte★

Fiore Umberto Casa Vinicola di Silvana & Mauro Fiore *(Gattinara), 1880.* The Fiore line encompasses a very wide range of wines, mostly mediocre, including whites from Veneto and the Oltrepò Pavese in Lombardy. Their spanna-based wines include Gattinara, Ghemme, Sizzano, and two Spannas—the regular Spanna del Piemonte and the fantasy-named Sogno di Bacco. We have found them all unimpressive. Gattinara 0; Ghemme 0; Sizzano 0; Spanna (both) 0

Fracchia Provino *(Grazzano Badoglio).* Fracchia produces two nebbiolo-based wines—a Gattinara and a Barolo.

Franchino Marco *(Gattinara).* Franchino owns a piece of the regarded Lurghe vineyard. Umberto Fiore has from time to time offered the Franchino Lurghe cru under his own label. Gattinara 0

Francoli. Francoli offers a Gattinara, a Ghemme, and a Spanna under his label. The only one we've tasted was the Spanna, and it was, while decent enough, not much else. Spanna★

Ioppa F.lli Gianpiero e Giorgio Az. Agr. e Vitivin. *(Romagnano Sesia).* Their Ghemme is highly regarded by other producers in the zone.

Kiola. This firm, in the Langhe, also sells a Gattinara. It is, like all of their wines, mediocre at best. Kiola is now owned by F.lli Dogliani. Gattinara 0

"Le Colline" Az. Agr. *(Gattinara), 1951.* The Monsecco winery produces from 80,000 to 95,000 bottles (600 to 700 hectoliters) a year of three nebbiolo-based wines—Barbaresco, Gattinara, and Ghemme—in about equal quantities. A few years ago they were buying about a quarter of their grapes, but told us that when all of their own vineyards are in full production, sometime in the mid-1980s, they expect to make all of their wines from their own grapes. They have 10 acres (4 hectares) in the Valferrana vineyard in Gattinara and 5 acres (2 hectares) in Pelizzane in Ghemme. They also produce a Barbaresco from their own grapes grown in the 12.5-acre (5-hectare) vineyard in Treiso. In all, they own 40 acres (16 hectares).

Besides these wines, they also produce a Borgoalto, mostly from their own grapes (60 percent). Their wines are given fairly long oak aging; the Barbaresco and Gattinara about five years in cask, and the Ghemme four. Their Gattinara is made from 100 percent spanna; the Ghemme contains 30 percent vespolina.

The estate derives its name from previous owner Conte Don Ugo Ravizza's "mon vin sec" ("my dry wine"). Until recently, Monsecco didn't use the name Gattinara on the label, proudly flying its own colors. The new owners (since 1979) added that denomination to their labels with the 1974 vintage.

The Monsecco Gattinara can be magnificent, but frequently overlong wood aging dries the wine out, robbing it of fruit and creating problems with volatile acidity. When it is good, there is no finer wine in the zone. As we haven't tasted any of the wines produced under the new ownership, we can't say how or if the wines have changed. The best vintages for Monsecco were 1964 and 1971; for Ghemme, 1974. Monsecco★★★

Monsecco. See "Le Colline" Az. Agr.

Nervi Livio *(Gattinara).* Besides their Gattinara, they also produce a Spanna. There is no connection with Luigi & Italo Nervi, which is another firm.

Nervi Luigi & Italo Casa Vinicola *(Gattinara), 1915.* Nervi has the largest vineyard holdings in Gattinara at 52 acres (21 hectares), which supplies 60 percent of their grapes. Their annual production of 140,000 bottles makes up about 30 percent of the total produced in the zone. Their vineyards include 20 acres (8 hectares) each in the crus of Molsino and Valferane. In 1978, they produced 1500 bottles of each. Since 1976, they've bottled their best Gattinara as Podere dei Ginepri. We generally prefer their regular Gattinara, especially the one sold in the Bordeaux-type bottle. And somewhat surprising, we find the Gattinara sold in the U.S. superior to the one sold in Italy.

Giorgio Aliata of Luigi and Italo Nervi

The Nervi wines can be among the best in the zone, but in some years they don't quite measure up. Their best vintages were 1970, 1974, 1978, 1982, and 1983; the worst were 1977 and 1984. Gattinara★★; Ghemme 0; Spanna★

Oleggio Cantina Sociale. See Cooperativa Intercomunale Oleggio.

Ormezzano Maurizio *(Mossa S. Maria)*. Ormezzano produces a fine Lessona from 100 percent spanna, aged for two years in cask. We've found no Lessona better. Lessona★★

Orsolani Casa Vinicola. Our experience with their Gattinara, although limited, has left a favorable impression. We haven't seen it for a few years. Gattinara★★

Patriarca Mario *(Gattinara)*. Their Gattinara is fairly good. Gattinara★+

Perazzi Luigi *(Roasio S. Maria)*. Perazzi has 12.4 acres (5 hectares) of vineyards from which he produces a Bramaterra made with the maximum nebbiolo allowed under the law (70 percent) and the minimum levels of the other three grapes (20 percent croatina and 5 percent each bonarda and vespolina). He also produces an Orbello, We've never tasted better Bramaterra than those produced by Perazzi. Bramaterra★★; Orbello★

Ponti Guido *(Ghemme)*. Ponti has the largest vineyard holdings in Ghemme, 42 acres (17 hectares), and at an annual production of 100,000 bottles they are the zone's largest producer. They also make Sizzano and Boca, as well as a Nebbiolo del Piemonte Rosato. We have found both their Ghemme and their Sizzano quite reliable. Ghemme★★; Sizzano★★; Spanna★

Rovellotti A. F. *(Ghemme), 1971*. Rovellotti owns 12.4 acres (5 hectares) of vines from which they produce a Ghemme and a white Greco. Their vineyards include the 2.5-acre (1-hectare) cru Baraggiole and 5 acres (2 hectares) of Civetta. They have bottled a Ghemme Baraggiole since 1974. The best vintages have been 1974, 1978, 1979, 1982, and 1983; this last vintage, Rovellotti feels, was exceptional. Ghemme★★

Rusca Attilio. Perhaps their Fara is better than our limited experience suggests. Fara 0

Sebastiani Giuseppe Az. Agr. *(Ghemme), 1896*. Sebastiani owns parts of the Baraggiole, Pelizzane, and Ronco Tavoline crus in Ghemme. Their Ghemme is quite good. Ghemme★★

Sella Lessona, Tenuta S. Sebastiano allo Zoppo *(Lessona Castello)*. This winery produces some 36,000 bottles of Lessona a year from 14.3 acres (5.8 hectares) of vines in that zone. From another 18.2 acres (7.4 hectares), they make about 10,000 bottles each of two other wines, Orbello and Piccone. They own 46.5 acres (18.8 hectares) of vineyards in total and have an average annual output of nearly 100,000 bottles, which includes the 42,000 bottles from their 14-acre (5.7-hectare) property in the Bramaterra zone. Bramaterra★★; Lessona★★; Orbello★; Piccone★

Sella Tenuta, Bramaterra *(Roasio)*. Sella owns 14 acres (5.7 hectares) of vines from which they produce about 42,000 bottles of Bramaterra each year. Bramaterra★★

Sizzano e Ghemme, Cantina Sociale di *(Sizzano), 1960*. This co-op has 244 members in Ghemme and Sizzano who provide them with the grapes to produce the characteristic wines of this area. We don't know their average production of the spanna-based wines, but we do know that in 1979 they produced 50,000 bottles of Ghemme, and 20,000 bottles of Sizzano in 1980. They also make a Spanna del Piemonte which is aged for two years before sale. Ghemme★ Sizzano★★; Spanna★

Travaglini Giancarlo *(Gattinara)*. Travaglini has 27 acres (11 hectares) of vineyards in Gattinara. We have never been impressed with their wines. Gattinara★; Spanna★

Troglia G. *(Torino)*. This merchant sells a wide range of wines from the Novara–Vercelli area in weird-shaped bottles. Troglia wines were better in the early to mid-1970s when he was selling vintages from the 1960s. Troglia also sells wines from the Langhe. We haven't had that much experience of late and so give then the benefit of the doubt. Gattinara★; Ghemme★; Spanna★

Vallana Antonio & Figlio *(Maggiore)*. Vallana used to produce six Spannas—Cinque Castelli and the crus Campi Raudii, Traversagna, S. Lorenzo, Montalbano, and del Camino—as well as Gattinara, Spanna, and Boca. The crus were labeled "Castello di" and the name of each, but as there are no actual castles the law no longer allows this terminology. Since the inauguration of DOC, Vallana has dropped their individual Spanna bottlings.

Spanna	Last vintage	Now used for
Campi Raudii	1973 or 1974	Gattinara
Cinque (5) Castelli	n/a	Spanna del Piemonte
Del Camino	n/a	Spanna del Piemonte
Montalbano	1980	Boca
San Lorenzo	1973 or 1974	Gattinara
Traversagna	1977	Boca

Vallana is a master blender who has produced some very fine and long-lived Spannas worthy of four stars. His wines underwent a change some time in the late 1960s or early 1970s; sadly, they are not at the same high level as previously. Rumor has it that Vallana used to blend aglianico grapes from Basilicata into his wines to give them the body and strength they needed to age and develop. (The law today requires Spanna to contain 85 percent of that grape variety.) Whatever he did, the wines were magnificent; today they are a mere shadow of their former glory. If the story is true, we think it would have been preferable to have dropped the denomination of Spanna from the label; the name Vallana meant much more.

Vallana has an annual production of 240,000 bottles: 20,000 bottles (150 hectoliters) of Boca, 6650 to 8000 (50 to 60) of Gattinara, and 80,000 (600) of Spanna del Piemonte, the balance being used for various other wines, red and white.

The old		The new	
Campi Raudii	★★★★	Boca	★★
Cinque (5) Castelli	★★	Gattinara	★★ +
Del Camino	★★	Spanna	★★
Montalbano	★★★		
San Lorenzo	★★★		
Traversagna	★★★★		

Villa Antonio. The few bottles from this producer that we've tasted were, to put it mildly, poor. Gattinara 0; Spanna 0

Villadoria Marchese. This firm is primarily a mediocre producer of Langhe wines. None of their wines has impressed us; some are worse than others. Spanna 0

Zanetta Ercolana in Giroldi. Our limited experience suggests they might be the best producer in the zone. Sizzano★★

Chapter 5

The Nebbiolo Wines
of the Valtellina

In the Valtellina in northern Lombardia, vines are planted on the steep terraced hillsides on either side of the Adda River valley up to altitudes of 2000 feet. On the north the vineyards are sheltered from the cold northern winds by the Rhaetian alps; to the south the Orobie pre-alps hold out the humidity and fog of the Padana plains. Situated at the northern end of Lake Como, the vineyards receive the benefit of the moderating winds from the lake which also help to dry the moisture on the vines after rain.

The growing zone of the Valtellina, entirely in the province of Sondrio, extends 24 miles (40 kilometers) east from Ardenno to Tirano, encompassing 3415 acres (1382 hectares). The vines produce an average annual yield of 4.7 million gallons, less than half of it—2.4 million gallons (90,000 hectoliters)—DOC Valtellina and Valtellina Superiore. The total production of the two DOCs is slightly less than that of Barolo and Barbaresco combined, from an area some two-thirds the size of Barolo alone (2075 acres, or 869 hectares). Overproduction is a problem.

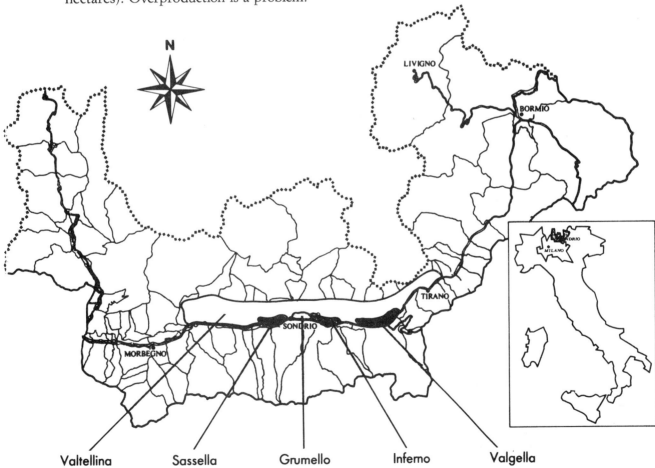

Valtellina   Sassella   Grumello   Inferno   Valgella

The vine is believed to have been cultivated in the Valtellina since before the Roman era. The wines of this general area, called Rhaetia by the Romans, were praised by Virgil. Svetonio recorded that Augustus counted these wines among his favorites. Pliny also wrote of the Rhaetian wines and very likely referred to the Valtellina wines in particular, which he should have known well since he was a native of Como. Leonardo da Vinci was more specific, noting in his Codice Atlantico that the "Volotolina...valley surrounded by high and terrible mountains makes powerful wines."

The defining grape, the one that gives character and personality to the Valtellina wines, is the nebbiolo, here known as chiavennasca, apparently taking its name from the town of Chiavenna, to the north and east of the DOC zone. The wines of the Valtellina are made from at least 70 percent chiavennasca; the Superiore is made from 95 percent. Brugnola, merlot, pignola, pinot nero (pinot noir), and rossola grapes, in varying proportions, make up the difference.

The regular Valtellina is a wine best drunk within one to three years of the vintage, though there are a few exceptions which will live a bit longer. The better, more serious wines from the area carry the designation *superiore* and generally speaking *are* superior to those labeled simply Valtellina. Unfortunately, though, they are rarely on a par with— never mind superior to—the other nebbiolo wines to the west, in Piemonte and the Valle d'Aosta.

Valtellina Superiore

The Valtellina Superiore wines have higher alcohol than the regular—12 percent—and are aged at least two years, one in oak. They have a fruity–floral bouquet, sometimes displaying nutlike notes. These wines are usually at their best between five to ten years of the vintage. The Superiore wines often carry the name of the subregion where the grapes are grown: Grumello, Inferno, Sassella, or Valgella. These vineyards are all on the right bank of the Adda facing south. Some 1200 acres (488 hectares) of vines are in the DOC zone. From 1977 to 1984, production here averaged 265,000 cases a year.

Grumello

The Grumello district, located between Sondrio and Montagna, has vineyards covering 257 acres (104 hectares). Average production is more than 56,500 cases.

Grumello has an aroma that recalls strawberries and, for some, faded roses. It is at its best about five to six years after the vintage.

The regarded crus of Grumello include Castel Grumello, Sassorosso, and Stangone. Enologica Valtellinese owns the 5.2-acre (2.1-hectare) Castel Grumello plot, from which they have been bottling a cru since 1975. They produce an average of 18,000 bottles a year.

> *Recommended producers*
> Enologica Valtellinese (Castel Grumello)
> Negri
> Pelizatti (Sassorosso)
> Rainoldi
> San Carlo (Stangone)

Grumello is a good wine to accompany pork roast and chops or poultry such as quail or guinea hen.

Inferno

The Inferno district extends from Poggiridenti east to Tresivio. With only 166 acres (67 hectares) of vines, it is the smallest of the four subregions. Average production of Inferno is 38,750 cases a year. It is perhaps also the warmest district, taking its name, they say, from the intense summer heat in its steeply terraced vineyards. Inferno has, in fact, the steepest slopes in the Valtellina.

The bouquet of the Inferno wines is noted for suggestions of strawberries, violets, and hazelnuts. It is at its best within six to eight years of the vintage.

Al Carmine and Paradiso are two regarded crus of Inferno. The Paradiso vineyard extends into Sassella as well. The wine is generally described as being more similar in character to the Inferno wines, though, than to those of Sassella. Enologica Valtellinese owns 8.9 acres (3.6 hectares) of the Paradiso vineyard, from which they have been bottling a Paradiso riserva since 1968. Production is about 35,000 bottles annually. The wine is aged for four years in slavonian oak casks.

Recommended producers
Enologica Valtellinese (Paradiso)
Negri
Rainoldi
San Carlo (Al Carmine)

Sassella

Sassella, the only subregion west of the town of Sondrio, takes in 376 acres (152 hectares) of vines between Castione Andevenno and Sondrio. Average annual production is about 77,200 cases. It is the fullest in body of the Valtellina wines and matures somewhat more slowly than the others; it is also the longest-lived. Sassella is at its best from about seven to nine years of the vintage. Some tasters find notes of hazelnuts and spice in these wines. Sassella makes a good accompaniment to pork or lamb chops and steak.

Regarded crus of Sassella include Ai Grigioni, Paradiso, and Sasso dal Corvo.

Recommended producers
Enologica Valtellinese
"La Castellina"
Negri
Nera
Rainoldi
San Carlo (Ai Grigioni)
Tona (Sasso dal Corvo)
Triacca (Paradiso)

Valgella

Valgella, the largest subregion with 408 acres (165 hectares) of vines, is in the *communes* of Chiuro, Tresenda, and Teglio. Average production is 94,200 cases a year.

The wines of Valgella mature within three to four years of the vintage. In aroma they are said to recall strawberries, hazelnuts, and *goudron,* or tar.

Valgella is the lightest in body of the Valtellina Superiore wines and the shortest-lived—many would also add the most variable in quality. About five or six years ago, when we were drinking a lot more Valtellina Superiore wines, however, we found Valgella, contrary to its reputation, to be the most consistent in quality and generally the best with the exception of some special selections from the other districts.

Valgella goes well with pork, veal, or turkey.

Caven is a regarded cru.

Recommended producers
Nera
Rainoldi
San Carlo (Caven)

Riserva

The term *riserva* on Valtellina Superiore indicates that the wine has been given four years of aging. The riservas tend to be fuller in body and richer in flavor than the regular Valtellina Superiore wines. We have enjoyed a number of fine riservas from Pelizatti, especially the '61 and '64 Riserva Della Casa, and many bottles of Nino Negri's Castel Chiuro Riserva. This last wine, because of a ruling by the Common Market bureaucrats in Brussels, can no longer be labeled Castel Chiuro but simply Nino Negri riserva, since Negri doesn't own an actual castle. (A *castel* must be a castle, it seems, but a *chateau* may be only a shed.) The wine, however, is none the worse for the name change.

Some other Valtellina special selections we've enjoyed are Nera's Signorie and Negri's Fracia.

The Perla Villa of Tona is a regular Valtellina (not a riserva), being produced from 70 percent chiavennasca and 30 percent pignola grapes. Pelizatti's Runchet Valtellina is a blend of all six allowable grape varieties, at least 70 percent being chiavennasca.

Sfursat

Sfursat, or Sforzato, is similar in some ways to an Amarone. It is made from late-harvested grapes—in this case mostly chiavennasca—which are left to dry on frames or mats for a month or two after the harvest, sometimes until the end of January or February. The very sweet, concentrated grapes are fermented until there is no sugar left, producing a dry wine of at least 14.5 percent alcohol.

A. D. Francis in *The Wine Trade,*[4] writes of a "Valtelline wine" from the seventeenth century made from dried grapes, but unlike the Sfursat of today, at least, this wine was aged quite differently. He notes that Gilbert Burnet, Bishop of Salisbury, described it as

> an aromatic wine tasting like a strong water drawn off spices and, though a natural wine, as strong as brandy. The grapes were left on the vines until November to ripen thoroughly and then kept in garrets for two or three months before pressing. The liquor was then put into an open vessel, where it threw off a scum twice a day for a week or a fortnight, after which it was put into a closed vessel and for the first year was very sweet and luscious, but at the end of the year about a third was drawn off and replaced with newer wine and so on every year. Every March it fermented and for a long time became undrinkable, but each year it slowly became stronger. Burnet met a lady named Madame de Salis who had kept such wine for forty years. It had become so strong that one could not drink more than a thimbleful.

Sfursat is full-bodied wine, tannic and robust, with richness of flavor and a complex aroma with suggestions of raisins, figs, nuts and spices. It can age for up to seven or eight years, occasionally longer. It is a good wine to accompany hearty stews, braised meats, and strong cheeses, especially gorgonzola.

Recommended producers
Enologica Valtellinese
Negri
Nera
Rainoldi

Vintages in the Valtellina

In rating the vintages in the Valtellina, we have had to rely on the evaluations of others more often than on our own sometimes very limited experience. We have noted where our own opinions differ. from the '67s on, we provide our own evaluations based on personal tasting experience, except where otherwise needed.

The most highly regarded vintages (four stars) since World War II have been 1947, 1952, 1964, and 1983. We have greatly enjoyed quite a number of '64s, including the Negri Castel Chiuro Riserva and Pelizatti Riserva della Casa and Grumello riserva, as well as the Inferno and Sassella riservas of Enologica Valtellinese. These wines were, in fact, the finest Valtellina wines we have tasted. We can't comment on the '47s and '52s except to say that most likely the wines are too old today. The '64s could still be holding their own if they had proper storage. As for the '83s, we haven't yet had the pleasure.

Vintages on the next level, rated very good (three stars), are 1954, 1957, 1959, 1961, 1969, 1970, 1971, 1978, and 1982. We are not familiar with the '54s. We've only tasted one bottle of '57, an Enologica Valtellinese Inferno Riserva—insufficient to judge the overall quality of the vintage. We've had a number of '59s and '61s and concur that these were very good years indeed, though they didn't quite come up to 1964. We have very much enjoyed the '59 Negri Castel Chiuro Riserva and the '61 Riserva della Casa, Grumello and Sassella of Pelizatti.

The Enologica Valtellinese lists 1954, 1957, 1961, 1964, 1969, 1978, 1980, and 1983 as excellent vintages and 1972 as the worst.

	Originally rated	Probable rating today	Comment
1984	?	?	Like elsewhere in Italy, it was a difficult vintage.
1983	★★★★	[★★★★]	Like the '82s, they are still too young to receive full marks.
1982	★★★	[★★★]	Too young to really judge yet.
1981	★★	[★★]	We can't comment, not having tasted them.
1980	★★	★★	The authorities rated this vintage ★★. Those we tasted seem to bear out that rating.
1979	★★	★★	There was some very good Sforzato made. The other wines were generally good and are still holding. The best Sassellas should still improve.
1978	★★★	★★★	Splendid wines, the best of the decade, and surely the best since the great '64s. The regular Valtellina Superiore are showing very well now. The riservas can still improve.
1977	0	0	Vintage that should have been declassified.
1976	★	0	Only 1977 was worse in the decade.
1975	★[★]	0	Most of the '75s are probably too old now. Sforzato, which should be still showing well, rates ★★.
1974	★★★	★★★	We found these wines better than others did. In fact, many of the '74s were the best Valtellinas we had tasted since the '64s. The best riservas should still be good, and there's a good chance that the better regular Valtellina Superiore are also holding, though there's probably no point in keeping them any longer.
1973	★[★]	0	Light wines overall. Though better than the Novara–Vercelli and Aosta–Torino nebbiolos, they still weren't much better than average. They're most likely too old now.
1972	0	0	Others gave the vintage ★, but judging from our experience, the '72s should never have been bottled.
1971	★★	[★]	Authorities gave this vintage ★★★. Based on our own experiences (numerous '71s though no Sforzato), many were high in acidity and rather thin. It's possible that some riservas have held; the Sfursats are probably still good★★[★].
1970	★★★	★★[★]	As with the other nebbiolo wines, this was a very good vintage for the Valtellinas. The best riservas could still be holding. As for the rest, probably not; fifteen years is too long for most Valtellinas, Superiore or no.

	Originally rated	Probable rating today	Comment
1969	★★★	★[★]	Some excellent Sforzato was produced. The best riservas could still be good. The regular Valtellina Superiore wines are most likely gone.
1968	★	0	We've enjoyed some very good bottles and at one time might have given the vintage ★★(★). Now the wines are probably too old.
1967	★★★	★★[★]	Authorities gave the vintage only ★★. We dissent; we've always considered it a very fine vintage. The best riservas should still be holding, but it is doubtful whether they will improve.
1966	★	0	
1965	0	0	
1964	★★★★	★★★	These were magnificent wines. The best riservas could still be if they were stored well.
1963	★	0	
1962	★	0	
1961	★★★	★[★]	A very fine vintage, on a par with 1967. In the decade, only 1964 was better. Given proper storage, the riservas could still be drinking well.
1960	0	0	
1959	★★★	★[★]	
1958	★	0	
1957	★★★	★	
1956	★	0	
1955	★	0	
1954	★★★	★	
1953	0	0	
1952	★★★★	★★[★]	
1951	★	0	
1950	★	0	
1949	★	0	
1948	★	0	
1947	★★★★	★★[★]	
1946	★	0	
1945	★★	0	

Tasting Notes

1980

Perlavilla, Tona di Gianluigi Bonisolo *(9/83)*. Light-bodied, light in tannin, simple, fruity, agreeable, ready.★

Sassella, Nera *(4/85)*. Small nose; not a lot of tannin, a bit light in body, tasty; needs two or three years yet to be at its best.★(★)

Sassella, Tona di Gianluigi Bonisolo *(9/83)*. Unexpectedly full in aroma and flavor; light tannin, good fruit; ready.★

Sforzato, Tona di Gianlugi Bonisolo *(9/83)*. Lacks the characteristic richness of a Sforzato though has nice enough flavor, light tannin, quite forward; more or less ready.★

Sfursat, Rainoldi *(9/83)*. Floral aroma with hints of raisins; a bit light but has a lot of flavor; quite nice and surprisingly ready.★★

1979

Sforzato, Enologica Valtellinese *(4/85)*. Concentrated aroma with a dried fruit character; a big wine, robust and flavorful; still tannic but enjoyable now.★★★ −

Sforzato, Nera *(6 times 7/84)*. Medium brick; an aroma of cherries and raisins; fairly full-bodied, good fruit; should be ready soon.★★

Valtellina "La Taberna" Tona di Gianluigi Bonisolo *(9/83)*. Pale garnet; small aroma; tasty, light tannin; a nice glass of wine now.★

Valtellina "Tellino," Nera *(4/81)*. Fresh, fruity, peppery aroma; simple, high acidity, moderate fruit; marred by alcohol on the aftertaste.

1978

Grumello, Rainoldi *(9/83)*. Full, rich bouquet with suggestions of nuts and flowers; moderate tannin, has the stuffing and backbone; drinks well now but can, and should, improve with two to three more years.★★(★)

Inferno, Nera *(9/82)*. Bouquet has notes of vanilla and fruit; well balanced, light tannin, lots of flavor; ready now though room for improvement★★

Inferno, Rainoldi *(9/83)*. Light garnet; well balanced, some tannin, light-bodied, tasty; ready but should improve yet.★★

Inferno Riserva della Casa, Enologica Valtellinese *(6/85; 10,600 bottles)*. Fairly rich, floral, nutty aroma; light tannin, flavorful; quite ready; tails off toward the end.★★ +

Sassella, Rainoldi *(9/83)*. Pale garnet; not much aroma; more forward on the palate than the Grumello or Inferno, nice fruit, light-bodied, even a bit simple.

Valgella, Rainoldi *(9/83)*. Nose has a suggestion of nuts; light tannin, well balanced, lots of flavor, enjoyable now.★★

Valtellina, Rainoldi *(twice 9/83)*. Small aroma; light-bodied, not a lot of tannin; enjoyable now and very ready. A bottle tasted one year earlier, though somewhat better, also merited ★.

1977

Sassella, Enologica Valtellinese *(9/81)*. Pale color; small nose; light-bodied, high in acid, some fruit, drinkable; finish is rather harsh.

1977

Sfursat, Negri (*twice 9/82*). Lacks the expected richness and intensity on aroma and palate, some glycerine, nice flavor, not to keep. A bottle tasted eighteen months earlier seemed to need more age; this one shows signs of fading.

1976

Grumello, Rainoldi (*3/81*). Floral bouquet with a nutlike note; very good for the vintage, fairly well balanced, nice flavor, some style; for present drinking.★

Inferno, Nera (*4/80*). Berrylike aroma; light-bodied, some tannin, fruity; very ready now, but it should hold for a year, possibly two.★

Sassella, Rainoldi (*9/82*). Small aroma; light-bodied, some tannin, lacks weight, unstructured.

1975

Inferno, Enologica Valtellinese (*11/79*). Pale color; hot, alcoholic aroma; more flavor than the nose suggests, but gives way to too much tannin; short, dull aftertaste; already too old.

Inferno, San Carlo Vigna Al Carmine (*6 times 12/83*). Brick red; some berrylike fruit on nose; high acid, drying out a bit, but still has some flavor and interest. Bottles tasted a few years earlier, though better, never amounted to a lot either.

Sassella, Nera (*4/80*). Fruity aroma marred by alcohol; light to medium body, somewhat off-balance with too much tannin.

Sassella, San Carlo Vigna Ai Grigioni (*6 times 12/83*). Brick red; small floral aroma; somewhat light in body, decent balance, some tannin, acid a trifle high but adds liveliness; in all, a nice bottle, but not one to keep.★

Sforzato, Nera (*7 times 2/85*). Tawny orange at rim; moderately intense aroma with a floral character and notes of nuts and raisins; fairly nice fruit, moderately rich, some alcohol intrudes; very ready.★

Sforzato, Tona (*10/78*). Fairly rich, concentrated bouquet that recalls raisins and figs; some tannin, a lot of fruit; touch of bitterness on the aftertaste; needs some time yet, but nice now.★★(+)

Valtellina, Nera (*4/80*). Floral aroma with fruit and a touch of tar; soft and fruity, but rather light; has held up rather well but is not to keep.★

1974

Grumello, Nera (*6 times 12/83*). Brick red; fruity, vaguely floral aroma, still has fruit but is beginning to dry out.★ (It was considerably better in 1980 and 1981, when we gave it ★★+.)

Grumello, San Carlo, Vigna Stangona (*9 times 12/83*). This wine was at its best from late 1979 through 1982 when it merited ★★★. The most recent bottle tasted had a fruity, berrylike aroma; still flavor interest, but showing signs of drying out.★

Inferno, Enologica Valtellinese (*10/79*). Light-bodied, soft, has fruit, quite ready, perhaps a bit too simple; finish is rather short.★−

Inferno, Nera (*10/79*). Characteristic aroma; well balanced, nice flavor, good quality; very nice wine.★★

Inferno, Rainoldi (*11/79*). Somewhat backward and closed in, but displays a lot of fruit, still has some tannin to shed.★(★)

1974

Inferno, San Carlo, Vigna Al Carmine (*10/79*). Pleasant, characteristic aroma; fuller than the Nera and more flavorful, some tannin but nice now, could even improve.★★(★)

Sassella, Nera (*10/79*). Has body, flavor, and balance, some tannin; nearly ready.★★(★)

Sfursat, Enologica Valtellinese (*twice 2/80*). Rich and intense on aroma but lacks intensity on the palate, surprisingly soft; not to keep.★ (It was better a year earlier.)

Sfursat, Negri (*11/83*). Deep, rich, intense bouquet, recalls almonds; full and robust with the concentrated character of dried fruit; fairly long on the finish.★★

Sfursat, Rainoldi (*10/82*). Raisiny, concentrated aroma; full-bodied, moderate tannin, some alcohol intrudes, but has a lot of fruit.★(★)

Valgella, Nera (*8 times 12/83*). This wine was at its best from 10/78 to 4/80, when it merited ★★+. The bottles tasted in 3/81 showed signs of fading; the last bottle was drying out, with noticeable volatile acidity, though still some flavor interest.

Valgella, San Carlo, Vigna Caven (*9 times 12/83*). This wine was at its best in 1979 and 1980, when it merited ★★+, by 1981, it was showing signs of senility. By 12/83, it was already somewhat oxidized, and although some flavor remained the wine was falling apart.

Valtellina, Nera (*10/78*). Seems too light, lacking substance and weight; probably was better a year or two ago.

Valtellina Superiore, Nera "Signorie" (*9 times 10/78–11/82*). The more recent bottles were better than the earlier ones, having the benefit of more age. Latest bottle: Color shading to tawny; lovely bouquet with some delicacy; smooth texture, well balanced, and stylish; a long finish; ready.★★★

1973

Grumello, Nera (*10/78*). Nice nose; medium-bodied, still some tannin to lose, seems to have the fruit to develop.★(★?)

Inferno, Nera (*10/78*). Some varietal character on nose; light- to medium-bodied, some tannin, nice flavor.★★

Inferno, Negri (*11/78*). Alcoholic nose; light to medium in body, some oxidation. Was it ever better?

Inferno, Pelizatti (*11/78*). Pale color; some oxidation.

Sassella, Nera (*twice 11/82*). Bottle of 10/78: Light-bodied, but has good flavor; at its peak.★★− Bottle of 11/82: Corked.

Sassella, Polatti (*3/81*). Color showing age; some fruit and oak on nose, but alcohol intrudes; palatal impressions are favorable, but lacks some style; acceptable, no more.

Sassella, San Carlo, Vigna Ai Grigioni (*4 times 7/81*). Bottle of 10/79: Well balanced with nice flavor, perhaps even a bit young.★★ Bottle of 7/81: Has developed a nice bouquet with a nutlike nuance; quite soft, a touch of tannin; good, but not up to the earlier bottles.★

Sforzato, Enologica Valtellinese (*11/78*). Big, rich, fruity aroma that brings up cherries; light-bodied, flavorful, some tannin; bitter finish.★

Sfursat, Negri (*twice 11/79*). Nice flavor, some concentration and tannin, nearly ready.★★−

159

1972

Sforzato, Pelizatti *(11/78)*. One-dimensional aroma with characteristic raisiny note; some tannin, perhaps too much, good flavor; touch of bitterness on finish.★

1971

Fracia riserva, Negri *(11/78)*. Note of hazelnuts on aroma, marred by some alcohol; has tannin and nice flavor, but where will it go? Some alcohol intrudes on the finish, which is short.★ −

Grumello, Rainoldi *(11/79)*. Some oxidation, thin, off-balance.

Sassella riserva, Nera *(twice 4/80)*. The more recent bottle was better; fruity aroma with hints of nuts; a mouthful of tannin but seems to have the fruit to outlast it, a knife-and-fork wine; try again in two, perhaps three years.★(★ +)

Sassella riserva, Pelizatti *(11/78)*. Lightish color; some oxidation, alcoholic, not a lot of fruit; bitter finish.

1970

Grumello riserva, Pelizatti "Sassorosso" *(11/78)*. Pale garnet; some oxidation and alcohol on the nose, little else; some flavor interest on entry, and then *nulla*.

Sassella riserva, Enologica Valtellinese *(4/80)*. Dried out!

1969

Sfursat, Negri *(6 times 11/82)*. Some oxidation, but also a dried, concentrated raisiny note, some tannin; drying out but not totally gone. Without question, it was better three to four years ago when it merited ★★ +.

1967

Valtellina Superiore riserva, Nino Negri *(11/78)*. This wine is made from a selection of Negri's best grapes from Grumello, Inferno, and Sasella. Fruity aroma, seems to have still more to give; a bit light in body, some tannin, a lot of fruit; should improve yet.★★(+)

1964

Grumello riserva, Pelizatti "Sassorosso" *(3/82)*. Intense, concentrated bouquet; follows through with the same richness on the palate, smooth and flavorful; very impressive indeed.★★★ +

Sassella riserva, Enologica Valtellinese *(3/80)*. Brick with orange reflections; floral aroma marred by some va; still some tannin and flavor, but beginning to dry out.★ −

Valtellina Superiore Negri "Castel Chiuro Riserva" *(12 times 3/82)*. The bottles from the 1970s were magnificent, meriting ★★★ +. Those tasted since 1980 still offered some interest but were on the way downhill. For the memory ★★★; the wine today 0.

1957

Inferno, Enologica Valtellinese *(11/79)*. Pale garnet; fragrant, nutlike aroma, quite lovely, but with a touch of oxidation; considerable tannin, some fruit; probably was better a few years ago.★★

The Producers of Valtellina Superiore

In all, fourteen producers bottle all four denominations of Valtellina Superiore; additionally, one producer bottles Grumello and Sassella, and one bottles only a Sassella.

Producer	Grumello	Inferno	Sassella	Sfursat	Valgella	Selections
Balgera Rag. Gianfranco	x	x	x	—	x	—
Bettini F.lli	x	Poggiridenti	x	Spina	x	—
Enologica Valtellinese	2: regular & Castel Grumello	x	2: regular & Paradiso	x	x	Riservas
Fay Sandro	x	x	x	—	x	—
"La Castellina" Az. Agr.	—	—	x	—	—	—
Negri Nino	x	x	x	x	x	2: Riserva & Fracia
Nera Pietro	x	x	x	x	x	Signorie
Pelizatti Arturo	2: regular & Sassorosso	x	x	x	x	2: Runchet & Riserva della Casa
Polatti F.lli	x	x	x	—	—	—
Rainoldi Guiseppe	x	x	x	x	x	2: Tzapei & Vecchia Valtellina
San Carlo	Stangone	Al Carmine	Ai Grigoni	—	Caven	—
Tona G.	x	Al Carmine	Sasso dal Corvo	x	—	Perla Villa Valtellina (70% Nebbiolo)
Triacca F.lli	x	x	Paradiso	x	—	—
"Villa Bianzone" Cantina Coop	x	x	x	x	x	2: Villa & Riservas

PART II

Sangiovese

Chapter 6

The Sangiovese Grape

Sangiovese, the grape of Brunello di Montalcino, Chianti, Carmignano, Vino Nobile di Montepulciano, Torgiano, and many of the new *barrique*-aged wines of Tuscany, is one of the world's noble varieties. Sangiovese is the prominent grape of the red wines of all central Italy. It is frequently mixed with other varieties, which is the tradition here, but it is the sangiovese that gives the character, perfume, and structure to these wines. The best tend to be made from sangiovese only, or a very high proportion of it.

This widely grown variety is believed to have originated in Tuscany. At various times known as sangioveto, San Gioveto, sangioghetto, and S. Zoveto, the name in general use for the grape today is *sangiovese*. This name, according to one theory, is derived from Sanguis Jovis ("blood of Jove"), though just why is not quite clear. The wines of the sangiovese tend to be medium in color, not dark red. And Jove, though a pleasure-loving deity—the original jovial type—was not the god of wine. However it came to be named, the sangiovese today stands for a red wine of medium body, dry and firm, with a tannic spine and a floral bouquet, a wine that ages moderately well.

There are a number of subvarieties of the sangiovese and no less than fourteen clones. Among the more noted are the sangiovese piccolo, or sangiovese, and the sangiovese grosso, known as prugnolo gentile in Montepulciano and as brunello in Montalcino. Biondi-Santi claim that their brunello is a clone of the sangiovese grosso. There is a special clone of the sangiovese in the vineyards of Badia a Coltibuono in Chianti Classico and another at Castello di Nippozano in Chianti Rufina. And the old sangiovese di Lamole clone can be found at Castellare. A few other Chianti estates also have particular clones. The sangiovese di Romagna grown in Emilia-Romagna is still another.

Sangiovese dominates the red grape plantings not only of Tuscany but of Umbria and Marches as well. It is used in nearly every red wine recognized under DOC in those regions. It is widely planted in Emilia-Romagna, Marches, and Lazio. There are a significant number of vines cultivated in the province of Avellino in Campagna and in Puglia. Sangiovese is also planted in the vineyards of Abruzzo, Basilicata, Calabria, Molise, Sardinia, and Sicily.

The sangiovese grosso is said to have been introduced into Abruzzo from Montepulciano, where it became known as montepulciano d'Abruzzo for the town it came from. If this is correct, then the sangiovese is the most important red variety in Abruzzo and Molise as well.

Though Sangiovese is generally blended with other varieties, as in Chianti, Carmignano, Vino Nobile, and Torgiano, it can stand very well on its own, as demonstrated by Brunello, Le Pergole Torte of Monte Vertine, and Sangioveto of Badia a Coltibuono. This noble variety has its own character; it doesn't need to be blended with other grapes to produce an excellent wine. The wines of the sangiovese have a certain subtlety, a delicacy that is lost in fact when some other, more aggressive varieties, such as cabernet, are mixed with it. The personality of the other, more assertive grape tends to dominate, even when only a small proportion is added. When vinified on its own, or with the local varieties traditionally added to it, the characteristic fruity, floral perfume and delicacy of

MAP OF THE TUSCAN WINES D.O.C. D.O.C.G.

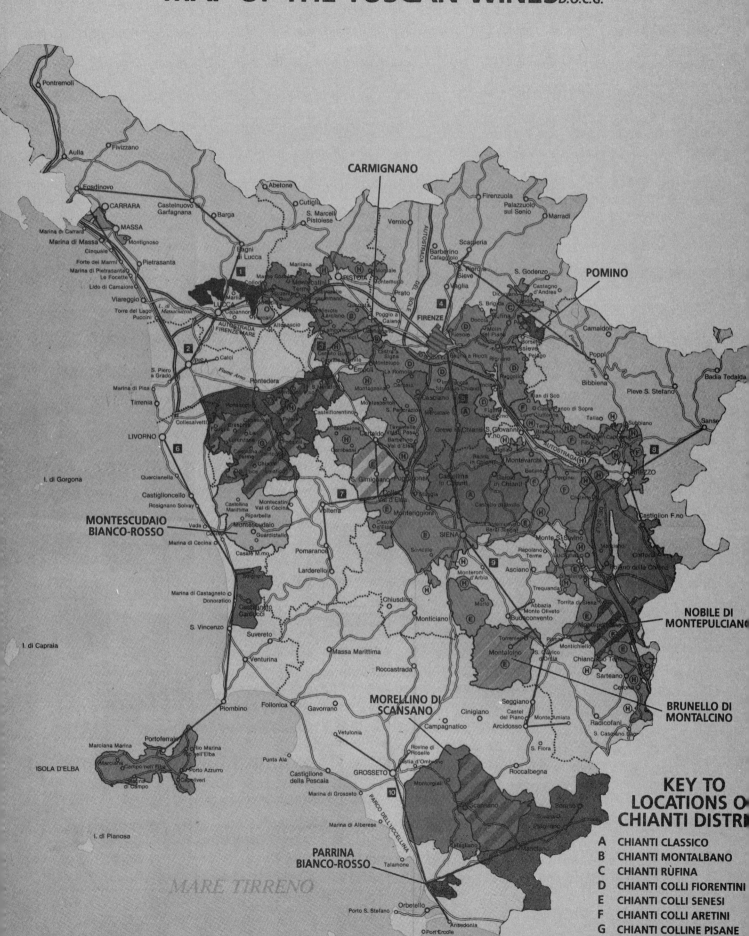

CARMIGNANO

POMINO

MONTESCUDAIO
BIANCO-ROSSO

NOBILE DI
MONTEPULCIANO

MORELLINO DI
SCANSANO

BRUNELLO DI
MONTALCINO

MARE TIRRENO

PARRINA
BIANCO-ROSSO

**KEY TO
LOCATIONS O
CHIANTI DISTRI**

A CHIANTI CLASSICO
B CHIANTI MONTALBANO
C CHIANTI RÙFINA
D CHIANTI COLLI FIORENTINI
E CHIANTI COLLI SENESI
F CHIANTI COLLI ARETINI
G CHIANTI COLLINE PISANE
H CHIANTI

the sangiovese grape shine.

In recent years a number of experiments have been made with aging sangiovese in *barrique,* which when done well adds an extra dimension to the wine. Besides interesting nuances of aroma and flavor, the tannin in the oak gives the wine a better capacity to age, developing a smoother texture and more complexity in the course of its evolution. Many of the new *barrique*-aged sangiovese wines, such as those created by enologists Maurizio Castelli and Vittorio Fiore, are especially fine wines (see Chapter 12). While we feel that the nebbiolo wines, for example, do not benefit from *barrique* aging, we find that those from the sangiovese can.

The sangiovese is the major or sole grape variety in all of the finest red wines of Tuscany, and some are very fine indeed.

Early History

Vine fossils have been discovered in Tuscany, to the west of the Chianti Classico zone, that are believed to be of the species *Vitis ausoniae,* related to the *Vitis vinifera* (wine grape) family. Before the arrival of man, the vine was growing wild in central Italy. It awaited only his talent and his ingenuity to cultivate and train it, to select and propagate its best varieties, and to harvest and vinify its fruit, to turn it into a beverage worthy of the paeans of poets. The first to recognize its possibilities were an Etruscan people, the Tuscans, who are believed to have been producing wine for their banquets and religious rituals as early as the ninth century B.C.

The Etruscans trained the vines on trees, a system that is still used in the traditional vineyards today, where the grapevines are supported, or garlanded, on wooden poles and small trees called *testucchi,*

During the dark ages after the fall of Rome, the monks who built the sturdy stone abbeys whose ruins form the nucleus of some of the wine estates of today planted monastery vineyards and kept viticulture alive, producing wine for solemn refectory meals and religious ceremonies.

From documents of the early middle ages, we learn that the white wines of the area were Trebbiano and Vernaccia, named after the grape varieties they were made from. The red wine was called Vermiglio for its bright red color. This wine was described as having a perfume of iris, the "Florence lily," or of violets, flowers that grow in colorful profusion in the countryside of Tuscany in spring.

A scent of irises is also noted in the aroma of the Chianti wine of today. Some folks say that it's typical of the sangiovese; others attribute it to a more exotic *uvaggio.* Raymond Flower[5], discussing winemaking in fourteenth-century Tuscany, records that "the practice of scenting the wine with iris flowers seems to have been very widespread"—truly a floral bouquet. It's a charming idea but seems more legendary than historical. It is surely not done any longer, yet there is still that fragrance in the Chianti wines. Many tasters find an aroma of tartufi in the bouquet of the nebbiolo wines of the Langhe, including the authors, but no one has ever suggested—at least not to our knowledge—that the winemakers of Piemonte shave tartufi into their wines!

Chapter 7

Chianti

Chianti is surely one of the most beautiful viticultural regions of the world. Her rolling hills reveal and conceal pink-roofed gray stone villas and *case coloniche*. On their slopes verdant rows of vines skirt the heights crowned with medieval villages and castles. Lines of dark cypresses stand like sentries overlooking valleys dotted with silvery-leafed olive trees, golden poplars, and broad umbrella pines. In the dusky bosks and scrub that fringe the woodlands, brightly feathered pheasants and shaggy wild boar, *cinghiale*, find refuge in the underbrush.

Chianti's fields and forests have been popular hunting grounds, and some people believe the name Chianti may be derived from this activity, first applied to the area where the hunting took place and later to the wine produced there. It's an idea that holds a certain charm for those of us who enjoy a fine Chianti with roast pheasant or *pappardelle* with game sauce, or one of the bigger styles with braised *cinghiale*.

One theory on the origin of the Chianti name, proposed by E. Repetti, suggests that it comes from the Latin word *clangere* or *clango* which referred to the sounds of the hunt—bird calls, cries of alarm, and the blast of the hunting horns. This later evolved into Clantum or Clanti, in Italian becoming Chianti.[6]

S. Pieri rejects this theory and offers another. He speculates that Clante was an Etruscan family name and that the land that was under their ownership or rule became known by their name, which later evolved into the modern Chianti.[7]

It seems a logical explanation. Historian Alessandro Boglione states, however, that the name of Clante has not been found on any of the Etruscan tombs in the area, sometimes marked with stones bearing inscriptions in the Etruscan language (still basically undeciphered) which are believed to be family names.

The first written reference to Chianti that has been found is in a twelfth-century copy of a document from A.D. 790 in the possession of the Badia di S. Bartolomeo at Ripoli. This parchment confirms a donation of land to the monastery, including a property in Chianti; *"curte in Clanti cum integro salingo."*[8]

Again in the twelfth century, a document from 1148, preserved at Badia a Coltibuono, records that Ildibrandino and his wife gave to his brother Bullitto property in the territory of Chianti inherited from his mother and granted him all rights on the estates and leased properties: *"Omnes terras et res quae dicti iugales habent per matrem in Clanti,"* and *"De omnibus libellariis, feodis e tenimentis suis qui habent in predicto territorio de Clanti."*[9]

A few other references from the twelfth and thirteenth centuries to the region of Chianti have been found in various deeds and documents, including what perhaps constitutes official recognition of the name in 1260, in the Libro di Montaperti, a register of official records of the Florentine Republic.[10]

Written reference to the name of Chianti being applied to wine is not found until more than a century later. In the book *Compagnia del Banco*, published in December of 1398, Francesco Datini and Bartolomeo Cambioni write of Francescho di Marcho and Stoldo di Lorenzo, who are in debt to Piero di Tino Riccio for 3 florins, 26 soldi, and 8 denari, the price of 6 casks of white Chianti wine.[11] So the first reference so far found to the wine of Chianti was of a white wine, which is rather ironic because the law does not allow the white wine of the region to carry the Chianti name since the inauguration of DOC in 1967.

According to Paronetto,[12] the wine of Chianti was named in the miracle play of San Antonio performed during the latter half of the fifteenth century with the lines:

Io n'ho di Chianti e vin di San Losino
Trebbian dolci, vernaccia e malvagia.
I have some Chianti and wine of San Losino
Sweet trebbiano, vernaccia and malvasia.

Written records of the wine being called Chianti, though they have been found, are rather rare. The wine continued to be more commonly known as Vermiglio or Vin di Firenze (Florence wine) into the seventeenth century.

In England, the wine of Chianti was known as Florence. A. D. Francis notes that in the 1590s

> the wines of Florence were well regarded, but were inclined to go off quickly and needed to be shipped promptly through the Strait of Gibraltar before the late autumn winds from the Atlantic held them up.[13]

André Simon cites an entry in Pepys' diary of January 8, 1661, recording that he was served Florence at Lady Sandwich's house. And he was apparently appreciative of it (or else remarked that it would be a wine that Mrs. Pepys could enjoy) as her ladyship, he noted, presented him with two bottles of the same wine for his wife.[14]

Others of Pepys's countrymen were less impressed, but the British were in many cases just looking for a temporary substitute for their beloved Claret while they were involved in another war with France.

Interesting Parallels

They could have done worse in their choice; there are a number of similarities between the wines of the two regions. Chianti, like Bordeaux, is made from a blend of grape varieties, which some wine drinkers feel adds to the wine's complexity. The best Bordeaux and the best Chianti are medium-bodied wines with a certain elegance, firm acidity, and a tannic backbone. They age gracefully, developing nuances of bouquet and flavor. The French wines take longer to soften and open up, but at their respective peaks the wines have a similar style. Both are made in two basic styles, one meant to be drunk young and fresh (though not as young for the Bordeaux) and the other to be aged.

The Chianti made for present drinking is light and fresh, simple and straightforward. It is meant to quench thirst and to accompany everyday meals. This style of Chianti is the most common, in both senses of the word. It is not the Chianti that concerns us here.

The second style of Chianti is a wine to sip and to savor, to pour at more important meals, at dinners with friends who appreciate fine wine, and on quiet evenings when one relaxes over a glass, giving full attention to the finished product of the winemaker's art.

The more serious style of Chianti is bottled in the shouldered Bordeaux bottle, designed to be laid down to age. It needs five or more years to mature and soften its youthful harshness. At its best—generally from five to eight years of the vintage—it is a stylish, aristocratic wine. From a good vintage it can age for ten to fifteen years. Some notable exceptions to this limit are the Monsanto Il Poggio, Castello di Nipozzano, Fattoria Montagliari, Villa Selvapiana, Badia a Coltibuono, and Ruffino Riserva Ducale gold label. These and a few others can live for decades, developing subtle nuances of aroma and flavor, mellowing to a velvety texture, and leaving a lingering impression on the palate and on the memory. Generally the best Chiantis for aging come from the Classico and Rùfina zones.

Chianti Vintages

Vintages in Chianti vary greatly from one area to another. The region is too vast and the exposures and microclimates too diverse to have consistent weather conditions for the year throughout any one zone, let alone the entire region.

Some clue to the quality of a vintage, however, seems better than no idea at all. So we offer here an overall evaluation of the wines of the last decade, with the note that they are and can be only generalizations. Since Chianti rarely lives beyond eight years of the vintage, we are including ratings only back to 1975. These refer to the probable condition of the wines today. Vintage information for the Chianti Classico and Rùfina zones is covered under those zones.

1984	★	1979	★★
1983	★★★	1978	★★
1982	★★	1977	★★
1981	0	1976	0
1980	★	1975	★★ −

The Chianti *Uvaggio*

From as early as we know, Chianti has been made from an *uvaggio,* or a blend of grapes, both red and white. At different periods and in the hands of different producers the mix has varied.

The Accademia dei Georgofili, a noted agricultural society, experimented with many combinations early in the nineteenth century and came up with a recommended blend using equal portions of canaiolo, San Gioveto, roverusto, and mammolo to produce a wine of body with a capacity to age, while a wine made from occhio di pernice, trebbiano, canaiolo, and mammolo in equal measure was advised for a more delicate wine for drinking young.

Barone Bettino Ricasoli, in the second half of the nineteenth century, developed his own formula. He got the most satisfactory results with a blend of seven to eight parts sangiovese and two to three parts canaiolo. If the wine was to be consumed young, he included a small amount of malvasia. Ricasoli noted in a letter to Professor Studiati of the University of Pisa that the sangiovese contributed bouquet and vigor, canaiolo added sweetness to soften the acidity of the sangiovese without diminishing the bouquet, and the malvasia added flavor and freshness and made the wine lighter and more accessible for everyday drinking. He noted, though, that this grape should be kept to a minimum in wines for aging.[15]

As tastes in wine change, the *uvaggio* in Chianti has also changed. In earlier days, a light, easy-drinking style was preferred, a young wine of the year that didn't require cellar aging to become soft and ready (one similar to the simple young Chiantis of today). Many modern wine drinkers prefer a more serious wine, a Chianti with more depth, character, and style, one to be laid away to develop complexity and finesse. This means a wine with more sangiovese and less trebbiano. Some canaiolo may still be added to mellow the sangiovese. But trebbiano (Italy's answer to California's ubiquitous thompson seedless) with a lot of juice and little character has no place here.

The producers, recognizing the shift in consumer demand, have fought for changes in the wine laws to reflect this change in tastes.

Many Chianti producers have openly admitted to us that they use only sangiovese in their wine. Despite the government regulations, they are not diluting their wines with other, lesser varieties, especially whites—a situation the rule makers in Rome have tacitly acknowledged and which is reflected in the nominal amount of white grapes now required in Chianti under the new regulations.

	DOCG		DOC
	Classico	Other	
Sangiovese	75–90%	75–90%	50–80%
Canaiolo	5–10	5–10	10–30
Trebbiano } Malvasia }	2– 5	5–10	10–20
Other red grapes	0–10	0– 0	0– 5

Canaiolo

Canaiolo nero, canajolo rosso, or canajuolo rosso, as it has variously been known, has been cultivated in Tuscany since at least the thirteenth century. Pier de Crescenzi, writing in his monumental twelve-volume *Ruralium Commodorum Libri Duodecum* on agriculture published in the thirteenth century, describes the canaiolo nero. Paronetto[16] cites Giovan Cosimo Villani of Florence, who wrote in the eighteenth century that Chianti was made predominantly from canaiolo nero plus small amounts of sangioveto, mammolo, and marzemino.

Malvasia del Chianti

Malvasia del Chianti, or malvasia toscana, is a white variety native to Chianti. It is fruity and perfumed, though less so than the malvasia of the south, which is another variety, and oxidizes easily.

Trebbiano

Trebbiano, grown in Tuscany since at least the thirteenth century, has been included in a number of Chianti blends, but not all. Barone Ricasoli, credited for inventing modern Chianti, recommended using a small proportion of white grapes and then only the malvasia variety. He did not advise using trebbiano at all, a grape he considered lacking in character.

Actually, trebbiano wasn't all that common in the *uvaggio* before the advent of DOC in 1967, when a number of producers and growers lobbied for a greater proportion of white grapes, including the trebbiano, to be required in Chianti. Today, with the emergence of Bianco della Lega, Galestro, and a few other new Tuscan whites to take up the slack, the DOCG commission has reduced the white grapes in Chianti to no more than Trebbiano toscano, the grape known in France and California as Saint Emilion or ugni blanc. (The trebbiano di Soave, trebbiano giallo, and trebbiano d'Abruzzo grown in other regions of Italy are different varieties.) The Tuscan trebbiano (with very rare exceptions, and those in the hands of some very talented winemakers) produces neutral wines that must be consumed while they are very young and fresh, before they lose their fruit or oxidize, which they do they do very easily. What does this grape add to the overall blend? You might say that the trebbiano adds elasticity—that is, it allows the wine to be stretched.

Governo

The use of *governo,* a second fermentation created by the addition of dried grapes or the must of dried or concentrated grapes, is traditional in Tuscany. It was recommended as early as the mid-fourtheenth century, though it probably wasn't in widespread use until much later. In a tract published in 1364, Ruberto di Guido Bernardi advised that winemakers employ a governing process, or "governo," to better control the quality of their vintages. He wrote that a small quantity of grape bunches from the trebbiano nero (a variety virtually unknown today) should be set aside in the *cantina* to dry, then added to the wine to initiate a second fermentation. His colleague, Francesco di Giovanni di Durante, was in basic agreement with the system but differed on the starter. Durante advocated using sun-dried white grapes that had been crushed and heated before being added to the wine.[17]

Governo was not a new idea, although, like many other "innovations" of the middle ages, it may have been reinvented. In the second century B.C., Cato advised winemakers to add a small portion of juice from grapes reduced by boiling to their wine. Pliny wrote in *Natural History* of the practice of adding cooked must to counteract harshness. And Columella, in *De Re Rusticus,* included a recipe for it.

What does governo do for the wine? It adds needed body, fruit, and glycerine to thin wines. The carbon dioxide it creates gives the wine freshness and lightness. And the sweet concentrated berries bring down the total acidity in the wine. It does tend to increase the volatile acidity, however, and produces a wine that is more susceptible to oxidation.

For the governo toscano, or *all' uso Chianti,* 10 to 15 percent of must from grapes gathered before the harvest and partially dried on *cannici* (reed trays) or *castelli,* (wicker frames) is added to the wine before December 31. The fermentation thus created continues until late January or February, even into March. A *rigoverno* is yet another induced fermentation done in March or April.

Governo is being used less and less commonly today for one reason or another. One of the reasons given is that wines made with governo don't age. We find a lot of evidence to contradict this point of view. Ruffino's especially fine Riserva Ducale gold label is made with governo, and it is a wine that can take a lot of age, judging by the '47, as well as others we tasted from the 1950s in recent years. The Montagliari Chiantis from the 1950s that we tasted recently, also made with governo, had aged very well. We could point to a number of Chianti Classicos from the '71 and '75 vintages made without benefit of governo that are falling apart already.

Fabrizio Bianchi of Monsanto, who produces some very long-lived Chianti Classico, used governo until 1968. He made the wine in the traditional manner, using the whole unstemmed bunches, crushed by foot in the first years and by hand with a nail-studded cudgel which only broke up a small portion of the grapes. To soften some of the harshness picked up from the stems, he added some white grapes and used governo (and made a lovely wine, by the way). When he eliminated the stems, he also stopped using the governo (and the white grapes as well in his Il Poggio riserva).

The colorino is regarded as a good grape to be used in governo. Both Cappelli and Ruffino, though, use selected bunches of sangiovese in their wines.

One reason generally not given for abandoning the procedure by those no longer using governo is the extra cost of the labor involved. We are inclined to believe that this has been more of a factor in most decisions to dispense with the process than the ageability of the wines. Many estates that still use governo are now adding grape concentrate rather than the grape bunches, gathered and sorted, laid out to dry and tended, collected and crushed, and added to the wine vats. The concentrate is considerably cheaper, particularly when bought from the south—up to 15 percent of wine or must from outside the zone is, or was until recently, allowed in Chianti. Just open the can, add to the wine, and stir!

Fine Chiantis are made both with the traditional governo (the Montagliari, Poggio al Sole, and Ruffino, for example) and without it (such as the Selvapiana, Nipozzano, and Capannelle).

Chianti Territory

Chianti is produced in the Tuscan provinces of Arezzo, Firenze, Pisa, Pistoia, and Siena. This area encompasses 8650 registered grape-growing farms with 1.2 million acres (466,000 hectares), nearly 150,000 (60,000) of which are in vines. The Chianti-growing region is one of large wine estates, as in Bordeaux, instead of small vineyards divided among multiple owners, as in the Langhe and Burgundy. Many of the vineyards in Chianti are planted in *coltura esclusiva,* in specialized vineyards, but there are also still many in *coltura promiscua,* in rows interspersed with olive trees and other crops.

Under *mezzadria,* the feudal system, which lasted up until 1967 here when it was prohibited by law, grapes were only one of the variety of crops a tenant farmer needed to provide for his family. When *mezzadria* died out, many vineyards were replanted exclusively to vines. But there were many that were not replanted, sometimes because of the olive trees, which were too valuable to pull out. (The olive tree, which lives for centuries, takes many years to bear fine quality fruit.) After the catastrophic freeze in the winter of 1984–1985, which destroyed most of the olive trees in Tuscany, the countryside will take on a bleaker aspect in years to come. The loss will be more than one of esthetic pleasure in the balanced beauty of the landscape; it will be gustatorial as well, with only the rare drop of Tuscany's liquid gold to be found until the extensively replanted *oliveti* once again resume production. (The full extent of the damage is yet to be fully assessed; hopefully it has been much overestimated.)

More than 40 million gallons (1.5 million hectoliters) of Chianti are produced a year, much of it young Chianti—light, simple, fresh, straightforward wine meant to be drunk within the year. This was the Chianti sold in the rustic straw-covered fiaschi. Some of it still is, through considerably less than previously, as the cost of the labor to wrap the flasks in straw is frequently more than the value of the wine inside. The baskets woven around the bottles, originally made to protect the fragile blown-glass containers as they were jostled about in shipment by oxcart, and perhaps also to hold the bulbous flasks upright when set on the table, were later maintained at least in part for their picturesque charm. They also made the two styles more obvious to distinguish on the merchant's shelf, as the fiasco was obviously not suitable for laying a wine down to age.

Chianti and the Law

Some authorities have predicted that the production of Chianti under the stricter DOCG regulations will drop to only 5.3 to 8 million gallons (200,000 to 300,000 hectoliters) from the current 13 million gallons (500,000 hectoliters).

Besides the reduction in allowable yields, there are also minimum vine age requirements for the wines in three zones: Classico, Colli Fiorentini, and Rùfina. The grapes used for

DOCG Chianti from those three zones must be from vines no less than five years old.

There is speculation that the new regulation requiring that wines be submitted for blind tasting to determine whether or not they are typical in character will further reduce the amount of wine sold as Chianti.

DOC/DOCG Requirements

| | DOC | | DOCG | | |
	Chianti	Classico	Chianti	Rùfina and Coli Fiorentini	Classico
Aging requirements[a]					
Regular	cannot be sold prior to March 1 after the harvest		same as DOC	cannot be sold prior to June 1 after the harvest	
Vecchio	2 years from Jan 1		no longer exists under DOCG		
Riserva	3 years from Jan 1		3 years	3 years	3 years
Minimum alcohol					
Regular	11.5	12.0	11.5	11.5	12.0
Vecchio	12.0	12.5	no longer exists under DOCG		
Riserva	12.0	12.5	12.0[b]	12.5	12.5
Maximum yield					
(gallons/acre)	935	861	748[c]	599[d]	561[e]
Addition of concentrate, must, or grapes allowed					
	15%	15%	15%	15%[f]	15%[f]

Notes: [a] The law does not stipulate the type of receptacle to be used; it can be woden casks or barrels, stainless steel or cement vats, bottles, or any combination thereof.

[b] If the label bears a geographical designation, minimum alcohol is 12.5 percent.

[c] 6.6 pounds (3 kilograms) of grapes per vine up to a maximum of 3.3 tons per acre (75 quintali per hectare).

[d] 6.6 pounds (3 kilograms) per vine up to 3.6 tons per acre (80 quintali per hectare).

[e] 11 pounds (5 kilograms) per vine up to 4.5 tons per acre (100 quintali per hectare).

[f] Can use only concentrated must from the production zone in question, or purified concentrated must can be added.

The Chianti Vineyards

The soil in Chianti is made up of schistous clay with admixtures of flint, limestone, pebbles, and sand. In the best vineyards there is much *galestro,* a friable rock that breaks easily, cracking from changes in temperature and crumbling into fragments. The maritime origin of the terrain, formed in the tertiary period, is evidenced by the fossilized shells of marine creatures that have been found in some of the vineyards.

The Chianti vineyards cannot be situated at altitudes higher than 1805 feet (500 meters) except in certain exceptional cases, where they are allowed up to 2135 feet (650 meters). The majority are planted between 820 and 1640 feet (250 and 500 meters).

There are seven delimited Chianti zones: Classico, Colli Arentini, Colli Fiorentini, Colline Pisane, Colli Senesi, Montalbano, and Rùfina.

The most famous, of course, is the Classico zone; it is also the largest.

Chianti Vineyard and Production Statistics

	Total Chianti	Classico	Other zones
Average annual production (millions of cases)	15.7[a]	3.7[b]	7.1[c]
Vineyard area (hectares)			
Specialized	n/a	6,925	12,955
Promiscuous	n/a	3,343	7,382
Total	58,805	10,268	20,337
Growers	n/a	1,172	1,519
Cooperatives	n/a	5	8
Bottlers	n/a	295	400

Source: These statistics were compiled from a variety of sources, including the Italian Wine Center in New York and the 2 Chianti Consorzi, 1985.

Notes: Average based on date from [a] 1978–1983

[b] 1974–1984

[c] 1974–1983

Chianti Classico

The Chianti Classico district covers 173,000 acres (70,000 hectares) in the area south of Firenze and north of Siena; 25,363 (10,268) are planted to vines, 2800 acres (6925 hectares) in specialized cultivation, and 8260 (3343) mixed. This district accounts for more than 15 percent of the total vineyard acreage in the Chianti region. There are 1172 growers and five co-ops in the zone; 295 of them bottle Chianti Classico. Average annual production is 3.7 million cases a year.[18]

The classico zone is the original or classic—not necessarily the best—vineyard area in the region. The towns of Radda in Chianti, Gaiole in Chianti, and Castellina in Chianti form the historic center of Chianti Classico. During the turbulent thirteenth century, when constant battles were being waged between Siena and Florence over control of this territory, these three localities formed a league, the Lega del Chianti, for mutual defense and administration of lands held in common. The league chose for its standard the symbol of a black rooster on a yellow ground, the crest of the *podestà* in charge of the Lega, whose headquarters were in Radda.

In 1932, a ministerial decree defined the modern borders of the Chianti region and the central, *classico*, zone. These borders were quite similar to those set down by the Grand Duke of Tuscany in his *bando* of 1716, *Sopra la Dichiarazione de' Confini delle quattro Regioni Chianti, Pomino, Carmignano, e Vald' Arno di Sopra:*

> *Per il Chianti è restato Determinato sia.*
> *Dalla Spedaluzzo, fino a Greve; di li a Panzano, con tutta la Potesteria di Radda,*
> *che contiene tre Terzi, cioè Radda, Gajole, e Castellina, arrivando fino al Confine*
> *dello Stato di Siena, &c.*

The region of Chianti took in Greve, Panzano, and the three parts of the *podesteria* of Radda—Radda, Gaiole, and Castellina in Chianti. Today, these areas plus San Casciano Val di Pesa, Barberino Val d'Elsa, Tavarnelle Val di Pesa, Castelnuovo Berardenga, and a small part of Poggibonsi make up the Chianti Classico production zone.

Il Gallo Nero

There is a rather picturesque legend surrounding the black rooster. According to the story, Firenze and Siena, at one point in their constant dispute over borders, agreed to accept a north–south dividing line established through a rather unusual procedure. They made a pact wherein it was agreed that the point where two horsemen met, one representing each city, would determine the extent of their respective domains. The riders were to set out on a specified day at cock's crow.

The proud Sienese selected a fine strutting cock to do the honors for their city, and they fed their champion well. The frugal Florentines secured a scrawny bird and gave him just enough to keep the creature alive and kicking. At daybreak on the appointed day, the overstuffed Sienese chanticleer dozed contentedly, while the hungry Florentine cock awoke early, crowing for chow. Needless to relate, when the riders met it was almost at the battlements of Siena, at Fonterutoli, where the limits of the zone still are today.

Consorzio Vino Chianti Classico

In 1924, thirty-three Chianti producers in the classic Chianti area formed a voluntary growers' organization, the Consorzio Vino Chianti Classico, to defend and promote the Chianti name. Today there are 714 members. This does not include three out of the four largest houses, though. Melini belongs to the consorzio, but Ruffino, Brolio, and Antinori do not.

The consorzio chose as their emblem the *gallo nero*, a black rooster on a gold background, the symbol of the thirteenth-century Chianti league. They point out that the Chianti League also set standards, as they do, to protect the wines of the area. The consorzio issues a neck label with their *bollino,* or seal, to members' wines that qualify. The border of the *bollino* indicates the category of the wine: a red rim for regular Chianti Classico, silver for vecchio, and gold for riserva.

The Lega del Chianti were the first to set down regulations on winemaking in the territory, along with all the other civil and criminal statutes for the region under the sway of the *podestà.* Their legislation included a decree setting the date when the harvest could begin. A statute from 1444 forbids the harvesting of the grapes before San Michele's day, September 29, because "the League is damaged by early gathering since the wines cannot be good and cannot be sold."[19]

This power over the picking is one of the methods that the Lega's modern-day counterpart, the Chianti Classico consorzio, also chose to enforce their standards for the classicos of their members. They used to decide when the harvest could begin for consorzio members. Judging by the fiasco of 1973, one wonders what auguries they used to determine when to set the date. It was surely not the ripeness of the grapes.

Fabrizio Bianchi told us that as his grapes reached full ripeness in the fall of 1973 and he was looking forward to what looked to be his best vintage yet, he kept waiting for the consorzio to give the approval to harvest, but they remained silent. Finally he called. Wait, they said. He waited. The grapes were perfect, ripe and ready. He called again. Wait, they said. He waited. Finally it started to rain and rain and rain. The vineyards were drenched, the grapes were diluted, and they began to rot. What should have been a vintage to crow over became one to cry over. Bianchi managed to make a good wine only by severe selection, producing only about one-fifth of his normal harvest for Il Poggio. Although Fabrizio laughs now at the consorzio's mulishness, he admits he sent them a strong letter at the time.

One has to give the consorzio credit for one thing at least—for learning a lesson, albeit at someone else's expense. The following year they decided that perhaps the growers could judge for themselves when their grapes were ripe. Now the decision on when to pick is left up to consorzio members.

While we readily admit that the standards maintained by the Classico Consorzio are higher than those set down in the DOC regulations and that they are trying to bring up the minimum level of quality for Chianti Classico, we must also point out that they seem to have a ceiling on quality as well. They have told us that certain wines—very fine wines, in fact—are rejected at their committee tastings because they are atypical, that is, not modest enough. They have told at least one producer we spoke with that his wine was too big, too full-bodied and flavorful, too rich. They suggested that he tone it down, blending in some thin, neutral wine to produce a more representative Chianti Classico. This producer refused to lower his own standards, so they refused to grant him the *bollino* for his wine.

Today, more and more producers are coming to realize that the consorzio is a hindrance to quality for the better producers. They don't need it, and they are leaving the organization. Recently, Capannelle and Castello dei Rampolla pulled out, and we spoke to many others who said they were thinking of doing the same.

Key to Quality

The consumer does need some sort of guideline to assist him or her in making the best selections among the different vintages, styles, and levels of Chianti Classico produced.

But neither the initials of a government agency nor the seal of a growers' association can guarantee quality. The safest gauge here, besides a good basic knowledge of the wines, is the name of the estate or the producer who stands behind the wine.

Naturally, the more knowledge and experience a wine drinker has, the better off he or she is. The grape variety, the region, the vintage—all have an effect on the wine. Whether or not you'll like it in the end depends on your personal taste and preferences, but having an idea of the type of wine you can expect when you pull the cork and pour is a very helpful base to start from.

The Character of the Communes

In Chianti Classico, the basic style of the wines from the northern part of the region differs from that produced in the southern districts. Going from Florence toward Siena, the wines become fuller in flavor, firmer in texture, and higher in alcohol and tannin. As a general rule, the Chianti Classicos from the province of Firenze are lighter and more delicate than those of Siena; they have less body and more perfume. Exceptions can be found, but they reflect more the proportions of red and white grapes and winemaking techniques than geography and climatic differences. All else being equal, one general principle applies: the bigger Chianti Classicos are produced in the southern part of the district, the lighter ones in the northern part.

San Casciano Val di Pesa, in the northwestern corner of the Classico zone, takes in the villages of Romala, Mercatale Val di Pesa, and Montefiridolfi. These wines tend to be light in body. The best of them, such as the Palazzo al Bosco, age fairly well. Serristori is another well-known producer in this district.

Greve, in the northeastern part of the zone, encompasses Strada in Chianti, Passo dei Pecorai, Dudda, Montefioralle, Lucolena, and Panzano. The wines of Greve are, by reputation, the most characteristic as well as the most harmonious of the Classicos. They are not supposed to be long-lived wines, but the Montagliari Classicos of Giovanni Cappelli contradict that notion. Other fine estates in this area include Savignola Paolina, Villa Cafaggio, Fontodi, Le Masse di S. Leolino, Castello dei Rampolla (uncharacteristic, because of its use of cabernet), Castello di Querceto, Vecchie Terre di Montefili, and Querciabella. The well-known estates of Nozzole, Castello Vicchiomaggio, Verrazzano, Villa Calcinaia, Castello di Uzzano, and Vignamaggio are also in the Greve district.

Radda in Chianti lies in the eastern central part of the Classico zone and includes the towns of Volpaia, Selvale, and Villa. The Chiantis of this zone are considered to be well-balanced wines, somewhat similar to those of Greve but fuller in body. They are also reputedly long-lived, a viewpoint we cannot confirm. Monte Vertine and Castello di Volpaia are two *aziende* in this area that produce good wines. Pian d'Albola, Vignale, and Vignavecchia are among the well-known estates in Radda.

Gaiole in Chianti is in the southeastern part of the Classico zone. The villages of Starda, Lecchi, and Monti are in this district. The wines of Gaiole are regarded for their richness of flavor and full body. They are fairly tannic, well-structured wines with the capacity to age well. Badia a Coltibuono is a good example. The very fine Capannelle *azienda* is in this *commune*. Riecine, Castello di S. Polo in Rosso, and Castello Brolio are located in Gaiole.

Castelnuovo Berardenga, in the southernmost part of the Classico zone, encompasses the villages of San Gusmè, Pianella, and Querciagrossa. This district is noted for producing full-bodied wines that are sometimes a bit low in acid but age quite well. Fine examples of this style of Chianti are produced at "Berardenga" Felsina, Pagliarese, Castell'In Villa, Villa Colombaio, and Poggio Rosso. Some other well-known estates here include San Felice, Le Lodoline, Valiano, and Catignano.

Castellina in Chianti, located in the western south-central part of the Classico zone, takes in the villages of Fonterutoli and Castagnoli. These Classicos are prized for their perfume. It is claimed that they have the capacity to age, but our experience suggests otherwise. The Castellina

LE STRADE DEL GALLO NERO

CARTA
DELLA ZONA
DI PRODUZIONE

CHIANTI
CLASSICO
GALLO NERO

Consorzio Chianti Classico
Firenze - Via de' Serragli 146 - Tel. 229351/2/3
Telex 574625 COGANE

Chiantis tend to be fairly full wines, somewhat similar to the wine of the neighboring *commune* of Radda. Regarded estates from Castellina include Castellare, Straccali, Lilliano, Castello di Rencine, Melini's Granaio estate, San Leonino, Castello di Fonterutoli, and Villa Cerna. Not one of our top-rated (three stars or higher) Classicos is produced in this area, but that could just be a coincidence.

Barberino Val d'Elsa, in the western central part of the Classico zone, boasts two of the top Classico estates: Monsanto and Isole e Olena. It seems reasonable to include in this grouping the small nearby portion of Poggibonsi that is in the Classico zone. It is a bit difficult to generalize about this area. The wines of Monsanto are among the fullest in body of all the Classicos, yet those produced close by on the estates of Quercia al Poggio and Casa Sola tend to be rather light.

Tavarnelle Val di Pesa, north of Barberino, is in the western central part of the Classico district. Sambuca, Badia a Passignano, and San Donato in Poggio are in this area. Again, we find it difficult to generalize about the character of the wines. The best estate here is Poggio al Sole, producing wines that age moderately well. Their wines are high in acid and somewhat austere in nature. La Ripa and Villa Francesca are two other well-known estates from the Tavarnelle district.

Chianti Classico★★★

The Chianti Classico Producers

Estate	Locality	Vineyards (hectares)	Production (cases)
Agricoltori del Chianti Geografico	Gaiole	500.0	277,750
Ancilli F.lli	Poggibonsi	0.0	55,500
Antinori	San Casciano VP	165.0	360,000
Baccio da Gaiuole (Gittori)	Gaiole	3.9	2,750
Badia a Coltibuono	Gaiole	47.5	30,000
Barberino	Barberino VE	n/a	9,500
Barfede-Certaldo	S. Donato In Poggio	5.0	21,000
Bartali Alberto	Castellina	0.0	33,000
Belvedere	Poggibonsi	12.5	7,750
Berardenga, Fattoria di Felsina	Castelnuovo Berardenga	52.0	22,000
Bertolli (*see also* Fizzano)	Castellina	0.0	78,000
Bibbiano	Castellina	27.0	22,000
Bossi	Castelnuovo Berardenga	0.0	39,500
Brolio	Gaiole	315.0	155,000
Cafaggio di Pesa	Castellina	0.5	450
Caiano	Castelnuovo Berardenga	10.0	5,500
Campacci	S. Gusmè	12.0	5,000
Campomaggio	Lucarelli, Radda	23.6	14,000
Candialle	Panzano	3.3	3,300
Cantagalli, Az. Agr. La Torre	Barberino VE	11.0	6,600
Capannelle	Gaiole	3.0	1,775
Carobbio	Greve	n/a	2,200
Carpineto	Dudda, Greve	8.4	6,550
Casa Nova della Cappella	Gaiole	4.4	3,300
Casa Sola	Barberino VE	24.5	19,000
Casalbelvedere	Greve	0.3142	150
Casalgallo	Querciagrossa	1.8	1,450
Casalino	Querciagrossa	22.0	15,500
Casa Volterrani	Vagliagli	32.0	20,000
Casavecchia di Nittardi	Castellina	6.3	4,000
Casilli, Az. Agr. Starda	Gaiole	6.3	550
Castel Ruggero	Strada In Chianti	6.2	1,300
Castelgreve, Soc. Coop. Castelli dei	Mercatale VP	900.0	550,000
Castellare	Castellina	15.0	8,300
Castell'In Villa	Castelnuovo Berardenga	55.0	44,500
Castellinuzza	Greve	3.2	1,825

Castello dei Rampolla	Panzano	38.0	17,750
Castello di Ama	Gaiole	67.0	27,500
Castello di Bossi	Castelnuovo Berardenga	51.0	16,500
Castello di Cacchiano	Gaiole	82.0	33,000
Castello di Castelvari	Mercatale VP	36.0	22,000
Castello di Cerreto, Emilio Pucci	Pianella	28.6	16,000
Castello di Fonterutoli	Castellina	32.2	18,000
Castello di Gabbiano	Mercatale VP	50.0	40,000
Castello di Meleto	Gaiole	208.0	133,000
Castello di Monterinaldi	Radda	72.0	55,500
Castello di Querceto	Lucolena, Greve	40.0	22,000
Castello di Radda (Montemaggio)	Radda	0.0	4,000
Castello di Rencine	Castellina	27.7	21,500
Castello di San Donato in Perno	Gaiole	63.1	40,000
Castello di San Polo in Rosso	Gaiole	23.5	20,000
Castello di Tizzano	S. Polo In Chianti	19.1	11,000
Castello di Tornano	Gaiole	8.5	7,000
Castello di Uzzano	Greve	65.7	43,000
Castello di Verrazzano	Greve	42.2	35,500
Castello di Vertine	Gaiole	n/a	33,000
Castello di Volpaia	Radda	31.8	18,000
Castello Vicchiomaggio	Greve	25.0	13,000
Catignano	Pianella	9.3	7,750
Cecchi Luigi (*see also* Villa Cerna)	Castellina	0.0	50,000
Cellole	Castellina	14.3	11,000
Cennatoio	Panzano	10.3	6,200
Cerbaiola (a label used by Barfede-Certaldo)			
Cispiano	Castellina	10.0	4,000
Coli	Sambuca VP	17.2	13,000
Colli d'Oro, Fattoria di Topina	Castellina	25.0	27,500
Conti Serristori	S. Andrea In Percussina	27.9	23,000
della Badia	Sambuca VP	0.0	110,000
Fattoria Barberino di Poggibonsi	Poggibonsi	n/a	33,000
Fattoria Belvedere Campoli	Mercatale VP	7.4	7,200
Fattoria della Aiola	Vagliagli	30.7	22,000
Fattoria delle Corti	S. Casciano VP	n/a	33,000
Fattoria delle Fonti	Poggibonsi	15.5	7,200
Fattoria delle Lodoline	Vagliagli	14.9	11,000
Fattoria di Cinciano	Poggibonsi	38.0	16,500
Fattoria di Monaciano	Castelnuovo Berardenga	46.7	22,000
Fattoria di Petroio	Querciagrossa	15.1	9,500
Fattoria di Selvole	Vagliagli	22.0	16,500
Fattoria di Trasqua	Castellina	54.8	33,000
Fattoria di Vistarenni	Gaiole	80.0	83,000
Fattoria Il Castagno	Querciagrossa	14.1	13,000
Fattoria La Loggia	Montefiridolfi	13.8	11,000
Fattoria La Ripa	S. Donato In Poggio	13.0	13,000
Fattoria Le Barone	Panzano	17.1	10,000
Fattoria Le Pici	S. Gusmè	8.3	4,500
Fattoria Le Ripe	S. Casciano VP	12.7	10,000
Fattoria Montagliari (Cappelli)	Panzano	38.0	19,000
Fattoria Morrocco	S. Donato In Poggio	9.3	8,300
Fattoria Poggiarello	Castellina	12.7	10,000
Fattoria Querciabella	Ruffoli, Greve	11.7	4,300
Fattoria Tregole	Castellina	1.9	1,750
Filetta, Socci Guido	Lamole, Greve	9.5	5,250
Fizzano (Bertolli)	Castellina	32.7	22,000
Fontodi	Panzano	21.0	9,000
Fossi	Campiobbi	0.0	5,500
Gaiello della Filgare	S. Donato In Poggio	8.2	3,600
Giorgio Regni	Gaiole	3.4	1,550

Granducato Enopolio di Poggibonsi	Poggibonsi	0.0	55,500
Grignanello	Castellina	9.2	5,500
Il Guerrino	Greve	8.9	n/a
Il Palagio	Mercatale VP	26.4	18,000
Isabella de' Medici	La Volpaia, Radda	0.0	7,750
Isole e Olena	Barberino VE	32.0	20,000
La Capraia	Castellina	59.0	33,300
La Casaccia	S. Gusmè	19.0	10,000
La Casaccia	Radda	1.6	n/a
La Castellina	Castellina	19.0	12,000
La Cerreta Soc. Coop.	Gaiole	46.0	33,000
La Mandria	Lecchi In Chianti	42.3	22,000
La Massa	Panzano	13.0	20,000
La Montanina	Monti In Chianti	2.2	1,650
La Pagliaia	Castellina	46.6	35,500
La Piaggia	Castellina	2.7	2,200
La Presura	Strada In Chianti	2.7	3,300
La Quercia (Cappelli Giovanni)	Panzano	0.0	33,000
Lamole, Fattoria Pile e Lamole	Greve	5.2	6,700
Le Bocce	Panzano	43.9	28,000
Le Chiantigiane, Cantine Sociali Consorziate	Tavarnelle VP	45.1	55,000
Le Lame	San Casciano VP	4.0	3,100
Le Masse di San Leolino	Panzano	3.1	2,000
Le Miccine	Gaiole	6.5	900
Le Piazze	Castellina	59.0	35,500
Leccio	Castellina	1.0404	825
Lilliano	Castellina	47.3	33,000
Lornano	Castellina	30.8	19,000
Luca della Robbia	Panzano	0.0	6,700
Luiano	Mercatale VP	25.0	16,500
Marcellina	Panzano	9.0	3,300
Melazzano	Greve	23.4	16,500
Melini	Poggibonsi	188.0	220,000
Mezzuola	Greve	2.4	1,300
Monsanto	Barberino VE	78.9	28,000
Monte Vertine	Radda	43.7	4,200
Montecchio	S. Donato In Poggio	21.2	6,600
Montemaggio	Radda	15.0	16,000
Montesassi	Castellina	5.1	4,500
Montiverdi	Gaiole	23.1	11,000
Montoro	Greve	2.8	1,300
Nittardi	Castellina	6.3	5,000
Nozzole	Passo dei Pecorai	90.0	60,000
Ormanni	Poggibonsi	32.3	22,000
Pagliarese	S. Gusmè	27.0	22,000
Pagni	Castelnuovo Berardenga	0.0	6,500
Palazzo al Bosco	La Romala	10.2	6,700
Petroio alla via della Malpensata	Radda	15.0	7,750
Pian d'Albola	Radda	28.0	22,000
Pietrafitta	Castellina	8.7	1,650
Podere "Casa Emma"	Barberino VE	9.2	5,500
Podere Castellinuzza	Greve	n/a	3,300
Podere Il Palazzino	Monte In Chianti	3.7	2,000
Poggio al Sole	Badia a Passignano	13.0	3,600
Poggio alla Croce	Castellina	15.4	12,000
Poggio Bonelli	Castelnuovo Berardenga	18.5	10,000
Poggio Rosso	Castelnuovo Berardenga	1.0	650
Poggiolino	Sambuca VP	7.8	3,900

Quercia al Poggio	Barberino VE	13.0	10,000
Querciavalle	Castelnuovo Berardenga	9.8	7,750
Quornia	Castellina	11.9	11,000
Riecine	Gaiole	2.6	1,550
Rignana	Greve	14.6	6,100
Ripertoli	Greve	3.0	1,650
Riseccoli	Greve	12.9	5,500
Rocca delle Maciè	Castellina	87.5	90,000
Ruffino	Pontassieve	230.0	n/a
S. Fabiano Calcinaia	Poggibonsi	8.6	4,500
S. Leonino, Fattoria I Cipressi	Castellina	53.0	40,000
S. Stefano a Collegalle	Greve	19.2	13,000
S. Valeria	Vagliagli	9.2	5,500
Sagrona e Faule	Greve	10.7	6,100
San Cosma, Podere Colle ai Lecci	S. Gusmè	9.0	7,000
San Fedele	Radda	12.0	11,000
San Felice	S. Gusmè	100.0	66,000
San Martino a Uzzano	Greve	5.7	3,300
San Vito In Berardenga	Castelnuovo Berardenga	23.0	13,000
Santa Caterina (a label used by Monsanto)			
Santa Cristina (a label used by Antinori)			
Santa Lucia	Mercatale VP	89.7	83,000
Savignola Paolina	Greve	6.0	1,900
Setriolo	Castellina	2.3	1,300
Signoria (a label used by Barfede-Certaldo)			
Sole di Gagliole	Castellina	2.0	900
Sommavilla	Castellina	2.2	650
Sonnino	Gaiole	1.1	3,300
Straccali	Castellina	0.0	17,000
Tenuta Colombaia	Chiocchio	21.0	n/a
Tenuta di Vignole	Panzano	7.8	5,500
Tenuta Le Corti	Greve	n/a	9,000
Tenuta Villa Rosa	Castellina	34.7	28,000
Tiorcia	Gaiole	0.95	650
Tomarecchio e Miscianello	Ponte a Bozzone	7.2	4,000
Valiano	Vagliagli	69.4	55,500
Vecchie Terre di Montefili	Greve	6.5	3,100
Vigna di Sorripa (a label used by Le Lame)			
Vigna Vecchia	Radda	23.0	13,300
Vignamaggio	Greve	33.5	12,500
Villa Antinori (a label used by Antinori)			
Villa Banfi	Montalcino	n/a	30,000
Villa Cafaggio	Panzano	27.0	14,250
Villa Calcinaia	Greve	40.0	20,000
Villa Cerna (Luigi Cecchi)	Castellina	75.0	44,500
Villa Colombaio	Querciagrossa	11.3	11,000
Villa Consuelo	Montefiriodolfi	58.6	39,000
Villa d'Arceno In Chianti	S. Gusmè	59.5	27,750
Villa Francesca	S. Donato In Poggio	0.3	1,650
Villa Montepaldi	S. Casciano VP	46.9	33,000
Villa Terciona	Mercatale VP	55.9	41,000
Vitiano	S. Polo in Robbiana	21.2	27,750
Viticcio	Greve	14.1	11,000
Vitignano	Pianella	25.1	16,500

Notes: 1 hectare = 2.4711 acres.

1 hectoliter = 26.42 gallons, 11.11 cases, or 133 bottles

Rating the Chianti Classico Producers

★★★★

Monsanto, Il Poggio

★★★

Badia a Coltibuono
Capannelle
Fattoria Montagliari, Cappelli Giovanni
Fattoria Montagliari e Castellinuzza, Giovanni
    Cappelli
+ Fattoria Montagliari, Vigna Casaloste, Giovanni
    Cappelli
Fortilizio Il Colombaio (Villa Colombaio)
Isole e Olena
Monsanto
Ruffino Riserva Ducale gold label
Savignola Paolina
Villa Cafaggio
Villa Colombaio

★★

Baccio da Gaiuole (Gittori) (most recent vintage
    tasted 1977)
+ Berardenga, Fattoria Felsina
Brolio Riserva del Barone
− Castellare
+ Castell'In Villa
+ Castello dei Rampolla
− Castello di Gabbiano
+ Castello di Querceto
+ Castello di S. Polo In Rosso
− Castello di Tizzano (most recent vintage tasted
    1971)
Castello di Uzzano (most recent vintage tasted
    1973)
+ Castello di Volpaia
Castello Vicchiomaggio, Prima Vigna riserva
Catignano
Conti Serristori, Machiavelli riserva
+ Fontodi
+ Le Bocce (most recent vintage tasted 1977)
Le Masse di San Leolino
Lilliano
Melini riserva
Monte Vertine
Nozzole (most recent vintage tasted 1977)
Pagliarese
+ Pagliarese, Boscardini riserva
Palazzo al Bosco
+ Poggio al Sole
+ Poggio Rosso
Querciabella
Riecine
Ruffino Riserva Ducale
San Felice, Il Grigio riserva
Straccali
Tregole
Vecchie Terre di Montefili
Vignamaggio
− Villa Antinori
Villa Antinori Riserva Marchese
Villa Terciona (most recent vintage tasted 1974)
− Vistarenni, Podere Bertinga
Viticcio

★

− Brolio
Brolio riserva
Campacci
− Campomaggio
Cappelli Giovanni, La Querce
Carobbio (most recent vintage tasted 1977)
− Carpineto (most recent vintage tasted 1975)
− Castelgreve
Castello di Ama
+ Castello di Cerreto, Emilio Pucci
+ Castello di Fonterutoli
+ Castello Vicchiomaggio
Castelpolo, Castello di S. Polo In Rosso
Cerbaiola di Barfede-Certaldo
Cispiano
Conti Serristori
Fattoria del Leccio, Fratelli Beccaro (most recent
    vintage tasted 1968)
+ Fossi (older vintages)
La Pagliaia Riserva Granduca Ferdinando III
La Ripa
Melini
Monsanto, Santa Caterina
− Monticelli (Viticola Toscana)
Pandolfini (most recent vintage tasted 1971)
Quercia al Poggio
Ruffino
S. Leolino, Fattoria I Cipressi
San Felice
− Santa Cristina, Antinori
Signoria di Barfede-Certaldo (most recent vintage
    tasted 1975)
− Tenuta La Colombaia (most recent vintage tasted
    1977)
Tenuta Villa Rosa
Verrazzano (most recent vintage tasted 1974)
Villa Banfi
Villa Cerna

0

Barberini (most recent vintage tasted 1977)
Bertolli (most recent vintage tasted 1978)
Burchino (most recent vintage tasted 1978)
Casa Sola
Castello di Cacchiano (most recent vintage tasted
    1977)
Castello di Meleto
Castello di Monterinaldi
Castello di Radda
Castello di Rencine (most recent vintage tasted
    1977)
Castello di San Donato in Perno
Cecchi Luigi (most recent vintage tasted 1976)
Cellole
Cepperellaccio, Principe Kunz d'Asburgo Lorena
Conti Capponi (most recent vintage tasted 1975)
Conti Serristori, Ser Niccolo riserva (most recent
    vintage tasted 1975)
Fattoria della Aiola
− Fattoria delle Barone
Fattoria delle Lodoline

Fattoria di Vistarenni
Fizzano (most recent vintage tasted 1971)
Fossi
Geografico, Agricoltori del Chianti
Granducato Riserva Corona (most recent vintage tasted 1978)
Il Guerrino (most recent vintage tasted 1977)
– Isabella de' Medici
La Loggia
La Mandria (most recent vintage tasted 1975)
Le Chiantigiane
Le Pici (most recent vintage tasted 1974)
Luiano
Mazzoni (bottled by Villa Cafaggio, most recent vintage tasted 1977)
Montemaggio
Montepaldi, Marchese Corsini (most recent vintage tasted 1976)

Pian d'Albola (most recent vintage tasted 1977)
Podere Il Palazzino
Ricasoli
Riseccoli
Rocca della Maciè
Rocca della Maciè, Zingarelli riserva
Saccardi (most recent vintage tasted 1977)
Selvole
Tizzano (most recent vintage tasted 1974)
Valiano
Vigna Vecchia
Vignale
Villa Calcinaia, Conti Capponi (better in the 1960s and early 1970s)
Villa Consuelo (most recent vintage tasted 1978)

Tasting Notes
1984 [★]

This was a difficult vintage. The spring was generally overcast, and the lack of sun which continued throughout the summer and most of September hindered the ripening process. Then heavy rains in early autumn created widespread rot and mildew on the vines. Producers who picked early, before the middle of October, got low sugars. Those who felt they could delay the harvest saw sugar levels rise. The best fruit was harvested in November. Quantity overall was down 25 percent; quality was mixed. In general, the vintage was rather poor. Careful selection was in order; those who selected carefully made some fairly good wines.

Fabrizio Bianchi and Minuccio Cappelli didn't produce any Chianti Classico under their Monsanto and Montagliari labels. Villa Calcinaia described the vintage as poor. Paolo di Marchi said that though their harvest was reduced, it was necessary to make a careful selection. Vignamaggio considered it a medium vintage.

Though 1984 was generally a poor year, the best wines have a certain elegance. Of the eight Chianti Classicos we tasted from cask in May 1985, we found the Villa Cafaggio the most successful, followed by the Savignola Paolina, Castellare, and San Polo In Rosso. The Fontodi, too, shows some promise.

Castellare (*ex-cask 5/85*). Dark color; cherries on aroma and malvasia character; acid a bit high, very fruity.★★
Castello di Cerreto, Emilio Pucci (*ex-cask 5/85*). Fairly full-bodied, has fruit, difficult to assess, but shows some potential.(★)
Castello di S. Polo In Rosso (*ex-vat 5/85*). A surprising amount of fruit, acid on the high side.★(★)
Catignano (*ex-cask 5/85*). Aromas of raspberries and spice; a bit light, acid on the high side, fruity.★

Fontodi (*ex-vat 5/85*). A bit rough and unready, high acid, light-bodied, fruity.★(+?)
Quercia al Poggio (*ex-vat 5/85*). Pale color; lightly fruity aroma; high acid, low fruit, thin.
Savignola Paolina (*ex-vat 5/85*). Fresh and fruity, cherries and berries; quite nice.★★
Villa Cafaggio (*ex-vat 5/85*). Richly fruited aroma and flavor, surprising body.★(★)

1983 [★★★★]

This vintage was characterized by a drought from June to August. In July temperatures soared to over 100° F, causing some uneven ripening. September rains brought welcome relief. The best grapes were harvested toward the end of October.

Paolo di Marchi of Isole e Olena said some of their grapes were burnt in the intense heat, giving the resulting wines a slightly raisiny flavor. Overall, he describes them as wines of good color, low acid, high alcohol, and soft tannins, round wines that will be ready early. Ruffino noted that the wines are very rich and high in alcohol. Villa Cafaggio, Castello di Vignamaggio, Castello di Gabbiano, Castello di Querceto, Pagliarese, Campomaggio, Vicchiomaggio, Castellare, Castello di Ama, Catignano, and Minuccio Cappelli of Giovanni Cappelli rate the vintage as excellent. Di Marchi puts it after 1982, but ahead of 1981. Villa Calcinaia, too, put it on the second level. Castell'In Villa said it was not one of their favorite vintages. Niederbacher rates the year three stars; the consorzio gives it four.

We tasted nearly three dozen Chianti Classicos from the vintage in April and May 1985 and were very impressed. In fact, we would rate it the finest vintage since 1971. We especially enjoyed the Capannelle, Monsanto and Monsanto Il Poggio (our favorite), Montagliari, and Villa Cafaggio. Badia a Coltibuono, San Polo in Rosso, Fontodi, and Vecchie Terre weren't far behind. We were unimpressed with the Castello di Meleto, Castello di Monterinaldi, Castello di S. Donato in Perno, Castello di Radda, and Montemaggio, Podere Il Palazzino, Fattoria di Selvole, and Vigna Vecchia.

While the '83s may not age as well as the bigger '82s, they should give more pleasure in their time, making up in elegance and style what they lack in endurance and strength.

Badia a Coltibuono (5/85). Fresh, berrylike aroma; moderate tannin, loads of flavor; young, but quality is evident.★★(★)

Campacci (ex-cask 5/85). Mushrooms on aroma; light and simple.★

Campannelle (ex-vat 5/85). Big, fruity aroma rises out of the glass; rich in flavor, sweet, style already evident; long finish.★★★(+)

Cappelli Giovanni, "La Querce" (5/85). Light, fruity aroma; some tannin, cherrylike fruit, flavorful, simple.★

Castellare (ex-vat 5/85). Simple and fruity, easy, soft, quaffable.★

Castello di Cerreto riserva, Emilio Pucci (ex-cask 5/85). Rich aroma; full-bodied, loads of flavor, somewhat astringent; shows promise.★★(+)

Castello di Meleto (5/85). Aroma lacks freshness; some tannin, shy of fruit, drinkable.

Castello di Monterinaldi (5/85). Fruity but dull; overly drying at end.

Castello di Radda (5/85). Simple, fruity, dull, astringent.

Castello di S. Polo In Rosso riserva (ex-cask 5/85). Aroma and flavor of sweet ripe fruit, well balanced, already displays style.★★(★)

Castello di San Donato in Perano (5/85). Odd nose, odd flavor, taste recalls filter paper.

Castello di Volpaia riserva (ex-vat 5/85). Cherrylike fruit; light tannin, lively, almost sweet.★★+

Castello Vicchiomaggio (ex-cask 5/85). Raspberries on aroma; a lot of flavor, moderate tannin; young.★(+)

Catignano (ex-cask 5/85). Fragrant and fruity, light and quaffable; quite agreeable.★★

Fattoria Montagliari riserva, Cappelli Giovanni (ex-cask 5/85). Aroma of cherries, vaguely floral; flavorful, fairly tannic, well balanced.★★(★+)

Fontodi (5/85). Oak and raspberries on nose; fruity, soft-centered, some tannin, well-knit; can be enjoyed today though rather firm on finish.★★(★)

Fontodi riserva (ex-cask 5/85). Raspberries, flowers, and some oak on aroma; tastes almost sweet, has some elegance; should make a splendid bottle, not as strong as the '82 but has more style.★★(★)

Isole e Olena (5/85). Fragrant aroma, vaguely berrylike; still some tannin to lose, fairly rich, supple center, has a roasted quality and a vaguely raisiny note.★★(+)

La Ripa (5/85). Aroma of mushrooms and fruit; light tannin, fruity, simple, agreeable. ★.

Monsanto, Il Poggio riserva (ex-vat 4/85). Rich aroma of ripe fruit and mushrooms; light tannin, rich ripe fruit, lots of flavor and lots of class.★★(★★).

Monsanto riserva (ex-vat 4/85). Some ripe fruit on nose; a lot of flavor, moderate tannin, seems a bit light.★★(★)

Montemaggio (4/85). Fruit and almonds up front, some tannin, dull.

Pagliarese (twice 5/85). Fresh aroma with berrylike fruit, some charm; light, fruity, simple and easy.★★

Podere Il Palazzino (ex-vat 5/85). Low acid, unbalanced, dull.

Quercia al Poggio (ex-vat 5/85). Fruity aroma with some tar; still rough and unready but quite a lot of fruit.★★(+)

Savignola Paolina (3 times 5/85). First bottle of 5/85: Loads of flavor, seems almost sweet, has delicacy, charm, and some length.★★(+)
Second time, ex-cask 5/85): Richly fruited aroma with a touch of tar; has tannin, flavorful, some delicacy; good quality.★★(+)

Selvole 5/85). Fruity and quaffable, but rather ordinary; a vague off note at the end.

Valiano (4/85). Fresh, berrylike aroma; light and fruity, acid a bit high, but drinkable enough.★

Vecchie Terre di Montefili (ex-cask 5/85). Perfumed aroma; flavorful, has style; some tannin at the end.★★(★)

Vigna Vecchia (5/85). Light and fruity, unbalanced, a bit shallow; dull finish.

Vignamaggio (ex-cask 5/85). Fruity aroma and flavor, seems almost sweet, light tannin.★(+)

Villa Cafaggio (ex-vat 5/85). Richly fruited aroma with suggestions of black cherries; sweet ripe fruit, has richness of flavor and lots of style.★★★(+)

Viticcio (6/85). Almost nouveau-like in its simplicity and berrylike character; a spritz throws the balance off.

1982 [★★★+]

This was a year destined for a small harvest. Hail fell in the spring before the flowering, curtailing the possible crop size; then again in early September hail reduced the actual harvest.

Paolo di Marchi describes the '82s as hard and tannic, Chianti Classicos to age, and, for them at least, better than the '83s. Minuccio Cappelli, Castello di Querceto, Pagliarese, Catignano, Castello di Ama, Castellare, Vignamaggio, and Campomaggio rate the wines very highly. Castell'In

Villa and Villa Calcinaia considered the wines very good. Both the consorzio and Niederbacher gave the vintage three stars.

After having tasted nearly four dozen '82s in April and May 1985, we believe that they will be long-lived wines, outlasting the '83s, for example. They do lack elegance, however; they're big wines but not great ones.

Our favorites among the '82s are the Isole e Olena, Villa Cafaggio, Badia a Coltibuono "Old Vines," Capannelle, San Polo in Rosso, Volpaia, Monsanto Il Poggio, and Montagliari. Some clinkers are Castello di Monterinaldi, Montemaggio, Podere Il Palazzino, Villa Calcinaia, and Vistarenni.

Badia a Coltibuono *(5/85)*. A lot of berrylike fruit up front; quite rich, a peppery character, and notes of spice; room for improvement.★★(+)

Badia a Coltibuono riserva *(ex-cask 5/85)*. Rich, ripe fruit on aroma, suggests blackberries; quite tannic, rich, sweet fruit, full-flavored; a lot of character.★★★

Badia a Coltibuono (old vines) riserva *(ex-cask 5/85)*. Very deep color; intense, floral aroma with berrylike aspect; enormous weight and extract; heaps of tannin; sure to make a very fine bottle in time.★★★(+)

"Berardenga," Fattoria Felsina *(5/85)*. Lovely aroma with notes of raspberries and flowers; acid a bit high, lively, fruity; tart finish.★

Campacci *(ex-cask 5/85)*. Small, vaguely floral aroma; light in body, fruity, simple.★ +

Campomaggio *(5/85)*. Notes of tobacco and cherries on aroma; light and fruity, some tannin, in an easy style, perhaps too much so.★ −

Capannelle vecchio *(twice 5/85)*. Fruity, floral aroma with cherries and berries; firm tannin, well-knit, flavorful; has style and class, needs further age. ★★(★)

Cappelli Giovanni, "La Querce" *(5/85)*. Aroma of flowers and cherries; sweet and fruity, simple, quaffable.★

Castellare *(3 times 5/85; 48,336 bottles)*. Bottle of 4/85: Nice aroma with floral notes, still a bit closed; well balanced, light tannin, tasty; nice now.★★ +

Tasting of 5/85 ex-vat: Fresh, fruity, simple, easy.★

Castell'In Villa *(twice 5/85)*. Very nice berryish aroma; some tannin, good body, flavorful; too serious for a quaffing wine.★ +

Castello dei Rampolla *(5/85)*. Light, fruity aroma, with cabernet character evident; well balanced, needs another year.★(+)

Castello di Ama *(5/85; 158,280 bottles)*. Fresh, berrylike aroma with a slight stalkiness; low acid, unstructured, though agreeable enough and easy to drink.★ −

Castello di Cerreto, Emilio Pucci *(5/85)*. Floral, fruity aroma, with raspberry notes; light tannin, could soften but nice now.★★ −

Castello di Monterinaldi *(5/85)*. Insufficient fruit, dull, flat.

Castello di Querceto *(5/85; 6 months in barrique)*. Oak up front with a cherrylike backnote; fruity flavor with an oak component, has style and structure; finish is all oak; nice now but should improve.★★ +

Castello di S. Polo In Rosso *(5/85)*. Soft, fruity, quaffable, berrylike; a touch of bitterness at the end.★ +

Castello di S. Polo In Rosso riserva *(ex-cask 5/85)*. A mouthful of ripe fruit; well structured, tannic, a big wine of good quality.★★(★)

Castello di Volpaia *(twice 5/85; 92–93% sangiovese, 7–8% canaiolo)*. Floral aroma with cherrylike fruit and some spice; some delicacy, soft and round, well made; a bit short.★★ −

Castello di Volpaia riserva *(ex-vat 5/85)*. Enormous concentration of ripe fruit, full-flavored; tremendous potential.★★(★)

Catignano *5/85)*. Flowers and berries on nose; fruity, raspberry-like flavor, light and easy.★★

Fattoria Montagliari riserva, Cappelli Giovanni *(ex-cask 5/85)*. Intense aroma of cherries and other fruit; surprisingly full-bodied and rich, rough edges, very young.★★(★)

Fontodi *5/85)*. Richer and more intense aroma than the '83; full-bodied, full-flavored, still has tannin to shed.★★(+)

Fontodi riserva *(ex-cask 5/85)*. Aroma of oak and raspberries; full and rich, has style; tannic finish; good potential to age.★★(★ −)

Isole e Olena riserva *(5/85)*. Lovely, fragrant aroma with a touch of oak; tannic, supple center, lots of character and lots of flavor; needs perhaps three more years.★★(★ +)

La Loggia *(4/85)*. Light aroma; astringent, some fruit, unbalanced.★ −

Le Masse di San Leolino *(4/85)*. Nice nose; fruity, easy, soft.★★ −

Monsanto, Il Poggio riserva *(ex-cask 4/85)*. Rich concentration on aroma with notes of cherries and flowers; heaps of tannin, richly flavored, enormous extract.★★★

Monte Vertine *(5/85)*. Delicate floral aroma; light tannin, fruity, well balanced, soft, very drinkable; a trifle short.★★

Montemaggio *(4/85)*. Aroma suggests amaretto; not a lot of fruit, astringent.

Pagliarese *(will be a riserva; twice 5/85)*. Fresh aroma recalls raspberries, still a bit closed; flavorful, sweet fruit; tannic finish.★★

Podere Il Palazzino riserva *(ex-cask 5/85)*. Nice fruit on nose and a hint of toffee; tannic entry, has fruit, lacking in structure.

Poggio al Sole *(twice 5/85; 34,559 bottles)*. Delicate floral aroma; well balanced, light tannin, lively, some elegance and length; ready.★★ +

Quercia al Poggio *(ex-vat 5/85)*. Fruity aroma; quite tannic but seems to have sufficient fruit.★(?)

San Felice *(4/85)*. Floral aroma; light tannin, fruity, a bit simple; a good quaffing wine.★

Savignola Paolina *(ex-vat 5/85)*. Fuller than the '83, has delicacy and some style.★★(+)

Tenuta Villa Rosa *(4/85)*. Floral aroma; fruity, firm vein of tannin, drinkable now, but should be better in a year.★(+)

Vecchie Terre di Montefili *(5/85)*. Floral perfume; fairly full, well balanced, light tannin; good quality.★★ +

Vigna Vecchia (5/85). Berrylike fruit, fresh, simple, quaffable.★

Vignamaggio (ex-cask 5/85). Fruity aroma and flavor; not quite together yet.★(★)

Villa Cafaggio (5/85). Rich, fruity aroma with blackberries, tar, and some spice; tannin to lose; shows potential.★★(+)

Villa Cafaggio riserva (ex-vat 5/85). Inky black color; intensely concentrated aroma recalls blackberries; full, rich, ripe, and concentrated, loads of tannin; one of the best '82s we've tasted.★★★(+)

Villa Calcinaia, Conti Capponi (4/85). Baked character, flat and dull.

Vistarenni (4/85). A small-scale wine with a touch of astringency.

Viticcio (6/85). Light floral aroma; fruity, agreeable, quaffable, and easy.★ +

1981 ★★

March and April, two very hot and dry months, were followed by a rainy May. The first two weeks of June were again dry and extremely hot; then, in the second half of the month, rainstorms hit more than once, and there was a significant drop in the temperature.

Producers who rated the vintage highly include Castello di Querceto, Minuccio Cappelli, Pagliarese, Catignano, Villa Cafaggio, and Castellare. Raffaele Rossetti of Capannelle said it was top class. Paolo di Marchi describes the '81s as very good wines that are ready now or soon will be. Villa Calcinaia rates them very good, and Castell'In Villa said the wines were not bad. The consorzio gives the year three stars; Niederbacher gives two.

The '81s are somewhat light-bodied and not for long aging. Of the more than thirty we've tasted, we especially like the Montagliari and Castello dei Rampolla; Monte Vertine is very close behind. The Badia a Coltibuono, Berardenga, Capannelle, Castello di Querceto, Fontodi, Isole e Olena, Monsanto Il Poggio, Savignola Paolina, Vecchie Terre, and Pagliarese are also good. We didn't think much of the '81 Chianti Classico from Podere Il Palazzino, Vigna Vecchia, or Villa Calcinaia.

Badia a Coltibuono riserva (ex-cask 5/85). Hints of tar and wood on aroma; a lot of fruit, seems sweet, well balanced, tannin to lose but should be ready early.★★(+)

"Berardenga," Fattoria Felsina riserva (5/85). Floral aroma with notes of raspberries; fruity, tart edge; vaguely bitter on finish.★★(+)

Capannelle riserva (twice 5/85). Lovely aroma suggests berries and cherries, some oak; light tannin, flavorful, balanced; has a tannic bite at the end.★★ +

Cappelli Giovanni, "La Querce" (12/83). Light, fresh, and fruity, with a berrylike character and some charm; very nice.★★

Castellare (ex-cask 2/83). Undeveloped aroma with some fruit evident; tart edge; agreeable, not much more.★

Castello dei Rampolla riserva (5/85). Oak and cabernet fruit on nose; well balanced, well made, has style and flavor but no Chianti character. As a red wine★★(★); as a Chianti★

Castello di Ama (5/85; 208,870 bottles). Light and fruity, rather simple, quaffable.★

Castello di Ama, Vigneto Bellavista (5/85; 13,424 bottles). Floral, fruity aroma brings up berries; moderate tannin, fairly nice fruit; finishes on a firm note.★

Castello di Cerreto riserva, Emilio Pucci (5/85). Floral aroma; good body, some tannin, should be ready in two or three years.★(★ +)

Castello di Querceto riserva (5/85; 8 months in barrique). Fairly rich aroma with some oak and a cherrylike back note; firm tannin and acid, lean, nice fruit, soft center; needs age, good potential.★★(+)

Castello di S. Polo In Rosso, "Castelpolo" (5/85). Lovely berrylike aroma, vaguely floral; light tannin, raspberry flavor, easy.★ +

Castello di Volpaia riserva (twice 5/85). Delicate floral aroma with a hint of pine; moderate tannin, fruity; room to improve.★★

Castello Vicchiomaggio (5/85; just bottled that day). Vaguely floral aroma with a touch of raspberries; some tannin, flavorful, a bit light; tannin builds up at the end.★(?)

Fattoria Montagliari riserva, Cappelli Giovanni (ex-cask 5/85). Lovely bouquet; sweet fruit with a honeylike back note, moderate tannin, well balanced; very good.★★(★)

Fontodi riserva (5/85; 15,500 bottles). Oak and a lot of fruit on the nose; some tannin, beginning to soften and come ready; finish is somewhat astringent.★★(+)

Isole e Olena riserva (5/85). Fragrant aroma with an oak component; light tannin, well balanced, soft and supple in the center, coming ready but still needs more time.★★(+)

La Ripa (5/85). Floral, berrylike aroma with a raisiny note; tannic entry, flavor of overripe fruit.★ −

Le Masse di San Leolino (twice 5/85). Fragrant floral bouquet with a touch of resin; elegant, a lot of flavor and a lot of style; could be longer on the finish; near its peak.★★

Luiano (7/85). Rubber-tire aroma, vague berry and floral notes; has fruit and a slight spritz, also sediment; refermented in the bottle; barely drinkable.

Monsanto, Il Poggio riserva (ex-cask 4/85). Floral, fruity aroma; light tannin, ripe, almost sweet fruit; has style.★★(+)

Monte Vertine riserva (5/85). Expansive, perfumed, floral bouquet, some oak; well-knit, soft center, some delicacy; ready though could improve.★★★ −

Monticelli (Viticola Toscana) *(5/85)*. Simple, fruity, quaffable.★ −

Pagliarese riserva *(twice 5/85)*. Fresh, raspberry-like aroma; good body, still some tannin, balanced; drinkable now but will improve.★★(+)

Podere Il Palazzino riserva *(5/85; 3160 bottles)*. Floral aroma with a hint of toffee; light tannin, has fruit, unstructured; not a success.

Poggio al Sole *(5/85; 30,087 bottles)*. Floral aroma with some delicacy; light tannin, tart, flavorful; lively finish.★ +

Querciabella vecchio *(6/85; 6000 bottles)*. Lovely floral aroma, brambly character; fruity, well balanced; somewhat light toward the end.★★

Ruffino *(11/83)*. Light, fruity, fresh, and quaffable; a good, easy-drinking glass of wine.★

San Felice *(3/85)*. Fragrant floral perfume; fairly high acid; has fruit, getting tired but still drinkable; age shows, especially toward the finish.★

Santa Cristina, Antinori *(twice 3/85)*. Light nose; unbalanced, high acid and alcohol intrude, has fruit but showing age; still drinkable. (Bottle of 10/83 was much more enjoyable, with more fruit and better balance.★) This bottle 0

Savignola Paolina *(twice 5/85)*. Nice aroma; flavorful, soft, smooth, has some delicacy and charm. The bottle of 10/83 was just as nice.★★ +

Vecchie Terre di Montefili riserva *(5/85)*. Nice nose, vaguely floral; well-knit, quite forward and ready, but room to improve yet.★★(+)

Vigna Vecchia riserva *(5/85)*. Low fruit, flat, shallow, dull.

Villa Antinori riserva *(5/85)*. Small aroma; astringent and harsh, young, firm structure, some potential evident; very harsh finish.★(★ −)

Villa Calcinaia, Conti Capponi *(4/85)*. Baked character.

Vistarenni, Podere Bertinga *(4/85)*. Nice fruit on the nose, vaguely floral; tannic vein, with the stuffing to support it.★★ −

1980 ★★

There was a short spring in 1980, and the flowering took place late. The summer was characterized by fluctuating temperatures and long periods of dry weather. It was a normal fall, but the harvest was brought in late, during the last week of October through the first week of November.

The wines are medium-bodied and have good color. They are fairly high in acid, more so than the '79s, similar to the '78s; they have less tannin than either. Paolo di Marchi found the wines light in body, perhaps even a bit thin. Castello di Gabbiano and Vicchiomaggio considered it an excellent vintage. Antinori gives it four points out of a possible five. Castello dei Rampolla and San Polo in Rosso described it as a good vintage, Villa Cafaggio places it about average, Castell'In Villa said it was all right but not one of their favorites, and Villa Calcinaia found it a medium year.

The best wines of the vintage, to our taste, were the Monsanto Il Poggio and Isole e Olena, followed by Castello dei Rampolla, Monsanto riserva, and Poggio al Sole. The least of them were the riservas of Campomaggio, La Loggia, Pagliarese, and Tenuta Villa Rosa.

Brolio *(twice 10/83)*. Characteristic aroma; light tannin; simple and quaffable, no more.★ −

Campomaggio riserva *(5/85)*. Aroma of tobacco and cherries, a bit corked; overly tannic for the fruit.

Capannelle riserva *(5/85)*. A touch of peppermint on the aroma; tannic entry gives way to nice fruit; well made, young, has potential; weak finish.★★

Cappelli Giovanni, "La Querce" *(5/82)*. Fresh and fruity, light and tasty; has some charm.★ +

Castellare *(2/83)*. Vaguely toasty note on nose, very little else; moderate fruit, tart edge, a bit thin; not a success; shows more age than the '79.

Castello dei Rampolla riserva *(5/85)*. Reticent aroma with hints of oak and cabernet fruit, vaguely floral; firm structure, cabernet herbaceousness more apparent as the wine airs, lean; somewhat austere but well made and distinctive, if not exactly our idea of a Chianti.★★(+)

Castello di S. Polo In Rosso riserva *(twice 5/85)*. Floral aroma; moderate tannin, drinkable now but should improve; tannic finish.★(★)

Castello di S. Polo In Rosso vecchio *(twice 5/85)*. Vaguely musty on aroma, some fruit; light tannin, fruity; a bit short.★ +

Castello di Volpaia riserva *(twice 5/85)*. Floral aroma with notes of almonds and a touch of pine; tasty, balanced, a nice mouthful of wine; could be longer on the aftertaste.★★

Castello Vicchiomaggio, "Prima Vigna" riserva *(ex-barrique, 5/85)*. Oak up front on nose, some fruit in the back; at this point the oak dominates, more tannin and body than the regular riserva.★(★)

Castello Vicchiomaggio riserva *(5/85)*. Floral aroma with toasty notes; flavorful, moderate tannin, well balance; short; needs a few years, shows promise.★(+)

Fattoria Montagliari riserva, Cappelli Giovanni *(ex-cask 5/85)*. Light nose with some fruit evident; fairly tannic, fruit is there; short, tannic finish.★(★)

Fontodi riserva *(twice 5/85; 13,480 bottles)*. Floral aroma still somewhat closed; some tannin, a bit light, flavorful; nearly ready, most likely won't keep.★★

Isole e Olena riserva *(5/85)*. Floral aroma with some oak; fairly tannic, supple center, well balanced; some length.★★(★)

La Loggia riserva *(4/85)*. Fruity aroma, astringent, unbalanced.

La Ripa *(5/85)*. Somewhat floral aroma; fairly tannic, has fruit; harsh finish.★

Le Masse di San Leolino riserva *(twice 4/85)*. Lovely floral bouquet with a touch of cherries; light tannin, a lot of flavor, some style and character; needs some time to soften.★★

Lilliano *(10/83)*. Very light though characteristic floral aroma; soft and tasty, most agreeable; very ready.★★

Luiano riserva *(7/85)*. Aroma has a baked character, jammy, overripe, heavy; light tannin, fruit on entry, then thins out; tannic aftertaste; not a success.

Monsanto, Il Poggio riserva *(ex-cask 4/85)*. Nice nose, some spice; fairly full and tannic, spicy and fruity, heaps of flavor.★★(★)

Monsanto riserva *(4/85)*. Expansive floral aroma with a touch of licorice; has tannin and the fruit to carry it; tart finish with a suggestion of berries.★★(+)

Monte Vertine *(10/83)*. Light floral aroma; some fruit, fairly well balanced, light tannin, good flavor; very ready.★★

Pagliarese riserva *(twice 4/85)*. Both bottles were oxidized.

Poggio al Sole riserva *(5/85; 4906 bottles)*. Delicate floral aroma, vaguely berrylike; firm, well balanced; lively finish.★★+

Querciabella riserva *(6/85; 6000 bottles)*. Spicy aroma, black pepper nuance; fruity, seems a trifle tired though quite drinkable.★★

Riecine *(10/83)*. Straightforward, fruity aroma; light tannin, tasty, balanced; quite nice.★★

Rocca della Macìe *(4/81)*. Fruity aroma with some spice; fresh and fruity; high acid, unbalanced.

Ruffino Riserva Ducale gold label *(ex-cask 7/82)*. Cherrylike aroma; considerable fruit, well structured; should make a nice bottle.★★(?)

San Felice, "Il Grigio" riserva *(4/85)*. Perfumed aroma with floral notes; tannic edge, fruit is evident in the center; tannic finish; has potential.★★

Tenuta Villa Rosa riserva *(4/85)*. Fruity aroma and flavor, rather astringent.

Viticcio riserva *(twice 11/84 and 6/85; 10,000 bottles)*. Bottle of 11/84: Floral scent, vaguely candylike; some tannin, has fruit; fairly well balanced; nearly ready; some firmness at the end.★★

Bottle of 6/85: Similar, but some age starting to show in the form of acid at the end; drink up.

1979 ★★+

The summer of 1979 was favorable and the harvest long. It was a very large crop, and some of the grapes came in overripe. Sergio Manetti of Monte Vertine considers this his best Chianti Classico vintage. Antinori gives it top marks, five out of five. Minuccio Cappelli (Fattoria Montagliari), Villa Calcinaia, Pagliarese, and Castello dei Rampolla found it a very good year. Castll'In Villa described it as good, San Polo in Rosso said very good, and Villa Cafaggio rated it average. Vignamaggio and Barone Ricasoli said it was not a good vintage. Paolo di Marchi said that because of overcropping his wines were light and thin, wines that won't age. Niederbacher gives the year three stars; the consorzio gives two.

Having tasted nearly four dozen Chianti Classicos, we find that overall it was indeed a very good vintage. The wines are for early drinking, though a few will age. The best we thought were the riservas of Capannelle, Monte Vertine, Monsanto Il Poggio, and Poggio Rosso; then Montagliari, Castell'In Villa, Rampolla, Isole e Olena, Monsanto, Vignamaggio, and Villa Cafaggio, also all riservas. We were very unimpressed with the Castello di Monterinaldi, Cellole, Montemaggio, Vicchiomaggio, and Vistarenni riservas, and the Isabella de' Medici.

Badia a Coltibuono riserva *(5/85)*. Vaguely floral aroma with a touch of pine; moderate tannin, firm, flavorful; some astringency at the end.★(★)

"Berardenga," Fattoria Felsina riserva *(5/85)*. Floral aroma with a raspberry note, seems older than its years; good body, tart edge, still some tannin to soften.★(★)

Capannelle riserva *(5/85)*. Peppermint and fruit on aroma; still some tannin, tasty; long finish that recalls pine and mint; will improve.★★(★)

Capannelle vecchio *(10/83)*. Fruity aroma with a touch of flowers; light tannin, fruity.★+

Cappelli Giovanni, "La Querce" *(twice 12/83)*. Fruity aroma and flavor, but has lost its freshness and charm. (Bottle tasted a year earlier was still fairly fresh, meriting.★)

Castelgreve riserva *(10/83)*. Still some tannin, decent balance; a bit young but drinkable now.★

Castellare *(2/83)*. Fragrant, characteristic Chianti aroma; soft and fruity, agreeable, some tannin but nice now.★+

Castell'In Villa riserva *(5/85)*. Complex bouquet with notes of flowers, pine, mint, and raspberries; some tannin, a lot of flavor, good body, quite ready; long, firm finish with notes of blackberries.★★+

Castello dei Rampolla riserva *(5/85)*. Herbaceous cabernet aroma, some fruit in the back; well made, firm tannin, cabernet character dominates. Is this a Chianti?★★(+)

Castello di Fonterutoli riserva *(10/83)*. Fragrant floral aroma; soft and smooth, balanced; quite nice now.★★

Castello di Monterinaldi riserva *(5/85)*. Some fruit, light tannin, unstructured, shallow; short.

Castello di S. Polo In Rosso (*3 times 5/85*). Vaguely woodsy, mushroomlike aroma with a touch of leather; tannin on entry gives way to nice fruit; tannic aftertaste, vaguely bitter. (Bottle tasted 7/83 seemed softer and more ready to drink.)★(★)

Castello di Volpaia riserva (*twice 5/85*). Floral, pinelike aroma with spicy notes, has delicacy; light tannin; ready now though can improve.★★

Catignano (*twice 1/83*). Pale color; fresh and quaffable, seems almost sweet.★

Cellole riserva (*twice 10/83*). Aroma, flavor, and structure recall a southern wine.

"Cepperellaccio," Principe Kunz d'Asburgo Lorena (*11/80*). A light, unbalanced wine; the most interesting thing about it is the name.

Cispiano Riserva della Serena (*4/85*). Perfumed scent with a spicy note; light-bodied, some fruit, lacks freshness; dull aftertaste.

Fattoria Montagliari riserva, Cappelli Giovanni (*5 times 5/85*). Floral perfume; somewhat astringent, a bit light, nice flavor; long finish, with a bite, needs more age.★★(+)

Fontodi riserva (*twice 5/85*). Floral notes and some berries on aroma, showing age; still some tannin, flavorful, a bit light, some tannin at the end; ready now.★★

Isabella de' Medici (*twice 4/83*). Pale, anemic color; some character on aroma; light, fruity, simple; could have more weight, but drinkable.

Isole e Olena (*5/85; magnum*). Lovely bouquet of fruit and a touch of oak; light tannin, soft and round, smooth, well balanced; light finish; near its peak.★★+

La Ripa riserva (*twice 5/85*). Bottle of 10/83: Lovely floral bouquet; balanced; some tannin, tasty, ready now.★★+
Bottle of 5/85: Small nose; overly tannic; alcoholic aftertaste.★−

Monsanto, Il Poggio riserva (*twice 4/85; 32,880 bottles*). Richly concentrated aroma with suggestions of flowers, berries, and apricots; moderate tannin, a bit light for Il Poggio but flavorful, with a sweetness to the fruit; long, lingering finish; should be ready in about two to three years.★★(★−)

Monsanto riserva (*4 times 4/85*). Flowers, spice, and fruit on aroma; still has tannin, fairly nice fruit; a trifle short; ready, though it could improve.

Monsanto, "Santa Caterina" (*10/81*). Fruity aroma with cherrylike notes; agreeable, fruity, touch of tannin; falls away quickly at the end.

Monte Vertine (*5 times 10/83*). Characteristic floral bouquet with some fruit; not to keep but quite enjoyable now.★+

Monte Vertine riserva (*10/83*). Has richness of bouquet and flavor that make it seem drinkable now, though it still has tannin to shed.★★(★)

Montemaggio riserva (*4/85*). Seaweed on aroma and flavor; awful.

Pagliarese, Boscardini riserva (*4/85*). Fruity aroma seems somewhat restrained, a touch of oak; firm tannic vein, has the structure and flavor; finishes short.★★

Pagliarese riserva (*3 times 5/85*). Floral aroma with raspberry-like fruit; light tannin, fruity, quite ready, soft; vaguely bitter at the end. (Perhaps was better in 10/83.)★★

Palazzo al Bosco (*ex-vat 11/80*). Heaps of flavor; well balanced; should make a nice bottle in time.★★

Poggio al Sole (*5/85; 40,942 bottles*). Pale garnet; light floral aroma with a suggestion of berries; light tannin, soft and flavorful, very ready; moderately long, lively finish.★★

Poggio Rosso riserva (special selection of San Felice) (*4/85; 7536 bottles*). Fruity aroma; well balanced, firm tannic vein, flavorful; real quality here.★★★−

Quercia al Poggio (*5/85*). Pale garnet; fragrant aroma; too much tannin for the fruit, but drinkable enough.★−

Querciabella riserva (*6/85; 2100 bottles*). Spicy aroma bears a resemblance to the '81, brambly note; light tannin, fruity, ready.★★

Riecine (*ex-vat 4/80*). Nice aroma; fruity; shows promise.★(★+)

Rocca della Macìe (*11/80*). Smallish nose; light-bodied, fresh, some fruit; very short.

Ruffino (*twice 11/80*). Fresh and fruity, a simple little quaffing wine, goes down easily.★

Ruffino Riserva Ducale (*11/83*). Fruity aroma with some freshness; lovely for current drinking, no need for further age.★★

Santa Cristina, Antinori (*twice 10/82*). Lovely nose; light to medium in body, soft and smooth, an agreeable little wine. (There has been bottle variation; the bottle of 11/80 was harsh and unbalanced and shy of fruit.)★

Vigna Vecchia riserva (*5/85*). Floral aroma with a touch of cherries; light tannin, low in fruit, unbalanced.

Vignamaggio riserva (*5/85*). Pretty floral aroma; some tannin, well balanced, a lighter style, still needs some time to soften; tannic ending.★★(+)

Villa Antinori riserva (*twice 5/85*). A vague harshness on the nose and some cabernet character evident; fairly soft though has some tannin, a good glass of wine, lacks style and definition but drinkable enough.★+

Villa Antinori Riserva Marchese (*5/85*). Herbaceous bell pepper aroma up front with some fruit in the back; moderate tannin beginning to soften, somewhat astringent, flavorful, bell pepper notes intrude; needs a few years to really soften.★(★)

Villa Banfi (*3/85*). Rather shy on aroma, some fruit; medium body, some acid throws the balance off, might soften a bit but hardly seems worth the wait; drinkable now but not a lot to it.★−

Villa Cafaggio riserva (*5/85*). Blackberries on aroma; heaps of flavor, light tannin, surprisingly big for a '79; tannic finish.★★+

Villa Colombaio (*ex-cask 4/80*). Light, perfumed bouquet; very soft and fruity; surprisingly forward; very good.★★

Vistarenni (*twice 10/83 and 4/85*). Both bottles were quite similar; a small, dull wine of no character or style.

1978 ★★

Barone Ricasoli rates this as one of the very best vintages. Castell'In Villa said it was a great one. Villa Calcinaia also puts in among the best. Antinori gives it four out of five points. San Polo in Rosso considers it very good, as does Vicchiomaggio. For Badia a Coltibuono it was better than 1977. Gabbiano and Catignano describe it as good, and Villa Cafaggio calls it about average. Paolo di Marchi finds the wines not well balanced, in some ways similar to the '80s. Niederbacher gives it four stars; the consorzio gives it three.

After having tasted more than four dozen different Chianti Classicos, we find the vintage doesn't live up to the press it received early on. While many wines still need more time, we suspect they won't turn out all that well. It has never been one of our favorite vintages. We did like a few wines, though, very much: Pagliarese Boscardini riserva, San Felice "Il Grigio" riserva, and Villa Banfi riserva.

Badia a Coltibuono riserva *(3 times 5/85)*. Perfumed bouquet with characteristic flowers and a hint of pine; supple center, needs more time to soften some rough edges but developing very well. (Considerably softer than a bottle tasted two years earlier.)★★★(+)

Bertolli riserva *(10/83)*. Small aroma; tasty, lacks somewhat in structure and length, but agreeable.

Brolio *(twice 2/85)*. Harsh and unbalanced, shallow, dull, thin; was better in 1/80; now too old.

Brolio riserva *(3 times 10/83)*. Simple aroma; some tannin and firmness, simple flavors; drinkable now, could improve.★

Brolio Riserva del Barone *(9/83)*. Splendid aroma, a lot of fruit, fresh; moderate tannin, well balanced, nice flavor, drinks well now; the best Brolio we've tasted in years.★★

Burchino *(8/82)*. Dull though characteristic aroma; flat, dull, and tired; too old.

Capannelle riserva *(5/85)*. Woodsy bouquet with notes of mushrooms; fairly rich and tannic, firm, well made; very long finish that recalls pine; needs age yet.★★(+)

Cappelli Giovanni, "La Querce" *(2/85)*. Floral aroma; almost sweet on entry, then thins out; too old.

Casa Sola *(11/79)*. Fresh and grapey, yet with a hot, baked character about it.

Casa Sola riserva *(3/83)*. Characteristic Chianti aroma; moderate fruit, some tannin, lacks style; not a lot to it.

Castellare *(10/83)*. Simple, fruity aroma with a hint of flowers; flavorful, balanced, light tannin; ready now.★+

Castell'In Villa riserva *(5/85)*. Floral aroma with a minty note and something vaguely odd; soft center with a lot of tannin around it; long finish.★(★★−)

Castello di Cerreto riserva, Emilio Pucci *(5/85)*. Floral, fruity aroma; fairly rich, tannin to shed; finishes on a tannic note.★(★)

Castello di Querceto *(twice 1/83)*. Nice aroma; balanced, fresh, and fruity, tasty, some style; quite good.★★

Castello di S. Polo In Rosso *(twice 5/85)*. Floral bouquet with berrylike notes; some tannin and a surprising amount of fruit, quite drinkable; finishes short with some tannic roughness.★★

Castello di S. Polo In Rosso riserva *(3 times 5/85)*. Same wine as the regular aged one year in oak; aroma of concentrated grapes and figs; some tannin, soft; vaguely bitter, overly tannic finish; drink up now.★★

Castello di Volpaia riserva *(5/85)*. Floral bouquet with a touch of pine; quite drinkable, light tannin; a bit short.★★−

Castello Vicchiomaggio riserva *(twice 5/85)*. Vague floral notes on nose; moderate tannin, fruity, angular; good, but seemed softer when tasted 10/83.★+

Cerbaiola di Barfede-Certaldo *(4/80)*. Lightly fruity aroma; a bit light, fruity, some tannin.★

Fattoria della Aiola riserva *(10/83)*. Small nose; small wine, not a lot of fruit, seems like more tannin than there is because of lack of fruit.

Fattoria Montagliari riserva, Cappelli Giovanni *(twice 7/85)*. Mineral aroma, vaguely floral; some tannin, nice fruit, a bit light, some tannin, should improve but lacks some style; not up to this producer, either bottle, and the first was tasted 10/83.★

Fossi *(2/85)*. Dull, boring; ho-humm.

"Granducato" Riserva Corona *(10/83)*. Light nose, seems closed; good fruit up front, a bit shallow; overly tannic finish; not bad, just unimpressive.

Isole e Olena riserva *(5/85)*. Floral bouquet with notes of leather and caramel on a background of oak; some tannin, fruity, some oak, supple; long.★★(+)

La Pagliaia Riserva Granduca Ferdinando III *(4/85)*. Perfumed bouquet; fruity, peppery flavor; tannic finish.★+

La Ripa riserva *(twice 5/85)*. Bottle of 10/83: Nice fruit initially on the nose gives way to a dullness; good fruit on palate; fair balance.★−

Bottle of 5/85: Aroma of prunes and raisins, jammy; overly tannic; alcoholic finish; drying out.

Luiano *(2/85)*. Thin, yeasty, flat, dull, unbalanced.

Monsanto, Il Poggio riserva *(twice 4/85; 38,650 bottles)*. Aroma somewhat reticent; hard, slightly astringent, closed in, very young, but quality is evident.★★(★−)

Monsanto riserva *(twice 5/82)*. Aroma somewhat closed, hints of tar and fruit; rich flavors, still somewhat backward, loads of flavor, some spiciness.★★

Pagliarese *(4/80)*. Lightly fruity aroma; easy to drink.★+

Pagliarese, Boscardini riserva *(5/85)*. Floral bouquet with raspberry-like fruit; full-flavored, well balanced, light tannin; long finish; very ready.★★★

Pagliarese riserva *(5/85)*. Reticent nose with some fruit; still a bit tannic, soft; short.★+

Palazzo al Bosco *(twice 6/81)*. Nose is rather subdued, hints of berries; smooth texture, moderate tannin; quite good; ready.★+

Poggio al Sole *(twice 5/81)*. Lovely perfumed aroma, with fruity overtones; lively acidity; clean, refreshing aftertaste.★★

Riecine *(4/80)*. Wild cherries leap out of the glass; well balanced, lots of fruit, some tannin.★★

Riseccoli *(4/80)*. A bit light in body, some tannin; short.

Rocca della Macìe *(11/80)*. Lacking in aroma; some freshness and fruit; rather short, dull aftertaste.

Ruffino *(11/80)*. Fresh, fruity aroma; some tannin, soft, pleasant drinking.★

Ruffino, Montemasso *(ex-cask 11/80)*. Nice nose; fruity, some tannin.★

190

"S. Leolino," Fattoria I Cipressi riserva *(3 times 2/85)*. Bottle of 10/83: Floral bouquet; tannin up front, with the fruit to support it; agreeable though not much else.★

Bottle of 2/85: Thin, some fruit, unbalanced; too old.

San Felice, "Il Grigio" riserva *(10/83)*. Lovely, fragrant bouquet; a nice mouthful of fruit; needs a few years but is drinkable now.★★(★)

Valiano riserva *(10/83)*. Small nose, some fruit; light tannin, moderate fruit, some dullness, but drinkable.

Vigna Vecchia riserva *(5/85)*. Seems a lot older than a '78.

Vignamaggio *(11/80)*. Floral, fruity aroma; light-to medium-bodied, fruity, some tannin, balanced; ready.★ +

Vignamaggio riserva *(5/85)*. Floral aroma with a toffeelike note; firm and tannic, needs time to soften; a bit short.★(★)

Villa Antinori riserva *(twice 10/83)*. Fruity aroma with a cabernet-like herbaceousness; tannic, moderate fruit, somewhat unbalanced; short.

Villa Antinori Riserva Marchese *(5/85)*. Weedy, herbaceous aroma, more like cabernet than sangiovese; moderate tannin, fairly well structured; again cabernet dominates on palate.★(★)

Villa Banfi *(twice 3/85)*. Fragrant, floral bouquet with a touch of oak; very well balanced, a lot of flavor, has character and style; one of the better '78s.★★★

Villa Calcinaia, Conti Capponi *(3 times 2/85)*. Bottle of 10/83: Very dull.

Bottle of 2/85: Oxidized.

Villa Calcinaia, Conti Capponi riserva *(4/85)*. Aroma and taste have a cooked quality.

Villa Cerna riserva *(10/83)*. Small nose; good fruit on palate, moderate tannin, drinkable, has room for improvement.★

Villa Consuelo *(twice 2/85)*. Anemic color; shows age, astringent, thinning out at end.

1977 ★★ +

This vintage was highly regarded from the start, and for good reason. Many fine wines were produced. In fact, it is possible that Fabrizio Bianchi's Monsanto Il Poggio was his finest to date, no mean feat when you consider the '75, '71, '66, '64, and '62 that preceded it.

Villa Cafaggio describes 1977 as excellent; Giovanni Cappelli, Pagliarese, Catignano, and Vicchiomaggio all consider it especially fine; La Ripa said for them it was perhaps the best ever. Antinori, Villa Calcinaia, and Castell'In Villa rate it very good. Paolo di Marchi said it was an easy vintage, with no problems, but the wines are now getting too old.

For us, some wines—too many, in fact—are showing age badly. But eight years is getting on for a Chianti Classico. Besides the really outstanding Monsanto Il Poggio, we were also impressed with the Capannelle and Berardenga riservas and Baccio da Gaiuole; Isole e Olena and Monsanto riserva were not far behind. The Castell'In Villa is pretty good as well.

Baccio da Gaiuole *(3/79)*. Youthful aroma with character; flavorful, tannin to shed, has structure and style. Out of a group of about thirty Chianti Classicos, this was clearly the best.★★★

Badia a Coltibuono riserva *(10/82)*. Unfortunately, the only time we tasted this wine the bottle was slightly corked, but the structure and flavor indicated its quality.★★(★?)

Barberini *(11/79)*. An undistinguished little wine.

"Berardenga," Fattoria Felsina *(9/79)*. Fresh, fruity Chianti aroma; a bit light but tasty; a good quaffing wine.★

"Berardenga," Fattoria Felsina riserva *(5/85)*. Floral bouquet; firm, flavorful, good body; still needs time, but has potential.★★(★)

Brolio *(3/82)*. Fragrant aroma; light-bodied, shows some signs of drying out, dull.

Capannelle riserva *(5/85)*. Woodsy bouquet with a touch of strawberries; light tannin, soft, sweet, tasty, impressive; long finish with notes of strawberries and mint.★★★ +

Cappelli Giovanni, "La Querce" *(twice 11/79)*. Fresh, fruity aroma and flavor, some spice on the finish.★ +

Carobbio vecchio *(10/80)*. Pretty nose, delicate and scented; soft, some tannin, good flavor; ready.★

Castelgreve riserva *(10/83)*. Has fruit, moderate tannin; very drinkable though an atypical Chianti.★ −

Castell'In Villa *(twice 5/85)*. Floral bouquet with a vaguely vegetal back note that adds complexity; light tannin, flavorful, soft, velvety, round; some tannin at the end, finish has a note of blackberries and a touch of mint; enjoyable now.★★★ −

Castello di Cacchiano *(twice 6/81)*. On aroma seems more like a California wine than a Chianti, slightly toasty, and a faint off note; soft-centered, harsh edges, something off on flavor.

Castello di Cerreto riserva, Emilio Pucci *(10/83)*. Smallish nose; some fruit on entry, then shallow.

Castello di Fonterutoli *(twice 6/81)*. Light nose, some fruit evident; moderate tannin, balanced, flavorful, almost sweet; a small-scale wine.★ −

Castello di Meleto riserva *(5/85)*. Not much aroma; low in fruit; drying out.

Castello di Rencine *(4/80)*. Floral, fruity aroma; a bit light for the tannin; slightly bitter aftertaste.

Castello di San Donato in Perano riserva *(5/85)*. Small nose; unbalanced, no particular character; grating aftertaste.

Castello Vicchiomaggio riserva *(twice 5/85)*. Aroma recalls a bakery shop, toffee notes that carry over on the palate; fairly tannic, seems to have sufficient fruit, an angular wine; short tannic finish. Will it develop?★(+)

"Cerbaiola" di Barfede-Certaldo *(4/80)*. Floral aroma with some fruit; light, fruity, simple.★

Cispiano *(11/79)*. Light aroma; unbalanced, some flavor; not much to it.

Fattoria delle Barone *(4/81)*. Floral aroma marred by volatile acidity and lactic overtones; light-bodied and shallow, lacks structure, flavor, and length.

Fattoria delle Lodoline *(3 times 6/81)*. Harsh aroma, some fruit but showing age; drying out. Even in 1979 it didn't amount to much.

Fattoria Montagliari e Castellinuzza riserva, Cappelli Giovanni *(4 times 5/84)*. Floral perfume; soft, light tannin, full of flavor, some elegance.★★(+)

Fattoria Montagliari riserva, Cappelli Giovanni *(5/85)*. Moderate tannin, well balanced, flavorful; still young but drinkable now.★★(+)

Fossi vecchio *(5/83)*. Nice nose; fruity entry but shallow.

Il Guerrino *(3/79)*. Hot nose; has weight in the mouth; seems clumsy.

Isole e Olena riserva *(5/85)*. Berrylike aroma with a roasted, toasty aspect; some tannin, soft-centered, drinkable but could improve over the next two years.★★★

La Pagliaia riserva Granduca Ferdinando III *(10/83)*. Light nose; nice flavor, moderate tannin; short.★

La Ripa riserva *(twice 5/85)*. Bottle of 10/83: Light, fruity aroma; some tannin, drinkable now, nowhere to go.★

Bottle of 5/85: Some oxidation, moldy, gone.

Le Bocce *(10/78)*. Very fresh and fruity; tart, lively, *beverino.*★+

Mazzoni (bottled by Villa Cafaggio) *(11/79)*. Hot nose; light-bodied; not much to it.

Monsanto, Il Poggio riserva *(7 times 4/85; 23,730 bottles)*. Big, richly fruited bouquet, expansive and complex, with nuances of flowers, blackberries, blueberries, apricots; enormous extract and weight, richly concentrated, exceptional balance, still quite tannic, full of life and style; superb; might just be the best Monsanto to date.★★★(★)

Monsanto riserva *(5 times 9/83)*. Big, rich aroma; lots of fruit with hints of spice, blueberries, vanilla, and flowers; moderate tannin, heaps of fruit; lovely now but could improve.★★★

Monsanto vecchio *(4/80)*. Perfumed bouquet; some tannin but good now, fruity, balanced; some length.★★

Nozzole riserva *(10/83)*. Light, characteristic floral bouquet; soft, ready though could improve.★★

Pagliarese *(3 times 5/81)*. Somewhat reticent aroma with hints of fruit and flowers; flavorful, soft, has style; a nice bottle.★★+

Pian d'Albola *(twice 6/81)*. Floral aroma with some fruit; almost sweet on entry, still has tannin, light-bodied, tart edge; ready now, not to keep.★

Poggio al Sole *(twice 9/82; 39,833 bottles, unfined, unfiltered)*. Nice floral aroma; fruity, agreeable flavors, but a harsh acidic edge, a little meager in body; some alcohol intrudes on the finish; old and tired, though still drinkable.

Riecine *(3 times 11/80)*. Characteristic flowers on aroma; refreshing, lively acidity, fruity, well made.★★

Riseccoli *(3 times 6/81)*. Aroma has hints of coffee, some oxidation intrudes; harsh edges, some fruit, but has seen better days, though we're not sure when. Even in March 1979, it seemed old and tired.

Rocca delle Macìe *(10/78)*. Fresh, fruity, and simple; low acid, good flavor.★−

Ruffino *(11/79)*. Fresh and fruity; tart, some tannin; quaffable.★

Saccardi *(1/82)*. Has some character and flavor but in all an unimpressive small wine.

Serrestori *(11/78)*. Light, fresh, and fruity; quaffable.★

Serrestori, "Ser Niccolo" riserva *(10/83)*. Smallish nose; unbalanced, not a lot of fruit, moderate tannin; altogether unimpressive.

Tenuta La Colombaia riserva *(2/83)*. Small nose; light-bodied, not a lot of flavor, lacks life, harsh edges; bitter aftertaste.

Valiano *(11/79)*. Pale; some fruit, vinous, undistinguished.

Vignale *(twice 2/80)*. Lovely, fragrant bouquet, and that's its one real virtue; a bit light, fruity but shallow.

Villa Antinori riserva *(9/83)*. Characteristic floral aroma with some fruit; well structured, some tannin to lose, firm acidity; probably needs three years to smooth out the harsh edges.★★(+)

Villa Antinori Riserva Marchese *(5/85)*. Weedy, bell pepper aroma with a touch of fruit and some oxidation; fruity, herbaceous flavor. Is this a Cabernet or a Chianti? Astringent aftertaste; seems older than its years.★

Villa Cafaggio *(3/79)*. Some fruit on aroma and palate; moderate length.★★−

Villa Colombaio *(twice 4/80)*. Perfumed bouquet; soft and fruity, some tannin, balanced, tasty.★★−

Viticcio riserva *(7/82; 10,000 bottles)*. Lightly perfumed aroma; light and soft, not a lot to it; shallow, thin; short.

1976 0

This vintage was without a doubt the worst of the decade. For the most part, it should never have been bottled. Bianchi didn't bottle a Monsanto. Minuccio Cappelli didn't offer a Montagliari. He did bottle a small amount of fairly agreeable wine for his personal use.

Of the two most successful '76s we tasted, both producers—Badia a Coltibuono and Cappelli—considered the vintage very bad if not downright poor. The best anyone had to say for it, in fact, came from Stefano Farkas of Villa Cafaggio, who said the vintage was "not good."

Badia a Coltibuono riserva *(5/85; 7600 bottles)*. Musty aroma with berrylike notes; a surprising amount of fruit, not to keep.★

Castello di Gabbiano *(3/79)*. Pale; oxidized; thin, alcoholic.

Cecchi *(3/79)*. Some tannin, lacks substance, weight, and length.

Fattoria Montagliari, Cappelli Giovanni *(5/85)*. From a single barrel bottled in 1979–80; still has fruit, suggestions of leather, very light and soft; thin finish.★

La Ripa *(5/85)*. Off flavors of rotten grapes.

Le Bocce *(10/78)*. Fruity, flavorful, light-bodied, a bit clumsy.★−

1976

Monte Vertine *(3/79)*. Small nose; fruity entry gives way to a harshness toward the end.

Montepaldi, Marchese Corsini *(3/79)*. Hot, alcoholic nose; touch of oxidation.

1975 ★★★

This vintage was highly acclaimed from the outset. Antinori once again gives it five out of five. Felsina said it was very, very good. Cispiano considers it one of the great years, and numerous other producers also rate it excellent.

During the harvest there was rain, and it made a difference when the grapes were picked. We've tasted some four dozen '75s; many were fine, but many others were tired, showing age, or poor from the start. The best, once again, was the outstanding Monsanto Il Poggio. Only second to the Il Poggio was the exceptional Montagliari Vigna di Casaloste, then the riservas of Felsina's Berardenga, Montagliari, Badia a Coltibuono, Poggio al Sole, Castell'In Villa, and the Fortilizio Il Colombaio. For the most part, these wines are ready now.

Badia a Coltibuono riserva *(7 times 5/85)*. Floral bouquet with notes of berries; firm, a mouthful of flavor and a lot of tannin; very young yet but has all the ingredients for a splendid wine.★★(★)

"Berardenga," Fattoria Felsina riserva *(5/85)*. Aroma still closed; rich in flavor, considerable tannin, needs another three or so years to soften, firm structure; a lot of quality here.★★(★ +)

Brolio *(11/79)*. Pale garnet; onionlike aspect to aroma; has body and flavor; ready.★

Brolio riserva *(twice 9/83)*. Fragrant floral aroma; not a lot of fruit, a fair amount of tannin, somewhat unbalanced; won't keep. A bottle tasted 1/80 seemed to be drying out.

Capannelle riserva *(5/85)*. Complex floral bouquet with woodsy notes; well balanced, full-flavored, still some tannin; fairly long finish with a suggestion of mint; tannin builds up at the end, too much?★★(?★)

Carobbio *(10/80)*. Tired, noticeable oxidation.

Casa Sola riserva *(11/79)*. A bit light; has tannin, fruit, and backbone; try again in two to three years.★

Castelgreve riserva *(10/83)*. Aroma of raisins, oxidation apparent; still has some fruit and tannin; lacks style.

Castell'In Villa riserva *(5/85)*. Delicate, floral bouquet with nuances of mint and pine; a rich mouthful of flavor, well structured; very long finish, some tannin at the end; room to improve but very nice now.★★★ −

Castello di Cacchiano *(twice 6/81)*. Characteristic aroma, floral and fruity; some tannin, tart edge; shows age, not to keep; was better in 3/79.

Castello di Fonterutoli *(3/79)*. Floral bouquet marred by intrusion of alcohol; light, flavorful; short, with some alcohol at the end.

Castello di Rencine *(twice 6/81)*. Small aroma with some fruit, some oxidation; nice entry, mellow, some tannin; a biting sharpness at the end; too old; was better two years earlier, but still didn't amount to much.

Castello di S. Polo In Rosso *(5/85)*. Floral aroma; flavorful, soft, somewhat rustic; has aged surprisingly well for a regular Chianti.★★ −

Cispiano *(11/79)*. Some fruit, some tannin, not much interest.

Conti Capponi *(twice 11/79)*. Pale; light-bodied; not much to it except some tannin.

Fattoria della Aiola riserva *(3/79)*. Some oxidation; light, harsh; showing age.

Fattoria Montagliari riserva, Cappelli Giovanni *(twice 5/82)*. Lightly floral aroma; still tannic but with the stuffing to support it; young yet; has potential.★★(★)

Fattoria Montagliari, Vigna di Casaloste riserva, Cappelli Giovanni *(5/85; 5500 bottles)*. Floral bouquet, refined and elegant; stylish, flavorful, smooth-textured, raspberry-like fruit; very enjoyable now but will improve yet.★★★(★)

Fortilizio Il Colombaio riserva *(4/80)*. Light, fruity aroma; well balanced, some tannin to soften, good fruit; give it three, perhaps four years.★★★

Fossi riserva *(5/83)*. Oxidation is evident, but the structure seems to indicate it was a good wine; could be an off bottle or perhaps just a bit too old.

Isole e Olena riserva *(5/85)*. Well-developed bouquet, floral with some fruit; light tannin, fairly soft, ready; some length; not to keep.★★ +

La Mandria *(2/82)*. Alcoholic nose; drying out.

Le Bocce vecchio *(10/78)*. Fruity aroma; flavorful, balanced, some tannin but ready.★★

Melini *(11/79)*. Light, fruity aroma; light- to medium-bodied, nice flavor.★ +

Monsanto, Il Poggio riserva *(8 times 4/85; 35,700 bottles)*. Richly concentrated aroma; lovely, rich, ripe fruit flavors fill the mouth, enormous weight and extract, considerable tannin, beginning to resolve itself and soften, impressive balance and structure; enormous length. This one is bigger and richer than the '77; what it lacks in elegance it makes up in richness.★★★(★)

Monsanto riserva *(5 times 10/83)*. Rich aroma with suggestions of blueberries and toasty notes; flavorful, light tannin, good balance, quite nice now; long finish.★★★ −

Nozzole riserva *(11/80)*. Blackberries on aroma; some tannin, but richness and concentration make it enjoyable now.★★★

Palazzo al Bosco riserva *(11/80)*. Somewhat subdued aroma with light fruit; a bit light in body, fruity, some tannin to lose.★(★ +)

Pian d'Albola riserva *(3/79)*. Hot aroma; some tannin, lacks substance and length.

Poggio al Sole riserva *(5/85; 1475 bottles)*. Berrylike fruit on aroma; flavorful, soft, round, and ready.★★★ −

Riecine *(7/79)*. Light body; a little acidic and thin; dull finish; too old.

Rocca della Macìe vecchio *(10/78)*. Not much aroma, jammy; some oxidation, unbalanced.

1975

Rocca della Macìe riserva *(twice 11/80)*. Light but characteristic aroma; light- to medium-bodied, some tannin, some fruit; overall unimpressive.

Ruffino Riserva Ducale *(4 times 11/80)*. Nose somewhat reticent; good body, a lot of fruit, some tannin to lose; in all, a good bottle.★★(+)

Ruffino Riserva Ducale gold label *(11/83)*. Perfumed bouquet; still has a tannic bite, richly fruited flavor, balanced; young, but quality is evident.★★(★)

"S. Leolino," Fattoria I Cipressi riserva *(2/80)*. Characteristic aroma; some tannin, flavorful, needs a few years yet.★(★)

Saccardi *(10/83)*. Oxidized; still some flavor interest, albeit very little.

"Signoria" di Barfede-Certaldo *(4/80)*. Rose color; floral, fruity aroma; some tannin; moderate length.★

Tenuta La Colombaia *(11/79)*. Small aroma; some tannin and fruity; not bad.★−

Tregole *(10/78)*. Touch of pine and floral notes in aroma; fairly well balanced, flavorful; quite nice.★★−

Vigna Vecchia riserva *(5/85)*. Floral aroma with a hint of toffee, seems older than its years; some fruit remains, but beginning to dry out.★−

Vignale riserva *(12/82)*. Nice nose, though showing some oxidation; flat, very dull.

Villa Antinori riserva *(3 times 5/85)*. Part of it was aged eighteen months in *barrique*. Bottle of 11/79: Herbaceous aroma with some harshness; a nice wine but no depth or class.★

Bottle of 5/85: Fruity aroma with an herbaceous back note; still has tannin, but beginning to soften and smooth out nicely, good fruit, well-knit, quite enjoyable now; an herbaceous note at the end.★★★

Villa Banfi *(twice 2/80)*. Pale; light-bodied, undistinguished.

Villa Cafaggio Vecchio *(3/79)*. Small, scented bouquet; balanced, tasty, some style, good weight and length.★★+

Villa Calcinaia, Conti Capponi riserva *(10/83)*. Corked.

Villa Colombaio riserva *(11/79)*. Lovely, perfumed bouquet; some tannin to lose, loads of flavor, good quality; needs some time yet.★★+

Viticcio riserva *(6/85)*. Nice nose, displays complexity and mellowness from bottle age; soft, round, and smooth; flavorful; very ready.★★+

1974 ★

This was a year with a very dry summer. The wines have body and tannin but lack somewhat in substance and fruit. They are reminiscent in some ways of the '78s; something is missing.

A few producers felt that the vintage for them was better than 1975. Paolo di Marchi of Isole e Olena feels the wines have aged better than the '75s. Certainly the Monsanto Il Poggio and Giovanni Cappelli's Montagliari challenge their '75s. For the most part, the '74s are getting on in age and are best drunk up now. Outside of these two, there is very little else we can recommend.

Badia a Coltibuono riserva *(5/85)*. Small nose; taste of old wood, moderate tannin, soft-centered; beginning to tire.★+

Brolio riserva *(11/79)*. Hot, alcoholic nose; some tannin, has substance, good body.★

Castello di Cerreto riserva, Emilio Pucci *(3/79)*. Some oxidation; could be the bottle.

Castello di Meleto *(3/79)*. Pale garnet; light nose; thin, without substance or length; barely drinkable.

Castello di Volpaia riserva *(5/85)*. Odd note on aroma; still some tannin, some flavor; drying out, but still good now.★

Castello Vicchiomaggio riserva *(5/85)*. Floral aroma; some tannin, soft-centered; shows signs of drying out at end.★+

Fattoria delle Lodoline riserva *(4/80)*. Pale; thin, alcoholic.

Fattoria Montagliari e Castellinuzza riserva, Cappelli Giovanni *(12 times 2/85)*. Tawny with orange reflections; lovely, fragrant bouquet; well balanced, tasty, elegant, and stylish; a real success; at its peak, where it's been for three years.★★★

Fattoria Montagliari riserva, Cappelli Giovanni *(5/85, at the winery)*. Perfumed bouquet; soft and round, has delicacy; at its peak.★★+

Fortilizio Il Colombaio riserva *(twice 10/81)*. Lovely, fragrant bouquet; well structured, tasty, soft; long finish; elegant.★★+

Isole e Olena *(5/85)*. Oxidized, though still has some interest.

La Ripa *(5/85)*. Alcoholic, some oxidation, drying out.

Le Bocce riserva *(10/78)*. Nice nose; balanced, flavorful, nice texture, some tannin to shed, has style.★★(+)

Le Pici riserva *(10/83)*. Nice fruit up front, then shallow; drying out.

Monsanto, Il Poggio riserva *(9 times 4/85; 34,600 bottles)*. Fairly rich bouquet with toasty, berrylike notes, vaguely floral; full of flavor, still some tannin to shed, a big wine, coming ready with still more to give; a slight touch of hotness at the end.★★+

Monsanto regular *(twice 6/83)*. Gallon of 6/83: Lovely, full, rich bouquet with suggestions of blueberries; full of flavor, smooth and round, still some tannin, but pretty much ready.★★+

Bottle of 5/83: Still good, but beginning to fade.★

Monsanto riserva *(twice 11/80)*. Fragrant bouquet though a bit reticent; still undeveloped, has some softness.★

Nozzole riserva *(3 times 4/81)*. Floral bouquet characteristic of Chianti; light-bodied and tart, lacks somewhat in fruit, still has tannin, but not a wine to keep.

Rocca della Macìe riserva *(10/78)*. Nice nose though a bit light; good flavor but unbalanced and harsh, especially at the end; not to keep.

Rocca della Macìe, Zingarelli riserva *(3/79)*. Oxidation apparent.

1974

Ruffino Riserva Ducale *(7 times 4/81)*. Bouquet displays some complexity from bottle age; good body and structure, some acidity and tannin, good fruit; should be better in a year or two.★★

Saccardi *(3/79)*. Not a lot of aroma; flavorful, has tannin and substance; a bit short.★

Serrestori, "Machiavelli" riserva *(11/78)*. Fragrant scent; a bit light, some tannin to lose, good flavor; enjoyable now.★★

Straccali riserva *(10/78)*. Bouquet shows development; soft and flavorful, some tannin; ready now.★★ +

Tizzano riserva *(3/79)*. Pale garnet; small nose with a slight dankness; has substance and weight; only the nose throws it off.

Valiano riserva *(11/79)*. Hot nose; light-bodied, some tannin and fruit; rather pedestrian.

Verrazzano *(twice 3/81)*. Fragrant aroma showing bottle age, but not much complexity; some tannin, low fruit, acidity on the high side; some alcohol at the end; getting on in age.

Villa Antinori Riserva Marchese *(5 times 5/85)*. Bottle of 5/83: Pale color, showing age; vegies on aroma that carry through on palate; showing age.

Bottle of 5/85 (tasted at winery): Pale brick color; weedy, herbaceous notes dominate aroma and palate; showing age but drinkable (was at its best in 1980 and 1981).★

Villa Terciona *(3/79)*. Small nose marred by intrusion of alcohol; a bit light, still has fruit; no need to hold longer.★ −

1973 0

Spring was mild, and the summer was hot and dry. Heavy rains close to the harvest only helped stretch an already large crop. Overall, the wines were light, even thin, lacking in body, weight, and structure. They matured early and faded fast. A big problem was the consorzio. This was the last vintage in which they interfered with the grower–producers, telling them when they could harvest. Bureaucratic meddling ruined what might have been a very great vintage. They withheld permission to harvest until too late. While they continued to refuse permission to pick the grapes, heavy rainstorms broke, drenching the vineyards and diluting the fruit.

Gabbiano felt the vintage was very good nonetheless. Minuccio Cappelli described his '73s as perfumed wines in which the bouquet makes up for what they lack in body. Cappelli's Montagliari riserva, the Monsanto Il Poggio, and Vignamaggio riserva are still drinking well. But most '73s are too old today.

Castelgreve riserva *(10/83)*. Some oxidation; showing age, but still has some interest and fruit.★ −

Castello di Uzzano *(11/80)*. Lovely bouquet; soft, nice texture, a bit light, but very drinkable.★★

Castello di Volpaia riserva *(5/85)*. Floral aroma with a touch of pine; still has flavor interest, but beginning to dry out.★ −

Castello Vicchiomaggio riserva *(twice 5/85)*. Dull nose; overly tannic; drying out.

Fattoria Montagliari riserva, Giovanni Cappelli *(3 times 5/85)*. Floral bouquet with a touch of black pepper; still has flavor; a bit drying at the end; not to keep but still good.★★

Fortilizio Il Colombaio riserva *(4 times 8/82)*. Floral bouquet; still has flavor and some fruit, but showing age, beginning to dry out. The bottles tasted in 4/80 were still good, meriting★ +

Le Bocce riserva *(10/78)*. Complex bouquet showing some development; soft and round, stylish; impressive, particularly for the vintage.★★★

Melini riserva *(twice 11/79)*. Small aroma with some volatile acidity and alcohol; nice in mouth, smooth-textured; as ready as it will ever be.★ +

Monsanto, Il Poggio riserva *(13 times 4/85; 6500 bottles)*. Brickish orange robe; floral bouquet with berries and a note of apricots; round, smooth, ready, and holding well; licorice at the end.★★ +

Monsanto riserva *(3 times 3/82)*. Moderately intense aroma with suggestions of blueberries; some harshness at edges; beginning to fade though still quite good; peaked perhaps two years ago.★★ −

Palazzo al Bosco riserva *(twice 12/80)*. Smallish nose; light-bodied, nice entry, soft.★ −

Straccali riserva *(10/78)*. Small nose; unbalanced; alcohol at the end.

Vignamaggio riserva *(5/85)*. Light floral aroma; still has fruit and tannin, some delicacy; shows signs of drying out at the end; drink them up.★★

Villa Banfi *(twice 3/79)*. Pale color; oxidized.

Villa Terciona *(10/78)*. Touch of oxidation on the nose; still some tannin but a surprising amount of fruit; quite good for the year and its age (not a riserva).★★

1972 0

The 1972 vintage was beat out for last place in the decade only by 1976. Many producers described the vintage as bad, others as poor. The Monsanto Il Poggio was the most notable exception—a big, rich, concentrated wine that has aged gracefully. It is still lovely. There should be no rush to drink them up. The Berardenga riserva is also still good, though starting to go.

1972

"Berardenga," Fattoria Felsina riserva *(5/85)*. Well-developed aroma with toasty, berrylike notes; sweet and ripe, soft-centered, flavorful; beginning to dry out at the end.★★ −

Castell'In Villa vecchio *(10/81)*. Still has fruit but is beginning to dry out; some alcohol at the end; considering the vintage and its age, not at all bad.★

Monsanto, Il Poggio riserva *(17 times 4/85; 12,770 bottles)*. Brickish orange robe; intensely rich bouquet with nuances of flowers and berries and a note of apricots; a big, richly concentrated wine with a sweetness of ripe fruit, well balanced; very ready; a resounding success for a vintage that was overall a disaster, or near disaster.★★★

Monsanto riserva *(9 times 3/82)*. Fragrant, characteristic bouquet with some delicacy; smooth and tasty, very ready, in fact a bit past its peak (which seemed to be in 1979 and 1980); has a slightly harsh edge to it; in all, very enjoyable.★ +

Villa Colombaio *(4/80)*. Small aroma that hints of fruit; light-bodied, some tannin, a surprising amount of fruit.★★

1971 ★★★★

The flowering took place early, in the second week of March for the sangiovese and a week later for the trebbiano. May was dry and sunny. July and August were mild and extremely dry; a scant 0.107 inches (2.2 millimeters) of rain fell the first month and 0.43 inches (8.8 millimeters) in August. In the first ten days of September, the vineyards were quenched with 2.34 inches (48 millimeters) of much needed rain. One week before the harvest, hail slashed the crop and made a selection among the damaged vineyards necessary.

Niederbacher and the consorzio both give the year their maximum points, four stars. Many producers agreed. Our recent tasting notes on more than a dozen '71s indicate that the best are still splendid, and some, like the Monsanto Il Poggio and Montagliari Vigna di Casaloste, can even improve. Others are at or near their peaks. The best Classicos are still good; the lesser ones, including riservas, have long since faded. The Badia a Coltibuono still has more to give. Montagliari and Castell'In Villa are at or near their peaks.

Badia a Coltibuono riserva *(3 times 5/85)*. Rich, intense bouquet with notes of berries and pine, a hint of flowers; round and smooth, almost velvety, has style and distinction, a lot of flavor, and still more to give. (This wine has opened up a lot since the previous bottle, tasted 10/82)★★★

"Berardenga," Fattoria Felsina riserva *(5/85)*. Earthy, mineral aroma; tannic, lacks stuffing; not to keep.★ −

Castell'In Villa riserva *(5/85)*. Brick, orange at rim; floral bouquet with berrylike notes; concentrated fruit, smooth and velvety, some tannin, well balanced; long finish; ready.★★★

Castello di Cacchiano *(4/80)*. Alcoholic nose with some fruit; light-bodied, no fruit left, dried out.

Castello di Fonterutoli riserva *(twice 12/81)*. Color showing age; light aroma with some interest; lacks flavor and structure. (The wine was better two and a half years ago.)

Castello di Volpaia riserva *(5/85)*. Some oxidation, not much left to it.

Fattoria Montagliari e Castellinuzza riserva, Giovanni Cappelli *(11 times 5/85)*. Medium garnet, orange reflections; lovely, perfumed bouquet; smooth-textured, full of flavor, stylish and elegant; a complete wine, at its peak, where it has been for at least four years.★★★ +

Fattoria Montagliari, Vigna di Casaloste riserva, Giovanni Cappelli *(twice 5/85; 5500 bottles)*. Delicate floral perfume; full-flavored, has delicacy, elegance, and style; good now and has a lot of potential.★★★(★)

Fizzano riserva *(11/80)*. Still has considerable tannin; some fruit evident. Is it drying out, or is the fruit masked?

Fossi riserva *(5/83)*. Dull and flat; shows age.

Isole e Olena riserva *(5/85)*. Age showing badly, drying out, though some interest remains.

Monsanto, Il Poggio riserva *(7 times 4/85; 36,700 bottles)*. Bottle of 10/82: Floral bouquet with blueberry-like fruit; enormous richness and concentration, still has more to give, should become a great wine.★★★(★)

Bottle of 4/85: Intense aroma with toasty, berrylike notes; heaps of tannin, loads of flavor, has depth and concentration; still very young.★★★(★)

Monsanto riserva *(10 times 8/84 and twice from gallon 5/84)*. From bottle 8/84: Lovely bouquet, rich and fragrant; heaps of flavor and concentration; well structured; most enjoyable.★★★

From gallon 5/84: Expansive floral bouquet with a note of blueberries; light tannin, soft and full-flavored, velvety, seems sweet; at its peak. (The earlier gallon tasted 3/79 seemed to be approaching its peak.)★★★ +

Monsanto, Uvaggio del Poggio a Sornano *(twice 4/85)*. This wine is actually a simple Chianti, the Sornano vineyard not being in the classic zone. Deep ruby, garnet at rim; expansive perfumed bouquet with notes of apricots and cassis; smooth-textured, full of flavor, a big, rich wine of very fine quality and enormous length; enjoyable now, will improve.★★★(+)

Pandolfini *(8/78)*. Characteristic Chianti nose; soft and tasty; a bit short.★

Poggio al Sole riserva *(5/85)*. Lightly perfumed bouquet with berrylike notes; some tannin, soft, smooth-textured; moderate length; holding but not to keep.★★

Quercia al Poggio *(twice 5/85)*. From vat: Pale; old, drying out.

From bottle: Some oxidation apparent, still has fairly nice flavor and some interest.★

Riseccoli riserva *(3/80)*. Perfumed bouquet, its one virtue; somewhat unbalanced, still some fruit and tannin, but showing age; slightly bitter finish.

1971

Rocca della Macìe riserva *(10/78)*. Characteristic aroma, somewhat light; high acid throws it out of balance.

Ruffino Riserva Ducale gold label *(8 times 9/83)*. Fruity overtones on bouquet and floral notes; still has tannin, rich and concentrated, very well balanced; should make a splendid bottle in four to five years.★★★(+)

Vignamaggio riserva *(5/85)*. Expansive floral aroma showing a lot of development; fairly tannic on entry, with a lot of fruit beneath, quite rich; tannic finish; needs more time.★★(★)

Villa Calcinaia riserva, Conti Capponi *(10/83)*. Vaguely mineral note on nose; some age shows, not much tannin left; not to keep.★

Villa Cerna riserva *(twice 10/83)*. Floral perfume with some berrylike fruit; still has tannin, soft and round, tasty, ready; a trifle short.★★ −

Villa Colombaio riserva *(4/80)*. Lovely, perfumed bouquet; good body, loads of flavor, well structured, still some tannin to shed; very good quality.★★★(+)

1970 ★★

This was a good vintage from the start but fell in the shadow of the outstanding 1971. For the most part, the '70s are wines to drink, not to hold. Niederbacher rated the year three stars; the consorzio gave it two.

The Berardenga and Castello di Querceto are as good as they'll ever be, which is very good indeed. Badia a Coltibuono and Monsanto Il Poggio will certainly improve. The '70 Il Poggio has always challenged the younger '71, though we do think the '71 will come out on top in the end.

Badia a Coltibuono riserva *(3 times 5/85)*. Pine, fruit, and old wood on aroma; light tannin, soft-centered, ready, with room for improvement.★★(+)

"Berardenga," Fattoria Felsina riserva *(5/85)*. Lovely, complex bouquet with toasty, floral, and berrylike nuances; some tannin, good fruit, soft and smooth; finishes on a tannic note.★★★ −

Castelgreve riserva *(10/83)*. Raisiny aroma (governo?), some intensity; heavy-handed, clumsy.

Castello di Cerreto riserva, Emilio Pucci *(4 times 1/84)*. Bottle of 9/82: Some oxidation, but nice flavor and balance, still very good.★★ Bottle of 1/84: Oxidized. (This wine seemed to peak in 1980; at that time it was very good.)

Castello di Gabbiano riserva, "La Cagnina" *(3 times 1/84)*. Brick, red, orange at rim; lovely, fragrant, characteristic bouquet; soft, smooth, and well balanced, some sweetness; at its peak.★★ +

Castello di Querceto riserva *(5/85)*. Floral bouquet with a suggestion of blackberries; tannic entry, then a rush of fruit across the palate, almost sweet, hints of leather; not to keep.★★★

Castello di Volpaia riserva *(5/85)*. Hints of tar and flowers on the nose; light tannin, a lot of flavor; showing signs of drying out.★

Fattoria Montagliari e Castellinuzza riserva, Giovanni Cappelli *(twice 1/84)*. Light brick red; lovely floral bouquet; light- to medium-bodied; soft, tasty, well balanced; at or near its peak, shows class.★★ +

Fortilizio Il Colombaio riserva *(4/80)*. Aroma is fairly closed but has a suggestion of fruit; tannin to shed, heaps of fruit; still undeveloped but shows impressive quality.★★(★ +)

Monsanto, Il Poggio riserva *(9 times 4/85; 18,630 bottles)*. Deep, rich, intense aroma with a concentration of blueberry-like fruit and toasty, woodsy notes; a big, rich mouthful of wine, enormous weight and extract, still has tannin, suggestions of leather and tobacco; very high quality.★★★(★)

Monsanto riserva *(20 times 11/84)*. From gallon 10/79: Has rounded out nicely, soft, flavorful; moderate length.★★★ Bottle of 11/84: Floral bouquet with a toasty aspect; fairly full and open, still has tannin, and good fruit; more or less ready, though it was better a couple of years ago.★★★ −

Rocca della Macìe riserva *(10/78)*. Browning; some alcohol apparent, overly tannic, low fruit; drying out.

Ruffino Riserva Ducale gold label *(twice 3/81)*. Color beginning to show age; floral bouquet with a raisiny note; still has tannin to shed, but the fruit is there to support it.★(★ +)

Saccardi riserva *(10/83)*. Lightly floral bouquet; drying out, though still has some fruit; a hint of oxidation on the finish.

Straccali riserva *(10/78)*. Lovely, characteristic bouquet; soft, a bit of tannin, tasty; ready, not to keep a slight harshness at the end bodes ill for the future.★★ +

Villa Antinori riserva *(11/79)*. Bouquet showing complexity of bottle age; good fruit, still has tannin, but quite ready.★★

Villa Colombaio riserva *(3 times 11/79)*. Lovely, perfumed bouquet; loads of flavor, has some tannin to lose but enjoyable now; has style.★★★ −

1969 ★★ −

The vintage was rated highly from the start; both Niederbacher and the consorzio gave it three stars. We never agreed. Today most '69s are too old. Badia a Coltibuono and Berardenga have peaked. But the Monsanto Il Poggio is still absolute perfection.

Badia a Coltibuono riserva *(6 times 5/85)*. Moderately intense floral bouquet, berrylike notes; nice texture, some sweetness, still has some tannin but very ready now; some alcohol mars the finish; no reason to keep any longer.★★ +

"Berardenga," Fattoria Felsina riserva *(5/85)*. Deeper in color than the '70 and '71; perfumed aroma with fruity notes; some tannin, soft and easy; tannic finish.★★

1969

Castello di Volpaia riserva *(5/85)*. Floral bouquet, some fruit in back; light tannin, a lot of flavor; for present drinking.★ −

Castello Vicchiomaggio riserva *(5/85; in half-bottle)*. Small aroma; some tannin, beginning to dry out.★

Fortilizio Il Colombaio riserva *(4/80)*. Lovely, perfumed bouquet; some tannin remaining, soft and round; near its peak.★★ +

Isole e Olena *(5/85)*. Barnyardy, awful.

Monsanto, Il Poggio riserva *(11 times 4/85; 13,420 bottles)*. Big, rich, expansive bouquet with nuances of berries, leather, and toast; soft, round, tasty, the richness makes it seem sweet; near its peak, where it's been for the past few years.★★★

Monsanto riserva *(twice 12/80)*. Lovely, perfumed bouquet with a suggestion of blueberries; soft and round, intense and flavorful; a touch of acid at the end.★★ +

Poggio al Sole riserva *(5/85)*. Nice aroma though showing age; flavorful; beginning to dry out.★ +

Quercia al Poggio *(5/85)*. Too old, faded.

Rocca della Macìe riserva *(10/78)*. Complex bouquet showing development; soft and velvety, good flavor; peak; the best Rocca della Macìe we've ever tasted.★★ +

Straccali riserva *(twice 11/82)*. Tawny color; delicate floral perfume; still has some fruit, but beginning to dry out.★ −

Villa Antinori riserva *(twice 9/83; 1.5-liter bottle)*. Tawny color, orange at rim; aroma displays some complexity from bottle age, a little light, vaguely floral; soft and smooth; a troublesome dryness at the end; as ready as it will ever be.★ +

1968 ★+

Niederbacher gave the year three stars; the consorzio gave two. Badia a Coltibuono said for them it was better than 1971. Giovanni Cappelli, on the other hand, found it not so good. Drink them up now if you have any. Monsanto Il Poggio is still splendid, but there's no need to keep it any longer.

Badia a Coltibuono riserva *(4 times 5/85)*. Onionskin; nice fruit on aroma over a background of old wood, some oxidation; considerable tannin remaining, very little fruit, astringent; drying out. (There seems to be bottle variation; one tasted six months earlier was very good, meriting ★★, while another tasted two years earlier showed signs of drying out.)★★ −

"Berardenga," Fattoria Felsina *(twice 5/85; not a riserva; tasted at the winery)*. Awful aroma; ditto on palate.

Castelgreve riserva *(10/83)*. Raisiny aroma and flavor, soft, lacks style, though drinkable enough.★

Fattoria del Leccio, "Fratelli Beccaro" riserva *(12/78)*. Characteristic Chianti aroma; still some tannin, a slight harshness, seems a bit shallow; some acid at end.

Fortilizio Il Colombaio riserva *(4/80)*. Pretty garnet robe; soft and smooth, a lot of flavor; very ready and very good.★★★

Monsanto, Il Poggio riserva *(9 times 4/85; 12,550 bottles)*. Lovely bouquet with toasty notes, tobacco, berries, and mushrooms; a complete wine that's now at its peak; rich and full-flavored, velvety texture. (There has been some bottle variation; the lesser bottles seemed to be drying out.)★★★

Monsanto riserva *(3 times 3/80)*. Well-developed, expansive bouquet; rich, soft, and velvety; very long finish; very good wine and very ready. (As with the riserva, we've encountered some bottle variation.)★★★ −

Nozzole riserva *(2/82; in half-bottle)*. Moderately rich bouquet with suggestions of cassis and tar; soft, round, and tasty, a touch of tannin, but very ready.★★

1967 ★★

Without question, 1967 was one of the best vintages of the 1960s. Niederbacher gave it three stars; the consorzio gave it four. At this point most have peaked. Monsanto Il Poggio and Giovanni Cappelli's Montagliari are splendid. The Villa Calcinaia is lovely. Many '67s are past their peaks and showing signs of senility.

Carpineto riserva *(10/83)*. Slight aroma; fairly well balanced; tasty and soft; very ready.★

Fattoria Montagliari riserva, Giovanni Cappelli *(5/85)*. Brick tending to orange at rim; expansive floral perfume; moderate tannin, sweet fruit, fairly full, soft and velvety; long finish.★★★

Fortilizio Il Colombaio riserva *(4/80)*. Perfumed bouquet with fruity notes; very soft and smooth, some tannin but good fruit; very ready.★★ +

Monsanto, Il Poggio riserva *(7 times 4/85; 8930 bottles)*. Light though characteristic bouquet with nuances of leather, toast, tobacco, and underbrush; full of flavor, some tannin; just coming ready.★★★

Monsanto riserva *(10/81)*. Intense, mushroomlike bouquet with a slight earthiness; flavorful; shows signs of drying out at the end.★★

Ruffino Riserva Ducale gold label *(10/80)*. Perfumed aroma; full-bodied, still has tannin and considerable fruit; surprisingly young, needs more time, though it has a troublesome dryness at the end.★★(?)

Villa Antinori riserva *(twice from bottle 1/82 and twice from 1.5-liter bottle 9/83)*. From bottle: Browning; some oxidation but also interesting nuances on bouquet; nice flavor, somewhat astringent; certainly on the decline but still a nice glass of wine.★★ − From 1.5-liter: Tawny; toasty overtones on aroma and a touch of volatile acidity add complexity at this point; well structured, still some tannin, very good drinking now.★★

Villa Calcinaia riserva, Conti Capponi *(twice 4/85)*. Onionskin; lovely, perfumed bouquet, with some age showing; light tannin, flavorful; very nice now, has held up well.★★

1967

Viticcio riserva *(6/85)*. Vaguely jammy aroma, berrylike fruit, shows age from bottle, old leather; light-bodied, virtually no tannin at all, very drinkable though it falls away at the end.★★ −

1966 ★

The 1966 vintage got a lot of bad press, and for good reason—the quality of the goods. There were some remarkable exceptions, though. Monsanto Il Poggio is superb, certainly among the greatest Chiantis we've tasted—and among the finest wines from anywhere. The Berardenga, too, is splendid.

Badia a Coltibuono riserva *(5/85)*. Light nose with some fruit evident; soft and smooth; rather short.★★

"Berardenga," Fattoria Felsina *(5/85; not a riserva; tasted at the winery)*. Perfumed bouquet; still has tannin, loads of flavor, well balanced; very ready.★★★

Monsanto, Il Poggio riserva *(8 times 4/85; 5370 bottles)*. Brick robe shading to orange; expansive bouquet with nuances of cassis, flowers, blackberries, almonds, apricots, toasty notes; exceptional balance, superbly crafted, liquid velvet on the palate; enormously long finish; a complete wine.★★★★

Straccali riserva *(12/81)*. Garnet robe orange at rim; some oak on aroma, very little fruit; still has flavor but showing obvious age; too bad—it was splendid in the mid to late 1970s.

1965 0

Our experience with the '65s is limited, but as the vintage never amounted to much to begin with, any bottles left now are probably best left.

Badia a Coltibuono riserva *(1/81)*. Some oxidation on aroma, berrylike fruit beneath; still flavorful, though overly tannic and drying out. +

1964 ★★

Niederbacher gave the year three stars; the consorzio gave it four. It was the best vintage of the decade for Chianti. The Monsanto Il Poggio is superb, at or near its peak. The Badia is very good, as is the Montagliari. And the Machiavelli riserva of Conti Serristori is still a nice glass. Many others are fading or have already faded.

Badia a Coltibuono riserva *(5/85)*. Floral aroma with toasty notes; smooth, round, full-flavored; moderately long; quite ready.★★★ −

Fattoria Montagliari e Castellinuzza riserva, Giovanni Cappelli *(12/84)*. Bouquet shows a lot of depth and complexity from bottle age; soft and smooth, some elegance, lovely now, perhaps even a bit past its peak, but very nice.★★ +

Fossi riserva *(4 times 1/83)*. Pretty, floral bouquet with some delicacy; light tannin, tasty; beginning to dry out; drink it now.★

Lilliano riserva *(10/83)*. Browning; bouquet is big and rich with a chocolate note and a touch of oxidation that adds complexity at this stage; nice flavor; drink up.★ +

Serristori, Machiavelli riserva *(3/85)*. Perfumed floral bouquet, has delicacy; supple center, some acid at the edges; just past its peak, but still very good.★★★ −

Monsanto, Il Poggio riserva *(5 times 4/85; 13,760 bottles)*. Beautiful brick robe with orange reflections; rich, fruity, floral bouquet with nuances of berries, tobacco, and leather; has richness of flavor, smoothness of texture, and fullness of body; very long finish recalls licorice, evergreen, and chocolate; a superb wine, at or near its peak.★★★★

Monsanto riserva *(twice 4/80)*. Bouquet is the essence of cassis; soft and velvety, enormous extract; very long; still young but so enjoyable now.★★★(+)

Palazzo al Bosco riserva *(11/80)*. Lovely bouquet with some elegance; soft and flavorful, some tannin, good structure, stylish; fairly long on the finish.★★ +

Ruffino Riserva Ducale gold label *(3/81)*. Well-developed, complex bouquet, moderately intense; nice flavor, some tannin to shed; overly drying on the finish.★★

Villa Antinori riserva *(1/83; 1.5-liter)*. Considerable fruit on aroma with suggestions of blueberries; a lot of tannin. Is there enough fruit? Drying at the end.★

1963 0

Niederbacher and the consorzio agreed. So do we; 0 it was, and 0 it is.

Fossi *(6/81)*. Complex bouquet with overtones of oak, then berrylike fruit and flowers; moderate tannin, moderate fruit; beginning to dry out.★

1962 ★

Only 1964 was better in the decade, though Niederbacher gave 1962 three stars and the consorzio four. The wines are, for the most part, too old now. Monsanto and Cappelli's single-vineyard Casaloste, though, are still very good.

Badia a Coltibuono riserva *(4 times 1/83)*. Brick tending to onionskin; well structured and flavorful; moderate tannin, good quality, can still improve. (A bottle tasted six months earlier and another one and a half years earlier seemed to be drying out.)★★

Fattoria Montagliari, Vigna di Casaloste riserva, Giovanni Cappelli *(11 times 5/85; 3500 bottles)*. Beautiful orange-garnet robe; expansive, floral perfume; silky texture, shows a lot of style and elegance; could be longer on finish. (Bottles have been variable. Some seemed to show a lot more age; many others were as fine as this.)★★★

Fossi *(6/81)*. Lovely, elegant, refined bouquet; still some tannin, nice flavor; has held up well, but drink them now.★★

Monsanto, Il Poggio riserva *(4 times 4/85; 5730 bottles)*. Lovely robe; deep, rich, perfumed bouquet; incredible richness and concentration, fine balance, showing no signs of age, complete. What more can we say? (It has been like this for close to 5 years now.)★★★★

Ruffino Riserva Ducale gold label *(3 times 3/81)*. Fragrant, floral bouquet; soft on entry, then shows noticeable tannin, well structured, room for improvement; has some length and style.★★(★)

1961, 1960, 1959 o

Niederbacher gave the '61s one star; the '60s and '59s zero. The consorzio gave one star to 1960 and two to 1961 and 1959. In our opinion, the vintages all started out poor and aged as badly. There are always exceptions; the '59 Badia a Coltibuono, tasted at the winery in May 1985, was still good.

1961

Badia a Coltibuono riserva *(1/81)*. Complex bouquet; considerable flavor, some tannin, well-knit, very nice, some style; a pleasant surprise.★★ +

Fossi *(twice 6/81)*. Cooked aroma; dried out.

1960

Brolio riserva *(3 times 9/83)*. Some interesting nuances on aroma, but oxidation intrudes; dried out, lacks interest.

Fossi *(6/81)*. Baked aroma reminiscent of a southern wine; some flavor, clumsy.

1959

Badia a Coltibuono riserva *(5/85)*. Aroma of old wood; soft, tasty; short; ready.★★

Fossi *(3 times 10/83)*. Medium brick, browning at edges; light floral aroma with a candylike note and some oxidation; some fruit; short, but enjoyable still; another surprise.★

1958 ★★★

We were always quite pleased with the '58s; we found them superior to the more highly regarded '57s. The few we've been lucky enough to taste in recent years indicate that they can still be very fine if stored properly. Niederbacher rated the year two stars; the consorzio gave it three.

Badia a Coltibuono riserva *(5/85)*. Fruity aroma recalls old wood, also a piney note; light tannin, soft and round, tasty, very ready; could have more length.★★★ –

Fattoria Montagliari e Castellinuzza Riserva Vino Vecchio, Giovanni Cappelli *(5/85)*. Label does not say Chianti; lovely bouquet, somewhat floral with berrylike notes; rich in flavor, velvety, extremely well balanced; sweet finish; a lot of class here.★★★ +

Fossi *(twice 6/81)*. Fragrant bouquet with some refinement; soft, moderate tannin, tasty; shows some signs of drying out at end; not to keep.★★

Ruffino Riserva Ducale gold label *(11/83)*. Floral, fruity bouquet with a note of cedar; considerable tannin and some astringency, but the flavor is there; needs more age yet.★★(★)

Villa Antinori riserva *(11/79)*. Lovely bouquet; lots of flavor, well structured, has style; at or near its peak.★★★

1957 ★

The vintage was highly regarded at one time, but based on the '57 Palazzo al Bosco and the Ruffino Riserva Ducale gold label tasted a few years ago, they're fading now. Niederbacher and the consorzio both gave the year three stars.

Palazzo al Bosco riserva *(11/80)*. Small nose; light tannin, nice flavor, well structured, some elegance; drying a bit at the end.★★

Ruffino Riserva Ducale gold label *(twice 11/83)*. Some oxidation over a wheatlike aspect and a hint of flowers; drying out, though still has some interest.★

1956 o

The '56s never amounted to much and are too old now. Niederbacher and the consorzio both gave 1956 one star.

1956

Ruffino Riserva Ducale gold label *(11/83)*. A surprising amount of fruit on aroma; still has flavor, but drying out. +

1955 ★★

The '55s were very fine. The vines benefited from a very hot summer and produced some very good fruit. But good as it was, thirty years is a long time; there is no reason to hold them any longer. Enjoy them now. Both Niederbacher and the consorzio rated the year at three stars.

Fattoria Montagliari e Castellinuzza Rosso Stravecchio, Giovanni Cappelli *(10/83)*. Deep color beginning to brown; fairly intense bouquet with some complexity; medium- to full-bodied, soft and round; fairly long.★★★ −

Ruffino Riserva Ducale gold label *(4 times 11/83)*. Deep garnet, brick at rim; lightly floral bouquet with some fruit; complete, well structured, round, full of flavor; very good condition, no signs of age.★★★ −

1954 ★★

Barone Ricasoli rated this vintage highly. Niederbacher gave it one star. The only '54 we've tasted recently, Giovanni Cappelli's Fattoria Montagliari (5/85), was splendid.

Fattoria Montagliari e Castellinuzza Chianti Rosso Stravecchio, Giovanni Cappelli *(5/85)*. Nice, delicate, floral aroma with a touch of decay in the back; soft and smooth, very ready; (Made with governo, 12 percent white grapes, thirty years ago!)★★★

1953 [0]

How is the vintage today? We couldn't say. It's been years, if in fact we ever tasted any. Niederbacher rates the year at one star.

1952 ★

At one time the wines were very good. Niederbacher gave the vintage three stars. Now the best of them are beginning to dry out. As for the others, we expect they have long since faded.

Badia a Coltibuono riserva *(11/80)*. Complex bouquet with just a trace of oxidation; still has tannin and considerable fruit; very good, though perhaps drying a bit at the end.★★★ −

Fattoria Montagliari e Castellinuzza Chianti Rosso Stravecchio, Giovanni Cappelli *(10/83)*. Intensely fruity bouquet; heaps of flavor, complete; superb.★★★

Ruffino Riserva Ducale gold label *(11/83)*. Lightly perfumed bouquet; round and smooth, loads of flavor, though beginning to dry out.★★

1951 0

The chances of coming up with a good bottle today are doubtful. Minuccio Cappelli considered it a poor year. Ruffino felt the opposite. Niederbacher gave the vintage a zero rating.

Ruffino Riserva Ducale gold label *(11/83)*. Brownish; oxidized.

1950 ★★

The only '50 we can recall tasting, Giovanni Cappelli's Montagliari (10/83), suggests the best can still be good. Niederbacher's rating was two stars.

Fattoria Montagliari e Castellinuzza Chianti Rosso Stravecchio, Giovanni Cappelli *(10/83)*. Floral bouquet; velvety texture; good flavor; very good quality.★★ +

1949 0

Barone Ricasoli said it was an excellent year. Minuccio Cappelli disagreed. Of the two we've tasted recently, both were getting old. Niederbacher saw 1949 as a three-star vintage.

Badia a Coltibuono riserva *(twice 10/82)*. Light color, browning; a nice bouquet despite some oxidation and some volatile acidity; starting to dry out, but still has flavor interest.★ +

Ruffino Riserva Ducale gold label *(10/80)*. Shows age in color, aroma, and flavor; going, though not totally gone.

1948

We haven't tasted any. For Niederbacher, it was a one-star vintage.

1947 ★★★

This vintage was always highly regarded, and the outstanding Ruffino Riserva Ducale we tasted on three different occasions suggests that if they were stored well they can still shine. Niederbacher gave the year three stars.

Ruffino Riserva Ducale gold label *(3 times 9/83).* Brilliant, tawny robe with orange edge; lovely, almost Claretlike bouquet, persistent and expansive, toasty, with a touch of blueberries; refined, a mouthful of wine, lots of class; a classic. ★★★★

1946 0

The '46s were never much regarded; now they're too old. Niederbacher rated it at one star.

Brolio riserva *(twice 9/83).* Pale brick; some floral notes, but a wet-dog smell in the background; drying out, acidic, very little flavor interest; very tired, old and feeble; a second bottle still had some sweetness.

Older Vintages

The 1937, 1931, 1929, and 1923 vintages were all highly regarded. As for today, who knows? A bottle direct from the *cantina* would stand a chance; from the wineshop shelf, we wouldn't be much tempted, unless the price was so irresistible that curiosity alone would satisfy. On the other hand, if you've got one in your cellar that you'd like an expert opinion on, we never turn down an opportunity to add to our experience! ("Indefatigable note-takers", did he call us?)

Colli Aretini

This production zone is in the easternmost part of the Chianti district, in the province of Arezzo. The Chiantis of Colli Aretini tend to be high in acidity, fresh and lively. They are best consumed young and with a light chill. Rating ★

Recommended Producers
Villa Cilnia (Podere di Cignano)
Villa La Selva

Tasting Notes

1984 Villa Cilnia *(4/85).* Fresh, berrylike aroma, light peppery note; a bit deficient in fruit; unimpressive, overly drying.

1983 Villa Cilnia *(4/85).* Fresh and fruity, some spice; an easy, simple style. ★

1982 "I Selvatici" *(4/85).* Old, dull, and tired; drying out.

1980 La Rovere *(twice 3/82).* Light, fresh, simple, quaffable; a bit austere on the aftertaste. ★

1980 San Fabiano Borghini Baldovinetti *(4/85).* Fresh, berrylike aroma; light tannin, dull, already drying out.

1979 "Mulino di Salmarega," Podere di Cignano *(5/81).* Pale, vinous, simple, mediocre.

Colli Fiorentini

This Chianti zone is located in the Florentine hills, south, east, and northeast of the city of Firenze. The best wines of the Colli Fiorentini are the most like those of the Classico zone, which it borders on the north. The Fiorentini wines, especially the better riservas, can be aristocratic, and they age moderately well. Generally, they're at their best between four and six years of vintage. Rating ★★ +

Recommended producers
Castello del Trebbio
Castello Guicciardini Poppiano
Fattoria Giannozzi
Fattoria Il Corno
Fattoria Lilliano
Fattoria Pagnana
Pasolini dall' Onda Borghese

Tasting Notes

1983

Castello del Trebbio *(4/85)*. Fresh and fruity with berrylike notes; easy and simple.★ +

Petreto *(4/85)*. Fresh and fruity, though a bit clumsy, slightly baked quality to it.★ −

Il Corno *(4/85)*. Surprisingly full-bodied, some tannin, a lot of fruit; should improve.★★

1982

Castello del Trebbio *(4/85)*. Low fruit, drying out, dull and flat.

1980

"Aldobrandini" Fattoria Antinoro Montelupo Fiorentino *(3/82)*. Pale; harsh, alcoholic aroma; some fruit upon entry, but that's about it.

"Aldobrandini" Fattoria Monte Murlo Terricciola *(3/82)*. Pale; vinous; tart, thin, uninteresting.

Fattoria dell'Ugo, F. & G. Amici Grosso *(3/82)*. High acid makes it unbalanced.

Il Corno *(6/82)*. Pale; off nose; thin, off flavors.

La Querce *(twice 4/84)*. Some oxidation; going. Might have been a good bottle at one time, but four years is too old for this style of wine; yet the wine was on the market in New York at the time of this tasting. No wonder Chianti has a bad reputation.

Pagnana *(3/82)*. Fresh, ripe fruit aroma and flavor, agreeable; a good quaff.★

Tenuta San Vito in Fior di Selva (Montelupo Fiorentino) *(3/82)*. Slight nose vaguely hints of fruit; modest flavors; bitter aftertaste.

1979

Castello Guicciardini Poppiano *(4/81; tenth)*. Fresh, berryish aroma; soft and fruity, quaffable, low acid.★

1977

Castello del Trebbio *(4/85)*. Too old. Why did they even pour it for us?

Lilliano *(10/78)*. Small nose; high acid, low fruit; fell apart in the glass.

Oscar Pio di Torricino riserva *(3 times 5/83)*. Anemic appearance; lacks aroma; and interest, some flavor.

Pasolini dall' Onda Borghese *(3/82)*. Fragrant; flavorful, light tannin; austere finish.★

Pasolini dall' Onda Borghese riserva *(4/85)*. Mellow, some tannin, well balanced, some quality; could use another year, perhaps two.★★

1976

Oscar Pio di Torricino *(4/80)*. Floral aroma; light, soft, and easy; a real surprise.★

1975

Giannozzi riserva *(twice 3/82)*. Stinky, candylike nose; unbalanced with high acid.

Pasolini dall' Onda Borghese riserva *(3/82)*. Has seen better days.

1973

Tegolato, Castello di Poppiano *(11/80)*. Browning; some oxidation, dried out. You really have to wonder if they actually like the style of this wine; they did pour it for us, and they didn't find any fault in it.

Colline Pisane

The Pisane production zone is in the westernmost part of the Chianti district, southeast of Pisa. The Colline Pisane Chiantis are wines to drink young and fresh, preferably with a light chill; they tend to be light and soft. Some tasters detect a scent of hawthorne flowers in the aroma of these wines. Rating★

Colli Senesi

Colli Senesi, the southernmost of the Chianti zones, is also the largest, reaching northeast, west, and south of Siena. The two southern portions of this district take in the production zones of Brunello di Montalcino and Vino Nobile di Montepulciano. Many producers of those wines also make a Chianti Colli Senesi. We expect, though, that this situation is about to change, especially in Montepulciano. With DOC approval for a Rosso di Montepulciano, this will become the second wine for many of the producers.

The Colli Senesi wines are generally fuller in body and higher in alcohol than most of the other Chiantis. They are generally best drunk young while they are still fresh; the best can take moderate age. Rating★★

Recommended producers
Agr. Ficomantanino
Barone Neri del Nero (Castel Pietraio)
Costanti Emilio
Fattoria Chigi Saracini
Fattoria del Cerro
Fattoria di Pietrafitta
Fattoria Felsina
Il Poggiolo
Majnoni Guicciardini
Podere Boscarelli
Villa Cusona (Guicciardini-Strozzi)

Tasting Notes

1983

Chigi Saracini *(4/85)*. Fresh, berrylike aroma; fruity and fresh; a good quaff.★★ –

Costanti *(5/85)*. Floral, fruity aroma; an easy, fruity wine with some character.★★ +

Fassati *(4/85)*. Surprisingly full, fruity, quaffable; some tannin at the end.★

Fattoria del Cerro *(twice 4/85)*. Floral, berrylike aroma; soft, round, and easy.★ +

Ficomantanino *(4/85)*. Floral, berrylike aroma and flavor, some acid, light tannin.★

Podere Boscarelli *(4/85)*. Ripe berryish aroma; fruity, light tannin, easy, quaffable.★★

1981

Il Poggiolo riserva *(twice 6/85)*. Fresh aroma with berries and flowers; flavorful, drinkable, though a bit tired.★ +

1980

Fattoria di Vico, Majnoni Guicciardini *(3/82)*. Candy aroma; tart edge, light, moderate flavor.

1979

Camigliano *(3/82)*. Light color, aroma, flavor, and body, lacking in fruit and interest.

Poggio alla Sala *(3/82)*. Barnyard aroma; still has flavor, though getting old.

Villa Cusona, Guicciardini Strozzi *(3/82)*. Pale color, beginning to brown; berrylike fruit; flavorful; somewhat austere on finish.★

1978

Castel Pietraio di Barone Neri del Nero *(10/79)*. Light, fresh, fruity, and quaffable★★

Il Poggiolo *(3/82)*. Pale color shows some age; getting old, but still drinkable.

1976

Villa Cusona, Guicciardini Strozzi *(11/79)*. Pale, nothing much of interest to offer.

1975

Castel Pietraio di Barone Neri del Nero *(5 times 1/80)*. This wine, from one of the zone's better producers, illustrates the point that most of these wines are at their best from one to two years of age and begin to decline shortly afterwards. Small but characteristic aroma; light-bodied, easy, still fruity; was at its best in 1978. Now★

1974

Villa Cusona, Guicciardini Strozzi riserva *(11/79)*. Vinous; some tannin, flavorful; bitter finish.★

Montalbano

The Montalbano zone, in the northwestern corner of the Chianti region, includes the production zone of Carmignano. It's not surprising, therefore, to see that some Carmignano producers also make a Chianti Montalbano. Generally, these wines are best drunk quite young, within a year or two of the vintage. In the better years—but rarely—some Montalbano is produced that can improve with age. Rating★★

Recommended Producers
Fattoria Artimino
Fattoria di Bacchereto
Fattoria Il Poggiolo
Tenuta di Capezzana

Tasting Notes

1984

Capezzana *(5/85)*. Cabernet fruit, cherries and berries, aroma and flavor, light, fruity, and fresh.★+

1983

Fattoria Artimino *(4/85)*. Fresh, berrylike aroma; a lot of fruit up front, some tannin, fairly full-bodied; could use another year.★

Fattoria di Bacchereto *(twice 4/85)*. Light aroma of berries; light, fresh, and fruity; a good quaff.★

Il Poggiolo *(5/85)*. Fruity aroma, fresh; easy, fruity, and agreeable.★

Rùfina

The Rùfina production zone, in the northernmost part of the Chianti district, takes in the *communes* of Rùfina, Dicomano, Londa, Pelago, and Pontassieve in the province of Firenze. Rùfina is the smallest of the Chianti zones. Of the 30,847 acres (12,483 hectares) in the district, 1829 acres (740 hectares) are in specialized vineyards; some 1236 (500) are in promiscuous cultivation. Production averages 250,000 cases a year, a drop in the bucket compared to the more than 15 million cases of Chianti.

The Chiantis of Rùfina are the highest in acid and by reputation are the fullest in body, though our own experience differs on the latter point. The Rùfina Chiantis are wines with a good capacity to age, as can be seen by our tasting notes on the '23 and '45 Nipozzano and the '47 and '48 Selvapiana. The Rùfina wines are the most consistent of the Chiantis. No zone produces higher overall quality. They are also among the best. Of all the Chiantis we've tasted, two of the top five estates—Nipozzano and Selvapiana—are in Rùfina. Rating★★★

Producers
★★★★
Castello di Nipozzano (Frescobaldi)

★★★
+ Montesodi (Frescobaldi)
+ Villa Selvapiana

★★
Poggio Reale (Spalletti)

★
Fattoria di Vetrice
Remole (Frescobaldi)
Tenuta di Poggio
Villa di Monte

0
Fattoria di Doccia
Le Coste
Villa Vetrice

Consorzio VitiRufina

This organization was founded in 1980 to defend, protect, and promote the wines of the Chianti Rùfina district. The following are members of the consorzio:

Cerreto	Il Poggiolo
Colognole	La Corte
Doccia	Lavacchio
Galiga e Vetrice	Le Coste
Gavignano	Petrognano
Grignano	Poggio Reale
I Veroni	Selvapiana

Vintages

	Based on our own tastings, in some cases of a single bottle, we offer the following evaluations for Chianti Rùfina.	Marchese de' Frescobaldi's evaluations of vintages at Castello di Nippozzano	Francesco Giuntini's ratings on the vintages at Villa Selvapiana
1984	[0]	—	poor; he won't produce a riserva
1983	none tasted	★★★★	first rate
1982	[★★★]	★★	first rate
1981	★★★ −	★★★	first rate
1980	★★★	★ +	very good
1979	★★ +	★★★	very good
1978	★★★	★★ +	very good
1977	★★ +	★	top-class vintage
1976	none tasted	0	very poor; he didn't bottle
1975	★★ +	★★	first class
1974	★★★	★★★	bad
1973	0	★	bad
1972	0	0	bad
1971	★★	★★	first rate
1970	★★ +	★★	very good
1969	★★ −	★★	very good
1968	★★ +	★ +	very good
1967	★★	★★	good
1966	★★ +	0	top flight
1965	★★ −	★	top flight
1964	★★	★★	good
1963	none tasted	★	bad
1962	★★★	★★★	first class
1961	★★	★★★ +	not bad
1960	none tasted		not bad
1959	★★ +	★★	not bad
1958	★★		excellent
1957	none tasted	★★	not bad
1956	★★ +		very good
1955	★★★		no opinion given
1954	none tasted		no opinion given
1953	none tasted		no opinion given
1952	none tasted		no opinion given
1951	none tasted		no opinion given
1950	none tasted	★★★	no opinion given
1949	none tasted		no opinion given
1948	★★★		excellent
1947	★★★ +		excellent

1946	none tasted		no opinion given
1945	★★★★	★★★★	no opinion given
1936	none tasted	★★	
1934	none tasted	★★★	
1923	★★★★	★★★★	
1917	none tasted	★★	
1908	none tasted	★★★	

Tasting Notes

1983

Fattoria di Doccia *(4/85)*. Oxidized.

Le Coste *(4/85)*. Dull, flat, uninteresting.

Remole, Marchese di Frescobaldi *(11/84)*. Light and fruity, low acid, somewhat shallow; short.

Villa Vetrice *(twice 5/85)*. Fresh, berrylike aroma; some tannin. Is there sufficient fruit?

1982

Le Coste *(4/85)*. Baked character reminiscent of a southern wine.

Selvapiana riserva *(ex-cask 5/85)*. Enormous richness and concentration, very young, a lot of potential.★★(★)

Villa Vetrice *(twice 5/85)*. Fruity aroma with a tarlike note; tannic and firm. Is there enough fruit?

1981

Selvapiana riserva (aged in wood) *(5/85)*. A touch of oak, less open on aroma than the other; sweet entry, has more tannin and, surprisingly, is younger than the version not aged in wood.★★(+)

Selvapiana riserva (no wood aging) *(5/85)*. Aroma has notes of underbrush, flowers, and cherries; well balanced, sweet, ripe fruit on palate, has delicacy and elegance, needs time to soften the tannin, though enjoyable now, soft-centered; tannic finish.★★(★)

Villa di Monte *(5/85)*. Tar and cherries on aroma; a bit unbalanced, fairly nice fruit.★−

1980

Castello di Nipozzano riserva *(twice 5/85)*. Complex bouquet, moderately intense, with nuances of flowers, fruit, and leather; well balanced, moderate tannin, flavorful, some delicacy and style, young; fairly long finish.★★★(+)

Montesodi *(ex-cask 5/85)*. Rich, intense aroma with berrylike fruit and a touch of tar; very well balanced, full and flavorful; very long on the finish.★★★(★)

Tenuta di Poggio riserva *(4/85)*. Some oxidation, dull and stale, drying out.

Villa di Monte riserva *(5/85)*. Cherrylike fruit, some tannin, agreeable if a bit young.★(+)

1979

Castello di Nipozzano riserva *(3/85)*. Fragrant, floral bouquet; well balanced, soft and round; surprisingly ready.★★

Fattoria di Vetrice riserva *(twice 5/85)*. Cherries and tobacco on aroma; flavor almost sweet, quite agreeable, and should improve.★(★)

Montesodi *(5/85)*. Reticent aroma; moderate tannin, full-flavored, well-knit, medium body, soft-centered, still young and a bit closed, but potential is quite evident.★★(★)

1979

Selvapiana riserva *(5/85)*. Woodsy aroma with notes of raspberries; ripe fruit flavors but overly soft, a bit dull; tails off at the end.★+

1978

Castello di Nipozzano riserva *(twice 11/83)*. Nice nose, some oak and fruit, and a vague suggestion of peanut shells; seems a bit rough at this point but well structured, tannic but with the stuffing to support it; give it a few years yet.★★(★)

Fattoria di Vetrice riserva *(5/85)*. Aroma a bit overripe and raisiny, with hints of tobacco and cherries; raisins follow through on palate; flat, tannic aftertaste.★−

Montesodi *(3 times 5/85)*. Richly fruited aroma with a lot of depth, nuances of flowers, tobacco and oaky notes; enormous richness and weight, has concentration and extract, gobs of fruit; long finish. When we first tasted this wine, in May 1983, it was so closed we were not sure where it was going; obviously it was in the right direction.★★★(★)

Selvapiana riserva *(5/85)*. Complex bouquet with hints of licorice and mint; somewhat rough and tannic, but the fruit is there.★★(★)

Tenuta di Pomino, Marchese di Frescobaldi *(4/81)*. Perfumed aroma with notes of fruit and spice; soft and fruity, could use more acid, a bit dull.

1977

Castello di Nipozzano riserva *(4/81)*. Perfumed bouquet with flowers and a touch of spice; some tannin, well balanced, seems to need more fruit, or else it's still closed; some potential evident.★(★)

Fattoria di Vetrice riserva *(5/85)*. Fruity, a bit simple, some tannin, light, drinkable, room to improve a bit.★+

Selvapiana riserva (no wood aging) *(5/85)*. Woodsy, berrylike aroma with a hint of peaches; well balanced, soft, concentrated, tasty; long, complex finish that brings up raspberries and blueberries.★★★

Villa Vetrice riserva *(4/85)*. Oxidized.

1975

Castello di Nipozzano riserva *(3/82)*. Nice nose with some complexity; flavorful, has tannin, needs age; showing good quality.★★(+)

Fattoria di Vetrice riserva *(5/85)*. Overripe, raisiny aroma; fairly tannic, fruity; harsh aftertaste.★

Poggio Reale riserva, Spalletti *(3/82)*. Stinky, barnyardy; tart edge, drying, and grating on the teeth.

Selvapiana reserva *(6 times 5/85)*. Floral bouquet with notes of mushrooms and underbrush; very well balanced, ripe fruit flavors, rich and sweet; needs age, but the richness makes it tempting now.★★★(+)

1974

Castello di Nipozzano riserva *(4 times 5/85; 198,000 bottles)*. Lovely, complex bouquet, with woodsy, floral, and tobacco notes and some delicacy; balanced, light tannin, soft-centered; very long finish with a slight hint of mocha; ready, but has room for improvement.★★★

Fattoria di Vetrice riserva *(5/85)*. Stinky; drying out.

Montesodi *(4/81)*. Lovely bouquet with notes of fruit and oak; well-knit, some tannin to shed, tasty, stylish.★★(★)

1973

Selvapiana riserva *(5/85)*. Brick, orange at rim; overripe aroma with a raisiny note; too old, drinkable but dull.

1972

Villa Vetrice riserva *(5/85)*. Never should have been bottled.

1971

Castello di Nipozzano riserva *(twice 11/83)*. Perfumed bouquet with floral notes and a hint of chocolate; still has tannin to shed, seems surprisingly closed in or else is beginning to decline; we suspect the former.★★(?)

A bottle tasted two years earlier also seemed closed, though the fruit was beginning to emerge.

Selvapiana riserva *(5/85)*. Concentrated aroma and flavor, rich and ripe, with notes of raisins and chocolate, lacking in style.★★

1970

Castello di Nipozzano riserva *(twice 5/85)*. Complex, fruity bouquet with a touch of tobacco in background; light tannin, velvety texture, rich fruit, complete; fairly long finish; ready now but room to improve further.★★★ −

Selvapiana riserva *(5/85)*. Brickish, orange at rim; lovely nose with strawberry notes; soft, round, sweet fruit, tasty; very nice and very ready.★★

1969

Selvapiana riserva *(5/85)*. Woodsy bouquet with a hint of tar; tasty, soft-centered; as ready as it will ever be.★★ −

1968

Selvapiana riserva *(twice 5/85)*. Woodsy, berrylike aroma; fairly tannic on entry, then ripe fruit, soft-centered; finish is rather tannic; perhaps fading a bit.★★ +

1967

Castello di Nipozzano riserva *(11/83)*. Perfumed bouquet with some delicacy; light and balanced, still a bit of tannin, nice flavor; beginning to dry out but still quite nice.★★ −

Selvapiana riserva *(5/85)*. Complex bouquet with suggestions of underbrush, flowers, and berries; soft-centered with tannin around it, loads of flavor; perhaps starting to dry out, but so good now.★★★ −

1966

Selvapiana riserva *(5/85)*. Delicate perfume with woodsy notes; soft and velvety, light tannin; good fruit and balance; could be longer on the palate.★★★ −

1965

Selvapiana riserva *(5/85)*. Berries and woodsy aromas; tannic entry, then soft and flavorful; blueberries on the somewhat tannic finish; beginning to dry out.★★

1964

Castello di Nipozzano riserva *(11/83)*. Vaguely floral bouquet; a bit light, still has a fair amount of tannin; closed when poured, but opened up in the glass.★★

Selvapiana riserva *(5/85)*. Brick, tawny at edges; lovely bouquet with a suggestion of underbrush; comes in and goes out with tannin, but soft in center and tasty.★★ +

1962

Castello di Nipozzano riserva *(twice 5/85)*. Brick, orange at rim; bouquet of flowers, mushrooms, underbrush, and tobacco; still some tannin, medium-bodied, flavorful, hint of raspberries, well structured, smooth; fairly long finish.★★★

Selvapiana riserva *(5/85)*. Perfumed bouquet, has delicacy, notes of pine, mint, and licorice, later toffee; some tannin still, fairly smooth-textured, tasty; tannic finish.★★ +

1961

Castello di Nipozzano riserva *(11/83)*. Expansive bouquet; soft and smooth, loads of flavor; impressive.★★★

1959

Castello di Nipozzano riserva *(twice 11/83)*. Floral bouquet, refined and elegant; soft and velvety, some tannin remains, but nearly resolved; a lovely glass of wine; no need to hold longer.★★★

1958

Selvapiana riserva *(5/85)*. Some decay up front on aroma, mint and mushrooms in back; drying out a bit, but still a lot of flavor; overly tannic on finish.★★

1956

Selvapiana riserva *(5/85)*. Complex aroma; rich and intense, sweet, ripe fruit flavors, smooth and round.★★★ −

1955

Castello di Nipozzano riserva *(5/85)*. Lovely tawny robe shading to orange; woodsy bouquet with suggestions of mushrooms and tobacco; ripe fruit, sweet, round, tasty, complete; long finish; real quality here, no signs of fading.★★★ +

1948

Selvapiana riserva *(5/85)*. Tawny robe shading to onionskin; lovely, complex bouquet with a suggestion of mint; velvety texture, tasty; very long; a complete wine, at its peak.★★★ +

1947

Selvapiana riserva *(5/85)*. Deeper color and richer aroma than the '48, seems younger as well; woodsy bouquet, loads of fruit, still has considerable tannin, velvety texture; very long finish; not peak yet.★★★(★)

1945

Castello di Nipozzano riserva *(twice 5/85)*. Beautiful brick robe, tawny at edge; expansive bouquet with notes of flowers and underbrush; still some tannin, full-bodied, liquid velvet, enormous weight and extract; can still improve, but nearly perfect now.★★★★

1923

Castello di Nipozzano riserva *(5/85)*. Beautiful brick robe shading to orange; full, complex bouquet with suggestions of underbrush and flowers (when it was decanted the bouquet filled the room); still some tannin, sweet and gentle, elegant; incredible length, a touch of tannin at the end.★★★★

The Chianti Putto Consorzio

This voluntary growers' association has 2000 members who cultivate some 32,000 acres (13,000 hectares) of vines in Chianti. Some 500 of them bottle their wine; the grapes from another 600 are vinified at co-ops. The Putto members produce 18.5 million gallons (700,000 hectoliters) of Chianti a year. The organization was founded in 1927. Today they have members in all of the Chianti zones except Classico, which has its own consorzio. The group grants to wines that meet its standards a neck label with the consorzio seal depicting a *putto*, or cherub, with a grapevine.

	DOC	Chianti Putto
Maximum yield *(gallons/acre)*	935	860
Minimum alcohol		
Regular	11.5%	12.0
Vecchio	12.0	12.0
Riserva	12.0	12.5

Regional Chianti

The Chianti region takes in all of the seven zones as well as some peripheral areas among and around them. Many wines sold simply as Chianti, though, are from one of the delimited zones and could carry that denomination on the label, but because the names of the Chianti zones are not well known, many producers don't bother putting the district name on the label. We hope to see more recognition for the better Italian wines in the future, and perhaps we can also look forward to seeing more definitive labeling as a consequence. The more information the wine drinker has available to him or her, the better.

Tasting Notes

1983

Montepetrognano *(4/85)*. Clean, fresh, and simple; a nice glass of wine.★ +

Sorelli *(4/85)*. Fruit and spice up front, Côte du Rhôneish.★

Trambusti Gonfalone *(4/85)*. Raspberry aroma and flavor; a good quaff.★ +

1981

Castello Le Portine *(4/85)*. A bit too simple, low fruit.

1980

Marco Tistaelli *(4/83)*. Some fruit and spice on the nose; dull and flat on the palate.

1979

"Boccaccio" di Barsottini e Fedeli *(twice 2/82)*. Pale, stinky, oxidized.

Borghese *(3/82)*. Too old, stinky.

Gotha, Fabrizio Bianchi dai Vigneti di Monsanto *(twice, 5/82)*. Cassis aroma; full and flavorful, soft and smooth.★★

Valdigallo *(bottled by Monsanto; 10/81)*. Floral aroma; low acid, soft, fruity, could use more personality, but agreeable.★

1978

Bardi Angelo *(3/82)*. Too old.

"Boccaccio" di Barsottini e Fedeli *(4/80)*. Candy nose, light and quaffable.★

1978

Graziosi *(3/82)*. Stinks to high heaven; thin, unbalanced.

Montione *(4/80)*. Stinky, unbalanced.

1977

Burati *(3/82)*. Simple, almost candy aroma and flavor, lacks weight and character.

Leonardo *(10/78)*. Some berrylike notes on the nose; fresh and flavorful.

Mirafiore *(3/82)*. Some fragrance; some fruit on entry, then shallow.

Tribuno "Corovin" *(4/79)*. Flat, light, and tart.

1976

Burati *(11/79)*. Pale, corky.

Chianti Producers

Agricoltori del Chianti Geografico *(Gaiole, Siena), 1964.* This *cantina sociale* has 137 members with some 1236 acres (500 hectares) of vines in Castellina, Gaiole, and Radda. They bottle more than half of their annual production, the equivalent of 277,750 cases. Their wines include Galestro, Vernaccia di San Gimignano, Vin Santo, and Chianti Classico. Their standard-quality Chianti Classico is bottled under four labels: Chianti Geografico, Castello di Fagnano, Contessa di Radda, and Lodovico da Montaione. Chianti Classico 0

Antinori *(San Casciano Val di Pesa, Firenze).* Antinori owns five estates, three wineries, and 5000 acres (2000 hectares) of land. Their 1000-acre (400-hectare) Santa Cristina estate has 270 acres (110 hectares) under vines. They recently bought the nearby 136-acre (55-hectare) I Peppoli vineyard from Villa Terciona. And it was only a few years ago that they almost sold out to Villa Banfi. (That deal was so close that it was announced in the Italian press.)

Antinori produces 900,000 cases of wine a year, including 360,000 of Chianti Classico. Nearly half of their production is exported. The Antinori wines are produced from their own vines as well as from grapes purchased from other growers. Their Chianti Classicos are made from sangiovese, canaiolo, trebbiano, and malvasia grapes, plus cabernet—both sauvignon and franc—in their riserva. They have included cabernet in their riservas since 1974 or 1975. We were told a few years ago that the '74 contained 3 or 4 percent cabernet; recently they told us the '75 was the first vintage with cabernet in the blend, some 2 to 3 percent.

Antinori produces three Chianti Classicos. The regular, sold under the Santa Cristina label, is a Chianti to be drunk young. It's dependable, if no more. A portion of the Santa Cristina is aged for one year in oak casks.

The riservas are sold under the Villa Antinori label. These wines are fermented longer—for fourteen instead of nine to twelve days as with the Santa Cristina—to extract more color, more flavor, and more substance. The riserva is aged for about sixteen months in a combination of *barriques* and 1320-gallon (50-hectoliter) casks of Slavonian oak, some of which is new wood. The casks are at most five to six years old. Less than 50 percent of the wine is aged in small barrels.

The Villa Antinori Riserva Marchese is their top Chianti. We were told the first time we went to the winery in May 1982 that this wine was exactly the same as the Villa Antinori Riserva except that it had more bottle age. Perhaps there have been some changes made; on our most recent visit we were told that it is, in fact, a different wine. The *uvaggio* is not the same, nor is the wood aging. For the Riserva Marchese, more than 50 percent of the wine goes into *barrique*. The first vintage to be given a significant period in small barrels was 1977; 65 percent of that wine was aged in *barrique*.

For a company this size, the quality of the Antinori Chiantis is not bad (not that a small production is any assurance of high quality). The Santa Cristina is drinkable, though not much more than that. But that's all it's supposed to be. Unfortunately, it's also somewhat variable.

The Villa Antinori Riserva is a good Chianti Classico, although not top level. Among the 1970s we found the 1975 vintage the best, although there was some variability among bottles.

The Villa Antinori Riserva Marchése has been somewhat more consistent, though to our tastes not necessarily a better wine. We preferred the regular riserva in 1977, for example. The '79 is a good wine and one that shows promise.

Among the older vintages, we remember the '58 riserva very well, truly a fine wine. The '64, too, was very good, though the last one we tasted, in 1983, was fading. The '67, now getting a bit old, also gave much pleasure in its time. We never thought much of the '68 or the '69. The '68 was, in fact, very poor, from the first time we tasted it in about 1972 or 1973. The '70 was quite good, as was the '71. But somehow these wines just didn't measure up to the vintage. It seems that the '67 was the last first-rate Chianti Classico the Antinoris made for some time, until the 1975 vintage.

While it could be argued that the Antinoris make better wines today than they used to, we don't care for that much cabernet in our Chianti. The percentage, as they point out, is not high. But the character is thrown off—perhaps their cabernet is too aggressive, perhaps the sangiovese they use is deficient in character. As the wine ages it takes on more of a pronounced herbaceous, weedy quality. They say the cabernet adds structure. We can't see that the sangiovese is a grape that lacks structure; look at the Monsanto Il Poggio, Le Pergole Torte, and Badia Sangioveto for just three fine examples. No, we like the cabernet too, but when we feel like drinking cabernet, we drink a Cabernet, not a Chianti. Chianti Classico: Santa Cristina★ − ; Villa Antinori★★ − ; Riserva Marchese★★

Artimino (*Artimino, Firenze*), *1936*. This Carmignano producer has 2160 acres (873 hectares), 300 (120) planted to vines, 86 (35) for Chianti. They produce 67,000 cases of wine a year, including a fairly good Chianti Montalbano. Chianti Montalbano★

Avignonesi (*Montepulciano, Siena*), *1978*. This producer of a very fine Vino Nobile also produces a Chianti Colli Senesi. It has not been given any wood age up until now, but they told us they plan to give it some in the future.

Bacchereto (*Bacchereto, Firenze*), *1925*. This Carmignano producer also makes a Chianti Montalbano, using a blend of 60 percent sangiovese, 25 percent canaiolo, and 15 percent trebbiano, malvasia, and occhio di pernice. Chianti Montalbano★

Baccio da Gaiuole (*Gaiole, Siena*). Gianfranco Innocenti has 15 acres (6 hectares) of vineyards on his Gittori estate, from which he produces 33,000 bottles of wine a year. Our experience with his "Baccio da Gaiuole" is very limited—to one bottle, in fact. It was at a tasting of about thirty Classico Chiantis, and the Baccio da Gaiuole '77 stood out in a lineup that included some quite illustrious names. On the strength of that one wine, we give Gittori★★.

Badia a Coltibuono (*Gaiole, Siena*). Badia a Coltibuono (the "Abbey of the Good Harvest") was founded in the middle of the eleventh century by monks of the Vallombrosian order, who are credited with planting the first vines in this part of Chianti. Today the abbey and property, of more than 2100 acres (848 hectares) are owned by Piero Stucchi-Prinetti. Surrounding the abbey and its outbuildings are some 1800 acres (728 hectares) of land ranging in altitude from 1300 to 2600 feet (396 to 792 meters). It is mostly forestland, with some olive groves, and vines on the lower elevations. At Monti in Chianti there are another 300 acres (120 hectares) at about 1300 feet (396 meters) where Badia has more vineyards. In all, only 117 acres (47.5 hectares) are planted to vines. There is a special clone of the sangiovese at Badia; some of the vines are more than 40 years old. In 1982, they produced a very fine Chianti Classico from these old vines.

Besides Chianti Classico, Badia produces a very good white wine from trebbiano and malvasia, a Coltibuono Rosso from sangiovese and canaiolo, meant to be drunk young and fresh, a Rosato, a Vin Santo, and an especially fine *barrique*-aged sangiovese, Sangioveto.

Average annual production of all their wines is about 30,000 cases. Badia also produces grappa, honey, vinegar, and an exceptionally fine extra virgin olive oil.

Up until a few years ago it was possible to have a tasting at Badia of a range of Chianti Classicos going back to 1958, from cask. This, however, has changed. In 1980, Stucchi-Prinetti brought in Dott. Maurizio Castelli, one of the region's, indeed Italy's, finest enologists, to be the winemaker at Badia.

Today the Badia Chianti is fermented in stainless steel and aged for considerably less time than previously in large and very old chestnut and Slavonian oak casks. Governo is not used.

We have frequently detected an aroma and taste of old wood in the Badia wines, but much less so today than previously. Badia's Chiantis are very fine wines, fairly full-bodied, and capable of aging better than most. Among their more recent vintages, we were particularly impressed with the 1983 and 1982, especially the "Old Vines," then 1978 and 1975, with 1981 and 1977 just behind. Chianti Classico★★★

Piero Stucchi-Prinetti
of Badia a Coltibuono

Barberino *(Barberino Val d'Elsa, Firenze)*. Fattoria Barberino produces some 9450 cases of Chianti Classico a year. The last vintage we tasted from this mediocre producer was the 1977, and we found it wanting. Chianti Classico 0

Barfede-Certaldo *(S. Donato In Poggio, Firenze)*. Barfede-Certaldo owns 12.3 acres (5.0 hectares) of vines, from which he produces 46,500 bottles of Chianti Classico a year. They bottle an additional 206,000 bottles of wine a year made from purchased grapes. We found both their '78 and '77 Cerbaiola and '75 Signoria reasonably good. Chianti Classico (both labels)★

Barone Neri del Nero *(Monteriggioni, Siena)*. Barone Massimo Neri del Nero, owner of Castel Pietraio, produces 4200 cases of a good Chianti. Chianti Colli Senesi★★

"Berardenga" Fattoria di Felsina *(Castelnuovo Berardenga, Siena)*. *1960.* The Felsina estate covers 865 acres (350 hectares), 130 (52) of which are planted to vines. Most of the vineyards, 67 acres (27 hectares), are in the Classico zone; another 23 (9.4) are in Colli Senesi. The vines are planted at an average altitude of 1150 feet (350 meters) facing south to southeast. Felsina produces about 22,000 cases of wine a year, including 12,000 of Chianti Classico and 5500 of Chianti Colli Senesi.

The first Classico they sold in bottle was from the 1966 vintage. Highlights of the fine tasting arranged for us at the *azienda* by Giuseppe Mazzocolin, director of the estate, showing most of the vintages that they have produced to date, included the 1977, 1975, 1970, and, surprisingly, the 1966, a rather mediocre year. The 1969, 1972, 1979, and 1981 were also good. We found a consistency of quality in these wines. Only the '68, '71, and '82 were disappointing. Chianti Classico★★ +

Giuseppe Mazzocolin
of Fattoria di Felsina "Berardenga"

Bertolli *(Castellina, Siena)*. Bertolli has 81 acres (32.7 hectares) at Fattoria di Fizzano, where they produce some 22,000 cases of wine a year. The company, though, sells about three and a half times that—about 78,000 cases, nearly half of which is Chianti Classico. Their best wine, which we have not tasted since the 1971 vintage, is sold as Fattoria Fizzano.

Our experience with the Bertolli wines of late has been quite limited; we've only tasted their less than impressive '78 recently. But we can't say the bottles tasted some years ago were much better. Chianti Classico 0

Boscarelli *(Cervognano, Siena), 1963*. Podere Boscarelli, a good Vino Nobile producer, has 11.1 acres (4.5 hectares) of vines for Chianti, from which they produce 30,000 bottles a year of a good Chianti Colli Senesi. Chianti Colli Senesi ★★

Brolio *(Gaiole, Siena)*. The Brolio castle, on the estate of Barone Ricasoli, creator of Chianti, dates from 1142. The Canadian liquor giant, Seagram's, has been the owner of the Ricasoli firm since 1959. There are 780 acres (315 hectares) of vineyards on the property, planted at an average altitude of 1185 feet (480 meters).

Vineyards	Acres	Hectares
Agresto	161	65
La Grotta	111	45
Torricella	74	30
Tremoleto	66	35

The average annual production of all the Ricasoli wines is more than 1 million cases. This includes 120,000 to 150,000 cases of Chianti Classico, plus 18,000 to 20,000 cases of the riserva, as well as regional Chianti and the other standard Tuscan wines, plus a line of Veronese wines. They produce a very good white wine, Torricella, made with 75 percent malvasia and 25 percent trebbiano grapes from their Torricella vineyard.

Under the Ricasoli label they sell Chianti and Chianti Classico. These wines are made basically from grapes that they buy. The Brolio Chianti Classico and Classico Riserva are made from their own grapes. In these wines there is some malvasia in the *uvaggio*, but no trebbiano. The original Barone Ricasoli felt that the malvasia was a variety with some character; the trebbiano, on the other hand, had none, and therefore it couldn't add anything to the blend. (We couldn't argue with him on that point.) The Brolio riservas are not made with *governo*.

Barone Bettino Ricasoli of Brolio

Their top wine is the Riserva del Barone, made from 75 percent sangiovese, 12 percent canaiolo, 8 percent malvasia, and 5 percent colorino. The '78 was their first, and a very good wine; they produced 546 cases.

The Brolio riserva is aged for one and a half years in casks of Slavonian oak; the Riserva del Barone for three years. Brolio hired a new enologist in 1975. Since the mid-1970s, their Chiantis have been given less wood age.

The present Barone Ricasoli told us that he feels Chianti Classico is not a wine that ages well; it rarely lasts more than twenty years and is generally best from about five to eight years.

Except for the Riserva del Barone, the last really good Brolio Chianti we've tasted was the '58. It was a stunning wine. That was, alas, some time ago. Though they're drinkable enough, these wines unfortunately have slipped badly.

Ricasoli Chianti and Chianti Classico 0; Brolio Chianti Classico, regular and riserva★; Brolio Riserva del Barone★★

Burchino. We haven't tasted the Burchino Chianti Classico in a while, not since the 1978 vintage, in fact, but somehow don't feel it has been a great loss. Chianti Classico 0

Camigliano *(Montalcino, Siena)*. This producer, who also makes a fairly good Brunello, has some 17 acres (7 hectares) of vines planted for the production of Chianti. They produce about 5500 cases a year of Chianti Colli Senesi. It's certainly on a different plane from their Brunello. Chianti Colli Senesi 0

Campacci *(S. Gusmè, Siena)*. Remo Migli owns 30 acres (12 hectares) of vines, from which he produces 5000 cases of wine a year. Most of it is Chianti Classico, regular and riserva; he also produces a tiny amount of Vin Santo.

His Chianti Classico (the pre-1984 vintages made from 60 percent sangiovese, 20 percent canaiolo, and 10 percent trebbiano and malvasia) is made with *governo* and aged in casks of oak and chestnut. The Migli Chianti Classicos are decent wines, not bad though not special either. Among recent vintages we found his 1982 preferable to the 1983. Chianti Classico★

Campomaggio *(Lucarelli, Radda, Siena). 1948.* Campomaggio has 58 acres (23.6 hectares) in Radda in Chianti. The vineyards are planted at altitudes of 1015 to 1280 feet (310 to 390 meters) and have a southeastern to southwestern exposure. The grapes for their riserva come from their Le Vecchie vineyards. The *azienda* has an annual production of 12,000 to 15,500 cases a year. Besides Chianti Classico they also produce a small quantity of Vin Santo.

The Campomaggio Chianti is vinified at their estate but bottled and marketed by Fattoria di Ama. Campomaggio has sold their Chianti Classico in bottle since the 1967 vintage. In our limited experience, we have found their Chianti Classico wanting. Chianti Classico★ −

Raffaele Rossetti of Capannelle

Capannelle di Raffaele Rossetti *(Gaiole, Siena), 1974.* Rossetti owns 7.4 acres (3 hectares) of vines, planted at an average altitude of 1180 feet (360 meters) facing southwest. He produces 21,300 bottles a year of very fine Chianti Classico and a *barrique*-aged Capannelle Rosso.

Before we visited the *cantina*, Rossetti spoke to us about his wines and his commitment to cleanliness, which includes sterilizing not just the bottles for his wines but every vat, tube, and machine that the wine will come in contact with. He proudly told us that when a famous surgeon visited his winery a few years ago, the man paid him the highest compliment he could receive; the doctor remarked that the *cantina* was cleaner than his operating room!

We had already accepted an invitation from this quite charming man to visit Capannelle but must admit we began to fear that his wines would be so clean that they would be free not only of all defects but of all personality and interesting nuances as well. Our trepidations were laid to rest when we tasted the wines. It's true that the Capannelle wines are free of defects, but they are as full of personality and character as the producer himself. In fact, they are among the finest Chiantis produced.

The wines are fermented in stainless steel and aged in fairly small oak casks. They rest again for a period in stainless steel before being bottled, needless to say, under sterile conditions.

Rossetti's Chianti Classico is made from red grapes only. His first wine was from the 1975 vintage.

Among the vintages we tasted at Capannelle, we found the 1983 to be particularly fine. The 1982, 1979, and 1977 are also very good, followed by 1981 and 1978. The 1975 was also fairly good. There was no '76 Capannelle.

Raffaele is proud of his wine, and his packaging reflects this. The wine is bottled with an elegantly simple hand-stamped label. The vecchio is available with a silver label, the riserva in gold—both done in the noble metal itself. There's surely a bottle one is not likely to soon forget. Fittingly, the wines inside are memorable as well.

Rossetti has dropped out of the consorzio, not the first good producer to do so, and told us he will stop using the Chianti Classico name on his wines. From now on he will fly his own colors. His red wines will be Riserva Capannelle and Capannelle Barrique. Chianti Classico★★★

Capezzana (*Carmignano, Firenze*). This fine Carmignano producer also makes a good Chianti Montalbano. They use an *uvaggio* of 75 percent sangiovese, 10 percent each of canaiolo and trebbiano, and 5 percent of other varieties. Chianti Montalbano★

Cappelli Giovanni (*Panzano, Firenze*), *1730.* Giovanni Minuccio Cappelli is the proprietor of the 500-acre (200-hectare) Montagliari farm. From these 94 acres (38 hectares) of vines, he produces the Montagliari and Montagliari e Castellinuzza Chiantis.

He also owns Casa Vinicola Socovitch and produces a line of wines under the La Quercia label from his own grapes as well as grapes he buys from other growers. The La Quercia Chianti is a good, fresh red wine meant to be drunk young. Besides the Chianti, he produces a very good sweet Vin Santo and a white wine under this label.

Cappelli has a total production of 29,000 cases of wine a year; 19,000 cases are Chianti Classico 1650, Vin Santo, including a very good dry Montagliari Vin Santo, 5500 white, 2200 rosé, and 650 a very good *barrique*-aged sangiovese, Brunesco di S. Lorenzo.

Cappelli's vineyards include Casalino, Casaloste (which is bottled as a single vineyard), La Quercia, and Montagliari.

The Montagliari and Castellinuzza estates were separated into two properties when Cappelli's grandfather died, leaving an estate to each of his two sons. When Minuccio took over, he reunited them. He produces 5500 cases a year of the Montagliari riserva, which is labeled either as Montagliari or as Montagliari Castellinuzza (in the U.S., to simplify the name for the American market!). This wine is made from an *uvaggio* of 90 percent sangiovese and 10 percent canaiolo, malvasia, and trebbiano in about equal proportions. He uses the same blend for his La Quercia Chianti.

Giovanni Cappelli of Fattoria di Montagliari

The Montagliari is fermented in oak uprights for seven to eight days on the skins, then continues for an additional fifteen days or more after being drawn off its lees. He adds sangiovese grapes, selected and semidried, for the *governo* to create a second fermentation, which lasts into February or March. He stopped fermenting with the stems for the vintages from 1973 to 1980, but has started adding them again. He finds that including the stems produces a wine with more perfume and body as well as tannin. In March, he racks the wine and moves it into oak casks, where it is aged for three to five years before bottling.

Cappelli produces a limited amount of the single-vineyard Casaloste Montagliari Chianti Classico in vintages that he feels justify it. To date he has produced a '62, a '71, a '75, and a '77; just 2000 bottles of the '75, and 3500 bottles each of the other three vintages. Casaloste is a 12.4-acre (5-hectare) vineyard in *coltura promiscua* planted to sangiovese and colorino grapes. The colorino is a grape used, as its name suggests, to add color to the wine.

Promiscuous cultivation is not as economically viable today as the specialized vineyards, but Minuccio says it is in some ways a better system. It is more beneficial to the vines, which, being spaced further apart, get more nutrients from the soil as well as better ventilation and more sun. Perhaps. Or perhaps there is a touch of nostalgic traditionalism in this brass-tacks businessman.

We recently tasted a wide range of vintages at Montagliari and must admit that, while we were very impressed, we were not surprised. Our experience with these very fine Chianti Classicos goes back over a decade. Among our favorites of the younger vintages are the '83, '82, '77, '75, and '71, particularly the Casaloste '75 and '71. Cappelli didn't bottle any Montagliari or La Quercia in 1984, 1976 or 1972.

Cappelli rates the vintages for his estate:

Top	1971, 1962
Second	1975, 1964, 1959, 1957, 1947, 1941, 1937
Third	1983, 1982, 1981, 1979, 1978, 1977
Fourth	1980, 1974, 1973, 1970, 1969, 1967, 1966, 1960, 1958, 1956, 1955, 1954, 1953, 1950, 1948
Least	1984, 1976, 1972, 1968, 1965, 1963, 1961, 1952, 1951, 1949

On the more recent vintages, he offers this assessment:

		Our rating
1981	very good (he picked before the rain)	★★(★)
1980	good	★(★)
1979	better than 1978	★★(+)
1978	might be very good	★
1977	very good	★★(+)
1976	bad, none was bottled commercially	★ (from a private bottling)
1975	only 1971 was better in the decade	★★(★); cru—★★★(★)
1974	not special	★★+
1973	the wines had good perfume	★★
1972	terrible, none made	
1971	outstanding, the best of the decade, and one of the best of all time	★★★+; cru—★★★(★)
1970	good	★★+

On our latest visit to Montagliari, Minuccio set up a fine tasting for us in one of the dining rooms of his *trattoria*. This research seemed to cause some distraction among the staff, at dinner on the other side of the room. Perhaps it wasn't the number of bottles that Minuccio, always a generous host, was opening that arrested their attention so much as the fact that though we were tasting them all we drank nary a one, and such fine wines too. But normalcy returned when the tasting was over. As we left to go into the other room for dinner, we each carried off a couple of bottles for the table. And the tasting broadened, with Minuccio ordering a little of everything on the menu (and off?) that we either expressed an interest in or that he thought we should sample, smiling with satisfaction at our compliments and laughing at the protest that there would be too much when we were so obviously enjoying the fine specialties of the region and of the house.

Friends to whom we recommended the *trattoria* and rooms at Montagliari were luckier than we, traveling in Italy on business on a tight-to-bursting schedule. They spent a few idyllic days there in a little house in the midst of the vines, visited *cantine* at a leisurely pace, ate at the *trattoria* every day, often with Minuccio, and polished their Italian (after the initial formalities, Cappelli wouldn't hear any English from the Scicolones, despite the fact that he speaks it very well when the occasion requires).

Cappelli is without question one of the finest producers of Chianti Classico. His Montagliari is a wine of delicacy, elegance, and balance, and it ages extremely well. This wine can be relied on for consistency at a high level. Chianti Classico: La Quercia★; Montagliari (e Castellinuzza) riserva★★★; Montagliari, Vigna Casaloste★★★ +

Carobbio *(Greve, Firenze)*. Carobbio produces the equivalent of about 33,000 bottles of Chianti a year; of this they bottle about 26,500. These are light, early-maturing Chiantis, both the regular and the riserva. We cannot say that we've been overly impressed with them, though we haven't tasted any since the 1977 vintage. Chianti Classico★

Carpineto *(Dudda, Greve, Firenze)*. Carpineto owns 20.7 acres (8.4 hectares) of vines. Their vineyards supply some of the grapes for the 6550 cases of wine they produce annually. We hear that these wines, in the opinion of some at least, have improved. It's been quite a few years since we've tasted them, and we must admit we weren't overly impressed, though they can be agreeable if not much else. Based on our personal, though admittedly past, tastings we can give them only★.

Casa Sola *(Barberino Val d'Elsa, Firenze)*. Casa Sola has 61 acres (24.5 hectares) of vines. They produce about 19,000 cases a year of fairly mediocre, though drinkable, wines including Chianti Classico. Chianti Classico 0

Casa Volterrani *(Vagliagli, Siena)*. Volterrani has 79 acres (32 hectares) of vineyards. They produce some 20,000 cases of wine a year, which includes Chianti Classico, Bianco della Lega, and Vin Santo. Their Chianti Classico is fermented in stainless steel and aged in *barrique*.

Casale. See Falchini Riccardo.

Casalino *(Querciagrossa, Siena)*. Tenuta di Angoris, a large producer of wines in Friuli, owns this Chianti Classico farm and its 54 acres (22 hectares) of vines. Casalino produces, on average, 15,500 cases of wine a year.

Castel Pietraio. See Barone Neri del Nero.

Castel Ruggero *(Strada In Chianti, Firenze)*. Castel Ruggero was an eleventh-century military fortress of the Guidi counts. The Alamanni family turned it into a villa in the fifteenth century. Today there are 15 acres (6.2 hectares) of vines on the estate. Annual production of Chianti Classico is 16,000 bottles. This wine is bottled only in the better vintages. It sounds hopeful, but as we have unfortunately never seen the wine, we can offer no opinion.

Castelgreve *(Mercatale Val di Pesa, Firenze), 1966*. The 190 members of the cooperative winery of Castelli del Grevepesa own 2225 acres (900 hectares) of vines. They have an annual production of some 555,000 cases of wine a year. One-third of this is exported. Some 100,000 cases is Chianti Classico; the balance is table wine. They own cellars in Badia a Passignano and Ponte di Gabbiano. The Castelgreve Chianti Classicos, produced with governo, are made from 80 percent sangiovese, 10 percent canaiolo, 10 percent trebbiano and malvasia, and 5 percent colorino.

They produce a Valgreve rosé and a white made from a blend of trebbiano and malvasia. Under the Castelgreve label they sell a regular and a riserva Chianti Classico as well as some special cru bottlings. They also produce a Vin Santo.

Cru	Tons of grapes	Bottles	Vintage
Lamole	77	45,000	1981
		59,827	1982
Montefiridolfi	99	59,960	1983
Panzano	99	51,000	1981
Sant'Angiolo Vico L'Abate	22	9,240	1980
		29,870	1982
Vigna Elisa	22	14,000	1980
		28,668	1983

Chianti Classico★

Castellare (*Castellina, Siena*), 1975. Milan publisher Paolo Panerai has 37 acres (15 hectares) of vines at his Castellare estate. The vineyards are planted at 1310 to 1575 feet (400 to 480 meters) with a south to southwestern exposure. Besides the standard grapes of this area, he also has cabernet sauvignon, sauvignon blanc, and semillon vines.

The average annual production at Castellare is some 100,000 bottles of wine. This includes, besides the Chianti Classico, a *barrique*-aged I Sodi di S. Niccolò, Bianco di Castellare, Vin Santo, and a fresh, light, fruity red, Governo di Castellare. Maurizio Castelli, enologist at Castellare, produced 10,000 bottles of this wine in 1983, their first vintage. Castellare's pre-DOCG Chianti Classico was made from a blend of about 70 percent sangiovese, 4 percent canaiolo, 13 percent trebbiano, 10 percent malvasia, and 3 percent other red grapes.

We have found the Chianti Classicos of Castellare rather uneven but expect more consistency since Maurizio Castelli became their winemaker in 1981. The '84, judging from our tasting ex-cask, looks like it should turn out fairly well; we also liked their '82. Chianti Classico (for now)★★ –

Castelli del Grevepesa. See Castelgreve.

Castell'In Villa (*Castelnuovo Berardenga, Siena*). Coralia Pignatelli della Leonessa produces some 44,500 cases of wine a year from the 136 acres (55 hectares) of vines on her Castell'In Villa estate. Of this, 75 percent is Chianti Classico, the balance consisting of a white wine and a Vin Santo. She also produces an excellent virgin olive oil.

Pignatelli has made the wine here from the first vintage in 1971. Since 1975, her Chianti has been made from sangiovese grapes only. She produces two Chianti Classicos, a young Chianti sold under the Montecastelli label, and the Castell'In Villa, both regular and riserva. In 1982, she produced as an experiment a *barrique*-aged sangiovese, Balsastrada.

The Castell'In Villa Chiantis are fairly full-bodied, and stylish, with a characteristic touch of mint in their bouquet. The '77, '78 and '79 are all worth looking for. Chianti Classico★★ +

Castello dei Rampolla (*Panzano, Firenze*), 1967. Principe Alieo di Napoli Rampolla is the proprietor of this castle and its 94 acres (38 hectares) of vines. In the vineyards, planted at altitudes of 985 to 1310 feet (300 to 400 meters), there are 54 acres (22 hectares) of sangiovese, 27 (11) of cabernet sauvignon, 5 (2) of malvasia and 2.5 (1) each of chardonnay, traminer, and sauvignon blanc.

The average annual production at Castello dei Rampolla is 213,000 bottles; 133,000 are of Chianti Classico—about 80,000 of regular and 53,000 of riserva—40,000 of Sammarco, a cabernet sauvignon/sangiovese blend, 20,000 of malvasia, and 20,000 of Trebianco, an interesting white wine made from three white varieties: chardonnay, traminer, and sauvignon blanc.

The vineyards were planted in 1969. They produced their first Chianti Classico, 15,000 bottles, in 1975. In 1976, they didn't make any wine. They began experimenting with *barriques* with the 1978 vintage. The following year they produced their first Chianti Classico riserva. That was also the first vintage when they included some cabernet sauvignon in the *uvaggio* for their Chianti—8 to 10 percent in the riserva and 5 percent in the regular. These percentages vary with the vintage. The '81 regular again had 5 percent cabernet sauvignon; in the '82 this was reduced to only 1 to 2 percent, while the '81 had a full 10 percent.

The regular Castello dei Rampolla Chianti Classico is aged for one year in stainless steel and one in fairly new oak casks of 660, 790, and 1320 gallons (25, 30, and 50 hectoliters). The riserva is given an additional year in cask.

The Castello dei Rampolla wines are quite good, although they are certainly not representative of Chianti. We find that, as in many of the other wines with cabernet sauvignon in the *uvaggio*, their flavor tends to be dominated by the cabernet, which overpowers the more gentle character of the sangiovese. These wines are Chianti Classico only by virtue of the fact that the vineyards are in the zone. In our opinion, Castello dei Rampolla should fly their own colors and drop the Chianti Classico name. They did recently drop out of the Chianti Classico consorzio.

All of the Castello dei Rampolla wines that we tasted, from 1979 to 1982, were very good, the 1981 in particular. But as well made as they are, as Chianti we cannot rate them higher than★★.

Castello del Trebbio *(Santa Brigida, Pontassieve, Firenze).* This 504-acre (204-hectare) estate in the Florentine hills has 79 acres (32 hectares) of specialized vineyards and one in promiscuous cultivation. They produce some 16,600 cases of wine a year, which includes a decent Chianti Colli Fiorentini plus a white, rosé and Vin Santo. They also produce a regional Chianti with the Torre dei Pazzi label. Chianti Colli Fiorentini★

Castello di Ama *(Gaiole, Siena).* Castello di Ama has 166 acres (67 hectares) of vineyards planted at an altitude of 1380 to 1610 feet (420 to 490 meters). Besides the Chianti varieties, they also have malvasia nera, chardonnay, pinot grigio, merlot, and pinot noir vines. Ama produces 300,000 to 350,000 bottles of wine a year, 200,000 to 220,000 of it Chianti Classico. The balance is red, white, and rosé table wines.

They bottled their first Castello di Ama Chianti Classico from the 1977 vintage. Their top wines are labeled for the cru where the grapes are grown.

Cru/vineyard	Hectares	Exposure	First vintage
Bellavista	27	se/sw	1978
La Casuccia	24	se/sw	—
S. Lorenzo a Ama	16	sw	1982

In 1982, the cru wines were given some *barrique* aging.

Our experience with these wines has been limited, but those we've tasted have been pretty good. Chianti Classico★

Castello di Cacchiano *(Gaiole, Siena).* Fratelli Ricasoli own this estate and its 203 acres (82 hectares) of vineyards. They produce 33,000 cases of wine a year. Despite their reputation, we have not been impressed with their Chianti. Chianti Classico 0

Castello di Cerreto *(Pianella, Castelnuovo Berardenga, Siena).* Marchese Emilio Pucci is the proprietor of this Chianti Classico estate and its 71 acres (28.6 hectares) of vines. There is no castle here, though there are the ruins of a tower nearby. Their annual production of 16,000 cases is made up of 12,000 to 13,000 cases of Chianti Classico, a Vin Santo, a white, a rosé, and the young red Graniolo.

In the 1940s, these wines were sold under the Pianella label, named for the district in which the estate is located. In the early 1960s, they changed the name to Castello di Cerreto.

The *uvaggio* used for the Cerreto Chiantis is 80 to 85 percent sangiovese, 10 percent canaiolo, 5 percent malvasia, and a small amount of trebbiano (a blend that will have to be changed under the new DOCG regulations, which don't allow more than 5 percent of white grapes in Chianti). The regular Cerreto is aged for one to two years in oak casks; the riserva for three to four.

At one time we found these wines considerably better than they are today, particularly in the 1960s and early 1970s. Their '81 is quite good, though, and the '82 and '83 are good wines although not really up to the level of vintages. These are full-bodied Chiantis, reflecting the style of the district where they are produced. Chianti Classico★ +

Castello di Fonterutoli *(Castellina, Siena).* Lapo Mazzei owns this estate encompassing 80 acres (32.2 hectares) of vines. He has an annual production of nearly 18,000 cases a year. Although these wines seem to enjoy a good reputation, we find them rather disappointing. Even the riservas mature quickly and fade shortly afterward. Chianti Classico★ +

Castello di Gabbiano *(Mercatale Val di Pesa, Firenze).* This estate, named for the twelfth-century castle of Gabbiano, encompasses 125 acres (50 hectares) of vineyards planted at altitudes of 655 to 720 feet (200 to 220 meters), facing southwest. Besides the typical Chianti varieties, there are also merlot, cabernet, and chardonnay vines. The annual production at Gabbiano averages 40,000 cases a year, which includes Chianti Classico, white, Rosato, and Vin Santo. It has been many years since we tasted their Chiantis; the '76 was the last, unfortunately. But we remember well enjoying many fine bottles from the 1970 vintage. Chianti Classico★★ −

Castello di Meleto *(Gaiole, Siena).* Viticola Toscana Agricola Immobiliare owns this estate and its 514 acres (208 hectares) of vines. They produce 133,000 cases of wine a year, which is stored at and sold by the Storiche Cantine. Their wine, like that of the others who belong to the Storiche Cantine, is mediocre at best. Chianti Classico 0

Castello di Monterinaldi *(Radda, Siena)*. Fattoria di La Pesanella owns this castle and its 178-acre (72-hectare) vineyard. They produce 55,500 cases of mediocre wine a year. Castello di Monterinaldi belongs to the Storiche Cantine, or as it is sometimes familiarly referred to, hysterical cantine, for reasons that will be obvious to anyone who's tasted their wines. Chianti Classico 0

Castello di Nipozzano. See Fresobaldi.

Castello di Poppiano. See Castello Guicciardini Poppiano.

Alessandro Francois of Castello di Querceto

Castello di Querceto *(Lucolena, Greve, Firenze), 1896.* The Francois family are the proprietors of this beautiful old castle dating from the time of the Lombards and its 500-acre (200-hectare) estate. Their 100 acres (40 hectares) of vines are planted at altitudes of 1150 to 1475 feet (350 to 450 meters).

Besides the usual grapes of the area, they also grow cabernet sauvignon, merlot, and chardonnay. They have a number of vineyards, or crus, some of which are bottled separately.

Cru/vineyard	Hectares
La Madonnina	4
Le Capanne	10
Le Corte	3
Le Giuncaie	10
Le Rabatte	3
Quercetino	6
Terreni	4

Alessandro Francois, in charge of the winemaking here since 1975, produces 22,000 cases of wine a year. Besides the Chianti, he also makes a *barrique*-aged Le Corte, Quercetino, a cabernet sauvignon/sangiovese blend; La Giuncaie, a cabernet sauvignon/merlot blend (since 1985); Bianco della Lega, charmat spumante, and Vin Santo. This *azienda* has three labels: Caratello for a fresh red wine to drink young, Le Capanne, and Castello di Querceto.

Francois ferments in temperature-controlled stainless steel tanks and ages his Chianti in a combination of oak casks and *barriques*. Even his regular Querceto Chianti, in the better years, is given some time in *barrique*. The regular '82, for example, had six months of *barrique* age. The '81 riserva was given eight months in *barrique*.

Castello di Querceto has been bottling Chianti since about 1900.

The fine enologist, Vittorio Fiore, though not a consultant here, offers recommendations from time to time as a friendly neighbor.

Our experience with these wines is unfortunately limited to just four vintages: 1970, 1978, 1981, and 1982. All were very good, Chianti Classicos with style. Chianti Classico★★ +

Castello di Radda *(Radda, Siena)*. Montemaggio produces 4000 cases a year of this Chianti, made from purchased grapes and/or wine. Our limited experience, based on a bottle from the exceptionally fine 1983 vintage, suggests a rating of 0.

Castello di Rencine *(Castellina, Siena)*. Around the eleventh-century ruin of the castle of Rencine on this estate are some 68 acres (28 hectares) of vines. The winery has an annual production of about 21,500 cases. We haven't tasted their Chianti since the 1977 vintage. Those we did taste, though, never lived up to their reputation. Chianti Classico 0

Castello di San Donato in Perano *(Gaiole, Siena)*. This winery has 156 acres (63 hectares) of vines. They produce 40,000 cases of rather mediocre wine a year. San Donato is one of the members of the Storiche Cantine. Chianti Classico 0

Katrin Canessa of Castello di San Polo In Rosso

Castello di San Polo in Rosso *(Gaiole, Siena), 1973*. Cesare and Katrin Canessa bought this castle and 1000-acre (400-hectare) estate a bit more than a decade ago to produce Chianti. Today they have some 58 acres (23.5 hectares) of vines in specialized cultivation, at an average altitude of 1310 feet (400 meters). There are another 25 acres (10 hectares) planted promiscuously.

Their annual production averages 20,000 cases. Chianti Classico makes up 70 percent, the remaining 30 percent is about evenly divided among their top-of-the-line Castello di San Polo in Rosso rosso, the Bianco, and the Rosa di Sanpolo.

Dott. Maurizio Castelli is the enologist at San Polo in Rosso. He uses the free-run juice only for the two Chiantis that carry the estate name; the Castelpolo contains some press juice. Castelli ferments the wines in stainless steel. When he feels it will add a benefit, he uses *governo*. These Chianti Classicos are made from mostly sangiovese. More than 85 percent of their vines are sangiovese, 8.7 percent are canaiolo, 5 percent trebbiano and malvasia, and just a bit more than 1 percent are other varieties.

The San Polo Chianti Classicos are very good wines, wines of style. We especially liked their '83 and '82; we also found the '84, '80, '79, and '78 quite good. Chianti Classico: Castello di S. Polo In Rosso★★ + ; Castelpolo★

Castello di Tizzano *(S. Polo In Chianti, Gaiole, Siena)*. Conte Filippo Pandolfini owns this eleventh-century castle and its 47 acres (19 hectares) of vines. He produces 11,000 cases of wine a year. We haven't tasted this Chianti in some time, but our memory is that it was a fairly good one. Chianti Classico★★ −

Castello di Uzzano *(Greve, Firenze)*. Uzzano owns 162 acres (66 hectares) of vines. They produce about 43,000 cases a year. We hear that they still use governo. The most recent vintage from them that we've tasted was the 1973; it was quite good. They have a good reputation. Chianti Classico★★

Castello di Verrazzano *(Greve, Firenze)*. Giovanni da Verrazzano, navigator, explorer, and possible pirate, was born here in 1485. (Today he is perhaps best known, in the U.S. at least, for the bridge named after him that spans the narrows in the New York City harbor, which he explored.) In Greve, capital of Chianti Classico, a memorial statue of Verrazzano dominates the naviform—ship-shaped, to the landlubbers—piazza in the center of town.

The Verrazzano estate has 104 acres (42 hectares) of vines. The *azienda* has an average annual production of 35,500 cases of wine, which includes Chianti Classico, white, rosé, and Vin Santo. The most recent Chianti we've tasted from them was from the 1974 vintage. We have had many bottles of previous vintages, though not for some time, and have always found the wines agreeable, if a bit simple. Chianti Classico★

Castello di Vertine *(Gaiole, Siena)*. This producer is a member of the Storiche Cantine. We've never tasted any of their wines that we can recall, but if they are at the general level of the other wines of the co-op, it has not been a great loss. On the other hand, one never knows, and should the occasion arise to taste them, we would certainly do our duty.

Castello di Volpaia *(Radda, Siena)*. Giovannella Stianti Mascheroni owns this tenth-century castle and its 79 acres (31.8 hectares) of vineyards. Her average annual production of 200,000 to 230,000 bottles is made up of 150,000 to 180,000 Chianti Classico, 20,000 to 25,000 Coltassala (a *barrique*-aged sangiovese), white wine and Vin Santo. These Chiantis, from past vintages at least, were not wines for long aging. We have noticed a definite improvement in the wine in the past few years. Dott. Maurizio Castelli, who has been the winemaker at Volpaia since 1980, produced fine wines in 1982 and 1983. The '78, '80, and '81 were also quite good. Chianti Classico★★ +

Castello Guicciardini Poppiano *(Montespertoli, Firenze)*. Conte Ferdinando Guicciardini has 593 acres (240 hectares) on his Poppiano estate; 198 (80) are in specialized cultivation, another 54 (22) are planted promiscuously. He produces 66,500 cases of wine a year, including a fairly good Chianti. Chianti Colli Fiorentini★

Castello Vicchiomaggio *(Greve, Firenze)*. This castello was built at least as early as the tenth century; it was described in a document of 957. The current owners bought the estate in 1966 and bottled their first wine from the 1969 vintage.

Vicchiomaggio has 62 acres (25 hectares) in vines. With the reduction of white grapes required now by DOCG regulations, only 54 acres (22 hectares) will furnish grapes for the Vicchiomaggio Chianti Classico. The vineyards are planted at altitudes of 620 to 950 feet (250 to 290 meters). Their 5-acre (2-hectare) Prima Vigna vineyard was planted, in promiscuous cultivation with other crops, between 1935 and 1940.

Vicchiomaggio uses *governo* for all their Chiantis, the riserva as well as the regular. They don't add grapes but unfermented grape juice, which is concentrated from their own grapes, to create the second fermentation. In their DOC Chianti Classicos, Vicchiomaggio used 15 to 20 percent of white grapes in their *uvaggio*; in their DOCG wines this will be limited to only 3 to 5 percent.

Their production of some 13,000 cases a year will also be reduced under the new regulations to 10,000 to 11,000 cases. In vintages when they make a riserva, this wine comprises 25 to 30 percent of the Chianti Classico they produce. Besides these two wines, Vicchiomaggio also produces a small amount of Vin Santo.

Prima Vigna, a *barrique*-aged Chianti Classico from this old vineyard, is their flagship wine. It was first produced in 1977, 3000 bottles. The wine was aged for ten months in previously used *barriques*. The next vintage they made was the 1980, aged for three months in new barrels.

The Vicchiomaggio Chianti Classico riserva, also aged for a time in *barrique*, is given at most two years in old oak barrels.

We find the Chiantis of Castello Vicchiomaggio lean, austere, and angular. For those who like this style, we would recommend the '80 and the '83. Chianti Classico★ + ; Prima Vigna★★

Catignano *(Pianella, Castelnuovo Berardenga, Siena).* This 121-acre (48.8-hectare) estate has 23 acres (9.3 hectares) in vines, which yield 93,000 bottles of red wine a year. Of this, 41,000 are Chianti Classico (regular only); the balance is *vino da tavola*, red table wine. They don't produce a riserva. Catignano has been bottling Chianti since about 1960. The pre-DOCG vintages are a blend of 80 percent sangiovese, 15 percent trebbiano and malvasia, and 5 percent canaiolo. The proportion of white grapes will perforce be reduced in their post-1983 Chiantis. They make their Chianti with *governo*. The wine is aged for two years in old Slavonian oak casks. While theirs is a Chianti Classico ready for early drinking, it can take moderate age. We found the '82 and '83 both quite good. Chianti Classico★★

Cecchi Luigi *(Castellina, Siena), 1893.* Cecchi produces 50,000 cases a year of what we've found overall to be mediocre wines, although it's been some time since we've tasted them. Their best wine comes from their Villa Cerna estate. Chianti Classico 0

Cellole *(Castelnuovo Berardenga, Siena).* Cellole has 35 acres (14 hectares) of vines from which they produce an average of 11,000 cases of Chianti Classico a year. Our experience with these wines, though limited, has left us less than impressed. Chianti Classico 0

Cepperellaccio *(Barberino Val d'Elsa, Firenze).* Kunz Piast d'Asburgo Lorena, owner of Fattoria Antico Castello di Poppiano in Barberino Val d'Elsa, produces this mediocre Chianti Classico. The most interesting thing about it is its rather curious name. Chianti Classico 0

Cerbaiola. A label used by Barfede-Certaldo.

Cerreto *(Pontassieve, Firenze).* Fattoria Cerreto owns 198 acres (80 hectares), 31 (12.5) of specialized vineyards and 7.4 (3) promiscuous in the Chianti Rùfina zone. They have a production of some 8300 cases a year.

Cispiano *(Castellina, Siena), 1972.* Alceca Corp. of Washington, D.C., an importer of some very good Italian wines, owns this Chianti Classico estate. The annual production from its 25 acres (10 hectares) of vineyards is 4000 cases of light, drinkable wines. Chianti Classico★

Coli *(Sambuca, Tavarnelle Val di Pesa, Firenze).* Coli owns 42.5 acres (17.2 hectares) of vines from which they produce 13,000 cases of wine a year. They also buy grapes to produce another 110,000 cases of Chianti Classico, which they sell under the della Badia and S. Carlo labels. They've been bottling their Chianti since 1926.

Conte Capponi. See Villa Calcinaia.

Conti Serristori *(S. Andrea In Percussina, Firenze).* The estate of the Conti Serristori, today owned by the Swiss conglomerate Winefood, has 69 acres (28 hectares) of vineyards. They have an annual production of about 23,000 cases of Chianti Classico. Their best wine is the Riserva Machiavelli. Although it's been some time since we tasted their Classicos, we remember them being fairly good, if a bit light in body. The '77 Ser Niccolo Riserva, though, was disappointing. Chianti Classico regular★; Machiavelli Riserva★★; Ser Niccolo Riserva 0

Costanti *(Montalcino, Siena).* This producer of a very fine Brunello also makes 2000 to 2650 bottles a year of Chianti Colli Senesi. If we can judge from the commitment to quality they display with their Brunello (and, for that matter, their extra virgin olive oil), plus the one Chianti of theirs we've tasted, the '83, we don't doubt it is a very good Chianti. Chianti Colli Senesi★★ +

Del Cerro *(Acquavina, Siena), 1922.* This producer of very fine Vino Nobile makes almost 25,000 cases of Chianti Colli Senesi from their 120 acres (48 hectares) of vines in the Sienese hills. Chianti Colli Senesi★ +

Della Badia. A label used by Coli.

Falchini Riccardo *(San Gimignano, Siena), 1830.* Falchini has 50 acres (20 hectares) of vineyards at his Casale farm. His annual production is some 15,500 cases of wine; 70 percent is a very good Vernaccia di San Gimignano; the remaining 30 percent is divided about equally among Chianti Colli Senesi, Vin Santo, and a champagne-method brut. Falchini has plans, like numerous other producers in Tuscany, to produce a cabernet aged in *barrique*. Considering the quality of his Vernaccia, we expect his Chianti to be good.

Fattoria Bossi (*Pontassieve, Firenze*). Marchese Bonaccorso Gondi produces 11,000 cases of wine a year from his 40 acres (16 hectares) of vines. He has 13.6 acres (5.5 hectares) in the Chianti Rùfina zone, from which he produces 3300 cases; 16 (6.5) in Chianti, which yields 5000 cases and 10 (4) in the Valdisieve area, from which he makes 2600 cases of other wine.

Fattoria Cusona. See Villa Cusona.

Fattoria della Aiola (*Vagliagli, Siena*). Aiola owns 76 acres (30.7 hectares) of vineyards in Castelnuovo Berardenga and Radda. They produce some 22,000 cases of wine a year. Chianti Classico 0

Fattoria delle Lodoline (*Vagliagli, Siena*). Lodoline owns 36.7 acres (14.9 hectares) of vines, from which they produce 11,000 cases of mediocre Chianti Classico a year. Chianti Classico 0

Fattoria di Ama. See Castello di Ama.

Fattoria di Calcinaia. See Villa Calcinaia.

Fattoria di Doccia (*Molin del Piano, Pontassieve, Firenze*). This 519-acre (210-hectare) Chianti Rùfina estate has 141 acres (57 hectares) under vines. Their annual production totals 44,500 cases. Chianti Rùfina 0

Fattoria di Felsina. See "Berardenga" Fattoria di Felsina.

Fattoria di Fizzano. See Bertolli.

Fattoria di Galiga e Vetrice. See Villa di Vetrice.

Fattoria di Petroio (*Querciagrossa, Siena*). This 371-acre (150-hectare) estate has 37 acres (15.1 hectares) in vines. They produce 9500 cases of Chianti Classico a year. Petroio has a fairly good reputation.

Fattoria di Selvole (*Vagliagli, Siena*). The Selvole estate boasts the eleventh-century Selvoli castle and Church of S. Martino a Selvoli, as well as 54 acres (22 hectares) of vines. They produce about 16,500 cases of wine a year. Our experience here is very limited, but a producer who could turn out a poor wine in an outstanding vintage like 1983 must be doing something—most probably many things—wrong. Chianti Classico 0

Fattoria di Vetrice. See Villa di Vetrice.

Fattoria di Vistarenni (*Gaiole, Siena*). Vistarenni has 740 acres (300 hectares) in Radda and Gaiole; 198 (80) are in specialized vineyards. Their annual production of 77,500 to 89,000 cases includes two white wines, a rosé, Vin Santo, novello, and a brut spumante, Fattoria di Lucignano, from the Val d'Arbia area, as well as three Chianti Classicos: Fattoria di Vistarenni, Fattoria di Corsignano, and the single-vineyard Podere Bertinga from the 30-acre (12-hectare) vineyard of that name. Their '81 was pretty good, but the '82 and '79 were not so. Chianti Classico Vistarreni 0; Podere Bertinga★★ –

Fattoria I Cipressi. See S. Leonino.

Fattoria Il Corno (*S. Casciano, Firenze*). This 210-hectare estate has 136 acres (55 hectares) of vines, planted at an average altitude of 655 feet (200 meters). The vineyards have a southeastern exposure. Their annual production of 500,000 bottles, all from their own grapes, includes 266,000 to 330,000 bottles of Chianti and 80,000 to 93,000 bottles of Chianti Colli Fiorentini. They also produce 66,000 bottles of white wine and 5300 of Vin Santo. Vittorio Fiore has been their consulting enologist since 1981. They consider the best vintages at Il Corno 1983, 1981, 1980, 1978, 1977, 1975, 1971, 1969, 1967, 1964, 1961, and 1958. We found their '83 quite good; their '80 left something to be desired. Chianti Colli Fiorentini (for now)★

Fattoria La Loggia (*Montefiridolfi, Firenze*). This Chianti Classico producer in the San Casciano district has 34 acres (13.8 hectares) of vines, planted at about 1150 feet (350 meters). Their annual production of 11,000 cases of wine includes a Chianti Classico sold under the Fattoria La Loggia label as well as white, rosé, and red wines under the Tena dei Greppi label. Neither the '82 nor the '80 Classico we tasted had much to offer. Chianti Classico 0

Fattoria La Ripa (*S. Donato In Poggio, Firenze*), 1939. La Ripa has 32 acres (13 hectares) of vines in the Tavarnelle Val di Pesa area of the Classico zone. The vineyards, facing southeast, are planted at an average altitude of 1475 feet (450 meters). In 1983, they put in 5 acres (2 hectares) of cabernet sauvignon. This wine will be aged in *barrique*.

Their average production of 13,000 cases of wine a year includes 8900 to 10,000 of Chianti Classico, occasionally as much as 11,000. The balance is Bianco della Lega and Vin Santo. The first Chianti Classico they bottled was the '67; their first riserva was the '80. Their riserva is aged for at least two years in chestnut casks. Of the vintages we've tasted recently, we preferred the '79. The La Ripa Chiantis are agreeable wines, though lacking in style. Chianti Classico★

Fattoria Le Barone *(Panzano, Firenze).* This *azienda* has 24.6 acres (10 hectares) of vines in specialized cultivation and 17.6 (7.1) farmed promiscuously. They produce nearly 10,000 cases of Chianti Classico a year. Admittedly, we have only tasted one vintage, 1977, but it was enough. The wine was barely drinkable, although conditions should have been optimal; it was served at the (mediocre) restaurant of this castle hotel. Chianti Classico 0

Fattoria Le Pici *(S. Gusmè, Siena).* Le Pici produce 53,000 bottles of Chianti Classico a year from their 20.5 acres (8.3 hectares) of vines. We haven't tasted this Chianti since the '74, so our rating may be a bit out of date, but that wine was nothing to write home about. Chianti Classico 0

Fattoria Querciabella *(Ruffoli, Greve, Firenze), 1971.* Giuseppe Mazzanti's Agricola Campoverde owns this 153-acre (62-hectare) estate. There are some 29 acres (11.7 hectares) under vines; 2.5 acres (1 hectare) are in *coltura promiscua.* The vineyards are planted at altitudes of 1540 to 1640 feet (470 to 500 meters), facing east to southeast. These vines produce the grapes for Querciabella's Chianti Classico riserva and their vecchio.

Vineyard	Planted in	Hectares
Il Borro	1960	1.20
Il Poggio	1964	0.50
Il Solatio	1959	1.94
Querciabella	1963	1.50
S. Lucia	1969	2.20

In all, Querciabella produces 52,000 bottles of Chianti Classico, from a blend of 78 percent sangiovese, 5 percent sangiovese grosso, 4 percent canaiolo, 5 percent cabernet sauvignon, 2 percent cabernet franc, 3 percent trebbiano, 2 percent malvasia, and 1 percent colorino. They age their regular Chianti Classico for one year in oak, the vecchio for two years, and the riserva for four. They also produce a *barrique*-aged wine from red grapes only, which they call Casaocci. Chianti Classico★★

Francesco Giuntini of Villa Selvapiana

Fattoria Selvapiana *(Pontassieve, Firenze), 1840.* Francesco Giuntini, genial proprietor of the 865-acre (350-hectare) Selvapiana estate, has 124 acres (50 hectares) in vines, 25 (10) planted in *coltura promiscua.* Giuntini's annual production of almost 27,000 cases includes 9000 to 13,000 cases of Chianti Rùfina. Of this 3300 to 8800 are a very fine riserva. The grapes for this wine, which contains 7 percent white grapes at most, are from the 25-acre (10-hectare) Torricella vineyard.

We had an opportunity to reassess these wines on our most recent visit to Tuscany in the spring of 1985. After meeting us at our previous appointment and taking us to the very interesting wine museum at Spalletti's Villa Poggio Reale, Francesco then stopped at another *cantina* which he thought might interest us and whose wines he described, with astonishing but typical modesty, as on about the same level as his. At our rather definite disagreement, he amended this to say that they should be at about the same level since they had vineyards in very good positions.

Finally, he took us to his own *cantina,* or rather to his house. He had "spared" us the usual visit through the cellar, bringing the wines to us instead. In the comfort of the drawing room, we tasted at our own pace from the lineup of bottles he had made ready for us, some ten wines. He had made a selection of vintages, he explained, not wanting to tire us with too many (too many?). It was a very good tasting. But during the fine dinner, accompanied by our favorites from among the bottles opened, our discussion of the Rùfina zone and of Selvapiana brought up other vintages, other wines not tasted. Well, if we wanted to taste them too, we were certainly welcome to, Francesco offered, pleased that we should be interested. And before the night was out he had gone down to the cellar to fetch another twelve bottles.

Giuntini's Selvapiana is among the top Chiantis produced. In fact, except for Monsanto's Il Poggio and the Castello di Nipozzano of Frescobaldi, there is no finer Chianti, in our opinion, Classico or otherwise. The Selvapiana is a wine with balance and class, full of flavor and style. It shows real quality, and consistently so. Our favorite among the recent vintages is the 1975, followed by the 1982, 1981, 1978, and 1977. Among the older wines, the '47 and '48 were very fine wines by any standard. The '56, '66, and '67 were also impressive.

Francesco provided us with the following vintage evaluation of his wines the morning after our tasting. We found it interesting to see how our evaluations stacked up against his own assessments.

top class	1947, 1948, 1958, 1962, 1965, 1966, 1971, 1975, 1977, 1981, 1982, 1983
very good	1956, 1968, 1969, 1970, 1978, 1979, 1980
good	1964, 1967
average	1957, 1959, 1960, 1961, 1984 (no riserva)
bad	1963, 1972, 1973, 1974, 1976 (not bottled)

Chianti Rùfina★★★ +

Fattoria Tregole *(Castellina, Siena).* Tregole produces an average of 21,000 bottles a year of Chianti Classico from their 4.7 acres (1.9 hectares) of vines. We haven't tasted any since the 1975 vintage, but we did find them overall fairly good. Chianti Classico★

Filetta, Socci Guido *(Lamole, Greve, Firenze).* Filetta has 23.4 acres (9.5 hectares) of vines, from which they produce some 60,000 to 66,500 bottles of Chianti Classico a year. This estate has a good reputation.

Fontodi *(Panzano, Firenze).* Domiziano and Dino Manetti bought the Fontodi estate in 1968. They replanted the vineyards between 1969 and 1974 and produced their first wine in 1970. They have 52 acres (21 hectares) in vines, including 5 (2) of sauvignon blanc, traminer, and pinot bianco and 2.5 (1) of cabernet sauvignon. They make a white blend from the first two varieties, which is aged in *barrique* as is their pinot bianco. Besides these two, they also produce a Bianco della Lega, a Vin Santo, a *barrique*-aged sangiovese called Flaccianello, and a regular and riserva Chianti Classico.

Their average annual production is about 106,000 bottles a year, 80,000 bottles of which are Chianti Classico. In 1981, 15,000 of these were riserva; in 1982, 20,000; and in 1983, 30,000. Their Chianti Classicos before the 1984 vintage (when DOCG regulations reduced the proportion of white grapes) are a blend of 80 percent sangiovese, 10 percent canaiolo, and 10 percent white grapes. Their riserva already included only 5 percent white grapes. Since 1981, about 2 to 3 percent of the wine in their riserva has been given some time in *barrique*.

Overall, we find the Fontodi Classicos to be well-made wines of balance and style. We especially liked their '83; the '82 and '81s are also quite good. Chianti Classico★★ +

Fortilizio Il Colombaio. See Villa Colombaio.

Fossi *(Campiobbi, Firenze)*. Duilio Fossi doesn't own any vineyards; he buys grapes and/or wine to produce some 5500 cases of Chianti Classico a year. He earned something of a reputation with his older wines. A few years ago we tasted the Fossi Chiantis from 1958 through 1964. The '58 and '62 were quite good, the best of the lot. The other vintages were uneven, some good, some not so good. Among his more recent wines, we were disappointed with the '78, '77, '75, and '71. Chianti Classico 0; older vintages★ −

Frescobaldi *(Pelago, Rùfina, and Pontassieve, Firenze)*. The Frescobaldis, who are among the largest landowners in Europe, own eight *poderi* in Chianti:

Estate	Hectares in vines	total	Altitude (feet)
Castello di Nipozzano	124	500	820-1310
Tenuta di Poggio a Remole	55	320	820- 300
Tenuta di Pomino	75	850	1310-2295

Others
Castiglioni
Corte
Montagnana
Montecastello
Valiano

They also have part interest in the Brunello di Montalcino estate of Castelgiocondo.

At Tenuta di Poggio a Remole in Pontassieve, Frescobaldi produces 400,000 bottles of wine a year. It is a simple young Chianti meant to be drunk young and fresh. This is no sipping wine; it is for drinking in draughts, the younger and fresher the better. Chianti Rùfina★

Their Chianti Rùfina riserva is produced at the Castello di Nipozzano farm in Pelago. (They do not produce a regular Chianti Rùfina from Nipozzano.) About half the vineyards on the estate face south, the rest to the west or east. The Nipozzano riserva is made from a blend of 80 percent sangiovese, 10 percent canaiolo, 5 percent trebbiano, and 5 percent of other varieties including a small portion of cabernet sauvignon. About 20 percent of the wine is aged for fifteen to eighteen months in new oak barrels; the rest spends up to two or three years in older oak casks. Frescobaldi produces some 200,000 bottles of this exceptionally fine Chianti a year. The Nipozzano riserva is known for its capacity to age, a reputation that is well deserved. In the spring of 1985, we had the pleasure of sharing a bottle of the '45 as well as a '23 from the cellar of the castle at Nipozzano with Marchese Leonardo Frescobaldi and their fine enologist, Dott. Luciano Boarino. The '23 had coated the sides of the old blue-green blown-glass bottle with sheets of sediment like a Port crust, but the wine retained a fine color as well as remarkable structure and flavor—an outstanding wine and a memorable experience. The very young '45 was also magnificent. Chianti Rùfina★★★★

The Montesodi Chianti Rùfina was first produced in 1974 from a special 25-acre (10-hectare) plot on the Nipozzano estate. The thirty-year-old vines in the Montesodi vineyard are planted at an altitude of 1150 feet (350 meters). They produce an average yield of no more than 320 gallons an acre (30 hectoliters a hectare). This wine is a sangiovese–canaiolo blend. The sangiovese is a special clone found here at Nipozzano. Montesodi is produced only in the better vintages. The wine is aged for two to four years in small oak barrels; the '78 was given three months of *barrique* age as well.

Vintage	Production (bottles)
1974	4,850
1978	15,570
1979	18,340

Montesodi is a richly flavored, intense, full-bodied, warm red wine. As impressed as we were with the few vintages we tasted, because of our limited experience we cannot give it full marks in our rating as yet. Chianti Rùfina★★★ +

The Frescobaldis produce a very fine white wine from grapes grown at Tenuta di Pomino in the Rùfina zone. It is made from a blend of chardonnay, pinot bianco, pinot grigio, and trebbiano. The grapes for the riserva, Il Benefizio, are from a 34.6-acre (14-hectare) vineyard of that name planted at altitudes of 1970 to 2300 feet (600 to 700 meters). This wine is fermented in wood.

Leonardo Frescobaldi

Frescobaldi did produce a red Pomino as well, made in the style to be drunk young, though it could take moderate age, but this wine is due for a change. With the recent DOC recognition for Pomino, the Frescobaldis have decided to create a new Pomino rosso. Leonardo, generally quite candid despite an aristocratic reserve, told us with perhaps an apologetic smile that he preferred not to divulge as yet just what sort of changes they had in mind. We suspect there is some experimentation still going on and wouldn't be surprised to see a wine with more cabernet and merlot in the blend. The use of a little cabernet in the Pomino wines goes back for many years.

Frigeni Dott. Giulio *(San Gimignano, Siena), 1960.* Dott. Frigeni owns 37 acres (15 hectares) of vines in the Colli Senesi, from which he produced 11,000 cases of wine a year, including Chianti Frigeni and Vernaccia di San Gimignano.

Geografico. See Agricoltori del Chianti Geografico.

Giorgio Regni *(Gaiole, Siena).* Regni's Fattoria Valtellina estate has 8.5 acres (3.5 hectares) of vineyards, from which he produces 18,650 bottles of Chianti Classico a year, as well as some white wine and Vin Santo. His wines have quite a high reputation.

Gittori. See Baccio da Gaiuole.

Granducato *(Poggibonsi, Siena).* Enopplio di Poggibonsi bottles some 55,000 cases a year of what is, based on our limited experience, a mediocre Chianti Classico. Chianti Classico 0

228

Grignano *(Pontassieve, Firenze)*. This 1236-acre (500-hectare) estate has 104 acres (42 hectares) of vines in specialized cultivation and 50 (20) in *coltura promiscua*. Their annual production averages 10,000 cases. They are in the Chianti Rùfina production zone.

Il Capitano *(Pontassieve, Firenze)*. Fattoria Il Capitano has 173 acres (70 hectares), 23 (9.2) in vines; 12.4 (5) are in *coltura esclusiva* and 44.4 (18) *promiscua*. They produce an average of 5500 cases of wine a year, including Chianti Rùfina.

Il Guerrino *(Greve, Firenze)*. This *azienda* owns 22 acres (8.9 hectares) of vineyards. We've had limited experience with these wines. The last bottle we tasted was the '77—a fine vintage, though you couldn't have proved it by this wine. Chianti Classico 0

Il Paradiso *(San Gimignano, Siena), 1972*. Graziella Cetti Cappelli is the proprietor of Fattoria Il Paradiso, an estate in the Colli Senesi zone. She has 39 acres (15.9 hectares) of vineyards; 22 acres (9 hectares) are planted to vines for Chianti, 15 (6) for Vernaccia di San Gimignano, and 2.2 (0.9) are in chardonnay. Cappelli produces 80,000 to 93,000 bottles a year of Chianti and 66,500 to 80,000 of Vernaccia di San Gimignano, including 5300 bottles of a brut spumante. She has plans to produce a wine from her Paterno II vineyard that will be called Rosso Paterno II. It will be from a familiar *uvaggio*: 80 percent sangiovese, 15 percent cabernet sauvignon, and 5 percent cabernet franc—the same formula as Antinori's Tignanello. She previously made a Chianti Paterno Secondo from those vines.

Il Poggiolo *(Carmignano, Firenze), 1800*. This producer of a fine Carmignano also makes a fairly good Chianti Montalbano from an *uvaggio* of 75 percent sangiovese, 10 percent each of canaiolo and trebbiano, and 5 percent of other varieties. Chianti Montalbano★

Il Poggiolo *(Monteriggioni, Siena), 1977*. Federico Bonfio has 31.6 acres (12.8 hectares) of vines, 16.8 (6.8) in the Il Poggiolo vineyard and 9.9 (4) in Le Portine. He has produced his Il Poggiolo Chianti Colli Senesi since 1977, the Le Portine since 1980. He has an average annual production of about 53,000 bottles of wine, all from his own grapes. Bonfio rates 1983, 1982, and 1981 as excellent vintages; 1980 as very good; 1979 as good; and 1978 and 1977 as very good. Our own tastings of the Bonfio wines have produced mixed results. He does seem to be a serious producer, so we think it is possible that we had some bad bottles. Based on our experience, though, we can only give him one star; we think, though that this is an estate worth watching.★

Graziella Cetti Cappelli of Podere Paradiso

Isabella de' Medici *(La Volpaia, Radda, Siena)*. This *casa vinicola* buys grapes and/or wine to produce over 7500 cases of really mediocre Chianti Classico a year. They also sell a pretty poor Brunello. Chianti Classico 0

Isole e Olena *(Barberino Val d'Elsa, Firenze), 1950*. The di Marchi family of Piemonte are the owners of this property, which includes the fourteenth-century village of Olena and the eighteenth-century Isole estate. They replanted the vineyards between 1967 and 1972. Today there are 79 acres (32 hectares) under vines, planted at an average altitude of 1265 feet (386 meters).

Isole e Olena bottled their first wine sold under their label from the 1969 vintage. Previously they had sold much of their wine to Antinori; they still sell a portion to that firm and to Ruffino.

The average annual production at Isole is 20,000 cases; this includes 10,000 cases of Chianti Classico, 1500 of the *barrique*-aged Borro Cepparello, 100 cases of a very good Vin Santo, plus a white, a rosé, and a fresh young red.

Since 1976, the estate has been run by Dott. Paolo di Marchi, who is also the enologist. The Isole Chianti Classico is made from mostly sangiovese and canaiolo and less than 5 percent white grapes. The must is fermented in stainless steel, and the wine is aged in tanks, casks of chestnut and oak, and *barriques*, in about equal distribution. Currently, one-third of their casks are chestnut. Di Marchi doesn't want a lot of wood character in the wine; he respects the variety and seeks to maintain its personality. He has been using *barriques* since the 1978 vintage.

At the fine vertical tasting di Marchi set up for us recently at the estate, we were quite impressed with the style, balance, class, and consistency of the wines. We found his '82 the best of all. The '79 and '77 are also quite fine, and we can also recommend his '83, '81, '80, and '78. The wines here have improved considerably since Paolo's arrival. The older vintages reflect a different style, or lack of it.

The di Marchi family also own the Villa Sperino property in Lessona. Paolo told us that he would like someday to restart the winemarking there. We look forward to tasting those wines. Chianti Classico★★★

Paolo de Marchi of Antiche Fattorie Isole e Olena

La Cerreta *(Gaiole, Siena)*. This social cooperative controls 114 acres (46 hectares) of vines. Their average annual production is some 33,000 cases of wine. They belong to the Storiche Cantine. We haven't tasted any of the La Cerreta wines, but considering their association, our expectations would not be high.

La Loggia. See Fattoria La Loggia.

La Mandria *(Lecchi In Chianti, Siena)*. La Mandria has 104 acres (42.3 hectares) of vines in the Gaiole area. They produce some 22,000 cases of Chianti Classico a year. The most recent vintage we've tasted was their 1975; it was quite mediocre. Chianti Classico 0

La Pagliaia *(Castelnuovo Berardenga, Siena)*, 1888. This *azienda* has 115 acres (46.6 hectares) of vineyards. Their average annual production is about 35,500 cases of wine, including, besides their Chianti Classico, a Bianco della Lega, a rosé, and a Vin Santo. Their top wine, Riserva Granduca Ferdinando III, is made from the best grapes from the best parts of their vineyards. Chianti Classico Riserva Granduca Ferdinando III★

La Pesanella. See Castello di Monterinaldi.

La Quercia. See Cappelli Giovanni.

La Ripa. See Fattoria La Ripa.

Le Bocce *(Panzano, Firenze)*. Le Bocce has 109 acres (44 hectares) of vineyards and produces almost 28,000 cases of wine a year. This includes a very good Chianti Classico, if we can judge it from previous experience. Unfortunately, we have not tasted it since the 1977 vintage. Their '73, '74, and '75 were very good; the '76 was passable (good for the year); and the '77 was also fairly good. Chianti Classico★★ +

Le Chiantigiane *(Sambuca, Tavarnelle Val di Pesa, Firenze)*. This *cantina sociale* bottles some 55,000 cases of wine a year; very little of it is Chianti Classico. The co-op is not in the classic zone, and their members have only 11 acres (45 hectares) of Classico vineyards. It's been a while since we tasted their Chianti Classico; those bottles we did were drinkable, though not much more. Chianti Classico 0

Le Lame *(San Casciano Val di Pesa, Firenze)*. This *fattoria* produces 3100 cases of Chianti Classico a year from their 10 acres (4 hectares) of vines. Their riserva, Vigna di Sorripa, is made from the grapes of that vineyard only.

Le Masse di San Leolino *(Panzano, Firenze)*. Wine production at this estate was mentioned in the property census of 1427. Today Norman Bain owns the estate and its 7.7 acres (3.1 hectares) of vines. He has an annual production of about 2000 cases. We found his '80, '81 and '82 all good Classicos. Chianti Classico★★

Le Miccine *(Gaiole, Siena)*. Half of the acreage on this 32-acre (13-hectare) farm is planted to vines. They use only organic fertilizer, from sheep, in the vineyards. They have an annual production of 10,500 gallons (400 hectoliters) of Chianti Classico but bottle only about 20 percent of it (900 cases).

Le Pici. See Fattoria Le Pici.

Norman Bain of Le Masse di San Leolino

Lilliano *(Castellina, Siena)*. Conte Ugo, Marquis of Tuscany, donated this property to the Abbey of Poggibonsi in A.D. 980. Today Lilliano has 117 acres (47 hectares) of vines, producing 33,000 cases of Chianti Classico and other wines. Their pre-DOCG vintages are made from 80 percent sangiovese, 6 percent malvasia, 5 percent trebbiano, 4 percent canaiolo, and 5 percent of other varieties. The Lilliano Principessa riserva is made from 100 percent sangiovese. The '80 was quite good. Chianti Classico★★

Lilliano *(Antella, Firenze), 1960*. Fattoria Lilliano, not to be confused with the Chianti Classico estate, has 178 acres (72 hectares) in the Colli Fiorentini zone; 43 (17.5) are planted to vines for Chianti. They will plant 5 acres (2 hectares) of chardonnay. Lilliano produces about 12,000 cases a year. They rate 1983, 1975, and 1970 as their best vintages and 1976 as their least. We haven't tasted these wines in some time, but with the exception of the '77 we've always had a fairly good impression. Chianti Colli Fiorentini★

Luiano *(Mercatale Val di Pesa, Firenze)*. This estate, in the San Casciano area, has 62 acres (25 hectares) of vines planted at altitudes of 820 to 985 feet (250 to 300 meters). They produce an average of nearly 16,500 cases of wine a year. This includes 10,000 bottles of two Chianti Classico riservas: Luiano and S. Andrea a Luiano. These wines are aged for two years in oak casks. The pre-1984 vintages of their regular Chianti Classico are made from 65 percent sangiovese, 15 percent canaiolo, 15 percent trebbiano, and 5 percent malvasia; their riserva from 70 percent sangiovese, 20 percent canaiolo, plus 10 percent of trebbiano and malvasia. This, of course, has changed with the new DOCG regulations. We were unimpressed recently with their '79, '80, and '82. Chianti Classico 0

Machiavelli. See Conti Serristori.

Marchese de' Frescobaldi. See Frescobaldi.

Mazzoni. We have tasted this Chianti Classico only once, the '77, bottled by the very fine Chianti Classico producer Villa Cafaggio. The wine left us wondering what went wrong. Chianti Classico 0

Melini *(Poggibonsi, Siena), 1705*. Melini, one of the largest producers of Chianti Classico, is owned by Winefood, the Swiss conglomerate. They have 1050 acres (425 hectares), including 464 (188) of vineyards and a number of *fattorie*.

Fattoria	Location	Hectares In vines	Hectares Total
Casalta	Castellina	n/a	n/a
Gaggiano	Castellina, Poggibonsi and Barberino Val d' Elsa	50.00	175
Granio[a]	Poggibonsi	17.89	[b]
La Selvanella[a]	Lucarelli and Radda	64.10	114
Terra Rossa[a]	Castellina	55.81	136
Valiano	Valiano	n/a	n/a
Total		187.80	425

Notes: [a]Bottled separately.
[b]Included in the 175 hectares of Gaggiano.
1 hectare = 2.4711 acres

Melini produces more than 110,000 cases of Chianti Classico a year and bottles twice that amount. They also sell a fairly good Vino Nobile. We haven't tasted any of their Chianti Classico since the 1975 vintage. Before that we tasted numerous bottles, mostly reliable and mostly good. Chianti Classico regular★; riserva★★

Fabrizio and Giuliana Bianchi of Fattoria Monsanto

Monsanto (*Barberino Val d'Elsa*), *1961*. Fabrizio Bianchi, proprietor of Fattoria Monsanto, bought the first part of the estate, then called Azienda Pallone, in 1961. He renamed it Monsanto, taking the name from the district where the property is located. This locality, known in ancient times as Scrutania, was the site of an Etruscan village. It was given the name of Monsanto some time in the early middle ages in honor of San Ruffiniano, who ended his evangelical mission in this locality. Monsanto is mentioned in ecclesiastical papers from A.D. 998.

Bianchi came to the area to attend the wedding of a friend, he recalls, and seeing the vineyards rekindled his love for the country. He decided he would like to buy some land and produce wine and olive oil for his family. Though he lived and worked near Milano, in the family textile business, as a boy he had spent many summers in the country with his uncles in Piemonte and had worked in their vineyards.

The Pallone property was owned by two sisters who were not on speaking terms and had divided everything, including the house itself, into two parts. The holdings of only one sister were on the market when Bianchi made his original purchase of about half the estate. This included the vineyards of Sornano, Il Poggio, La Chiesa, and part of Fonte del Latte and Scanni. A year later he was able to buy the rest of the property.

At that time the estate was worked under the old system of *mezzadria*. The *mezzadro* who ran the property made the '61 Monsanto as he had previous vintages; the wine was not bottled but sold in demijohns, except for a small portion that Bianchi took for his personal use and to give as gifts to friends.

In 1962, Fabrizio made the wine with the assistance of his uncle, "in true *contadino* fashion," dumping the grape bunches, whole berries, stems, and all into large wooden tubs and bashing them about with a wooden club stuck with nails, which broke up only a small portion of the grapes. He recalls that he and his uncle found it funny at the time, but they did it that way, using the local methods. He laughs now at the memory of it.

The must was put into wooden uprights, *tini di legno*, for the fermentation, with the stems, which lasted for fifteen days. Wine made by this method tends to pick up harsh tannins from the stems and becomes rather rough. To soften the wine, they added white grapes and used *governo*. This system of winemaking was employed at Monsanto up through the 1967 vintage. In 1966, Fabrizio did some experiments with fermenting without the stems and was pleased with the results. In 1968, he initiated some new vinification methods—no white grapes, *governo*, or stems, and a reduced period of skin contact. Today the Monsanto Chianti Classico is fermented for one week on the skins, the Il Poggio for eight to ten days.

Bianchi taught himself to make wine. With a natural enthusiasm and an eagerness to learn, he read books in French on winemaking and notes that he basically learned as he went along. Experience, he feels, is the real teacher. You learn from the wine itself; every vintage is different. Perhaps as a consequence he has more of an open mind about making wine. He was, and still is, willing to experiment, to try new ideas. But he is slow to change; he makes many tests first to be sure of the results and to understand the reasons behind them.

He sends samples out for analysis and tastes frequently. Tasting, he says, is 90 percent in the aroma; the palate confirms it. When his business requires him to be in Gallarate, he has samples sent up from the farm and is on the phone following the progress of the wine intently. Fabrizio is not an absentee landlord (the bane of many a Chianti *fattoria*); when he can't be at Monsanto in person, he is on the phone, avidly following every phase of the wine's development.

The most important consideration in making a fine wine, Bianchi believes, is the quality of the fruit. You can't overcrop. While he might get 3 tons of grapes per acre (70 quintali per hectare) for the regular Monsanto, the Il Poggio averages 1.8 to 2 (40 to 45). The Il Poggio vineyard is harvested two weeks later than those for the regular Monsanto. The sweeter must attains ¾ to 1 percent more alcohol than the riserva. Fabrizio echoes the belief of all the finest producers in pointing out that you have to select very carefully and reject all but the best grapes.

The winemaker, he feels, is less important; he should do as little as necessary and keep the wine as natural as possible. A good wine, Fabrizio says, needs little interference. The less you do, the better. He notes that the farmers made good wine here—surprisingly good considering what they had to work with, using traditional methods and without benefit of technology. Enology, he feels, has sometimes gotten in the way of good winemaking, taking away the character of the wine.

He does, though, use stainless steel tanks and cultured yeast. The stainless tanks give him better control over the temperature of the fermentation, which is extremely important. He experimented with using cultured yeast in lieu of the wild yeast that forms on the grapeskins and found that while it made no difference in the wine, it was a lot more convenient.

The essential things, he says, are to plant the right grapes in the right place, to have a good fermentation, and to bottle at the right time.

The grapes are pressed gently in a vaslin press. (No press juice is used in the Il Poggio.) Both Chianti Classicos spend one to two years in stainless after the fermentation, and from there they are moved to oak. The Il Poggio is aged for two to three years in oak casks, the Monsanto for two.

Bianchi doesn't induce the malolactic. He waits for it to happen, which it always does, sooner or later—sooner when the must is lower in alcohol, later when the gradation is higher. He doesn't fine or filter the wine; he clears it by racking only, twice the first year and once a year after that.

When Fabrizio took over the farm, the vines were in promiscuous cultivation with olive trees. In 1963 and 1964, he began replanting the vineyards. Barone Ricasoli, then president of the Classico Consorzio, was one of the first to make the changeover to specialized vineyards and advised others to do so also. In 1964, Bianchi replanted the top of the Il Poggio vineyard; two years later he replanted the slope. He had to dynamite to break up a large stratum of solid rock under part of the vineyard to allow the vines to reach deep into the soil for nutrients and moisture.

The Monsanto estate covers more than 395 acres (160 hectares), 50 (20) in Poggibonsi and 345 (140) in Barberino Val d'Elsa. The 195 acres (78.9 hectares) of vines produce some 35,000 cases of wine a year.

Crus/vineyard	Hectares	Altitude (meters)	Exposure	Vines	Planted	Zone
Fonte del Latte	3.87	290/305	ne	85% sangiovese	67,68	BVE
Il Poggio[a]	5.32	280/320	sw	90% sangiovese	63,64,69,70	BVE
				7% canaiolo		
				3% colorino		
La Chiesa	1.80	295/305	ne	75% sangiovese	66,67	BVE
				25% malvasia nera		
Mulino[b]	1.90	250/260	sw	100% cabernet s.	76	BVE
	1.00			100% trebbiano t.	71,72	BVE
Salcio	2.15	260/280	sw	50% trebbiano t.	66,67	PGB
				50% vermentino		
Scanni[c]	3.34	275/300	sw	100% sangiovese	69,70	BVE
Sornano[d]	4.73	280/300	sw	95% sangiovese	66,67	PGB
				5% malvasia nera		
Val di Gallo	6.66	260/280	ne	100% sangiovese	70,71,74	PGB
	1.00			100% chardonnay	81	
Total	31.77					
Other vineyards	11.93					
Promiscuous	35.20					
Total in vines	78.90					

Notes: [a] Used for Monsanto, Il Poggio riserva.
    [b] Used for Cabernet Sauvignon, Vigna Mulino.
    [c] Used for Sangioveto Grosso.
    [d] Bottled as a Chianti cru in 1971.
    BVE = Barberino Val d'Elsa
    PGB = Poggibonsi
    1 hectare = 2.4711 acres
    1 meter = 3.281 feet

Besides Chianti Classico, Bianchi produces two whites, a rosé, a small amount of a fine sweet Vin Santo, a Sangioveto Grosso, a Cabernet Sauvignon, a sangiovese–cabernet blend called Tiscvil, and two champagne-method sparklers—a rosé and a white Bianco di Bianchi. On rare occasions he has produced a botrytised Trebbiano.

Chianti Classico	Cases
Monsanto vecchio	6000
Monsanto riserva	7500
Monsanto Il Poggio	3250
Santa Caterina	3000
Chianti	
Valdigallo	7500
Other wines	
Cabernet Sauvignon	500
Sangioveto Grosso	400
Sangiovese di Monsanto	2000
white	800
Vin Santo	100
Bianco dei Bianchi spumante	2000
Brut Spumante	1000

Overall, they are good, even very good wines. But the real star is the Monsanto Chianti Classico riserva from the Il Poggio vineyard. It is in our considerable experience without question *the* single finest Chianti and one of the world's vinicultural treasures. There are two reasons: its very high level of quality and its very high level of consistency. The least of the Il Poggios that we've tasted are better than most other Chianti Classicos.

When we say consistency, we are not speaking of a dozen or so bottles, but scores, and not one vertical tasting, but five—of every vintage of Monsanto Il Poggio from the first in 1962 through the most recent at the time tasted along with a number of other Monsanto Chianti Classicos (missing only two vintages, 1963 and 1965, of which there were only a couple of bottles, one cache saved for sentimental reasons—it was the year of his son's birth—and the other strictly to have a complete library of vintages).

At a tasting of that kind with wines of that level, the tendency is to be more than usually critical. A defect tends to stand out. But we didn't find one wine that was less than good.

At our most recent vertical tasting at Monsanto this spring, we were joined by Alfredo and Luciana Currado of Piemonte. At the Vietti *cantina* earlier in the trip, Alfredo had said something that rather took us aback: that he found the best wines of Tuscany to be—did he say the whites?! Not possible. No, he laughed, not *"i vini bianchi, i vini di Bianchi."* Ah, that was more like it.

Fabrizio's wife, the gentle Giuliana, a fashion model before her marriage, came in from the garden in old jeans, her blond hair casually tied back from a face adorned only with a healthy glow and a warm welcoming smile. She joined us just briefly, offering friendly greetings but putting off pleasant conversation until later, not to distract anyone from serious tasting. Giuliana, Fabrizio notes, has a very fine palate, and he has a high regard for her opinion. She doesn't care, though, for the harsh young wines, preferring a smooth, round, and ready vintage.

We all enjoyed the older vintages later at the dinner Giuliana had prepared. She has a light touch in the kitchen and shares her husband's belief in the importance of the *materia prima*, selecting the best ingredients available and preparing things simply and naturally.

Production and Ratings of Monsanto, Il Poggio

Year	Bottles	Our rating	Bianchi's rating	Comments
1962	5,730	★★★★	★★★★	Generally hard wines, ready now
1963	—	—	0	Decent wines that have faded now
1964	13,760	★★★★	★★★	Lighter than 1962, with more perfume
1965	—	—	0	Poor
1966	5,370	★★★★	★★★★	Light body, high alcohol, from young vines
1967	8,930	★★★	★★★	A medium year, lacked body; the last Monsanto with white grapes, stems, and *governo*
1968	12,550	★★★	★★★	A medium year, very low acid
1969	13,420	★★★	★★★★	Similar to 1962, needed age but very soft now
1970	18,630	★★★(★)	★★★★	Excellent, close to 1971 in quality, maybe better, and should last longer
1971	36,700	★★★(★)	★★★★	Excellent
1972	12,770	★★★	★★★★	A success, some botrytis, a lot of rain, but Bianchi waited to pick and the sun came out
1973	6,500	★★+	★★	Soft, not to age, the least in quality
1974	34,600	★★+	★★★	Excellent, to age
1975	35,700	★★★(★)	★★★★	Excellent
1976	0	—	0	Terrible, none bottled
1977	23,730	★★★(★)	★★★★	Best of all
1978	38,650	★★(★−)	★★+	Good
1979	32,880	★★(★−)	★★★	Better than 1978
1980	34,550	★★(★)	★★★	Similar to 1978

At the tasting, of all the Il Poggios from 1962 to 1983, not one vintage was fading, though a few had peaked and probably shouldn't be held much longer. Among the more recent vintages, we recommend laying down the '77 and '75 and, when they are available, the '83 and '82. Most, in fact, will improve with further age, but these two will need more than most. We preferred the '79 to the '78; the '80 is also very good. Both the '70 and the '71 can improve yet. The '73 should probably be drunk up.

While we rate the Monsanto riserva highly, there are other fine Chiantis on that level. The Il Poggio riserva is simply in a class by itself. This is not a classic Classico, you might say; no, it is rather the epitome of what a Classico can be. It is darker in color, fuller in body, richer in flavor and extract, lower in acid, higher in alcohol, more harmonious, more complex, and just downright more impressive overall. This is a wine for contemplation.

We could sit, with the greatest of pleasure, in the *caminetto* at Monsanto on the cushioned benches by the fire—and have, on frosty spring and autumn evenings—catching the burnished reflections of the ruby wine held up to the flames, inhaling its rich perfume, and savoring its nuances.

Lovely as an old vintage is by itself as an after-dinner glass, this wine is an excellent complement to roast meat, *bistecca alla fiorentia* (*"bue americano"* Fabrizio adds with an appreciative grin), with pigeon or duck, or game, *cinghiale,* even venison. And tempting as it is to drink young, owing to its depth of fruit and fine balance, Il Poggio should be given age to develop its full potential, at least eight years and in the best vintages ten to twelve.

It's worth mentioning again that the regular Monsanto Chianti Classico riserva is also a very fine wine, far better than most Chianti Classicos. It has only one real problem; its position, standing as it does in the shadow of the great Il Poggio.

Chianti Classico Santa Caterina★; Monsanto riserva★★★; Monsanto Il Poggio★★★★

Montagliari. See Cappelli Giovanni.

Montagliari e Castellinuzza. See Cappelli Giovanni.

Monte Vertine (*Radda, Siena*), *1967.* Sergio Manetti, the proprietor of this estate, has 108 acres (43.7 hectares) of vines planted at an average altitude of 1395 feet (425 meters).

Manetti produces 50,000 bottles of wine a year, including two Chianti Classicos, a regular and a riserva. The former is aged for one and a half years in oak casks, the latter for three. There are no white grapes in either wine today. Until recently, though, the Monte Vertine Chiantis were made with 80 percent sangiovese, 15 percent canaiolo, and 5 percent malvasia and trebbiano.

The first Chianti Classico produced here was the '71; the first riserva was from the 1974 vintage. Manetti feels that his best Chianti Classico to date was the '79. We were impressed with it ourselves, the riserva especially. The '82, '81, and '80 were also quite good.

Manetti produces two crus: Il Sodaccio from a 1.2-acre (0.5-hectare) plot, and Le Pergole Torte from the 6.9-acre (2.8-hectare) vineyard of that name. He also makes a very fine white wine. "M." This quite atypical trebbiano–malvasia blend was first produced in 1982.

Chianti Classico★★

Montemaggio (*Radda, Siena*). This *azienda* has 37 acres (15 hectares) of vines planted at altitudes of 1475 to 1740 feet (450 to 530 meters). They produce more than 16,000 cases of Montemaggio Chianti Classico a year from their own vines plus 4000 cases of Castello di Radda from purchased grapes. They ferment their wines in stainless steel tanks and age them in old chestnut casks. The '83 Castello di Radda, from that outstanding vintage, was not very good. The Montemaggio Chianti Classicos we tasted in April 1985—the '83, '82, and '79—were equally unremarkable. Chianti Classico (both labels) 0

Montesodi. See Frescobaldi.

Monticelli. Our experience here is limited to the '81 Monticelli. While it was nothing special, it was drinkable. This wine is produced by Storiche Cantine member Viticola Toscana, which also owns Castello di Meleto.

Chianti Classico★ –

Montoro (*Greve, Firenze*). Principessa Sobilia Palmieri Nuti in Carafa di Roccella has 6.9 acres (2.8 hectares) of vines on her Montoro estate, from which she produces 16,000 bottles a year of a highly regarded Chianti Classico.

Nozzole *(Passo dei Pecorai, Greve, Firenze).* This 1235-acre (500-hectare) Chianti Classico estate is owned by Ruffino. There are 222 acres (90 hectares) of specialized vineyards on the property. Their annual production of Chianti Classico is 60,000 cases. Up to and including the 1977 vintage—the most recent we have tasted—we have found the Nozzole Chiantis to be reliable and fairly good, and characteristic of the Greve style. Chianti Classico★★

Pagliarese *(S. Gusmè, Siena), 1810.* The family of Alma Biasiotto in Sanguineti have been the owners of the Pagliarese estate since 1965. There are 67 acres (27 hectares) of vines on the property, planted at an average altitude of 1150 feet (350 meters). The vineyards have a south, southwesterly exposure. Pagliarese produces 22,000 cases of wine a year, as well as virgin olive oil and honey.

They make a regular Chianti Classico sold under the Pagliatello label and two riservas, one a cru from their Boscardini vineyard. Their Classicos produced before the new DOCG status for Chianti are from 80 percent sangiovese, 12 percent other red varieties, and 8 percent white grapes. They have some cabernet sauvignon in the vineyard and have included 4 to 5 percent in their Chianti for the past few years. Pagliarese bottled their first Chianti Classico under their own label from the 1965 vintage.

The first Boscardini riserva was the '78. Today they are producing 12,000 bottles a year. This wine, from sangiovese, canaiolo, and trebbiano grapes grown in their 12.4-acre (5-hectare) Boscardini vineyard, is aged for six months in Alliers *barriques* and another two years in cask. It is their best Chianti Classico. Besides these wines, they make Camerlengo, a *barrique*-aged sangiovese grosso.

The Chiantis of Pagliarese are good wines and quite reliable. Among recent vintages we can recommend the '78 and '79 Boscardini, also the '83, '82, '81, '79, and '78 Classicos. We found only the '80 not up to par. Chianti Classico★★; Boscardini Riserva★★+

Pagnana *(Rignano sull' Arno, Firenze).* This 630-acre (255-hectare) Colli Fiorentini estate has 172 acres (70 hectares) of vines in specialized cultivation and 17.2 (7) mixed. They produce between 16,500 and 22,000 bottles of wine a year. Their '80 Chianti was quite agreeable. Chianti Colli Fiorentini★

Palazzo al Bosco *(La Romala, Firenze).* This estate, located in the San Casciano district in the northwestern part of the Classico zone, has 25 acres (10.2 hectares) of vineyards. They produce about 6700 cases a year of good and reliable Chianti Classico. We have enjoyed many bottles of the Palazzo al Bosco Chianti in the vintages from the 1960s and early 1970s. Their '79 was good and the '75 very good. Chianti Classico★★

Parga *(Molin del Piano, Firenze).* Fattoria Parga, covering 222 acres (90 hectares), has 69 acres (28 hectares) or vineyards, 40 (16) in specialized cultivation. They produce 6500 cases of wine a year, including a Chianti Rùfina.

Pasolini dall'Onda Borghese *(Imola, Bologna) 1760; (Barberino Val d'Elsa, Firenze), 1573.* Pasolini has 148 acres (60 hectares) in Barberino Val d'Elsa, from which they produce 40,000 to 45,000 cases of wine a year, Chianti and Chianti riserva. These are reliable wines and generally represent quite good quality. Though the estate is in the Colli Fiorentini zone, the wines are sold simply as Chianti, without a more specific denomination. Pasolini also has 104 acres (42 hectares) in Emilia Romagna, from which they produce 33,000 to 40,000 cases of wine a year, including Sangiovese, Trebbiano, and Albana di Romagna. Chianti★★

Petriolo *(Rignano sull' Arno, Firenze).* The 346-acre (140-hectare) Petriolo farm has 153 acres (62 hectares) of vineyards; 62 (25) are in mixed cultivation. They produce some 22,000 cases of wine a year.

Pian d'Albola *(Radda, Siena).* This *fattoria* has 69 acres (28 hectares) of vines, from which they produce about 22,000 cases of Chianti Classico a year. Their present output, we have heard, will shortly be expanded to 50,000 cases. An increase in quality would be a better plan in our opinion. Chianti Classico 0

Pietrafitta *(San Gimignano, Siena), 1500.* Pietrafitta has nearly 100 acres (40 hectares) of vines, 44 (18) planted for Chianti and 54 (22) for Vernaccia di San Gimignano. Their average annual production is 30,500 cases, 13,000 of Chianti Colli Senesi and 17,500 of the Vernaccia.

In some vintages they bottle a Chianti cru from their Campidonne vineyard. Pietrafitta name 1983 and 1975 as their two best vintages. Chianti Colli Senesi★

Pietraserena *(San Gimignano, Siena), 1966.* This *azienda* has 40 acres (16 hectares) of vines; 25 (10) for Chianti Colli Senesi and 15 (6) for Vernaccia di San Gimignano. Their annual production of more than 13,000 cases breaks down to about 7700 for the red and 5500 for the white.

Podere Castellare. See Castellare.

Podere di Cignano *(Pieve al Bagnoro, Arezzo), 1958.* Giovanni Bianchi owns this 57-acre (23-hectare) farm in the hills of Arezzo. His annual production at Cignano is 220 tons (2000 quintali) of grapes, 20 percent of which becomes Chianti Colli Aretini.

Bianchi produces more than 20,000 bottles of Villa Cilnia Chianti Colli Aretini a year from an *uvaggio* of 70 percent sangiovese, 15 percent canaiolo, 8 percent malvasia nera, and 7 percent trebbiano. He also produces Chianti Colli Aretini with the Mulino di Salmarega label, some special white wine, an interesting red Le Vignacce, and three single-vineyard wines:

Cru	Hectoliters	Bottles
Campo del Sasso	85	11,300
Poggio Cicaleto	130	17,300
Poggio Garbato	280	37,300
Total	495	65,900

Chianti Colli Aretini★

Podere Il Palazzino *(Monte In Chianti, Siena).* The Sderci brothers have 9.1 acres (3.7 hectares) of vines at their *fattoria,* including the 3.7-acre (1.5-hectare) Grosso Senese cru. In 1974, they replanted their promiscuous vineyards. Their annual production is 24,000 bottles of wine. This includes 13,000 bottles of Chianti Classico, 3000 of Grosso Senese, and 2000 of white wine.

Their Chianti Classico from vintages before DOCG was made from an *uvaggio* of 70 percent sangiovese, 10 percent canaiolo, and 20 percent white grapes. Since 1984, they use a blend of 85 percent sangiovese, 10 percent canaiolo, and 5 percent malvasia. The 1977 was the first vintage bottled under their own label. Their bottling is done by a mobile bottling unit. Previously they made wine on an amateur level for their own consumption; now they offer it for sale. Chianti Classico 0

Poggio a Remole. See Frescobaldi.

Poggio al Sole *(Badia a Passignano, Firenze), 1969.* The Poggio al Sole farm of Aldo Torrini and family in the Sambuca Val di Pesa area of Chianti Classico not far from Greve is on the grounds of the eighteenth-century Vallombrosian Abbey of Passignano. Reportedly there were vines and olive trees growing here in the twelfth century. Torrini put in his first vines in 1969, the year he purchased the 100-acre (40-hectare) estate. Today there are 17 acres (7 hectares) of vines in specialized cultivation and 15 (6) in *coltura promiscua.* The vineyards are planted at an average altitude of 1650 feet (500 meters) with a southern exposure.

While waiting for their vines to come into production, they bought grapes to produce a wine that they sold in demijohns. Today they produce 35,000 to 40,000 bottles of regular Chianti Classico annually and 4000 to 5000 of riserva, as well as 4000 bottles of Vino della Signora, a white wine from traminer grapes, plus a few other wines.

Their pre-1984 Chianti Classico is made from 75 percent sangiovese, 10 percent canaiolo, 10 percent trebbiano and malvasia, plus 5 percent colorino, mammolo, and ciliegiolo.

Aldo Torrini of Az. Agr. Poggio al Sole

The wine is fermented for four to five days on the skins; ten days later they add dried grapes for the *governo*. They use *governo* for all of their Chianti Classico including the riserva. The second fermentation lasts for about two and a half months. The regular Chianti is aged for two years, the riserva for three.

Their Chianti Classico is reliable and good. It has a lively, rather austere nature owing to higher than average acidity. The '82 and '80 were the best of their recent vintages; the '78 and '79 were also quite good. Chianti Classico★★ +

Poggio Reale. See Spalletti.

Poggio Rosso *(San Felice, Castelnuovo Berardenga, Siena)*. Poggio Rosso has a mere 2.5 acres (1 hectare) of vines. From these they produce about 8000 bottles of wine a year, not exactly a viticultural outpouring. But while their quantity is modest, judging from the single vintaged we tasted (1979), their quality is another story. It was quite a good wine. The first Poggio Rosso was bottled in 1978. These wines are distributed by San Felice. Chianti Classico★★ +

Prunatelli *(Pontassieve, Firenze)*. Fattoria Prunatelli has 52 acres (21 hectares) of vines, 50 (20) cultivated promiscuously. They produce 40,000 bottles of wine a year, including a Chianti Rùfina.

Pucci Emilio. See Castello di Cerreto.

Quercia al Poggio *(Barberino Val d'Elsa, Firenze)*. This *fattoria* has 32 acres (13 hectares) of vines. They produce the equivalent of 120,000 bottles of wine a year, most of which is sold *sfuso*. They only bottle about 26,500. Besides their temperature-controlled stainless steel tanks and cement vats, they have three chestnut casks. They don't believe in giving their wines much wood age but hold some of it in vat for an unusually long duration. In May 1985, we tasted two '71s at the *cantina,* one from bottle and the other from vat. The cellarman said that the latter was being aged for a client, a restaurant in Rome where they go for that sort of wine. We couldn't get excited about either of the '71s, but the '79 and '82 were acceptable. As for the '84 and '83, maybe if they leave them in vat long enough, they can get the restaurant to take them off their hands. Chianti Classico★ −

Remole. See Frescobaldi.

Ricasoli. See Brolio.

Riecine *(Gaiole, Siena)*. This farm, with 6.5 acres (2.6 hectares) of vines, is owned by Palmina Abbagnono Dunkley; her husband, John Dunkley, makes the wine. They produce some 19,000 bottles of Chianti Classico a year. This wine has a rather high reputation and prices to match. The wine itself is on a somewhat more modest plane. The Riecine Chiantis are reasonably consistent and fairly well-made wines, not exciting, but we liked the '77, '78, '79, and '80 that we tasted a few years ago. Chianti Classico★★

Ripertoli *(Greve, Firenze), 1979*. Records of this estate date back to the late tenth century. There are 7.4 acres (3 hectares) of vines on the property, planted at 1475 to 1640 feet (450 to 500 meters) with a south to southwesterly exposure. Ripertoli produces two wines: about 6700 bottles of a cabernet sauvignon–sangiovese blend and 13,300 bottles of Chianti Classico. They told us that the first vintage they sold in bottle was the 1973.

Riseccoli *(Greve, Firenze)*. Riseccoli owns 32 acres (13 hectares) of vines and produces 5500 cases of Chianti Classico a year. The most recent vintages we've tasted of these wines were the '77 and '78. Neither amounted to much. In fact, they only confirmed our previous dim opinion. Chianti Classico 0

Rocca delle Macìe *(Castellina, Siena)*. This *azienda* produces an average of 50,000 cases of wine a year. They have 216 acres (87.5 hectares) of vines. They also buy grapes and perhaps wine as well; they bottle a total of nearly 90,000 cases a year. That's a lot of mediocre wine from a single source. We have tasted a range of their Chiantis, from the '69 to the '80, and, except for the '69, all qualified as rather dreary duty. Chianti Classico 0; Zingarelli Riserva 0

Ruffino *(Pontassieve, Firenze), 1877*. Italo and Franco Folonari bought Ruffino in 1913. Today they are the largest producers of Chianti Classico and have the greatest holdings in the region, nearly 3000 acres (1200 hectares) of land, 570 (230) under vines.

Fattoria	Locality	Hectares	
		Vineyard	*Total*
Montemasso	S. Polo di Greve	80	495
Nozzole	Passo dei Pecorai	90	500
Zano	Montefiridolfi	60	200
Total		230	1195

Ruffino also has production facilities and cellars in Brescia and Cellatica in Lombardy and Negrar in the Veneto. Among their other wines are a Barolo sold under the Anforio label and a line of Veronese wines.

They produce three Ruffino Chianti Classicos as well as the Nozzole, and the Torgaio di San Salvatore. This last is Ruffino's Fresco di Governo Chianti, a light and quaffable wine meant to be drunk young and fresh. Their regular Ruffino Classico is also best drunk young and fresh, though it can take a bit more age than the Torgaio. It is reliable and agreeable, no more no less, and they produce a lot of it.

Their Riserva Ducale, bottled with the beige label, is quite good. It is produced in good vintages only. Their top wine is the Riserva Ducale gold label, and it is very good indeed, in fact among the best of the Chianti Classicos. This wine is produced only in the best vintages. The gold label, like all their Classicos, is made with *governo*. They named this wine for the Duke of Aosta, who, when he visited their cellars many years ago, liked their wine. The first Riserva Ducale that was sold worldwide was the '51; some 30,000 to 35,000 to 35,000 bottles were produced.

Their three Chianti Classicos (pre-1984) are made from an *uvaggio* of 70 percent sangiovese, 15 percent canaiolo, 10 percent malvasia and trebbiano, plus 5 percent colorino, ciliegiolo, and cabernet. They were using the cabernet long before it became trendy.

The differences among the three wines lie in the selection and aging. The best grapes from their own vineyards only are used for Riserva Ducale, which is aged at least three years in large oak casks. The gold label is a selection from the best lots of the best vintages of the riserva.

We have had many bottles of these Chianti Classicos through the years and have rarely been disappointed. Ruffino has been able to maintain a level of quality and consistency unusual for a company their size. And in that regard they are in a class by themselves, in Chianti Classico at least.

The Riserva Ducale gold label is a full-bodied, full-flavored, well-balanced wine that requires age (*governo* notwithstanding) and rewards those with the patience to wait. We have particularly enjoyed the '47, '55, '58, '62, '71, and '75.

Chianti Torgaio★; Chianti Classico regular★; Riserva Ducale★★; Riserva Ducale gold label★★★

S. Andrea a Luiano. See Luiano.

S. Leonino *(Castellina, Siena).* Fattoria I Cipressi is a 282-acre (114-hectare) estate with 131 acres (53 hectares) of vineyards. They have an annual production of nearly 40,000 cases. Their S. Leonino Chianti Classico can be quite agreeable, rarely more. Chianti Classico★

Saccardi The most recent vintage of this Chianti we've tasted is the '77, and, like the '75 before it, it left a lot to be desired. Chianti Classico 0

San Felice *(S. Gusmè, Siena), 1967.* This 1060-acre (430-hectare) farm has 247 acres (100 hectares) of vines, planted at altitudes of 1245 to 1310 feet (380 to 400 meters). The vineyards have a south to southwesterly exposure. San Felice produces about 66,000 cases of wine a year.

Wine	Cases	Hectoliters
Chianti Classico	36,6000	3300
Chianti Classico Il Grigio Riserva	9,300	840
Cru bottlings	3,300	300
White and rosé	15,500	1400
Vin Santo[a]	1,600	150
Total	66,300	5990

Note: [a] Varies from 1100 to 1600 cases (100 to 150 hectoliters).

The San Felice Chianti Classico, in pre-1984 vintages, is made from 75 percent sangiovese, 10 percent canaiolo, and 15 percent trebbiano and malvasia. (Under the new regulations, this proportion of white grapes will be reduced to not more than 5 percent.) The Il Grigio riserva is made with the best grapes from their 44-acre (18-hectare) Chiesamanti vineyard. Their Vigorello is made from sangiovese and canaiolo. Besides these wines, they also produce Poggio Rosso Chianti Classico, a cabernet sauvignon, a champagne-method spumante, three white wines including the Citerno chardonnay, a Flamma rosé, and Santuccio, a dessert wine.

San Felice owns the Brunello di Montalcino estate of Campogiovanni.

The best wine we've tasted from San Felice is without a doubt their Chianti Classico Il Grigio. Chianti Classico★; "Il Grigio"; Chianti Clasico★★

Santa Caterina. See Monsanto.

Santa Cristina. See Antinori.

Savignola Paolina *(Greve, Firenze), 1780.* Savignola has 15 acres (6 hectares) of vines planted at altitudes of 1150 to 1245 feet (350 to 380 meters). Only one-quarter of the vineyards are in specialized cultivation; the other 11 acres (4.5 hectares) are planted in the traditional way, mixed with other crops. They produce about 22,600 bottles of wine a year: 14,600 of the regular Chianti Classico, 4000 riserva, 3300 red and rosé vino da tavola, and 660 bottles of white wine.

The winemaker at Savignola is Paolina Fabbri, a tiny, eighty-seven-year-young dynamo whose engagingly enthusiastic yet logically practical outlook is reflected in the quality of her wines. Signora Paolina takes advantage of the services of a consulting enologist, Dott. Cortovesi, but she takes charge of making the wines herself. In the past she made the wines with *governo,* but she doesn't do so any longer. She has just purchased a filter, though she hasn't used it yet. Her riserva is aged for three years in wood, mostly chestnut.

Paolina Fabbri of
Az. Agr. Savignola Paolina

The 1942 vintage was the first Chianti Classico she bottled under her label. On the way down to the cellar for a tasting from barrel and bottle conducted at a thoughtfully expeditious pace to keep us on schedule, she made a brief detour to show us some bottles of the older vintages which, though a bit low in fill, seemed to have maintained remarkably good color.

The Savignola Paolina wines are delicate, gentle Chiantis with real style, a characteristic they share with the lady who produces them. They are among the better Chianti Classicos. The '83, '82, and '81 we tasted were all very good. Chianti Classico★★★

Serristori. See Conti Serristori.

Setriolo (*Castellina, Siena*). American Desmond Crawford has 5.7 acres (2.3 hectares) of vines on his Setriolo farm. He produces 16,000 bottles of Chianti Classico a year. We've heard that it is a pretty good wine but have not had the opportunity to taste it.

Signoria. A label used by Barfede-Certaldo.

Socovich. See Cappelli Giovanni.

Spalletti (*Rùfina, Firenze*), *1912*. This *azienda* has 185 acres (75 hectares) of vines, which supply them with about 35 percent of the grapes for their wines. They produce a wide range: Veronese wines, Orvieto, a few different Tuscan whites, and Chianti Rùfina. Spalletti owns two estates in the Rufina zone:

Estate	Altitude Feet	Production cases
Colognole	1150–1310	22,000
Poggio Reale	330–655	33,000

Their Poggio Reale riserva is made from 75 percent sangiovese, 12 percent canaiolo, 3 percent colorino, and 5 percent each of trebbiano and malvasia.

They consider the best vintages for Poggio Reale riserva to be 1983, 1982, 1981, 1979, 1977, 1975, 1971, 1967, 1964, 1959, 1958, 1957, 1955, 1952, 1950, 1949, 1948, and 1946; worse were 1984, 1973, 1966, 1963, 1956, and 1951.

The wine museum at their Poggio Reale villa is worth a visit.

Their Chiantis are quite good and fairly reliable. Chianti Rùfina★★

Storiche Cantine Radda In Chianti (*Lucarelli, Radda, Siena*), *1971*. This cooperative aging cellar stores and markets the wines of its seven members. The *cantina* has a storage capacity of more than 1 million bottles. Their members own some 1236 acres (500 hectares) of vines and produce more than 300,000 cases of wine a year.

Chianti Classico brand	Cases produced
Castello di Meleto[a] (owned by Viticola Toscana)	133,000
Castello di S. Donato in Perano[a]	55,500
Castello di Vertine[a]	n/a
La Cerreta[a]	40,000
Castello di Monterinaldi[a] (owned by La Pesanella Monterinaldi) (Fattoria La Pesanella)	55,000
Montecasi (owned by Viticola Toscana)	n/a
Monticelli[a] (owned by Viticola Toscana)	n/a
Other wines	
Podere Ferretto Vino Nobile di Montepulciano (owned by Fattoria delle Maestrelle)	
Podere Scansanaccio	

Note: [a] See individual entries.

As a group, these wines are consistent though consistently rather mediocre.

Straccali (*Castellina, Siena*). Casa Vinicola Giulio Straccali buys grapes and/or wine to produce some 17,000 cases of wine a year. In the 1960s we found these Classicos to be quite good. Then the quality slipped and for a time was uneven. We haven't tasted any since the 1974 vintage, which was quite good. We've heard, though, that they have returned to form. From our past experience we can still rate them★★.

Tenuta di Poggio a Remole. See Frescobaldi.

Tenuta di Pomino. See Frescobaldi.

Tenuta di San Vito in Fior di Selva *(Loc. Camaioni, Montelupo Fino, Firenze), 1958.* Roberto Drighi has 54 acres (22 hectares) of vines on his San Vito farm. He produces 12,500 cases of wine a year, including almost 11,000 of Chianti from the Colli Fiorentini zone. This wine is made from a blend of 69 percent sangiovese, 9 percent canaiolo, and 22 percent trebbiano.

Tenuta La Colombaia *(Chiocchio, Firenze).* Our experience with this producer is somewhat limited. The only wines we've tasted were the '75 and the '77. Neither came up to the vintage. Chianti Classico★ −

Tenuta Villa Rosa *(Castellina, Siena).* Villa Rosa owns 86 acres (34.7 hectares) of vines and produces almost 28,000 cases of wine a year. We found their '82 decent enough but didn't think a lot of their '80. Chianti Classico★

Torgaio di San Salvatore. See Ruffino.

Torre dei Pazzi. See Castello di Trebbio.

Torricino *(San Martino alla Palma, Firenze).* Oscar Pio of Torricino produces Chianti in the Colli Fiorentini zone. His '76 was fairly nice, his '77 unimpressive. The Torricino Chianti is made with *governo;* the *uvaggio* used is 60 percent sangiovese, 5 percent canaiolo, and, rather surprisingly, 35 percent white grapes (which is more even than DOC allowed)—25 percent trebbiano and 10 percent malvasia. Chianti Colli Fiorentini★

Tregole. See Fattoria Tregole.

Valiano *(Molin di Piano, Firenze).* This 128-acre (52-hectare) estate in the Rùfina zone (not to be confused with the Classico) has 35 acres (14 hectares) of vineyards; 27 (11) in specialized cultivation. They produce 93,000 cases of wine a year.

Valiano *(Vagliagli, Siena).* Valiano has 170 acres (69.4 hectares) of vines and produces some 55,500 cases of wine a year. We've heard good things about these wines, but our experience doesn't confirm the rumors. Chianti Classico 0

Vecchie Terre di Montefili *(Greve, Firenze), 1980.* Roccaldo Acuti is the proprietor of this estate, which was once a farm owned by the Badia a Passignano monastery. He currently has 16 acres (6.5 hectares) of vineyards, part in promiscuous cultivation, planted at altitudes of 1475 to 1640 feet (450 to 500 meters) with a southwest exposure.

His first wine was from the 1980 vintage. The winery is a hobby for Acuti but one that he takes very seriously. He has engaged the noted enologist Vittorio Fiore as consultant.

Vecchie Terre has an annual production of about 30,000 bottles of regular Chianti Classico, 3000 of riserva, and 3000 of Bruno di Rocca, a sangiovese-cabernet sauvignon blend aged in *barrique.* The Vecche Terre Chianti is made basically from sangiovese with the addition of 3 percent cabernet sauvignon. The wine is made with *governo,* for which they use dried grapes, Acuti points out, not concentrate, as is now becoming fairly common practice in the area. The wine is fermented in stainless steel and aged in oak casks of 795 gallons and in *barriques.*

Of the three vintages we've tasted—'81, '82, and '83—all were good, especially the '83. This is an estate that bears watching. Chianti Classico★★

Vigna di Sorripa. See Le Lame.

Vigna Vecchia *(Radda, Siena), 1876.* This *azienda* has 57 acres (23 hectares) planted to vines, at altitudes of 1640 to 1805 feet (500 to 550) meters, and another 5 acres (2 hectares) in promiscuous cultivation. For the most part the vineyards have a southerly exposure; a small portion faces west.

Vigna Vecchia has sold its wine in bottle since the 1960 vintage. They produce some 12,500 cases of wine a year, most of it Chianti Classico. They also make a small amount of white wine and Vin Santo, plus a *barrique*-aged sangiovese called Canvalle, and Picchio Rosso, a fizzy 100 percent sangiovese with 16 percent alcohol (concentrate is added at bottling to create a second fermentation in the bottle).

This estate has had a fine reputation for years, but we are hard pressed to explain it. Of the six vintages we tasted recently, the '82 and '75 were agreeable, but the '83, '81, '79, and '78 were not. Chianti Classico 0

Vignale *(Radda, Siena)*. We can recall tasting only two wines from Vignale—the '75 and the '77, two very good years. Neither wine came close to the quality of the vintage. Chianti Classico 0

Vignamaggio *(Greve, Firenze), 1910*. This estate was owned by the Gherardini family in the 1400s, when Francesco Datini, a successful wine merchant and connoisseur of wine, was one of their best clients. A famous descendant of the Gherardinis, Monna Lisa, had her portrait painted by an artist who is said to have had an appreciation for the wines of Chianti, which was perhaps not entirely a sentimental predilection since he was born in the village of Vinci in the Chianti region.

Conte Ranieri Sanminiatelli, the proprietor of the Vignamaggio estate, has 83 acres (33.5 hectares) of vineyards; this includes 2.5 acres (1 hectare) of cabernet sauvignon vines, some of them seventeen years old. His annual production averages 150,000 bottles, of Chianti Classico only. Two-thirds is the regular, one-third riserva. The minuscule amount of white wine and excellent Vin Santo he makes are for family use only.

The first Chianti Classico sold in bottle with the Vignamaggio label was the '26.

Sanminiatelli ferments his Chianti in oak uprights. It is aged in oak and chestnut casks. In a move toward modernity, he will be getting some *barriques*. He has not made his wine with *governo* since 1952, with the exception of a couple of weak vintages, the 1976 and 1984, for example. When he does, he adds concentrate from white grapes to start the second fermentation. He began to reduce the amount of white grapes in the *uvaggio* also in 1952.

The Vignamaggio Chianti Classicos are quite good; they have balance and some style. We can recommend the '82 in particular; the '83, '79, and '78 are also good. Chianti Classico★★

Villa Antinori. See Antinori.

Villa Banfi *(Montalcino)*. At one time Rocca della Macìe produced a mediocre Chianti Classico sold under this label for Banfi, the American importing giant based in the Brunello district. Today Banfi is producing its own Chianti Classico, some 30,000 cases of a riserva only, from grapes purchased in the zone. The '78 was one of the best Chiantis we tasted from the vintage. The '79, on the other hand, was disappointing. Our rating, then, is rather tentative. Chianti Classico★

Villa Cafaggio *(Panzano, Firenze), 1966*. This estate is in the San Martino In Ceccione district near Greve. The oldest part of the villa is the thirteenth-century turret, the rest of the building dating from the sixteenth and seventeenth centuries. The property was bought by the Farkas family in 1965. Stefano Farkas, winemaker and director of the *azienda,* points out that the name Cafaggio is a Longobard word for "enclosed cultivated fields"—in their case, fields of vines.

The Cafaggio vineyards are planted facing south at an altitude of about 1575 feet (480 meters). They have 54 acres (22 hectares) in specialized cultivation and 12.4 (5) promiscuous in their Solatio Basilica vineyard.

Vineyard	Hectares
Cafaggiolo	3.0
Canfera	4.5
Cipressi	2.5
Vigna Cantina	1.5
Vigna Nova	4.5
Villa	6.0
Total	22.0

The '67 was the first Chianti Classico they bottled under the Villa Cafaggio label. They have an annual production of 13,000 to 15,500 cases, which includes 10,250 of DOCG Chianti. They also produce Solatio Basilica, a 100 percent sangiovese wine from the grapes of that single vineyard.

The modern winery, with its tile floors and stainless steel tanks, presents a marked contrast to the lovely old villa; it appeals to the practical, rather than the romantic in one. The Cafaggio wines, however, satisfy the whole man.

*Stefano Farkas
of Villa Cafaggio*

Farkas uses a vaslin press and ferments in temperature-controlled stainless tanks. He ages his Chianti Classico in Slavonian oak casks. He used to use *governo,* on occasion but doesn't any longer.

We tasted a number of the newer wines in the *cantina,* evaluating the vintages and reevaluating our previous impression of the *azienda.* Stefano was ready to draw samples from whichever vintage or vat we chose, and we were as willing to taste as many as we reasonably had time for. Our tasting of vintages from bottle at the villa reconfirmed our impressions from the winery. Our experience with these wines goes back many years, and the wines were as we remembered them—very good and consistently so. A couple of times we had heard the opinion that these wines were not up to their previous high level. We were surprised; this has not been our experience. Since our tasting at Cafaggio we are even more surprised.

We can highly recommend their '83, '82, and the '79, '77, '75, and '84 (this last tasted from three different vats) were all very good. The Villa Cafaggio Chiantis are Classicos with body, structure, balance, and style. There are very few finer Chianti Classicos produced. Chianti Classico★★★

Villa Calcinaia *(Greve, Siena), 1523.* Conte Neri Capponi is the proprietor of this estate. He has 99 acres (40 hectares) of vines: 74 (30) of sangiovese, 15 (6 of canaiolo, and 10 (4) of trebbiano and malvasia. Annual production ranges from 19,000 to 21,000 cases; 11,000 to 14,500 are Chianti Classico, which includes a young Chianti sold as Conti Capponi. They also produce 1650 cases of Casarza and 2200 of Vindunano, as well as a white wine and a Vin Santo. These Chiantis were better in the 1960s and early 1970s. Chianti Classico Conte Capponi and Villa Calcinaia 0

Villa Cerna *(Castellina, Siena), 1962.* Luigi Cecchi is the proprietor of the 2575-acre (1042-hectare) Villa Cerna estate, at one time the residence of Benedictine monks. From its 185 acres (75 hectares) of vineyards, Cecchi produces an average of 44,500 cases of wine a year: 10,000 of white and the balance red.

It's been some time since we tasted the Villa Cerna Chianti, but they did produce a decent if unexciting wine. Chianti Classico★

Villa Cilnia. See Podere di Cignano.

Villa Colombaio *(Querciagrossa, Siena).* This estate was owned until recently by Contessa Isabella Bonucci Ugurgieri della Berardenga. Because of the poor reputation of Chianti wine, the land became worth more for homesites, and a short time ago the Villa Colombaio winery and vineyards were sold for that purpose. From the point of view of a winelover, this was very unfortunate turn of events. The Colombaio wines were without question among the most consistent and best of the Chianti Classicos.

Production from their 28 acres (11.3 hectares) of vines was 11,000 cases of wine a year; half was bottled as Chianti Classico. They produced a regular Villa Colombaio (sold as a riserva in some markets) and a riserva Fortilizio "Il Colombaio."

If you're lucky, you might still find some of these fine, full-bodied Chiantis on the market; they're worth looking for. We've tasted the Colombaio Classicos, from the '67s through the '79s, and can recommend every vintage. Chianti Classico★★★

Villa Consuelo *(Montefiridolfi, Firenze).* The Fattoria di S. Andrea a Fabbrica estate covers 145 acres (58.6 hectares) in the San Casciano Val di Pesa area in the northwestern part of the Classico zone. They produce some 39,000 cases of wine a year. Our limited experience with their Villa Consuelo Chiantis has left us less than impressed. Chianti Classico 0

Villa Cusona Fattoria di Guicciardini-Strozzi *(Loc. Cusona, San Gimignano, Siena).* Robert Guicciardini and Girolamo Strozzi own 148 acres (60 hectares) of vineyards at Villa Cusona in the Colli Senesi zone, from which they produce 250,000 bottles a year of Vernaccia di San Gimignano, 150,000 of Chianti, and 7000 of Vin Santo. They name as the best vintages for their Chianti 1983, 1981, 1979, 1977, 1975, 1971, 1970, 1969, 1967, 1964, 1961, and 1958. Noted enologist Vittorio Fiore consults here. Chianti Colli Senesi★★ –

Villa di Monte. See Villa de Vetrice.

Villa di Vetrice *(Rùfina, Firenze).* The Grati brothers own 1153 acres (462 hectares). They have two estates in the Rùfina zone—Galiga and Vetrice—as well as another 250 acres (100 hectares) of vines. Their average production is 111,000 cases of wine a year. Besides the standard white and rosé wines of the area, they produce Chianti Rùfina under a number of labels: Artemide, Fattoria di Vetrice, Villa di Monti, and Villa di Vetrice. These wines vary considerably; some are fair, others good. The best wines seem to be sold under the Fattoria di Vetrice label. Chianti Rùfina Fattoria de Vetrice★; Villa di Vetrice and Villa di Monte 0

Villa La Selva *(Montebenichi, Bucine, Arezzo), 1958.* Sergio and Riccardo Carpini have 111 acres (45 hectares) of vineyards on their La Selva farm in the Colli Aretini zone, from which they produce some 35,000 to 40,500 cases of wine a year. This includes three Chiantis, a rosé, and a spumante. They make one Chianti meant to be drunk young. The second is aged for two to three years and will live for a few more. Their best wine is the riserva, which ages fairly well. Reportedly, La Selva uses *governo* for all its Chiantis. They use the services of consulting enologist Vittorio Fiore. It's been some time since we've tasted their wines, but we did enjoy them. Chianti★★

Villa Montepaldi *(S. Casciano Val di Pesa, Firenze).* Montepaldi have 116 acres (47 hectares) of vines, from which they produce 41,000 cases of wine a year. The estate is owned by Marchese Corsini. It's been some years since we tasted this Chianti Classico, but those we did left us unimpressed. Chianti Classico 0

Villa Terciona *(Mercatale Val di Pesa, Firenze).* This estate in the San Casciano area has 138 acres (56 hectares) of vineyards. They produce about 41,000 cases of wine a year. We found both their '73 and '74, the most recent we've tasted, surprisingly good for the vintages. They recently sold some vineyard land to Antinori. Chianti Classico★★ –

246

Vistarenni. See Fattoria di Vistarenni.

Viticcio *(Greve, Firenze).* This *azienda* produces 11,000 cases of Chianti Classico a year from its 35 acres (14 hectares) of vines. Our overall experience with these wines has been favorable, although we were disappointed with the '83. Chianti Classico★★

The Smallest Chianti Classico Estates

Estate	Locality	Vineyards (hectares)	Production (bottles)
Cafaggio di Pesa	Castellina	0.5000	5,330
Casalbelvedere	Greve	0.3142	1,735
Casilli Az. Agr. Starda	Gaiole	1.0618	6,665
Leccio	Castellina	1.0404	10,000
Le Miccine[a]	Gaiole	6.5000	10,665
Poggio Rosso[a]	Castelnuovo	1.0000	8,000
Sole di Gagliole	Castellina	2.0000	10,665
Sommavilla	Castellina	2.1680	8,000
Tiorcia	Gaiole	0.9500	8,000

Notes: [a] See entry under producer.

1 hectare = 2.4711 acres

1 hectoliter = 26.42 gallons, 11.11 cases, or 133 bottles

Chapter 8

Brunello di Montalcino

The history of Brunello di Montalcino is very short, going back a little more than one hundred years, but the tradition of winemaking in Montalcino is a long one. The Etruscans may have cultivated the first vines here; many artifacts and tombs from that era have been discovered in the region. Or it may have been the Romans who first planted vineyards on Monte Alcino, which they called Mons Ilcinus. The town takes its name from the holm oak—*ilex*—common in these hills and a symbol on the city's crest and on the seal of the Brunello di Montalcino consorzio.

Montalcino was settled by inhabitants of a nearby village seeking refuge from Saracen invaders early in the tenth century. Some believe it was they who terraced its slopes to plant vineyards on the stony hillsides. Their wines would have been quite different, however, from the Brunello of today. Until the 1500s, all mention of the wine of Montalcino refers to white wine. And Francesco Redi in his poem *Bacco in Toscana*, written in 1685, praises the Moscadaletto, or "pleasant little Moscadello," which he considered the best wine of the area.

White wine continued to dominate in Montalcino at least until late in the last century. And the red wine made here included a proportion of white grapes, as the Chianti does today. But that was all changed with the emergence of Brunello, and this red wine, from only red grapes and only the grapes of a single variety—the sangiovese grosso—would become not only the most noted wine of Montalcino but perhaps the most famous wine of Italy.

This grape is a subvariety of the sangiovese called sangiovese grosso, or *brunello*, for the brownish cast to its berries. The first reference to Brunello wine, according to Guglielmo Solci, is in a note written in 1842 by Canon Vincenzo Chiarini of Montalcino, in which he had high praise for the wine from the brunello grape.[20]

At Biondi-Santi, they claim that their brunello vines are a special clone of the sangiovese grosso isolated in the Il Greppo vineyard by Clemente Santi, who recognized its superior qualities and propagated its growth. Nothing has been found in the Biondi-Santi archives noting when he discovered the brunello clone or produced the first wine exclusively from this grape. But by 1860, Santi was producing a wine he called Brunello, and apparently a good one. In 1869, the agrarian committee of the district awarded Santi a silver medal for his Vino Rosso Scelto (Brunello) 1865.

The subvariety, sangiovese (or sangioveto) grosso was gaining some recognition outside the region as well. In a technical book on winemaking published in 1871, Alessandro Bizzarri refers to the "Sangioveto grosso and piccolo."[21]

The Birth of Brunello di Montalcino

Credit for producing the first Brunello wine as we know it today—a 100 percent varietal made without the use of *governo*, traditional in this region—goes to Santi's grandson, Ferruccio Biondi-Santi, who is credited with perfecting Brunello in the 1870s. He planted new vineyards exclusively to this variety and improved the winemaking techniques to produce a wine for long aging. A few bottles of his 1888 and 1891, two exceptional vintages, are still preserved in the *sacristia* of the *cantina* at Fattoria Il Greppo. In 1970, at the second recorking ceremony (Tancredi Biondi-Santi had had the '91 recorked, after thirty years, in 1927), the dignitaries and journalists present are reported to have been impressed with the wine's capacity to age.

Ferruccio Biondi-Santi's son, Tancredi, carried on his father's work and is responsible for establishing an enviable reputation for the wine through judicious marketing and promotion emphasizing its importance and quality.

At the Siena Exposition of 1933, there were four Brunellos presented: the Biondi-Santi plus that of Guido Angelini, the Barbi of Giuseppe Colombini, and Roberto Franceschi's Sant'Angelo. According to Emanuele Pellucci,[22] Angelini was the only other producer besides Biondi-Santi bottling a Brunello at that time. Except for occasional special bottles, the others were selling their wine in cask or demijohns. Franceschi began bottling, on a limited basis, in 1936. Colombini was also among the first to offer Brunello in bottle. Later, Costanti, Casale del Bosco, Lovatelli, Lisini, Mastropaolo, Camigliano, Castiglion del Bosco, and others began doing the same.

Yet, into the 1950s, only Biondi-Santi made a practice of vintage dating and laying down older vintages in his cellars. The other producers were selling the wine of the year, frequently in *fiaschi*.

The Biondi-Santi Brunello '55 received international attention when it was selected to be poured at a state dinner in honor of Queen Elizabeth hosted by Italian President Giuseppe Saragat in 1969. The reputation of Brunello was made.

The Brunello Production Zone

Brunello di Montalcino is produced in the hilly region within the Chianti Colli Senesi district, south of Siena, bordered by the Orcia, Ombrone, and Asso rivers. The Montalcino production zone covers 60,200 acres (24,362 hectares); 50 percent of the zone is woodland; large tracts of brush, fields, pastureland, and olive groves make up a major portion of the remaining area. At most, 2500 acres (1000 hectares) can be planted to vines for Brunello di Montalcino. According to 1984 statistics, there are 1992 acres (806 hectares) under vines, including 25 (10) in promiscuous cultivation. There are more than 100 growers with Brunello vineyards in the zone and 53 producers who bottle an average of 230,000 cases of Brunello a year.

The acreage under vines has been increasing steadily since the recovery from *phylloxera*, which arrived late in this part of Italy, in the 1930s, virtually wiping out the vineyards, which had reached a high of 2286 acres (925 hectares) specialized and 3072 acres (1243) mixed in 1929. In 1969, there were just 115 acres (46.6 hectares) of specialized vineyards and 95 (38.4) promiscuous; by 1974, these figures were 637 (258) and 173 (70); a decade later, in 1979, there were 1513 (612) and 151 (61), respectively.

The grapes for Brunello di Montalcino are harvested between the latter part of September and the middle of October.

The climate in the Brunello production zone is Mediterranean. On the lower slopes the soil is clayey marl; higher up, a combination of limestone and marl with some tufaceous volcanic stone. The best soils are galestro alberese-clay with carbonate of lime and friable rock.

Sub Districts of the Brunello Zone

Claudio Basla of Altesino points out that the Brunello production zone can be divided into three districts. The first district takes in the area north and to the east of the town of Montalcino, including the town of Torrenieri. This district, Basla says, is noted for producing the most elegant Brunellos. Among the better producers here are Costanti, Caparzo, and Altesino.

The second district, the smallest, is a wedge extending southeast from Montalcino and around the town of Castelnuovo. Biondi-Santi, Colombini, and Mastrojanni are located here. This area, the most protected, is considered to be the most favored.

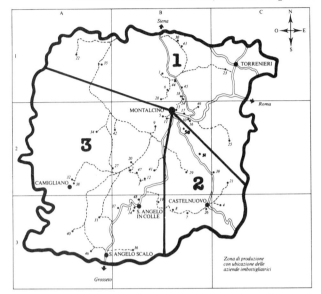

	Loc.	Producer	Azienda		Loc.	Producer	Azienda
1	B1	Baricci Nello	Colombaio-Montosoli	27	B2	Salvioni M. Grazia	Quercecchio
2	B2	Bartolommei Alfo	Caprili	28	B1	Sassetti Livio	Pertimali
3	B2	Bellini Roberto	Chiesa S. Restituta	29	B2	Schwarz Herbert	La Magia
4	C3	Benocci Annina	S. Giorgio			**Società**	
5	B2	Berni Domenico	Pietroso	30	B1	-Altesino S.r.l.	Altesino
6	B1	Cencioni Giuseppe e figli	Capanna	31	A3	-Argiano S.r.l.	Argiano
7	B3	Ciacci Bellocci Elisa	Poggio agli Olivi	32	A2	-Camigliano S.r.l.	Camigliano
8	B3	Ciacci Giuseppe	Sesta	34	A2	-Castelgiocondo S.p.A.	Castelgiocondo
9	B2	Cosimi Roberto	Il Poggiolo	35	A1	-Castiglion del Bosco S.p.A.	Castiglion del Bosco
10	B2	Costanti Andrea	Colle al Matrichese				
11	B2	Daviddi Enrico	Due Porti	36	B3	-Col d'Orcia S.p.A.	Col d'Orcia
12	B2	Fattoi Ofelio	Capanna S. Restituta	37	B3	-Fertigea S.p.A.	Campogiovanni
				38	A2	-Fontevino S.r.l.	Fontevino
13	B3	Franceschi C. e R.	Casello	39	C2	-La Poderina S.a.s.	La Poderina
14	B3	Franceschi C. e R.	Poggione	40	A3	-P.A.M. Comp. Agr. S.A.	Poggio alle Mura
15	B2	Fuligni Eredi	Cottimello				
16	B2	Giannelli Carli Ernesta	Il Colle 2°	41	B2	-Poggio Antico S.p.A.	Poggio Antico
17	B2	Focacci Gino Antonio	I Comunali	42	B2	-Poggio Salvi S.S.	Poggio Salvi
18	B1	Lambardi Silvano	Canalicchio (S. Giuseppe)	43	B1	-Tenuta Caparzo S.p.A.	Tenuta Caparzo
19	B3	Lisini F.lli	Lisini	44	B1	-Valdicava S.a.s.	Valdicava
20	B2	Machetti Renata	S. Carlo	45	B1	-Valdisuga S.p.A.	Valdisuga
21	C2	Mastrojanni Gabriele	Mastrojanni	46	A3	-Villa Banfi S.p.A.	Poggio all'Oro
22	A1	Nardi Silvio	Casale del Bosco	47	B2	Soldera Gianfranco	Case Basse
23	C1	Neri Giovanni	Casanuova	48	B3	Talenti P. Luigi	Pian di Conte
24	B1	Pacenti Primo e R.	Canalicchio di Sopra	49	B2	Zannoni Gioberto	La Fortuna
25	C2	Rosi Ermanno	S. Filippo	50	B2	Biondi Santi	Il Greppo
26	B3	Poggi Fabbri Marusca	Le Presi	51	B2	Colombini	I Barbi

Based on a map by Consorzio del vino Brunello di Montalcino (1985)

The third zone, the southwestern part of the Brunello region, encompasses the towns of Camigliano, S. Angelo In Colle, and S. Angelo Scalo. This area reportedly produces the most robust Brunellos. Among the best known vineyards of this district are those of Castelgiocondo, Pian di Conte, Lisini, Il Casello, and Villa Banfi; among the best are Il Poggione and Case Basse.

Brunello and Italian Wine Law

When Brunello was granted DOCG (Denominazione di Origine Controllata e Garantita) status in 1980, some of the regulations regarding its production under DOC were changed.

The Brunello producers were previously allowed to add up to 10 percent of grapes, must, or wine from outside the Brunello production zone to bring up the alcohol in poor years when conditions are less than favorable. Under the new regulations, the correction can be done only with an older vintage of Brunello; up to 15 percent is allowed.

One controversial regulation concerned aging requirements. Under DOC, Brunello had to be aged for no less than four years in oak or chestnut casks. Some producers protested, and rightly so, that this regulation, especially in the weaker vintages, caused the wine to dry out and be robbed of its fruit. They argued that the producers should be allowed to decide for themselves how long to leave the wine in wood. Other producers, in favor of long cask aging for Brunello, countered that the problem wasn't the time in cask but the wood itself, claiming that if the casks were old enough and large enough there was no problem. The regulation was kept but modified somewhat. The aging requirement was reduced to three and a half years.

Obviously, government officials are not interested in lessening their authority by eliminating regulations, even unnecessary ones. The better producers don't need a government committee to tell them how to make wine; they will continue to make fine wines despite their regulations. And those producers lacking ability or integrity will manage to make poor wines regardless.

We report the DOC and DOCG regulations as part of the description of the wine in general but are confident that the wine buyer will learn from his or her own experience that the only guarantee of quality is surely not the official government stamp but the name of the producer responsible for the wine. The vintage also affects the quality of the wine, and by vintage dating the wine the producer gives the consumer a further indication of what to expect, although in the worse cases the top-flight producers will not bottle. If the wine doesn't measure up to their own high standards, they will not sell it as Brunello, although it legally qualifies, and if the wine of a particular vintage can't take the required wood aging, they will declassified it.

DOC Requirements

	Minimum age (years)		Minimum Alcohol	Maximum yield (gallons/acre)
	cask	total		
DOC Regular	4	4[a]	12.5%	748
Riserva	4	4[a]	12.5	748
DOCG Regular	3.5	4[b]	12.5	599/556[c]
Riserva	3.5	5[b]	12.5	599/556[c]

Notes: a. Aging period from Nov. 1 the year of the harvest.

b. Aging period from after Jan. 1 after the harvest; cask aging from April 1.

c. When picked, 599 gallons/acre (56 hectoliters/hectare) are allowed; after aging, only 556 gallons/acre (52 hectoliters/hectare)

Rosso di Montalcino

At one time many of the producers of Brunello di Montalcino sold a younger, second wine made also from sangiovese grosso grapes, labeled Rosso dei Vigneti di Brunello, or with some such similar name. Since 1983, this wine, too, has come under DOC regulation, and is now officially called Rosso di Montalcino.

DOC Requirements

Minimum alcohol	Maximum yield (gallons/acre)
12%	599

Rosso di Montalcino is made from the grapes of younger vines, and/or in the case of the better producers from wines that don't quite measure up to the high standards they set for their Brunello.

Rosso di Montalcino is generally given six to eighteen months of cask aging. It can be quite a good wine. Though not one for aging, it can take three to five years. Among the better Rosso di Montalcinos we've tasted are those from Altesino and Il Poggione.

Rosso di Montalcino is a good wine to serve with turkey, cornish hen, quail or pheasant, cutlets, or chops.

Brunello in the Glass

Young Brunello di Montalcino has a deep ruby-red color which shades to garnet with age as its harsh, youthful tannins mellow to a velvety texture. It has a rich aroma of cherries and berries which develops nuances of flowers, spices, underbrush, and nutlike notes; chestnuts in particular are considered characteristic. It is a firmly structured wine, full in body with a dry, warm flavor displaying a richness of extract and concentration of fruit. Its finish is long and lingering.

This is Brunello at its best. Unfortunately, such Brunello is not a common enough occurrence. But from producers such as Colombini (in the great vintages), Il Poggione, Costanti, and Altesino, Brunello di Montalcino can be truly one of the world's viticultural gems, particularly after seven to eight years of aging.

Brunello makes a fine accompaniment to roast beef, pigeon, duck, or goose, and especially to game, feathered or furred, such as venison or wild boar.

A good place to taste a wide range of Brunellos is La Cucina di Edgardo, Il

Montalcino, in the town of Montalcino; they offer at least one vintage of all or nearly all the Brunellos bottled.

Rating: Rosso di Montalcino★★; Brunello di Montalcino★★★★

Rating the Montalcino Producers

★★★★
Altesino
Colle al Matrichese (Costanti)
Il Poggione (Franceschi)
★★★
Case Basse
Fattoria dei Barbi (Colombini)
− La Casa (Tenuta Caparzo)
La Gerla
Tenuta Caparzo (since 1980; previously★)
★★
Biondi-Santi
Campogiovanni
Canalicchio di Sopra
Capanna (G. Cencioni)
Castelgiocondo
I Comunali (Bartoli-Giusti Focacci)
Il Casello (Franceschi)[1]
La Fortuna[1]
Lisini
+ Mastrojanni
S. Filippo (Rossi Ermanno)
Tenuta Col d'Orcia
★
Camigliano[1]
Canalicchio (Lambardi Silvano)[1]
Cappana di S. Restituta (Fattoi Ofelio)[1]
Caprili[1]
Casanuova

Castiglion del Bosco[2]
Colombaio di Montosoli (Baricci Nello)[1]
Le Presi
Tenuta Caparzo (prior to 1980; currently ★★★)
Val di Suga (since 1982; previously 0 −)[3]
0
Argiano
Casale del Bosco (Nardi Silvio)[3]
Cecchi Luigi
Il Colle[1]
− Isabella de' Medici (Val di Suga)
La Chiesa S. Restituta (Bellini Roberto)
La Magia[1]
La Poderina[1]
Olivieri (Val di Cava)
− Poggio alle Mura[4]
Poggio Antico
Riguardo (Tosco Vinicola)
Val di Cava
− Val di Suga[3]
Villa Banfi

Notes: 1. Based on one vintage only
2. Worth watching since Altesino manages the estate.
3. Worth watching since Vittorio Fiore consults for them
4. Now owned by Villa Banfi, who will retire the label after the 1979 vintage.

Tasting Notes

1984

This was a very difficult year. Biondi-Santi, for one, didn't produce a Brunello. Judging from the seven cask samples we tasted in May 1985, it appears that with much care and strict selection it was possible for a number of producers to make a good, even a very good, wine in 1984. Not one of the seven wines we tasted was bad, and a couple were remarkable. Costanti's Brunello at this stage shows great promise.

Altesino *(ex-cask 5/85)*. A surprising amount of fruit considering the vintage; still harsh and tannic.★(?)

Caparzo *(ex-cask 5/85)*. Surprisingly fruity and well balanced.★★

Case Basse *(ex-cask 5/85)*. Cherries and blueberries on aroma; a bit light, but nice fruit.★★

Comunali, Bartoli-Giusti-Focacci *(ex-cask 5/85)*. Fruity aroma with notes of cherries; a tart edge, a bit simple, nice fruit; should be ready early.★(+)

Costanti *(ex-cask 5/85)*. Enormous richness on nose, suggestions of blueberries, tar, and licorice; a bit light-bodied but loads of flavor; some acid at the end; the best '84 we tasted.★★(+)

Il Poggione *(ex-cask 5/85)*. Aroma somewhat reticent, some fruit, hints of licorice and raspberries; a bit light for a Brunello, but balanced and flavorful; will be ready early.★★

La Gerla *(ex-cask 5/85)*. Cherrylike fruit on aroma, peppery notes; a bit light, well balanced, though not quite together.★(★)

1983 [★★★★]

This was a vintage of elegant, stylish wines. Many are stunning, particularly the Il Poggione and Altesino. The wines lack the richness and fullness of the '82s, but for their sheer elegance and beauty they will be hard to beat. It is probably true that they won't live as long as the '82s, but that is not the final test of quality. Though their peak should be sooner, it should also be higher. Of the ten cask samples we tasted, we found, besides the Il Poggione and Altesino, the Carpazo, Case Basse, Costanti, and La Gerla impressive. The Biondi-Santi was a disappointment.

Altesino *(ex-cask 5/85)*. Aroma has aspects of licorice, nuts, and flowers; full of flavor, medium- to full-bodied, fairly tannic, cherrylike fruit; real quality here.★★(★ +)

Biondi-Santi *(ex-cask 5/85)*. Moderate concentration of fruit, a firm tannic vein, seems a bit light, lacks some style.★(★)

Canalicchio di Sopra *(ex-cask 5/85)*. Expansive

1983

aroma of nuts and cherries; fruity, somewhat light-bodied.★(★)

Caparzo (*ex-cask 5/85*). Rich aroma with notes of champignons, fruit, nuts, and pine; full-flavored, some astringency; vaguely sweet.★★(★)

Case Basse (*ex-cask 5/85*). Surprisingly bigger and richer than the '82 and more tannic.★★(★)

Comunali, Bartoli-Giusti-Focacci (*ex-cask 5/85*). Lovely aroma; seems sweet, a bit light and simple.★(★−)

Costanti (*ex-cask 5/85*). Already displays elegance and delicacy, should make a splendid bottle.★★(★+)

Il Poggione (*ex-cask 5/85*). Opaque color; a suggestion of licorice on nose; full, rich fruit flavors, tannic, less body than the '82 but more elegance, more style.★★★(★)

La Gerla (*ex-cask 5/85*). Cherries and peppery notes on aroma; tannic entry, rich fruit flavors, lots of potential.★★(★)

S. Filippo (*ex-cask 5/85*). Sweet fruit under moderate tannin, young; shows promise.★(★)

1982 [★★★+]

Altesino, Il Poggione, Colombini, and Castiglion del Bosco rate 1982 as a top-flight year.

The Brunellos of 1982 are big, fat, rich wines of concentration and extract. What they lack in elegance they make up for in power. While they should be long-lived and outlast the '83s, they'll never match the sheer elegance and beauty of that vintage. Of the ten wines we tasted from cask, Il Poggione was the standout. On nearly the same level, though, were Altesino, Caparzo, Case Basse, Costanti, and La Gerla. Biondi-Santi again failed to come up to the vintage, or so it seems at this stage.

Altesino (*ex-cask 5/85*). Intense aroma; a big, rich, tannic wine, full of flavor, richer and fuller though less elegant that the '83, should be long-lived; already long on the aftertaste.★★(★)

Biondi-Santi (*ex-cask 5/85*). A big aroma with suggestions of berries and vanilla; tannic, but has the stuffing; a good wine that's just not up to the level of the better '82s we tasted.★(★)

Canalicchio di Sopra (*ex-cask 5/85*). Aroma of ripe fruit, nuts, and cherries; moderate tannin, a bit astringent, loads of flavor.★(★−)

Caparzo (*ex-cask 5/85*). Mushroom and fruit aromas; seems almost sweet, shows refinement and class.★★(★)

Case Basse (*ex-cask 5/85*). Delicate, floral aroma with some fruit; sweet, rich, and ripe, a lot of quality here and some elegance.★★(★)

Comunali, Bartoli-Giusti-Focacci (*ex-cask 5/85*). At this point harsh, not quite together, but has the stuffing and the potential.★(★?)

Costanti (*ex-cask 5/85*). Mushroomy aroma; nice flavor, though lacks the intensity expected from the vintage, has some style.★★(★)

Il Poggione (*ex-cask 5/85*). Woodsy aroma with notes of berries and chocolate; a rich, concentrated mouthful of wine, one for long aging.★★★(+)

La Gerla (*ex-cask 5/85*). Pepper, cherries, and flowers on nose; ripe, concentrated fruit under the firm tannic structure; lots of character and potential.★★(★)

S. Filippo (*ex-cask 5/85*). Chestnuts all over the aroma; heaps of flavor, fairly tannic, not much style, but a good wine.★(★−)

1981 [★★+]

Capanna considers 1981 one of the top vintages. Altesino described it as very good. Colombini and Biondi-Santi also said it was good.

We find the '81s to be good wines, though a trifle light. They should be ready early. Those of Costanti and Il Poggione impressed us the most. Altesino, Case Basse, La Gerla, and S. Filippo also produced good Brunellos.

Altesino (*ex-cask 5/85*). Toasty aroma with a floral aspect; somewhat closed, with a sweetness to the fruit, fairly tannic, a bit light; shows promise.★★(+)

Canalicchio di Sopra (*ex-cask 5/85*). Aroma of nuts and fruit; light tannin, surprisingly forward, even a bit simple.★

Caparzo (*ex-cask 5/85*). Light nose; fruity, a bit astringent, somewhat light-bodied, but well balanced; some quality evident.★★

Case Basse (*ex-cask 5/85*). Fruity, perfumed aroma; soft, some tannin; good quality.★★(★−)

Colombini (*ex-cask 5/82*). Loads of fruit on nose and palate, some style already evident, acid on the high side.★★

Comunali, Bartoli-Giusti-Focacci (*ex-cask 5/85*). A bit light, but has the fruit.★(★−)

Costanti (*ex-cask 5/85*). Lovely, berrylike aroma; sweet, stylish, and elegant, sure to make a splendid bottle.★★(★)

Il Poggione (*ex-cask 5/85*). Intense aroma with surprising richness of fruit, also licorice and tarlike notes; rich and flavorful, chewy; shows impressive quality.★★(★)

La Gerla (*ex-cask 5/85*). Lovely aroma up front; some tannin, seems a bit light, but the structure and fruit are there.★★(+)

S. Filippo (*ex-cask 5/85*). Perfumed aroma, pretty, vaguely of pine; well balanced, almost sweet, has some delicacy, should be ready early.★★(+)

1980 ★+

Altesino, Castiglion del Bosco, La Fortuna, and Colombini rated the year highly. Biondi-Santi didn't produce a riserva. Niederbacher gave it three stars.

We found the vintage mixed. These are wines for early drinking. Of the twenty-one Brunellos

1980

tasted, Costanti produced the star; Colombini was close behind. Altesino and Capanna were also very good. The Biondi-Santi, again, was wanting.

Altesino (*3 times 5/85*). Loads of fruit on nose and some oak; moderate tannin, young and flavorful, well balanced, a bit light, but lots of flavor; will be ready early.★★(+)

Argiano (*4/85*). Light nose with vague off note; tannin seems rather high for the fruit.

Biondi-Santi (*ex-cask 5/85*). Smallish nose; rather light and simple, lacks character.

Canalicchio Az. Agr., Lambardi (*4/85*). Aroma is somewhat restrained, with hints of flowers and mint that carry across the palate, somewhat astringent, a sense of fruit evident.

Canalicchio di Sopra (*5/85*). Floral, fruity aroma; light tannin, fruity, in an easy, simple style.★(+)

Capanna, G. Cencioni (*5/85; 13,500 bottles*). Expansive aroma of flowers and fruit with suggestions of tobacco and licorice; moderate tannin, lots of fruit, firm structure, can be enjoyed now but has potential for improvement.★★(+)

Caparzo (*5/85*). Fruity aroma with a pinelike note; moderate tannin, a bit light, well balanced, flavorful; should be ready early.★(★)

Caprili (*twice, 4/85*). Some fruit on aroma and vague mineral and floral notes; tannin to shed, good fruit, a bit light, lacks some intensity, but a nice glass of wine.★ +

Casanuova (*4/85*). Reticent aroma; light to moderate tannin; lacks some weight and richness, though a pleasant wine; nearly ready.★ +

Case Basse (*ex-cask 5/85*). Floral aroma; a vague sweetness, loads of flavor; light finish.★★

Castiglion del Bosco (*ex-cask 5/85*). Reticent aroma with notes of fruit and nuts; well balanced, not a lot of tannin, soft-centered, a bit light, some style.★ +

Col d'Orcia (*4/85*). Aroma hints of nuts and minerals; ripe fruit, moderate tannin, lacks some style.(★)

Colombaio di Montosoli "Baricci" (*twice 4/85*). Fruity aroma; a richness of flavor under the moderate tannin, but no real style; should be ready in two to three years.★★ —

Colombini (*twice 5/85*). Floral aroma, warm with a nutlike nuance; not a lot of tannin; light-bodied, forward, some elegance and style; long; for early drinking.★★★ —

Costanti riserva (*ex-cask 5/85*). Licorice, tar, and floral aroma; well balanced, tannin to shed, has delicacy and style.★★(★)

Il Poggione (*twice 5/85*). Reticent aroma with suggestions of licorice and flowers; moderate tannin with nice fruit beneath, could have more length on palate; should mature early.★★

La Chiesa di S. Restituta (*3 twice 4/85*). Nose a bit restrained; nice fruit; some tannin, lacks character, a bit simple.(★)

La Gerla (*5/85*). Mineral note on aroma; tannic entry, rough and unready, but the flavor is there.★(+)

S. Filippo (*4 times 5/85*). Aroma of nuts and fruit; light tannin, soft center, an easy style; room for further improvement.★(+)

Villa Banfi (*4/85*). Some oak, also fruit on nose; a fair amount of tannin. Is there enough fruit? At this stage, it's difficult to say.?

1979 ★★ +

Altesino and S. Filippo characterized 1979 as a very good year. La Fortuna, Castiglion del Bosco, Castelgiocondo, and Colombini said it was a good vintage. Biondi-Santi didn't produce a riserva.

There were many splendid wines produced and unfortunately many not so splendid. The Altesino is stunning. Close behind are Costanti, both the regular and the riserva, Il Poggione, Caparzo's La Casa, Il Casello, and La Gerla. We also like the La Fortuna, I Comunali, and Mastrojanni. And there were a number of disappointments.

Altesino riserva (*10 times 5/85*). Some oak, a lot of fruit, and a vaguely nutty note; tannic, with heaps of flavor to support it; a chewy wine that needs four to five more years to smooth out, but will make a splendid bottle.★★(★ +)

Biondi-Santi (*5/85; bottle 26,968*). The bottle was decanted two hours before tasting according to Biondi-Santi's instructions. Aroma recalls nuts and vaguely flowers; moderate tannin, astringent at edges, surprisingly forward, and a bit simple. As the evening wore on, the wine became quite astringent.★(?)

Campogiovanni (*4/85*). Flowers and nuts on aroma; has tannin and a lot of flavor, with a nutlike note; finish recalls almonds.★★

Canalicchio di Sopra (*4/85*). Nutlike aroma; some tannin, approachable now, should improve; a bit short.★(★)

Capanna di S. Restituta, Az. Agr. Fattoi (*3 times 4/85*). Vaguely floral aroma; fairly nice fruit on the palate, light tannin, a bit light in body and simple; short.★(+)

Capanna, G. Cencioni riserva (*5/85; 720 bottles*). Aroma recalls fruit and nuts; moderate tannin, good fruit, light; somewhat tannic finish, seems overly drying at the end, perhaps too long in wood.★★ —

Caparzo (*twice 5/85*). Aroma of pine and fruit; tannic entry, fruit in the center, nice until the end when it tails off and thins out.★(+)

Castelgiocondo (*twice 5/85*). Aroma somewhat reticent, hints of fruit and vaguely of licorice; some tannin, a bit light, some tannin at the end; will be ready early.★(★)

Castiglion del Bosco (*5/85*). Nutty aroma; some tannin, nice fruit, lacks style, a bit pedestrian.★ —

Colombini (*6 times 4/85*). Small aroma; light tannin, light-bodied, quite agreeable; nearly ready.★★

Comunali, Bartoli-Giusti-Focacci (*3 times 5/85*). Bottle of 4/85: Lovely, complex aroma with nuances

1979

of cherries, nuts, flowers, and spice; some tannin to shed, a bit young but approachable.★★(+) Bottle of 5/85: Expansive, floral bouquet, vaguely nutlike; light tannin, surprisingly forward, perhaps a bit simple, some tannin at the end.★+

Costanti (5/85; 11,700 bottles). Lovely bouquet recalls cherries, flowers, vanilla, and berries; has delicacy, well balanced, almost sweet, elegant, well made; long finish with a suggestion of nutmeg.★★(★)

Costanti riserva (5/85; 4400 bottles). Pretty bouquet of vanilla, flowers, and spice; lacks the sweetness of the regular, but has more weight and structure; good length, though a touch of astringency at the end.★★(★?)

Il Casello, prop. Franceschi (twice 5/85). Floral aroma, a bit closed; well balanced; soft-centered, round, flavorful, tannin to lose; give it perhaps three more years.★★(+)

Il Colle (4/85). Tar and nuts on aroma; a fair amount of tannin, with a sense of fruit beneath, lacks style.(★)

Il Poggione (twice 5/85). Intense aroma with hints of licorice, tar, and spice; tannic entry, full-flavored, fruit on middle palate, soft-centered; needs another three to four years.★★(★)

La Casa, Caparzo (5/85). Fruity aroma with a hint of toffee and overtones of oak; rich, toasty oak flavors on entry, give way to tannin, fairly rich; firm, tannic finish; should soften in about three years.★★(+)

La Fortuna (3 times 4/85). Aroma of mushrooms and flowers; some tannin, a lot of flavor, soft-centered; young but approaching drinkability.★★(+)

La Gerla riserva (5/85). Closed in and tannic, but shows promise; the stuffing is there, and the structure; finish is a bit light.★(★+)

La Magia (4/85). Stinky aroma (mercaptans?); overly tannic for the fruit; harsh finish.

La Poderina (4/85). Notes of chocolate and Marsala on nose, and on palate under the tannin.

Le Presi (4/85). Mineral aroma with suggestions of volcanic earth and black pepper notes; tannic entry gives way to heaps of flavor; short, tannic ending.★(★−)

Mastrojanni, Podere Loreto (4/85). Aroma has a pleasant touch of resin, some flowers and fruit; sweet ripe fruit under the tannin, has style, balance, length; shows real quality.★★(★)

Nardi (4/85). Oxidized.

Poggio Antico (3 times 4/85). Lacks structure, weight, and definition. This was the best bottle of the three.

S. Filippo (3 times 5/85). Aroma a bit reticent, hints of nuts, fruit, and flowers; still has tannin to soften, with the fruit to carry it; a nice wine, but could have more style.★★

Val di Cava (4/85). Nutty aroma; a chocolatey flavor. Is there enough fruit for the rather considerable tannin?

Val di Suga (twice 5/85). Hot nose; some tannin, shy of fruit, dull and flat.

Villa Banfi (3/85). Some oak, some fruit on aroma; straightforward, rather simple, an agreeable small-scale Brunello with room to improve.★

1978 ★★

Right from the start, this vintage received a lot of good reviews. We always felt the wines were less good than the acclaim. At this point, based on twenty-one different Brunellos, our evaluation seems to have been proved correct. It was a mixed vintage. Biondi-Santi, once again, didn't bottle a riserva.

The Altesino Brunello and the Il Poggione riserva shine. Among the other good ones are La Fortuna, the Colombini riserva, Capanna, the Caparzo La Casa, and Mastrojanni.

Altesino riserva (3 times 5/85). Floral aroma with notes of hazelnuts and cherries; moderate tannin; flavorful, more forward than the '79, though still young, has style and balance; long tannic finish.★★(★)

Altesino, Vigna Altesino (6/84). Aroma somewhat closed, but some richness of fruit comes through; moderate tannin, rich, ripe fruit flavors; vaguely bitter on finish.★★(+)

Argiano (1/84). Not much on nose; light-bodied, unbalanced; altogether unimpressive.

Camigliano (11/83). Aroma a bit closed, but gives hints of fruit and oak; fairly tannic and astringent, moderate fruit. Is there enough? Seems so.(★)

Canalicchio di Sopra (5/85). A lot of fruit on aroma and a nutlike aspect; light tannin, fairly rich; could have more length, but will make a nice glass and rather soon.★★

Capanna, G. Cencioni (1/84). Full, rich aroma; flavorful, moderate tannin, well structured, a big wine; quite nice.★★(+)

Caparzo (4 times 5/85). Woodsy aroma with a nutlike aspect; moderate tannin, a trifle shy on fruit; vaguely bitter aftertaste that tails off at the end; shows some potential.★(?)

Castiglion del Bosco (3 times 6/84). Ripe cherries on aroma, fairly open; a mouthful of flavor, still has tannin, nearly ready but will improve.★★

Castiglion del Bosco riserva (5/85). Aroma of licorice, tar, nuts, and fruit; a lot of flavor up front, soft-centered, light tannin, a bit coarse but agreeable.★

Cecchi Luigi, bottled by A.A.T.C. (twice 6/84). Mineral aspect to aroma; lacks weight, definition, and flavor; flat and dull though drinkable.

Colombini (1/84). Floral aroma with a nutlike component; tannic, rather closed, but holds out some promise; very short, tannic aftertaste.★(★?)

Colombini riserva (5/85). Floral bouquet with some delicacy and a vague nutlike note; tannic entry, some astringency and firmness; quite young.★★(★)

Comunali, Bartoli-Giusti-Focacci riserva (5/85). Chestnuts and vanilla on aroma; well-knit, a bit light, tasty, chestnuts on palate; tannic finish; could improve.★★

Il Poggione (twice 1/84). Nutty aroma with berrylike notes; well balanced, sweet fruit flavors, supple center.★★(+)

Il Poggione riserva (twice 3/85). Rich, intense floral bouquet with cherrylike notes; surprisingly for-

1978

ward and supple, stylish; has length; still needs age.★★(★)

La Casa, Caparzo *(twice 5/85)*. Hints of toffee on aroma and flavor; fuller, richer, and more intense than the '79, also rounder; still young.★★(★ −)

Lisini *(5/84)*. Floral, nutty aroma with a vague note of tobacco; fairly well balanced, though alcohol mars it somewhat, especially toward the end.★★

Mastrojanni, Podere Loreto *(5/85)*. Some oak and a lot of fruit on nose, vaguely floral with nutlike notes; still undeveloped, fairly rough and tannic, but the fruit is there, rich and flavorful.★★(★ −)

Nardi riserva *(5/85)*. Mineral aroma; lacks structure and length; rather simple, though drinkable.★ −

Poggio Antico *(3 times 4/85)*. Quite a lot of bottle variation here; the best one was the most recent. Per-

fumed bouquet; almost sweet on entry, gives way to an astringency, has flavor; some alcohol and a tannic bite on the finish.(★)

S. Filippo *(5/85)*. Aroma of nuts and flowers; quite tannic, though with the reserves to carry it; a nice glass, though a bit young yet.★(+)

Tenuta di Riguardo, bottled by Tosco Vinicola *(7/85)*. Warm, fruity aroma, slight suggestion of nuts; light tannin, fruity, overly simple; drinkable now, lacks style.★ −

Val di Suga riserva *(5/85)*. Candylike aspect to aroma; fairly tannic, insufficient fruit; hot finish.

Villa Banfi *(6/84)*. Characteristic aroma, flowers and cherries beneath overtones of oak; fairly tannic, lacks structure and definition; not a success.

1977 ★★★

Without question, 1977 produced the best wines between 1975 and 1982. Altesino, Castiglion del Bosco, Biondi-Santi, and La Fortuna rated the vintage highly. Colombini said it was a good year.

Of the thirteen Brunellos we tasted, Altesino comes out on top. We were impressed also with the Colombini and Lisini. Close behind were the Biondi-Santi riserva and Caparzo's La Casa. Among the top producers, only Costanti was wanting.

Altesino riserva *(5/85)*. Floral, fruity bouquet, vaguely nutty; moderate tannin, a complete, well-structured wine of style and elegance; needs two or three years.★★★(+)

Argiano *(twice 6/84)*. Hot nose, with overripe fruit and a mineral aspect; nice fruit, moderate tannin.★

Biondi-Santi *(5/83)*. Full of flavor, round and smooth, surprisingly forward.★★

Biondi-Santi riserva *(5/85)*. Decanted two hours earlier following Biondi Santi's instructions. Aroma a bit reticent, some fruit evident; moderate tannin, well-knit, surprisingly soft; a bit short; should improve.★★(+)

Caparzo *(3 times 5/85)*. Fruity aroma, vaguely woodsy; tannic entry, seems to have sufficient fruit, but lacks somewhat in weight.★(+)

Col d'Orcia *(twice 2/83)*. Unyielding on nose; fairly well balanced though a bit astringent, a tannic roughness, but has the stuffing to support it. The bottle tasted a year earlier seemed more forward and softer.★(★)

Colombini *(3 times 6/84)*. Lovely aroma with overtones of cherries and flowers; moderate tannin, well structured, elegant and stylish, good flavor and

length.★★(★)

Costanti riserva *(twice 5/85; 4000 bottles)*. A bit dull and uncharacteristic; the only disappointment we've ever had from this outstanding producer.

La Casa, Caparzo *(5/85)*. Vaguely toffeelike aroma; moderate tannin, well-knit, has a sweetness and lots of fruit; tannic finish; needs a few more years yet.★★(★ −)

La Chiesa di S. Restituta *(twice 6/84; 9200 bottles)*. Browning; some oxidation over a hot, baked aroma; better in the mouth, light tannin, lacking in fruit, nowhere to go. This describes the better bottle. The one tasted eight months earlier was even duller.

Lisini *(6/84)*. A bit reticent on nose, though shows some fruit; a mouthful of flavor, light to moderate tannin, well balanced, has style; impressive.★★(★)

Riguardo, bottled by Tosco Vinicola *(6/84)*. Browning; a vaguely caramel back note; light tannin, fruity, simple, agreeable.

Val di Suga riserva *(twice 5/85)*. Hint of mushrooms on aroma; more tannin than fruit, unstructured; lacks interest.

1976 0

Altesino, S. Filippo, Il Poggione, Campogiovanni, Castiglion del Bosco, Biondi-Santi, Costanti, and Capanna listed this vintage among the worst ever. Biondi-Santi, much to his credit, didn't bottle. Costanti and Il Poggione produced a limited quantity of surprisingly good wine. Altesino and Canalicchio di Sopra also produced pleasant surprises.

The best are holding, but barely. Signs of senility are beginning to creep in.

Altesino, Vigna Montosoli *(6 times 1/84)*. Characteristic floral bouquet with fruity overtones; soft, acid a touch high, but in all a good glass of wine; not to keep.★ +

Canalicchio di Sopra *(5/85, at the winery)*. Aroma shows development and some complexity, nutlike, a hint of fruit; beginning to dry out a bit, but still has a lot of nice fruit; quite drinkable.★ +

Caparzo *(3 times 5/85, at the winery)*. Pine on aroma that's showing age; still has tannin and a lot of

fruit; finish is all tannin, drying out, but still good.★ −

Costanti *(5 times 3/83)*. Light-bodied, tasty, very well made, shows some quality; not to keep.★★ −

Il Poggione *(3 times 3/85)*. Fragrant aroma with a touch of tar and tobacco; still has tannin and a surprising amount of fruit; well made, has held up very well, shows no signs of deterioration.★★

Riguardo, bottled by Tosco Vinicola *(3/82)*. Butterscotch and vanilla on aroma which carry through on the palate; lacks structure and weight, but drinkable.

1975 ★★★+

Il Poggione rates the vintage among the all-time greats, better ever than 1970. Colombini, Biondi-Santi, Costanti, Caparzo, Altesino, Castelgiocondo, Campogiovanni, La Fortuna, Camigliano, Castiglion del Bosco, and Capanna agree it was top flight, one of the very best.

No question about it, there were some outstanding wines produced in 1975, but the vintage was no guarantee; there were also some losers. The best need more age.

Our favorite '75s are the Il Poggione and Colombini, especially their riservas. Close behind is the Biondi-Santi riserva, his best wine of the decade. It has flashes of brilliance that show what his reputation was all about. Other fine '75s are Altesino (the regular and the two crus, especially the Montosoli), the Col d'Orcia riserva, and the Costanti. The real disappointment here was Caparzo.

Altesino (*3 times 1/80*). Deep aroma, rather closed; flavorful, well structured, very young, with a lot of promise.★★(★)

Altesino, Vigna Altesino (*3 times 4/81*). Chestnuts on aroma, rich and intense, though a bit subdued; still has tannin, elegant, well-knit, stylish.★★★(+)

Altesino, Vigna Montosoli (*3 times 1/82*). A stylish wine with loads of fruit and flavor; displays real quality, though still somewhat closed.★★★(+)

Argiano (*twice 4/81*). Some fruit on the nose; a bit pedestrian, nearly ready.

Argiano riserva (*twice 11/83*). Tawny at rim; some oxidation; better on palate, though low in fruit and a bit shallow.

Biondi-Santi (*3 times 5/83*). Real quality, one of the few times the wine has equaled the reputation; not the wine of the vintage, but certainly one of the best.★★★

Caparzo (*6 times 5/85*). Vaguely piny aroma showing development and age; some tannin, nice entry and middle palate, has ricnhess of flavor, but going off; not to keep.★

Caparzo riserva (*3 times 11/83*). Pale color; aroma is a bit light, with hints of fruit and flowers; still tannic, flavorful, not up to the vintage; short.★

Castiglion del Bosco (*3 times 11/83*). Seems to have too much tannin for the fruit. Where will it go?

Col d'Orcia (*4 times 2/83*). Floral, fruity aroma, seems somewhat young; almost sweet, some tannin to shed, well balanced, displays style and class.★★(★−)

Col d'Orcia riserva (*twice 11/83*). More flavor and better structure than the regular, will make a splendid bottle with time.★★(★)

Colombini (*6 times 11/80*). Intense, fragrant perfume with floral notes; an elegant, stylish wine with lots of style; young yet, shows a lot of promise.★★(★)

Colombini riserva (*5 times 9/83*). A wine with everything—richness, elegance, balance, style, flavor, and length; it has to be the wine of the vintage.★★★(★)

Costanti riserva (*5/85; 1200 bottles*). Lovely, complex bouquet, with nuances of vanilla, toffee, flowers, pine, berries, ripe fruit; sweet, some tannin, beginning to resolve itself, finely honed, elegant.★★★(+)

Il Poggione (*5 times 5/85*). Richly perfumed bouquet of flowers, tan, and licorice; sweet and ripe, not a big wine but an elegant one, balance is nearly perfect, exudes style; ready, but still some room for improvement.★★★★

Isabella de' Medici, Val di Suga (*4 times 6/84*). We kept trying, but one bottle was worse than the other.

Lisini riserva (*3 times 11/83*). Baked character to aroma, mineral notes; moderate tannin, a bit coarse; a disappointment.

Nardi riserva (*5/85*). Hot, cooked, overripe aroma; tannic. Is there enough fruit? Harsh.

Olivieri, Martini Bramante, Tenuta Val di Cava (*twice 3/82*). Soft and easy, lacks style and distinction, though pleasant enough; a Chianti-style Brunello.

Poggio alle Mura riserva (*3 times 11/83*). Pale; unstructured, lacks flavor, weight, and definition.

Val di Suga riserva (*3/83*). Rather a nice nose; good flavor, surprisingly soft and easy; ready.

1974 0

At one time the '74s offered pleasant drinking, although many were somewhat low in fruit. Nearly all are too old today. Surprisingly, the Caparzo riserva is an exception. Biondi-Santi didn't produce a riserva. It's not a vintage to hold. Drink them up, or pour them out.

Argiano (*twice 4/80*). Aroma displays some fruit, though a bit closed; light-bodied, some tannin and flavor; very short.

Biondi-Santi (*11/79*). Pale; lacks aroma; thin, low in flavor; a short, sharp finish, and this only five years after the vintage.

Caparzo (*6 times 12/82*). Fruity aroma with a nutty aspect; lacks substance and somewhat in structure; short finish with noticeable volatile acidity. This wine peaked in 1980 and in fact was enjoyable until early or mid-1981, when it started to decline.

Caparzo riserva (*twice 5/85, at the winery*). Rich aroma with a suggestion of leather, vaguely of figs; surprisingly full, seems younger than the '75, almost sweet.★★+

Castelgiocondo riserva (*4/81*). Perfumed scent, with notes of ripe fruit; some tannin, flavorful, a bit light, has some style; a bit young yet, but a nice glass. It has probably faded by now.★★

Castiglion del Bosco (*twice 3/82*). Vanilla and ripe fruit on aroma, quite nice, but something unpleasant lurks in the background; considerable tannin; drying out.

Col d'Orcia (*3 times 10/80*). Perfumed aroma, some fruit and complexity; considerable tannin. Is there enough fruit? We think so. It is probably too old today.★(★)

Colombini (*3 times 9/81*). Perfumed aroma with a nutlike component; nice flavor, a bit light, some style.★★−

1974

Colombini riserva *(11/83)*. Fruity aroma with cassis and floral notes; light tannin, soft and flavorful, quite ready; a bit short; a pleasant small-scale wine.★ +

Nardi *(10/80)*. More like a Chianti than a Brunello, a lightweight, small-scale wine.

Olivieri, Martini Bramante, Tenuta Val di Cava *(twice 12/80)*. Another Chianti-like Brunello, small-scale and overly simple, with harsh edges.

1973 0

Camigliano rated the year highly. Once again, the Biondi-Santi riserva wasn't produced. For the most part, the '73s were light wines and are fading fast; many have already gone. A real surprise is the Biondi-Santi regular, without question the star of this mediocre year and considerably above the vintage. Lisini made quite a good '73, though we haven't tasted it in some time.

Altesino *(5 times 11/83)*. Fragrant, vaguely floral bouquet; beginning to dry out, was better in 1979, but still has flavor and interest.★

Biondi-Santi *(6/84)*. Surprisingly deep color, garnet; lovely bouquet; some class, has an uncommon richness, well structured, full of style and class; perhaps Biondi-Santi's finest wine of the 1970s after his especially fine '75.★★ +

Campogiovanni riserva *(3 times 11/83)*. Vague coffeelike notes on aroma; some tannin, modest flavors, still good but drying out.★ −

Caparzo *(twice 5/85)*. Beginning to brown; shows a lot of age on nose; still has nice flavor and interest, but drying out. It was at its peak in 1979 and 1980.

Colombini *(8 times 5/83)*. Well-developed aroma with some complexity; still drinkable, but beginning to dry out. It was at its best from 1978 to 1981.★

Il Poggione *(6 times 2/84)*. Light but characteristic aroma; fairly well balanced, light-bodied, soft and tasty; moderately long finish with a tannic component; still good, though past its peak, which was from 1979 to early 1983.★

Lisini *(twice 11/79)*. Nice aroma of cherries; light, some tannin, has fruit; short. By now it has probably faded.★ +

Poggio alle Mura *(11/79)*. Best forgotten. (This producer has trouble in great years.)

1972 0

By reputation, 1972 was among the worst of the Brunello vintages. The only one we tasted, the Colombini, while a decent enough wine, should not have been bottled as a Brunello.

Colombini *(twice 10/83)*. Fragrant, floral scent with some spice; the aroma is the best part, and then there's some flavor, a bit light, not bad for the year, but doesn't do anything for the reputation of the house. +

1971 ★★ −

Castiglion del Bosco, Campogiovanni, Capanna, Biondi-Santi, and Camigliano rate the 1971 vintage highly.

High acid and a meagerness of body characterize the '71s, although there were some exceptions. The best are holding well. The Il Poggione was a real knockout. Colombini also produced a good '71 Brunello. The Biondi-Santi riserva, while good, is a bit too high in acid to be really enjoyable.

Biondi-Santi riserva *(7 times 2/84)*. Bottle of 2/84: Shot, and at $171.50 a bottle the loss becomes grievous.

Bottle of 11/83: The best of the seven bottles tasted since 5/79. Perfumed bouquet, vaguely nutlike; fairly well balanced, still some tannin, beginning to soften and round out, though a troublesome touch of oxidation intrudes; a good but not great bottle. (The price, on the other hand, is quite the opposite.)★★

Campogiovanni riserva *(10/80)*. Color showing age; some oxidation; still has considerable tannin, but fairly well matched with fruit. Too old by now.★(+)

Castiglion del Bosco *(4/80)*. Nice aroma, still a bit closed; tannin to lose, shows some promise.★(+)

Col d'Orcia *(3 times 11/78)*. Fragrant scent; light, some tannin, lacks substance and weight.

Colombini riserva *(21 times 11/84)*. Vaguely floral bouquet with nutlike notes; soft, smooth, and round, some style, very ready, as good as it ever was; a vague touch of alcohol mars the finish.★★ +

Il Poggione *(3 times 8/83)*. Complex, floral bouquet with a nutlike nuance; full of flavor, elegant and well-knit, exudes style and class; very long on finish. Surely the wine of the vintage, in fact a fine Brunello by any standard.★★★

Poggio alle Mura riserva *(3 times 5/83)*. Tawny; aroma offers some interest; still some tannin; as ready as it will ever be.

1970 ★★★★

Biondi-Santi, Colombini, Caparzo, Il Poggione, Castiglion del Bosco, Costanti, and La Fortuna rate this year as one of the very best. Il Poggione places it after 1975. Judging from the wines we've tasted, the vintage was outstanding, the best in our experience. The Colombini was magnificent, a wine with uncommon elegance and style. The Il Poggione and Costanti aren't far behind. Among the big names, only Biondi-Santi was disappointing; this is not just one bottle we're talking about, but a number of them.

Production in 1970 was considerably less than today, as were the number of producers selling Brunello in bottle.

Biondi-Santi (*16 times 4/85*). Unbalanced, high acid, very little fruit remaining; it was worth a lot more before we opened it. Of the sixteen bottles we tasted only one was good, and that was in 1977. The bottles came from at least three different shipments, and more than half a dozen sources. And this vintage is considered one of the greatest of all time!

Biondi-Santi riserva (*twice 10/80*). First bottle: Completely oxidized.

Second bottle: Some oxidation, but still offers some interest.

Castiglion del Bosco (*5/80*). Color is browning; volatile acidity on aroma; dried out.

Col d'Orcia (*twice 10/80*). Rich, berrylike aroma; loads of flavor, soft, elegant, stylish; room to improve.★★★

Colombini riserva (*14 times 3/82*). Superb bouquet—deep, rich, and complex, with floral overtones; a complete wine, has an uncommon elegance, full of flavor and style; long finish; still room to improve.★★★★

Costanti riserva (*4 times 5/85; 2600 bottles*). Deep color; intense bouquet, with nuances of vanilla, toffee, flowers, resin, and leather; still some tannin to shed, but heaps of flavor make it tempting now; round and smooth, velvety; real quality here.★★★(★)

Il Poggione (*4 times 5/85*). Woodsy, floral bouquet with a note of mushrooms; velvety, full-flavored; enormously long finish; a complete wine that is quite ready but has room to improve further.★★★★

Nardi (*12 times 7/83*). Hot, almost baked aroma; harsh edges, drying out. This wine was at its best from 1979 to 1980; it started to go over the top in 1981.

Poggio alle Mura (*10 times 12/80*). At one time this was a drinkable little wine, with no real character or virtues and no real defects; since 1979, it has shown marked signs of deterioration.

1969 ★ –

Castiglion del Bosco described 1969 as a poor year. Biondi-Santi said it was very good. Overall, the vintage wasn't highly thought of. The only one we've drunk recently is the Il Poggione, tasted at the winery in May and it showed signs of fading. If you have any in your cellar, drink them up.

Il Poggione (*5/85*). Deep garnet; complex bouquet with berrylike undertones; beginning to dry out, though still has flavor interest.★★ –

1968 ★ –

Castiglion del Bosco, Biondi-Santi, and Camigliano described 1968 as a good to very good year. Overall, it was a medium vintage, and judging from those we tasted recently the wines are getting tired.

Colombini (*5/80*). Dried out.

Colombini riserva (*5 times 5/85*). Bottle of 9/83: Light brick color; lovely bouquet, moderately intense; still some tannin, full of flavor; drinkable now, though room for improvement.★★(+)

Bottle of 5/85: Tawny, orange at rim; some oxidation, but still has interesting nuances of aroma; soft and tasty; short; still good, but going.★★ –

Nardi riserva (*5/85*). Totally oxidized.

1967 ★ –

Camigliano and Costanti called 1967 a very good vintage. Colombini and La Fortuna said it was good. Castiglion del Bosco rated it poor. The '67s are not wines to hold any longer, although it was considered a three-star vintage at one time. Even the Costanti, tasted at the winery in May, showed signs of tiring.

Costanti riserva (*5/85*). A trace of oxidation on aroma; still has flavor, though drying out.★ +

Poggio alle Mura riserva (*3/81*). Cooked, somewhat oxidized aroma; unbalanced, poorly made.

1966

Castiglion del Bosco found 1966 rather poor. Biondi-Santi didn't produce their riserva. La Fortuna and Colombini, on the other hand, considered it a good year. We can't recall tasting any.

1965

Castiglion del Bosco said that 1965 was very good. Biondi-Santi didn't bottle any wine in 1965. We don't believe we've ever tasted a '65 Brunello.

1964 ★★ –

The consensus was that 1964 was a first-class vintage. Biondi-Santi, Castiglion del Bosco, Colombini, Costanti, Il Poggione, and La Fortuna all gave it high marks. Our experience with the Colombini and Costanti recently and Biondi-Santi a few years ago suggests the wines are getting on in age; they're showing signs of senility.

Biondi-Santi riserva (*4 times 5/83*). Noticeable oxidation, but with some nice nuances beneath; flavorful and soft, acid edges, tails off at the end with a harshness to remind you it's going.★ +

Colombini riserva (*4 times 5/85*). Bottle of 11/80: Deep color; rich, complex bouquet; still has tannin, soft and round, well structured, enjoyable now, though can improve yet.★★(★)

Bottle of 5/85: Orange, tawny at edge; warm, nutlike aroma, with some oxidation apparent; drying out, though some flavor remains.★

Costanti riserva (*5/85*). Brick red; some oxidation, and a vague figlike note; a lot of age showing, but it still has flavor interest.★ +

1961

Biondi-Santi, Colombini, and Il Poggione considered 1961 a first-class vintage. Niederbacher gave it his top marks of four stars.

1958

La Fortuna said 1958 was a very good year. Biondi-Santi and Colombini agreed that it was good. Niederbacher rated it three stars.

1957

La Fortuna rated the year as very good. Colombini said it was a good vintage.

1955

This was considered a first-class vintage. Biondi-Santi, Colombini, Il Poggione, and La Fortuna gave it top marks. Niederbacher gave it his top rating, four stars.

Biondi-Santi riserva (*11/79*). Bouquet has depth and complexity; still has considerable tannin and a richness of flavor; well balanced, has depth, style, and length on the palate.★★★(+)

1951 and 1946

Biondi-Santi and Colombini characterized these two years as good vintages. Niederbacher rated them three stars.

1945

The year was rated top flight by Biondi-Santi, Colombini, Il Poggione, and La Fortuna. Niederbacher rated it four stars.

Other Vintages

Niederbacher didn't rate 1963, 1962, 1960, 1959, 1957, 1956, 1954, 1953, 1952, 1950, 1949, 1948, or 1947. Biondi-Santi didn't produce a '62 or a '60.

The Montalcino Producers

Altesino (*zone 1*), *1970*. Giulio Consonno, a Milanese businessman, is the proprietor of Altesino. There are 84.4 acres (34.1 hectares) of vineyards on the estate. 7.8 (3.1) in mixed cultivation.

Cru/vineyard	Hectares	Altitude (meters)	Exposure
Altesino	6.0	250	s
Gauggiole	21.1	300	ne & sw
Montosoli	7.0	400	nw & s

An additional 17 acres (7 hectares) of vines came into production in 1985. Besides the sangiovese grosso and standard white grapes of the zone, they have a little chardonnay and 1.2 acres (0.5 hectare) of four-year-old cabernet sauvignon vines.

Altesino produces 17,750 cases of wine a year, including 4450 to 5550 cases of Brunello, 22,000 bottles of a *barrique*-aged sangiovese called Palazzo Altesi, 25,000 bottles of a white from

Claudio Basla and
Giulio Consonno of Altesino

90 percent trebbiano and 10 percent malvasia, and a small amount of Cabernet Sauvignon. The balance is Rosso di Montalcino.

Claudio Basla manages the estate with a watchful eye on quality. Enologist Piero Rivella produces the wine. Angelo Solci provides valuable insights and innovations as a second consulting enologist.

They believe in quality at Altesino and pay the price in reduced quantity. They never plan in the vineyards for the Rosso di Montalcino, for which DOC allows a yield of 748 gallons per acre (70 hectoliters per hectare). Instead they make the wine as a Brunello at the maximum yield of 599 gallons per acre (56 hectoliters per hectare). Then, after the wine is made and tasted, they select the best for their Brunello and declassify the rest to Rosso di Montalcino. If the wine is not considered up to their standards for Rosso, they sell it off *sfuso*, unlabeled.

The Altesino Brunello is put initially into large, 3300-gallon (125-hectoliter) Slavonian oak casks for the initial aging period, being moved to smaller and smaller sizes down to 790 gallons (30 hectoliters).

In years that justify it, they bottle their crus, Vigna Altesino and Vigna Montosoli. In the best years they also produce a limited amount of riserva, 3000 bottles at most.

They made a very good '84 Brunello at Altesino, by a very careful selection, using only 1.3 tons per acre (29 quintali per hectare) of grapes, in place of the maximum yield of 3.6 tons per acre (80 quintali per hectare).

From their first Brunello in 1972, Altesino has established a reputation for both quality and consistency. We've found their Brunellos to be wines of style and real personality. They are among the top wines of the zone year after year. Their Rosso di Montalcino is also among the best.

The '75 Brunello is very good, the '77 is top flight, and the '79 might just be the best of the vintage. We can also recommend the '78, '80, and '81. Their '82 and '83 are bound to be stand-outs, the '83 particularly. Rosso di Montalcino★★ + ; Brunello★★★★

Argiano *(zone 1)*. Argiano has 741 acres (300 hectares); 40 (16.2) are planted to brunello. Since 1981, they have been connected with the Cinzano group. We have found their wines uneven. At their best, which is unfortunately not often enough, they can be quite good. Brunello 0

Bartoli-Giusti-Focacci. See Comunali.

Biondi-Santi *(zone 1), 1840*. Franco Biondi-Santi, third-generation proprietor of Fattoria Il Greppo, produces an average of 40,000 to 50,000 bottles a year of his regular Brunello di Montalcino and 15,000 bottles of the riserva. There are years when he makes no Brunello at all, such as in 1984, 1976, 1972, 1965, 1962, and 1960. In other years he produces a regular Brunello but no riserva; there was no riserva in 1980, 1979, 1978, 1974, or 1973.

The difference between the two Brunellos, Biondi-Santi points out, is in the grapes. The regular Brunello is from sangiovese grosso vines ten years old or older; the vines for the riserva are at least twenty-five years old. Biondi-Santi also produces a mediocre, overpriced red table wine, labeled Il Greppo, from the vines younger than ten years.

Franco Biondi-Santi of Fattoria Il Greppo

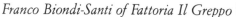

The 116-acre (47-hectare) estate has nearly 37 acres (15 hectares) planted to vines at altitudes ranging from 655 to 1315 feet (200 to 400 meters), facing south. There are 30 acres (12.1 hectares) of sangiovese grosso vines for Brunello di Montalcino, 3.4 acres (1.37 hectares) of twenty-five-to thirty-five-year-old vines, and 25.5 acres (10.75 hectares) planted from 1968 to 1970. Biondi-Santi also has a 5.9-acre (2.4-hectare) vineyard from which he produces Chianti Colli Senesi. Signora Biondi-Santi owns the 262-acre (106-hectare) I Pieri estate.

According to Biondi-Santi, the great vintages at Il Greppo were 1888 (regarded as the greatest vintage of all), 1891, 1925, 1945, 1946, 1951, 1955, 1958, 1961, 1964, 1968, 1969, 1970, 1971, 1975, 1977, 1981, 1982, and 1983. It's interesting to note that it took from 1888 until 1964, seventy-six years later, to reach the midpoint in their great vintages, while the second half were produced in the less than twenty years that followed.

The Biondi-Santi Brunello has without a doubt the greatest reputation, not only for Brunello di Montalcino but for any wine produced in Italy. Is it deserved? Since 1970, we have tasted Biondi-Santi Brunellos from ten vintages. The '80, '74, and—if you can believe it—'70 were all rather poor wines. The '70, in fact, was a disgrace. This vintage was one of the greatest of all times, yet of the eighteen bottles we've tasted over the course of nearly ten years all but one were undrinkable. They were oxidized, and this wasn't a matter of a couple of cases that had been hurt by bad storage. The bottles came from three different importers and four or five different shops. On two occasions the wines were bought within two weeks of their arrival in the U.S.

It is true that when the Biondi-Santi Brunello is good there are very few better—the '75 was in that class—but these wines should not be the exception; they should be the rule. There is a great need for some quality control here. For the prices they charge, the winelover should be assured of getting more than a famous label for his or her money; he or she should be getting an excellent bottle of wine. When one looks at the price–quality ratio (the '71, for example, at $171.50 a bottle and only a two-star Brunello) one can only conclude that no producer in the world of wine has more fitting initials.

The Biondi-Santis appear to be very proud of their reputation. A little more pride in the quality of the product would do the family name more honor. Jacopo Biondi-Santi proudly showed us a bottle of the 1888 in the *sacristia* of their cellar, holding it up to the light to display its still remarkably good color. But they are less eager to open the bottles, even of the newer, highly touted vintages. Perhaps they are not unaware themselves that their wines are worth more in the cellar than they are in the glass. Il Greppo 0; Brunello★★

Camigliano *(zone 3), 1934.* This 2470-acre (1000-hectare) estate is located near the medieval village of Camigliano. Of their 173 acres (70 hectares) of vines, 114 (46) are planted to sangiovese grosso, 35 (14) are for red table wine, 7.5 (3) are for white, and 17 (7) are for Chianti Colli Senesi. They have an annual production of 37,775 cases: 28,900 of Brunello di Montalcino, 5550 of Chianti, and 1665 of white wine. The balance is *vino da tavola*. They also have some cabernet sauvignon, chardonnay, and pinot vines.

They bottled their first Brunello with the 1967 vintage. Piero Rivella, the enologist at Camigliano, also consults for some other fine Brunello producers, including Altesino.

Our tasting experience with these Brunellos is limited to the 1978 vintage. Brunello★

Campogiovanni *(zone 3).* Campogiovanni is owned by the Chianti Classico producer San Felice, which oversees the winemaking. Their 25-acre (10-hectare) vineyard of sangiovese grosso is planted at 920 feet (280 meters), with a southern exposure. Campogiovanni produces some 5325 cases of wine a year: the Brunello, which they have bottled since 1971, and a Rosso di Montalcino, which is aged for eighteen months in barrel. Rosso di Montalcino★; Brunello★★

Canalicchio *(zone 1).* Silvano Lambardi, proprietor of Canalicchio, had 8.6 acres (3.5 hectares) of sangiovese grosso vines. In our limited experience, this Brunello has been a good one. Brunello★

Canalicchio di Sopra *(zone 1), 1969.* The Pacenti brothers, Primo and Rosildo, planted their Brunello vineyards in 1969. today they have 11.1 acres (4.5 hectares) under vines, from which they produce Brunello and Rosso di Montalcino. The Brunello makes up 30 to 35 percent of their production, the Rosso about 30 percent, and the balance is sold *sfuso*.

To ensure better-quality fruit, workers make a pass through the vineyard before the harvest, picking off the bad bunches to concentrate the vine's strength in ripening those that remain, thereby producing better bunches of riper fruit. The best grapes are used for their Brunello. A few figures show the seriousness of their selection. In 1970, 1971, and 1972, they produced a mere 200 to 300 bottles. In 1974, their production had grown to 3000 bottles, but in 1976, a poor vintage, it dropped to 1000. Their annual output is increasing as their vineyards come into full production. In 1980, they produced nearly 7000 bottles, in the following year 8000.

Our experience with these wines, over six vintages, shows them to be fairly consistent. Even their '76 was good. Brunello★★

Capanna di S. Restituta (*zone 3*). Ofelio Fattoi has 6.9 acres (2.8 hectares) of Brunello vines. The '79, the only vintage of Capanna di S. Restituta we've tasted, was fairly good. Brunello★

Caparzo. See Tenuta Caparzo.

Caprili (*zone 1*). This 5.9-acre (2.4-hectare) vineyard is owned by Alfa Bartolomei. The only vintage we've tasted, the 1980, was pretty good. Brunello★

Capanna, G. Cencioni (*zone 1*), *1957*. Giuseppe Cencioni owns 23.5 acres (9.5 hectares) of vines, some in mixed cultivation with other crops; 19.2 acres (7.8 hectares) are planted for Brunello, the other 4.2 (1.7) for *vino da tavola*. They have two crus of Brunello: Cerro with 8.6 acres (3.5 hectares) and Capanna with 10.6 (4.3). The vineyards, which face south to southeast, are planted at altitudes of 985 to 1150 feet (300 to 350 meters).

Besides the Brunello, produced since 1970, Cencioni also produces a Rosso and a Vin Santo. Their average production at Capanna is about 56,000 to 60,000 bottles a year; 10,000 to 14,000 bottles of this are Brunello. Cencioni's '78 Brunello was particularly good; we also liked his '79 and '80. Rosso di Montalcino★; Brunello★★

Caparzo. See Tenuta Caparzo.

Caprili (*zone 1*). This 5.9-acre (2.4-hectare) vineyard is owned by Alfa Bartolomei. The only vintage we've tasted, 1980, was pretty good. Brunello★

Casale del Bosco (*zone 1*). Nardi has 111 acres (45 hectares) of vines on his Casale del Bosco estate, from which he produces 11,000 cases of Brunello a year. Nardi has bottled a Brunello since 1955. For the most part, these wines lack character and style; they tend to be decent wines, nothing more. And we've had a few bottles that were considerably less.

In 1982, Nardi took a significant step in the direction of quality when he engaged the services of a talented consulting enologist, Vittorio Fiore. We look forward to the new Brunellos of this estate from the 1982 vintage on; perhaps even the 1981 and 1980. Brunello (for the present) 0

Casanuova (*zone 1*). Giovanni Neri owns 15 acres (6 hectares) of vines. Our experience is very limited—we've tasted only the '80—but we think it shows promise. Brunello★

Case Basse (*zone 3*). Gianfranco Soldera now owns about 17.5 acres (7 hectares) of vines but expects to increase this to 30 (12). He has 15 acres (6.1 hectares) of Brunello and 2.5 acres (1 hectare) of white grapes. Most of Case Basse's annual production of 5000 cases is Brunello; they also make a small quantity of Rosso di Montalcino, a wine that left us totally unimpressed. Although they have been bottling their wine since 1975, their first Brunello sold in bottle was from the 1977 vintage.

Case Basse has a very good reputation, and, judging from our own experience, for their Brunello it is well justified. Rosso di Montalcino 0; Brunello★★★

Castelgiocondo (*zone 3*). This 2150-acre (870-hectare) estate has 545 acres (220 hectares) in vines. The vineyards, which have a southern exposure, are planted at an altitude of 1150 feet (350 meters). Some 340 acres (137 hectares) are planted to sangiovese grosso for the Brunello and Rosso di Montalcino. They produce a Campo ai Sassi Rosso di Montalcino that is quite good.

Their first Brunello was the '74. This wine was rather light, even a bit weak. As the vines have matured, the improvement in the fruit has been reflected in the wines. We expect to see continued improvement. Among the owners of the Castelgiocondo estate are the Frescobaldis, who have long demonstrated their commitment to quality with their other wines. We think this will be a Brunello worth watching. Rosso di Montalcino★★; Brunello (for now)★★

Castiglion del Bosco *(between zones 1 and 3), 1946.* This firm owns some 5000 acres (2000 hectares), 198 (80) in vines, which includes 91 (37) planted to Brunello. They produce 6650 to 7750 cases of Brunello a year plus a Rosso di Montalcino, some white wine, and a Chianti. Most of the casks they use for aging are made of chestnut, of 660-gallon (25-hectoliter) capacity; a few are only 80 gallons (3 hectoliters). Castiglion del Bosco also produces Dei Roseti Brunello, which they began selling in Italy some five or six years ago. Today it is also sold in the U.S. They bottled their first Brunello from the 1964 vintage.

While these Brunellos can be good, for the most part they are unexciting. But there are changes afoot. Under the new ownership, Altesino, one of the finest producers in the zone, has been enlisted to improve the quality here. Altesino produced the 1982 vintage and was involved to an extent with the 1980 and 1981. Rosso di Montalcino 0; Brunello★

Cecchi Luigi. This Chianti firm sells an undistinguished Brunello. It is more like a Chianti, albeit an overpriced one, than a real Brunello. The wine is bottled for Cecchi by A.A.T.C. Brunello 0

Cencioni Giuseppe. See Capanna, G. Cencioni.

Col d'Orcia. See Tenuta Col d'Orcia.

Colle al Matrichese. See Costanti.

Colombaio di Montosoli *(zone 1).* Nello Baricci owns 5 acres (2 hectares) of vines, from which he produces some 4000 bottles of Brunello and 1500 of Rosso di Montalcino a year. His first Brunello was produced from the 1971 vintage. Thus far we've tasted only his '80, which was pretty good. Brunello★

Colombini *(zone 1), c.1700.* The Colombini estate takes in the 1000-acre (400-hectare) Fattoria dei Barbi and del Casato properties. They have 420 acres (170 hectares) of grain and 400 (163) of woods as well as 77.4 acres (31.3 hectares) of vines planted. Fifty acres (20 hectares) are Brunello. Donna Francesca Colombini Cinelli, proprietor of the Colombini farm, is also the winemaker.

Colombini produces 20,000 cases of wine a year: 7775 to 12,225 Brunello, which in the better vintages includes a very small amount, a mere 200 to 450 cases, of riserva, plus 2200 to 3300 cases each of Rosso di Montalcino, Brusco dei Barbi, and red *vino da tavola*, 550 to 1100 of Bianco del Beato, and 300 to 650 of Vin Santo.

In the great vintages, years like 1970 and 1975, the Colombini Brunellos have an uncommon elegance and finesse as well as extraordinary balance and style. In vintages like

Francesca Colombini Cinelli of Fattoria dei Barbi

these there is no finer Brunello produced. Indeed, very few, if any, equal. Those who have tasted Colombini's magnificent '70 and '75 will know what we mean. She produced a very good '71, '77, '78 riserva, and '80. But there are many years when the wines are disappointing. In lesser vintages—years like 1972, 1973, and 1974, to name some of the more notable examples—the wines just don't seem to be able to rise above the vintage. We find her '78 regular and even her '79 wanting.

We have praised the Colombini Brunello in many articles. For us to consider lowering a producer's rating is serious business, but in this case we feel we must. We want to emphasize that these ratings reflect our personal experience over thirteen years of serious tasting of Italian wines, and they represent an attempt to evaluate the producers as fairly as possible in the context of the wines we cover. This being the case, and with a review of our tasting notes at hand, we feel we cannot give this producer our top rating of four stars; the wines are unfortunately too variable. Brunello★★★

Comunali di Bartoli-Guisti-Focacci *(zone 1), 1938.* Az. Agr. Comunali has more than 10 acres (4 hectares) of vineyards planted at altitudes of 985 to 1475 feet (300 to 450 meters). They produce from these vines 15,000 bottles each of Brunello and Rosso di Montalcino a year. Their first Brunello, sold in bottle, was the '38. Overall, we find their wines quite good. Their '79 in particular is very good. Brunello★★

Andrea Costanti of
Il Colle al Matrichese

Costanti *(zone 1), 1964.* There are about 7.5 acres (3 hectares) of vines on Costanti's Il Colle al Matrichese estate, planted at altitudes of 1475 to 1640 feet (450 to 500 meters). The vineyards have an east–southeastern exposure. Costanti produces from 19,300 to 22,000 bottles of wine a year: 14,650 to 16,000 bottles of Brunello, from 2000 to 2650 of Chianti Colli Senesi (made from 70 percent sangiovese plus canaiolo, trebbiano, and colorino), and 2650 to 3350 of Vermiglio from Brunello vines.

Emilio Costanti produced his first Brunello in 1964. From that vintage he established a reputation not only for exceptional quality but also for consistency. We've found only one other producer as consistent as Costanti, and that is Il Poggione. Even in a year like 1976, he produced a good Brunello—in our opinion, the best of the vintage. His '77 never came up to the vintage; in face it was not very good. This was quite a surprise until we learned that Costanti had been seriously ill and couldn't give the wines his usual care and attention. Costanti died a few years ago, leaving the estate to his young nephew, Andrea Costanti, and Maria di Biasi. They had a high esteem for the wines Emilio Costanti produced, so they wanted to maintain the quality. Enologist Vittorio Fiore was hired as a consultant in 1983. Fiore finished the '78 Brunello and made the '83.

When the vintage justifies it, Costanti produces up to 3000 bottles of Brunello riserva. The grapes for the riserva come from their Paretaio vineyard. Their Baiocco vineyard furnishes the grapes for their regular Brunello.

We found the Costanti '70 and '75 to be top notch, among the very best. The '83 and '82 show great potential. The '80 Brunello was the best wine of the more than twenty we tasted from that vintage. The '79 and '81 were also good. Even the '84 shows a lot of promise. Of the '84s we tasted from barrel in May 1985, this was the one that impressed us most. Brunello★★★★

Dei Roseti. See Castiglion del Bosco.

Il Casello *(zone 3).* This estate is leased by the Franceschis, producers of Il Poggione. Part of the vineyard—5.7 acres (2.3 hectares) of sangiovese grosso vines—is located close to the Il Poggione estate. Pierluigi Talenti, the fine winemaker at Il Poggione, makes this Brunello as well. Il Casello produces only one wine, Brunello. Their annual production is about 1325 cases. The only Il Cassello Brunello we've tasted thus far, the '79, was among the best of the vintage. Our rating system doesn't allow us to give a higher evaluation than we have based on a single vintage, but our expectations for the future are quite high. Brunello★★

Il Colle *(zone 1).* Il Colle has 4.6 acres (1.9 hectares) of vines, from which they produce a Brunello. Their '79 was unimpressive. Brunello 0

Il Poggione *(zone 3), 1890.* The Franceschi family bought this estate in Sant'Angelo In Colle in about 1900. It was then part of Azienda Sant'Angelo. Upon the death of Comm. Franceschi in 1959, the *azienda* was divided between his two sons. The Il Poggione farm went to Leopoldo, and Col d'Orcia went to Stefano. When Leopoldo died in 1979, Il Poggione became the property of his sons, Clemente and Roberto.

The estate covers 3460 acres (1400 hectares), 153 (62) in vines; 91.4 acres (37 hectares) are planted to Brunello, at altitudes ranging from 490 to 1245 feet (150 to 380 meters). In 1953, they put in their first specialized vineyards; previously all had been in *coltura promiscua*, with other crops.

Wine was being produced at Il Poggione in the 1920s, but the first Brunello to be sold commercially from the estate was the '65. Previously their Brunello was either drunk at their own table or sold unlabeled.

Dott. Pierluigi Talenti and Clemente Franceschi of Tenuta Il Poggione

Il Poggione has an annual production of about 265,000 bottles: 160,000 of Brunello and 105,000 of Rosso. The less satisfactory wine is sold *sfuso*, in bulk. They also produce a small quantity of Moscadello—20,000 bottles—produced from grapes grown in their 6.24-acre (2.5-hectare) vineyard, and an excellent extra virgin olive oil.

The winemaking at Il Poggione has been in the very capable hands of enologist Pierluigi Talenti since 1959. Quality control at Il Poggione begins with a careful selection in the vineyard. There is a second selection after the wine is made. Any wine that is judged below their high standards is sold *sfuso*. In the spring, after the fermentation, Talenti makes a third selection to decide which wine will become Brunello and which will be sold as Rosso di Montalcino. Both wines start out the same, but the Rosso is aged for five to six months in cask while the Brunello is given at least three years longer in large Slavonian oak casks.

The Rosso di Montalcino of Il Poggione is, for us, the best in the zone. In 1982, which was exceptional, they produced 5000 cases.

Until 1978, they produced only a regular Brunello. Talenti doesn't believe in overlong wood aging. In that vintage he produced a scant 300 cases of a very fine riserva.

On our visit in the spring, we were generously invited to select any bottle we wanted to taste from the fine collection of vintages in the *cantina*. They certainly had no cause for concern about our choosing an off vintage; they don't produce off vintages at Il Poggione. Every year, the Brunellos of this producer are among the very best produced in the zone. They have never, to our knowledge, produced a Brunello that was less than good. Even in a year like 1976 they made good wine, by careful selection and a sharp eye on quality. In 1984, by limiting their production to about 25 to 30 percent of normal, they again produced a good Brunello, judging from our cask tasting.

Of the ten '83 Brunellos we tasted from cask in Montalcino, the Il Poggione was a standout. The '82, a real standout, was again one of the top Brunellos of that very fine vintage. The '81 was in the top two, their '80 and '79 are both quite good, and the '78 riserva is one of the best produced that year. We've never tasted their '77. Their '76 is holding well. The '75 is stunning; ditto the '70. Their '71 was without question the star of the vintage. Rosso di Montalcino★★★; Brunello★★★★

Isabella de' Medici. Val di Suga produces the Brunello for this mediocre Chianti Classico producer. It is perhaps not surprising, considering its source (Val di Suga) and its destination (de' Medici), that it is among the worst in the zone. Brunello 0 –

La Casa. See Tenuta Caparzo.

La Chiesa di S. Restituta *(zone 3), 1972.* Roberto Bellini, proprietor of the 104-acre (42-hectare) La Chiesa di S. Restituta estate, put in 20 acres (8 hectares) of vines in 1972. Today there are 25 acres (10 hectares): 16 (6.5) of brunello vines and 9 (3.5) of trebbiano and malvasia. The vines are planted at altitudes ranging from 1000 to 1150 feet (330 to 350 meters). Total annual production at S. Restituta is about 4450 cases; 2750 is Brunello with the balance divided among Rosso di Montalcino, their white wine, and Vin Santo. Bellini produced his first Rosso di Montalcino in 1974 and his first Brunello the following year.

These Brunellos enjoy a good reputation, especially in Germany. Some of the other producers in Montalcino also hold them in regard. We have been unimpressed with the wines we've tasted from both the 1977 and 1980 vintages. Brunello 0

La Fortuna *(zone 1), 1967.* Gino and Gioberto Zannoni own 6.2 acres (2.5 hectares) of vines, 3.2 (1.3) in sangiovese grosso for Brunello. They produce 8000 to 9325 bottles of Brunello a year and 10,500 to 13,300 bottles of *vino da tavola.* We rate them on their '79 alone. It was a very good wine. Brunello★★

La Gerla, *1978.* Dott. Sergio Rossi has 6.2 acres (2.5 hectares) of vines on his La Gerla estate. The vineyard, planted at an average altitude of 820 feet (250 meters), has an east to northeast exposure. La Gerla has an annual production of about 15,000 bottles: 7000 of Brunello and 8000 of Rosso di Montalcino. In 1984, 80 percent of the grapes for these two wines were from the vines on the estate; in 1985, all were.

Vittorio Fiore, a fine enologist, has been consulting here since 1979. Our experience with their Brunellos, which includes every vintage from 1979 to 1984, indicates that they are one of the top new estates. Brunello★★★

La Magia *(zone 1).* Herbert Schwarz, proprietor of La Magia, owns 38.5 acres (15.6 hectares) planted to sangiovese grosso vines for Brunello. His 1979 was rather mediocre. Brunello 0

La Poderina *(zone 2).* La Poderina has 0.5 acres (0.2 hectare) of Brunello vines. The one vintage we have tasted from this estate was unimpressive. Brunello 0

Dott. Vittorio Fiore, consulting enologist

Le Presi *(zone 2).* Fabbri Marusca Poggi has 1.5 acres (0.6 hectare) of Brunello vineyards. The one wine we tasted of Le Presi, the '79, was a good Brunello. Brunello★

Lisini *(zone 3).* Elina Lisini's 495-acre (200-hectare) Casanuova estate has 30 acres (12 hectares) of vines for Brunello. Some of the vines were put in between 1930 and 1940, others in 1967. In the oldest part of the vineyards are 200 vines planted in 1880. These plants, unlike the others, which have all been grafted onto phylloxera-resistent root stock, are still on their own roots.

In 1983, they made a special bottling of 300 liters from the old vines. Lisini has an annual production of 30,000 bottles of Brunello and 50,000 to 60,000 of Rosso di Montalcino. They also produce some 3000 to 4000 bottles of Brunello riserva. Lisini's first Brunello sold in bottle was from the 1967 vintage. Her '73 was one of the best produced that year. The '75 was disappointing. The '77 was, again, one of the best. Overall, the Lisini Brunellos are quite good though somewhat variable. Brunello★★

Mastrojanni *(zone 2).* Gabriele Mastrojanni owns 27.4 acres (11.1 hectares) of vines at Podere Loreto. To date, we have only tasted two vintages, 1978 and 1979. Both were very good and indicate that Mastrojanni might, in fact, be a three-star producer, although we couldn't give that rating from such limited experience. Rosso di Montalcino★★; Brunello★★ +

Nardi. See Casale del Bosco.

Olivieri. Marcello Olivieri, who used to be a producer of a fine Chianti Classico, sells 15,000 to 20,000 bottles a year of a simple, almost Chianti-like Brunello produced for him by Martini

Bramante of Val di Cava. The wine is reliable if unexciting. Brunello 0

Pian di Conte *(zone 3)*. Pierluigi Talenti, the fine enologist at Il Poggione, had 0.5 acre (0.2 hectare) of Brunello vines at Pian di Conte. The first Brunello he produced here was from the 1981 vintage. We haven't tasted it, but judging from his other wines, we expect it to be a very good one. Their annual production, Talenti told us, will eventually reach 20,000 bottles a year.

Poggio alle Mura *(zone 3)*. There are 272 acres (110 hectares) in vines on the 4050-acre (1639-hectare) Castello Poggio alle Mura farm, 130 (52.5) planted to brunello. There are also 717 acres (290 hectares) of olive trees (since reduced by the severe freeze of 1984–85), orchards, and cereals, not to mention livestock. Besides all this, the *fattoria* also produced Brunello, Rosso di Montalcino, Chianti, Moscadello, white wine, and Vin Santo. Perhaps their other products were of a higher quality; their wines were without a doubt the worst in the zone. We were told by a noted Brunello producer that Poggio alle Mura used to be one of the two major problems in Montalcino. Fortunately for the other producers, Villa Banfi solved this one by buying the estate. They are retiring the label; 1979 will be the last vintage. Brunello 0 –

Poggio Antico *(zone 3), 1968*. The vineyards on the 495-acre (200-hectare) Poggio Antico estate were for the most part planted in 1970. Of the 54 acres (22 hectares), some 50.2 (20.3) are planted to brunello. Poggio Antico produced their first Brunello in 1974. Their annual production averages 8800 cases of wine: 6600 of Brunello and 2200 of Rosso. Although these wines seem to have a fairly good reputation, we have been totally unimpressed with them. Rosso di Montalcino 0; Brunello 0

Riguardo. Tosco Vinicola bottles this Brunello. It is rather pedestrian, lacking in distinction and class, though admittedly it is drinkable. Brunello 0

S. Filippo *(zone 1), 1972*. Ermanno Rosi, proprietor of S. Filippo, owns 12 acres (4.9 hectares) of vines. The vines in the 10-acre (4-hectare) brunello vineyard are planted at an average altitude of 1000 feet (305 meters). Rosi produces 26,650 to 30,650 bottles of wine a year: 18,000 bottles of Brunello and 10,000 to 12,000 of Rosso di Montalcino, plus a small amount of white and Vin Santo.

Overall, they are good wines. The first S. Filippo Brunello sold in bottle was the '77. Their '81 is one of the better Brunellos we've tasted from that vintage. Rosso di Montalcino★; Brunello★★

Svetoni. Cantina Svetoni, producer of Vino Nobile di Montepulciano, sells 10,000 bottles a year of what is probably a mediocre Brunello at best. We haven't tasted it, but they bought the wine from the zone's worst producer, Poggio alle Mura.

Tenuta Caparzo *(zone 1), 1964*. This 125-acre (50-hectare) estate located in the Torrenieri area has 37 acres (15 hectares) of brunello vines. The vineyards, planted at an altitude of about 985 feet (300 meters), have a southeastern exposure. Their annual production is more than 200,000 bottles of wine: 50,000 bottles of Brunello, 20,000 of Ca'del Pazzo, 90,000 of Rosso di Montalcino, 30,000 of a white wine, and 20,000 of a sparkling rosé.

They produce two Brunellos: the Tenuta Caparzo (42,000 bottles) and the cru, La Casa (8000 bottles). La Casa is a 25-acre (10-hectare) plot on the Montosoli hillside north of Montalcino; only 7.5 acres (3 hectares) are in vines. Altesino, Biondi-Santi, and Capanna also own a piece of this highly regarded hillside.

Sante Torone
of Tenuta Caparzo

The first Caparzo Brunello was from the 1972 vintage. The La Casa premiered in 1976. The grapes for the La Casa, besides coming from a special vineyard, are also handled somewhat differently. This wine spends at least five months of its aging period in French *barriques*.

When Caparzo started out, they showed a lot of promise. But they proved inconsistent. One year their wines would be good, the next not so good. The basic material was there, but direction was lacking. In 1980, they hired a consulting enologist, Vittorio Fiore, who has made a significant improvement in these wines. Today the Caparzo Brunellos are not only consistent but very good as well. The '82 and '83 in particular show a lot of potential. Caparzo also produces a good Rosso di Montalcino. Rosso di Montalcino★★−; Brunello La Casa★★★−; Tenuta Caparzo (pre-1980)★; Tenuta Caparzo (since 1980)★★★

Tenuta Col d'Orcia *(zone 3)*. Tenuta Col d'Orcia was at one time part of Franceschi's Azienda Sant'Angelo. When Comm. Franceschi died in 1959, his estate was divided between his two sons, Leopoldo and Stefano. Leopoldo inherited Il Poggione, and Stefano got the 1485-acre (600-hectare) Col d'Orcia estate. To our knowledge, this Brunello has been sold in bottle, with the Col d'Orcia name, since 1965.

In 1973, Tenuta Col d'Orcia was sold to Cinzano. Today they have 131 acres (53 hectares) in vines for Brunello, making them one of the larger estates in Montalcino.

Enologist Piero Rivella, brother of Ezio Rivella, consults for Col d'Orcia. This Brunello is made in the lighter, more elegant style. The wine in our opinion is better than its reputation. Rosso di Montalcino 0; Brunello★★

Tosco Vinicola. This *azienda* bottles a mediocre Brunello for Riguardo and one for Spalletti. Though we haven't tasted the Spalletti, we tend to doubt that it is much better.

Val di Cava *(zone 1)*. Bramante Martini has 14.5 acres (5.9 hectares) on his 500-acre (200-hectare) Val di Cava farm planted to sangiovese grosso vines, from which he produces a Brunello and a Rosso di Montalcino. To our knowledge, he produced his first Brunello in 1968. Martini also bottles an undistinguished Brunello for Marcello Olivieri. Brunello 0

Val di Suga *(zone 1), 1970*. Val di Suga has 57 acres (23 hectares) of vines, planted at an altitude of about 490 feet (150 meters) from which they produce some 11,000 cases of wine a year: 50,000 bottles each of Brunello and Rosso di Montalcino and 30,000 of Rosso del Merlo. They bottled their first Brunello in 1971.

The Val di Suga Brunellos used to be among the zone's worst. When the new owner, Leonello Marchesi, took over recently, he brought in Vittorio Fiore as consulting enologist. We had the opportunity to taste some barrel samples from their 1982 and '83 vintages; Fiore's hand was evident. Brunello (pre-1982) 0−, (since 1982)★

Villa Banfi *(zone 3), 1977*. The Mariani brothers, John and Harry, best known for their Riunite Lambrusco, have built a very large, very expensive, and very modern winery in Montalcino. With 7040 acres (2850 hectares) they are probably the largest landholders in the area. There are 1730 acres (700 hectares) of vineyards at Villa Banfi; this will eventually reach 2225 acres (900 hectares). The vines, planted at altitudes ranging from 655 to 1150 feet (200 to 350 meters), have a southern exposure. Their vineyards are planted 50 percent to moscadello; of the other half, chardonnay and cabernet sauvignon account for 15 percent each, 10 percent is sangiovese grosso, and another 10 percent is made up of other varieties including pinot grigio and sauvignon blanc. They also buy grapes.

Villa Banfi owns another Brunello estate, Poggio alle Mura, which they acquired a few years ago. That label, we are told, will be retired after the 1979 vintage.

Enzio Rivella of Villa Banfi

Their planned annual production at the Montalcino winery is 1 million cases of Bellagio, a light, sweetish white wine, and nearly 600,000 cases of other types, including 100,000 Moscadello, 70,000 each of Chardonnay and Cabernet Sauvignon, 60,000 Pinot Grigio, 50,000 Novello, 30,000 Chianti Classico riserva, and 20,000 each of Brunello and Rosso di Montalcino.

Their first Brunello, from the 1973 vintage, was sold in Italy only. They entered the U.S. market with their first estate-bottled Brunello, the '78.

Based on the 1978, 1979, and 1980 vintages, we are unimpressed with the Villa Banfi Brunello, but in all fairness to the Marianis and to their chief enologist, Ezio Rivella, it could be that the vines were too young. Thus far, their '79 was their best wine; it was also the best vintage. They do seem determined to produce a world-class Brunello, but at this point they have a ways to go. Brunello 0

Chapter 9

Carmignano

The Carmignano wine region has a very old history. The Etruscans are believed to have cultivated vines in this area in the eighth century B.C. Later, Caesar gave grants of land with vineyards in Carmignano to veterans of his legions.

Francesco Datini, the successful fourteenth-century merchant and connoisseur of wines, writes of the wine of Charmignano in his letters. He obviously held it in high esteem; he paid four times more for the Carmignano wines than for the others listed in his cellar records.

In the poem *Bacco in Toscana,* written in 1685, Aretine poet and noted medical doctor Francesco Redi sang the praises of Carmignano with these lines:

> *Ma se giara io prendo in mano*
> *di brilliante carmignano*
> *cosi grato in sen mi piove*
> *ch'ambrosia e nettar non invidio a Giove.*

> But if *I* hold a cup in hand
> of brilliant Carmignano
> so much pleasure does it bring to my heart
> that ambrosia and nectar *I* do not envy of Jove.

In 1716, Grand Duke Cosimo III de' Medici issued his Decreto Moto Proprio, which protected the name of Carmignano, followed by a *bando* proscribing the boundaries of the zone and establishing rules of wine production in Carmignano. Cosimo is said to have sent a gift of Carmignano wine to Queen Anne of England.

The Carmignano Production Zone

The Carmignano production zone covers a small area, a little more than 12 miles (20 kilometers) northwest of Florence, bordered by Monte Albano on the southeast and the Arno and Ombrone rivers on the west. The vineyards are in the *communes* of Carmignano and Poggio a Caiano on the western edge of the Chianti Montalbano zone. Vines are planted on the slopes of the hills in marly, calcerous, clayey shists and sandstone soils.

There are 213 acres (86 hectares) under vines in Carmignano. Production of the red wine has been on the increase since the inauguration of DOC in 1975. From just over 10,000 cases in 1975, output had more than doubled by 1983, reaching 25,000 cases. There are fourteen growers in Carmignano, eight of whom bottle the wine and sell it under their own label.[23]

The Carmignano Uvaggio

Carmignano, like Chianti, is made from a mixture of red and white grapes: 45 to 65 percent sangiovese, 10 to 20 percent canaiolo nero, and 6 to 10 percent cabernet or, as it is better known locally, uva francesca, plus 10 to 20 percent canaiolo bianco, trebbiano toscano, and/or malvasia and up to 5 percent of other grapes (mammolo, colorino, occhio di pernice, S. Colombano, montepulciano, and/or merlot). Most of the cabernet plantings in Carmignano are in fact cabernet sauvignon. Cabernet franc has problems of ripening in this area in some vintages, producing very little fruit.

DOC Requirements

	Minimum age (years)		Minimum alcohol	Maximum yield (gallons/acre)
	Cask	Total		
Regular	1	1.5ᵃ	12.5	599
Riserva	2	3.0ᵇ	12.5	599

Notes: a. Cannot be sold before June 1 of the second year after the harvest.
b. Aging begins from September 29.

The Rebirth of Carmignano

In 1932, when the boundaries for the Chianti region were set, including Carmignano in the Chianti Montalbano zone, the wines of this area began to be sold under the better-known Chianti name. This practice continued up until the late 1960s when the producers realized that their wines represented a higher level of quality than Chianti and therefore they would do better to sell their wine as Carmignano.

Although the wines of Carmignano had been recognized for centuries, the producers had to demonstrate to government officials significant differences from Chianti in the regulated aspects of the wine's production in order to be granted a separate DOC. There was a tradition in the zone of using foreign grape varieties, originally introduced into the area by the Medicis, so the producers decided to use cabernet sauvignon to give their wines a different *uvaggio,* or mixture of grape varieties, from that used in Chianti. Count Ugo Contini Buonacossi may have been the first to plant cabernet sauvignon in his vineyards at Tenuta Capezzana. If there was any of that variety planted in the area previously, it was very little indeed.

Since 1975, the wines of the Carmignano zone may be labeled as either Chianti Montalbano or Carmignano. The producers generally take advantage of this situation to make a selection, using their best grapes for their Carmignano.

The Other Wines of Carmignano

Besides Carmignano and Chianti Montalbano, many producers in this area also make Barco Reale and Vin Ruspo. *Barco Reale* is a younger, lighter version of Carmignano. It is made from the same grapes, but in a style to be drunk sooner.

Vin Ruspo is a rosé wine made from the free-run juice of the same grapes used to produce Carmignano. The must is left for a few hours in contact with the skins, just long enough to pick up a little color. This is an old, traditional wine in Carmignano, made by the farmers under the old system of *mezzadria.* The *mezzadri* would secretly draw off a portion of the must from the harvested grapes for themselves before they made the wine which would be divided with the *padrone* of the estate. This "stolen wine" was drunk while young and fresh in the spring following the harvest.

The Character of Carmignano

Of all the DOC wines of Tuscany, those of Carmignano are possibly the most consistent. The wines are very similar to Chianti but generally represent a higher-quality product with some refinement. They are noted for a characteristic floral aroma with suggestions of violets and irises; the cabernet frequently adds an herbaceous note.

Carmignano drinks well from its third or fourth year up to its tenth or twelfth, though it can live much longer, depending on the vintage and the producer. Rating★★★

Vintages

In general, the vintages in Carmignano are quite similar to those of Chianti, though microclimatic differences create some variations. Our personal experience with these wines is insufficient to provide a comprehensive view, but from our survey of some of the more important producers we can offer the following guide:

1984   A difficult year that required careful selection; very little riserva will be produced.
1983   Very good; the best of the decade so far.
1982   Very good, just a shade below 1983 in quality.
1981   Elegant wines for early drinking.
1980   Good wines, though not first flight.
1979   A top-flight vintage, one of the best.
1978   A good vintage.
1977   Elegant wines, similar to the 1981s.
1976   Very poor; some producers didn't bottle a Carmignano.
1975   An outstanding year, the best in modern times.
1974   Average wines that are beginning to show age.
1973   Rather light-bodied wines of average quality.
1972   Generally very poor, though some exceptions can be found.
1971   Very good.
1970   Good.
1969   Excellent.

Tasting Notes
1984

Tenuta di Capezzana *(ex-cask, 5/85)*. Fresh, fruity aroma; has a surprising amount of fruit and body for the vintage; light aftertaste.★(★)

1982

Artimino, Vino del Granduca *(4/85)*. Loads of flavor, with a richness of fruit in the center; needs a few more years yet, but promises well.★★(+)

Bacchereto *(twice 5/85)*. Aroma is closed; light to moderate tannin, fruity; a short, tannic finish.(★)

Calavria *(4/85)*. Seaweedy, oxidized.

Tenuta di Capezzana *(twice 5/85)*. Somewhat closed aroma, though with some cabernet fruit evident; well structured, a lot of flavor; needs a year or two to show itself.★★(+)

1981

Bacchereto *(5/85)*. Cherry aroma with floral notes; lightly tannic; fruity, but a bit simple; short.★

Il Poggiolo riserva *(twice 5/85)*. Floral, berrylike aroma with a touch of oak; medium-bodied, firm acidity, some tannin, flavorful, berrylike fruit; finishes on a tannic note.★★(+)

Tenuta di Capezzana *(5/85)*. Fruity, a bit simple, some oak; soft and fruity.★★ −

Villa di Capezzana riserva *(twice 5/85; 45,570 bottles)*. Loads of fruit on nose and across the palate; moderate tannin, well-knit, has style and some length.★★(★)

1980

Artimino, Riserva del Granduca *(twice 4/85)*. Fragrant aroma; quite tannic, but the fruit is evident beneath and is sweet.★(★)

Bacchereto *(twice 5/85)*. Rich, cherrylike aroma with an herbaceous back note; tannin up front, seems a bit shallow; tannic finish.

Il Poggiolo riserva *(3 times 5/85)*. Light aroma, herbaceous cabernet component evident on both nose and palate, perhaps even a bit overbearing at this stage; fruity, almost sweet, fairly well balanced; finish is a bit weak.★★

Tenuta di Capezzana *(9/83)*. Somewhat reticent aroma with a vague cherrylike note; firm, some tannin to shed, somewhat astringent, flavorful though still a bit young; in all, a nice bottle.★(★)

1979

Bacchereto *(5/85)*. Small aroma, but nice; tannic entry, fruit follows; give it two or three years.★(★)

Il Poggiolo riserva *(6 times 5/85)*. Fragrant, berrylike aroma; well balanced, flavorful, medium-bodied, good structure, has some class, well made; a light herbaceousness at the end.★★(★)

Tenuta di Capezzana *(twice 5/83)*. Moderately rich aroma with notes of tobacco, tea, chocolate, and hints of cherries in the back; tasty, light tannin, well made; needs two years or so, though it can be enjoyed now.★★(★)

Villa di Capezzana riserva *(twice 5/85; 40,850 bottles)*. Cabernet fruit and cherries on aroma; loads of flavor, some oak, a firm vein of tannin; shows a lot of class, though still quite young.★★(★ +)

Villa di Trefiano riserva *(5/85; 7045 bottles)*. Fruity aroma with flowers and cabernet character; well balanced, moderate tannin, flavorful; still a bit young.★★ +

1978

Tenuta di Capezzana *(1/84)*. Aroma has floral and fruity aspects; some acidity, fruity, a bit light but tasty, somewhat simple.★ +

Tenuta di Capezzana riserva *(twice 5/83)*. Some age evident on aroma, mellow; still has tannin to shed, flavorful, a nice bottle; give it two or three years.★★(+)

Villa di Capezzana riserva *(3 times 1/84)*. Richer and fuller than the regular, has tannin to lose, needs time, but the quality is already evident.★★

273

1977

Tenuta di Capezzana *(4/80).* Some oxidation apparent, perhaps a bad bottle.

1975

Tenuta di Capezzana riserva *(3 times 9/83).* Berrylike fruit on aroma; still has a fair amount of tannin, but has the fruit beneath to support it; notes of dried apricots and blueberries on this rich mouthful of fruit.★★

Villa di Capezzana riserva *(twice 5/85; 61,200 bottles).* Beautiful floral bouquet; already nice to drink, though with room for further improvement, still has some tannin to shed, well-knit, richly flavored, finely honed; long finish; a classic wine.★★★(★)

1974

Villa di Capezzana riserva *(4/80).* Tarry notes on aroma and a touch of oxidation, but the fruit is there; well structured, still has tannin; in all, good quality, though somewhat off.★★ −

1969

Il Poggiolo *(7/82).* Rich, intense bouquet; thick and full, with heaps of flavor.★★ +

Villa di Capezzana riserva *(5/85; 21,600 each of bottles and half-bottles).* A lovely floral bouquet; medium-bodied, soft and sweet, moderate tannin, room to improve, fruit is a trifle overripe; long, tannic finish.★★★ −

1938

Capezzana Chianti Very Old Riserva *(5/85).* Onionskin; woodsy, vaguely floral bouquet suggests autumn leaves; still has life left, body and flavor, though drying out, shows no signs of decay. For its stamina★★

*Giovanni Cianchi Baldazzi
of Fattoria Il Poggiolo*

*Conte Ugo Contini Bonacossi
of Villa Capezzana*

1937

Villa di Capezzana *(5/85)* Onionskin, moldy; over the hill.

1930

Villa di Capezzana *(5/85).* Onionskin; a lovely floral bouquet with delicacy; sweet and gentle, soft and velvety, elegant, a touch of tannin; long finish; a bit tired, but still very, very good.★★★★ −

Carmignano Producers

Artimino *(Artimino)*, 1936. This 1810-acre (732-hectare) estate has 250 acres (100 hectares) of vines planted on the hills at altitudes ranging from 330 to 920 feet (100 to 280 meters). Their Carmignano vineyards cover 111 acres (45 hectares), those for Chianti 86 (35). The remaining 49 (20) are in vines for various other Tuscan wines. New and future plantings will increase their production of Carmignano. They currently produce 46,000 to 53,000 cases of wine a year.

Their top wine is the Carmignano Riserva del Granduca. They produce a Rosso di Artimino from sangiovese, cabernet sauvignon, and montepulciano d'Abruzzo grapes and a Chianti Montalbano, plus the usual Vin Ruspo, Barco Reale, Vin Santo, and a Novello, as well as some whites. Their Carmignano is aged for two to three years in oak casks; the Chianti Montalbano for six months, and the Rosso for six to eight months. Artimino round out their line of wines with two styles of Artimino spumante, which they don't produce but buy from others. Their Carmignano is quite good. Carmignano★★

Bacchereto *(Bacchereto)*, 1925. The Bacchereto farm has an annual production of 93,000 bottles of wine, all from their own grapes. They have 38.6 acres (15.6 hectares) of vines planted at altitudes of 655 to 985 feet (200 to 300 meters). Their Carmignano is made from a blend of 60 percent sangiovese, 15 percent canaiolo nero, 10 percent cabernet sauvignon, 10 percent trebbiano toscano and malvasia, plus 5 percent mammolo, San Colombano, and occhio di pernice. The *uvaggio* for their Chianti Montalbano is 60 percent sangiovese, 25 percent canaiolo nero, and 15 percent trebbiano toscano, malvasia, and occhio di pernice.

crus/vineyards	hectares	used for
Bosco del Martini	5.0	Carmignano, Barco Reale, Vin Ruspo, Vin Santo
Santuaria	1.5	Chianti Montalbano
Vigna Sparse	6.0	Barco Reale
Vigna Vecchia	2.5	Chianti Montalbano

Carmignano★

Il Poggiolo *(Loc. Poggiolo, Carmignano)*, 1800. Giovanni Cianchi Baldazzi has 74 acres (30 hectares) of vineyards, 20 (8) in vines for Carmignano. He produces 133,000 bottles of wine a year, which includes 35,000 bottles of Carmignano.

Vineyard	Hectares
Calcinaia	7.0
Campisalti	7.0
Valle	1.0

Il Poggiolo has bottled a Carmignano since the 1860s. Until a few years ago it was made from a blend of 65 percent sangiovese, 15 percent canaiolo nero, 10 percent cabernet sauvignon, and 10 percent white grapes (trebbiano toscano and canaiolo bianco). Now the white grapes have been eliminated, and since 1979 the cabernet sauvignon for the Carmignano is being aged in small, used Port barrels. Their Carmignano is aged for two to three years in a combination of oak and chestnut casks, mostly oak. The Chianti Montalbano is a blend of 75 percent sangiovese, 10 percent canaiolo nero, 10 percent trebbiano, and 5 percent other varieties.

Il Poggiolo also produces a small quantity of very fine Vin Santo, as well as Vin Ruspo and Barco Reale. Like many others in Tuscany, they are experimenting at Il Poggiolo with cabernet sauvignon in *barrique*. Baldazzi considers 1969 his best vintage. This Carmignano is a very fine one; in our experience, only Capezzana produces a better one. Carmignano★★+

Tenuta di Capezzana *(Carmignano)*. Capezzana traces its name to a Roman legionnaire, Capitus, who received a land grant in Carmignano from Julius Caesar in about 60 or 50 B.C. Wine is believed to have been produced at Capezzana since at least that time, if not earlier.

Wine is known to have been produced here during the time of Longobard rule, "in the twenty-first year of [Charlemagne's] reign," when his son Pepin was king of the Longobards and lord of northern Italy. A parchment (now in the archives of the city of Florence) that was found on the Capezzana estate records an agreement made on 16 December 804 between Dardano, priest of the church of San Pietro in the region called Capezzana ("...*ecclesie in loco qui dicitur Capetiana...*") and Martino, son of Johannis, in which Martino gives the priest a lease on the buildings and church land with forests, gardens, vineyards, and olive groves for an annual payment in services and goods including half the olive harvest and half of the wine produced. ("...*ecclesie sancti Petri exinde per singulos annus censum reddere deveatis vino et oliva medietate....*")

The annual production at Conte Ugo Contini Bonacossi's Tenuta di Capezzana is 67,000 cases a year. The 247 acres (100 hectares) of vineyards on the estate are planted at altitudes ranging from 200 to 720 feet (60 to 220 meters). Of this, 99 acres (40 hectares) are planted for Carmignano and Barco Reale, another 66 acres (20 hectares) for Chianti Montalbano. His 7.4-acre (3-hectare) Ghiaie della Furba vineyard is planted to cabernet and merlot vines.

Vittorio Fiore, one of Italy's leading enologists, consults for Capezzana.

They produce three styles of Carmignano: Tenuta di Capezzana, Villa di Capezzana riserva (40,000 to 60,000 bottles), and Villa di Trefiano riserva (5000 to 8000 bottles). The Villa di Trefiano contains a higher proportion of cabernet. This last wine, though produced at Capezzana, is the wine of Conte Ugo's son Vittorio.

Capezzana also produces 10,000 bottles of chardonnay, 5000 to 8000 of the Ghiaie della Furba cru, and 2000 bottles of a champagne-method sparkler, as well as a Vin Ruspo rosé made from sangiovese, cabernet, and canaiolo nero, and a Vin Santo.

Without question, Villa di Capezzana is the finest Carmignano of all. In certain vintages it reaches exceptional heights of excellence. Carmignano Villa di Capezzana★★★ Tenuta di Capezzana★★ Villa Trefiano★★

Other Carmignano producer–growers

    Azienda Agricola Landini (Carmignano)
    Fattoria Ambra (Carmignano), 20 acres (8 hectares)
    Fattoria di Calavria (Comeana), 12.5 acres (5 hectares), 2.5 acres (1 hectare) of Carmignano
    Fattoria di Castello (Carmignano)
    Fattoria "La Farnete" (Comeana)
    Podere "L'Albanella" (Vergherto di Carmignano)
    Podere Le Poggiarelle (Fontanaccio di Carmignano)
    Podere Sasso (Santa Cristina a Mezzana di Carmignano), 7.5 acres (3 hectares)

Chapter 10

Vino Nobile di Montepulciano

Vino Nobile di Montepulciano is produced around the walled hilltop town of Montepulciano in the province of Siena in the southern part of Tuscany. The village of Montepulciano is of ancient origin; it may originally have been an Etruscan settlement, although no positive proof of this has been found. In the sixth century, inhabitants from Chiusi, fleeing barbarian invaders, found safety on this hill, which was then called Mons Politicus.

When vines were first planted is not known, but documents dating from the eighth and ninth centuries record the sale of lands with vineyards and payment of rents in terms of money and of wine. The earliest document found with evidence of vineyards on Montepulciano, written in 789, records the donation of land to the church, including a vineyard at "castello pulciani" on the hill known then as Mons Pulciano, which became in Italian Montepulciano.

The wine of Montepulciano was noted outside the zone as early as the 1500s. Sante Lancerio, wine steward to Pope Paul III (1534–1549), recorded the prelate's perigrinations and viniferous preferences. Among those the pontiff esteemed highly was the wine of Montepulciano. Sante Lancerio obviously shared his opinion, writing:

> The wine of Montepulciano is absolutely perfect as much in winter as in summer.... Such wines as these have aroma, color and flavor and His Holiness drinks them gladly, not so much in Rome where they were delivered in *fiaschi* but more so in Perugia.[24]

In the following century, Francesco Redi elevated the wine to regal status. In his poem *Bacco in Toscana,* the god of wine, quite overcome by a cup of Montepulciano, declares that "Montepulciano d'ogni vino è re" (Montepulciano of all wines is king).

Emanuele Pellucci[25] cites a note written by Giovan Filippo Neri in the mid-1800s referring to "il vino portato da Monte Pulciano" (the wine brought from Monte Pulciano), in which it is described as "vino nobile," the first reference found using this term for the Montepulciano wine. This is a description, however, not a name. The origin of the name Vino Nobile di Montepulciano is uncertain. Some think that there were probably two qualities of wine being produced in Montepulciano, and the finer one was referred to as the noble wine. Others theorize that the name came from the fact that it was the wine drunk by the nobility. It's not unlikely that these two went hand in hand. It's only natural that the nobility drank the better wine, in Montepulciano as well as everywhere else.

It seems more likely that the name came from the description of the wine of Montepulciano as "the king of all wines" in the famous and much cited poem by Redi.

Whether the better wines of Montepulciano were ever officially referred to as Vino Nobile in times past, we don't know. On the oldest labels it is simply Rosso Scelto di Montepulciano (selected, or choice, red wine of Montepulciano). In our century Adamo Fanetti was the first to use the name Vino Nobile for the red wine he made at Tenuta Sant' Agnese.

In 1933, a wine exhibition was organized at Siena. Fanetti brought some of his best wine to the show, where he shared a stand with Tancredi Biondi-Santi, a friend and producer whose wines he esteemed. Fanetti's wine attracted favorable attention and was sold there at auction for an unusually high price for Montepulciano wine. Encouraged by its reception, he began bottling the wine, labeling it Vino Nobile.

Observing the success of his wine, other producers of Montepulciano began calling their wines Vino Nobile as well. Fanetti sued for the exclusive right to the name, but the judgment went against him. At the second Siena Exhibition a few years later, a number of other poliziani producers also presented Vino Nobile, including Baiocchi, Bologna, Bracci Testasecca, Bucelli, Contucci, Pilacci, Ricci Paracciani, and Waldergan.

Important foreign recognition came when the Fanetti Vino Nobile won a gold medal in 1937 at the Grand Prix de Paris.

The Vino Nobile Production Zone

The vines for Vino Nobile are planted at altitudes ranging from 820 to 1970 feet (250 to 600 meters). There are approximately 1630 acres (660 hectares) of vineyards, which are cultivated by 161 growers; another 1655 (670) are under vines for Chianti Colli Senesi. Today there is virtually no room for further expansion in the vineyards. The average annual production of Vino Nobile di Montepulciano in the period from 1974 to 1983 was 230,000 cases. There are thirty-two producers in the zone who bottle their wine.

The Uvaggio of Vino Nobile

DOC required an *uvaggio* of 50 to 70 percent prugnolo gentile, or sangiovese grosso, a subvariety of sangiovese; 10 to 20 percent canaiolo nero; 10 to 20 percent trebbiano toscano and/or malvasia del Chianti; and up to 8 percent of mammolo and/or pulcinculo, also known as grechetto bianco. The mammolo vine, fairly common here, gives to the wine, they say, its characteristic scent of sweet violets *(mammola)*.

Vino Nobile di Montepulciano, then, was a red wine that could be made from as much as 28 percent white grapes, and that was before the allowance of 10 percent of must or wine from outside the zone, of unspecified color, that could be added. Under the new DOCG regulations, the percentage of mammolo and/or pulcinculo has been reduced to 5 percent, and the limit on white grapes is being changed; in the future not more than 5 percent will be allowed. The regulation on correcting with must or wine to bring up the alcohol has also been amended; it can be made now only with Vino Nobile (up to 15 percent, from another vintage).

DOC Requirements

	Minimum age (years)		Minimum alcohol	Maximum yield (gallons/acre)
	cask	total		
DOC regular	2	2[a]	12.0%	748
riserva	2	3[a]	12.0	748
riserva speciale	2	4[a]	12.0	748
DOCG regular	2	2[b]	12.5	599/556[c]
riserva	2	3[b]	12.5	599/556[c]

Notes: [a] Aging period from November 1 the year of the harvest.
      [b] Aging period from January 1 after the harvest; cask aging from April 1.
      [c] When picked, 599 gallons/acre (56 hectoliters/hectare) are allowed; after aging, only 556 gallons/acre (52 hectoliters/hectare).

Consorzio del Vino Nobile
di Montepulciano

Carta delle Zone di Produzione

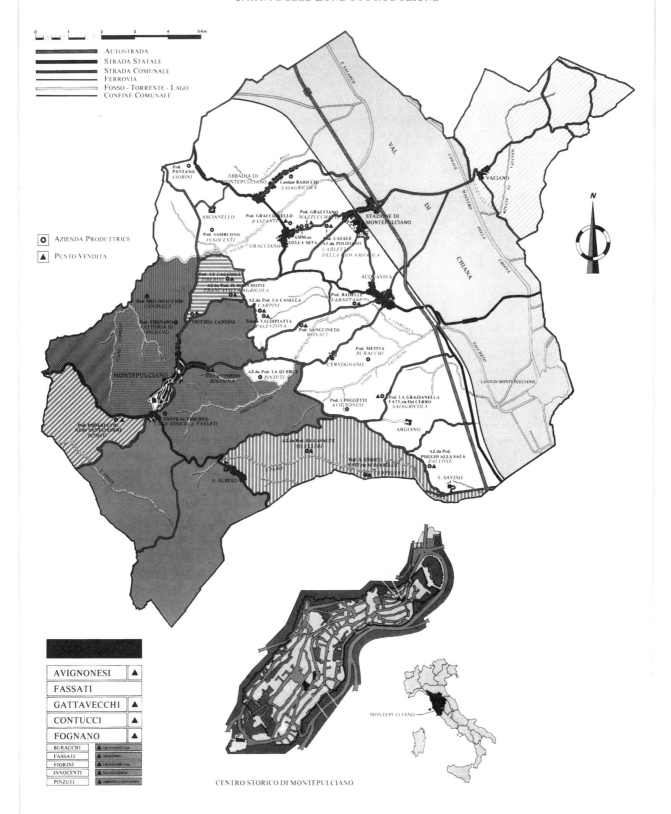

Autostrada
Strada Statale
Strada Comunale
Ferrovia
Fosso - Torrente - Lago
Confine Comunale

0   1   2   3   4   5 Km

○ Azienda Produttrice
▲ Punto Vendita

AVIGNONESI	▲
FASSATI	
GATTAVECCHI	▲
CONTUCCI	▲
FOGNANO	▲

BURACCHI		▲ CHIUSI CITTÀ
FASSATI		▲ SINALUNGA
FIORINI		▲ CHIANCIANO T.me
INNOCENTI		▲ Soc. POLCIANO
PINZUTI		▲ ABBAZIA S. SALVATORE

CENTRO STORICO DI MONTEPULCIANO

279

The Character and Quality of Vino Nobile

Vino Nobile in its youth can be rough and tannic but, given five to eight years of aging, mellows to a soft, velvety wine, complex in aroma and rich in flavor. At its best it is a wine to accompany roast meats—beef and lamb—and game birds. This is Vino Nobile at its best; unfortunately, the wine rarely comes up to this level.

Vino Nobile di Montepulciano is produced from a blend of grapes similar to that for Chianti, and the Montepulciano region is within the Chianti Colli Senesi zone. In fact, this wine, despite its name, is generally very common. For too many years it has been no more than an overrated, overpriced, variable Chianti, and not much else. But changes are afoot. Since 1982, there seems to have been a dramatic improvement in overall quality in Montepulciano. We were told that this is due to a more serious effort on the part of the better producers, who came to the realization that the wine wasn't living up to its title.

To begin with, it seems there's a more careful selection of the grapes being made at harvest. The more serious producers are using the best fruit only in their Vino Nobile and declassifying the rest to Chianti Colli Senesi, Rosso di Montepulciano (soon to be DOC), *vino da tavola,* or, in the worst cases, selling the wine off in bulk, unlabeled. The changes can be noted in the marked improvement in quality. In some cases outside help has been brought in. Able enologists such as Maurizio Castelli (consulting for Boscarelli and Poliziano) and Vittorio Fiore (for Tre Rose) are also sure to make a difference.

Regrettably, not all the producers have pulled themselves up as firmly. Some of the respected names of the past, such as Contucci and Fanetti, while still producing good wines, have slipped noticeably in recent years. The zone's finest producer, Bologna Buonsignori, is unfortunately no longer making wine, having retired due to advanced age. There are some bright new lights appearing on the horizon: Poliziano, since 1982 under the able hand of Dott. Federico Carletti, and Avignonesi, for two. Saiagricola's Fattoria del Cerro and Cantine Baiocchi are also top flight. Although Boscarelli, a long-time favorite, has had its ups and downs, we feel they are a producer to keep an eye on. Casalte, Pantano, and Raspanti, three producers new to us, also show promise.

The basic material is there. With the new expertise and renewed emphasis on quality, we look forward to more really fine wines from Montepulciano, Vino Nobiles worthy of the name. Rating pre-1982 ★★ − ; since 1982 ★★★

Rating the Producers

★★★★	★	0
Bologna Buonsignori	Buracchi	Bigi Luigi
	Casella	− Bordini
★★★	Fassati	Caggiole (Podere Il Macchione)
Avignonesi	Fattoria Gracciano	− Cantina del Redi
Cantine Baiocchi (Saiagricola)	di Mazzucchelli Franco	Cecchi Luigi
Fattoria del Cerro (Saiagricola)	Fattoria Fognano	Gattavecchi
Poliziano (from 1982; previously ★) +	Melini	La Querce
	Poliziano (pre-1982; since ★★★)	Podere Ferretto
★★	Santavenere	(Fattoria delle Maestrelle)
Boscarelli	Scopetello	− Poggio alla Sala
Casalte	Tenuta di Gracciano	Sanguineto
Contucci	di Della Seta Ferrari Corbelli	Tistarelli Mario
Fanetti	Vecchia Cantina	Tripusa
Pantano		
Raspanti Giuseppe		
Valdipiatta		

Tasting Notes
1984

It's too soon to say with certainty, but prospects are not good. It was a difficult harvest. Boscarelli, Del Cerro, Poliziano, and Fanetti produced no Vino Nobile, and Avignonesi made no red wine of any kind. Fassati produced what appears, from cask, to be a fairly good Vino Nobile.

Fassati *(ex-cask 4/85).* Very deep, purplish color; intense, cherrylike aroma; heaps of flavor, almost sweet, high acid.★+

1983 [★★★★]

We were quite impressed with the style and elegance of the few '83s we tasted from cask in April 1985. Niederbacher gives the vintage three stars. Boscarelli and La Querce, among others, rate it highly. Fassati, however, said the weather was too hot for them and that there wasn't enough rain.

Avignonesi *(ex-cask 4/85).* Fruity aroma rises out of the glass, touch of oak up front followed by notes of tar, flowers, and cherries; rich, ripe, sweet fruit, well balanced, not as full as the '82, but has more style and elegance.★★(★)

Fassati *(ex-cask 4/85).* Floral aroma with some oak; seems rather light, acid on the high side, flavorful.★

Poliziano *(ex-cask 4/85).* Aroma displays loads of fruit and some tarlike notes; fairly tannic, but with the stuffing to support it, chewy; tannic finish.★★(★)

Valdipiatta *(ex-cask 4/85).* Dark, almost opaque; enormous richness on nose; incredible concentration on palate, tannic, a wine of huge proportions.★★(+)

1982 [★★★+]

Niederbacher rates the year at three stars, on the same level as 1983. Most producers also place it about equal to the previous vintage. The wines are fuller, richer, and more concentrated, and they will probably be longer lived. But we prefer the style and elegance of the '83s.

Avignonesi *(ex-cask 4/85).* Some oak, with vague cherry and floral notes; well balanced, has almost a sweetness to it, moderate tannin; some length.★★(★)

Baiocchi *(twice 4/85).* Richly concentrated aroma with floral overtones; some tannin to shed, flavor of ripe blackberries, licorice notes from the aroma through the flavor and the finish, richly concentrated, a big wine.★★(★)

Boscarelli *(4/85).* Reticent aroma, but with some fruit evident, a touch of oak in back; a mouthful of tannin gives way to sweet vanilla flavor followed by fruit; a firm, tannic finish★★(+)

Del Cerro *(4/85).* This is supposed to be the same wine as Baiocchi; we find a slight difference. Floral, fruity aroma; seems sweet fruit is so rich and ripe, acid seems a bit low, has less complexity than the Baiocchi.★★(+)

Fassati *(ex-cask 4/85).* Fairly nice fruit on the nose, vaguely cherrylike; fairly full-bodied, a mouthful of flavor, moderate tannin.★★

Poggio alla Sala *(4/85).* Light nose; has tannin and fruit; recalls Marsala.

Poliziano *(ex-cask 4/85).* Oak dominates the initial aroma, but richly fruited in background; loads of tannin, with the fruit to back it up; the best of the '82s tasted.★★(★)

Valdipiatta *(ex-cask 4/85).* Berrylike aroma with a hint of tar; heaps of tannin and heaps of fruit; very young.★(★)

1981 ★★+

Niederbacher ranks the year at three stars, equal with 1982 and 1983. At Fassati, they consider it the best vintage since 1967. Boscarelli places it after 1982 and 1983. Dott. Federico Carletti of Poliziano said that while the grapes in 1981 were the best of any vintage in the 1980s thus far, temperatures were too hot during fermentation, and consequently their wines didn't achieve their full potential.

Avignonesi *(twice 4/85).* Fruity, floral aroma with some oak and notes of cherries; well structured, has style, a wine of character.★★★

Boscarelli riserva *(4/85).* Richly fruited aroma, fairly intense; moderate tannin, a nice mouthful of flavor, well balanced, has some style; give it about three more years.★★(+)

Casalte *(twice 4/85).* Nice aroma of spice and berries, recalls a Côtes du Rhône wine; ditto on the flavor, moderate tannin and fruit, shows quality; an off note mars the finish.★★(+)

Del Cerro riserva *(twice 4/85).* Floral bouquet with ripe berries in the background; seems more tannic than the '82 and somewhat lighter in body, loads of flavor; jamlike, overripe fruit on finish.★★

281

1981

Fanetti (4/85). Richly fruited aroma with hints of flowers and tar; astringent, fairly tannic, but has the fruit to back it up; a bit harsh at the end.★(★ +)

Fassati (ex-cask 4/85). Licorice and rich fruit on aroma; fairly tannic, with loads of flavor beneath, very well balanced.★★(+)

Fattoria di Gracciano, Podere Cervognano riserva (twice 4/85). A fairly reticent aroma that hints of fruit; light tannin, shallow; tannic finish; a dull wine.

Fognano riserva (twice 4/85). Peppery, fruity aroma reminiscent of a Côtes du Rhône; follows through on the palate, light tannin, nice fruit, young; some quality evident.★(★)

La Querce Az. Agr. di Pinzi Pinzuti Lido (twice 4/85). Both times there was some oxidation; dull and flat.

Podere Le Caggiole (4/85). Small aroma, some fruit evident; dull, wheat-like flavor, astringent; tannic finish.

Poggio alla Sala (4/85). Has as cooked fruit character; shallow; short.

Poliziano (ex-cask 4/85). Lots of nice fruit on the nose, also a touch of licorice and a tarlike note; less impressive on the palate, nice entry, then shallow; rather short.★

Poliziano riserva (twice 4/85). Complex bouquet with nuances of licorice and cherries; nice entry, then a bit shallow; tannic finish.★

Raspanti Cav. Giuseppe (twice 4/85). Pretty, floral aroma with notes of pine; has a sweetness to the flavor, a bit light, some tannin, very nice until the finish, which is somewhat bitter.★★

Santavenere (twice 4/85). First bottle had a problem with hydrogen sulfide.

Second bottle: Flowers, cherries, and spice on aroma; some tannin, fruity flavor, perhaps too fruity, lacks Vino Nobile character.★★★ (as a light, fresh, fruity red); ★ (as a Vino Nobile)

Valdipiatta (ex-cask 4/85). Tar and fruit on aroma; heaps of tannin, very young yet, but shows promise.★(★)

1980 ★ +

This was a mixed vintage; they won't be long-lived wines. Niederbacher gives it two stars. Boscarelli said it was poor and didn't bottle. We find it sort of in between the two evaluations.

Buracchi riserva (4 times 4/85). Two bottles were corked. Another was overly tannic for the low fruit and lacking in character. The best bottle had a nice aroma of fruit with chocolate and spicy aspects; fruity, lacking in length and style.★

Casella (twice 4/85). Cherrylike fruit on aroma, vaguely floral; tannic, but with sufficient fruit to carry it, the fruit seems almost sweet.★(★)

Contucci (twice 4/85). First bottle: Stinky, reeking of mercaptans; a disgusting flavor of barnyard and rubber tire.

Another bottle: Tarry aroma; tannic with a core of almost sweet fruit beneath.★(★)

Fassati, Podere Fonte al Vescovo (3 times 4/85). As with many other Vino Nobiles, there was bottle variation. Best bottle: cherrylike fruit with a note of tar; moderate tannin, enough fruit to support it, needs a few years yet, should make a good bottle.★(★)

Fognano riserva (4/85). Light aroma with fairly nice fruit, somewhat reminiscent of a Côtes du Rhône wine; carries through on palate, moderate tannin; needs another year or two.★(★ −)

Gattavecchi (3 times 4/85). No variation here— all were unbalanced, low in fruit, and lacking personality.

Sanguineto riserva (4/85). Vaguely floral, fruity aroma; overly tannic, shallow; short.

Scopetto (twice 4/85). Lightly floral bouquet; some tannin, good fruit in the center, fairly well balanced; a bit simple.★(+)

Tenuta di Gracciano (4/85). Quite tannic, doubtful if there's enough fruit.

Valdipiatta (ex-cask 4/85). Tar, fruit, and oak on aroma; short, tannic finish. Where will it go?

Vecchia Cantina riserva (4/85). Light aroma with fairly nice fruit; ditto the flavor; marred by an off note at the end.★ −

1979 ★★★

This was a very good vintage for many producers.

Avignonesi (4/85). Expansive, floral bouquet with a vague cherrylike note; very well balanced, an elegant, stylish wine, velvety; very long finish; has room for improvement yet.★★★

Bologna Buonsignori riserva (4/85). Pretty nose of ripe fruit and flowers, cherry and tarlike notes; sweet flavor of ripe berries and cherries, soft and round, some tannin, has real style.★★★

Boscarelli (3 times 9/83). Rich aroma, though not fully open, ripe fruit is evident; flavorful, still needs time to soften.★(★)

Boscarelli riserva (4/85). Aroma displays some oak over a lot of fruit with a tarlike aspect and a vaguely floral note; loads of tannin, but the fruit is there to carry it; has a sweetness to it; a rough, tannic finish.★★(★)

Carletti della Giovampaola (second label of Poliziano) (4/85). Not much nose, but a lot of flavor, cherrylike fruit, moderate tannin, fairly well balanced.★★(+)

Casella riserva (4/85). Tar and fruit on aroma; fairly nice fruit on entry gives way to tannin. Is there enough fruit? We suspect not.

Del Cerro riserva speciale (4/85). Aroma shows some development, with vague tarlike and floral nuances; light tannin, fairly fruity, some spice; a vague off note at the end.★★

Fanetti riserva (twice 5/85). Malvasia character on aroma, some flowers, tar, also cherries; light tannin, a bit simple, drinkable, but no real character.★

Fassati (11/84). Reticent aroma; some tannin to lose, flavorful, quite young.★(+)

1979

Fassati, Podere Fonte al Vescovo *(twice 4/85)*. Floral aroma with cherrylike notes; somewhat astringent, acid seems a bit high, flavorful; shows some promise.★★

Fognano riserva *(4/85)*. Spicy, cherry aroma; well balanced, moderate tannin, flavorful; short.★(+)

Gattavecchi *(twice 5/85)*. Unbalanced, too much tannin for the fruit.

Le Pietrose riserva (produced by Fattoria del Cerro) *(4/85)*. Nice nose, vaguely floral; overripe, pruny taste; not as good as the del Cerro.★

Tistarelli Mario (bottled by CA.VI.O.T.) *(4 times 3/85)*. Oxidized. The bottles tasted in 1983 were not oxidized but had very little to offer.

"Tripusa," Enoteca Europea riserva *(4/85)*. Astringent, low in fruit, unbalanced.

Valdipiatta *(twice 4/85)*. Perfumed aroma with notes of tar and cherries; light tannin, loads of flavor, soft-centered; needs more age.★★

Vecchia Cantina *(twice 4/85)*. Light nose; has tannin and the fruit to carry it; somewhat astringent on aftertaste.★

1978 ★★

The wines of 1978 were more variable than those of 1979.

Avignonesi *(4/85)*. Floral bouquet, has delicacy; well balanced, light- to medium-bodied, flavorful, quite ready, soft and smooth, room for further improvement; light tannin at the end, which is a bit short.★★+

Boscarelli *(6 times 8/82)*. Cherrylike aroma marred by a slight harshness; nice fruit, still needs a few years to soften; short finish. We have found considerable bottle variation with this wine.★(+)

Boscarelli *(4/85; aged in barrique)*. Some oak on the nose and a lot of fruit; falls down on palate; tannic and lacking in fruit.

Cantina del Redi *(4/85)*. Baked, cooked, awful.

Casella riserva *(4/85)*. Overly tannic for the fruit.

Cecchi Luigi *(twice 1/84)*. Awful. A bottle tasted a few months earlier was unstructured and shallow.

Del Cerro riserva speciale *(3 times 4/85)*. Aroma shows complexity of bottle age, with nuances of flowers and cherries; well balanced, soft and smooth, some style, ready now; very good indeed.★★★

Fanetti *(10/81)*. Nose is somewhat muted; some tannin, soft, a bit light-bodied, tasty; some style and length.★★

Fanetti riserva speciale *(twice 1/84)*. Fruity floral bouquet; firm and tannic, has structure and fruit; needs two to three more years.★(★)

Fassati *(11/84)*. Small nose; astringent, not a lot of fruit. Where will it go?

Fognano riserva *(1/84)*. Almondlike notes on aroma; unbalanced, dull, not a lot to it.

Gattavecchi *(twice 5/85)*. Unbalanced with tannin, coarse, no real character.

Poggio alla Sala *(5 times 1/84)*. None of the bottles amounted to much; all had a baked, cooked character reminiscent of a southern wine (could the 10 percent from outside the zone by showing its nature, or did they use concentrate?); dull, unbalanced, flat.

Poliziano riserva speciale *(4/85)*. Floral bouquet with some nice fruit in the back; moderate tannin, nice entry; tannic finish that tails off at the end.

Valdipiatta *(twice 5/85)*. Fragrant though light aroma; medium-bodied, fruity, a bit simple perhaps, but drinkable enough; short.★

Vecchia Cantina riserva *(twice 3/84)*. Nice nose, though has a bit of an overripe character; flat and shallow. The bottle tasted two months earlier was considerably better and merited★.

1977 ★★

The '77s are good wines, but fail to live up to their original acclaim.

Bologna Buonsignori riserva *(5/85)*. Woodsy bouquet with floral and berrylike nuances; still has tannin to lose, well balanced, flavorful, elegant, and stylish; needs two years or more, but approachable now.★★★(+)

Bordini riserva (bottled by L.B.&F. of Orvieto) *(9/83)*. Nice nose up front, but with an off-putting note lurking in the back; off flavors, thin.

Boscarelli *(3 times 8/82)*. As with the '78 Boscarelli, we found considerable bottle variation. In this bottle mercaptans were painfully evident.

A bottle tasted three weeks earlier: Lovely bouquet; nice flavor, well balanced; shows promise.★★

Buracchi *(4/85)*. Some oxidation; reminiscent of a wet dog.

Carletti della Giovampaola riserva (second label of Poliziano) *(4/85)*. Showing age on aroma; very shallow and a bit thin toward the back.

Contucci *(4/80)*. Aroma is still closed, but fruit and oak evident; nicely balanced, some tannin, a bit light, good structure; nearly ready.★(+)

Del Cerro riserva speciale *(4/85)*. Complex bouquet, toasty and fruity; well balanced, soft and round, vaguely sweet; rich, blackberry-like fruit; some length.★★+

Fassati *(3 times 5/84)*. Cherrylike aroma with a floral aspect; good fruit on entry, low acid, has an overripe quality; dull finish.

Fassati riserva *(5/85)*. Dull and flat, with a somewhat cooked character.

Fognano riserva *(4 times 9/83)*. Pale color shows considerable age, browning; some fruit on nose marred by a vague off note; lacking in structure, weight, and definition.

Pantano *(4/85)*. Corked.

Podere Ferretto, prop. Fattoria delle Maestrelle (bottled by Storiche Cantine) *(5/85; 61,100 bottles)*. Toffee notes on aroma, vaguely medicinal; lacks weight, structure, and definition.

Podere Il Macchione, Le Caggiole *(4/85)*. Stinky; unbalanced, bitter.

1977

Tenuta di Gracciano (*3 times 8/82*). Nose a bit closed, but already shows some fruit; has tannin and the stuffing to support it, lacks style; needs a few years yet.★

Valdipiatta (*twice 4/85*). Lovely bouquet of flowers, fruit, and vanilla; light to moderate tannin; fairly nice fruit; short, tannic aftertaste.★

1976 0

This year was very bad from the start. Fassati bottled; Boscarelli and del Cerro did not.

1975 ★★

Niederbacher gives 1975 four stars, calling it one of the all-time greats. It's amazing how few wines lived up to expectations. For the most part they are ready for present drinking and can only decline from here.

Bologna Buonsignori riserva (*4/85*). Vague off note mars a very nice aroma; some tannin to shed, well structured, heaps of flavor, young; shows a lot of quality.★★(★)

Boscarelli (*4 times 3/85*). Vaguely floral aroma; some tannin and acid, fairly good fruit; alcohol mars the finish. It was better between two and four years ago when it merited ★★ + , it has aged.★

Carletti della Giovampaola riserva speciale (second label of Poliziano) (*4/85*). Corked.

Contucci (*4/80*). Floral bouquet; well balanced, tasty, quite nice.★★

Fanetti riserva (*3 times 8/82*). Fruity aroma; fairly well balanced, flavorful, better on palate than on nose, but a bit pedestrian.★

Fassati (*4 times 3/82*). Mineral notes on aroma; some tannin, some fruit; ok, not special.

Fassati riserva (*5 times 5/85*). Bottle variation here. The best and most recent was soft, fruity, easy, and agreeable.★ +

Fattoria di Gracciano (*10/80*). Aroma has a hint of chestnuts and a harshness; considerable tannin, some potential.★

Fattoria di Gracciano riserva (*9/79*). Vaguely floral aroma; nice fruit, needs more time, lacks depth.★

Fattoria di Gracciano riserva speciale (*12/80*). Some complexity on nose; shallow; some alcohol mars the finish.

Fognano (*twice 4/85*). A big zero; very little to it, lacks character and structure.

Fognano riserva speciale (*twice 3/82*). Good fruit on aroma, some oak; flavorful, fairly well balanced, has tannin to lose; a bit short.★

Melini riserva speciale (*3 times 9/83*). Fragrant perfume; good fruit, some tannin to lose, medium-bodied; in all, a nice glass of wine.★★ −

Poggio alla Sala (*4/85*). Disgusting aroma and flavor.

Poliziano riserva (*twice 10/81*). Fragrant; some tannin, tasty; ready now.★ +

Tenuta di Gracciano (*4/85*). Odor of mercaptans; overly tannic, low fruit; unimpressive, to say the least.

Vecchia Cantina riserva (*4/85*). Toasty, fruity aroma; moderate tannin, flavorful entry; tails off toward the end.★ −

1974 ★−

Most '74s are approaching senility; they should be drunk up without delay. The Bologna Buonsignori riserva is still very good. If you're lucky enough to have any, you don't need to be concerned.

Bologna Buonsignori riserva (*4/85*). Delicate floral bouquet with a berrylike aspect; sweet and velvety, round and smooth, a wine of quality, balance, and style.★★★

Bordini (*twice 3/82*). Slight oxidation mars the nose, which has a raisiny note; taste of overripe, raisined grapes.

Del Cerro riserva speciale (*4/85*). A lot of age apparent on the nose; tannin on entry; still a lot of flavor, but not to keep, drinkable now; somewhat off at the end.★

Fanetti riserva (*3 times 3/82*). Floral aroma with tarry notes; overly tannic for the fruit.

Fassati, Podere Fonte al Vescovo (*4/85*). Honey and berries on the aroma; ripe, berrylike fruit; near its peak, surprisingly good.★★

Fattoria di Gracciano riserva (*4/80*). Light, fragrant aroma; nice flavor, still has tannin to soften.★

1973 ★

This vintage was highly acclaimed at one time. Niederbacher rated it at three stars. Drink them up now.

Baiocchi (*4/85*). Medium garnet, brick at rim; light nose; some fruit, light tannin, very soft and smooth; some tannin at the end; quite ready, not to hold.★ +

Bigi Luigi riserva speciale (*11/78*). Light color; small nose; light-bodied, not much tannin, drinkable.★

Bologna Buonsignori riserva (*5/85*). Woodsy, berrylike aroma; well balanced, still some tannin, but soft and ready, strawberrylike fruit; fairly long on finish.★★★

1973

Fanetti (*4 times 8/82*). Awful cardboard smell (dekkra?). Bottles tasted three years earlier were quite nice, with a fragrant bouquet and a hint of sweetness; they merited ★★; this one 0.

Fanetti riserva speciale (*4/85*). Off odors, dank.

Fassati (*12/79*). Light, perfumed aroma; high acid; shallow.

Fassati, Podere Fonte al Vescovo (*4/85*). Floral bouquet with some fruit, but showing age; still has tannin, nice fruit up front, drying out.★

Fattoria di Gracciano riserva (*9/79*). Some volatile acidity; light fruity; bitter finish.

Poliziano riserva (*4/80*). Nutty aroma, some fruit; light and tasty, balanced, some tannin.★

Valdipiatta (*5/85*). Corky.

Vecchia Cantina (*8/82*). Pale garnet; light, fragrant aroma; a bit light in body, tasty, no tannin remains, almost sweet; at its peak.★

1972 0

This was a hopeless vintage. The wines didn't stand a chance.

1971 0

The 1971 vintage was another poor one. The wines are too old now.

Fassati (*twice 8/82*). Tart, lacks flavor; shot.

Fassati, Podere Fonte al Vescovo (*4/85*). Dried, berrylike fruit on aroma; tannic, some fruit; drying out.

Fattoria del Pantano (*4/85; 500 bottles*). Vaguely floral bouquet; nice entry; moderate tannin, some sweetness; not to keep, but nice now.★★ −

Fattoria di Gracciano riserva (*10/80*). Browning; alcohol mars the nose; not much flavor left.

Poliziano riserva speciale (*11/80*). Pale; nutty, fruity aroma; light, some tannin, and not much beneath it.

1970 ★★

This was a highly acclaimed vintage, and the wines have lasted well. There is, however, no need to keep them any longer. Niederbacher gave it four stars.

Baiocchi (*4/85*). Floral, vaguely toasty aroma that shows some age; soft and flavorful, a bit past its peak, but quite nice now; touch of tannin at the end.★★

Contucci riserva speciale (*twice 4/85*). Aroma of flowers and fruit; shows a lot of development; well balanced, heaps of flavor, soft, lovely now, has some style; could even improve.★★★

Fanetti riserva speciale (*8 times 1/84*). Vaguely floral bouquet; loads of flavor, quite ready; not to keep.★★

Fassati (*4 times 8/82*). Still some fruit on the nose; nothing left on the palate. It was better a few years ago; in fact, it was quite nice.

Fassati, Podere Fonte al Vescovo (*4/85*). Small nose with some fruit; drying out, though there's still some fruit left.

Melini riserva speciale (*6 times 3/83*). Some oxidation on the nose; drying on the palate. In 1979 and 1980, this was a very good bottle of wine meriting ★★. Today it's too old.

Poliziano (*twice 4/85*). Floral aroma; light, drying out, fruit on entry, then nothing.

Poliziano, Fattoria Casale riserva (*10/81*). Shows age on nose but very little complexity; some dullness, beginning to dry out.

1969 [0]

Niederbacher gave 1969 two stars. Most likely the wines are too old now.

1968 0

The '68s are long gone.

Fassati (*3 times 8/82*). Some fruit still evident, but the wine has dried out.

Fassati, Podere Fonte al Vescovo (*4/85*). Aroma of an old wine; still some flavor interest, though drying out.

1967 0

Originally 1967 was one of the all-time great vintages, perhaps deserving four stars. The few we've tasted recently were completely gone.

Contucci riserva speciale (*4/85*). Faded.

Fassati (*twice 8/82*). Nothing of interest remains.

Fassati, Podere Fonte al Vescovo (*4/85*). Oxidized.

Older Vintages

Most, if not all, older vintages are too old now. But for the record, here is how authorities in the zone rated them:

★★★★   1958

★★★   1964, 1962, 1954, 1952, 1947
★★   1966, 1961, 1957, 1951, 1949, 1945
★   1960, 1956, 1955, 1953, 1950, 1948, 1946
0   1965, 1963, 1959

1965 Baiocchi riserva *(4/85).* Nose shows a lot of age; vaguely jammy, drying out, but still has flavor interest and fruit.★ −

1964 Baiocchi riserva *(4/85).* Floral bouquet, vaguely honeyed; light tannin, some delicacy, smooth textured; some age shows, but still very good.★★

1957 Fratelli Baiocchi riserva *(4/85).* Brick-red robe, orange rim; bouquet has delicacy and floral notes; velvety, round and sweet, very ready, light tannin, complex; long finish with notes of blueberries; perhaps just beginning to dry out.★★★

1953 Fratelli Baiocchi riserva *(4/85).* Orangish brick robe; toasty, floral bouquet, vaguely berrylike with a hint of leather; soft and round, sweet and delicate; very long finish has a touch of tannin.★★★

Vino Nobile di Montepulciano Producers

Alberto Falvo, Adriana Avignonesi, Ettore Falvo of Avignonesi

Avignonesi *(Montepulciano), 1978.* Avignonesi owns 195 acres (93 hectares) of vines; 45 (18) in Montepulciano and 150 (60) in Cortona. Their vineyards in Montepulciano are planted for Vino Nobile and Chianti Colli Senesi. They also have 10 acres (4 hectares) of cabernet franc. Most of their vineyards were replanted in 1972, and a few in 1973 and 1974.

Vineyard	Acres	Hectares	Total yield tons	Total yield quintali
Caprile	15	6	39	350
Marmo	10	4	24	220
Poggio di Sopra	20	8	49	440
Total	45	18	112	1010

Avignonesi produces 30,000 to 40,000 bottles of Vino Nobile a year and 10,000 to 12,000 of Chianti Colli Senesi. Their Chianti, which is not aged in wood, will in the future, like many of the Chiantis of this area, become Rosso di Montepulciano. Their Vino Nobile is aged in fairly new oak casks, and they are experimenting with *barriques.* Since the 1978 vintage, their Vino Nobile has been made without white grapes.

Avignonesi also produces 15,000 to 18,000 bottles a year of the *barrique-*aged sangiovese–cabernet blend, Grifi; two white wines—100,000 to 120,000 bottles of Bianco Vergine Valdichiana and 18,000 to 20,000 of Malvasia—as well as what is without a doubt the finest Vin Santo we have ever tasted. They produce a scant 600 to 800 bottles a year of this outstanding dessert wine. Beginning with 1985, they have added a Chardonnay to their repertoire.

There is currently no finer producer in the zone. The Avignonesi Vino Nobile is definitely one of the best. Vino Nobile★★★

Baiocchi. See Del Cerro.

Bigi Luigi. The Bigi Vino Nobile can be good, though unexciting. There are many better Chiantis available. Vino Nobile 0

Bologna Buonsignori Nobili F.lli Luigi e Leopoldo, Fattoria Comizio *(Montepulciano).* The few wines we've tasted from this producer have been outstanding wines of style and balance. They are, or were, the zone's finest. Unfortunately, Sig. Bologna Buonsignori has retired, and the wine is no longer being produced. The last vintage he bottled was 1979. Vino Nobile★★★★

Bordoni. The bottles we've tasted from Bordoni thus far have been quite mediocre, if not downright poor. They are bottled by L.B.&F. of Orvieto. Vino Nobile 0

Boscarelli *(Cervognano di Montepulciano), 1963.* Boscarelli is considered by many to be the top estate in the zone. We have found their wines, like nearly every other Vino Nobile di Montepulciano, to be variable. They are nevertheless among the zone's better producers.

They have 22 acres (9 hectares) of vines planted at an altitude of about 655 feet (200 meters). Half the acreage is planted to grapes for Vino Nobile, the other half for Chianti Colli Senesi. They produce about 30,000 bottles of each. Since the 1979 vintage, their wines have been bottled by a mobile unit, a service used by a number of small producers in the zone. On this bottling-line-on-wheels, the wines are filtered before bottling. Previously their wines were not filtered.

At Boscarelli they make a careful selection of the grapes, using only the best for the Vino Nobile. The next quality goes into their Chianti, and the balance is used to produce a wine which is sold unlabeled in bulk.

The white grapes will be eliminated from Vino Nobile after the 1985 vintage, Signora Corradi de Ferrari told us. With the 1978 vintage, at the urging of their agent, they experimented with *barrique* aging but were not happy with the results.

The first wine sold in bottle under their label was the '68.

Since the beginning of 1985, enologist Maurizio Castelli has been consulting for Boscarelli; we have high expectations for future vintages. Vino Nobile★★ (for now)

Buracchi *(Montepulciano Stazione).* Buracchi owns 20 acres (8 hectares) of vineyards, 8.6 (3.5) in vines for Vino Nobile. From the rest they produce the other typical wines of the area: Chianti, Vin Santo, and a white wine. Their annual production of Vino Nobile is 20,000 to 26,500 bottles. The wine is aged in a combination of oak and chestnut casks. Vino Nobile★

Cantina del Redi *(Montepulciano)*. The wines we've tasted from this producer are a disgrace to the name. *Povero* Redi! Vino Nobile 0 −

Caggiole Podere Il Macchione. We didn't like their '77 Vino Nobile, nor did we like their '81. Vino Nobile 0

Carletti della Giovampaola. This is a second label used by Poliziano.

*Paola Silvestri Barioffi
of Fattoria Casalte*

Casalte *(Sant' Albino di Montepulciano), 1975.* Paola Silvestri Barioffi owns 20 acres (8 hectares) of vineyards: 6 (2.5) for Vino Nobile and 9 (3.7) for Chianti. The first Vino Nobile they bottled was the '79 (2000 bottles). They currently produce about 66,500 bottles of wine a year, 20 percent of which is Vino Nobile, 50 percent Chianti; the balance is white and rosé wine. They appear to be a producer to watch. Vino Nobile★★

Casella *(Gracciano), 1969.* Alfio Carpini, who also makes the wine for Valdipiatta, has 12.4 acres (5 hectares) of vines on his Casella estate, from which he produces about 31,000 bottles of wine a year. The wines thus far have been fairly good. Vino Nobile★

Castellani, Tenuta La Ciarliana *(Gracciano), 1962.* This firm owns 42 acres (17 hectares), one-third of which is planted to vines for Vino Nobile. The wines are aged in a combination of oak and chestnut casks.

Cecchi Luigi. This Chianti Classico producer markets a Vino Nobile that is drinkable enough, though rarely more than that. Vino Nobile 0

Contucci *(Montepulciano), 1789.* Contucci has 52 acres (21 hectares) of vineyards: 34 (13.7) are in vines for Vino Nobile, 9.3 (3.9) for Chianti Colli Senesi. They produce 105,000 to 120,000 bottles a year of Vino Nobile and 33,000 to 39,000 of Chianti, as well as 20,000 bottles of *vino da tavola*, red and white. Contucci also make a Vin Santo from 100 percent malvasia grapes. Their Vino Nobile is aged in a combination of oak and chestnut casks.

Contucci was among the first to bottle a Vino Nobile and until recently sold the wine under the name Cantine Riunite, Cav. Mario Contucci. At one time we found their wines among the zone's best. Now it's not only the label that has changed, but the wine in the bottle as well, and the change was unfortunately not for the better. Vino Nobile★★

Del Cerro *(Acquavina), 1922.* Originally founded as F.lli Baiocchi and later renamed Cantine Baiocchi, this winery has been owned since 1978 by Saiagricola, a company with large land holdings in Umbria, Piemonte, and Tuscany.

Del Cerro has 290 acres (117 hectares) of vineyards, planted at altitudes of 885 to 1115 feet (270 to 340 meters); 141 acres (57 hectares) are planted for Vino Nobile and 119 (48) for Chianti. They have an average annual production of 20,000 cases of the Nobile and 25,000 of the Colli Senesi Chianti. From their other vineyards, they produce 17,500 cases of other wines typical of the zone: Vin Santo and *vino bianco*. All of their wines are made from their own grapes.

Winery director Marcello Majani told us that the Fattoria del Cerro and Cantine Baiocchi Vino Nobiles are the same wine, with different labels for different markets. There is a difference in the other wines, however: the del Cerro Rosso contains 15 to 18 percent white grapes and the Chianti 7 to 8 percent; the Baiocchi wines contain little or no white grapes. Le Pietrose is another Vino Nobile produced by this firm.

The first Vino Nobile of del Cerro we tasted was the '78, the first sold under that label; for us it was the best of the vintage. Since then we've tasted many others, and for the most part they have also been first rate. Vino Nobile Baiocchi and del Cerro★★★

Marcello Majani of Saiagricola's Fattoria del Cerro and Baiocchi

Fanetti, Comm. Adamo e Giuseppe, Tenuta "S. Agnese" *(Montepulciano), 1921.* Fanetti, proprietor of the 306-acre (124-hectare) S. Agnese estate, has forty-four acres (18 hectares) in vines; approximately 35 (14) for Vino Nobile, from which he produces 80,000 bottles a year, and 10 (4) for Chianti, which yields 26,000 bottles. He also makes Vin Santo, white wine, and a unique Principesco. Fanetti's total production is about 120,000 bottles a year. From his 2.5-acre (1-hectare) Vin del Sasso vineyard, planted in 1981, he plants to produce approximately 2500 bottles of a *barrique*-aged cabernet. Fanetti, the estate that "made" Vino Nobile, enjoys quite a high reputation, but we find that too often their wines fail to live up to it. On rare occasions, when they do, these wines are among the best in the zone, but too often they are mediocre. Vino Nobile★★

Fassati *(Pieve di Sinalunga), 1913.* This winery is owned by Fazi Battaglia of Verdicchio fame. They have two facilities for their Vino Nobile: one in Montepulciano itself where the cellars are and one in Sinalunga for bottling and stockage. Their 37 acres (15 hectares) of vines at Podere Fonte al Vescovo are planted at altitudes of 1310 to 1575 feet (400 to 480 meters). The oldest vines are forty years old. Their most recent plantings were put in in 1976. Since 1977, their entire production of Vino Nobile has been from their own grapes.

Fassati recently bought 50 acres (20 hectares) in the Chianti zone. From 1986, they will produce a Chianti from their own grapes; thus far they have bought wine from Chianti and Chianti Classico and aged it in their cellars. They will continue to buy from the Classico zone.

Their first Vino Nobile was produced in 1967, and except for 1972 they have bottled one every year since. They make a selection of the grapes, using the best in their riserva.

Since 1979, Fassati has been treating its vines against mold with an antibotrytis spray which they say they were the first in the area to use. This treatment, their enologist Amedeo Esposito points out, made it possible for them to produce a Vino Nobile in 1984—and it's a good one—while many other producers had to declassify.

Their grapes are pressed in basket presses, and the wine is aged first in chestnut casks before being moved to oak for the final phase of aging. Currently, one-third of their casks are chestnut, and two-thirds, oak.

Fassati produces on average 93,000 bottles of Vino Nobile a year and 25,000 bottles of Chianti.

Our fairly extensive experience with these wines has left us less than impressed. They are fairly good wines, but unexciting. Vino Nobile★

Fattoria di Gracciano (*Gracciano*). Franco Mazzucchelli owns 50 acres (20 hectares) of vineyards: 17 (7) planted for Vino Nobile and 32 (13) for Chianti Colli Senesi. He produces about 50,000 bottles a year, which also includes a white wine and a Vin Santo. These wines, sold under the Fattoria di Gracciano, Cantina Svetoni label (not to be confused with Tenuta di Gracciano, which is another estate), have been known since the nineteenth century. They can be quite good, though we find them generally unexciting. Vino Nobile★

Fognano (*Montepulciano*), *1873*. Fognano has 160 acres (65 hectares), 86 (35) of which are in vines. Two-thirds are planted for Vino Nobile and one-third for Chianti Colli Senesi. The average 93,000 bottles a year of Vino Nobile and 40,000 of Chianti. Besides these two, they produce about 13,000 bottles of white wine and Vin Santo. They also plan to produce, like numerous others, a wine aged in *barrique*. After a rocky start they seem to be on the right track now. The best vintages at Fognano, according to them, were 1983, 1981, 1979, 1975, and 1973. Vino Nobile★

Gattavecchi (*Montepulciano*), *1958*. This firm has no vineyards. They buy wines, blend them, age them, and bottle them under their label, an average of 30,000 bottles a year. We've been less than impressed with their Vino Nobile di Montepulciano, their Chianti Colli Senesi, or, for that matter, any of their other wines. Vino Nobile 0

Innocenti Vittorio (*Montefollonico*), *1981*. Innocenti's first Vino Nobile di Montepulciano was produced at Podere Sambono in 1981; they made 500 cases. The wine is aged in chestnut casks. They also produce a Chianti Colli Senesi and a Vin Santo.

La Querce (*Madonna della Querce*), *1970*. Lido Pinzi Pinzuti has 25 acres (10 hectares) on his La Querce farm: 17 (7) planted to grapes for Vino Nobile and 3.7 (1.5) for Chianti. His Vino Nobile is aged for three years in oak casks. He also produces a white wine. Average annual production at La Querce is 7700 cases. Our experience with these wines has been limited, and unimpressive. Vino Nobile 0

Melini. We have found the Vino Nobile of this Chianti Classico producers to be quite reliable. They bottle it only in the best vintages. Vino Nobile★+

Pantano (*Chianciano*). Pantano own 27 acres (11 hectares); 18.5 (7.5) are planted to vines for Vino Nobile. They also produce a Chianti and a Vin Santo. Our limited experience suggests that this is a producer worth watching. Vino Nobile★★

Podere Ferretto, Fattoria delle Maestrelle. Storiche Cantine member Fattoria delle Maestrelle produces this wine. They produced over 5000 cases of a mediocre Vino Nobile in 1977. Vino Nobile 0

Poggio alla Sala (*Montallese*). This firm has 50 acres (20 hectares) of vines in the Montepulciano zone, plus many other vineyards in Umbria and Lazio. Their annual production at Poggio alla Sala averages about 54,000 cases, of which some 7500 are Vino Nobile. We can't say they're the worst producer in the area, but they're not far from it. Vino Nobile 0−

Poliziano (*Gracciano*), *1965*. Poliziano took its name from a noted local poet, Angelo Ambrogini, called Il Poliziano ("the man of Montepulciano").

They own 185 acres (75 hectares) of vines: 124 (50) for Chianti, from which they produce 22,000 cases a year, and 47 (19) for Vino Nobile, yielding nearly 9000 cases. From the remaining 15 acres (6 hectares) they make 5500 cases of Bianco Vergine Valdichiana.

Vineyards	Hectares
Caggiole	10
Casale	2
Vitaroccia	7

They use only 70 percent of the quantity allowed by law for their Vino Nobile, selecting the best grapes to obtain higher quality. At one time the Poliziano wines were rather variable. But since 1982, when Dott. Federico Carletti took charge, there has been a marked improvement. Their '82 Vino Nobile promises to be a very fine wine; it was the best we tasted from that vintage. Their '83, also tasted from cask, might be even better. Enologist Maurizio Castelli has been consulting for Poliziano since 1983, but it's Carletti who makes the wine.

Carletti della Giovampaola is another label they use for their Vino Nobile. Carletti told us that this wine is exactly the same as that sold under the Poliziano label.

Their Vino Nobile is aged in fairly new oak casks, none more than ten years old. In 1983, they began experimenting with *barriques*. Their *barrique*-aged wine will be bottled under the name of Elegiae. Vino Nobile pre-1982★; since 1982★★★

Raspanti Giuseppe. Raspanti owns 3.5 acres (1.4 hectares) of vines. Our limited experience with this producer's Vino Nobile (we tasted only the '81) leads us to conclude that this producer is worth looking for. Vino Nobile ★★

Sanguineto *(Montepulciano).* This estate has 12.4 acres (5 hectares) of vines, from which they produce 10,000 bottles of Vino Nobile a year. They also make a Chianti Colli Senesi. Our limited experience with the wines has not been particularly favorable. Vino Nobile 0

Santavenere *(Montepulciano), 1979.* Santavenere owns 22 acres (9 hectares) in Montepulciano, from which they produce some 30,000 bottles a year. Vino Nobile★

Scopatello *(Chianciano).* Scopatello has 160 acres (65 hectares) of vineyards from which they produce both Chianti and a fairly decent Vino Nobile di Montepulciano. Vino Nobile★

Tenuta di Gracciano, di Della Seta Ferrari Corbelli *(Gracciano).* Corbelli owns 27 acres (11 hectares); 10 (4) are planted to vines for Vino Nobile and 17 (7) for Chianti. He bottles his Vino Nobile under the Tenuta di Gracciano label, which should not be confused with Fattoria di Gracciano, which is a different wine. There is not a great difference in quality, however; like the other Gracciano wines, these can be fairly good. Vino Nobile★

Alex Palenzona of Tenuta Valdipiatta

291

Tenuta Valdipiatta *(Gracciano), 1969.* Alex Palenzona has 86 acres (35 hectares) at Valdipiatta, 30 (12) in vines. His annual production is about 54,000 bottles of Vino Nobile di Montepulciano per year. As Palenzona's work requires him to spend much of his time in Milano and Venezuela, Alfio Carpini, proprietor of the neighboring property, Casella, produces the wines at Valdipiatta as well as his own. Both wineries share the same cellar facilities. The first wine at Valdipiatta sold in bottle under their label was from the 1973 vintage. Overall, their Vino Nobile is quite good. Vino Nobile★★

Tistarelli Mario. This wine is produced for Tistarelli by a firm that identifies itself on the label only as CA.VI.O.T. Perhaps Casa Vinicola O.T. has reason to prefer to be semianonymous, considering the quality of the wine in the bottle. Vino Nobile 0

Tripusa. Enoteca Europea produces a mediocre Vino Nobile from our rather limited experience. Vino Nobile 0

Vecchia Cantina *(Loc. Cicolina, Montepulciano), 1937.* This 300-member cooperative winery controls 2500 (1000 hectares) of vines; 1000 (400) are planted to vines for Vino Nobile and 1235 (500) for Chianti. They produce about 56,000 cases of wine a year. The first wines they sold in bottle were from the 1940 vintage.

This Vino Nobile di Montepulciano is reliable and can be quite good, though unexciting. Vino Nobile★

Chapter 11

Torgiano

Torgiano is produced around the walled city of that name between Assisi and Perugia in Umbria. The town takes its name from the ancient Tower of Janus—Torre di Giano, the roman god with two faces—that watches over the town and the vineyards outside.

The excellent wine museum in Torgiano, put together by the gracious Maria Grazia Lungarotti, wife of the fine producer, traces the history of the wine in the region from earliest times. Old tools, equipment, and documents as well as a large selection of wine-related pottery and artifacts from many periods fill two well-organized floors of museum rooms.

Though references to the wine of Torgiano have been found dating back to the fourteenth and fifteenth centuries, the wine as we know it today is of fairly recent origin.

The Torgiano Production Zone

The vineyards are planted at altitudes of 950 to 1050 feet (290 to 320 meters). In 1975, there were 510 acres (206 hectares) of vines in the Torgiano zone, with a maximum allowable production by law of 154,000 cases of wine, both red and white. By 1984, this had increased to nearly 1500 acres (600 hectares) under vines with a maximum yield of 450,000 cases. Actual production in 1984 was, according to the Italian Wine Center in New York, considerably less than that, however—just under 100,000 cases. For the past ten years production has averaged 178,000 cases a year.

Torgiano rosso is made from a blend of 50 to 70 percent sangiovese, 15 to 30 percent canaiolo nero, 10 percent trebbiano toscano, and up to 10 percent ciliegiolo and montepulciano.

DOC Requirements

	Minimum age (years)	Minimum alcohol	Maximum yield (gallons/acre)
Regular	—	12%	834
Riserva	3	12%	834

Lungarotti, the zone's major producer, has an average annual production of 160,000 to 180,000 cases of Torgiano (red and white), 90 percent of it from his own grapes. He has nearly 470 acres (187 hectares) of vines in Torgiano and buys grapes from another 210 acres (85 hectares) or so.

Lungarotti Torgiano Vineyards

	hectares	acres
Red	126.55	312.7
White	60.77	150.2
Total	187.32	462.9

Lungarotti began bottling his wine on a commercial basis only in 1962, at that time just the Rubesco and Torre di Giano. He did bottle small amounts of wine in the 1950s but sold virtually all of his production in cask to restaurants in the area. Two cooperative wineries, or *cantine sociali,* sell Torgiano in bottle under their own labels. A number of small producers also bottle, but mostly for their own use.

Vintages

Lungarotti supplied us with the following vintage information:

★★★★	1983, 1982, 1980, 1975, 1971, 1970, 1968, 1966
★★★	1981, 1979, 1978, 1977, 1974, 1973, 1969, 1967, 1963, 1962, 1956
★★	1972, 1965, 1964
★	1960, 1959, 1957, 1955
0	1976, 1961, 1958

Rating★★★★

Torgiano Producers

Cantina Lungarotti *(Torgiano), 1962.* Dott. Giorgio Lungarotti graduated in 1935 from the university at Perugia, where he studied enology and specialized in viticulture. He had worked in the vineyards and the cellars of his father and uncle since he was a boy, and he continued to do so while he was studying, creating dust storms on the country roads, he recalls with a smile, as he sped from classes to *cantina* and back.

His enthusiasm for the wine is no less today. And it, along with his sincere dedication to quality, is shared by his daughter, Maria Teresa Severini Lungarotti, also a graduate of Perugia, where she was the first woman to receive a degree in enology in 1979. Teresa began working at the winery in the lab but has since taken on much greater responsibilities, including marketing.

Dott. Giorgio Lungarotti of Cantine Lungarotti *Teresa Lungarotti of Cantine Lungarotti*

The Lungarottis have a refreshing attitude toward wine. Dott. Lungarotti says that to open the wine in advance is not very important; if it needs aeration, decanting it will take care of that. They make no excuses if the wine arrives at a tasting shaken up from a recent journey. If the wine is well made, it is sound; there is no reason for concern, they feel. Only a very old wine or one with sediment to stir up will be hurt by such treatment, and then only temporarily. We agree (our experiments with a number of battered-about bottles have borne this out).

The Lungarotti winery has a capacity of 1.6 million gallons (666,000 cases). Annual production of the major wines varies from about 184,000 to 210,000 cases a year, of which 70,000 to 80,000 are Rubesco, 90,000 to 100,000 the white Torre di Giano, 15,000 to 20,000 chardonnay, 5000 to 6000 Cabernet Sauvignon, 2000 San Giorgio, and other 2000 a champagne-method brut. He also produces a Vin Santo, a rosé, and a sherry-type aperitif wine, Solleone, as well as small amounts of a few other wines. Lungarotti exports more than 60 percent of his production.

His chardonnay and cabernet sauvignon vines are grown in the Miralduolo area near the Tiber River, outside the DOC zone, at an altitude of about 820 feet (250 meters). The sangiovese and canaiolo nero are planted higher up on the hillside at 1150 feet (350 meters); the trebbiano toscano and grechetto are lower down at 655 to 820 feet (200 to 250 meters).

Lungarotti's average yield is about 855 gallons per acre (80 hectoliters per hectare) for the white grapes, 748 (70) for sangiovese, 513 (48) for canaiolo nero, and 428 (40) for cabernet sauvignon.

Cru	Hectares	First bottled	Production (cases)
I Palazzi	12	1983	2500
Il Pino	10	1970	2500
Monticchio	12	1964	5000
Vineyard			
Belvedere	20		7000-8000
Montescosso	16		-
Montespinello	20		4000

Rubesco, for as long as we can remember, has been an underrated wine. While it does receive some recognition today, when you compare its quality to other wines at the same price level, its fine value is even more obvious. And it challenges many that are priced much higher.

The first time we tasted this wine it made a memorable impression. That was in 1974 and not under the best of circumstances. We were finishing our first book on Italian wine and had been invited to a private tasting by a small importer of Italian wines. That was good. Then, a few days before the tasting, a heat wave struck. That was not so good.

When the day arrived, the heat had not abated, and we frankly would have preferred to go swimming. But there was a deadline to meet, and the appointment apparently couldn't be rescheduled. So we went, feeling that we'd give the wines a fair chance. When you taste at the winery or at the importer's you don't have to be concerned about how long the bottles have been sitting on the merchant's shelf or how they may have been stored.

The heat was sizzling on the asphalt griddle of 125 Street as we approached the importer's office, and we prepared ourself for the shock of the air conditioning as we pushed open the door. Shock: there was no air conditioning. We were greeted by a modest drop of perhaps 10 degrees. Fortunately, most of the wines were not served at room temperature (optimistically in the high 80s) but at the temperature of the somewhat cooler warehouse.

There was one wine, though, that must have been in the office for a while. When the first wines were poured, the Torgiano from Lungarotti stood out. It was the wine with the steam rising out of the glass; not only were the esters in the wine volatizing, but alcohol and acidity as well—our first introduction. The importer noticed it too; he pulled the bottle off the table and jostled it into the fridge with the whites, saying that it should really be tasted under better conditions. We didn't object.

What was this wine, anyway? we asked, never having heard of Torgiano or of Lungarotti. (We had heard of an Italian region called Umbria.) He filled us in with some background, and we went on through the rest of the tasting. What the other wines were, we can't recall at this point, but they were probably good. The '66 Rubesco, when they remembered to retrieve it from the icebox, had dipped a few degrees. In fact, it was rather frosty. But, despite the less than perfect presentation, its quality shone through. We were impressed. It says a lot for the wine, we think, and for the producer.

Rubesco is made from a blend of about 65 percent sangiovese, 35 percent canaiolo nero, and 5 percent other red grapes. The regular Rubesco is aged in oak for about 12 months, the riserva for fifteen to eighteen months, partly in new oak. Lungarotti's Cabernet Sauvignon, San Giorgio, Rubesco riserva, Chardonnay, and white Torre di Giano riserva are all given some *barrique* aging. Only a small amount—less than 10 percent—of the Rubesco is riserva.

Rubesco has a floral bouquet, often with fruity overtones; it is full-flavored and smooth in texture. The riserva is fuller and richer. While it is enjoyable to drink when first released, it ages well for ten to fifteen years, taking on nuances of aroma and flavor; in the best vintages it can live even longer.

Rubesco is a fine wine to accompany roast meats, duck, pigeon, or goose; it also goes well with feathered game such as pheasant or quail.

Among recent vintages we can especially recommend the '75 Rubesco riserva, a very fine wine, one of the best Rubescos we've tasted (and we've tasted quite a few). Rubesco★★★★

Tasting Notes

1981 (will be a riserva) *(ex-cask 5/82)*. A mouthful of fruit and tannin; should make a fine bottle in time.★★(?)

1979 *(11/84)*. Vague mineral notes on a somewhat floral aroma; light tannin, a lot of fruit; good now, but should improve.★(★)

1978 *(6 times 9/82)*. Rich aroma with suggestions of cassis and blueberries; some tannin to shed, a touch of acid toward the finish, but overall well balanced, richly fruited.★★

1977 *(twice 10/84)*. Fragrant, floral aroma, with some fruit; well balanced, some tannin to lose, good fruit, good quality.★★(+)

1977 Monticchio riserva *(11/84; 13,250 bottles)*. Slightly floral aroma with notes of oak and fruit; a bit light in body, very well balanced, young, but quality is evident, an elegant wine.★★(★)

1975 *(3 times 2/82)*. Fragrant, floral bouquet; smooth-textured, flavorful, vaguely bitter on aftertaste.★★(★)

1975 Monticchio riserva *(8 times 3/85; 11,850 bottles)*. Floral with cherries and a spicy, peppery aspect; exceptional balance, a mouthful of flavor, so much so it's tempting to drink it now; it will be superb with proper age, say two to three more years.★★★(★)

1974 Monticchio riserva *(18 times 11/84; 29,750 bottles)*. Complex bouquet with nuances of flowers, blueberries, and black pepper; still has tannin, lovely flavors, round, refined; shows some signs of drying out on the finish. This wine was at its best through early 1984★★★. The last three bottles all seemed to be beginning to dry out, though they were still very good.★★ +

1973 *(twice 2/81)*. The bottle of 2/81 was beginning to dry out. Bottle of 11/80: Complex bouquet of cherries and flowers with a touch of licorice; full-flavored; has length and style.★★★ +

1973 riserva *(4 times 11/84; 15,820 bottles)*. Medium garnet with orange reflections; lovely bouquet has some

spice; round and flavorful; a long finish; a wine of quality, ready now, but could still improve further.★★★

1971 riserva *(5 times 11/84; 13,850 bottles)*. Complex bouquet with floral and fruity nuances; well balanced, light tannin, full-flavored, smooth texture over a firm frame; a wine of real quality, at or near its peak.★★★ +

1970 *(2/82)*. Deep, rich bouquet brings up almonds and cassis; like velvet on the palate, refined and elegant.★★★ +

1969 *(2/82)*. Floral bouquet; velvety texture; at its peak.★★★

1969 riserva *(11/84; 8920 bottles)*. Beautiful brick-red robe; intense bouquet of flowers and fruit with a tarlike note; soft, round, flavorful, light tannin; peak now.★★★ −

1968 *(twice 1/83)*. Considerable fruit on nose; well balanced, moderately rich, still some tannin; very enjoyable now, can improve.★★

1966 riserva *(11/84; 8920 bottles)*. Beautiful brick-red robe; big, richly fruited bouquet with floral notes and a suggestion of tar; velvety texture; very long finish; a complete wine.★★★ +

1964 riserva (the first year a riserva was produced) *(11/84)*. Brick robe tending to orange; touch of mint on the bouquet, which is beginning to show age; round and smooth, lovely flavors, full yet subtle, gentle; very long on finish; very close to its peak.★★★ +

1962 *(11/84)*. Color shows a lot of age; also the aroma; tasty upon entry, then very little in the center; age evident on finish; tired, but still some interest and quality evident.★

1956 *(11/79)*. This wine was presented at a tasting of about a dozen old vintages organized by the Italian Wine Center in New York. There were some big names present. For us and many others, this was the best wine of the show. Lovely bouquet, floral, delicate; soft, smooth, and stylish; an elegant wine of real character.★★★ +

Chapter 12

More Sangiovese-Based Wines

For the past few years there has been a growing trend toward producing 100 percent sangiovese wines aged in *barrique,* sangiovese–cabernet blends aged in *barrique,* and some other nontraditional combinations using sangiovese as the base. Most of the new wines are from the Chianti area, which is not surprising considering the number of producers in the district and the marketing problems Chianti is experiencing.

Many producers, recognizing the tarnished image that Chianti has today, have decided to strike out on their own with their best product, without benefit or, in this case, hindrance of the Chianti name and the DOC regulations that go with it. The fame and high prices attained by Tignanello, one of the first to make a big splash in this sphere, did much to accelerate the trend toward the use of cabernet and *barrique* aging, but that wasn't the only impetus. As the market for Italian wine has become stronger worldwide, the pressures to produce wines of international character have also.

Among the many new entrants into the market, some are more successful than others. A number are of very fine quality. They deserve serious consideration and international attention. Of all of these new wines, the one we consider the most important is Sergio Manetti's Le Pergole Torte, for its judicious use of oak and its emphasis on Italy's own noble sangiovese.

In discussing the many wines made from the sangiovese, *in toto* or in part, we have attempted to make our coverage as complete and as up to date as possible, but it is a task we have come to consider next to impossible. We have no doubt that new wines are being created even as we write these lines.

We also cover here some wines that are not new and may even be quite traditional, wines that are not major enough to merit a separate chapter, such as Sangiovese di Romagna and Parrina, but are too important not to be included in our discussion of sangiovese-based wines.

The Wines

BALSASTRADA *(Tuscany).* Castell'In Villa, a good Chianti Classico estate, produced this *barrique*-aged wine from 100 percent sangiovese experimentally in 1982. They used the best grapes from their 10-acre (4 hectare) vineyard of Balsastrada. Considering their other wines, we expect it to be a success.

BORRO CEPPARELLO *(Tuscany).* This *barrique*-aged sangiovese wine is produced at Isole e Olena, a fine Chianti Classico estate, under the able hand of Paolo di Marchi. The wine is made with the best grapes selected from their own vineyards and is aged for about one year in *barrique.* Borro Cepparello is named for a spring torrent *(borro)* that runs across the estate. In 1980, the first vintage, about 8000 bottles were produced. As di Marchi was not satisfied with the '81 Borro Cepparello, it was blended into their Chianti. In 1982, production was nearly double that of the first vintage. Paolo will make a Borro Cepparello from the 1983 harvest, but considering the kind of year it was in 1984, it is doubtful whether there will be one from that vintage. The wines we tasted were actually better than our overall rating would indicate, but we feel one bottle and two barrel samples are insufficient to give it higher marks. Rating ★★ +

Tasting Notes

1984 (*ex-barrique 5/85*). Fruity aroma recalls freshly crushed grapes; quite a lot of flavor, acid is on the high side; shows some promise.★(★ −)

1983 (*ex-barrique 5/85*). Richly flavored, full of tannin and extract; very good potential.★★(★?)

1982 (*5/85; 14,490 bottles, 265 magnums*). Richly fruited aroma overlaid with oak; a mouthful of tannin gives way to a supple center, well structured; a long, tannic finish; impressive.★★★(★)

BRUNESCO DI SAN LORENZO (*Tuscany*). Giovanni Cappelli, proprietor of the fine Montagliari estate in Chianti Classico, produces this 100 percent sangiovese wine at his estate in Panzano. He uses only sangiovese because, as he says, "This is the area of sangiovese, it's a fine variety, why imitate the French with cabernet?" In 1980, the first vintage, he produced 3000 bottles; in 1981 and 1982 there were 3500 each year, and in 1983 7000. There won't be an '84 Brunesco di San Lorenzo. This is one of the more successful of the new *barrique*-aged wines. Rating★★★

Tasting Notes

1983 (*ex-cask 5/85*). Richly fruited aroma overlaid with oak; well balanced, a firm vein of tannin, sweet oak and fruit flavors, soft-centered; finish is long and tannic; has a lot of class.★★(★ +)

1982 (*5/85*). Aroma of oak up front on a fruity background; rich in flavor, sweet and ripe; very long finish; a very young wine.★★(★)

1981 (*5/85*). Aroma is closed, but has hints of oak and fruit, perhaps a touch overripe; sweet and fruity, oaky; long finish; needs age.★★(+)

1980 (*5/85*). Original sensation of oak on the aroma gives way to a cherrylike fruit with a vaguely floral aspect; softly fruited center, loads of tannin, flavor of sweet oak and fruit.★★(★)

BRUNO DI ROCCA (*Tuscany*). Enologist Vittorio Fiore produces this *barrique*-aged wine at the Chianti Classico estate of Vecchie Terre de Montefili. It is made from a selection of their best sangiovese and cabernet sauvignon grapes in a 50–50 blend and aged for about a year in small French oak. In the first vintage, 1983, some 4000 bottles were produced. There won't be an '84. Rating★★

Tasting Note

1983 (*ex-barrique 5/85*). Aroma of flowers and cherries with overtones of oak, cabernet fruit seems a bit restrained at this point; fruity, well balanced.★★

BRUSCO DEI BARBI (*Tuscany*). Brusco dei Barbi is made from a blend of approximately 80 percent sangiovese grosso and 20 percent canaiolo; in some vintages there is also some trebbiano used. *Governo* is used to add glycerine. This wine was first made in 1970 by Giovanni Colombini as a wine to accompany cheese, especially aged pecorino. It is a full-bodied, robust wine, rather high in alcohol (14.5 percent). It has a dry, raisiny character, similar to an Amarone. Brusco is a wine to drink with hearty fare. Although it can last for six to eight years, we don't find that it improves with age. Brusco dei Barbi is a rustic red, as the name suggests (*brusco*—"blunt, brusque"), of no particular distinction, although it is priced—in the U.S., at least—on a more lofty level. Colombini makes an excellent Brunello, but her name is insufficient to justify this price in our opinion. Rating★

Tasting Notes

1981 (*5/85*). Dried, concentrated fruit character, rustic, fruity.★ +

1978 (*9 times 1/84*). Dark color; aroma has a dried, raisiny character, (from *governo*?), quite rich; a mouthful of flavor, the dried fruit flavor recalls Amarone, as does the bitter finish.★

1977 (*3 times 5/83*). Off notes like a rubber tire smell mar the aroma; flavor is better, though an off character is still evident.

1976 (*9 times 5/85*). Bottle of 4/83: Dried fruit on aroma similar to an Amarone; full of flavor, somewhat rustic nature, some tannin, but no need to hold it.★

Bottle of 5/85: Tawny color; some oxidation, old, dull, and tired.

1975 (*3 times 4/81*). Aroma of nuts and raisins; some tannin, alcohol intrudes a bit; to drink now.

1974 (*4 times 6/81*). Aroma suggests figs and almonds; a dried, grapey character, some tannin; a rustic country wine.★

CÀ DEL PAZZO (*Tuscany*). Enologist Vittorio Fiore created this wine for noted Brunello di Montalcino producer Tenuta Caparzo from a 50–50 blend of sangiovese grosso and cabernet sauvignon. The wine is aged for about eight to ten months in French oak—a combination of Limousin, Alliers, and Nevers barrels. In the first vintage, 1982, 20,000 bottles were produced. Rating★★ +

Tasting Notes

1983 *(ex-barrique 5/85)*. Oaky aroma with notes of cherries, tar, and cabernet fruit; tannic, a bit rough, but the structure and fruit are there.★★(★)

1982 *(5/85)*. Aroma of oak, cabernet fruit, and cigars; well balanced, cabernet more dominant than the sangiovese grosso; slightly astringent finish; needs age.★★(+)

CAMERLENGO *(Tuscany)*. Pagliarese, a producer of good Chianti Classico, makes this *barrique*-aged wine from the best sangiovese grosso grapes in their 8-acre (3.25-hectare) Camerlengo vineyard. The wine is put first into large casks, then moved to small barrels for three to four months of further aging. From the initial vintage in 1979, 3500 bottles were produced; production has since doubled. Rating★+

Tasting Note

1979 *(5/85)*. Oak and fruit on aroma; some tannin, big and flavorful, but a bit too obvious, lacks subtlety.★(★)

CANVALLE *(Tuscany)*. Vigna Vecchia, in Chianti Classico, first produced this wine in 1982 from an 80–20 blend of sangiovese and cabernet sauvignon. It was aged for three and a half months in *barrique*. They produced nearly 5000 bottles in 1982 and again in 1983.

CAPANNELLE ROSSO *(Tuscany)*. Raffaele Rossetti produces this *barrique*-aged wine from 100 percent sangiovese grapes. In 1979, the first vintage, there were some 2000 bottles produced. That wine was aged for three months in *barriques* of Limousin oak, then for a further year in oak casks. There was no '80. In 1981 and 1982, he produced 3000 bottles from each vintage. Currently, the Capannelle Rosso is aged for four months in *barrique*, followed by five to six months in fairly new oak casks; from the casks it goes to stainless steel tanks before bottling. Rossetti is enthusiastic about the '83, feeling that it will really be something special; at this point we agree. Rating★★★

Tasting Notes

1983 *(ex-barrique 5/85)*. Aromas of oak and fruit rise out of the glass before swirling; the tannic entry gives way to sweet, ripe fruit; style and class are already evident.★★★(+)

1982 *(ex-cask 5/85)*. Fruity aroma of cherries overlaid with oak; well balanced, heaps of flavor; a long tannic finish.★★(★)

1981 *(twice 5/85)*. Deep red; lovely aroma, blending components of oak and fruit; sweet oak and fruit flavors beneath moderate tannin; drinkable now, but give it a few years; has style and length.★★(★)

CASAOCCI *(Tuscany)*. The good Chianti Classico producer Fattoria Querciabella makes this wine from a blend of 75 percent sangiovese, 5 percent sangiovese grosso, and 10 percent each cabernet sauvignon and cabernet franc. It is aged for eighteen to twenty four months in *barrique*. Their first vintage was 1982.

CASTELLO DI SAN POLO IN ROSSO *(Tuscany)*. Enologist Maurizio Castelli produced 15,000 bottles of this wine from a special selection of mostly sangiovese grapes for Cesare and Katrin Canessa, proprietors of this fine Chianti Classico estate. It represents 10 percent of their production. Rating★★

Tasting Note

1981 *(twice 5/85)*. Toasty, berryish aroma; soft and mellow, suggestion of sweetness, some tannin, loads of flavor.★★(+)

CASTELLUCCIO AZ. AGR., DI GIAN MATTEO BALDI *(Emilia Romagna), 1975*. The Castelluccio estate has 15 acres (6 hectares) presently in vines and another 15 (6) planned. The vineyards, cultivated at altitudes of 1235 to 1575 feet (376 to 480 meters), have a south to southeastern exposure.

Vittorio Fiore has been their consulting enologist since 1980. He oversees the production of three single-vineyard, *barrique*-aged wines from sangiovese grosso grapes grown on their estate at S. Maria in Casale: Ronco Casone, Ronco dei Ciliegi, and Ronco delle Ginestre. They have an annual production of 50,000 to 60,000 bottles per year of sangiovese grosso wines plus another

600 to 900 bottles of Ronco del Re, an outstanding white wine from sauvignon blanc grapes. They produced their first wine here in 1979. They consider 1979, 1981, and 1983 to be their best vintages to date. Rating★★★

Tasting Notes

1982 Ronco Casone *(5/85).* Black pepper, spice, and cherries on the aroma; light tannin, lots of flavor, well balanced; a bit young yet, but stylish; a long finish.★★★ −

1982 Ronco dei Ciliegi *(5/85).* Loads of fruit on aroma overlaid with oak, also a touch of spice and cherries; sweeter and rounder than the Casone, well balanced, flavorful; long.★★★

1982 Ronco delle Ginestre *(5/85).* Aroma has notes of spice annd cherries; the fullest, richest, and most tannic of the three crus, also the youngest and most closed, cherry flavors across the palate, lots of style.★★(★)

1981 Ronco delle Ginestre *(12/84).* Floral bouquet with some delicacy and refinement; balanced, lightly tannic, good flavor, almost seems sweet, oak apparent; has length and style.★★★

COLLE PICCHIONI AZ. VIT. DI PAOLA DI MAURO *(Latium), 1974.* Paola di Mauro owns this estate and its 10 acres (4 hectares) of vines. Her annual production averages 50,000 bottles a year. This estate, located in the Marino zone of the Castelli Romani hills about 12 miles (20 kilometers) southeast of Rome, produces three very good white wines and three good red wines. The Colle Picchioni Rosso is made from merlot and sangiovese with a small amount of montepulciano and cesanese. Vigna Due Santi is made from cesanese and merlot grapes from the Due Santi vineyard. Colle Picchioni Rosso, Vigna del Vassallo, is made from sangiovese (30 percent), montepulciano (40 percent), and merlot (30 percent) grapes grown in the 2.5-acre (1-hectare) cru of that name. That wine, which is most likely the best red of the Castelli Romani, is aged in small, 130-gallon (5-hectoliter) casks. In 1982, 3460 bottles were produced. The noted winemaker Giorgio Grai has been their consulting enologist since 1982. Rating Vigna del Vassallo★★

Tasting Note

1983 Vigna del Vassallo *(11/84).* Deep color; big, rich, fruity aroma with notes of cherries; has an uncommon richness for a Roman red, very well balanced, has style and length.★★★ −

COLTASSALA *(Tuscany).* Maurizio Castelli, consulting enologist for the Chianti Classico estate of Castello di Volpaia, first produced this *barrique*-aged wine in 1980. It is named for the 9-acre (3.6-hectare) vineyard where the grapes are grown. Coltassala is made from selected grapes, mostly sangiovese, but also about 5 percent of mammolo, a variety noted for a perfume of sweet violets *(mammola).* The wine is aged in French oak from three regions. In 1980, 19,000 bottles were produced; in 1981 22,000 bottles, and in 1982 about 30,000. Rating★★★ −

Tasting Notes

1983 *(ex-barrique 5/85).* Ripe cherry aroma overlaid with a light touch of oak, also has a blueberrylike note; quite fruity at this stage, some tannin; tannic finish.★★(?)

1982 *(twice 5/85).* Aroma of cherries and oak; firm tannin, somewhat astringent, flavorful, very young, but shows a lot of potential.★★(★?)

1981 *(5/85).* Oak up front on aroma, fruit in the back; firm and tannic on entry, oak followed by the fruit, a bit light but well balanced; potential is evident.★★(+)

1980 *(5/85).* Cherrylike aroma over an oaky background; sweet oak flavor mingled with fruit, moderate tannin, well-knit; should be ready fairly soon, perhaps two years.★★(+)

FLACCIANELLO DELLA PIEVE *(Tuscany).* This 100 percent sangiovese wine is produced by the fine Chianti Classico estate of Tenuta Fontodi from the best grapes grown in the vineyards of Pieve di San Leolino at Flacciano. The wine is given eight to nine months in *barriques* of French oak plus an additional eight to ten months in oak casks. Flaccianello was first made in 1981, some 5000 bottles. In 1982, production was doubled, and in 1983 there were some 13,500 bottles made. They didn't make Flaccianello in 1984. Rating★★ +

Tasting Notes

1983 *(ex-cask 5/85).* Richly fruited aroma with some oak; moderate tannin, soft-centered, hints of raspberries, has style.★★(★)

1982 *(ex-barrique 5/85).* All oak up front, on a richly fruited background; a rush of oak across the palate with a sense of fruit beneath, very rich, very full, very young; very long, needless to say, also very

good.★★(★)

1981 *(twice 5/85).* Oak up front on the aroma, raspberrylike fruit in the background; fairly rich and full, with some style and a lot of flavor beneath the oak, which provides an oaky sweetness and vanilla; could be longer on the aftertaste.★★(+)

FONTALLORO *(Tuscany)*. Felsina, the fine producer of Berardenga Chianti Classico, produces this wine from sangiovese grapes grown in the 5-acre (2-hectare) Fontalloro vineyard. The wine, somewhat surprisingly considering the current trend, is not put into *barrique* but is aged in small oak casks; they have six of 160-gallon (6-hectoliter) capacity and one of 1160 (44). They produced their first Fontalloro in 1983. Rating★★

Tasting Note

1983 *(5/85)*. Deep purplish color; intensely rich, concentrated aroma of flowers, cherries, and oak; vague notes of licorice and tar; sweet, rich, and flavorful, full-bodied and tannic; very young.★★(★)

GRANVINO DI MONTEMAGGIO *(Tuscany)*. Giampaolo Bonechi produced 6000 bottles of this *barrique*-aged sangiovese from the 1981 vintage. Rating 0

Tasting Note

1981 *(4/25)*. Oak, oak, and more oak; has a touch of fruit, for interest perhaps.

GRIFI *(Tuscany)*. Avignonesi, the fine producer of Vino Nobile di Montepulciano, produces this *barrique*-aged wine from a blend of 85 percent prugnolo gentile (as the sangiovese grosso is known locally) and 15 percent cabernet franc. The first Grifi, the '81, was aged for about a year in French *barriques*; they made more than 1000 cases. Production is due to increase, as will the proportion of cabernet. In the future, cabernet sauvignon will be used. Rating★★ +

Tasting Notes

1983 *(ex-barrique 4/85; in barrique since 6/84)*. Oak dominates the aroma, though some fruit is apparent in the background; fairly tannic on entry, oak flavor dominates, some fruit evident.★(?)

1982 *(4/85)*. Aroma of oak up front over a background of ripe cherries and flowers; liquid velvet on the palate; a complete wine that will certainly improve but is good right now; the single finest sangiovese–cabernet blend we've tasted to date.★★★ +

1981 *(4/85)*. Cabernet and oak aromas dominate, with some tobacco and fruit; a bit light-bodied, fairly well balanced; a nice wine.★★

GROSSO SENESE *(Tuscany)*. Podere Il Palazzino, a *fattoria* in Chianti Classico, produces this *barrique*-aged wine from 100 percent sangiovese. It is aged for one year in small barrels and another year in cask. Some 3000 to 4000 bottles are produced annually; the first vintage was 1981. Rating 0

Tasting Note

1982 *(ex-vat 5/85)*. Deep color; notes of mint, pine, and oak on aroma, with a suggestion of resin in back; oak and resin follow through on the palate, fairly tannic. Is there enough fruit? Seems over-oaked.?

I SODI SAN NICCOLÒ DI CASTELLARE *(Tuscany)*. This wine is produced from a blend of about three-quarters sangiovese di Lamole, a very old sangiovese clone, and one-quarter malvasia nera grapes grown in the I Sodi San Niccolò vineyard of Podere Castelare. This wine was first made from the 1977 vintage, then again in 1979, 1980, 1981, 1982, 1983 and 1984; in 1984, only 2650 bottles were produced. The malvasia nera, according to consulting enologist Maurizio Castelli, adds color, sweetness, and its personal character to the wine. In 1979, a part of the I Sodi was aged in *barrique*. Today it is put into a combination of new and slightly used French (half from Alliers) and Slavonian oak *barriques* for an average of about eight months. Rating★★ +

Tasting Notes

1983 *(ex-barrique 8 months 5/85)*. Ripe fruit and oak on aroma; moderate tannin, oak flavors on entry, followed by loads of fruit, still young, but shows potential.★★(+)

1982 *(twice 5/85; 18,400 bottles)*. Some oak and a lot of fruit; almost sweet, well-knit, tannic but soft-centered.★★(★)

1981 *(3 times 5/85; 11,450 bottles)*. Floral, fruity aroma with oak and malvasia character the most evident at this stage; moderate tannin, almost sweet, well-knit; needs age.★★(+)

1979 *(2/83; 2662 bottles)*. A fairly rich, fruity aroma; medium-bodied; flavorful entry, could use more depth, good now, though a bit young.★

IL SODACCIO *(Tuscany)*. Sergio Manetti of Monte Vertine, producer of a very good and reliable Chianti Classico as well as the outstanding Le Pergole Torte, created this wine for Giorgio Pinchiorri, proprietor of the noted Enoteca Pinchiorri in Florence. Manetti first produced Il Sodaccio in 1980 from an 85–15 blend of sangiovese and canaiolo nero grapes grown in his 1.25-acre (0.5 hectare) Il Sodaccio vineyard. The wine is aged in two-year-old 210- to 265-gallon (8- to 10-hectoliter) oak casks. Production is about 300 cases a year, when it is made. No Il Sodaccio was produced from the 1984 vintage. Rating★★

Tasting Note

1982 *(5/85)*. Cherrylike fruit and some oak on the aroma; moderate tannin, good fruit and structure, has delicacy and flavor; moderate length.★★ +

ISOLE E OLENA *(Tuscany)*. Paolo di Marchi produces this sangiovese–canaiolo blend at this fine Chianti Classico estate. It is not aged in wood and is best drunk young and fresh. Rating★

LA CORTE *(Tuscany)*. La Corte is produced by Allesandro Francois at his fine Chianti Classico estate of Castello di Querceto. Enologist Vittorio Fiore offers occasional professional advice. The wine is produced from selected sangiovese grapes (98 percent) grown in their 7.4-acre (3-hectare) La Corte vineyard, planted in 1973. It is aged for eight to nine months in a combination of new and slightly used French *barriques*. In 1978, the first vintage, 6000 bottles were produced. This has since doubled. Rating★★ +

Tasting Notes

1981 *(5/85)*. An aroma of cherries and berries over oak; sweet fruit, moderate tannin; young, but enjoyable now; a fairly long finish with a tannic bite.★★(★)

1980 *(5/85)*. Oaky notes overlay the cherries and flowers of the sangiovese grosso; moderate tannin, firm texture, full of flavor, not a big wine but a very pleasant one; needs age, but enjoyable now; could have a bit more length.★★ +

LE PERGOLE TORTE *(Tuscany)*. This wine is produced from the fourteen-year-old sangiovese vines in the 6.9-acre (2.8-hectare) Le Pergole Torte vineyard on Sergio Manetti's Monte Vertine estate in Chianti Classico. The wine is aged in a combination of French *barriques* (about three months) and 185- to 265-gallon (7- to 10-hectoliter) Slavonian oak casks; Manetti doesn't want the oak to overpower the subtle character of the sangiovese. In the first vintage, 1977, less than 5700 bottles were produced. Today production averages 20,000 bottles.

Le Pergole Torte is a medium-bodied, stylish dry red wine with a bouquet of flowers and fruit and a touch of oak. It drinks well from its fourth to sixth year on. Manetti told us that 1979 was the best vintage thus far. The wine is not made every year; he didn't produce Le Pergole Torte in 1984.

Le Pergole Torte is, in our opinion, one of the finest of the new Tuscan wines. It is made solely from the noble sangiovese variety, without the addition of lesser varieties, and shows how fine a purely Italian wine can be with no need to imitate the oaky California wines or the cabernets of France. Rating★★★★

Tasting Notes

1982 *(5/85)*. Beautiful ruby robe; an expansive aroma of cherries and flowers with a touch of oak; a mouthful of flavor, intense, cherrylike, youthful fruit, a firm tannic vein, soft-centered, finely honed.★★★(+)

1980 *(twice 12/84)*. Floral bouquet with a touch of oak; well balanced, somewhat firm, fruity, some elegance; ready now. Will it improve?★★ +

1979 *(3 times 5/83)*. More oak than fruit at this point, though the fruit is evident; well balanced, has flavor and style; could have more length.★★(★)

1978 *(2/82; 9840 bottles)*. Aroma is still backward, but suggestions of flowers and fruit evident; still somewhat tannic, but with the flavor and structure to carry it; a bit short.★(★ +)

1977 *(4/81; 5642 bottles)*. Lovely bouquet of fruit and flowers; well structured, some delicacy, moderate tannin; needs another year or two.★★(★)

Sergio Manetti of Fattoria di Monte Vertine

LE VIGNACCE *(Tuscany).* Giovanni Bianchi, proprietor of Villa Cilnia in the Chianti Colli Aretini district, produces this single-vineyard wine from a blend of sangiovese grosso, montepulciano d'Abruzzo, and cabernet sauvignon grapes, in equal proportions. It is aged for twelve to fifteen months in ten- to fifteen-year-old Slavonian oak casks of 660 gallons (25 hectoliters). Bianchi produced nearly 7000 bottles in the first vintage, 1982. Le Vignacce is a fairly full-bodied dry red wine that seems to have the capacity to age moderately well. Rating★

Tasting Note

1982 *(4/85).* Fruity aroma, some oak; cherrylike fruit evident, although the wine is still a bit closed.★

LOGAIOLO DI FATTORIA DELL'AIOLA *(Tuscany).* This wine is produced from red grapes only, which are grown on the Vagliagli hills in the Chianti Classico zone. Rating★

Tasting Note

1982 *(10/84; 13,930 bottles).* Floral bouquet similar to a Chianti; medium-bodied, soft and round, lacks some backbone, but flavorful; quite ready.★

MONSANTO SANGIOVETO GROSSO *(Tuscany).* Fabrizio Bianchi first produced this wine in 1974 from vines planted in 1969 and 1970. It is the product of 100 percent sangiovese grosso grapes grown at an elevation of 900 to 985 feet (275 to 300 meters) in his 8.3-acre (3.3-hectare) Scanni vineyard in Chianti Classico. Bianchi made 5200 bottles the first year. While it is a very good wine, we don't find it up to the admittedly lofty level of his riserva del Poggio Monsanto. Rating★★★

Tasting Notes

1977 *(4/85).* Floral aroma with a fruity background; exceptionally well balanced, heaps of flavor and style, tannic, though at first it almost seems ready; the best Monsanto Sangioveto Grosso thus far.★★★(+)

1975 *(twice 4/85; 3700 bottles).* Blueberries and vanilla on the bouquet, along with a touch of flowers; full-bodied and rich, still has considerable tannin; quite young, but the quality is evident.★★(★)

1974 *(6 times 4/85; 5200 bottles).* Superb bouquet with suggestions of cassis, cherries, and blueberries; considerable tannin. Is it beginning to dry out? It's difficult to say, though sensations of fruit are evident; it seemed more enjoyable two years ago when we gave it ★★★. For this one ★★.

MONTE ANTICO *(Tuscany).* This wine is produced close to the Brunello zone, in the province of Grossetto, from 95 percent sangiovese grosso grapes. Castello di Monte Antico, the zone's best producer, has 125 acres (50 hectares) of vines, 115 (45) planted to sangiovese grosso. They have an annual production of about 20,000 cases of red wine and another 1000 of rosé.

They make two reds: a regular and a riserva. The Monte Antico regular is often a good value. Both the regular and the riserva are quite similar to Chianti in character. The Monte Antico riserva is from vines at least fifteen years old; it is aged for about four years in cask. Reputedly, it can age for up to twenty years; our experience suggests otherwise. Rating★★

Tasting Notes

1980 *(4/85).* Floral aroma with a touch of oak; tannic on entry, fruit follows.★(+)

1979 *(6 times 10/83).* Light garnet; small aroma similar to a Chianti; a nice little wine, quite drinkable and correct.★

1975 riserva *(twice 2/82).* Delicate bouquet with some refinement; good structure, light tannin, tasty; some length; quite ready now.★★

MONTESCUDAIO *(Tuscany).* This medium-bodied dry red wine from the Livorno area of Pisa is quite similar in character to Chianti, which shouldn't be all that surprising considering the *uvaggio* it is made from: 65 to 85 percent sangiovese, 15 to 25 percent trebbiano toscano and/or malvasia del chianti, and up to 10 percent other varieties. Montescudaio is at its best between two and four years of the vintage.

DOC Requirements		
Minimum age	Minimum alcohol	Maximum yield *(gallons/acre)*
none	11.5%	823

Rating★ +

MORELLINO DI SCANSANO *(Tuscany)*. Morellino is a Chianti-type wine made from a minimum of 85 percent sangiovese grapes plus up to 15 percent other varieties grown in Scansano and parts of six other *communes* in the province of Grosseto. The riserva, which must be aged at least two years, is best drunk between its third and sixth years; we've heard that it will last well for up to seven or eight, but that has not been our experience.

DOC Requirements			
	Minimum age	Minimum alcohol	Maximum yield (*gallons/acre*)
Regular	none	11.5%	898
Riserva	2 years	12.0%	898

Recommended Producers
Banti Erik
Fattoria Coltiberto
Fattoria Le Pupille
Mantellassi Ezio
Poggiolungo
Val delle Rose
Rating★

Tasting Notes

1983

Fattoria Coliberto *(4/85)*. Corky, but the fruit and structure are still evident.★(?)
Cantina Coop. *(4/85)*. Cooked, southern character.
Cantina Coop. del Morellino di Scansano *(4/85)*. A big zero.
Erik Banti (2-bird label) *(4/85)*. Fresh, cherrylike fruit and berries on aroma; simple, fruity flavor with a touch of spice.★+
Erik Banti (4-bird label) *(4/85)*. Aroma displays oak (110 days in *barrique*); light tannin, simple, fruity, and quaffable.★
Fattoria Le Pupille riserva *(4/85)*. Light floral aroma; light tannin, fruity, fairly ready, though can improve some. A riserva with less than two years of age—a pre-release perhaps?★★−
Mantellassi Ezio riserva *(4/85)*. Label says "2 years in oak"! (plans for the future, maybe?) How can this be a riserva? A riserva must be aged for at least two years; the wine isn't even two years old. The wine couldn't have spent two years in oak, but that's what the label says. Oaky; some fruit and tannin; the regular is better.

Poggiolungo *(4/85)*. Tar, cherries, and fruit on aroma; light tannin, simple, quaffable.★
Val delle Rose *(4/85)*. Nose offers the most interest of the Morellinos tasted—cherries and floral notes; loads of fruit, somewhat tannic, in all, a very nice bottle; some tannin on finish.★★

1979

Fattoria Palazzaccio *(4/80)*. Stinky on nose; dull, off flavors, though a cherrylike character is evident.
Mantellassi Ezio *(4/80)*. Cherrylike aroma that carries through on palate; medium body, fruity, enjoyable now, though it can improve.★

1978

Poggiolungo *(4/80)*. Cherries on aroma; medium body, light tannin, soft and fruity.★
Val delle Rose *(4/85)*. Oxidized.

NV

Azienda di Poggio alla Mozza (Fattoria Moris) *(4/85)*. Oxidized.

PALAZZO ALTESI *(Tuscany)*. Angelo Solci, consulting enologist for Altesino, created this *barrique*-aged, 100 percent sangiovese grosso wine. The wine is made with whole berries fermented in a closed container. In the first vintage, 1980, 3000 bottles were produced. That wine was aged in a combination of Slavonian and French oak *barriques;* now they put it all in French oak. The grapes for Palazzo Altesi are from Altesino's Montosoli vineyard. Rating★★★

Tasting Notes

1984 *(ex-barrique 5/85)*. A lot of oak (heavy toast), but also a lot of fruit.★★(+)
1982 *(twice 5/85)*. Nuances of tobacco, cherries, and fruit under overtones of oak; oak flavors rush across the palate; a supple core of sweet, ripe fruit, moderate tannin; a long finish with a tannic bite.★★(★)
1981 *(5/85)*. Ripe fruit over vanilla and oak; well balanced; firm, moderate tannin, real quality here, oak adds a layer of complexity; needs a few years yet.★★★

Angelo Solci, consulting enologist

PARRINA *(Tuscany)*. This Chianti-style red wine is produced from 80 percent sangiovese and 20 percent canaiolo nero, montepulciano, and/or colorino grapes. DOC allows up to 10 percent wine and/or must from outside the zone to be used to correct a weak vintage. The grapes are grown in Parrina and in part of Orbetello in the province of Grosseto.

DOC Requirements

Minimum age	Minimum alcohol	Maximum yield (gallons/acre)
Until Dec. 1 the following year	12%	823

Parrina is best drunk between three and five years of the vintage.

Recommended Producer
Vino Etrusco La Parrina di Marchese Spinola Giuntini

Rating★★

Tasting Notes

1982 La Parrina Vino Etrusco *(4/85)*. Fruity, light tannin, balanced, some character; needs another year or two.★(★)

1976 La Parrina Vino Etrusco *(4/80)*. Floral aroma with a touch of mint; medium-bodied, some tannin, nice flavor and texture; has some style.★★

POMINO *(Tuscany)*. This recent DOC covers both a red and a white wine. We actually prefer the white, which is, in fact, one of Italy's top white wines, the one from Frescobaldi in particular. The Pomino red, up until 1983, was a Chianti Rùfina. There are some differences in the wine under DOC, though. The *uvvagio* is now 60 to 75 percent sangiovese; 15 to 25 percent, canaiolo nero, cabernet sauvignon, and/or cabernet franc; 10 to 20 percent merlot; and up to 15 percent other varieties.

DOC Requirements

	Minimum age (years)		Minimum alcohol	Maximum yield (gallons/acre)
	cask	total		
Regular	0.5	1	12.0%	786
Riserva	1.5	2	12.5%	786

Leonardo Frescobaldi told us that the '82 will be their last Pomino Rosso for at least two years. They are experimenting with a new wine and at this point are not sure of its ultimate character. We wouldn't be surprised if it contained a greater proportion of cabernet and merlot than previously, as this is the trend today in Tuscany.

PRINCEPESSA *(Tuscany)*. In 1982, the Chianti Classico producer Lilliano of Castellina in Chianti made 2200 cases of this wine from 100 percent sangiovese grapes. We've yet to taste it.

PRINCIPESCO *(Tuscany)*. This wine is made by Fanetti, the Vino Nobile di Montepulciano producer, from a blend of 90 percent sangiovese, 5 percent canaiolo nero, and 5 percent trebbiano and malvasia grapes. It was first produced from the 1979 vintage; they made 11,600 bottles. The wine is aged for at least five and a half years in rather unusual casks, of mulberry wood, one of 605 gallons (23 hectoliters) and another of 1690 (64). The second Principesco was produced in 1982. It is currently being aged in two mulberry casks, of 820 and 845 gallons (31 and 32 hectoliters). Rating★★

Tasting Note

1979 *(ex-cask 4/85)*. An interesting aroma, probably from the mulberry; round, a bit closed, tannin to shed, fairly fairly full-bodied, more flavorful and rounder than their '79 Vino Nobile.★★(+)

QUERCETINO *(Tuscany)*. The fine Chianti Classico estate, Castello di Querceto, has plans to produce this wine from a blend of 50 percent sangiovese and 50 percent cabernet sauvignon grapes grown in their 15-acre (6-hectare) Quercetino vineyard. The cabernet will be from an 11-

acre (4.5 hectare) plot planted in 1981. The first vintage of Quercetino will be 1985. The wine will be aged in *barrique*.

ROSSO ARMENTANO (*Emilia Romagna*). F.lli Vallunga produces this medium-bodied dry red wine from a blend of approximately two-thirds sangiovese and one-third cabernet franc. Rating★★ −

Tasting Note

1974 Vallunga (*4/80*). Fruity aroma; well balanced, some tannin, cabernet character evident; a nice wine that could use more character.★ +

ROSSO PATERNO II (*Tuscany*). Graziella Cetti Cappelli, proprietor of Fattoria Il Paradiso in the Chinati Colli Senesi zone, produces this Tignanello clone from 80 percent sangiovese, 15 percent cabernet sauvignon, and 5 percent cabernet franc. We have yet to taste it.

SAMMARCO (*Tuscany*). This 75–25 blend of cabernet sauvignon and sangiovese is produced by Castello dei Rampolla in Chianti Classico.

SAN GIORGIO (*Umbria*). This wine is the creation of the fine winemaker Dott. Giorgio Lungarotti. It is made from a blend of 55 percent sangiovese and 20 percent canaiolo nero, with 25 percent cabernet sauvignon added, he says, to provide backbone and structure. (Though no one who has tasted Lungarotti's Rubesco (*sans* cabernet) will think that wine lacks structure.) The cabernet does add a firmness to the San Giorgio, which is a fairly full-bodied wine. It is aged for about eighteen months in *barriques* of Slavonian oak. Lungarotti produces 2000 cases of the San Giorgio a year.

In some ways the wine can be compared to the Tignanello of Antinori; both are *barrique*-aged sangiovese–cabernet blends. But in the San Giorgio the cabernet adds firmness and a subtle nuance, while in the Tignanello it takes over the wine. Rating★★★

Tasting Notes

1979 (*11/84*). Medium dark red; aroma, though somewhat reticent, offers suggestions of mushrooms and fruit; richly flavored, some firmness, fairly long aftertaste; still quite young.★★(★)

1978 (*4 times 11/84*). Expansive bouquet with a note of mushrooms and some oak; still has tannin, but approachable now, mouth-filling flavors.★★★

1977 (*7 times 11/84*). Perfumed bouquet, intense and rich, mushroomlike back note; rich in flavor, a complete wine, lovely now, though it will improve.★★★

SANGIOVESE DI ROMAGNA (*Emilia Romagna*). These flavorful dry red wines range from medium- to full-bodied. They are best drunk with about two to three years of age. Most Sangiovese di Romagna is rather common, but a few producers make very good ones.

DOC Requirements

	Minimum age	Minimum alcohol	Maximum yield (gallons/acre)
Regular	Until April 1	11.5%	764
Riserva	2 years from January 1	11.5%	764

The sangiovese grapes for these wines are grown in the provinces of Bologna, Forlì, and Ravenna. Bruno Roncarati said that the best ones come from around Predappio near Forlì. Those of Rimini and Cesena are also good. Wines with the *superiore* designation come from more delimited areas.

Recommended Producers
Fattoria Paradiso
Giuseppe Marabini
Pasolini dall'Onda
Spalletti Rocco di Ribano
Vallunga

The most highly regarded vintages are 1977, 1961, 1957, and 1956. Also good were 1979, 1978, 1974, 1971, and 1970. Anything older is sure to be of academic interest only.

Mario Pezzi produces two single-vineyard Sangiovese di Romagna wines at Fattoria Paradiso that are among the finest in the zone, if not the finest: Vigna del Molino superiore (from sangiovese grosso), which is best within five years of the vintage, and Vigna delle Lepre riserva, ready from three to four years and can last, Pezzi says, for up to ten. Rating (for the better producers)★★

Tasting Notes

1980 Fattoria Paradiso superiore, Vigna delle Lepri riserva *(twice 4/85).* Floral, fruity aroma with suggestions of cherries and peanuts; soft, light tannin, fruity; very ready.★★ +

1978 Vallunga *(4/80).* Cherries on aroma; light tannin, light body, fruity.★

1977 Fattoria Paradiso superiore, Vigna del Molino *(10/78).* Smallish aroma; light tannin; flavorful, bitter almond finish.★

1977 Vallunga *(twice 11/78).* Floral aroma; flavorful, some tannin; ready.★ +

1976 Fattoria Paradiso superiore, Vigna delle Lepri riserva *(twice 4/85).* Pretty bouquet of cherries and flowers; soft and tasty; one of the best Sangiovese di Romagnas we've tasted.★★★ −

1975 Fattoria Paradiso superiore, Vigna delle Lepri riserva *(10/78); 2500 cases).* Aroma brings up cherries; a big wine, full of flavor, not a lot of tannin; needs another year or two.★★(★)

SANJOVETO *(Tuscany).* Enologist Maurizio Castelli created this *barrique*-aged wine at Badia a Coltibuono in 1980. It is made from 100 percent sangiovese, the best grapes from a vineyard of forty-year-old vines. Sanjoveto is aged about nine months in new and slightly used French *barriques,* about half and half. In 1980, 12,000 bottles were produced. Today the production is up to 20,000 bottles. Rating★★★★

Tasting Notes

1983 *(ex-vat 5/85).* A lot of sweet, ripe fruit, moderate tannin, potential evident, though it's difficult to fully assess (the wine has just finished malolactic fermentation).★★(?)

1982 *(ex-cask 5/85).* Aroma is closed; a mouthful of flavor, richly concentrated, a wine of large proportions and structure.★★(★★)

1981 *(5/85).* Reticent aroma reveals nuances of oak and fruit; loads of tannin and flavor; not quite together, but potential is evident.★★(+ ?)

1980 *(twice 5/85).* Berries, flowers, and oak on aroma; oak flavors on entry give way to rich fruit, well-knit; long.★★(★)

SOLATIO BASILICA *(Tuscany).* The very fine Chianti Classico producer, Villa Cafaggio, produces this wine from 90 percent sangiovese grapes selected from the fifty-year-old vines grown promiscuously in their 12.5-acre (5-hectare) Solatio Basilica vineyard. The wine is aged for one year in oak casks of about 790-gallon (30-hectoliter) capacity. The first Solatio Basilica was produced in 1981; 7866 bottles were made. It was produced again in 1982 and 1983, but not from the 1984 vintage. Production varies from 8000 to 10,500 bottles today. Without question, Solatio Basilica is one of the best of the new-breed sangiovese-based wines. Rating★★★ +

Tasting Notes

1983 *(ex-cask 5/85).* Enormous richness and concentration, lots of tannin and lots of style.★★★(★)

1982 *(ex-cask 5/85).* Black color; enormous weight and concentration, sweet, rich, and ripe.★★★(★)

1981 *(5/85).* Deep color; aroma of cherries, flowers, and berries; moderate tannin, well balanced, sweet, ripe fruit, rich and flavorful.★★(★)

TEGOLATO *(Tuscany).* This wine is, in fact, a Chianti, but it is sufficiently different—one might even say peculiar—to get its own entry. The name of this wine is from the word *tegole,* ("roof tiles"). Prinz Kunz Piast d'Asburgo Lorena ages this wine at his Antico Castello di Poppiano estate in small barrels under the *tegole,* from August to December. No, it's not a Vin Santo; it's an oxidized red wine. Rating 0

Tasting Note

1973 Tegolato, Castello di Poppiano *(11/80).* Browning; some oxidation, dried out. You really have to wonder if they like the style of this wine; after all, they did pour it for us and they didn't find any fault in it!

TESTUCCHIO *(Tuscany).* Massimo Schiavi produces this fairly full-bodied dry red wine from a blend of red grapes, basically sangiovese, with the addition of occhio di pernice, mammolo, ciliegiolo, and prugnolo. The vines are reputedly quite old. Perhaps they're even trained *a testucchio,* in the Etruscan style, four to five vines supported on a tree. We can offer no rating on the wine as we have not tasted it.

TIGNANELLO *(Tuscany).* If any one wine can be credited with promoting the fad for *barrique*-aging in Italy, it has to be this one. In 1971, Antinori produced 127,000 bottles of this wine from the 86-acre (35-hectare) Tignanello plot in their Santa Cristina vineyard in the Chianti Classico zone.

The first vintage was made from sangiovese and canaiolo nero plus a small amount of malvasia. The wine was aged in new 60-gallon (225-liter) French oak *barriques* until it was bottled in February 1974. The malvasia caused the wine to age faster than Piero Antinori liked, so it was replaced by cabernet sauvignon and cabernet franc. In the 1975 and 1977 vintages, the proportion of the two cabernets was about 10 percent; by 1978, it had been increased to 12 percent; in 1979, it was up to 15 percent; and today, it has reached 20 percent. Of the two cabernet varieties, three-quarters is cabernet sauvignon.

The wine today is given up to two years of *barrique*-aging. The French oak barrels used originally for aging the wine were later combined with some Slavonian *barriques;* then more and more of the Slavonian oak was used. Now they're going back to the French oak.

The Antinoris say that Tignanello is produced only in the best vintages. So far there has been a '71, '75, '77, '78, '79, '80, '81, '82, and '83. Since 1977, the popularity of the wine has been such that every vintage, it seems, is a best vintage for Tignanello.

Piero Antinori told us that in 1967 or 1968, Emile Peynaud, the noted enologist from Bordeaux, consulted at Antinori and in some ways helped to create Tignanello.

At the tasting we had this spring at Antinori of a number of vintages of Tignanello and their *barrique*-aged Chianti Classico, which also contains some cabernet, Piero Antinori launched into a most ironic commentary on the state of Italian viniculture. He told us that he thought the trend toward using cabernet and *barrique* aging that is so fashionable today in Tuscany is a dangerous one. Dangerous, one wonders, to whom. Italy, he said, is in danger of becoming a second-rate France or California imitator. He went on to say that the Italians should improve what they have and not copy other countries. One expects that he would like to see the other Italian producers take this advice.

The Tignanello is certainly a well-made wine; it has structure, balance, and style. The only problem, for us at least, is that the cabernet sauvignon and cabernet franc get in the way. The sangiovese is supposed to be the defining grape, but its character is submerged beneath the aggressive cabernet, even at only 15 to 20 percent.

Tignanello is best drunk from its fifth to eighth year; it can last longer, but at that point the cabernet becomes even more dominant. Rating★★

Tasting Notes

1982 *(ex-barrel 5/85).* Notes of oak and cherries over a vague cabernet background; well-knit, richly flavored, with oak and cabernet fruit dominant, showing real quality, young; at this stage the cabernet is more evident on the finish than on aroma.★★(★)

1981 *(twice 5/85).* Aroma a bit reticent, oaky vanilla notes; firm and flavorful, lacks the richness of the '82, but should develop into a good glass of wine in a few years.★(★)

1980 *(twice 5/85; 224,500 bottles plus larger sizes, eighteen months in barrique).* Cabernet and oak dominate on aroma and palate; firm structure; harsh aftertaste.★(+)

1979 *(4 times 5/85; 187,000 bottles).* Cabernet and oak up front on aroma; still has some tannin to shed, supple center, bell pepper flavors across the palate.★(★)

1978 *(7 times 5/85; 149,000 bottles).* Cabernet up front, oak in back; fairly well balanced, some tannin, coming ready; the least of the Tignanellos to date.★(+)

1977 *(5 times 5/85; 116,334 bottles plus larger sizes, seventeen months in barrique).* Cabernet is the most obvious component, fairly well-knit, somewhat astringent at the edges, fairly nice flavor.★(★)

1975 *(twice 3/82; 31,200 bottles).* Oak and fruit on aroma, suggestion of mint; fine balance, smooth-textured; fairly long finish marred by a touch of alcohol.★★(+)

1971 *(7 times 5/85; 127,000 bottles).* Aroma shows a lot of age, some oxidation, but still has interest, quite soft; beginning to dry out at the end. Was better a few years ago.★★ −

TISCVIL *(Tuscany).* Fabrizio Bianchi, proprietor of the very fine Chianti Classico estate of Monsanto, produced 6000 bottles of this wine with the Etruscan name in 1980. It is a blend of grapes—85 percent sangiovese and 15 percent cabernet sauvignon—and of vintages. The sangiovese was from the 1979 harvest, and the cabernet sauvignon, which was aged for one year in *barrique,* was from the 1980 crop. Bianchi points out that the cabernet sauvignon vines in 1980 were young and the fruit was not strong, while the sangiovese from 1979 was a robust wine, which made for a good balance between the two, with each variety contributing to the overall character of the blend. Tiscvil has not been produced again. Rating★★ +

Tasting Note

NV Tiscvil *(ex-cask 4/85)*. Aroma shows some age, honey, apricots, and floral notes; very soft, though has light tannin, loads of flavor, round, well balanced, cabernet character in the background; has style.★★★

VIGORELLO *(Tuscany)*. San Felice, the Chianti Classico producer, blends 80 percent sangiovese with 10 percent each of canaiolo and cabernet sauvignon. The result is aged for three years in oak casks followed by six months in *barrique* and six months in vat. They have produced this wine, albeit with some differences in its production and aging regime, since 1968. They produce on average some 40,000 bottles a year. Rating★

Tasting Note

1979 *(4/85; 38,880 bottles)*. Nice fruit on the nose, rich, though somewhat closed; nice fruit on entry gives way to gobs of tannin. It there enough fruit? We doubt it.★?

VINATTIERI ROSSO *(Tuscany)*. The fine enologist, Maurizio Castelli, created this wine from a blend of sangiovese grapes from two areas, 60 percent from Chianti Colli Senesi and 40 percent from Montepulciano. It is aged for one year in *barrique*. Vinattieri was produced for the first time from the 1982 vintage. That year Castelli made 7000 bottles, hardly enough to last him, his friends, and curious journalists until the next harvest. There will be a Vinattieri from 1983 but none from 1984. Rating★★ +

Tasting Note

1982 Vinattieri Rosso *(4/85)*. Lovely bouquet of cherries and berries, with a nice touch of oak; tannic entry, well-knit, sweet fruit and oak flavors; quite young; a well-made wine with real class.★★★

Chapter 13

Montepulciano d'Abruzzo

The montepulciano d'Abruzzo grape is said to be the sangiovese grosso, or prugnolo gentile, introduced into Abruzzo in the early nineteenth century from Montepulciano and named by the Abruzzesi for its town of origin. Whether or not this variety was indeed the same sangiovese grosso as was growing in Montepulciano when it was imported into Abruzzo and then to other neighboring regions, after a century and a half the vine has adapted to a different environment, creating new clones and becoming transmuted into a different subvariety at least, if not another variety altogether, although closely related to the sangiovese.

The montepulciano is the most important red variety of Abruzzo and Molise. It is the major variety in the Rosso Conero wines of Marches and is also used in the wines of Rosso Piceno. In Molise it makes up a part of the *uvaggio* in Biferno Rosso and Pentro di Isernia Rosso. It is used also in Cerveteri, Cori, and Velletri in Latium, San Severo in Apulia, and Colli Bolognesi Monte San Pietro in Emilia-Romagna, as well as in many non-DOC wines in those regions and a number of others.

Montepulciano d'Abruzzo is frequently blended with sangiovese. Masseria di Majo Norante in Molise, for example, blends 80 percent montepulciano and 20 percent sangiovese to produce a good Montepulciano del Molise, a wine that is ready to drink within two to four years of the vintage. Montepulciano, though, is a variety that can stand very well on its own, as demonstrated by the fine Montepulciano d'Abruzzos of Edoardo Valentini and Emidio Pepe.

The Montepulciano d'Abruzzo Production Zone

There are 7500 growers in Abruzzo, with close to 100,000 acres (40,000 hectares) of vines, including more than 22,000 (9000) in mixed cultivation.

Montepulciano vines are planted in the hills at altitudes up to 1640 feet (500 meters) in the coastal district and in the valleys near L'Aquila. The best grapes come from the hillside vineyards in the provinces of Aquila, Chieti, Pescara, and Termano. Of these four provinces, Chieti is the most important, with more than two-thirds of the region's total acreage under vines.

Forty-one cooperatives, thirty-one in the province of Chieti alone, vinify 65 percent of the grapes in Abruzzo. Bruno Roncarati, a noted and knowledgeable writer on Italian wines, considers the best Montepulciano d'Abruzzo to come from Francavilla al Mare in Chieti and Sulmona and Pratola Peligna in Aquila.

Montepulciano d'Abruzzo and Italian Wine Law

DOC regulations for Montepulciano d'Abruzzo allow up to 15 percent sangiovese grapes in the wine, but the better producers rarely blend, preferring a 100 percent montepulciano.

DOC Regulations

Category	Aging	Alcohol	Gallons/acre
Normal	until March 1 after the vintage	12%	1050
Vecchio	2 years	12%	1050

The Montepulciano Wine of Abruzzo

The Montepulciano wines in general are light- to medium-bodied, fruity, and common. But in the hands of a producer like Edoardo Valentini or Emidio Pepe, this variety can reach uncommon heights.

On our first visit to Abruzzo some years ago, we stopped for dinner at Albergo di Rocco on the Chieti-Penne highway and ordered, as always, local wine to accompany our meal. This wine was about as local as you can get. The restaurant (rooms upstairs, gas station and car wash out front) had a *cantina* below, where the proprietor produced his own Montepulciano and Trebbiano. We ordered some of each. When we commented on the food and wine (both good) to the waiter, he told us where we could find the best wine in the area. Having just begun to learn the language, we didn't quite catch the name, but it sounded like he said the Tini Valley. On a subsequent visit to the region we realized that what he had said was that the best wine from the area was that of Valentini. This was no slight to his employer, who agreed with the evaluation.

Recommended Producers

Barone Cornacchia	★+
Casal Thaulero	★
Duchi di Castelluccio	★+
Illuminati Dino	★+
Nicodemi Bruno	★★
Pepe Emido	★★★
Pietrantori Italo	★+
Rosso della Quercia	★★
Tollo Cantino Sociale	★
Rubino	★★
Valentini Edoardo	★★★+

Montepulciano d'Abruzzo★, the best producers★★★

Vintages

Edoardo Valentini, the foremost producer of Montepulciano d'Abruzzo, told us a few years ago that his best vintages were 1975, 1971, 1970, 1968, 1960, 1958, and 1956. The least were 1978, 1976, and 1972; in those vintages, he didn't produce any wine.

Emidio Pepe, the other first-flight producer of Montepulciano, told us that the best years for him were 1979, 1975, 1974, 1970, and 1967; the worst were 1976, 1972, and 1969. The 1978, 1973, and 1971 vintages were medium.

Because of the extensive growing region, it is difficult to generalize about vintages; differences can be significant. But on the theory that some information is better than none at all, we provide the following evaluations as a basic guideline. It applies to the small quantity of better wines only; most of the rest are best drunk within a year or two of the vintage. Outside of the three- and four-star vintages, we have included only the years from 1970 to 1983; anything older, with the exception of the Valentini and Pepe wines, would surely be too old today.

From Niederbacher's vintage chart:
★★★★ 1968, 1958, 1948
★★★ 1982, 1979, 1977, 1975, 1974, 1973, 1965, 1963, 1957, 1956
★★ 1983, 1981, 1980, 1978
★ 1976, 1972, 1971, 1970

Tasting Notes

1982

Priore *(4/85)*. Fruity, agreeable, no personality, a few defects. Why did we include it? It's better than most, and by that it illustrates a point: while most of these wines are common, a few rise above the ordinary and are worth the serious attention of winelovers everywhere. Tasting notes on many of those wines follow.

1981

Rosso della Quercia *(ex-cask 5/82)*. Aroma of chocolate-covered cherries; a little rough, but has the fruit.★(+)

1980

Barone Cornacchia *(5/84)*. Richly fruited aroma recalls cherries; full-bodied, richly flavored; a touch of alcohol mars the finish; not to keep.★+

Fattoria Bruno Nicodemi, Colli Venia *(4/83)*. Rich, cherrylike aroma; full of flavor, some tannin; good quality, good value.★★

Pepe *(ex-vat 1/81)*. The color is so dark it's like ink; a nice mouthful of fruit.★★(★)

Rosso della Quercia *(10 times 4/85)*. Fruity aroma with a dried-fruit nuance; still quite fruity, but seems to be near the end of its useful life. This wine was considerably better two years ago.★

Rosso della Quercia riserva *(3 times 4/85)*. Cherrylike aroma and flavor, vague mushroomlike note; a touch more fruit than the regular, but like that wine getting on in years; drink up.★+

Valentini *(ex-cask 4/81)*. Cherries all over the nose; some tannin, a bit light, will be ready early.★★

1979

Barone Cornacchia *(4/83)*. Fairly full, quite rich, fairly tannic, has the fruit to back it up; cherry notes from the nose through the finish.★★−

Duchi di Castelluccio *(2/81)*. Cherry aroma; fruity, some acidity; could use more age, but good.★+

Pepe *(ex-vat 1/81)*. Lacks the richness and intensity of the '81, but a good wine.★(★)

Rosso della Quercia *(8 times 6/82)*. Strawberry, cherry aroma; fruity, quaffable, most agreeable.★★

1978

Pepe *(ex-vat 1/81)*. Very dark color; some tannin, some astringency, not up to the other wines.★−

Rosso della Quercia *(13 times 4/83)*. Still has fruit, but beginning to fade; this wine was at its best in 1980 and 1981.

Valentini *(1/81; bottled 10/80)*. Intensely fruited, cherrylike aroma; full-flavored, full-bodied, well structured; young.★★(+)

1977

Duchi di Castelluccio *(10/78)*. Inky black; aroma leaps out of the glass, cherries; richly flavored; young, but drinkable now.★★

1977

Pepe *(5 times 5/81)*. Cherrylike aroma; some tannin, loads of flavor; moderate length.★★

Rosso della Quercia *(3 times 10/82)*. Still has fruit on the nose and palate, though it's getting on in years. It was at its best in 1980 and 1981.★+

Tollo, Rubino *(10/83)*. Fruit carries from the aroma across the palate, some firmness; a wine for serious drinking, not serious contemplation, but honest and with some character.★★

Valentini *(1/81)*. Rich, cherrylike aroma; still with tannin to soften, but the fruit is there to carry it, well balanced; some length.★★(★−)

1975

Duchi di Castelluccio *(twice 4/80)*. A big wine, richly fruited, lacks subtlety, but the flavor compensates.★★

Pepe *(8 times 5/81)*. Aroma of cherries; rich flavor, overall fairly well balanced, though marred slightly by a touch of alcohol; a nice wine that needs more age. There was some bottle variation. For the best bottles.★★★−

Valentini *(1/81)*. Black as ink; so big you could cut it with a knife, but not clumsy or lacking in style; a lot of quality and quite young.★★(★)

1974

Pepe *(10 times 11/81)*. Ripe fruit aroma; soft, round, and fruity; ready, though room for improvement; a big, rich wine.★★+

Valentini *(15 times 5/85)*. Opaque color belies its age (it was in our cellar for years); intense, cherrylike aroma; enormous weight and extract, intensely fruited, perhaps lacks some subtlety, but makes up for that with its richness of flavor; figlike note at the end.★★★

1973

Pepe *(twice 10/79)*. Cherry notes, vague, yeasty backnote; loads of fruit; moderate length; some style.★★+

Valentini *(1/81)*. Lovely aroma of cherries; still has tannin, seems to be losing its fruit; somewhat light toward the end.

1971

Pepe *(11/79)*. Fragrant, kirschlike aroma; still has tannin, but the fruit is there to carry it.★★+

Valentini *(1/81)*. Complex bouquet, with the characteristic cherrylike note; soft, round, well structured, and tasty; very long finish; very ready.★★★

1970

Pepe *(3 times 1/81)*. Cherries all over the aroma; flavorful, still has tannin; a bit short.★★+

Valentini *(1/81)*. Youthful color shows very little age; deep, rich, complex aroma; full-bodied, full-flavored; the finish is marred by a touch of alcohol.★★+

Older vintages

1969 Valentini *(1/81)*. Another deeply colored wine that appears younger than its years; complex bouquet, rich and intense; full-bodied, soft, round and tasty; long on the palate.★★ +

1968 Valentini *(1/81)*. Lovely nose, fragrant and fruity; soft, round, and velvety; has style.★★★

1967 Pepe *(twice 1/81)*. Complex bouquet, cherry note; soft and velvety; some style, very ready.★★★

1965 Valentini *(1/81)*. Floral bouquet, suggestion of toasted almonds; low acid, tasty; some age beginning to set in.★★ −

1961 Valentini *(1/81)*. Nose shows age, some va; harsh edges, beginning to fall apart.

1958 Valentini *(1/81)*. Did we say that Montepulciano d'Abruzzo should be drunk young, or that it is an unserious quaffing wine to wash down hearty fare? Did we also say there are exceptions? Here is one that is exceptional indeed. Rich and complex, on both the nose and the palate; a complete and well-structured wine of real quality, smooth-textured and velvety; very long finish.★★★ +

Montepulciano Producers

Pepe Emidio *(Torano Nuovo)*. Emidio Pepe owns 17.3 acres (7 hectares), 7.4 (3) in vines, 4.9 acres (2 hectares) of which are planted to montepulciano.

Pepe produced his first wine from the 1964 vintage. His average production of Montepulciano d'Abruzzo is some 20,000 bottles a year.

Production of Montepulciano d'Abruzzo

Year	Bottles	Year	Bottles
1967	12,000	1975	18,000
1970	18,000	1977	14,000
1971	15,000	1978	23,000
1973	20,000	1979	33,000
1974	20,000	1980	30,000

Pepe also produces a Trebbiano d'Abruzzo, which undergoes malolactic in the bottle. It's premeditated; that's the way he likes it. Pepe has some rather atypical ideas about wine and winemaking.

He doesn't like the taste of wine aged in wood, and he doesn't drink it. In fact, he doesn't drink any producer's wine but his own. At one of the dinners during a wine fair at Foggia, we sat with Pepe. We offered to pour him some wine from the bottles that had been chosen to accompany the buffet. He passed them all up. He had brought a few bottles of his own. He offered to pour us some. We accepted.

Emidio Pepe must be the most unusual winemaker we've ever met (and we've met quite a few), unusual in the way he makes his wine in particular. He doesn't believe in using machines of any kind, if at all possible.

The grapes for his Montepulciano are first destalked by being pushed by hand through a grid. His wife, Rosa, and daughters help out with the hand labor. Next the grapes are crushed by feet. Pepe did mention the possibility of being forced to use a hand-operated basket press in the future because of the difficulty of finding men willing to do the treading.

The must is fermented in glass-lined cement tanks, is allowed to settle, and is then racked. After about a year, the wine is racked again and then bottled. Pepe doesn't believe in wood aging, you recall. And he doesn't bother with much tank aging either. It's right into the bottles, which are stacked horizontally in long rows, where they stay for two or three years (a visit to this part of the *cantina* creates a bit of *deja-vu à la Champagne*).

At the end of the aging period, the bottles are stood upright and the sediment allowed to settle. A couple of months later they are moved to a small room in a corner of the *cantina* for the final and most curious phase in their rather original handling. Enter a woman with a winged corkscrew. She uncorks the bottle and proceeds to decant it into a fresh bottle. In doing so she pours, without benefit of a funnel, holding the bottle to the light filtering in through a small window. Not surprisingly, a fair amount of wine misses the bottle. It is caught in a demijohn topped with a large funnel on the floor at her feet. Do they let the wine left in the bottles settle again and redecant to lose less of it? We asked Pepe. Only at the table, where it is drunk by his family and by the workers; that wine is not bottled for sale.

We watched the operation in amazement for a while, then suggested to Emidio that things might go a bit faster if he attached a one-arm cork puller to the bench for the woman. *"Mai,"* he protested, that would disturb the wine. It must be opened by hand.

You have to see it to believe it, and if we hadn't we would be writing about the legend of Emidio Pepe and his twice-bottled Montepulciano, not ever daring to tell you that it is true.

With all the care and concern he invests in his wines, Pepe is bound to produce a fine Montepulciano d'Abruzzo, and he does. To our taste, only Valentini produces a better one, and Pepe's is very close to it in quality. Of all the vintages of Pepe's wines we've tasted, we liked his '70 and '71 the best. Montepulciano d'Abruzzo★★★

Giuseppe de Camillo of Vinicola Cascanditella (above right)　　　—photo by Tom Abruzzini

Rosso della Quercia *(Casacanditella)*. Giuseppe di Camillo, proprietor of Vinicola Casa-canditella, has no vineyards. He selects grapes from top-quality sites. They are crushed at a nearby cooperative under the direction of his enologist, and the must is brought to his *cantina,* Vinicola Casacandidella near Chieti. There it is fermented and the wine aged in oak casks.

The winery has a capacity of 600,000 bottles of wine. Giuseppe's young son, Bruno, helps out in the winery; the older, Peter, handles an important part of the sales. Di Camillo produces red, white, and rosé. His first wine, the *rosso,* was from the 1975 vintage. He didn't make a '76.

The name Rosso della Quercia ("red of the oak tree") does not refer to the origin of the fruit, nor to the type of cooperage used. The *quercia* of the name is a 900-year-old oak tree growing not far from the winery in the village of Casacanditella in the foothills of La Maiella.

Giuseppe is a warm, generous man with a love for his village and for his region. A few years ago he arranged a special dinner of regional specialties for a small group of journalists and a few other producers attending a wine fair in the area. For the highlight of the meal, he hired a man who could prepare *maccheroni al mugnaio,* a dish that takes all day to make. While the pork, veal, and beef simmered with tomatoes and seasonings in a large kettle on the fire, the man—originally he would have been a miller, as the name of the dish indicates—worked a large mound of flour into a long strand of pasta, adding only water, kneading it and rolling it between his palms, to form one long piece—more than 165 feet (50 meters) long—and coiling it into a

315

tall beehive. This dish was first made, they tell us, at the court of Count Robert d'Anjou at Fiume Fino in 1684.

Our pasta maker cut the *maccherono* with a wooden blade and draped it over his arm to carry it into the kitchen. Then the pasta, cooked perfectly *al dente,* was spread on a large wooden table, topped with the sauce, and all were invited to dig in, in the traditional manner, eating with the fingers. In our case they made an exception, and those who preferred to be neat and modern were invited to break with tradition and use forks. And to drink the wines passed around from glasses (saves spills from bottles bobbled with slippery fingers).

Giuseppe's Rosso della Quercia was one of the Montepulciano d'Abruzzos served with the *maccheroni;* it went very well.

Rosso della Quercia is made in two styles: regular and riserva. The riserva, from special vineyards, is aged in Limousin oak casks for about one year. Overall, these are good wines that emphasize the cherrylike fruit of the montepulciano grape. They age moderately well, reaching their peak before their fourth year. Montepulciano d'Abruzzo.★★

*Edoardo
Valentini*

—photo by Sheldon Wasserman

Valentini Edoardo *(Loreto Aprutino).* Valentini produces the finest red and white wines of the region, wines whose quality goes far beyond the borders of Abruzzo. His Montepulciano d'Abruzzo stands with the best wines of central Italy. His Trebbiano d'Abruzzo is in a class by itself, the finest Trebbiano we've ever tasted, and a very good white wine by any standard; surprisingly, it also ages very well. We've tasted some bottles that were still good after a decade.

Valentini, a lawyer by profession but a *vignaiolo* or "little ol' winemaker" by preference, gave up a career in law and the city life and moved to the family home in the country in the village of Loreto Aprutino to tend his vines, *oliveti,* and orchards, which he does with a passion, a passion for the land. In one sense, it seems strange that this scholar and intellect would prefer the isolated country life to the activity of the city. But here he has his books, stacked not only by his chair but on the shelves, tables, cabinets, and all other available spaces not covered with papers, unanswered correspondence, and so on.

The farm, when he took over, was worked under the old system of *mezzadria,* and produced a variety of crops. Edoardo reduced this to three: vines, olives, and fruit trees, all planted in specialized cultivation.

Valentini has 150 acres (60 hectares) of vines, 80 percent planted to montepulciano at altitudes of 920 to 985 feet (280 to 300 meters). When we visited him a few years ago, he said he planned to put in another 25 acres (10 hectares).

Cru	Hectares	Planted	Used for
Camposacro	12	recently	white
Castelluccio	14	1964 & 1971	all three
Cava Sorge	3	1965	red and rosé
Colle Cavaliere	12	1974 & 1975	all three
Colle Mantello	22	1978	red and rosé

From these vines he selects, in the years when he produces wines, about 5 percent of his best grapes and sells the rest. At most, he makes 30,000 bottles of wine a year: about 20,000 to 21,000 bottles of Trebbiano and Montepulciano d'Abruzzo Cerasuolo (rosé) and 7000 to 8000 bottles of Montepulciano d'Abruzzo *rosso.*

Production of Montepulciano d'Abruzzo

Year	Bottles	Year	Bottles
1970	8,775	1975	12,967
1971	8,182	1976	0
1972	0	1977	4,637
1973	13,027	1978	0
1974	12,779	1979	4,132

The first wine Edoardo bottled was either the '56 or '57; we've tasted them back only to 1958.

The first time we visited Edoardo at Loreto, we tasted a few wines from cask and some very fine vintages from bottle. He promised that if we gave him a couple of days' notice he would set up a tasting for us of all the vintages of Montepulciano d'Abruzzo and Trebbiano d'Abruzzo in his cellar, and wife Adriana would prepare "la lingua di pappagallo" and other such delicacies. We gave him ten days' notice.

When we returned ten days later, he had done as he had said. And Adriana, a lovely lady whose smile lights up her whole face and those of the people she smiles at, had prepared a menu of regional and house specialities, one dish more impressive than the last. But before we sated our appetites on the dinner, we had an excellent tasting.

Edoardo had lined up a dozen bottles of his Trebbiano and another dozen of Montepulciano. Edoardo says he doesn't care much for the red wine personally. One wonders what this wine would be like if he did—the only four-star Montepulciano d'Abruzzo? He has raised Trebbiano to heights none would have believed possible if they hadn't tasted his. He claims he has a special subvariety, the *true* trebbiano d'Abruzzo. (He has all the research and proofs among his papers, and someday when we have lots of time on our hands we've promised to plow through them. In the meantime, we'll take his word for it.)

For each wine Edoardo had a sheet listing all the statistics from the analyses made, as well as much other data in his journal, including the phases of the moon when the wines were racked and bottled. Edoardo is a man of the twentieth century, but he has deep roots in the past. Among his books are the texts of the ancients in the original Latin. (English will be his next language, he assured us.) He spoke of his wines with an enthusiasm that didn't let up for a minute—nor, unfortunately, did his description and explanation, even long enough for a translation. But we couldn't protest too strongly, as the wines themselves spoke volumes, and directly to the tongue.

Valentini's Montepulciano d'Abruzzo is aged for one year in old casks and is always sold as Vecchio. Of those we've tasted, we were most impressed with the '77, '75, '74, '71, '68, and '58. Valentini's wines have an uncommon richness and complexity. They are very well balanced and age extremely well, developing nuances of flavor and aroma found only in first-class wines. Montepulciano d'Abruzzo★★★ +

PART III

Aglianico

Chapter 14

The Aglianico Grape

Aglianico is the third of Italy's excellent native varieties. It is the noble vine of the south, considerably less known and less appreciated than the nebbiolo or the sangiovese. In one sense, the wines of the aglianico are to Italian wines what Italian wines are to the wines of the rest of the world. Edgar Rice Burroughs wrote a book entitled *The Land That Time Forgot.* The aglianico could be called the grape the world forgot.

There are only two really important wines made from the aglianico: Aglianico del Vulture and Taurasi. Outside of these, aglianico is used in Falerno and as a part of the *uvaggio* for Lacryma Cristi, Lettere, Solopaca, Pollino, Biferno, Pentro di Isernia, and a number of other wines.

Aglianico is grown in Basilicata, Campania, Calabria, Lazio, and Molise. Though the variety is a noble one, there are only a few wines made from it that demonstrate its great potential, and even fewer people who recognize its pedigree. To those who are wondering what the aglianico is all about, we recommend that they try d'Angelo's Aglianico del Vulture or Mastroberardino's Taurasi; then we think they will realize its possibilities.

The aglianico vine was reputedly introduced into the Vulture area of Basilicata by Hellenes from ancient Greece who settled in southern Italy in pre-Roman times. They planted the vine in volcanic soil on the sunny slopes of Monte Vulturino. Some authorities say that the aglianico may have been the first vine brought to Italy by the Greeks. This variety was called *Vitis hellenica* after them. Later this became Ellenico, and in the fifteenth century aglianico, as it is known today. From Basilicata, the aglianico was introduced into Calabria, Campania, and other neighboring regions.

Basilicata

Basilicata, the Lucania of the ancients, is the poorest region of Italy. And it is a land of natural disasters. On November 22, 1980, a major earthquake—not the first, but surely one of the most devastating—brought death and destruction to much of the area, a solemn reminder of the difficulty of ekeing out a living here. The tremors were felt as far north as Tuscany, where chandeliers swayed from the ceilings. Two nights later at the Altesino *cantina* in Montalcino, we met a young man from Basilicata who was on his way south to help the victims of the disaster and to be sure that his relatives were all right. While he waited for a friend to join him in the early morning hours to make the trip down, we stayed late in front of the fireplace singing traditional Italian songs as Claudio Basla accompanied us on the guitar.

Some of the medieval hilltop villages, with their communal ovens and narrow by-streets formed from a series of steps, which we had visited on our trip to the south the previous spring, no longer exist.

There are nearly 54,000 growers in Basilicata tending 40,000 acres (16,000 hectares) of vines in specialized cultivation and perhaps twice that in *coltura promiscua.* Production averages 12.2 million gallons (460,000 hectoliters) of wine a year. By far the most of it—8.7 million gallons (330,000 hectoliters)—is produced in the province of Potenza, an area with more than 30,000 acres (12,300 hectares) of vines in specialized vineyards and 60,000 (24,000) promiscuous. A shade over 2 percent of the regional production is DOC wine, and all of that is Aglianico del Vulture.

Aglianico del Vulture

Aglianico del Vulture is produced from grapes planted in volcanic soil at altitudes of 650 to 2300 feet (200 to 700 meters) in the *communes* of Acerenza, Atella, Banzi, Barile, Forenza, Genzano di Lucania, Ginestra, Lavello, Maschito, Melfi, Palazzo S. Gervasio, Rapolla, Rionero in Vulture, Ripacandida, and Venosa, and the localities of Caldare, Giardino-Macarico, Iatta, Piano Regie, Ponzi, Quercie, S. Croce, S. Maria, and S. Savino in the Vulture area of Basilicata, about midway between the cities of Potenza and Foggia in neighboring Apulia.

The best locations for the vines are on the southeastern slopes of the now extinct volcano, Monte Vulturino. The soil is rocky and poor. The vines in the best vineyards are trained *al alberello,* as individual head-pruned vines standing separately like "little trees."

There are some 590 acres (239 hectares) under vines in the Aglianico del Vulture DOC zone. Annual production, which varies considerably, averages just over 100,000 cases a year.

Vintage	Cases	Vintage	Cases
1976	71,104	1980	58,883
1977	61,105	1981	188,870
1978	48,851	1982	96,657
1979	142,208	1983	106,656

Source: Italian Wine Center, New York, 1985.

Italian Wine Law

DOC recognizes Aglianico del Vulture rosso, rosato, dry and semisweet, still and sparkling. The only styles of interest to us here are the still, dry reds. (The subject *is* noble wines.)

	DOC Requirements		
	Minimum age (years)	Minimum alcohol	Maximum yield (gallons/acre)
	Cask	Total	
Regular	0	1	11.5%	748
Vecchio	2	3	12.0%	748
Riserva	3	5	12.0%	748

The aging period for all three types is calculated from November 1; regular Aglianico del Vulture, then, cannot be sold before November 1 of the year following the harvest.

The Producers

There are seven individual producers and six cooperatives bottling Aglianico del Vulture. Of the wines we've tasted, those of Fratelli d'Angelo are clearly in a class by themselves. D'Angelo is not only the best producer in the zone, but a fine producer by any standard.

Recommended Producers
Botte
Consorzio Viticoltori Associati del Vulture
D'Angelo
Miali
Paternoster
Torre Sveva

Armando Martino and F.lli Napolitano also have good reputations.

The Quality of Aglianico del Vulture

Vulture is generally best from five to eight years of the vintage. It makes a good accompaniment to lamb or kid, either chops or roasts; it also goes well with stews and braised red meats.

Poverty, lack of recognition for the wine, and consequent low prices discourage many producers from making the sacrifices necessary to create a noble wine from the aglianico. With some recognition, we hope that this situation will change, and we can look forward to tasting a lot of excellent Aglianico del Vulture in the future. Rating★★ (the quality is potentially much higher).

Vintages

According to Donato d'Angelo, 1982, 1981, 1977, and 1973 were the best vintages for Vulture. Niederbacher basically agrees:

★★★ 1982, 1981, 1978, 1977, 1975, 1973
★★ 1983, 1980, 1979, 1974, 1971, 1970
★ 1976, 1972

Of the years we've tasted, we liked the '73 the best; it's doubtful, though, if any bottles of that splendid vintage are still available today.

Tasting Notes

1981 D'Angelo *(11/84)*. Big, richly fruited aroma; well structured, tasty, good quality.★★

1980 D'Angelo *(ex-vat 1/81)*. Expansive aroma of fresh cherries, acid on the high side (it hadn't gone through malolactic fermentation yet), loads of flavor.[★★]

1979 D'Angelo riserva *(3 times 12/84)*. Ripe cherry aroma; a forward rush of ripe fruit, medium body, balanced; long finish.★★ +

1978 Consorzio Viticoltori Associati del Vulture *(6/82)*. Cherry aroma; balanced, fruity, a bit light; ready.★ −

1978 D'Angelo *(ex-cask 5/80)*. Has the structure and the flavor, should make a nice glass with time, though not up to the '79.[★★]

1978 Paternoster *(5/80)*. Fruity aroma, fennel-like note; some tannin, drinkable now.★

1977 Cantina Coop. della Riforma Fondiaria *(5/81)*. Stinky; has tannin, shallow and bitter. This was better than the '78 (enough said about that wine.)

1977 D'Angelo riserva *(8 times 6/83)*. Bottle of 4/83: Characteristic cherry aroma; richly flavored, quite young; good quality.★★(★) Bottle of 6/83: Some oxidation, also some flavor; we suspect an off bottle is the culprit.

1975 D'Angelo *(8 times 7/85)*. Cherrylike aroma, vague floral notes; has a rustic side to it, light tannin, a lot of flavor, some astringency setting in; drink up.★★ −

1974 Centrale Cantine Coop. *(6/82)*. Pretty aroma, fruity, fresh, fragrant; stop. After that it is awful, tastes of filter paper.

1974 D'Angelo riserva *(5 times 2/81)*. Cherries all over this wine from the nose through the palate and the long finish, richly flavored and intense.★★ +

1973 D'Angelo *(3 times 5/80)*. Richly fruited aroma and palate, loads of quality here; very long finish.★★★

The Zone's Top Producer

F.lli d'Angelo *(Rionero in Vulture), c 1920*. Rocco d'Angelo and his sons, Donato and Lucio, produce 266,000 bottles of wine a year. They plan to double that by 1988. When we visited them a few years ago, their production was about 60 percent of what it is today. We don't know, though, if they are making more of their Aglianico del Vulture, which did range from 45,000 to 75,000 bottles a year. They also make three spumanti, plus Moscato, Malvasia, and a semisweet red aglianico, as well as a Sansavino red and a white Lucanello.

The fratelli d'Angelo don't own any vineyards. They buy their aglianico grapes from some of the best districts in the zone: Querce, San Sevino, Piano Dell'Altare, and Santa Maria. Enologist Donato d'Angelo makes the wine.

Up until 1958, d'Angelo, like nearly all the other producers here, sold their wine *sfuso*. When they began to bottle the wine, they sold it as Rionero Rosso or Vino di Basilicata. In 1964, they began labeling the wine D'Angelo Aglianico del Vulture.

Donato told us that although the wine wasn't labeled as Aglianico del Vulture until 1964, the name was used locally for the wines in the 1940s, although not by them. In 1971, Aglianico del Vulture was granted official DOC status under Italian wine law.

D'Angelo was among the first wineries, if not *the* first, to export wine from Basilicata to the U.S. From 1926 to 1929, they shipped the wines abroad in 55-gallon barrels.

Today, F.lli d'Angelo is to our knowledge the finest producer in Basilicata. Aglianico del Vulture★★ +

Falerno

Falerno was known in its heyday as Falernian. This was the legendary Roman potation. William Younger describes it as "the Great First Growth of the Roman Empire and...the most famous wine in ancient history."[26]

As with the Falernian of ancient times, both red and white Falerno are produced. There was also a sweet version in that age, but if there is one made today we are not aware of it.

The grapes for this wine, today as then, are grown in the region along the border of Latium and Campania, but the modern Falerno is a far cry from the most famous and highly regarded wine of its country.

Latium

The Falerno produced in Lazio tends to be lower in alcohol—generally under 12 percent—lighter in body, and somewhat earlier maturing than the version south of the border. In Lazio, the aglianico grapes are blended with barbera.

Though it has been some time since we tasted the Falerno of Leone Nannini, he used to make a good one.

Campania

In the Falerno of Campania, aglianico is often blended with sangiovese, negro amaro, and/or per'e palumbo. Generally, the higher the proportion of aglianico, the better the wine. At its best, this wine is dry, full-bodied, and somewhat rough when young, requiring a few years of bottle age to soften and mellow. It attains 13 percent or more alcohol. The only producers we can recommend are Michele Moio, especially for his fine black label Falerno, and Fattoria Villa Matilde.

Tasting Notes

nv Moio Michele (12%) *(5/80).* Floral perfume with honeyed notes; light-bodied, some tannin, fruity; a bit short.★ +

nv Moio Michele (15%) *(5/80).* Dark purple; floral bouquet; some tannin, full-bodied; balanced.★★ +

Taurasi

Taurasi takes its name from that village on the site of the ancient Oscan city of Taurasia in the center of the production zone. Wine has been produced here since before 80 B.C. Roman historian Titus Livy, writing of the area a few decades later in his *History of Rome,* referred to it as a "land verdant with abundant vines."

The DOC growing zone encompasses all or parts of the townships of Bonito, Castelfranci, Castelvetere sul Calore, Fontanarosa, Làpio, Luogosano, Mirabella Eclano, Montefalcione, Montemarano, Montemiletto, Paternòpoli, Pietradefusi, S. Angelo all'Esca, San Mango sul Calore, Taurasi, Torre Le Nocelle, and Venticano.

Aglianico vines are cultivated at altitudes of 1475 to 2460 feet (450 to 750 meters) on slopes with south and southeastern exposures. Good soil for the aglianico vines, according to Mastroberardino—perhaps the zone's only producer, certainly the most important—is volcanic earth rich in potassium. This provides higher sugars, though acid levels tend to be a bit low, which limits the wine's capacity to age. The best soil, they feel, is clay and clay-limestone mixtures in hillside locations.

Production of Taurasi averages 10,500 to 12,600 cases a year.

The Uvaggio

DOC regulations allow the addition of up to 30 percent of any combination of piedirosso, sangiovese, and barbera grapes. The piedirosso is reputedly the *Columbina purpurea* referred to by Pliny. Mastroberardino uses only aglianico in their Taurasi. They point out that the other varieties not only detract from the character of the wine but shorten its aging potential as well.

DOC allows up to five percent concentrated must to be used to bring up the alcohol in weak vintages.

DOC Requirements

	Minimum age (years)		Minimum alcohol	Maximum yield (gallons/acre)
	Cask	Total		
Regular	1	3	12%	823
Riserva	1	4	12%	823

Taurasi is aged in either oak or chestnut casks. Mastroberardino uses both. They age their riserva for four years, for the first year in the traditional large chestnut casks and then in casks of Slavonian oak ranging in capacity from 795 to 1320 gallons (30 to 50 hectoliters).

At Mastroberardino they pick their grapes late to produce wines with more richness and character. The aglianico is a late ripener, normally reaching maturity in the last ten days of October. When the picking is put off until the middle of November—a harvest between the 15th and 25th of November is normal for Mastroberardino—it is not rare for the first snow to fall while the harvest is still going on.

The Quality of Taurasi

Taurasi is a fine wine; in top-flight vintages it can achieve real distinction and class. It is a wine that deserves more recognition.

Taurasi goes well with roast meats, especially beef and lamb; it is also a fine accompaniment to steak or venison chops. A well-aged Taurasi goes very well with a good piece of not too potent provolone and good conversation. Rating★★★

Vintages evaluated by Mastroberardino

1984	0	Very bad, among the worst.
1983	★★★★	One of the best ever.
1982	★★★	Very good.
1981	★★★	Very good.
1980	★	Difficult.
1979	★★ +	Quite good, better than 1978.
1978	★★	Medium.
1977	★★★★	One of the best ever.
1976	0	Very bad, among the worst.
1975	★★★	Only 1977 and 1973 were better in the decade.
1974	★★	Medium quality.
1973	★★★	Only 1977 was better in the decade.

1972	★★	Fair.
1971	★★★	Very, very good.
1970	★★★	Very good.
1969	★★	Quite good.
1968	★★★★	One of the best ever; only 1961 was better in the decade.

Older vintages

★★★★	1961, 1958
★★★	1967, 1966, 1964, 1960, 1956, 1955, 1951, 1948
★★	1965, 1959, 1954, 1952, 1950, 1949, 1946
★	1957, 1953, 1947
0	1963, 1962, 1945

Antonio and Walter Mastroberardino

The Zone's Best Producer

Mastroberardino (*Altripalda, Campania*), *1878.* The winery founded by Michele Mastroberardino in the last century is today owned and operated by Antonio and Walter Mastroberardino. Antonio is the winemaker, Walter the viticulturist.

Mastroberardino has some 125 acres (50 hectares) of vineyards, which supply them with 50 percent of their grapes.

Tasting Notes

1981 (*6 times 7/85*). Characteristic cherrylike aroma with spicy, black pepper notes; tannic and rough, but seems to have sufficient fruit to carry it; try again in three or four years.★★(+)

1980 riserva (*8 times 4/85*). Floral aroma with a hint of almonds, volcanic nuance; a lot of flavor beneath the tannin, quite young, well structured, has potential.★★(★)

1979 riserva (*9 times 2/85*). Floral aroma, vaguely cherrylike back note; firm and tannic, closed.★★

1978 riserva (*twice 2/85*). Almonds, cherries, and flowers on aroma, volcanic back note; moderate tannin, flavorful, more forward than some of the other vintages, but still needs age.★★ +

1977 riserva (*7 times 4/85*). Floral bouquet, with notes of cherries and almonds; a mouthful of fruit beneath the tannin, well-knit, intense; a lot of class here, has style and real quality.★★★(+)

1975 (*twice 1/82*). Aroma of cherries and flowers; still has some tannin to lose, but drinkable now, well balanced; good quality.★★(★)

1974 (*12 times 12/84*). Characteristic floral, cherrylike bouquet; full-flavored, has an edge to it, no point in keeping it any longer.★★ −

1973 riserva (*17 times 7/85*). Aroma of almonds, cherries, flowers; still some tannin to be resolved, but quite drinkable now, with a lot of distinction and class; quite long; sure to improve; it displays style; give it another two or three years to be at its very best.★★★

1972 (*11/79*). Aroma lacks, some alcohol intrudes; not bad for the year, has body, some tannin, and flavor; very short.★ −

1971 riserva (*10 times 9/83*). Almonds and flowers on bouquet; well structured, still has considerable tannin as well as lots of fruit, young.★★(★)

1969 riserva (*5 times 9/83*). Light, fruity aroma with notes of cherries and flowers; still has a fair amount of tannin, but balanced with fruit.★★ +

1968 riserva (*11 times 7/85*). Bottle of 2/85: Cherries from the first sniff; a rush of fruit across the palate, cassis and floral notes; still firm and tannic, but with the fruit to carry it. It's surprising how slowly this wine is developing. When we first tasted it in 1978, we felt it needed a few more years to soften. Now it's been more than a few, and we will wait a few more.★★(★) Bottle of 7/85: Vaguely floral aroma, cherry notes, some va; still has tannin, and a lot of it, also a smoothness of texture; some alcohol intrudes on the finish.★★

1968 riserva, Montmarano (bottled after almost seven years in wood) (*twice 10/78*). Aroma of cassis; deep, rich flavors under the tannin; shows a lot of potential.★★(★)

1968 riserva, Piano d'Angelo (*4/85*). Rich bouquet with floral notes, showing a mellowness and complexity from bottle age; loads of tannin over loads of fruit, very young still; real quality evident.★★(★ +)

1961 riserva (*11/79*). Rich, expansive perfume, with nuances of walnuts, cherries, figs; velvety texture, complexity of flavors; ready.★★★

1958 riserva (*11/79*). Lovely aroma; considerable tannin, lots of flavor, still young; could be longer on the aftertaste.★★ +

Cru	Hectares	First bottled as a cru
San Gregorio	5	—
San Michele	10	—
Vigna Della Corte	5	—
Vignadangelo	20	from 1983
Vignadora	10	from 1983

In the better vintages Mastroberardino bottles selected lots from the best vineyards.

Cru	First bottled	Bottles
Castelfranci	1968	8,100
Montemarano	1968	7,950
Piano d'Angelo	1968	8,250
Tampenne in Argo di Montemarano	1971	2,123

Production at Mastroberardino varies from a bit over 55,000 to just under 75,000 cases a year. They expect to increase this to 100,000 within five years.

Wine	Type	Cases
Fiano di Avellino	white	3,000-5,000
Greco di Tufo	white	25,000-30,000
Hirpinia	white	2,000
	red	1,500
Lacrima d'Irpinia	rosé	2,000
Lacryma Christi del Vesuvio	white	10,000
	red	2,000
Taurasi	red	10,000-20,000
Taurasi riserva	red	1,000-1,500

They specialize at Mastroberardino in producing wines from the ancient varieties and the traditional grapes of the area: aglianico; greco, originally the Aminea gemina of Tessaglia; coda di volpe, the alopecis vine called by Pliny *cauda vulpium* ("tail of the fox"); fiano, referred to as *Vitis apiana* ("the bee vine") in Pliny's *Natural History* and the grape of the Roman Apianum wine; and the sangionoso or olivella grape known to Pliny as *Vitis oleagina.*

They also produce an aglianico rosé called Lacrimarosa d'Irpinia. Antonio discovered that the ancients had produced a similar wine, and he reintroduced this wine in 1966. It is quite a good rosé, with more character than most. It is firm and dry and goes quite well with food, especially luncheon dishes and white meats.

The Mastroberardinos are serious about producing fine wines and preserving the ancient tradition of the proud aglianico variety, as well as the other traditional vines of the area. But while they believe in tradition, they are not enmeshed in the past. Where they feel the wines will benefit from it, they take advantage of modern technology. Contrary to the ever-growing trend to use French grapes such as cabernet and French methods such as aging in *barriques,* they are intent on preserving their heritage.

Taurasi★★★

PART IV
Other Noble Reds

Chapter 15

Recioto della Valpolicella Amarone

According to archeological evidence, vines were growing in the Valpolicella area some 40 million years ago. Winemaking in the zone is not quite that ancient. It is known that the Arusnati people living around Tagus Arusnatium, now known as Fumane, were producing wine there in the fifth century B.C. Pliny refers to the Retico wine produced in the territory of Verona. Other Roman writers—Martial, Suetonius, Strabo, and Virgil— also wrote of the wines of this region.

The sweet Acinatico was already produced during the Roman era. In the sixth century it came in for high praise from Cassiodorus, minister to the Ostrogoth King Theodoric. Cassiodorus—scholar, connoisseur, and wine critic—was in charge of ordering provisions for the Veronese court at Ravenna. In a letter to his agents in the countryside, he sent an urgent demand for supplies of this rare wine. It was produced, albeit in very limited quantities, in both red and white versions. Of the red he had this to say:

> It has a pure and exceptional taste and a regal colour, so that you may believe either that purple got its colour from the wine or that the wine is the epitome of purple. Its sweetness is of incredible gentleness, its density is accompanied by an indescribable stability and it swells over the tongue in such a way that it seems either a liquid made of solid flesh or else a drink to be eaten.

He drew their attention also to the Acinatico bianco:

> Nor must you neglect to find that other wine which shines like a milky drink, since it is more marvellous but also more difficult to find. There is in it a beautiful whiteness and a clear purity, so that whilst the other one may be said to be born of roses, this one seems to be born of the lily.[27]

To his list of credits, we must add poet. One can imagine his agents, after having read such praise, insisting on trying a few glasses of the wine once located, just to be sure they had the real thing.

Based on our single experience with this wine, today even rarer than in Cassiodorus' day, the '28 Acinatico from Bertani tasted in April 1985, we can appreciate his enthusiasm.

> The color of the wine, after more than half a century, had taken on a warm mahogany hue—born of roses, as the poet would say. Its complex bouquet offered a medley of scents—licorice, berries, chocolate, dried grapes, coffee, nuts, and toffee. It was rich and concentrated, like a liqueur, in some ways reminiscent of an old Madeira, a wine to be sipped and savored. The finish lingered long on the palate, reflecting some of the aromatic chords struck on the aroma. It was a complete wine, very impressive indeed.★★★★

Gaetano Bertani told us the wine had 16 to 17 percent alcohol; it was quite well balanced. The high natural sugar content of the wine was caused by the fermentation being blocked when the alcohol got too high for it to continue.

Origin of the Valpolicella Name

Valpolicella, according to some accounts, means "valley of many cellars," which seems fitting. It is derived, they say, from the Greek word *poli* ("many") and the Latin *cella* ("cellar"). The name Val Polesela used in reference to this area is found, according to Giovanni Vicentini, in a decree issued by Federico Barbarossa on August 24, 1177.[28]

The Growing Zone

The Valpolicella area is a district 27 miles (45 kilometers) long and varying from 3 to 5 miles (5 to 8 kilometers) in breadth, north of Verona and extending from the Adige River to the Cassano Valley. Bardolino and Lake Garda lie to the west and Soave to the east. The land ranges in altitude from 490 to 1150 feet (150 to 350 meters).

Some parts of Valpolicella bring to mind the countryside of Tuscany, with their vineyards, olive groves, and cypress trees.

There are roughly 15,000 acres (6000 hectares) under vines in the nineteen *communes* of Valpolicella. More than half the vineyards are in Valpolicella Classico, the classic or oldest part of the zone, which takes in the villages of Fumane, Marano, Negrar, S. Ambrogio, and S. Pietro Incariano in the western part.

The area around Sant' Ambrogio is considered the heart of the Amarone production zone. Within this area, north of Gargagnago, is a district called Amaròn, which may have given the wine its name.

The Valpolicellas and Amarones of Sant' Ambrogio, including those of San Giorgio and La Grola, have been described as having a bouquet reminiscent of irises. These Amarones have more alcohol and are bigger in body and smoother in texture than most. They are generally ready to drink from their third or fourth year, though those of San Giorgio reputedly require more time—seven or eight years—to be at their peak. The Valpolicellas and Amarones of Fumane are said to display an aroma of violets; those of Negrar, especially from Jago and Moròn, to have a scent of roses.

The Wines of Valpolicella

Average annual production of the Valpolicella wines is more than 4.1 million cases. Of this, more than 50 percent is produced in the Classico zone. Less than 5 percent, or 200,000 cases, is Recioto della Valpolicella, including Amarone.

The wine of Valpolicella is made in various styles. The most common is the light-bodied, dry fruity red. This wine is most appealing drunk young and cool. It is at its best before the end of its second year, in some cases before its third.

Some producers make a more serious style, using a sort of *governo*. In the spring, occasionally later, the new Valpolicella is refermented on the lees from the Amarone. Foremost among the wines of this style is the Campo Fiorin of Masi. Allegrini also uses this traditional method to produce their Valpolicella. We've tasted ten-year-old Campo Fiorin and Valpolicella from Allegrini that was still drinking very well. Le Ragose is another fine producer who uses this technique.

Valpolicella is also made as a full-bodied, semisweet wine, Recioto della Valpolicella; as a semisweet sparkling wine, Recioto della Valpolicalla spumante; and as a full-bodied, robust, characteristically bitter dry wine, Recioto della Valpolicella Amarone.

Regardless of the style, Italian wine law sets regulations on the allowable grape varieties.

The *Uvaggio*

The wine must be made from 40 to 70 percent corvina veronese, 20 to 40 percent rondinella, and 5 to 25 percent molinara; up to 15 percent negrara trentina, rossignola, barbera, and/or sangiovese can also be added. Dindarella is another variety used by some producers. Up to 15 percent of grapes, must, or wine from outside the zone may be added to correct a weak vintage, deficient in alcohol and body.

The corvina, or cruina as it is also known, has a few different clones; these include corvinone, corvina rizza, and corvina gentile. This grape is said to contribute color, body, bouquet, and the basic Valpolicella character to the wine. Rondinella is added for color, strength, and vigor. Molinara or mulinara, also known as rossara veronese and rossanella, is blended in to make the wine lighter and more drinkable. Negrara, they say, adds softness, freshness, and early drinkability.

DOC Requirements

	Minimum age	Minimum alcohol	Maximum yield (gallons/acre)
Valpolicella	none	11%	898
Superiore	1 year	12%	898
Recioto	none	14%	513

The aging period for the superiore is calculated from January 1. Recioto must contain no less than 14 percent potential alcohol, the level it would reach if fermented dry; actual alcohol must be no less than 12 percent (the balance being unfermented sugar). To qualify as Amarone under the law, this wine cannot contain more than 0.4 percent residual sugar; it is often even drier.

The term *classico* on the label indicates that the grapes came from an area of five villages considered the classic zone. Recioto della Valpolicella Valpantena comes from the Valpantena valley to the east of the *zona classica,* in the center of the Valpolicella zone.

Recioto

According to Vicentini, the term *recioto* was first used for this wine in the middle of the nineteenth century. There are various theories regarding the origin of the name. The most commonly held says that it is derived from the dialect word *recia* ("ear"), because only the upper parts of the grape bunches, which are left to ripen longer on the vine, are used to produce the wine. Another explanation points to a possible derivation from the Latin word *racemus* ("grape cluster"), or *recis,* a harvested cluster hung to dry. Yet another view speculates that recioto comes from the ancient name Retico.

Cassiodorus also described the practice of drying the grapes for recioto:

> The grapes are selected from the trellises around the houses, hung up and turned and then preserved in special jars and kept in ordinary containers. The grapes become hard and do not liquefy. Then the juices seep through, gently sweetening. This process continues until the end of December when the winter weather makes the grapes liquefy and by a miracle the wine begins to be new whilst the wine in the cellars is already old. . . . It stops bubbling at its origin and when it becomes mature it begins to seem forever young.[29]

The method was not much changed from that used when Pliny the Elder recorded the method of making the Retica wine from semidried grapes stored in covered *amphorae.*

The process and the aging potential are noted again in the eighteenth century. Scipione Maffei explains the process for making the Recioto bianco:

> Store the carefully selected grapes until December; press them delicately during the cold winter season, and decant the must without fermenting. It is the method we are honored to use to this day. . . . The wine . . . can be sweet or not sweet, and has the property of remaining unspoiled however it is kept; it is much like the famous wine of Tocai, and it is often served with this name north of the mountains.[30]

Amarone

The first dry Amarone, according to writer Cesare Marchi, was the result of a fortunate accident. As he tells it, a certain Adelino Lucchese discovered a barrel of wine in his cellar that had been overlooked and neglected for some time. Sure that it had spoiled, he was about to dump it out when curiosity prompted him to take a taste just to see what had happened to it. He was astonished to discover that

> the forgotten wine had a velvety and penetrating perfume, an all-pervading [but not unpleasant] bitter taste and an austere rounded strength not to be found in the other barrels.[31]

The grapes for Recioto are harvested toward the end of September. They are spread out on *graticci,* trellises, or bamboo trays in large, well-ventilated rooms to evaporate their moisture and concentrate their sugars. During this period of four to six months, the grape clusters are periodically turned and examined for the appearance of unwanted molds. Those bunches that will be used for Amarone are left to raisin until January, by which time they have reduced to three-quarters or two-thirds of their original weight. The bunches destined for the sweet Recioto continue to concentrate until April.

At Bolla they told us that while they feel it is not necessary to have botrytised grapes to make Amarone, it is necessary for a good Amarone. Bertani also said they want some, though not a lot of botrytis on the grapes for their wine. At Bertani they keep the grapes from the different vineyards separate during the drying, fermentation, and aging. Their Amarone undergoes a slow fermentation for one month. It is aged for no less than eight years before being offered for sale. At Speri they dry the grapes until January, when they are fermented slowly in stainless steel tanks for one and a half months. After settling, the wine is moved to 528-gallon (20-hectoliter) ccasks; at that point it still contains some unfermented sugar. The wine is left in the casks until September, by which time it has fermented out and become a dry wine, which is then aged for three years in Slavonian oak.

Amarone in the Glass

On aroma, Amarone brings up notes of dried fruit, almonds, and occasionally flowers. Almonds are a quality prized in the bouquet of the best Amarones. This wine has a characteristic bitterness. Some say the wine takes its name from this attribute (*amaro,* "bitter").

Amarone is full-bodied, dry, rich, and concentrated, a big but not overbearing wine. Though it is quite dry, it hints at sweetness. A good Amarone contains a lot of glycerine, which makes it quite attractive with four or five years of age, when it develops a silky texture.

Many *amatori* of Amarone in Verona believe that is at its best consumed in its youth, from four to five years of the vintage, while it has all of its fruit. At Bolla they consider that their Amarone peaks before its tenth year.

To our taste, good Amarone needs ten years to really shine. We've had some bottles thirty years old that were still very good. With this kind of age the Amarone admittedly becomes a different wine; its forthright, fruity nature becomes less obvious, and it develops a more subtle, mature mellowness and complexity.

Young Amarone is a good wine to serve with hearty fare like braised meats, stews, even game. An aged wine makes a marvelous accompaniment to gorgonzola, stilton, or other creamy marbled cheeses, also walnuts, hazelnuts, or toasted almonds. The ultimate combination would also include a roaring fire and some good conversation. Zeffiro Bocci suggests it

> between meals [when] it is an energetic, invigorating and "solo" wine, the highest expression of Valpolicella's role as a "philosopher's wine." . . . If one abandons oneself to the wine's evocative power, it helps in the clarification of ideas and aids lucid and stimulating meditation.[32]

The best Amarones are among Italy's vinicultural gems. Rating★★★

Recommended Producers of Recioto della Valpolicella

★★★
+ Allegrini, Vigna Fiorgardane
Tedeschi, Capitel Monte Fontana
Tedeschi, Capitel San Rocco delle Lucchine Rosso

★★
+ Allegrini
Masi, Mezzanella
Venturini

★
Bergamini
Lenotti
Masi
Tedeschi

Recommended Producers of Recioto Bianco
Allegrini, Fiorgardane Vigna Campogardane
Anselmi Recioto di Soave dei Capitelli
Masi, Campociese
Pieropan, Recioto di Soave
Tedeschi, La Fabriseria de San Rocco

Rating the Amarone Producers

★★★
Allegrini
+ Allegrini, Fieramonte
Le Ragose
− Masi
Masi, Campolongo Torbe
+ Masi, Mazzano
+ Masi, Serègo Alighieri, Vaio Armaron
Tedeschi, Capitel Monte Olmi

★★
+ Bertani
− Bolla
− Longo
Tedeschi
Tommasi
Quintarelli
+ Venturini

★
Guerrieri-Rizzardi
Sartori
Scamperle
+ Speri
Tramanal
Villa Girardi
Zenato
Zeni

0
Barberini
− Burati
Castagna
Fabiano
Farina
La Colombaia
Lamberti
Montresor
Pasqua
+ Santa Sofia
Tre Rose

Tasting Notes
1984

In this difficult vintage, production was about half of normal. Acid levels were very high.

1983

Masi said that 1983 was a great vintage, Lamberti considers it the best since 1969. For Tedeschi, it was one of the very best, top flight. Speri said it was a good year.

1982

Evidently 1982 was a variable vintage, judging from the producers' comments. For Lamberti, it was a medium vintage. Masi noted there was a lot of rain, fog, and humidity after the regular harvest for Valpolicella, and the grapes left to dry developed some mold. Speri found it a good year. Tedeschi ranks it among the least.

1981

Lamberti described 1981 as a medium vintage. Tedeschi considers it very good. Masi declassified its crus because of hail damage.

1980 ★★+

Lamberti rates 1980 very good. Speri calls it good. Those from the better producers still need more age. Masi's Vaio Armaron is lovely.

Bolla (4/85). Typically full, rich, intense aroma and flavor; robust, characteristic bitter finish; needs another two years to round off the rough edges.★★

Le Ragose (4/85). Characteristic dried fruit on aroma and flavor; full-bodied, richly flavored, intense and concentrated; long finish with the typical bitter note; still has more to give.★★★

Masi, Campolongo Torbe (twice 7/85; 6300 bottles). Floral aroma with notes of dried grapes and raisins; richly concentrated; full-flavored, still has tannin to soften.★★★ −

Masi, Serègo Alighieri, Vaio Armaron (4/85). Cherrylike notes and a touch of licorice on aroma; tannin on entry softens out in the middle, full-bodied, well balanced, flavorful; a more gentle style of Amarone, and very good too.★★★

1979 ★★★

Masi ranks 1979 as excellent. Tedeschi is pretty much in accord. Many fine wines were produced that can be enjoyed now, though there is no need to rush to drink them. The Allegrini cru and Masi's Vaio Armaron are sure to please Amarone lovers; they are both very fine wines.

Allegrini classico (4 times 4/85). Intense aroma with suggestions of figs and dried fruit; full of flavor, good weight; bitter almonds on finish.★★★ −

Allegrini classico, Vigna Fieramonte (3 times 7/85; 10,600 bottles). Expansive aroma of almonds, flowers, figs, raisins, and prunes; robust, firm, full-flavored, smooth-textured; very long finish with a touch of bitter almonds.★★★

Guerrieri-Rizzardi classico (12/83). Aroma of almonds and raisins; dry, some firmness, light tannin, nice flavor, some alcohol intrudes.★ −

La Colombaia (7/85). Hot nose; dull, unbalanced with alcohol, thin, stale.

Lamberti (4/85). Mushroomlike notes on the aroma; unstructured, lacks weight and concentration; tastes old and stale.

Le Ragose (twice 7/85). Dried fruit on aroma; still firm and with tannin to shed, seems to have the fruit to carry it; a nice but disappointing bottle from a generally very fine producer.★★ −

They cannot have tasted our 79 La Colombaia!

Masi classico (4/85). Dried fruit on aroma, with floral and pinelike notes; robust and rich, nuance of black pepper, still has some tannin, though nice now; quite long.★★★ −

Masi, Serègo Alighieri, Vaio Armaron (4/85). Complex bouquet recalls tobacco, tea, dried fruit, and other goodies; dry, but with an impression of sweetness, enormous richness of flavor, lots of style; has a lot going for it; some tannin on the finish says it needs another two years or so.★★★(+)

Montresor (7/85). Flavorful, but no real character or style.

Santa Sofia classico superiore (7/85). Dried fruit character, overall fruity.

Sartori classico superiore (7/85). Off-putting, stinky nose; lacks weight and richness; drinkable.

Tedeschi, Capitel Monte Olmi (4/85). Aroma of figs and raisins, still somewhat reticent; light tannin, gives an impression of sweetness; very long; room for improvement yet.★★★

1978 ★★+

Lamberti didn't produce an Amarone in 1978. Masi considered it quite a good vintage. For Speri, it was good. The better ones need more age.

Masi classico (4/85). Lovely aroma of almonds and dried fruit; full-flavored, peppery, still has tannin to shed; the richness makes it enjoyable now, but it will improve.★★★

Scamperle classico (twice 7/85). Pruny, overripe aroma; straightforward fruitiness, some spice.★

Tre Rose (4/80). Raisins and dried fruit on aroma; alcoholic, tannic, insufficient fruit.

1977 ★★★

Masi found the vintage very good. For Tedeschi it was one of the best. Allegrini rates it tops. For the most part, these wines are quite drinkable now. We especially liked the Masi and Tedeschi crus and, although we haven't tasted it in a few years, the Allegrini.

Allegrini classico (4 times 4/81). Aroma quite intense, but still somewhat closed; still has tannin to shed, smooth-centered, a lot of glycerine; shows style.★★(★)

Barberini (12/83). A cooked, overripe character, overly alcoholic, unbalanced.

Bolla classico (twice 12/83). Characteristic almondlike aroma; a mouthful of fruit, some tannin, astringent edges, less than expected from this usually good, reliable producer. A bottle tasted fourteen months earlier, though better, was still below expectations.

Guerrieri-Rizzardi classico (4 times 7/85). Rich and concentrated aroma; could use more weight.★

Le Ragose (twice 5/83). Intense and rich, so rich it's almost sweet; loads of style.★★★ −

Masi, Campolongo Torbe (4/85; 5700 bottles). Floral aroma with a licorice note; soft-centered, well balanced, tasty; very long.★★★

Masi classico (3 times 7/85). Dried fruit and almonds on aroma; flavorful and concentrated; seems a bit tired on the aftertaste. Was much better in December 1983.★ +

Masi, Mazzano (12/83). Flowers on aroma and a hint of wheat; a mouthful of flavor, some astringency at the end; will improve yet.★★ +

Pasqua classico (3 times 7/85). Simple and fruity, uncharacteristic.

Sartori classico superiore (12/83). Almonds and flowers on aroma; lots of flavor, medium body; a bit short.★ +

Tedeschi (3 times 7/85). Richly flavored, has a lot of character; bitter almonds on finish.★★

1977

Tedeschi, Capitel Monte Olmi *(4/85)*. Aroma of almonds, figs, and dried fruit; some tannin, full-bodied, and full-flavored, chocolate notes, has a lot of character.★★★

Tommasi classico *(12/83)*. Slight, almondlike aroma; balanced, flavorful; a nice bottle of wine.★★

Villa Girardi classico superiore *(4 times 7/85)*. A fruity wine that lacks the weight and concentration expected of an Amarone.

Zenato classico *(twice 7/85)*. Dried fruit and chocolate notes; a bit lacking in character, drinkable.★ −

Zeni classico superiore *(4/80)*. Aroma of dried fruit, figs, and raisins; a lightweight but agreeable Amarone.★

1976 ★★+

For Masi it was a first-flight vintage. Bertani didn't produce an Amarone. The '76s are ready to drink, though the best ones will last. Masi's Mazzano is superb, a real classic in both weight and structure.

Allegrini classico *(ex-cask 10/78)*. Rich and concentrated; quality quite evident.★★

La Colombaia *(7/85)*. A waste of time and effort.

Le Ragose *(4/80; 960 bottles)*. Aroma is somewhat closed but suggests considerable fruit to come; some tannin, lots of flavor.★★

Masi, Campolongo Torbe *(3 times 1/82; 3800 bottles)*. Almonds and flowers on aroma; a bit light, but characteristic Amarone; typical bitter almond finish.★★

Masi classico *(4/85)*. Almond notes on floral aroma; a mouthful of flavor, smooth; finish is a trifle weak and overly drying with tannin.★★

Masi, Mazzano *(4/85; 5950 bottles)*. Intensely perfumed, floral bouquet, with licorice notes, also peaches and a hint of botrytis; soft tannin, richly flavored; very long and very good.★★★ +

Santa Sofia classico superiore *(twice 12/83)*. Small nose; weak, even a bit thin, some flavor; harsh aftertaste.

Speri classico superiore *(4 times 7/85)*. Bottles tasted in 1983 were clearly superior to the most recent tasted, which was totally uninteresting.

Tommasi classico *(4/80)*. Dried fruit and raisins; moderate richness, some alcohol evident at the end.★

1975 ★+

Masi said 1975 was very good year. Bertani made one-tenth their normal production, only 6000 bottles. Tedeschi says it was among their least vintages. There is no need to hold the '75s any longer.

Allegrini classico *(twice 4/80)*. Rich aroma of figs and dried grapes; a rich, full-bodied wine, well structured, robust.★★ +

Farina *(4/80)*. A lightweight, small-scale wine, shallow.

Lamberti *(11/81)*. Tawny color, some oxidation; too old.

Masi, Campolongo Torbe *(10/78)*. Floral perfumed bouquet, hints of figs and dried fruit; flavorful, seems almost sweet.★★

Masi classico *(4/80)*. Some almond notes on the nose; shows a lot of age; either it's the bottle, or it's too old.

Masi, Mazzano *(3 times 1/82; 3900 bottles)*. Char-acteristic almond note on the nose; a concentrated wine with loads of flavor; slightly hot at ending.★★ −

Quintarelli classico, brown label *(11/81)*. Nice nose; harsh and shallow on palate, volatile acidity painfully evident.

Quintarelli classico, green label *(twice 3/83)*. Bottle of 11/81: Overly drying; more to it than the brown label.

Bottle of 3/83: Rich and intense, full of flavor, almost sweet.★★ +

Tommasi classico *(twice 7/85)*. Chocolaty, full of flavor, good weight, a lot of character.★★ +

Tramanal *(11/81)*. Aroma of raisins, almonds, and cherries; flavorful; a bit short.★ +

1974 ★★★+

Bertani characterized the 1974 vintage as exceptional. Tedeschi puts it among the best. Speri rated it good. Masi's Mazzano is a real knockout that will certainly improve. Tedechi's cru is also very good. Nearly all the others are ready, though they will certainly last, those from the best producers at least.

Allegrini classico *(twice 10/78)*. Almondlike aroma; full-bodied and robust, loads of flavor; very long; a lot of quality here.★★★

Bolla classico superiore *(3 times 7/85)*. Rich and concentrated, dried fruit character, some tannin, characteristic bitterness.★★ +

Boscaini *(11/84)*. Awful. We suspect a bad bottle here, but we never had a chance to retaste it.

Fabiano classico superiore *(twice 7/85)*. Too old, but it didn't offer very much when last tasted (11/81) either.

Lamberti *(7/85)*. Overly simple, some oxidation; on the way down.

Le Ragose *(10/79)*. Expansive, aromatic aroma; well-balanced, flavorful; good quality.★★★

Masi, Campolongo Torbe *(10/78; 4000 bottles)*. Some oxidation, vaguely corky.

Masi classico *(3 times 4/85)*. Complex aroma recalls figs, raisins, prunes, vaguely floral; dry with an impression of sweetness, some tannin, velvety; long finish. ★★★

337

1974

Masi, Mazzano *(4/85; 3900 bottles)*. Intense bouquet, dried fruit, vaguely floral; a big wine with loads of flavor and glycerine; still seems young, impressive quality now, with a lot more to give.★★★(★)

Montresor classico superiore *(twice 12/83)*. Baked character, shallow, vegetal notes.

Quintarelli classico *(twice 9/84)*. Aroma of almonds and dried fruit; loads of flavor, full-bodied, but unbalanced and alcoholic.★ +

Santa Sofia classico superiore *(11/81)*. Off notes, shallow, dull.

Sartori classico superiore *(11/81)*. Lush, open aroma with fruit, almonds, raisins; drying out.★ −

Speri classico superiore *(twice 2/82)*. Characteristic dried fruit and almonds on aroma; smooth, flavorful, has style; typical note of bitterness at the end.★★ +

Tedeschi *(12/83)*. Raisins, almonds on aroma; fairly well balanced, characteristic Amarone, good; could be a bit longer on aftertaste.★★ −

Tedeschi, Capitel Monte Olmi *(4/85)*. Woodsy aroma, with nuances of mushrooms and berries; soft and smooth, gives an impression of sweetness, round, harmonious, complete; stylish, a grand wine.★★★ +

Venturini *(10/78)*. Big, rich, full, and concentrated; a lot of quality here.★★★

1973 ★ −

Bertani produced very little Amarone in 1973. Masi rated the vintage fairly good. We advise drinking them if you have any left; many are fading or already have.

Anselmi *(2/81)*. Color shows age; typical note of almonds on nose; a bit thin and drying out.

Bertani classico superiore *(12/83)*. Nice nose of almonds, dried fruit, and raisins; flavorful, some tannin, could be longer on aftertaste.★ +

Castagna *(10/78)*. A lightweight little wine lacking in flavor, concentration, and character.

Masi *(10/78)*. Aroma of almonds and raisins; balanced, flavorful, somewhat light.★★ −

Tedeschi, *(12/83)*. Caramel candy on aroma, almondlike notes; dried character to the fruit; very short aftertaste.★

Tedeschi, Capitel Monte Olmi *(4/81)*. Typical almond aroma; a lightweight Amarone, fairly nice flavor.★

Tommasi classico *(4 times 7/85)*. Fairly nice nose; good fruit in the mouth; thins out at the end. It was better two years ago.★ −

1972 0

Masi didn't bottle an Amarone in 1972, nor did Lamberti. Speri considers the vintage the worst. Tedeschi puts it among the worst. Allegrini said it was the worst vintage in memory. The only one we've tasted in recent years, the Bertani, indicates these Amarones should have been drunk up already.

Bertani classico superiore *(5/83)*. Has some flavor, but lacks the expected richness and weight of an Amarone.★ −

1971 ★★ +

Masi gives 1971 full marks. Tedeschi puts it among the finest vintages. Lamberti said it was a very good year. Speri also rated it good. Some wines are beginning to show age. There's no reason to hold them any longer. The Bertani should continue to improve.

Allegrini classico *(5 times 12/83)*. Bottle of 4/80: Richly intense aroma; full-flavored, balanced, a lot of quality.★★★

Bottle of 12/83: Oxidation beginning to set in; either getting old or an off bottle.

Bertani classico superiore *(5 times 4/85)*. Concentrated aroma recalling berries and dried fruit; firm and tannic, still a bit rough, full of flavor; surprisingly young.★★ +

Bolla *(11/79)*. Lacks weight, flavor, and definition; a big disappointment from a firm that usually makes a fairly good Amarone.

Burati *(2/80)*. Awful, from the aroma through the bitter end.

Longo *(10/78)*. Characteristic, with dried fruit and almonds all across the wine, flavorful.★★

Montresor *(10/78)*. A lightweight wine lacking in flavor and structure.

Santa Sofia classico superiore *(7/85)*. Stinky aroma; no improvement on flavor.

Tedeschi *(2/83)*. Richly intense aroma of raisins and almonds; falls down on palate, overly simple and one-dimensional.★

Tommasi classico *(5 times 12/83)*. Typical aroma of raisins and almonds; some tannin, moderate fruit; alcohol at the end. Getting a bit old; it was better from 1978 through 1981.★ −

1970 ★★

Masi considered 1970 a good vintage; Lamberti rated it very good.

Bertani classico superiore *(twice 12/83)*. Dried fruit character, raisins and almonds; a nice mouthful of fruit, chocolaty and rich; fairly long.★★ +

1969 ★★

All the producers we spoke to or received replies from on our questionnaire rate this year at the very top, none better. Some '69s, if stored properly, could still make splendid drinking, but we don't advise holding them.

Bertani classico superiore *(twice 11/81)*. Almondlike aroma; shows signs of age (same for both bottles, tasted eight months apart), overly drying, though still has some flavor interest.

Bolla *(10/82)*. Lovely, complex aroma from bottle age; intense, dry, and firm, richly flavored; could have more length on aftertaste.★★

Masi *(4/85)*. Dried fruit aroma, vaguely floral; soft, almost velvety, full-bodied, tasty; long finish with chocolaty notes.★★★

Santa Sofia classico superiore *(twice 11/81)*. Bad.

Sartori *(10/84)*. Some oxidation, but some quality still evident.★

Tommasi classico *(3 times 12/83)*. Aroma of almonds and raisins; a mouthful of rich fruit, moderate tannin; some alcohol throws the balance off.★

1968 ★★

Masi considered 1968 a very good vintage. And the one we tasted from them recently shows how accurate they are; it was superb.

Bertani classico superiore *(twice 12/83)*. Slight nose, but a big, rich mouthful of wine, dried fruit character; some alcohol at the end.★

Masi *(twice 4/85)*. Floral, woodsy bouquet, with mushroomy notes; so smooth and velvety it almost seems sweet, tasty; a very long finish with a hint of chocolate.★★★ +

1967 ★★ −

Masi puts this vintage just behind 1969 in quality, Tedeschi considers it among the best, Speri rated it good. The wines are ready now; there's no reason to hold them any longer.

Bertani classico superiore *(twice 4/81)*. Rich, raisiny aroma, overlaid with almonds; loads of flavor, quite nice; noticeable alcohol at the end, not to keep.★★ −

Tommasi classico *(5 times 12/83)*. Light nose with almond and vanilla notes; a flavorful wine with some tannin; typical bitterness on finish.★ +

1966 [0]

Bertani, for one, didn't produce an Amarone in 1966.

Older Vintages

The following ratings apply to the vintages as they were originally considered to be. It is doubtful, of course, that they will correspond to the status of the wines today. Our tasting experiences with these vintages are rather limited.

★★★★	1964
★★★	1962, 1961, 1958
★★ +	1963
★★	1959
★ +	1965
★	1960

1965 Bertani classico superiore *(twice 11/81)*. Some oxidation, but the richness and intensity of the bouquet shine through; a full-flavored wine with more tannin than we'd expect at this stage; doesn't seem to be drying out.★ +

1964 Bertani classico superiore *(5 times 12/83)*. Floral aroma with notes of almonds and a peachlike nuance; a mouthful of rich flavors, some tannin; fairly long finish★★★ −

1964 Tommasi classico *(3 times 12/83)*. Aroma of fruit and almonds, wheatlike notes; round and tasty, very ready, has a lot of character; fairly long, with a touch of bitterness at the end.★★ +

1963 Bertani classico superiore *(4 times 4/84)*. Beautiful robe, garnet with orange reflections; intense bouquet, characteristic; robust and flavorful, full and rich, smooth-textured; very long finish.★★★

1962 Bertani classico superiore *(5 times 12/82)*. Aroma of almonds, dried fruit, figs, prunes, green olives; a big, rich mouthful of wine; finish is rather short and overly drying, vaguely bitter.★★

1960 Bertani classico superiore *(5/79)*. Some oxidation apparent, but still has flavor and some character.★

1959 Bertani classico superiore *(4 times 5/85)*. Bottle of 4/85, at the winery: Bouquet has a lot of complexity and mellowness from bottle age, berry notes; still a lot of tannin, not a lot of fruit left, shows signs of drying out; still some interest left.★

Bottle of 5/85, in the U.S. from a private cellar: Concentrated bouquet, vaguely floral; richly flavored, intense,dry, but almost seems sweet; long, lingering finish.★★★

1958 Bertani classico superiore *(4 times 2/84)*. Beautiful brick robe shading to orange; concentrated aroma, with dried fruit; gives an impression of sweetness, smooth-textured, richly flavored; a long, bitter finish.★★★

The Amarone Producers

Allegrini *(Fumane di Valpolicella), 1886*. This very fine producer specializes in Valpolicella; they do not make Soave or Bardolino. Allegrini has 82 acres (33 hectares) of vines, from which they produce some 300,000 bottles of fine wine a year. This includes 150,000 bottles of a very good Valpolicella (no Valpolicella is better), 98,000 of a fine Amarone, 40,000 of Recioto, 5000 of the single-vineyard Pelara, 4200 of a still, dry white, and a scant 1200 of the very fine white Recioto Fiorgardane-Campogardane.

Marilisa Allegrini of Az. Agr. Allegrini   —photo by Tom Abruzzini

Allegrini is family owned and operated. Walter oversees the vineyards, Franco is the winemaker, and Marilisa is in charge of exports and administration. When Marilisa makes a marketing trip to the U.S., Allegrini's sales multiply. This outgoing and enthusiastic young woman could sell her wines on charm alone. But as her charm is based on a sincerity and integrity, she would not be able to do so if they were not excellent wines to begin with—which they are.

Allegrini's vines, planted at altitudes of 470 to 865 feet (190 to 350 meters), are mostly in Fumane; all are in the Classico zone. The vineyards are planted to approximately 70 percent corvina (the maximum allowed by law), 17 percent rondinella, 3 percent molinara, and 10 percent sangiovese— the basic composition of their regular Valpolicella and Amarone. The crus differ, and these wines vary according to the makeup of the individual vineyards. The Palazzo della Torre vineyard is planted 60 percent to corvina, 28 percent to rondinella, and 12 percent to molinara. The Amarone from their Fieramonte cru is 70 percent corvina, 20 percent rondinella, and 10 percent molinara. Allegrini's Fiorgardane Recioto is made from the same combination of grapes.

Cru/vineyard	Commune	Hectares	Planted	Used for	Cru since	Cases
Carpanè	Fumane	0.30	1954	Amarone, Recioto and Valpolicella	—	220
Fieramonte	Fumane	2.50	1975	Amarone	1978	900
Fiorgardane	Fumane	1.40	1942	Recioto	1969	110
				Valpolicella	—	350
Campogardane				Recioto, white	1971	110
				white, dry	—	350
Giara	Fumane	0.54	1970	Valpolicella	—	350
La Grola	Sant' Ambrogio	7.77	1980/84	Amarone and Recioto	6200	—
Lena	Fumane	4.46	1978	Amarone	3200	—
Mulino	Fumane	0.60	1963	Amarone and Valpolicella	—	400
Palazzo della Torre	Fumane	7.16	1967	Valpolicella	1980	2000
				Amarone	1980	900
Progni	Fumane	4.73	1953/63	Valpolicella	—	3600
Ca'del Paver		(0.52)	1968	Pelara	1979	440
Scornocio	Fumane	0.31	1957	Valpolicella	—	220
Volta	Fumane	3.55	1958/75	Amarone and Valpolicella	—	2200

The harvest at Allegrini normally begins about the last week of September. The pickers harvesting for the Valpolicella cut off the lower third of the grape bunches of those clusters that will be used for Recioto and Amarone, leaving the top part, in the traditional manner, to ripen longer on the vine before it is gathered.

Their Valpolicella is fermented for eight to ten days, the Amarone and Recioto for twenty to twenty-five. In March, Franco referments the Valpolicella on the Amarone lees to produce a bigger, richer, fuller wine, with a better capacity to age. We've tasted Allegrini Valpolicellas with ten years that were still very good. Their Valpolicella is aged for a minimum of one year in oak casks, quite a long time by modern standards. But this is not a modern Valpolicella; it is in the traditional style.

Each of the Allegrini wines—Valpolicella, Recioto, and Amarone—is among the best of its type; very few are their equal, and none is better. Amarone★★★; Amarone, Fieramonte★★★+; Recioto ★★+; Recioto Fiorgardane ★★★+; Recioto bianco, Campogardane ★★★+; Valpolicella ★★★

Bertani *(Verona), 1857.* Bertani has long been a regarded producer of Veronese wines. Their line includes a Valpolicella from Valpantena, a Recioto spumante, and a very fine Amarone.

They produce 120,000 to 150,000 cases of wine a year, 5000 of which are Amarone. Bertani, perhaps more than any other Veronese firm, believes in aging its Amarone. Before it is released for sale, it has been aged for no less than eight years. They have supplies of Amarones back to 1958 that are still offered for sale, although in very limited quantities, from time to time. Bertani's Amarones age very well. We have tasted some with thirty years of age that were still very good. Generally, we find their Amarones to be in a fuller-bodied style that ages very well. Amarone★★+; Valpolicella★★

Bolla *(Verona), 1883.* This firm produces well over a million cases of the full range of Veronese wine, including a pretty good Amarone as well as white and red Rhetico fortified dessert wines. They produced their first Amarone in 1949 or 1950. It was put on the market in 1955—the first, they claim, to be sold commercially by any firm. Generally, the Bolla Amarone is quite good. They feel it is at its best drunk before its tenth year. Amarone★★−; Valpolicella★

Le Ragose *(Arbizzano di Negrar di Valpolicella).* Marta Galli has 30 acres (12 hectares) of vines, including the 8.6-acre (3.5 hectare) Le Sassine vineyard planted with very old vines. In this vineyard, Marta says, there are nine different clones of molinara.

Besides producing a very good Valpolicella, which is refermented on the Amarone lees, she also makes 4000 bottles of Recioto spumante and a very fine Amarone, one of the best in fact. Amarone★★★; Valpolicella★★★

Masi Agricola *(Gargagnago di S. Ambrogio), 1790.* The Masi wineries and vineyards are owned by the Boscaini brothers. Sandro Boscaini, the eldest, is the director of the firm. They have 235 acres (95 hectares) of vines, which include some of the finest vineyards in Valpolicella.

Cru	Commune	Hectares	Exposure	Age of Vines (years)	Yield	Used in
Campo Fiorin	Valgatara (near Negrar)	5	n/a	n/a	n/a	Campo Fiorin
Campociesca	Negrar	3	ese	n/a	n/a	Recioto bianco
Campolongo di Torbe	Negrar	8	sw	15	250/280	Amarone
Mazzano	Negrar	5	w	13	200	Amarone
Mezzanella	Negrar and Marano	4	se	12	150	Recioto
Serègo Aligheri	S. Ambrosio loc. Gargagnago	15	ssw	20	300/350	Valpolicella
Vaio Armaron	S. Ambrosio loc. Gargagnago	10	n/a	30	n/a	Amarone

Masi also buys grapes. They produce 1.3 million bottles of very good Veronese wine a year, including a few specialties from local grape varieties. More than half of their production is of the normal Veronese wines. The remainder is Amarone, Recioto red and white, and a couple of proprietary wines. Some 85 percent of the grapes for their Valpolicella, in all of its forms, are from their own vineyards; they buy 80 percent of the grapes they use for their other wines.

Masi produces two Valpolicellas: the regular, which is quite good, and the cru, Serègo Aligheri, which is excellent. They first produced the Serègo Aligheri from the 1980 vintage. Production averages 24,000 bottles a year. The vineyard is cultivated under Masi's direction but is owned by the Alighieri family, descendants of Dante Alighieri, father of modern Italian and author of the *Divine Comedy.* We have never tasted a finer Valpolicella than this one.

The very fine Campo Fiorin was first produced in 1964 from the best grapes selected from Masi's Campo Fiorin vineyard. The *uvaggio* is approximately 55 percent corvina, 25 percent rondinella, 10 percent molinara, and 10 percent rossignella and sangiovese. The grapes are generally harvested during the first two weeks of September. In March, enologist Nino Franceschetti referments the wine on the lees of the Amarone.

Nino notes that the refermentation results in a wine of greater body and better structure, a richer and more complex wine with more alcohol. The wine attains an alcohol level of 13.5 to 14 percent. He pointed out that Campo Fiorin is released when they consider it ready, not necessarily in vintage sequence. Campo Fiorin is ready to enjoy from its fifth or sixth year until between its tenth and fifteenth.

Sandro Boscaini rates 1964, 1967, 1970, 1974, 1978, and 1983 as first-flight vintages. In the worst years—1972 and 1982—the Campo Fiorin was not produced. The following are Masi's ratings of those vintages that have been released:

★★★★	1978
★★★	1976, 1971, 1969, 1967
★★	1979, 1977, 1975, 1974, 1968
★	1973, 1970
0	1972

The label on the Campo Fiorin carries the phrase *nectar angelorum hominibus,* "nectar of the angels for men." We couldn't put it any better.

Tasting Notes—Campo Fiorin

1979 *(twice 4/85).* Peppery aroma, vague almond and cherry notes; seems a little stemmy, has a dried fruit character, a lot of flavor; some length.★★

1978 *(4/85).* Complex bouquet of almonds, dried fruit, and black pepper, with a note that hints of chocolate; richly flavored and full; long finish recalls peanuts; this wine has a lot of strength and needs age to tame it.★★(★)

1977 *(3 times 4/85).* Aroma of dried fruit, raisins, figs, prunes, and some flowers; richly flavored, soft, almost like velvet; long finish is somewhat drying.★★★ –

1976 *(ex-cask 10/78).* Big, perfumed aroma; loads of flavor, well structured; has a lot of potential.★★(★)

1975 *(6 times 4/85).* Dried fruit and chocolate, touch of oxidation; somewhat tired, still has flavor interest.★

1974 *(3 times 4/85).* Garnet, orange rim; nose displays a lot of complexity with suggestions of dried fruit, almonds, oranges; richly flavored, light tannin, velvety, some age beginning to creep in; very long finish recalls almonds.★★ +

Masi produces three Recioto della Valpolicellas: a regular, a Riserva degli Angeli, and a Mezzanella cru. The Riserva degli Angeli is made from an *uvaggio* of 65 to 70 percent corvina, 5 to 15 percent molinara, 25 to 30 percent rondinella, and no more than 10 percent of dindarella, rossignella, and negrara grapes from vineyards on the Valgatara hillside. The harvest generally takes place toward the end of September or beginning of October. The wine is aged for two years in oak casks.

Masi also produces the golden Recioto bianco from Campociesca, in very limited quantities. It is very rare and very fine. The Campociesca is made basically from garganega and trebbiano di Soave grapes, with the addition of some cortese and malvasia.

Masi rate the vintages for their Reciotos, in those years that have been released, as follows:

★★★★	1980, 1979, 1977
★★★	1978, 1976
★★	1981, 1974, 1973, 1970
★	1975, 1971
0	(1972 none made)

Masi produces four Amarones: a regular and three crus. The Campolongo di Torbe is made from a blend of corvina, rondinella, and molinara, plus some negrara, rossignella, and dindarella grapes. The vineyard is harvested at the end of September or beginning of October. This wine is aged for at least four years in old oak casks. The Mazzano Amarone is made from the same six grapes plus a small amount of raboso veronese. This wine is given no less than five years of oak aging and achieves a level of 15.8 to 18.8 percent alcohol.

The Campolongo di Torbe Amarone is made in a more gentle, sweeter style. It achieves an alcohol level of 15.5 to 16.5 percent. This wine, according to Franceschetti, Masi's very fine enologist, is shorter-lived than the Mazzano. He describes Mazzano as "the perfect expression of Amarone." No doubt he knows quite well whereof he speaks; we certainly cannot disagree.

The Vaio Armaron is aged for only three years in oak. This wine is sweeter, softer, and gentler than the Campolongo Torbe Amarone. Masi first made this exceptionally fine single-vineyard wine in 1979; production is now 12,000 bottles a year.

Masi evaluate the vintages for their Amarones, in those years that have been released, as follows:

★★★★	1979, 1976, 1974, 1971, 1969, 1967
★★★	1978, 1977, 1975, 1968
★★	1973, 1970
0	(none made) 1972

Masi is one of the most serious and dedicated producers of Veronese wines. Their Amarones are not surpassed by any one. Amarone★★★ − ; Amarone, Campolongo di Torbe★★★; Amarone, Mazzano★★★ + ; Amarone, Vaio Amaron★★★ + ; Campo Fiorin★★★; Recioto★; Recioto, Mezzanella★★; Recioto bianco, Campociesca★★★ + ; Valpolicella★★; Valpolicella, Serègo Alighieri★★★

Speri *(Pedemonte), 1874* F.lli Speri owns 100 acres (40 hectares) of vines, from which they produce 55,000 cases of wine a year, including 23,000 cases of Valpolicella and 8000 of Amarone. The grapes for their Amarone come from the higher elevations.

Cru	Locality	Altitude	Cases	Produced since
La Roverina	Negrar	490 feet	23,000	1978
Monte Sant' Urbano	Fumane	985 feet	8,000	1980

The Speri Amarone enjoys a good reputation. In our experience, though they can be very good, they have been rather uneven. We have to call them the way we see them. Amarone★ +

Tedeschi *(Pedemonte), 1890.* Renzo Tedeschi has 30 acres (12 hectares) of vines planted at an altitude of about 820 feet (250 meters). This supplies him with 70 percent of his grapes. More than two-thirds of his production is Valpolicella. The balance is made up of a fine Amarone, an exceptionally fine Recioto, and a sweet, luscious, golden Recioto bianco.

Tedeschi has sold his wines in bottle since 1960. He bottles his best wines under the cru names.

The Tedeschi wines can be quite good, but where they really shine is in their single-vineyard bottlings. At their best, these are surely among the zone's finest wines, whether Amarone or Recioto. Amarone★★; Amarone, Capitel Monte Olmi★★★; Recioto, Capitel Monte Fontana★★★; Recioto, Capitel San Rocco delle Lucchini Rosso★★★; white Recioto, La Fabriseria de San Rocco★★ +

Renzo Tedeschi of Az. Agr. Tedeschi

Cru	Hectares	Production (bottles)	Used for
Capitel San Rocco delle Lucchine	4	25,000/30,000	Recioto
Capitel Monte Fontana	2	2,500/3,000	Recioto
Capitel Monte Olmi	6	4,000/5,000	Amarone
La Fabriseria de San Rocco	n/a	n/a	white Recioto

Tenuta Villa Girardi *(San Pietro Incariano)*. Villa Girardi has 125 acres (50 hectares) of vines, which provide them with 70 percent of their grapes. They produce more than 75,000 cases a year of a full range of Veronese wine, including Amarone. They produce 5500 cases of the Amarone cru, Bure Alto. Amarone★

Chapter 16

Cabernet and Cabernet Blends

In the early part of the nineteenth century, the Bordeaux varieties—cabernet franc, cabernet sauvignon, merlot, and malbec, and perhaps some of the other, minor varieties, were introduced into Italy, where they were planted in the Tre Venezie (Fruili Venezia Giulia, Trentino Alto Adige, and Veneto). And Malbec was brought to Apulia from Bordeaux in the middle of the century.

After *phylloxera* wiped out the vines of the northeastern regions in the early part of this century, many vineyards were replanted with grafted Bordeaux varieties, especially merlot and cabernet franc. Today merlot is the major red variety of Fruiuli Venezia Giulia and perhaps the Veneto as well.

Cabernet, especially cabernet sauvignon, is becoming more widespread in Italy with the new plantings in Piemonte and Tuscany. More and more Tuscan producers are introducing some cabernet into their Chianti or blending it with the noble sangiovese to create new wines to satisfy a growing international market with a taste for Cabernet aged in *barrique*. And so, as the planting of the Bordeaux varieties becomes more widespread, Italian wine becomes more international in character. Though we certainly hope that Italian wine will not lose its own identity as a result, with xenophilic producers eschewing their nobile native varieties in favor of the more exotic, foreign-born, we can't overlook the fact that there are many wines from the Bordeaux varieties being produced in Italy. They make up a significant proportion of the total output; a number of these wines are very fine ones, and in some areas they are indeed traditional at this point as well. Not that a traditional wine is necessarily better than a new and perhaps more innovative one. In the final analysis, it's what's in the glass that counts. In a choice between drinking sentiment and drinking fine wine, we'll take the latter without hesitation.

In the hands of skilled craftsmen like Giorgio Grai, Maurizio Zanella, Fausto Maculan, or Boncompagni Ludovisi Principe di Venosa, these varieties achieve splendor in Italy as well.

Sometimes the varieties are blended, as in Grai's Alto Adige Cabernet, from cabernet sauvignon and cabernet franc. Sometimes one is used alone to produce a varietal wine such as Maculan's Palazzotto, from 100 percent cabernet sauvignon. In some wines cabernet is combined with merlot, as in the Fiorano of Boncompagni Ludovisi. In others they are blended with native varieties, as in the Torre Ercolana of Colacicchi-Anagni, a cesanese, cabernet, merlot blend.

The Grape Varieties

Cabernet. Cabernet, which in Italy may mean either cabernet sauvignon or cabernet franc, is recognized under DOC for all six zones of Friuli Venezia Giulia, two of the zones in Trentino Alto Adige, and five in the Veneto. It is used as a component in a number of other wines, in both Lombardia and Toscana, for example.

Zones Producing DOC Cabernet Wines

Alto Adige	Isonzo
Aquileia	Latisana
Breganze	Montello e Colli Asolani
Colli Berici	Piave
Colli Orientali del Friuli	Pramaggiore
Collio (Cabernet Franc)	Trentino
Grave del Friuli	

By far the majority of Italian Cabernet wines should be drunk young, within a year or two of the vintage, at most three. While some can last longer, they generally don't improve with age, and they lose their appealing youthful fruit. The best, though, can live a decade or more.

Cabernet Franc. This is the most widely planted of the cabernet varieties in Italy. Whenever the name Cabernet appears unqualified on a label of an Italian wine, it is virtually always cabernet franc, though in some cases there might be some cabernet sauvignon blended in.

Cabernet franc dominates the cabernet plantings in the Tre Venezie; it is planted as far south as Apulia, also further north in Lombardia, Emilia-Romagna, and Piemonte.

The cabernet franc wines tend to be similar in aroma to those from cabernet sauvignon, but with a more pronounced bell-pepper character. The franc wines are generally softer and rounder, with perhaps more body and less refinement.

Cabernet Sauvignon. This cabernet is less popular in Italy than cabernet franc, possibly because of its lower yields and the fact that its wines require more aging. Cabernet sauvignon is more frequently blended, with cabernet franc or with merlot, than it is used on its own as a straight varietal, a situation that is just as true in Bordeaux as well.

Cabernet sauvignon produces deeply colored wines that are hard and tannic in their youth, requiring time to soften and round out. In aroma these wines frequently offer suggestions of green olives, cassis or black currants, or cedar. In the right climate and the right soil, it produces wines of refinement and breed.

Cabernet sauvignon is the major variety of the Medoc and Graves regions of Bordeaux. In Italy it is planted throughout the three northeastern regions—Trentino Alto Adige, Friuli Venezia Giulia, and the Veneto—as well as in Lombardia, Piemonte, Emilia Romagna, Toscana, and Umbria.

Malbec. This Bordeaux variety is grown mostly in northeastern Italy, in the regions of Friuli Venezia Giulia and the Veneto; there are some plantings in Trentino Alto Adige and Lombardia. It is used mostly in combination with cabernet and merlot. A few producers make a varietal Malbec, or Malbeck as it is sometimes spelled. The one from Duca Badoglia in Friuli Venezia Giulia, though we haven't tasted it in a few years, was quite good and recommendable.

Malbec is grown as far south as Apulia in the Cerignola district between Foggia and Bari. It is a major grape in the *uvaggio* of the very good Torre Quarto of Fabrizio Cirillo-Farrusi.

Malbec produces wines with good color that tend to be rather soft. It's a variety being grown less today, even in Bordeaux.

Merlot. This variety, the most important grape in the Bordeaux districts of St. Emilion and Pomerol, is the major red variety in the northeastern corner of Italy. Merlot wines are recognized under DOC in all six zones of Friuli Venezia Giulia, in six zones in the Veneto (including two where its not labeled as Merlot but as Rosso), in two zones in Trentino Alto Adige, in Emilia Romagna, and in one zone in Lazio. Merlot is used as a supplemental variety in numerous Italian DOC wines and even more independents.

Zones Producing DOC Merlot Wines

Alto Adige	Collio
Aprilia	Grave del Friuli
Aquileia	Isonzo
Breganze ("Rosso")	Latisana
Colli Berici	Montello e Colli Asolani
Colli Bolognesi	Piave
Colli Euganei ("Rosso")	Pramaggiore
Colli Orientali del Friuli	Trentino

The merlot vine tends to be more productive than cabernet.

The wines made from the merlot variety tend to be softer, smoother, and rounder than those from cabernet, with less tannin and perhaps more alcohol. The Merlot wines tend to mature sooner than the Cabernets of the same area. As a rule of thumb, most Italian Merlots should be consumed before the end of their second year. The aroma of Merlot, at its textbook best, is reminiscent of tobacco or tea.

Petit Verdot. There are a few scattered plantings of petit verdot in Italy. This Bordeaux variety produces wines that are high in alcohol and acidity. We are not aware of any Italian wines made exclusively from this grape.

The Wines

ALTESINO CABERNET SAUVIGNON *(Tuscany)*. This fine Brunello producer has been experimenting with Cabernet Sauvignon. We tasted a cask sample of their '84, which showed potential. They expect to market their first Cabernet Sauvignon from the 1986 vintage.

ALTO ADIGE *(Trentino Alto Adige), DOC.* There are 13,600 acres (5500 hectares) under vines in the Alto Adige, or Süd Tyrol as the region is known locally. Most of the vineyards are on the slopes and hillsides of the Etsch Valley (Valle d'Isarco) between Meran and Salurn and in the Eisacktal (Val d'Adige) between Bozen (Bolzano) and Brixen. Two-thirds of the plantings are the prolific vernatsch or schiava (also known as trollinger) variety.

Twenty-one cooperatives process 54 percent of the grapes, and fifty fairly large wineries account for another 42 percent. The remaining four percent is vinified by small producers. Total yearly output of all wine in the region averages 6.1 to 6.7 million cases a year.[33]

When we think of this region, like many other winelovers, we tend to think of the fine white wines from rulander, gewurztraminer, weissburgunder, and riesling. The Alto Adige does indeed produce some of Italy's finest white wines, but red varieties also do well here, including such international favorites as cabernet sauvignon, cabernet franc, and merlot. These grapes, in the hands of a talented winemaker such as Giorgio Grai, can be the basis of an especially fine wine. These varieties are regulated under the wine law for the Alto Adige.

DOC Requirements

	Minimum varietal	Minimum age	Minimum alcohol	Maximum yield *(gallons/acre)*
Cabernet riserva	95%	none 2 years from Nov. 1	11.5	823
Merlot riserva	95%	none 1 year from Nov. 1	11.0	973

The official DOC vineyard area covers 4760 acres (1927 hectares) in thirty-three *communes*; of this, 175 acres (71 hectares) are planted to merlot and 72 (29) to cabernet. The red varieties must be planted at altitudes above 2300 feet (700 meters). The maximum yearly output is equivalent to nearly 2 million cases. Merlot accounts for 71,000 and Cabernet for 24,000—hardly a great production, when one compares it to the total output of some wineries that are considered rather small.

Cabernet sauvignon, cabernet franc, and merlot vines were introduced into the Süd Tyrol more than a century ago, so the growers here have had time to find out where each variety fares best.

Cabernet

The major cabernet plantings are in the Bozner Unterland in the southern part of the zone. The best Cabernets, according to Alois Lageder, who makes a good one, come from Magreid (Magre), an area with a soil composition of sand, limestone, and gravel. This area is almost at the southernmost extent of the vineyards in the region.

Lageder feels that his Cabernet is at its best about ten years after the vintage. He ages it for a year and a half in 530- to 790-gallon (20- to 30-hectoliter) oak casks, not of new wood. Since 1984, though, he has begun using *barriques*. Herbert Tiefenbrunner of Schloss Turmhof has also started giving his Cabernet some *barrique* aging, as have some of the cooperative wineries

Tom O'Toole, who is associated with the Bozen chamber of commerce, told us that 40 percent of the Cabernet in the Alto Adige is produced by Schloss Schwanburg; all they make is riserva.

Franco Kettmeir is unusual for the region in producing Cabernet Sauvignon. He produces 50,000 bottles of this wine a year and half that amount of Merlot. These two wines make up 30 percent of Kettmeir's red wine sold in bottle. He ages the Cabernet for a year to a year and a half in large, 2100-gallon (80-hectoliter) casks. Beginning with the 1982 vintage, he has given the Cabernet Sauvignon riserva six months in *barrique*. He produced 2500 bottles of that wine.

Recommended Cabernet Producers
Giorgio Grai, who has three labels:
>> Cantina Bellendorf
>> Herrnhofer
>> Kehlburg

> Bauernkellerei
> Josef Hofstatter
> Kellereigenossenschaft Magreid, Magre
> Kettmeir (Cabernet Sauvignon)
> Laimburger
> Lageder, Alois (particularly from the Wurmbrand vineyard)
> Martini, Karl (Kellermeistertrunk brand)
> Schloss Schwanburg
> Schloss Turmhof (Tiefenbrunner)

The Legendary Giorgio Grai

Giorgio Grai

Giorgio Grai has become something of a legend in Italy, both for his extraordinary palate and for his ability to craft outstanding wines from the grapes of many different regions. He is frequently asked to consult and is currently winemaker for *cantine* in Piemonte, Lombardia, Marche, and Lazio. There might be even more positions, but as one of his very satisfied clients puts it, Giorgio can be a *rompiscatole*, or something of a wearisome nitpicker.

We once asked him what his secret is, what he does to create an excellent wine from an area known for its mediocre wines or from a vineyard that was previously the source of nothing more than quite ordinary stuff. "I just make some small changes," he understates. But the small changes he makes are the ones that make the biggest difference. He is very exacting at the wineries where he consults, insisting first of all on simple cleanliness where it counts. "Do you think this barrel is clean?" he asks. "Yes" the reply. "No. Do you think these hoses are clean?" "Yes." "No." Giorgio is a stickler for taking care of the important details.

Grai has three *cantine* of his own in the vicinity of Bolzano, where he produces 100,000 to 150,000 bottles of finely honed wines a year. Grai's wines reflect his belief that a wine should have color, body, aroma, flavor, substance, balance, length, and character. The taster's first reaction, he says, should not be "What is this wine?" but "This wine is good." The second reaction should be to ask for another glass. Then, "What variety is it? From where?" Only if the wine is good does the question matter. "It's like when you meet a person. First they must be a good person, later you ask who are they? where are they from?"

Giorgio refers to a dinner he attended not long ago. There were a number of other producers and growers present whose wines were being poured. Some of Giorgio's friends asked him if he had any of his wines in the car. He did have a few that had been in the back for about a week or so jostling about as he maneuvered the curves of the mountain road to the house and the intricacies of parking in Bolzano, not that he was concerned about the condition of the wines. ("To say the wine was shaken up is just a matter of justification if it's not good.") But, he noted, there was plenty of wine on the table. He was urged nevertheless to bring in a few bottles, which he did, and they were poured. The director of a large *cantina sociale* criticized Grai's wines "for being too good" Giorgio explains; "they had too much flavor, too much aroma, they were not typical." He didn't reply to the comment. Some of those present felt he should defend his wines. "What can I say to this man?" responded Giorgio. "He is a big important director; I am just a small producer." With a hint of an ironic smile he continues, "So I only pointed out that I arrived late to the dinner, and the other wines had all been poured. 'But if you'll look at the bottles,' I said to them, 'you'll notice that those bottles are all half full. My wines were just poured, and all are finished'. And I sat down."

Grai studied at Conegliano in the late 1940s. After graduating with a degree in enology, he did some consulting, at first offering his services without pay to friends and recommended *cantine*. He felt that it furthered his own experience and allowed him the opportunity to follow the progress of a wine and verify his advice.

In 1962, he opened an enology lab, where he did analyses. At that time, he says, he overrated the value of technology. "I may do analyses," he notes, "and I may take down all of the statistics, but I can't tell if a wine will be good without tasting it." He didn't realize until after many mistakes, he says, that technology and analysis weren't the whole story. "Only when the material is bad is technology important; you can improve bad wine. But you can't make it good. The most important thing is to have good material. That's 50 percent; then you give your best effort."

It's important for a winemaker to know wine and to be honest, and he must taste often. Giorgio frequently tries wines from other parts of Europe.

Tasting, he considers, is 90 percent nose. The palate generally just confirms the original impression gained from the aroma of the wine. We visited one winery with him where he had been asked to consult, at a time when Giorgio was just coming down with a head cold. We were tasting the wines from cask when Giorgio looked at us and asked softly, "Do you taste the Sicilian wine?" "It does seem to have some southern wine in it," we noted. "Perhaps about 15 percent," he commented. "How much Sicilian wine was added to this wine?" he asked the cellarmaster quite matter-of-factly (not "Did you?" but "How much?") *"Che cosa?"* came the astonished reply. Giorgio repeated the question. "Fifteen percent," the *cantiniere* answered.

Timing is also very important, he feels; first to determine when to make the harvest, then when to bottle. "If you bottle the same wine at three different periods of the year, you get three different wines. You must understand how the wine will evolve in the bottle. It can't be bottled when it's ready to drink; it must be too early.

"You can't force the wine; you can't ask it to do what you want. You work with it. It has to come naturally. You don't fight nature; you work with her. You may assist her, but only with her cooperation. Everything is harmony. You have to find in life the balance."

Grai produced small lots of wines for himself in the early years, buying barrels of wine when he found good ones. He left the wine in the cellars as he had no facilities of his own yet. Kehlburg was his first label. In 1968, he bought Cantine Bellermont Wangen in Appiano. Later he bought the Herrnhofer *cantina* in Caldaro for more space. In the mid-1970s, he began to use that label for the wines he sold to Enoteca Solci in Milan. Currently, he has three labels: Bellendorf, Herrnhofer, and Kehlburg. The wines of the same variety from each of the three are the same.

Grai doesn't own any vineyards. At one time he bought grapes; today he buys new wines and blends them. It's better, he says, to buy young wine, as you have more control and can choose what you want. He selects lots from different producers in the region and from various casks and vats. One might be low in acid, he notes, another may be too high. One might have a lovely perfume, another better body. He takes some from each of those that have something to offer, perhaps from four or five different samples, maybe more, and comes up with a balanced blend. This blending also adds complexity to the wine, he feels.

We were with him at his bar when he was putting together a Gewurztraminer from six different lots. He poured us a glass from each of the bottles and asked our opinions of each. Then he gave his impressions. As we talked, he was pouring some of the wine from one of the glasses into a measured vial, then adding a little from another, and another. Then he poured that into a glass and offered it for us to taste. It was surely the best of the lot—balanced, interesting, good. Not too bad, he agreed, but it could still be better. He poured that out and made a slightly modified blend—better balanced, more interesting, very good. He had noted the amounts he needed and would buy those quantities from the producers.

Out of Grai's annual production of 100,000 to 150,000 bottles, 15,000 to 20,000 are his Cabernet, a wine of character and style, harmony and breed. It is made from 40 to 60 percent cabernet sauvignon and 60 to 40 percent cabernet franc. For us, it is the single finest Cabernet produced in Italy. And we are not alone in that opinion. We were asked recently by another producer of a fine Cabernet if we were going to award four stars to any Italian Cabernets—outside of Grai's, he added.

A few years ago we arranged a tasting in New York of some of Italy's finest cabernet and cabernet–merlot blends. There were thirty wines, including nearly all the best from Trentino Alto Adige, Friuli Venezia Giulia, the Veneto, Tuscany, and Umbria. Two fine California winemakers were there. When asked to name their favorite from the group, they chose, we were not surprised to see, the Herrnhofer Cabernet. Nor were we surprised at the reason they gave: the wine is a classic of balance and style.

There is only one problem with these wines, as we've told Giorgio many times. He must admit we are right, but... The defect, a grave one: availability or, to be more specific, the lack of it. Once the challenge of making the best wine he possibly can is met, he seems to lose interest in selling it.

Must we go all the way to Bolzano or to Fiè to get these wines? It's a good excuse to spend a few days with Giorgio and Elfi and the girls, but not really the most convenient method of stocking one's cellar. It's a problem shared by winelovers, restaurant owners, and wine merchants. The patient and good-natured Solci brothers have been known to throw their hands in the air in exasperation.

Gualtiero Marchese, maestro of the excellent restaurant that carries his name in Milano, told us his secret when we noted with astonishment a number of Grai's wines on his list. "I called on an angel in Fiè." (Giorgio's sweet wife, Elfi, a lady who might intercede more often if she had the time.)

Does she get frustrated with him too, like the rest of us? we wondered. She smiles. "You can't change Giorgio," she responds in her soft, pretty voice. You get the impression that she really wouldn't want to, although she may tease him. "If you don't stop complaining, I'll throw you down a deep hole," she says, undermining her threat with an involuntary smile as Giorgio laughs. "And I'll keep complaining all the way down," he answers with a kiss.

Giorgio doesn't decant his wines or open the bottles in advance to give the wine air. He enjoys following the wine's progress as it changes in the glass throughout the meal, inevitably getting better as it goes. When he smiles and gives a short, approving nod over the last drops of a wine, you wish you had had the forbearance to drink a little more slowly and still had some left in your own glass to savor.

Cabernet★★★★

Merlot

The most important of the merlot plantings in the Alto Adige are in Magreid, Kurtinig, Salurn, Terlan, and Andrian. Tom O'Toole, who is quite knowledgeable about the wines of this, his adopted region, considers that the best Merlots are produced in Siebeneich, near Terlan. Franco Kettmeir agrees with this point of view; he bottles a Merlot from that area.

Paolo Foradori of J. Hofstatter

Recommended Merlot Producers
Hofstatter, Josef
Kellereigenossenschaft Gries, Steinhof
Liebeneich Kellereigenossenschaft, Schreckbichl
Lageder, Alois
Kettmeir, Siebeneich

The Vintages

Giorgio Grai told us that 1969 was surely the finest vintage for Cabernet and 1975 and 1971 were on the next level. Tiefenbrunner picks 1983, 1981, 1979, and 1976 as the best vintages and 1982 and 1980 as the worst. Franco Kettmeir rates 1983 as the best of the recent vintages and 1981 as the least.

The Quality

Some of Italy's finest Cabernets are produced in this area, Cabernets that age better than most of those produced elsewhere in the country. There are also some good Merlots made in the Alto Adige, though we have considerably less experience with them. Cabernet★★ + ; Merlot★★ −

Cabernet Tasting Notes

1984

Bauernkellerei *(ex-barrique 4/85).* Bell peppers and new oak on aroma and flavor, with sweet vanilla adding an interesting component.★ −

Lageder, Magreid *(ex-cask 4/85).* (100 percent cabernet sauvignon) Herbaceous, varietal aroma, somewhat grassy; at this point overly fruity, needs to be tamed, fairly well balanced.★

1983

Lageder, Wurmbrand *(75 percent cabernet sauvignon, 25 percent cabernet franc, 4/85).* Light, undeveloped aroma; some herbaceousness carries through on the palate; some harshness and astringency, but a lot of flavor and potential; needs time to really show its quality. For now★(★).

1982

Lageder *(4/85).* Notes of cassis and grass on aroma; soft, touch of tannin, well-balanced.★★ −

Lageder riserva, Wurmbrand *(70–75 percent cabernet sauvignon, 25–30 percent cabernet franc, 4/85).* Light, varietal aroma, some cassislike notes; nice fruit on entry, light tannin; lacks some length.★(★)

Kellereigenossenschaft Magreid, Magre *(4/85).* Restrained bell-pepper aroma; more aggressive on the palate, though nice fruit as well.★

Kettmeir, Cabernet Sauvignon *(3 times 4/85).* Restrained grassiness on a varietal aroma; light tannin, soft, fruity, fairly well balanced.★

Schloss Schwanburg riserva (Rudolf Carl Erben). *(4/85).* Bell-pepper and cassis aroma; fairly well balanced, light tannin, fairly soft; some character.★ +

1981

Lageder riserva, Wurmbrand *(4/85)*. Tar and cassis on aroma, lightly grassy notes; medium-bodied, fairly well-knit; could be longer on palate, finishes with a touch of tannin.★(+)

Lun, H., *(non-D.O.C, 11/84)*. Herbaceous; low acid, unbalanced, some fruit.

Tiefenbrunner riserva *(70–30 percent cabernet sauvignon–cabernet franc, 11/85)*. Refined cabernet aroma, elegant; well structured, soft, round and flavorful; some length.★★+

1980

Bauernkellerei *(4/85)*. Herbaceous aroma with cassis notes; flavorful, light tannin, soft-centered, fairly well balanced; a bit short.★+

Brigl, Josef *(4/85)*. Varietal bell peppers; wine lies in the mouth with low acid and hangs at the end.

Kettmeir, Cabernet Sauvignon *(3 times 6/83)*. Light, fruity aroma; light tannin, soft and fruity.★

Lageder *(4 times 7/85)*. Refined cabernet aroma, some herbaceousness, fruity nuances; soft, perhaps too green tasting, but drinkable enough.★+

Lageder riserva, Wurmbrand *(4/85)*. Lovely bouquet, some cassis over light grassiness; smooth and round, tasty; ready, though no need to rush to drink it, it will hold for some time.★★

1979

Brigl, Josef *(twice 4/85)*. Bell peppers and still more bell peppers, some nice fruit beneath the veggies.

Lageder riserva *(70 percent cabernet sauvignon, 30 percent cabernet franc, 4/85)*. Bell pepper character, flat; harsh finish; a surprise from a usually quite good producer.

1978

Bauernkellerei *(4/85)*. Restrained bell pepper aroma, licorice and cassis notes; nice flavor, soft; finish has a vague dankness.★

Kettmeir, Cabernet Sauvignon *(4/85)*. Cassis aroma, some mint; still has tannin, seems to be losing its fruit, drying out.

1977

"Baron Widmann Kurtatsch," Kellereigenossenschaft Girlan *(10/79)*. Characteristic bell pepper aroma, one-dimensional; soft and fruity on entry, shallow; short, harsh, metallic aftertaste.

Grai, Bellendorf and Kehlburg labels *(50–50 of the two cabernets, 3 times 4/85)*. Richly fruited aroma with an herbaceous touch and an undertone of cassis; fairly full-bodied, still some tannin to soften, supple center; refined and stylish.★★(★)

1975

Grai, Bellendorf, Herrnhofer, and Kehlburg labels *(8 times 4/85)*. Intensely rich bouquet recalls cassis and blueberries; soft, round and velvety, light tannin, lots of flavor and lots of style; enormous length; enjoyable now, but has potential for further development.★★★+

1974

Lageder riserva *(85–90 percent cabernet sauvignon, 4/85)*. Nice nose, fruity with a cassis note; flavorful; drink up; age shows at the end, but still good.★★

1973

Grai, Herrnhofer and Kehlburg labels *(two parts cabernet franc, one part cabernet sauvignon, 6 times, 4/81)*. Bottle of 4/80: This wine was opened three days previously in Verona and left in the trunk of our car half full. It was retasted in Abruzzo after being jostled around for many kilometers. Expansive aroma rises out of the glass, showing more of an herbaceous aspect than when tasted in Verona; seems softer and smoother as well.★★+

Bottle of 4/81: Herbaceous aroma, with a note of cassis; still some tannin, richly flavored; very long finish.★★★−

Lageder riserva, Wurmbrand *(85 percent cabernet sauvignon, 15 percent cabernet franc, 4/85)*. Rich bouquet, light grassiness over cassis; light tannin, velvet center, loads of flavor, well-knit; quite long; impressive, some elegance.★★★

1971

Bauernkellerei riserva *(4/85)*. Light but nice aroma, licorice and cassis; still flavorful, though beginning to dry out a bit.★★−

Grai, Herrnhofer label *(twice 2/84)*. Richly fruited aroma with the characteristic varietal herbaceousness; rich, ripe fruit flavors, soft and round; fairly long; some age shows at the end, which is vaguely bitter.★★+

1970

Lageder riserva *(85–90 percent cabernet sauvignon, 15–10 percent cabernet franc, 4/85)*. Cassis, bell-pepper undertone; flavor almost sweet, tastes of ripe fruit, some delicacy; thins out at the end.★★

1969

Grai, Bellendorf label *(3 times 4/85)*. Beautiful garnet robe shading to orange; intense bouquet, cassis with an herbaceous back note; full of style, flavor, and elegance, sumptuous; shows no age.★★★★

Lageder riserva, Wurmbrand *(4/85)*. Richly fruited aroma recalls cassis; flavorful, light tannin; beginning to dry out at the end, still good.★★−

1967

Grai, Kehlburg label *(3 times 1/84)*. Beautiful brick robe, orange at rim; lovely bouquet recalls mint and cassis; liquid velvet, smooth and supple, richly flavored, a touch of tannin adds life; very long finish; real quality here.★★★+

Schloss Schwanburg riserva (Rudolf Carl Erben) *(4/85)*. Bouquet of concentrated cassis; loaded with flavor, no sign of age, well balanced, light tannin; very ready.★★+

1966

Grai, Kehlburg label *(twice 11/84)*. Color shows more age than the rest of the wine; bouquet has an enormous richness, with nuances of blueberries, vanilla, and herbaceous elements; finely structured, liquid velvet, full of flavor; enormous length, exudes style and balance.★★★+

Merlot Tasting Notes

1983 Liebeneich Kellereigenossenschaft, Schreck-bichl *(4/85)*. Characteristic varietal aroma; fair balance, fruity, good overall, though has some harsh edges.★ −

1982 Kettmeir *(4/85)*. Cherrylike fruit, grassy, spicy aroma; light tannin, somewhat unbalanced.

1981 Lageder *(4/85)*. Grassy aroma; lacks some structure, light and simple, fruity.★ −

1980 Lageder *(4/85)*. Fruity aroma, lightly grassy back notes; well balanced, quite nice now; drink up, starting to show some senility on the finish.★ +

1979 Kettmeir *(4/85)*. Berry, fruity aroma; light tannin, easy to drink; not to keep.★

1978 Kettmeir, Siebeneich *(11/84)*. Varietal aroma, a bit light; fruity; shows signs of age.★ −

1971 Hofstatter *(3/80)*. Rich nose, rich flavor, still has some tannin, well balanced, fine quality.★★ +

APRILIA *(Lazio), DOC*. The Merlot of Aprilia is made from a minimum of 90 percent merlot grapes. This wine at its best is soft and fruity, an everyday, quaffable red wine, no more. It is a wine to drink young, before its second or, at most, third year. Merlot 0

AQUILEIA *(Friuli Venezia Giulia), DOC*. Red varieties make up more than two-thirds of the plantings (800 out of 1200 acres) in this region, which encompasses all or part of seventeen villages in the province of Udine. Cabernet and Merlot account for more than fifty percent of the production of DOC wine. Yearly production of the Cabernet averages 33,000 cases; of the Merlot 70,000.

DOC Requirements			
	Minimum varietal	Minimum alcohol	Maximum yield *(gallons/acre)*
Cabernet	90%	11.5	898
Merlot	90%	11.0	973

A wine from Aquileia labeled Cabernet can be made from any combination of cabernet sauvignon and/or cabernet franc grapes.

Vanni Tavagnacco, the fine enologist at I Mòros, told us that this area is better for red wines than for whites. There is a salty character to some of the wines, more pronounced in the whites, which is attributed to the proximity of the sea.

The only producer from Aquileia that we can recommend is Ca' Bolani. They produce both a Cabernet and a Merlot.

Aquileia Cabernet is generally best drunk before its third year, Merlot before its second. Both wines can still be good with an additional year of age. Cabernet★; Merlot★

BARBAROLA *(Trentino Alto Adige), DOC*. Raffaelle Rino produces this merlot–cabernet blend. It is a wine that ages moderately well. Rating ★★ −

Tasting Note

1977 *(4/80)*. Aroma of varietal fruit and vanilla; fruity, acid on the low side, some tannin.★★ −

BELLAGIO *(Lombardy)*. This medium-bodied dry red is produced in the Como area from cabernet franc, malbec, merlot, and a small amount of pinot noir. It drinks well from its second to fourth year.

BELLAVISTA SOLESINE *(Lombardy)*. This fine producer of champagne-method spumante in the Franciacorta zone produces three *barrique*-aged wines: a chardonnay, a pinot noir, and this cabernet–merlot blend. The Solesine, like the others, is given 18 months in new oak. They produced 850 bottles (about three *barriques*) of their first Solesine from the 1982 vintage. Rating★

Tasting Note

1982 *(4/85)*. Understated bell-pepper aroma overlaid with new oak; firm vein of tannin at this stage, beginning to approach drinkability.★ +

BORGO CONVENTI ROSSO *(Friuli Venezia Giulia)*. Gianni Vescovo produces this wine from a blend of 40 percent cabernet sauvignon, 30 percent cabernet franc, and 30 percent merlot. The grapes are from a 2-acre (0.8-hectare) vineyard in Farra d'Isonzo in the Collio production zone. His first cabernet-merlot blend was from the 1979 vintage. That wine was made from 85 percent merlot and 15 percent cabernet franc. Like its more recent counterpart, it was also aged in small oak barrels. Vescovo gives the Borgo Conventi Rosso about one year in *barrique*. He produces about 5000 bottles when he makes it, which is only in the better vintages. This is a medium-bodied, dry wine with a fruity aroma of cherries and blackberries over an herbaceous background. Rating★★ +

Tasting Notes

1983 *(4/85)*. Characteristic herbaceousness over oak; a lot of flavor; some harshness suggests it is still young, though not a lot of tannin; finish is a bit short; needs two more years yet.★(★−)

1982 *(4/85; 2810 bottles)*. Richly fruited aroma, some cassis and oak, slightly grassy; full of flavor, supple, light tannin, well balanced; could be longer on the finish.★★(+)

1979 *(4/81)/* Lovely nose, light herbaceousness, suggestions of cherries and blackberries; well structured, lots of flavor, some tannin; some style evident.★★(★)

BREGANZE *(Veneto), DOC.* The Breganze production zone encompasses the villages of Breganze, Fara, Mason, and Moluena and parts of nine others, all in the province of Vicenza. There are some 25,000 acres (10,000 hectares) under vines in Breganze, about half on the hillsides and half on the plains.

Two DOC wines from this zone concern us here: Breganze Rosso and Cabernet. The Rosso must contain at least 85 percent merlot; the remaining 15 percent can be both or either of the cabernets, marzemino, groppello, and/or freisa. Not all producers follow that regulation, though, and in some cases, at least, their wine is no less for it. The Cabernet must be from 100 percent cabernet—cabernet sauvignon and/or cabernet franc.

DOC Requirements

	Minimum varietal	Minimum alcohol	Maximum yield *(gallons/acre)*
Cabernet	100%	11.5	903
superiore	100%	12.0	903
Rosso (Merlot)	85%	11.0	973

Annual production averages 85,000 cases of the Rosso and 22,500 of the Cabernet, not a lot of wine. And, not surprisingly, the best ones are even scarcer. The Cabernet is best before its fourth year, the Merlot before its third. Cabernet★/★★★; Merlot★

Recommended Producers
Bartolomeo
Maculan
Villa Magna

The Zone's Finest Producer

The finest producer in the zone, and the most innovative, is Maculan. Enologist Fausto Maculan produces a number of very fine wines, white and red, sweet and dry. Among them is the exceptionally fine *barrique*-aged dessert wine, Torcolato, and the fine white, Prato di Canzio. He also makes a few red wines of real quality: Fratta, Palazzotto, and Brentino

Maculan has 30 acres (12 hectares) of vines, which supply 25 percent of their grapes.

The *Brentino Breganze rosso* is a blend of both cabernets plus some merlot grapes from various vineyards, the proportions depending on the vintage. The '81 was made from 40 percent cabernet sauvignon and 30 percent each of cabernet franc and merlot. For the '80, Maculan used those same three varieties in a 25/35/45 blend. A small portion of the wine, at most 10 percent, is aged in *barrique*. In some vintages it is possible, Fausto told us, that none of the wine will be put into *barrique*. It depends on the grapes. Fausto doesn't make wine by a cookbook; he judges his material and works accordingly. Production in 1981 was nearly 2400 cases, and in 1982, 900 cases. Rating ★

Fausto Maculan of Maculan

Tasting Notes

1982 Brentino *(4/85)*. Light but fruity aroma; some tannin, nice fruit, good balance; the tannin on the aftertaste says it could use another year of age.★(+)

1981 Brentino *(3 times 7/85)*. Aroma of cabernet fruit, vague bell-pepper character; light tannin, fruity, soft and round; short; ready, a nice glass of wine.★ +

1980 Brentino *(twice 4/85; 14,870 bottles)*. Light, herbaceous aroma; fruity, more to it than the '81 or '82; moderate length.★★

The Breganze Cabernet regular is made from 60 percent cabernet sauvignon and 40 percent cabernet franc. They produced 360 cases in 1983. Maculan also produces two Breganze cabernet crus: Palazzotto and Fratta.

The *Palazzotto* is made from 100 percent cabernet sauvignon grapes grown in this 6.4-acre (2.6-hectare) vineyard in Mirabella di Breganze; the vineyard is not yet in full production. In 1981, Fausto produced 958 cases of regular bottles and 65 of magnums; in 1982, he made 950 cases of bottles and 60 of magnums. The '82 had 12.2 percent alcohol and was aged for twelve months in *barrique*. The '81, with 12.0 percent, was also *barrique*-aged for a year. Fausto rates the vintages for Palazzotto as follows:

★★★★	1983
★★★	1980
★★	1982, 1981

If it wasn't for the Fratta, there is no question that the Palazzotto would be the finest red wine of the zone. Rating★★★

Tasting Notes

1983 Palazzotto *(4/85)*. Aroma of oak gives way to cabernet fruit; finely crafted with loads of flavor, has tannin to soften; style quite evident.★★(★)

1982 Palazzotto *(twice 4/85)*. Aroma of cassis and oak with a tobaccolike note; lots of flavor, well balanced; fairly long finish, still young.★★(+)

1981 Palazzotto *(7/85)*. Lovely bouquet, refined and elegant, characteristic cassis and oak nuances; very well balanced, still some rough edges to smooth out, but a lot of flavor, in a somewhat understated style; elegant and stylish, sure to improve over the next two or three years, but lovely now. Fausto only gave the year★★. We gave the wine★★★

1980 Palazzotto *(4/85; 2768 bottles)*. Richly intense aroma of cassis over oak; richly flavored and tasty, smooth-textured.★★★

The *Fratta* is made from 50 to 60 percent cabernet sauvignon and 40 to 50 percent cabernet franc grapes grown in that 2.5-acre (1-hectare) vineyard. Maculan produced 364 cases of Fratta in 1981, 325 in 1982, and 500 in 1983. The wine achieves about half a degree of alcohol more than the Palazzotto. The first Fratta produced was from the 1977 vintage. The '79 was the first aged in *barrique*; it spent six months in Slavonian oak barrels. The '80 was aged for a year in Alliers oak, as was the '81.

Fausto said that thus far 1983 is the best vintage for Fratta. He rates the years as follows:

★★★★	1983, 1980, 1979
★★★	1982
★★	1981, 1978
★	1977

Fratta is without question one of the finest Cabernet wines produced in Italy. Rating ★★★ +

Tasting Notes

1983 Fratta *(4/85)*. Very deep color; incredible richness on the nose, cabernet fruit and oak; enormous concentration and weight, well-honed, supple center; very long, very young, and very good.★★★(+)

1982 Fratta *(4/85)*. Concentrated bouquet of cassis, licorice, and oak; richly flavored, though a leaner frame than the '83; tannic finish.★★(★)

1981 Fratta *(4/85)*. Richly fruited aroma, refined; firm with an astringent edge; still young, good potential.★★(+)

1980 Fratta *(4/85; 4427 bottles)*. Intense bouquet suggesting cassis, vague raspberry note, and some oaky vanilla; flavorful, balanced; still needs time for some more tannin to resolve itself.★★(★)

1979 Fratta *(4/85; 3985 bottles)*. Initial oak aroma gives way to an herbaceous character; nice fruit on entry, firm, lot of flavor; long; needs another year or two.★★ +

1978 Fratta *(4/80)*. Shy nose, some cabernet fruit evident; some tannin with an underlying softness; dull finish.★

1977 Fratta *(4/85)*. Fruity aroma, vague herbaceousness; some tannin, but soft and flavorful, quite nice; no need to hold any longer.★★

BRENTINO. See Breganze.

CAMPAGNANO *(Lazio)*. This wine is made from a blend of the two cabernets and the local cesanese variety. It is a medium-bodied dry red wine best drunk young.

CAMPO DEL LAGO. See Colli Berici.

CANTALEONE *(Trentino Alto Adige)*. Giovanni Visentin produces this wine from a blend of merlot, teroldego, and cabernet grapes grown in the S. Michele d'Adige area. It is a medium-bodied dry red of about 12.5 percent alcohol that ages moderately well.

CASTEL S. MICHELE *(Trentino Alto Adige)*. The Istituto Agrario Provinciale S. Michele produces some 16,000 to 18,000 bottles a year of this wine from 40 to 45 percent merlot, 35 to 40 percent cabernet sauvignon, and 20 percent cabernet franc. It is dry, soft, and flavorful, with a characteristic herbaceous aspect. Castel S. Michele is at its best from its third to sixth year. Rating★★

Tasting Notes

1983 *(4/85)*. Restrained bell-pepper aroma; soft, light tannin, strong flavor of peppers gives way to some nice fruit.★★ –

1980 *(10/83)*. Complex aroma with hints of black pepper and spice, herbaceous background; low acid, bell-pepper flavor, agreeable, though one-dimensional.★

1976 *(4 times 11/82)*. Fruity aroma with an herbaceous background; fruity, still has a fair amount of tannin; starting to dry out, at its best in 1980 and 1981.★

1975 *(twice 11/78)*. Fragrant aroma of oak and cabernet fruit; very soft and flavorful; ready; short.★★

1974 *(3/80)*. Some oak along with fruit on the nose; well structured; tasty, ready, though still some tannin.★★

CASTEL SAN GIORGIO *(Lazio)*. This wine is made from a blend of cesanese, merlot, and montepulciano grapes grown in the Maccarese area west of Rome. It is a medium-bodied dry red wine that ages moderately well. Castel San Giorgio is available in the vicinity of Rome, if it can't be found further afield.

CASTELLO DI QUERCETO *(Tuscany)*. This good Chianti Classico producer has a 7.4-acre (3-hectare) vineyard planted to cabernet sauvignon and merlot, from which he produces a *barrique*-aged wine. This wine was first produced from the 1984 vintage.

CASTELLO DI RONCADE *(Veneto)*. Barone Ciani Bassetti produces this wine from cabernet sauvignon, cabernet franc, merlot, and malbec grapes grown on his Villa Giustiniani farm in the Piave river area of Treiso. It is a medium-bodied dry soft red with an underlying herbaceous character. According to some reports, he also adds a little petit verdot. The labels we've seen list the first four grapes but not the last. We'll take his word for it. Bassetti ages the Castello di Roncade in small barrels for two years. The wine drinks well from its fourth to eighth year; in the best vintages, it can live for as much as ten. Rating★★

Tasting Notes

1979 *(9/81)*. Almost perfumed aroma, pretty, vague nutlike note; some tannin, flavorful; some style; still a bit young.★★ +

1969 *(5 times 11/82)*. Interesting aroma, hazelnut back note, vague off note; still has flavor interest, though beginning to lose its fruit, soft; at its best perhaps three to five years earlier, though the bottles did vary.★

CASTELVECCHIO *(Veneto)*. This wine is made from cabernet and merlot grapes grown in the Portogruaro area west of Friuli. It is a medium-bodied wine of about 12 percent alcohol that can take moderate age.

COGNO *(Trentino Alto Adige)*. Carlo Rossi (no connection to the California wine) produces this wine from a blend of 50 percent merlot and 50 percent of the two cabernets grown in the Mezza Prada district of Cimone in Trentino. Cogno drinks well from its third or fourth year.

COLLE DEL CALVARIO *(Lombardy)*. Tenuta Castello blends 30 percent merlot with 70 percent cabernet sauvignon grapes grown in Grumello del Monte near Bergamo to produce this medium-bodied dry red wine. It is aged for about two years in oak barrels. It is a wine that ages moderately well. Drink it within four to five years of the vintage.

COLLI BERICI *(Veneto)*, *DOC*. The Colli Berici zone encompasses all or part of twenty-eight *communes* between the Lessinian mountains and the Berici hills south of the city of Vicenza.

Among the wines of this district covered under DOC regulations are Cabernet and Merlot. Both wines must be made 100 percent from the named variety. The Cabernet can contain either of the two cabernets, alone or in combination.

DOC Requirements

	Minimum varietal	Minimum age	Minimum alcohol	Maximum yield (gallons/acre)
Cabernet	100%	none	11.0	834
riserva		3 years from Jan. 1	12.5	
Merlot	100%	none	11.0	973

The vine has quite an ancient history in the Colli Berici. Grape seeds from the wild species *Vitis silvestris* found here date from the Bronze age more than 3000 years ago. Grape growing is referred to in church documents from the eleventh century. And it is known that by 1250, Monte Berico was covered with vineyards producing highly regarded wines. In the seventeenth century, Zeffiro Bocci reports, Andrea Scoto wrote about the wines of Barbarano, Costozza, and Lonigo in his *Italian Itinerary*.[34]

Bordeaux varieties were grown here in the last century, but it wasn't until *phylloxera* devastated the vineyards in 1929 that these varieties became widely planted. Today the production of Cabernet is more than 30,000 cases a year, of Merlot more than 100,000 cases.

With few exceptions, Colli Berici Cabernet is best before its fourth year. The Merlot matures a year or two earlier. Cabernet ★/★★; Merlot ★/★★★

Conte da Schio's Costozza is a noteworthy wine which is sometimes sold as a Colli Berici DOC.

The best wines in the zone are produced by Lazzarini.

The Zone's Finest Producer

Lazzarini bought the Villa dal Ferro estate located in San Germano dei Berici in 1960. He has 32 acres (13 hectares) of vines. The Lazzarini wines are made by enologist Pamela Porro Lazzarini, his daughter.

Cru	Variety	Production (in bottles)
Bianco del Rocolo	pinot bianco	13,300
Busa Calcara	riesling	2,700
Campo del Lago	merlot	17,300
Costiera Granda	tocai	5,300
Le Rive Rosse	cabernet	17,300
Rosso del Rocolo	pinot nero	8,000

The *Le Rive Rosso* is made from both cabernets. It drinks well at four to seven years of the vintage. Rating ★★ +

Tasting Notes

1978 Le Rive Rosse (Cabernet) *(4/80)*. Raspberry aroma, characteristic herbaceous background; loads of fruit, some tannin, concentrated.★★ +

1977 Le Rive Rosse (Cabernet) *(3 times 11/82)*. Cabernet fruit aroma, light floral note in the back; soft and smooth with light tannin; a bit short.★★

1974 Le Rive Rosse (Cabernet) *(twice 4/80)*. Nice nose of fruit and spice, bell-pepper note in the back; soft, flavorful, light tannin, acid a bit deficient.★★

Lazzarini's *Campo del Lago,* is a dry, medium-bodied red wine with a lot of character. It is, in our opinion, the finest wine of the zone and just might be the finest Merlot produced in Italy. This wine is a good accompaniment to steaks and chops. It is at its best drunk between three and six years of age, though it can last eight. Rating ★★★

Tasting Notes

1980 Campo del Lago (Merlot) *(1/83)*. We tasted this wine at a tasting of about three dozen Cabernet and Merlot wines from the Tre Venezia. It was the only real wine at that tasting. Fruity, soft, very ready, which seems somewhat of a surprise.★★ +

1978 Campo del Lago (Merlot) *(3 times) 11/82)*. Light, herbaceous aroma, fruity background; firm texture, flavorful; only defect is a somewhat short finish.★★

1977 Campo del Lago (Merlot) *(3 times 11/82)*. Plummy aroma, herbaceous note; firm-textured, full of flavor, a very nice glass of wine.★★ +

1975 Campo del Lago (Merlot) *(3/80)*. A bit light, but tasty and very ready, quite enjoyable.★★ +

1972 Campo del Lago (Merlot) *(11/78)*. Big and rich on the nose, surprisingly so, green-olive notes; soft and flavorful; shows real quality, and from a not very highly regarded vintage.★★★ −

COLLI BOLOGNESI, MONTE SAN PIETRO, CASTELLI MEDIOVALE *(Emilia Romagna)*
DOC. This production zone is located southwest of Bologna. It covers ten villages centered around Monte San Pietro. The local Merlot wine is recognized and regulated by Italian wine law. In recent years production of this wine has varied considerably, from a trickle of 1150 cases in 1981 to 1980's flood of 4050.

DOC Requirements		
Minimum varietal	Minimum alcohol	Maximum yield *(gallons/acre)*
Merlot 85%	11.5	898

When DOC status was granted to Merlot, there was some discussion of also including Cabernet Sauvignon in the discipline. This variety, in fact, yields the best red wine of the district. And it seems that although the Cabernet is still not recognized, it soon will be. The cabernet sauvignon vine does fairly well in this area. Enrico Valliana produces both a red and a rosé, neither aged in oak. Both are good wines. Bruno Negroni is another good producer. Marchese Malaspina produces good Merlot and Cabernet Sauvignon. He also makes a Cabernet from 80 percent cabernet sauvignon and 20 percent bonardas, which we can recommend.

As a rule, these are wines to drink young—the Merlot before its third year, the Cabernet perhaps a year older. Cabernet★★ − ; Merlot★

COLLI EUGANEI *(Veneto), DOC.* This production zone comprises all or part of seventeen villages in the district southwest of Padova. The Colli Euganei Rosso is made from a base of 60 to 80 percent merlot; the other grapes in the *uvaggio* may be either or both of the two cabernets, barbera, and/or raboso veronese.

DOC Requirements		
Minimum varietal	Minimum alcohol	Maximum yield *(gallons/acre)*
Normal none	11.0	1050
Superiore 1 year	12.0	1050

Production averages more than 165,000 cases a year. This wine may be still or sparkling, dry or semisweet. (Make ours dry; we'll take our sweet peppers roasted, thanks.) Some varietal Cabernet and Merlot wines, not recognized under DOC, are also produced here.

The best wine of the Colli Euganei, by reputation, is Luxardo de' Franchi del Venda's Sant'Elmo. This wine is made from a blend of merlot, cabernet franc, and barbera. It is aged for about two years in oak casks. It is best at about four to six years of the vintage. The La Principesa Colli Euganei Rosso can also be quite good. Like most wines from this district, it is best drunk within two years of the vintage, while it still has its youthful fruit. Rating★/★★

COLLI MORENICI MANTOVANI DEL GARDA *(Lombardy), DOC.* This minor red wine from Mantua is made with 20 to 40 percent merlot grapes. It is at best an agreeable everyday beverage wine, to be drunk within two years of the vintage. Rating★

COLLI ORIENTALI DEL FRIULI *(Friuli Venezia Giulia), DOC.* This district takes in the towns of Attimis, Buttrio, Cividale del Friuli, Faedis Manzano, Nimis, Povoletto, Tarcento, and Torreano on the hills east of Udine. Some 40 percent of the 3800 acres (1534 hectares) of vines, or 1460 acres (591 hectares), are the red varieties, including 1045 (423) of merlot and 228 (92) of cabernet. Both Cabernet and Merlot wines are recognized under DOC for this production zone.

DOC Requirements			
Minimum varietal	Minimum age	Minimum alcohol	Maximum yield *(gallons/acre)*
Cabernet 90%	none	12.0	823
riserva	2 years from Jan. 1		
Merlot 90%	none	12.0	823
riserva	2 years from Jan. 1		

Production of Merlot averages nearly 140,000 cases a year; for the Cabernet production is less than one-third of that.

Recommended Producers
Cantine Florio, Tenuta Maseri Florio (Cabernet and Merlot)
Dorigo Girolamo (Cabernet and Merlot)
I Mòros di Nello Tavagnacco (Cabernet di Ippilis and Merlot)
Rodero (Cabernet Franc)
Specogna Leonardo (Cabernet Sauvignon and Merlot)
V. Nascig di Angelo Nascig (Cabernet Sauvignon and Merlot)
Villa Belvedere di Taddei (Cabernet Franc and Merlot)
Zamo Tullio di Ipplis (Merlot)

The Merlot regular is at its best before its second or perhaps third year; the riserva can be good for up to four. The Cabernet, made from either or both varieties, is best within four years of the vintage. The riserva can age for two, perhaps three years beyond that. Cabernet★★ − ; Merlot★ +

COLLIO or **COLLIO GORIZIANO** *(Friuli Venezia Giulia), DOC.* This zone, at the border of Yugoslavia, takes in the hills west of Gorizia. The soil here is of sandstone and marl. Collio is much more highly regarded for its white wines than its reds, and for good reason. But there are some good reds produced here. Both Merlot and Cabernet are recognized under DOC. Unlike the other zones of Friuli, here only cabernet franc grapes are allowed in the Cabernet.

DOC Requirements

	Minimum varietal	Minimum age	Minimum alcohol	Maximum yield (gallons/acre)
Cabernet	100%	none	12.0	823
Merlot	100%	none	12.0	823

There are almost 28,000 acres (11,280 hectares) of vines, which include 413 (167) of merlot and 131 (53) of cabernet franc. About 15 percent of the DOC output of more than 800,000 cases, or 120,000 cases, is Merlot and Cabernet; approximately 70 percent of this is Merlot.

The best red wines of Collio, according to Vanni Tavagnacco, the fine enologist at I Mòros in Colli Orientali, are from the vineyards on the lower altitudes in the area of S. Floriano del Collio.

The best reds of Collio, which can be quite good, have a definite varietal herbaceousness, but one that is not overbearing. In our experience, the Merlot wines tend to be more successful here than the Cabernets. Both wines tend to be soft and fruity. Collio Merlot is best before its second year, the Cabernet before its fourth. Cabernet★ + ; Merlot★★ −

Recommended Collio Producers
Berin Fabio (Cabernet Franc)
Borgo Conventi (Merlot)
Ca' Ronesca (Cabernet Franc and Merlot)
Conti Formentini (Cabernet Franc and Merlot)
Eno Friulia (Cabernet Franc)
Felluga Livio (Cabernet Franc and Merlot)
Gradnik (Cabernet Franc and Merlot)
Marco Felluga (Merlot)
Russiz Superiore (Cabernet Franc and Merlot)
Schiopetto Mario (Cabernet Franc and Merlot)
Scolaris Giovanni (Merlot)
Villa San Giovanni, Marco Felluga (Cabernet)

Besides some very fine white wines, Gianni Vescovo also produces a fine red wine from a blend of cabernet and merlot and a good DOC Merlot from grapes grown on his 26-acre (10.5-hectare) Borgo Conventi estate in Farra d'Isonzo.

Conti Formentini produces three good reds from his 240 acres (97 hectares) of vines at San Floriano del Collio: a Cabernet Franc, a Merlot, and a Merlot–Cabernet blend.

Mario Schiopetto produces a fine Merlot from vines cultivated in a district where the variety does particularly well. In the best vintages this wine was labeled Riva Rossa; in normal years it is simply Merlot. Today Riva Rossa is a blend of cabernet, merlot, and pinot nero. Schiopetto is an exceptional winemaker, producing some especially fine white wines. All of his wines, though, while they tend to be difficult to find, are worth the search. Schiopetto's '79 Riva Rossa was the single finest red wine we have tasted to date from Collio.

COSTA DELLE PERGOLE ROSSO (*Veneto*). Col Sandago produces this wine from a blend of 60 percent cabernet franc, 20 percent merlot, and 10 percent wildbacher grapes plus a small amount of other varieties including pinot noir and malbec. It is a medium-bodied dry red with an herbaceous, cherrylike character. This wine is best drunk from two to three years of the vintage. Rating★★ −

COSTOZZA CABERNET FRANK (*Veneto*). Conte da Schio produces this wine from cabernet frank grapes grown in the Colli Berici area. It is best drunk between three and four years of the vintage. His '74 carried the DOC blurb on the label; the '77 did not. The bottles we've tasted from both vintages were equally variable. Rating★★ −

Tasting Notes

1977 (*3 times 6/83*). Bottle of 6/83: Pungent bell-pepper aroma and flavor—and then some.0
 Bottle of 3/81: Oak and herbaceousness on aroma, a touch of mint, and bell peppers in the back; lean and austere, somewhat astringent, fairly nice fruit.★ +

1974 (*twice 11/80*). Refined, cabernet aroma; soft and smooth, acid a trifle low, full of fruit and cabernet character. (A bottle tasted some months earlier was not up to this level.)★★ +

Attilio Simonini of Favonio

FAVONIO CABERNET FRANC (*Apulia*). Attilio Simonini grows chardonnary, pinot blanc, trebbiano toscano, pinot noir, zinfandel, and cabernet franc on his 41-acre (16.5-hectare) Favonio estate in Donadone on the plains of the Capitanata northeast of Foggia. He has 10 acres (4 hectares) of cabernet franc, which he was told wouldn't grow here (nor would the other French varieties, he was warned). He wasn't deterred.

By pruning closely to keep yields low, utilizing extra crop cover to shade the grape clusters, training the vines on wires high from the ground, using a modified drip irrigation system to spurt just enough moisture on the vines at periodic intervals, and picking early, Simonini is able to harvest ripe, but not overripe, healthy bunches of grapes. Any fruit that doesn't meet his standards is not used in his wines.

Simonini established the vineyard and winery in 1970 and produced his first wines commercially in 1974. Today he produces nearly 20,000 cases a year; 5000 of these are Cabernet. He is happy to say that his daughter, Roberta, who is studying viticulture at the University of Padua, will join him at the winery after graduation.

In making his wines, Attilio aims for the type he enjoys drinking himself. He prefers a crisp style for his whites (he produces a remarkable Pinot Blanc) and a well-balanced, fruity red with character and style, quite unlike the vast majority of southern reds. Simonini is an innovator. He sets high standards and works with cheerful determination to achieve them.

He ages his Cabernet for six months to a year in large Slavonian oak casks. His riserva is aged for at least a year longer. The regular Cabernet is a medium-bodied, warm dry red wine with an aroma and flavor of bell peppers. The riserva is a different matter. This is a wine of some refinement; the extra aging in oak tones down the herbaceousness and brings out a character of oak and cassis.

Though a jovial and good-natured man, inclined to laugh at adversity, Attilio is also very serious about quality and committed to producing the best wine possible. His wines are getting better every year. Regular★; Riserva★★

Tasting Notes

1978 (*18 times 4/81*). Cassis, vanilla, and a touch of bell peppers; soft and smooth, tasty, light tannin; quite nice, ready, Simonini's finest regular Cabernet to date.★★

1974 riserva (*3 times 4/81*). Aroma of cassis, pine, and a vague bell-pepper back note; well balanced, soft and flavorful, acid a touch low, very ready and nice too.★★ +

FIORANO *(Lazio)*. Boncompagni Ludovisi Principe di Venosa produces a scant 110 cases a year of this wine from a blend of merlot and cabernet grapes. It is aged for two years in barrel. Fiorano is an elegant, stylish wine that ages gracefully for eight, even ten years. In our experience, there is no finer merlot–cabernet blend produced in Italy. Rating★★★

Tasting Notes

1980 *(8/85; barrel #1 403 bottles)*. Cabernet fruit with cherry and tobacco notes on aroma; some tannin, lighter and softer than the 1978 and rather more forward; somewhat light on the finish but well made; displays some class, nearly ready though sure to improve with another 2 years.★★ +

1978 *(8/85; barrel #2 1366 bottles)*. Deep color is still quite youthful; intense, refined aroma hints of cassis; still full of tannin, well structured, heaps of flavor; quite young but has real class, hold until at least 1988.★★★(+)

1973 *(twice 9/80; 1398 bottles)*. Deep color; refined bouquet recalls flowers, fruit, and oak; well-knit, tasty; lingers long on the palate; has elegance and a lot of style.★★★

FOIANEGHE ROSSO *(Trentino Alto Adige)*. Conti Bossi Fedrigotti produces this soft, round red wine from 40 to 60 percent of the two cabernets and 40 to 60 percent merlot grapes grown on his Foianeghe estate near Rovereto. It is aged for eighteen months to two years in small oak barrels. The wine can take moderate aging, from four to six years, perhaps longer in the better vintages. Rating★★

Tasting Notes

1979 *(5/83)*. Bell-pepper notes come through on the nose; agreeable and very drinkable, though it could improve a bit.★ +

1977 *(4/80)*. One-dimensional varietal herbaceous aroma; low acid, overly soft, fruity; moderate length.★ +

1975 *(4 times 11/82; 88,750 bottles)*. Herbaceous aroma has a definite but not overbearing green-pepper character; still has nice fruit, but the bell-pepper character is becoming dominant; it had a more pronounced fruity character a few years ago.★★ −

1971 *(3/80)*. Some oxidation starting to intrude, but flavor and character are still quite evident.★★ +

FORMENTINI ROSSO *(Friuli Venezia Giulia)*. Conti Formentini produces this 60 percent merlot, 40 percent cabernet sauvignon blend from vines grown in his San Floriano del Collio estate in the Collio production zone. The wine is aged for about two months in small oak barrels. It is a fairly nice, rather easy style of dry red wine with about 12 percent alcohol. The ones we tasted were not vintage dated. Rating★ +

FRANCIACORTA ROSSO *(Lombardy), DOC*. The Franciacorta zone near Brescia, an area best suited to the production of white wines and champagne-method sparklers, also produces red and rosé wines. The red wines are made from a rather interesting combination of varieties, two from Bordeaux and two from Piemonte. The wine itself is less so. DOC requires a blend of 40 to 50 percent cabernet franc plus 20 to 30 percent barbera, 15 to 25 percent nebbiolo, and 10 to 15 percent merlot. Ten percent of wine and/or must from outside the zone may be used to correct a weak vintage. The grapes are planted at an altitude of at least 1300 feet (400 meters). Maximum yield is 910 gallons an acre (85 hectoliters per hectare); minimum alcohol is 11 percent. Franciacorta Rosso cannot be sold before June 1 of the year following the harvest.

This medium-bodied, fruity red wine is made in two basic styles. One has a definite character of bell peppers. The Longhi-di Carli Franciacorta is a good example of this type. The second style is less obvious and melds better the diverse characters of the different grape varieties. The Ca' del Bosco is perhaps the best example of this type. Neither style ages well. These wines are best drunk within two, at most three years of the vintage.

Recommended Producers
Ca' del Bosco
Catturich Ducco
Lancini Luigi, Vigna Cornaleto
Longhi-di Carli
Monte Rossa

Rating★

FRATTA. See Breganze.

GAJA CABERNET SAUVIGNON *(Piemonte)*. Angelo Gaja produced his first Cabernet Sauvignon in 1982 from vines grown in his Darmagi vineyard in the Barbaresco zone. Production currently ranges from 6500 to 7000 bottles a year. Rating★★

Tasting Notes

1983 *(ex-barrique 11/84)*. Refined, toasty, fruity aroma of moderate intensity; tannic, but with the fruit to carry it; already displays some character.★★(+)

1982 *(11/84)*. Some cassis on aroma overlaid with oak; tannin and oaky, with the fruit to back it up.★★(+)

GHIAIE DELLA FURBA *(Tuscany)*. The very fine Carmignano producer, Conte Ugo Buonacossi, makes this single-vineyard wine from a blend of 40 percent cabernet sauvignon, 30 percent cabernet franc, and 30 percent merlot grapes grown in a 7.4-acre (3-hectare) plot on his Villa Capezzana estate. In the first vintage, 1979, he produced about 16,000 bottles. In years like 1984 he doesn't produce Ghiaie della Furba. The wine is aged in 550- to 790-gallon (25- to 30-hectoliter) casks. Since 1983, he has been experimenting with aging in *barriques*. Rating★★

Tasting Notes

1983 *(ex-cask 5/85)*. Harmonious blend of oak and fruit; well structured, displays some style, nice fruit.★★(+)

1980 *(5/85)*. Fruity aroma on an herbaceous back-ground; well balanced, soft, tasty, light tannin; could be longer on the palate.★★

1979 *(3 times 5/85)*. A soft, nicely fruited wine, herbaceous varietal notes; short; a bit simple.★ +

GIURAMENTO *(Lombardy)*. Cabernet, merlot, barbera, and schiava gentile grapes are the *uvaggio* for this medium-bodied wine from the Bergamo area. It can take moderate aging.

GRAVE DEL FRIULI *(Friuli Venezia Giulia)*, *DOC*. As in the other DOC zones of Friuli, the Italian wine law recognizes Cabernet and Merlot wines also from Grave. These wines are produced from vines grown on basically flat terrain in gravelly and sandy clay soils in the provinces of Udine and Pordenone. The soil here is quite porous, and irrigation is commonplace. Plantings of red varieties comprise more than two-thirds of the total acreage in Grave. Merlot, with more than 8300 acres (3364 hectares), represents more than half of the 16,150 acres (6536 hectares) of vines here. Cabernet plantings total 1512 acres (612 hectares), or almost 10 percent of the vines in this DOC zone.

DOC Requirements

	Minimum varietal	Minimum alcohol	Maximum yield (gallons/acre)
Cabernet	90%	11.5	898
Merlot	90%	11.0	973

Annual production of Merlot averages more than 1 million cases, that of Cabernet nearly 300,000. Together they account for more than half of the DOC wine produced in Grave del Friuli. Reputedly the best reds of the zone—the Cabernet, Merlot, and Refosco in particular—come from the zone near Casarsa.

Recommended Producers
Antonutti (Cabernet)
Casarsa Coop., "La Delizia" (Cabernet, Cabernet Sauvignon and Merlot)
Duca Badoglia (Cabernet and Merlot)
Friulivini Cantina Sociale (Cabernet Sauvignon and Merlot)
"La Boria," Cantina del Friuli Centrale (Cabernet and Merlot)
Lis Gravis (Cabernet Sauvignon)
Pighin F.lli (Cabernet and Merlot)
Pradio, Tre Pigne (Cabernet Franc)
Villa Ronche (Cabernet Franc and Merlot)

The red wines of Grave tend to be somewhat deficient in acid; they are fruity and overly soft and have a pronounced herbaceousness. They are, however, moderately priced and can make a good accompaniment to meals. The Cabernet is best before its fourth year, the Merlot before its second. Cabernet★; Merlot★

GRENER *(Trentino Alto Adige)*. F.lli Dorigati blends merlot and cabernet grapes with the local teroldego to produce this soft, fruity, medium-bodied dry red. It is at its best within three to four years of the vintage.

Tasting Note

1975 *(4/80)*. Age beginning to creep in in the form of oxidation; the acid is very low.

GRIANTINO *(Lombardy)*. Griantino is produced from a blend of cabernet, malbec, merlot, and pinot noir grapes grown in the Como area. It is a medium-bodied dry red wine that can take moderate aging of four to five years.

ISONZO *(Friuli Venezia Giulia), DOC.* The Isonzo production zone takes in the *communes* of Gradisca d'Isonzo, Romans d'Isonzo, Marino del Friuli, Medea, Moraro, San Pier d'Isonzo, Turriaco, Villese, and parts of thirteen others in the province of Gorizia. The soil here is rather similar to that of Grave del Friuli. Almost half of the nearly 1600 acres (650 hectares) of plantings in Isonzo are of the red varieties.

The red wines of this region, however, are well regarded by a number of producers in Friuli whom we spoke with.

DOC Requirements			
	Minimum varietal	Minimum alcohol	Maximum yield *(gallons/acre)*
Cabernet	90%	11.0	898
Merlot	90%	10.5	973

Annual production averages approximately 150,000 cases of Merlot and more than 50,000 of Cabernet, nearly 50 percent of the entire DOC output of the zone.

Recommended Producers
Angoris Riserva Castello (Cabernet)
Conti Attems

These reds, like those of the Grave zone, are at their best within two or three years of the vintage. There is no reason to cellar them. They don't improve, and since they are soft and ready when released they might as well be enjoyed while they still have all their fruit. Cabernet★; Merlot★

LATISANA *(Friuli Venezia Giulia), DOC.* Latisana includes all or part of thirteen *communes* in the province of Udine, an area of rolling hills and coastal flatlands close to the Adriatic. The soil here is sandy, and as in Aquileia the wines are said to take on a salty character from the sea's proximity, the whites in particular. Consequently, the red wines are more highly regarded.

More than two-thirds of the total acreage under vines in Latisana is planted to red varieties. Cabernet and Merlot account for more than 60 percent of the DOC wines. Annual production of these two averages nearly 100,000 cases; almost two-thirds of this is Merlot.

DOC Requirements			
	Minimum varietal	Minimum alcohol	Maximum yield *(gallons/acre)*
Cabernet	90%	11.5	898
Merlot	90%	11.0	973

Recommended Producer
Isola Augusta (Cabernet and Merlot)

These wines are best consumed young while they still have all their youthful fruit, which is indeed their only virtue. Cabernet★; Merlot★

LE RIVE ROSSO. See Colli Berici.

LUNGAROTTI CABERNET SAUVIGNON *(Umbria)*. This fine producer of Rubesco planted cabernet sauvignon vines in 1971 in his vineyards in the Miraduolo district, one of the cooler areas around Torgiano. He produced his first Cabernet Sauvignon from the 1974 vintage. Today Lungarotti produces 5000 to 6000 cases a year of this wine. Lungarotti gets only 430 gallons an acre (40 hectoliters a hectare) from the cabernet sauvignon, as compared to 835 (78) from his sangiovese vines. His Cabernet is aged in oak, including five to six months in new oak barrels. The '78 was given one month in *barrique*.

This deeply colored wine has a rich, intense aroma with a characteristic herbaceous aspect. It is full-bodied and soft, having rather low acidity. It ages fairly well, however. Rating★★

Tasting Notes

1978 *(11 times 7/85)*. Herbaceous, varietal aroma; some though not a lot of tannin, fairly soft and round, could use more acid, tasty; room to improve, though drinks well now.★★

1977 *(twice 11/84)*. Cassis and oak aroma; soft and flavorful; a bit short.★★

1975 *(11/84)*. Aroma brings up cassis, some oak in the back; a fair amount of tannin, fruity.★★

1974 *(twice 11/84)*. Nice nose, characteristic, with notes of tobacco, tea, and bell peppers; still has fruit, but starting to dry out a bit; drink up now.★

MASO LODRON ROSSO *(Trentino Alto Adige)*. Cantina Letrari-Palazzo Lodron produces this wine from a blend of cabernet, both cabernets, and merlot. It is aged for about a year and a half in oak barrels and needs one to three years of bottle age to be at its best.

MAURIZIO ZANELLA *(Lombardy)*. Maurizio Zanella, the young producer of the highly esteemed champagne-method Ca' del Bosco spumante, also produces a line of *barrique*-aged wines from French varieties. These wines are made by Zanella himself—a fine chardonnay, a very good pinot noir, and a fine Bordeaux blend made from 40 percent cabernet sauvignon, 30 percent cabernet franc, and 30 percent merlot.

The wines are not named for the grape varieties but carry simply the signature of the producer. The wines are described on the back labels, which also note Maurizio's gratitude to enologist Angelo Solci with whom the idea for these wines was developed.

The signature wine from the Bordeaux varieties is aged for about a year in *barriques* of Troncais and Limousin oak. In 1981, the first vintage for this wine, Maurizio made 1600 bottles and 300 magnums. He was pleased with the wine and has since nearly quadrupled the production to 7000 bottles. He told us the demand is such that he could nearly triple that amount to 20,000 bottles a year if he chose, but he prefers to put a hold on quantity and concentrate on the quality.

The "Maurizio Zanella" is a well-balanced wine of real character and style, clearly one of the finest new wines of Italy. Rating★★★

Tasting Notes

1984 *(ex-barrique 5/85)*. Fruity, herbaceous aroma, still undeveloped; richly fruited, still a bit rough; good potential.★★(+)

1983 *(twice 5/85)*. Aroma of fruit, oak, and mint; well balanced, smooth in center, surrounded with tannin, lots of flavor; already shows style.★★(★+)

1982 *(twice 5/85)*. Lovely nose, with suggestions of cassis and mint and an oaky nuance; tannic, rich and ripe, well structured; has personality.★★(★)

1981 *(11/84)*. Pronounced varietal herbaceousness plus oak; acid a bit low, some tannin, soft and flavorful.★★+

Maurizio Zanella of Ca' del Bosco

MONSANTO CABERNET SAUVIGNON *(Tuscany)*. Fabrizio Bianchi produces this Cabernet Sauvignon from grapes grown in the Mulino vineyard on his Monsanto estate. It is aged for one year in *barrique*. The '80 was his first vintage; today he produces about 500 cases a year. It is a good wine, although it doesn't attain the heights of his excellent Chianti Classico. Rating★★+

Tasting Notes

1984 *(ex-vat 4/85)*. A surprising amount of fruit, fairly tannic, rises above the image of the vintage.★+

1983 *(ex-cask 4/85)*. Herbaceous aroma; rich and concentrated with a lot of fruit and a lot of tannin, very well balanced; holds out a lot of promise.★★(★)

1982 *(3 times 4/85; 6400 bottles)*. Herbaceous aroma; enormous weight and extract, light tannin, rather forward though needs a couple of more years yet.★★+

MONT QUARIN *(Friuli Venezia Giulia)*. This wine is produced from cabernet and merlot grapes grown in Cormons, Gorizia. It is fairly characteristic for its type and ages moderately well.

MONTELLO E COLLI ASOLANI *(Veneto), DOC.* This growing zone in the province of Treviso in the eastern part of the Veneto encompasses the Asolano and Montello hills around the towns of Montebelluna and Asoli. Documents record that the vine was cultivated in this area as early as A.D. 980.

According to Bocci, the best wine "comes from the Montello side, the hills of Montebelluna and Valdobbiadene."[35]

As elsewhere in Veneto, cabernet and merlot grapes became more widely planted here after recovery from *phylloxera*, which destroyed the vineyards in this district in the period following World War I.

DOC Requirements

	Minimum varietal	Minimum age *(years)* cask	total	Minimum alcohol	Maximum yield *(gallons/acre)*
Cabernet	85%	none	none	11.5	748
superiore		1	2	12.0	
Merlot	85%	none	none	11.0	898
superiore		1	2	11.5	

The aging period for the superiore is calculated from November 1 in the year of the harvest.

The Cabernet must be made from no less than 85 percent cabernet, which may be either or both varieties, and the balance merlot. The Merlot wine may contain, besides the named variety, up to 15 percent malbec and/or cabernet.

Annual production of the cabernet has ranged from less than 5000 cases a year to just over 11,000 cases. There is somewhat more merlot produced, from 25,000 to 32,000 cases a year.

Az. Agr. Loredan Gasparini, the zone's finest producer, has 125 acres (50 hectares) of vines on their Venegazzù estate. They produce a good DOC Cabernet Sauvignon as well as two other wines made from Bordeaux grapes.

Montelvini also makes fairly good wines. This *azienda,* located in Venegazzù di Volpago, has 1250 acres (500 hectares), 840 (340) in vines. They buy a large proportion of grapes to produce more than half a million cases of wine a year. Of this, 40 percent is Cabernet and 10 percent Merlot. They rate 1982 and 1971 as their best vintages, 1983 and 1976 as the least.

These wines are among the more interesting varietal wines of the Veneto, perhaps because they have more character than most. We have enjoyed a number of bottles of Cabernet Sauvignon from Venegazzù. The Merlot and Cabernet of Montelvini can also afford good drinking. Neither of these wines ages very well, though. Some authorities have recommended drinking the Cabernet with between three and six years and the Merlot from two to five. Our experience and taste suggest an earlier timetable. We find the Merlot is at its best within a year of two of the vintage, perhaps three. The Cabernet can take an additional year. Cabernet★ + ; Merlot★ +

MONTEVECCHIA *(Lombardy)*. This fairly full-bodied wine comes from the area around Cernusco and Montevecchia north of Milan and west of Bergamo. It is produced from a blend of grapes very similar to that used in Franciacorta—barbera, nebbiolo, and merlot; only cabernet franc is missing.

MONTSCLAPADE *(Friuli Venezia Giulia)*. This *barrique*-aged Bordeaux variety blend of merlot, cabernet sauvignon, cabernet franc, and malbec has been produced since 1982 by Girolamo Dorigo, a fine producer of wines in the Colli Orientali zone.

MORI VECIO *(Trentino Alto Adige)*. Lagariavini, or Lagaria as it is labeled for the U.S., produces this wine from 50 percent merlot and 25 percent each of the two cabernets. The wine was named for the *azienda*'s 5-acre (2-hectare) vineyard in Mori, Trento. They first produced this wine in 1967. Currently they are producing some 70,000 bottles a year, though not all of the grapes are from the original vineyard. Mori Vecio is given some *barrique*-aging.

Lagaria rates 1969 as the best vintage for this wine and 1972 as the worst. Mori Vecio is ready to drink from its third year and ages well for another three or four. Rating★★ +

Tasting Notes

1979 *(7/85)*. Complex aroma; mellow, smooth and round, good body, nice flavor; marred by a slight harshness at the end.★★ −

1977 *(3 times 11/80)*. Quite a lot of nice fruit, bell-pepper note, some tannin, some style; needs one, perhaps two more years.★★(+)

1976 *(10/79)*. Has an herbaceous aspect; balanced, soft, some tannin, good fruit.★★

1975 *(10/78)*. Distinct varietal character, good quality, flavorful, some length.★★ +

1974 *(3/80)*. Herbaceous nature, some tannin, seems to lack some distinction, though drinkable.★

1971 *(2/79)*. Small nose, some fruit evident; flavorful; age beginning to show.★

MORLACCO *(Trentino Alto Adige)*. F.lli Pedrotti produce this wine from a blend of cabernet sauvignon, marzemino, and pinot noir grapes. It ages moderately well, reputedly for up to five or six years.

NAVESEL *(Trentino Alto Adige)*. Armando Simoncelli produces this wine, one of the many Bordeaux blends from Trentino, of cabernet and merlot grapes. It can be enjoyed from its third year. Rating★

Tasting Note

1978 *(4/80)*. Characteristic herbaceous aroma; light tannin, nice fruit, acid on the low side; hangs at the end.★

NOVALINE RUBINO *(Trentino Alto Adige)*. Liberio Todesca produces the Novaline Rubino from a blend of 60 percent cabernet sauvignon and 40 percent merlot. It is aged for about a year and a half in barrel. The wine drinks well from three to four years of the vintage, till about six or seven.

PALAZZOTTO. See Breganze.

PIAVE *(Veneto), DOC*. Historical records show that the vine was cultivated in this region during the Roman era, from at least the first century A.D. Today DOC regulates the production of four varietal wines from Piave: two whites and two reds, Cabernet and Merlot.

The vineyards are planted in the lowlands on both sides of the Piave river from Conegliano to the Adriatic sea in the provinces of Treviso and Venezia in the eastern part of the Veneto. As elsewhere in the region, cabernet and merlot vines were introduced here in the nineteenth century but didn't become widespread until after recovery from *phylloxera,* which devastated the vineyards here in the 1920s.

DOC Requirements

	Minimum varietal	Minimum age	Minimum alcohol	Maximum yield (gallons/acre)
Cabernet	100%	none	11.5	823
riserva		3 years	12.5	
Merlot	90%	none	11.0	973
vecchio		2 years	12.0	

Aging for the Cabernet riserva and the Merlot vecchio is figured from January 1 after the harvest. The Merlot may contain up to 10 percent cabernet and/or raboso grapes. Up to 10 percent of concentrate, if made from grapes grown in the zone, may be used to bring up the alcohol in a weak vintage.

Annual production of Cabernet averages about 275,000 cases a year. The output of Merlot exceeds 1.25 million cases.

> *Recommended Producers*
> Enetum (Cabernet and Merlot)
> Kunkler Bianchi (Cabernet and Merlot)
> Ponte Cantina Sociale (Cabernet Sauvignon and Merlot)
> Roncade (Cabernet)
> Silvestrini (Cabernet)
> SO.VI.VE., Societa Vini Veneti (Merlot)

Silvestrini's Cabernet is, from our experience, the finest DOC wine of the zone. Kunkler produces some fairly good Piave wines.

We must disagree with those who suggest that these wines will live for five or six years. From our experience, the Cabernet is at its most enjoyable before its third year, though it can last for one year beyond that. The Merlot is best before it is two years old. Cabernet★; Merlot★

PRAMAGGIORE *(Veneto), DOC.* The Pramaggiore growing zone is the easternmost in the Veneto. It takes in all or part of nineteen *communes* between the Livenza and Tagliamento rivers in the provinces of Venezia, Pordenone, and Treviso.

Cabernet and merlot vines were introduced here after World War I. Most of the cabernet plantings are cabernet franc, but there is some cabernet sauvignon.

DOC Requirements

	Minimum varietal	Minimum age	Minimum alcohol	Maximum Yield *(gallons/acre)*
Cabernet	90%	none	11.5	748
riserva		3 years	12.0	
Merlot	90%	none	11.5	823
riserva		2 years	12.0	

The aging period for the riserva is figured from November 1 after the harvest. Up to 10 percent merlot is allowed to be blended into the Cabernet, and the Merlot may contain 10 percent cabernet. Either wine can be made with concentrate—no more than 5 percent and only that made from grapes grown within the zone—to bring up the alcohol to the required minimum in difficult vintages.

Annual production of the Cabernet averages about 80,000 cases a year; that of the Merlot approaches 325,000.

Recommended Producers
"Gruarius," Cantina Sociale di Portogruaro (Merlot)
Guarise (Cabernet)
Lorenzi, Paolo de (Cabernet)
Morassutti Giovanni Paolo (Cabernet and Merlot)
Osvaldo (Carbernet)
Santa Margherita (Cabernet and Merlot)
Tenuta Agr. di Lison (Cabernet and Merlot)
Tenuta Agr. "La Fattoria" Gli Abbazia Benedettina di Summaga (Merlot)
Tenuta Sant'Anna (Cabernet and Merlot)

Santa Margherita produces a DOC Cabernet Sauvignon from Pramaggiore, as well as a Cabernet Franc. They bottle a single-vineyard Merlot from Selva Maggiore. They rate 1983, 1982, 1979, 1978, 1974, and 1971 as the best vintages for these wines.

The Pramaggiore wines tend to be low in acidity. They can take a couple of years of aging, no more. They are generally best within two or three years of the vintage. These wines start out with a fairly herbaceous nature which seems to become more aggressive with age. As with the Piave river wines, we feel these wines should be drunk earlier than is generally suggested—between one and three, at most four years for the Cabernet, and one to two, perhaps a year longer for the Merlot is about right. Cabernet★; Merlot★

QUARTO VECCHIO *(Veneto).* Cantine Petternella produces this wine from a blend of 70 percent cabernet sauvignon and 30 percent merlot. It is best drunk before its sixth year. Rating★★

Tasting Note

1978 Vigna Pezzelunghe *(7/85).* Characteristic herbaceous aroma; on the palate very green and acid; a real surprise. Although it had been quite some time since we tasted this wine, we remembered it being quite good. We base our rating of ★★ on our past experience, not on this wine, which gets 0.

QUATTRO VICARIATI *(Trentino Alto Adige).* Càvit, the large Trentino cooperative, makes this wine from cabernet and merlot grapes from the Quattro Vicariate hills of the Lagarina Valley in Trentino. It is aged for up to two years in oak casks. Quattro Vicariati is a soft, fairly herbaceous wine of no particular distinction. It is best drunk young, say within three years of the vintage; while it can last beyond that, there's not much point in keeping it longer. Rating ★

RAUTEN *(Trentino Alto Adige)*. The Salvetta brothers make this wine from 60 percent cabernet sauvignon and 40 percent merlot grapes grown on their farm in the Calavino area of Trentino. It is a fairly good red wine, best drunk between three and six years of the vintage. Rating★★ −

Tasting Note

1977 *(4/80)*. Herbaceous aroma with vanilla notes and cherries; nice fruit, acid a bit low, flavorful; short.★★ −

RIVA ROSSO. See Collio.

ROSSO DEL RIVOLTELLA *(Lombardy)*. This wine is produced by Az. Agr. La Tassinara from merlot and cabernet grapes; both cabernets are used. These grapes are grown on their estate near Desenzano del Garda. It is aged for a year in cask. The Rivoltella is at its best drunk between two and three years of the vintage.

SAMMARCO *(Tuscany)*. Castello dei Rampolla has 25 acres (10 hectares) of cabernet sauvignon vines in their 89-acre (36-hectare) vineyard. They produce Sammarco from a blend of 75 percent cabernet sauvignon and 25 percent sangiovese. The wine is aged in *barrique* for about two years. In 1980, the first vintage for this wine, they made 6500 bottles; in 1981, production was nearly double at 12,500 bottles. The 1981 vintage was given twenty-two months of *barrique* aging. Rating★★

Tasting Note

1981 *(5/85)*. Cabernet dominates the nose and palate, oaky background; seems a bit disjointed, not quite together, but the elements are all there; has a lot of tannin and a lot of fruit; be patient, perhaps in two more years its quality should begin to really show.★★(+)

SAN COLOMBANO AL LAMBRO *(Lombardy)*, DOC. This new DOC from the Milan area is for a red wine made from a blend of merlot, cabernet, and malbec.

SAN LEONARDO *(Trentino Alto Adige)*. This regarded Bordeaux blend is produced by Marchese Anselmo Guerrieri Gonzaga. It is made from 70 percent cabernet—both types—and 30 percent merlot grapes grown in the Toblino area of Trentino. San Leonardo is best drunk between four and six years of the harvest. Rating★★

SAN ZENO *(Trentino Alto Adige)*. La Vinicola Sociale Aldeno blends 40 percent merlot with 30 percent each of the two cabernets to produce this wine. It ages more gracefully than their other Bordeaux blend, Sgreben—until its fifth or sixth year, though it is enjoyable sooner. Rating★★ +

Tasting Notes

1976 *(4/80)*. Characteristic herbaceous aroma with nice fruit and some oak; some tannin, nice flavor, some style; moderately long finish.★★ +

1974 *(10/78)*. Herbaceous aroma, some oak; soft and fruity, flavorful; good quality.★★ +

SANTA GIULIA DEL PODERACCIO *(Lazio)*. Conte Vaselli, a noted producer of Orvieto, uses merlot and cabernet grapes grown in the Viterbo area to produce this wine. It ages moderately well.

SASSICAIA *(Tuscany)*. Marchesi Incisa della Roccheta, proprietor of the Tenuta San Guido estate in the Bolgheri zone, first produced Sassicaia in the 1950s, but the wine wasn't offered commercially until 1968 by the firm of Antinori. Piero Antinori told us that Sassicaia was always made from a blend of 95 percent cabernet sauvignon and 5 percent cabernet franc. The wine is produced at the estate and was, until the 1982 vintage, bottled and marketed by Antinori. It is aged in a combination of French and Slavonian oak barrels. The bottling from 1982 will be done by Marchese Incisa at the estate.

Annual production of this Cabernet is 5000 cases a year, double that of a few years ago.

Piero Antinori rates the vintages as follows:

★★★★	1981
★★★	1982, 1978, 1977, 1975, 1974
★★	1979, 1973, 1971
★	1980, 1976
0	1972

He told us that the 1969 was never released because it didn't achieve the level of quality they require. It's interesting to note that at a recent tasting in London of all the Sassicaia wines, the '80 (a vintage that Antinori considered rather mediocre) was rated best by the tasters present—which just goes to prove, *de gustibus non est disputandum,* there's no disputing about taste. It wouldn't have been our choice either. Rating★★ +

Tasting Notes

1980 *(5/85).* Aroma still somewhat closed, some nice nuances beginning to emerge; well structured, flavorful; finish is rather firm.★★ +

1979 *(twice 5/85).* Richer but more reticent aroma than the '80; well-knit, rich flavor; quite young, but holds out real promise.★★(★)

1978 *(4 times 11/82; 19,027 bottles).* Aroma still closed and undeveloped, some fruit and oak evident; firm-textured, a bit clumsy at this stage, quite a lot of flavor.★(★)

1977 *(5/83).* Rich aroma, though still somewhat closed, a note of tobacco; tannic and astringent, a lot of flavor; very young.★(★)

1976 *(twice 3/83).* Lacks fruit, balance, or style, though drinkable; both bottles were similar, allowing for the difference in age, though tasted a couple of years apart.

1975 *(twice 3/80).* Aroma of tar and oak; heavy-handed with oak dominating the flavor, overly tannic for the fruit. Will it develop?

1970 *(twice 4/81; 9850 bottles).* Richly intense aroma suggestive of cassis; well balanced, full of flavor, still has considerable tannin.★★(★ −)

1968 *(5/81).* High volatile acidity, tarry notes; cabernet character evident, full-flavored. Where will it go from here?★(?)

SGREBEN *(Trentino Alto Adige).* This wine, produced by La Vinicola Sociale Aldeno, is made from a blend of 40 percent merlot and 30 percent each of the two cabernets. It is best drunk before its sixth year. Rating★ +

Tasting Note

1976 *(4/80).* Aroma somewhat closed, herbaceous notes evident; could use more acid, nice flavor; short.★ +

SIMONINI, ATTILIO. See Favonio.

SOLAIA *(Tuscany).* Antinori first produced this wine from the 1978 vintage. They made 5000 bottles, which they felt was too few to put on the market. In 1979, they tripled their production and commercialized the wine. In 1980 and 1981, they didn't produce any Solaia, preferring instead to use the cabernet grapes in their more profitable Tignanello. In 1982, they produced Solaia again, about 2000 cases. Eventually they expect to reach an annual production of 4000 to 5000 cases.

The cabernet sauvignon (75 percent) and cabernet franc (25 percent) grapes for this wine come from the Solaia vineyard on their Santa Cristina property. The wine is aged for eighteen to twenty-four months in French and Slavonian oak barrels.

We've only tasted two vintages of Solaia but find it to be Antinori's most interesting wine. In some ways it is more reminiscent of a Bordeaux than the regarded Tuscan Cabernet blend, Sassicaia, which resembles more a California Cabernet. Because of our limited experience with this wine, we are more conservative in our rating than we would be otherwise, wanting to see if it will maintain the level of quality that we have seen thus far. Rating★★

Tasting Notes

1979 *(twice 7/85).* Oak apparent on the nose with some cabernet evident in the back, chocolate notes; a leaner, firmer style of Cabernet than Sassicaia, well-knit though not quite together, has the ingredients to make a splendid bottle.★★(★)

1978 *(5/83).* Nice cabernet fruit up front on the nose, bell-pepper back note; light tannin, well balanced; fairly nice.★★ −

SÜD TYROL. See Alto Adige.

TAVERNELLE CABERNET SAUVIGNON *(Tuscany)*. The large American importing firm, Villa Banfi, produces this wine from vines grown at an altitude of 1100 feet (340 meters) on their Montalcino estate in the Brunello zone. Their first Cabernet Sauvignon was produced from the 1982 vintage. It was aged for one year in *barriques* of Troncais oak. Eventually Banfi plans to produce 70,000 cases a year of this California-style Cabernet. Rating★(?)

Tasting Note

1982 *(twice 7/85)*. Oak on aroma, some cabernet fruit evident; grapey flavor on entry gives way to loads of tannin, has a lot of oak on the palate as well. Where will it go from here?(?★)

TORRE ALEMANNA *(Apulia)*. This wine is produced from the French malbec and native negro amaro and uva di Troia grapes grown in the Cerignola area between Foggia and Bari. Torre Alemanna is a full-bodied wine of 13 percent alcohol that can take a few years of age.

TORRE ERCOLANA *(Lazio)*. Cantina Colacicchi-Anagni produces a scant 1200 to 1400 bottles a year of this wine. It is made from a blend of cesanese del piglio, cabernet, and merlot grapes grown on their estate in the Frosinone area and aged for about two years in oak casks. Torre Ercolana is a rich, flavorful, full-bodied, smooth red wine that in our experience ages magnificently for up to ten years and can probably last longer. Rating★★★

Tasting Notes

1975 riserva *(twice 3/82; 1184 bottles)*. Rich, full bouquet, cassis notes; some tannin, full of flavor, well balanced, very rich, has style.★★ +

1973 riserva *(3/81; 1496 bottles)*. Richly fruited aroma recalls cassis; full-flavored and velvety.★★★

TORRE QUARTO *(Apulia)*. This estate is named for the ruins of a tower dating from A.D. 850 on the property. In 1847, Duc de la Rochefoucauld brought cuttings of the malbec vine from Bordeaux and planted a 2500-acre (1000-hectare) vineyard here. Marcello Cirillo-Farrusi, who bought the estate in the early 1930s, restored the winery and replanted part of the vineyard. Today the property is owned by his son, Fabrizio Cirillo-Farrusi. (We've heard recently that controlling interest has been bought by the regional government.)

There are 150 acres (60 hectares) of vines at Torre Quarto planted at 30 feet (9 meters) above sea level. Annual production averages nearly 30,000 cases. More than 60 percent of this is red, which includes Torre Quarto and Rosso di Cerignola. The estate also produces a bianco and a rosé.

Torre Quarto is made from 75 percent malbec and 25 percent uva di Troia grapes. The regular is aged for two years in oak casks, the riserva for an additional year. That wine is only made in the better vintages and not more than 2000 cases a year.

Fabrizio rates as his best vintages 1981, 1979, 1977, 1973, and 1971, with 1981 being especially fine and 1977 better than 1979. He said 1975 was good, 1974 and 1970 were average years and 1968 was also a good year.

Torre Quarto is a richly flavored, full-bodied wine that can seem a bit coarse in its youth. But given sufficient time, it can develop into a very impressive wine, with a richness of flavor and a complexity of character found only in top-quality wines. Torre Quarto drinks well from its fourth or fifth year for up to two decades or more. We have tasted thirty-year-old vintages that were still in fine condition; they had, in fact, improved with the years. Rating★★★

Tasting Notes

1980 *(ex-cask 4/81)*. Has fruit, but rasping at edges, not up to the level we expect from this wine.

1979 *(ex-cask 4/80)*. Pruny, raisiny aroma; rich extract, seems a trifle overripe; should make a nice glass of wine with sufficient time.★(★)

1977 *(14 times 7/85)*. Richly fruited aroma, notes of figs and prunes and a touch of vanilla; still some tannin, soft-centered, richly flavored; good now, but has a lot of potential.★★(★)

1975 *(5 times 7/85)*. Nose shows a lot of development and complexity from bottle age, mellow, toasty notes; loads of flavor, full-bodied; still has a lot of life left, no sign of age except in its mellowness.★★(+)

1975 riserva *(4/80; from tenth)*. Very soft, some tannin, and a lot of flavor.★★

1974 riserva *(5 times 7/85; 20,000 bottles)*. Toasty, woodsy aroma, with berry notes; tannin up front gives way to a load of fruit; goes out with tannin; seems like it's beginning to dry out, but still quite good.★★ −

Tasting Notes

1973 *(twice 5/80)*. Fruity aroma, some oak beneath; balanced, tasty, full-bodied; could use more age; it seemed younger than the '75 we tasted with it.★★ +

1971 riserva *(4 times 7/85)*. Richly fruited and intense aroma, vague raisiny note, also prunes; smooth-textured, full and flavorful, though a bit overripe; finish lingers.★★ +

1970 riserva *(4 times 1/81)*. Lovely, complex bouquet of fruit and flowers; rich in extract and flavor; good quality.★★ +

1968 *(8/78)*. Fruity aroma, some oak; soft, tasty, balanced.★★ –

1961 riserva *(4 times 4/83)*. Beautiful garnet robe, orange at rim; lovely bouquet, mellow and complex; soft, smooth and round, tasty; very ready, as it has been for at least the past five or six years.★★★

1957 riserva *(twice 3/85)*. Beautiful robe; expansive bouquet recalling cassis and toast; velvety texture, full of flavor; very long, has style.★★★ +

1953 riserva *(3 times 9/83)*. Intense, complex bouquet with nuances of figs, blueberries, cassis, and apricots; soft and smooth, flavorful; very good and very long.★★★ +

TRENTINO *(Trentino Alto Adige), DOC*. The major part of the Trentino growing zone is along the Adige river from Mezzocorona north of Trento to Belluno Veronese some 15 miles (25 kilometers) north of Verona, in the Lagarina valley around Rovereto, in the lower Sacra valley from Vezzano to north of Lake Garda, and in the Cembra valley. There are some 27,000 acres (11,000 hectares) planted to vines; more than 85 percent of the plantings are of the red varieties.

The Trentino DOC covers Cabernet and Merlot wines. The Cabernet can be made from either franc, sauvignon, or both. An update to the DOC regulations, effective from 1984, allows a blend of cabernet and merlot. These wines will be denominated "Cabernet e Merlot del Trentino" or some such similar phrase.

DOC Requirements

	Minimum varietal	Minimum age	Minimum alcohol	Minimum yield *(gallons/acre)*
Cabernet	100%	2 years	11.0	823
riserva		3 years		
Merlot	100%	1 year	11.0	935
riserva		2 years		

The aging period is calculated from January 1.

Reputedly, the best cabernet is grown in the Adige and Sario valleys. Cabernet franc, it is said, fares better on the lower slopes, while cabernet sauvignon does best at the higher elevations. The best merlot vines are considered to be those from the vineyards on the valley floors in the southern part of the region.

Recommended Producers
Barone de Cles (Cabernet)
Barone Fini (Cabernet)
Conti Bossi Fedregotti (Cabernet and Merlot)
Dorigati (Cabernet)
Endrizzi F.lli (Cabernet and Merlot)
Istituto S. Michele (Cabernet)
Kupelwieser (Cabernet)
La Vinicola Sociale Aldeno (Cabernet)
Lagaria, I Vini del Concilio (Cabernet and Merlot)
Lechthaler (Cabernet)
Letrari (Cabernet)
Pedrotti (Cabernet)
Pisoni (Cabernet)
Rino Raffaelli (Cabernet)
Salvetta F.lli (Cabernet)
Simoncelli Armando (Cabernet)
Tenuta San Leonardo (Cabernet and Merlot)

The best Cabernets of Trentino are as good as those from any of the other DOC zones. They tend to be fuller in body and not as long-lived as those from the Alto Adige. The Merlots are less interesting.

Niederbacher's vintage ratings:

Cabernet

★★★★ 1970, 1969, 1964, 1959, 1949, 1947
★★★ 1983, 1971, 1957
★★ 1982, 1980, 1979, 1977, 1976, 1975, 1967, 1966, 1963, 1961, 1958, 1954, 1952, 1946
★ 1981, 1978, 1974, 1973, 1972, 1968, 1962, 1956, 1955, 1951, 1950, 1948, 1945
0 1965, 1960, 1953

Merlot

★★★★ 1969, 1959
★★★ 1975, 1971, 1964, 1961, 1957
★★ 1983, 1980, 1976, 1974, 1970
★ 1982, 1981, 1979, 1978, 1977
0 1973, 1972

There are also a number of interesting cabernet–merlot blends produced in Trentino, such as Castel S. Michele, Foianeghe, and Rauten, and we may see more since the recent DOC recognition. Cabernet★★; Merlot★

VALCALEPIO (*Lombardy*), *DOC*. This wine is produced in the Bergamo area from a blend of from 55 to 75 percent merlot and 25 to 45 percent cabernet sauvignon grapes.

DOC Requirements

Minimum age	Minimum alcohol	Maximum yield (*gallons/acre*)
none	12.0%	695

Production of Valcalepio averages about 20,000 cases a year.

The Bergamasca cooperative cellars, with about 150 members, is the zone's most important producer, and in our limited experience one of the best.

They age their Valcalepio for two years, one in oak casks. They also produce a varietal Merlot meant to be drunk young. The wines of Conte Medolaga Albani can be fairly good. Caselle Alte and Tenuta Castello, producers of some other good wines, enjoy a good reputation, as does Tenuta La Cornasella and Bortolo Locatelli.

Valcalepio is best drunk within four years of the vintage, thought it can last beyond that. When we visited the zone in 1981, we tasted three vintages: 1978, 1976, and 1975. The '75 was getting on in age; the other two were fairly enjoyable. The Valcalepio wines are light-bodied reds that display the characteristic herbaceousness of the grape varieties they are produced from. Rating★ +

VALTREBBIOLA (*Emilia Romagna*). Az. Agr. Vigneti Casa Rossa blends 50 percent merlot, 40 percent cabernet sauvignon, and 10 percent malbec grapes to produce this wine, which is aged in cask for a year or two.

VECCHIA CASA ROSA (*Emilia Romagna*). Az. Agr. Vigneti Casa Rossa produces this wine from a blend of 30 percent each of merlot, cabernet sauvignon, and cabernet franc, plus 10 percent malbec and pinot noir. It is aged for about two years in oak casks.

VENEGAZZÙ (*Veneto*). Count Loredan Gasparini, former owner of Venegazzù in the Montello e Colli Asolani area planted French varieties on the estate in the 1930s. Today the 125-acre (50-hectare) Az. Agr. Ca' Loredan Gasparini estate produces from 44,000 to 55,000 cases of wine a year, 11,000 of the red Venegazzù.

The two Venegazzù Riserva della Casa wines, a white and a black label, are made from a blend of cabernet sauvignon and franc, merlot, and malbec grapes.

Neil Empson, agent for the wines, describes the rather unusual method employed to produce the black label. Following the fermentation, 50 percent of the wine is bottled with 5 percent malbec concentrate and is left for three years in bottle during which time it referments. At the end of this period, the bottles are opened and emptied into a tank where the wine is combined with the other 50 percent. This wine is then aged in oak for several months.

At Venegazzù, they list as their best vintages 1980, 1976, 1972, 1971, 1968, 1964, and 1961.

The Riserva della Casa wines, among the first, are also among the more interesting of Italy's Bordeaux blends. Of the two, the black label offers more interest and quality; it also ages better than the white label. White label★★; Black label★★ +

Tasting Notes

1979 white label *(7/85)*. Aroma shows some refinement, herbaceous notes evident; well-knit and flavorful, still some tannin, though quite nice now; moderately long finish; some style.★★ +

1978 black label *(3 times 3/83)*. Pretty nose, characteristic herbaceousness; tasty, has personality and balance.★★ +

1978 white label *(3 times 3/83)*. Some age beginning to show, but still has flavor interest.★

1977 black label *(5/84)*. Drinking very nice now, though has some roughness.★★ −

1977 white label *(3/83)*. Herbaceous aroma; acid on the low side, nice flavor; some dullness at the end.★

1976 *(11/80)*. Lovely nose, oak and characteristic herbaceousness; well structured, tasty, still some tannin; has style.★★★ −

ZUITER ROSSO *(Veneto)*. Montelvini produces this wine from merlot, cabernet, marzemino, and pinot noir grapes grown in the Le Zuitere area of Montello e Colli Asolani. Production is 40,000 bottles a year. The name is the dialect word for owl; this area was at one time densely populated by these nocturnal flyers. (We don't imagine, though, that they gave a hoot for the area's wines.)

Chapter 17

Other Noble Reds

Besides the wines produced from Italy's three noble grape varieties—nebbiolo, sangiovese, and aglianico—the fine Amarones, and the wines from the Bordeaux grapes, cabernet and merlot, there are a number of other excellent wines produced in Italy.

There are wines that could have been included here but were not. Undoubtedly, there are noble red wines produced in Italy that we have not yet discovered. Those are pleasures to look forward to.

There are others that we have heard of but don't have enough information about to discuss them. And there are still others for which our information is too out of date. In this last group are the Groppello Amarone of Frassine (no longer produced), Gabiano (a barbera-based wine from Piemonte that has recently been recognized under DOC) especially the one from Castello di Gabiano, and the Barbarossa Vigna del Dosso from Mario Pezzi's Fattoria Paradiso in Emilia-Romagna. That's future business.

There are some other worthwhile reds that we haven't included although a case could be presented for doing so. These include:

> Barbera d'Alba and Barbera d'Asti from top-quality producers such as Vietti, Bruno Giacosa, and a few others
> Castel del Monte riserva, Rivera's Fasciarossa, and Il Falcone
> Clastido, Angelo Ballabio
> Copertino Rosso riserva, Barone Bacile Castiglione
> Doxi Vecchio
> Marzemino, especially from Giorgio Grai
> Narbusto, Angelo Ballabio
> "Notarpanaro" Rosso del Salento, Cosimo Taurino
> Pignola (a grape claimed by some authorities to produce the finest red wines of Friuli)
> "Portulano" Rosso del Salento, Giuseppe Calò
> Roche or Rouchet, from Scarpa
> Rossese di Dolceacqua, especially the Vigneto Curli of Emilio Croesi and perhaps also those from Lelio Tornatorre and Michele Giuglielmi
> Teroldego Rotaliano

The Wines

BRICCO DELL'UCCELLONE. See Uccellone.

CHAMBAVE ROUGE *(Aosta)*. Ezio Voyat, producer of Passito di Chambave, one of the finest sweet wines we've ever tasted, also makes a Chambave Rouge. This medium-bodied dry red has an alcohol level of close to 13 percent, high for this region. It reputedly ages very well. This wine is made from a blend of the local gros vien variety with the addition of some dolcetto and barbera. We haven't had it in some time, but what we have tasted was very fine indeed. Rating ★★

CREME DU VIEN DE NUS *(Aosta)*. Don Augusto Pramotton produces this wine from a blend of the local vien du Nus variety plus pinot nero grapes from the vineyards of the church of Nus. We've heard that a small amount of merlot and petit rouge are also included in the blend. The wine is aged for about one year in oak casks. Creme du Vien de Nus is a full-bodied, full-flavored, mellow dry red with a richness and level of glycerine that give it an impression of sweetness. The wine is also known as Vin de la Cure de Nus (wine of the parish priest of Nus). Rating ★★ +

Tasting Note

1973 *(10/80)*. Floral bouquet; soft and tasty, velvet texture, hints of sweetness; very long.★★★ −

FRANCONIA *(Friuli Venezia Giulia).* The franconia variety of Fruili, also known as blaufraenkisch or limberger, is said to be the pinot noir. In Austria, blaufraenkisch is another name for the gamay. Pierre Galet in his monumental ampleography *Cepages et Vignobles de France* does not make any tie-in with either the pinot or the gamay, though he does say that the other two names, as well as a few others, are synonyms for this variety.

The Cormons district of Gorizia and the Rocca Bernarda and Corno di Rosazzo areas of Udine are highly regarded for their Franconia wines. Angelo Nascig, a fine producer who makes a scant 165 to 220 cases of this wine a year at his cantina in Corno di Rosazzo, produces a very good one. Some other regarded producers of Franconia are "Il Castello" di Gianfranco Fantinel in Buttrio, Francesco Lui in Corno di Rosazzo, Az. Agr. della Roncada in Cormons, and Giuseppe Toti of Prepotto.

The Franconia wines are at their best between two and three years of the vintage and last well for four or five. Rating ★★

LAGREIN *(Trentino Alto Adige).* The lagrein grape is used to produce rosé, called Lagrein Kretzer or Lagrein Rosato, and red wines, Lagrein Dunkel or Lagrein Scuro. There are 907 acres (367 hectares) of lagrein planted in the recognized DOC zone in the Alto Adige—8 percent of the vines cultivated in the region—which yield some 400,000 cases of wine a year. Most of the plantings are in the province of Bozen (Bolzano) in the area from Meran to Salurn in the Etschtal (Valle Isarco). The main growing areas are in Gries, Fagen, Bozen Dorf, Auer, Eppan, Kurtatsch, Neumarkt, and Andrian.

The Lagreins from Fagen and Bozen Dorf are particularly prized; those of Auer, Eppan, and Kurtatsch are also regarded. The Lagrein, red and rosé, produced from vineyards on the red cliffs of Gries and Mortizing on the edge of Bozen, may be denominated Grieser Lagrein. The Kellereigenossenschaft Gries produces a Grieser Lagrein as does the Klosterkellerei Muri-Gries.

DOC regulations for Lagrein allow 1048 gallons an acre and require an alcohol level of at least 11.5 percent. If the wine is aged for a year (from November 1) it may be labeled riserva.

Good vintages for Lagrein were 1964, 1969, 1971, 1974, and 1976. Giorgio Grai rates the 1975 and 1974 vintages highly, and his own Lagreins support that view.

The wines from this variety have a similar structure to those from cabernet. Lagrein has a fruity aroma with hints of almonds. It is generally at its best from four to six years of the vintage, but we've had some at ten years that were still in fine condition. Rating ★★

Recommended Producers
Barone de Cles, from Trentino
Conti Martini, from Trentino
Grai, Giorgio (Bellendorf, Herrnhofer, Kehlburg)
Hofstatter, J.
Kaufmann
Kellereigenossenschaft Gries, Greiser Lagrein
Klosterkellerei Muri-Gries, Greiser Lagrein
Lageder, Alois, Lindenburg
S. Margherita
Schlosskellerei Turmhof, especially the Schmalz
Schloss Schwanburg

Tasting Notes

1984 Lageder, Lindenburg *(ex-cask 4/85).* Undeveloped aroma; fairly tannic, but the fruit seems sufficient to carry it.★(★?)

1983 Grai *(ex-vat 11/84).* Intense aroma, notes of cherries; very rich, very full, very young, and very good.★★(★)

1983 Schlosskellerei Turmhof *(11/84).* Vaguely cherrylike aroma; well balanced, some firmness, well made; moderately long.★★ +

1981 Lageder, Lindenburg *(4/85).* Cherries and tar on aroma, vaguely floral; balanced and flavorful, light but nice; ready now, with room for improvement.★★(+)

1976 Grai, Kehlburg label *(4/85).* Lightly herbaceous aroma with notes of cherries; firm acid, lots of flavor.★★

1976 Schlosskellerei Turmhof, Schmalz *(11/84).* Lovely bouquet, some refinement, cherry notes; a lot of flavor and a tannic vein; some class here.★★★

1975 Grai, Herrnhofer label *(2/84).* Perfumed floral, fruity bouquet, almond and vaguely herbaceous notes; soft, round, and tasty; very long finish.★★★

1974 Grai, Bellendorf, Herrnhofer, and Kehlburg labels *(10 times 4/85).* Big, rich, intense aroma, refined, cherry notes; some firmness, round, soft, and flavorful, light tannin; showing no age.★★★ −

Tasting Notes

1973 Lageder, Lindenburg *(4/85)*. Cherrylike fruit on aroma, tar, and vague mushroom notes; still some tannin, tasty; some astringency at the end.★★

1969 Lageder, Lindenburg *(4/85)*. Fairly rich, mushroom aroma; full of flavor, sweet fruit, smooth-textured; long, chocolate notes at the end.★★ +

MONSUPELLO, PODERE 'LA BORLA *(Lombardy)*. Carlo Boatti, at Az. Agr. Monsupello, produces what are for us the finest wines of the Oltrepò Pavese. He has an annual production of 90,000 to 120,000 bottles of wine including a very good white—Friday's White Wine—and a good spumante. He makes about 21,000 bottles a year of Monsupello, Podere 'La Borla. Boatti has 27 acres (11 hectares) of vineyards, most in Torricella Verzate.

The cantina was founded in 1893. Boatti has produced his Monsupello since 1961. It is made from a blend of 45 percent barbera, 25 percent croatina, 24 percent uva rara (bonarda novarese), and 6 percent pinot noir. Boatti uses the free-run juice only and ages the wine for two years in oak casks. 'La Borla needs at least four years of age to soften and smooth out and can live for up to a decade, developing interesting nuances of aroma and flavor. Rating★★

Tasting Notes

1979 *(3 times 9/83)*. Some complexity on aroma, floral and fruity nuances, a vague cherrylike note; well structured, tasty, ready.★★

1976 *(4/80)*. Fruity aroma; soft, balanced, flavorful; some length.★★ −

1974 *(twice 4/81)*. Cherry notes on a fruity aroma; tart edge, lively, a bit light, flavorful.★★

1971 *(9/81)*. Bouquet displays a mellowness and complexity from bottle age, hints of blueberries; soft and round, some age beginning to show, but still has a surprising amount of flavor.★★

PINOT NERO or PINOT NOIR. When the pinot noir attains its glorious best there are no finer wines in the world—a situation, alas, as rare as it is rarefied. Even in its native Burgundy, where the variety yields its finest wines, the quality it is famous for often eludes wine producers. Innovative winemakers in California, who have had great successes with the other French varieties, have yet to master this difficult variety.

Italian winemakers have also attempted to produce excellent wine from the noble pinot noir, often to have their efforts treated to its high-born scorn. But occasionally, as elsewhere including Borgogne, they have succeeded. Giorgio Grai has had some successes. Lazzarini in the Colli Berici has also managed to produce a few pinot noirs that demonstrated the nobility of the variety. The talented young winemaker, Maurizio Zanella, has made a few surprisingly good pinot noirs and in fact seems to be setting new standards for the wine in Italy.

Most of the plantings of pinot noir in Italy are in the northeastern regions of Trentino Alto Adige, the Veneto, and Friuli, and in the Oltrepò Pavese and Franciacorta districts of Lombardia. A significant portion of those vines are used for the production of some of the better Italian sparkling wines. Among the best growing zones are the Alto Adige, Colli Berici in the Veneto, Franciacorta in Lombardy, and the Valle d'Aosta.

In the Alto Aidge, or Sud Tyrol, where the pinot noir is known as blauburgunder, there are 546 acres (221 hectares) of pinot noir, yielding an average production of more than 200,000 cases of wine a year. Most of the plantings are between Miran and Salurn.

The best vineyards are considered to be in the Bressanone and Appiano districts. The grapes from Mazzon in the Unterland are also highly prized. Other regarded areas for the pinot noir are Girlan, Pinzon, and Schreckbichl.

DOC sets the maximum yield at 898 gallons per acre and the minimum alcohol at 11.5 percent. To qualify as riserva the wine must be aged for at least one year, calculated from November 1.

In Trentino, the best wines by reputation are from Mezzocorona. DOC recognizes and regulates the Pinot Noirs of Trentino. The maximum yield allowed is 748 gallons an acre; the minimum alcohol, 11.5. Trentino Pinot Nero must be aged at least one year from January 1; with an additional year, it can be labeled riserva.

Maurizio Zanella, proprietor of the fine champagne-method spumante house Ca' del Bosco, made his first still red Burgundy-style Pinot Noir from the 1982 vintage, and it's a darned good one. He is currently producing 3000 bottles a year and could easily more than double that to

7000. Zanella also makes a very fine cabernet–merlot blend and a chardonnay, in fact Italy's best. Maurizio has made a number of pilgrimages to Burgundy in his attempt to master the intricacies of this enigmatic variety. Given Zanella's commitment to quality, it should come as no surprise that his Pinot Noir is as fine as it is.

Only one other Pinot Noir, in our opinion, has managed to match his for Burgundian finesse. That wine is Lazzarini's Rosso del Rocolo, which has sometimes achieved real heights.

A few years ago we went to a dinner with friends at a BYOB restaurant. Each had brought a bottle of Pinot Noir. Burgundy-lover Patrice Gourdin brought a fine Bourgogne. We selected an Italian Pinot Noir. Other wine-knowledgeable friends brought some other fine bottles. Had we known what wines Patrice, Carlo Russo of Ho-Ho-Kus Wine & Spirit World, and Willy Frank of Vinifera Wine Cellars were going to bring, we might have chosen a Burgundy cru rather than Lazzarini's Rosso del Rocolo, excellent as it was. One the other hand, we don't think that Sig. Lazzarini would have been unhappy; though the others did bring some beautiful bottles, including some lovely Burgundies, his fine Pinot Noir stood up to the competition admirably— not that it was the best wine of the night, but neither was it out of its league.

Recommended Producers
Brigl, Josef, especially Kreuzbichler (Alto Adige)
Grai, Giorgio (Bellendorf, Herrnhofer, and Kehlburg labels)
Hofstatter, J. (Alto Adige)
Kellereigenossenschaft Girlan (Alto Adige)
Lageder, Alois (Alto Adige)
Lazzarini, Rosso del Rocolo (Pinot)
Schloss Schwanburg (Alto Adige)
Tenuta Schlosshof, Barone Felix Longo (Alto Adige)
Vignoble du Prieure de Montfleury, Sang des Salasses de Moncenis (Aosta)

Tasting Notes

1984 Maurizio Zanella *(ex-barrique 5/85)*. Surprising richness and weight, a lot of varietal character evident, and a lot of potential.★(★★)

1983 Brigl *(4/85)*. Vaguely mushroomy aroma; almost sweet, flavorful; a bit short.★+

1983 Grai *(ex-vat 11/84)*. Undeveloped aroma; well balanced, flavorful, needs time to show its quality.★(★)

1983 Maurizio Zanella *(twice 5/85)*. Characteristic pinot noir fruit and champignons aroma, touch of volatile acidity adds complexity as it does in Burgundy; soft and smooth-textured, well balanced; lacks some follow-through at the end.★★+

1982 Maurizio Zanella *(5/85)*. Berries and oak on aroma, with a mushroomlike note in the back; seems somewhat heavy-handed, nice flavor.★

1979 Brigl, Kreuzbichler *(4/85)*. Lovely aroma, berries and flowers; nice flavor; marred by some harshness at the end.★

1979 Grai, Herrnhofer label *(twice 2/84)*. Characteristic strawberries on aroma; nice flavor but a bit simple; an agreeable wine.★+

1978 Brigl, Kreuzbichler *(4/85)*. Varietal mushroomlike aroma with berry notes; good fruit, light tannin, a nice glass.★★−

1978 Lazzarini, Rosso del Rocolo (Pinot) *(3 times 2/83)*. Expansive varietal aroma of berries and mushrooms; smooth-textured and supple, a lot of flavor; has some style.★★+

1977 Grai, Bellendorf label *(4/80)*. Rasberry aroma; seems a little low in acid; fruity.★

1977 Lazzarini, Rosso del Rocolo (Pinot) *(twice 5/83)*. Characteristic pinot aroma, berries, underbrush, tar; some tannin, nice flavor; vaguely bitter finish.★★

1977 Sang des Salasses, de Moncenis, Vignoble du Prieure de Montfleury **(8/79)**. Lovely, perfumed bouquet, hints of berries and mushrooms; lively acidity, nice flavor, a bit light.★★+

1976 Lazzarini, Rosso del Rocolo (Pinot) *(twice 12/82)*. Typical strawberries and mushrooms on aroma; soft, round and smooth, harmonious, elegant and stylish, a bit light but full of quality.★★★

1974 Lazzarini, Rosso del Rocolo (Pinot) *(8/79)*. Deep color; expansive bouquet, intense; flavorful; displays style; long finish.★★★

1973 Grai, Kehlburg label *(twice 9/81)*. Nice aroma, with a note of strawberries; fruity, soft.★+

1971 Brigl *(4/85)*. Toasty, berry aroma; light tannin, tasty, very nice; signs of drying out at the end; drink up.★+

1969 Brigl, Kreuzbichler *(4/85)*. Lovely aroma, toasty, berrylike, age apparent; flavorful, beginning to dry out, still good.★+

1969 Grai, Herrnhofer and Kehlburg labels *(twice 4/85)*. The bottle of 2/84 seemed to be drying out.

This bottle: Beautiful brickish-orange robe; champignonlike aroma, complex, toasty notes; liquid velvet, tasty, full of style and class; quite long; impressive indeed.★★★

1964 Brigl *(4/85)*. Light, varietal aroma, some vegie notes; a lot of tannin. Is there enough fruit left? It seems so.★(★)

1961 Brigl *(4/85)*. Lovely pinot bouquet with a berrylike quality; has a sweetness on the palate which gives way to a drying note at the end.★★+

1959 Brigl *(4/85)*. Toasty, berry notes, lovely bouquet; full-flavored, soft; long; showing no signs of age.★★★

1955 Brigl *(4/85)*. Berry, mushroomy aroma; loads of flavor; a bit drying out at the end, but still good.★★

1951 Brigl, Kreuzbichler *(4/85)*. Deeper color than the younger wines; lovely bouquet recalls mushrooms, berries, and underbrush; smooth-textured, well balanced; thinning out a bit toward the back.★★★

PRIMITIVO DI MANDURIA *(Apulia).* Following the outbreak of *phylloxera* in Apulia at the end of the last century, many grape varieties from other regions and other countries were introduced in hopes of renewing the vineyards. Among these, according to the late Dott. Piero Garoglio in his monumental eight-volume *Enciclopedia Vitivinicola Mondiale,* was a variety that became known as primitivo, or primativo.

This vine was planted in the Murge hills of Gioia del Colle, Acquaviva delle Fonti, Casamassima, Turi, and S. Michele. From there it traveled south to the Tarantino plains. Today 70 percent of the vines in the province of Taranto are primitivo.

Vines transplanted from the Gioia del Colle zone were called primitivo di Gioia. Those from other districts were named for their locality—primitivo di Lizzano, primitivo del Tarantino.

As this is an early-ripening variety that produces a mature crop of grapes in the second or third week of August, it became known as primitivo, from the dialect word *primativus,* "early ripener."

The primitivo, in fact, yields two crops, the first in August and another at the end of September or the beginning of October. The name, it seems, is not used just for a single early-ripening variety but for a number of varieties or subvarieties. One, at least, unlike the vast majority of grapes, yields red juice, not clear as is normally the case.

The wine produced from the primitivo, especially when the vines are judiciously pruned and trained *al alberello,* individually like "little trees" rather than spread out on wires, is inky black in color, robust, and powerful, achieving a high degree of alcohol. It is made in dry and semisweet styles. On occasion it is fortified, to increase the natural high levels of alcohol, sometimes approaching 20 percent, and produce a primitivo *liquoroso.*

DOC regulates the production of Primitivo di Manduria, which must be 100 percent from primitivo grapes grown in the area around the ancient Mesapican town of Manduria and sixteen other *communes* in the province of Taranto and three in Brindisi.

DOC Requirements

	Minimum age total	Minimum alcohol potential	Minimum alcohol actual	Maximum sugar	Maximum yield (gallons/acre)
Regular	June 1	14.0%	14.0%	1%	673
Dolce naturale	June 1	16.0	13.0	—	673
Liquoroso (fortified)	2 years	17.5	15.0	—	673
Dolce naturale secco	2 years	18.0	16.5	—	673

The aging period for the liquoroso wines is figured from the time when the wine is fortified.

One of the best zones in the Mandurian district for the Primitivo di Manduria wine is the area around the village of Sava, where there are some vineyards with vines more than fifty years old. Vittorio Librale's Azienda Vinicola Amanda, in Sava, is the zone's most important winery, both for quantity and for quality. Production at Amanda is about 50,000 cases a year.

Vittore Librale of Amanda

Librale produced his first wine, which he labeled Rosso di Sava, in the middle 1960s. Today the Rosso di Sava Primitivo is labeled Primitivo di Manduria. He also produces other wines from a blend of primitivo plus other local varieties.

Vittorio doesn't own any vineyards; he buys all the grapes for his wines, mostly from Sava and the nearby villages. He told us that the best vineyards in the area are Casale di Aliano, Contrada Petrose, Pasano, and Contra da Casa Rossa.

From those sites he was able to produce, three times in the 1970s, a wine he calls "Ventuno" for its 21 degrees of potential alcohol (18 degrees of actual alcohol plus the potential alcohol of the unfermented sugar). In 1973, he produced 5496 bottles from Casale di Aliano and 4752 from Contra da Casa Rossa. In 1974, he made 13,578 bottles. The third was from the 1979 vintage, which actually attained 22 percent. He made 19,840 bottles of that one. In 1980, Vittorio made a "21" and a "22" as well.

This is a wine to enjoy with fruit and nuts, aged pecorino piccante, or the local fermented cheese, ricotta ascante. Vittorio also pours it with his wife Nella's homemade *biscotti* seasoned with almonds and fennel.

The Amanda Primitivo has something the others lack: personality and style. As big and full-bodied as this wine is, and it is, it is not coarse.

The regular Amanda Primitivo is at its best from three or four years of the vintage till about eight. This wine, with a touch of sweetness (less than 1 percent) and a robust fruity nature, goes well with hearty stews, braised red meat or game, and assertive cheeses.

We found it also went reasonably well with *cozzimateddi,* some local wildlife hunted down in the vineyards—black snails, actually, that Vittorio found while we were looking over the primitivo vines, wondering if they could be related to the zinfandel. The snails were not exactly needed as a supplement to the banquet of local specialties that Nella, sister Pompea, and Mama had prepared, but Vittorio knew we'd find them interesting, so another side dish was added.

The subject of zinfandel came up again at the table where brother-in-law Gregorio Contessa spoke about his research into the history of the primitivo. Though they all liked the popular theory that relates it to the zinfandel, he had been unable to find any proof despite a thorough examination of all the old documents and manuscripts in the local archives.

A number of people believe that the primitivo was brought to the U.S. from Apulia in the last century and planted in California where it became known as zinfandel. The two varieties do have some characteristics in common.

A few years ago we organized a blind tasting of Zinfandels and Primitivos. None of the tasters knew how many bottles of each varietal there were. Interestingly, with the exception of a single person, no one there was able to identify the grape variety correctly for all the wines. Matching up was even more difficult when the wine was a Zinfandel made in the late harvest style.

Dott. Garoglio notes, however, that primitivo wasn't planted in Apulia until 1890 or 1892, fifty years after zinfandel was established in the vineyards of our own West Coast. So, although the primitivo is not the missing ancestor of the zinfandel, that's not to say that the zinfandel couldn't be the progenitor of the primitivo. Perhaps along with the American rootstock brought to Italy for the battle against *phylloxera,* a few zinfandel cuttings also made it to Gioia del Colle.

Rating Amanda★★ Amanda 21 or 22★★★ –

Tasting Notes

1983 *(4/85).* Dried fruit character on aroma; full of fruit and concentration, with a richness of flavor that makes it attractive now though it is still quite young, some tannin.★★

1980 Liquoroso Secco *(18 percent complete, 16.5 percent actual) (5/82).* Opaque color; chocolate, cherry aroma; full-bodied and robust, noticeable sweetness, cherry flavor with a suggestion of chocolate; needs another two years or so.★★

1980 "21" *(21 percent complete, 17.8 percent actual) (ex-vat 1/81).* The black wine of Sava—if we had a fountain pen we could write indelible tasting notes with it. Raisins and nuts on aroma; very full, very rich, very young, has both sweetness and tannin, as thick as fava puree.★★(+)

1980 "22" *(22 percent complete, 18 percent actual) (ex-vat 5/81).* Blacker even than the "21"; aroma recalls chocolate, cherries, figs, raisins, nuts, and blackberries, and this is a baby yet; sweet and intense, full-bodied and rich, a knife-and-fork wine.★★(★)

Tasting Notes

1979 "22" *(22 percent complete, 18 percent actual)* *(4/85)*. Opaque, dense; concentrated, raisiny notes, semisweet.★★

1978 Liquoroso Secco *(18 percent complete, 16.5 percent actual)* *(6 times 4/85)*. Inky; chocolate, cherry aroma; robust and chewy, noticeable sweetness; tannic finish.★ +

1977 *16.5 percent alcohol (twice 1/82)*. Very dark; flavor like cherries, very full, very ready.★

1976 *17 percent alcohol, 1 percent sugar (6 times 1/81)*. Deep purple; rich, concentrated aroma recalls figs and raisins; some tannin, sweetness gives it a mellowness, full-bodied and robust.★★ +

1974 "21" *(21 percent complete)* *(1/81)*. Aroma suggests blueberries and raisins; interesting flavors, concentrated.★★

1973 *17 percent (1/82)*. Opaque; chocolate, cherry aroma; intense, some sweetness, very full.★★ +

1973 Contra da Casa Rossa "21" *(21 percent complete, 17 percent actual)* *(6 times 7/82)*. Sweet and grapey, reminiscent of freshly crushed grapes, chocolate notes; beginning to dry out on the finish; was better in 1980.★★

1973 Vigneti dell' Antico Casale di Aliano "21" *(21 percent complete, 18 percent actual)* *(6 times 5/81)*. Opaque; complex bouquet recalls black cherries, chocolate, figs, nuts, and raisins; lovely texture, full of flavor and personality; went perfectly with the anise biscuit.★★★

1972 *18 percent complete, 17 percent actual (5/81)*. Deep ruby; fruity aroma recalls raisins; noticeable sweetness, but beginning to lose its fruit; an almost rasping aftertaste.★

1971 *18 percent complete, 17 percent actual (1/81)*. Still has sugar, round, full-bodied and full-flavored; alcohol starting to intrude at the end.★

REFOSCO *(Friuli Venezia Giulia)*. The refosco grape has seven or eight subvarieties, the most common two being the refosco dal peduncolo rosso and refosco nostrano. The former, also known as pecol ross, is considered the best, and the refoscone is just behind it in quality.

Refosco is recognized under DOC for Aquilea, Colli Orientali del Friuli, Grave del Friuli, and Latisana. There are some good Refoscos produced around Casarsa in the Grave del Friuli zone.

Colli Orientali del Friuli is considered the best district for this variety, and the most highly regarded wines are said to come from the *communes* of Savorgnano and Nimes. Some producers of Refosco in Colli Orientali make wines of distinction.

Paolo and Dina Rapuzzi have 20 acres (8 hectares) of vines on their Ronchi di Cialla farm in Prepotto; 7.5 (3) are planted to refosco. Since his first vintage in 1977, Rapuzzi has used new *barriques* of Slavonian oak to age all his wines. He produces 2750 to 3325 cases of wine a year: two whites and two reds, all from native grape varieties—Picolit and Verduzzo, Refosco and Schioppettino. All are very good, and each is among the best of its type made.

Angelo Nascig, in Corno di Rosazzo, has 6.2 acres (2.5 hectares) of vines at Az. Agr. V. Nascig, from which he produces 1200 cases of very good wine a year, including 220 cases of Refosco. He produces two, one from refosco dal peduncolo rosso, the other from refosco nostrano. In 1980, he blended the two together.

Giovanni Dri, at Nimis in Udine, who produces the exceptionally fine Verduzzo di Ramondolo, one of Italy's finest dessert wines, also makes a very good Refosco. When we visited him in 1981, he had 10 acres (4 hectares) of vineyards, 7.5 (3) planted to verduzzo, 0.7 (0.3) of tocai, and 1.7 (0.7) of refosco dal peduncolo rosso. He told us he had plans to put in another 3.7 acres (1.5 hectares) of verduzzo and refosco. His vines are planted at 1215 feet (370 meters), the highest vineyards in Friuli, he told us. His annual production at that time was 14,650 to 16,000 bottles of Verduzzo, 1325 of Tocai, and 2650 to 5325 of Refosco.

Dri feels his Refosco is at its best between four and seven years. His best vintages, he said, were 1979, 1978, 1974, and 1972; average years were 1980, 1977, and 1976.

Other good Refoscos are produced by Girolamo Dorigo and Villa Belvedere di Taddei also in the Colli Orientali del Friuli zone.

Generally, Refosco has a vinous character with some herbaceousness, sometimes with a touch of spice. It is full-bodied, fruity, and somewhat rustic. The finer ones have real character. Rating (for the better ones)★★ +

Tasting Notes

1980 Nascig *(ex-cask 4/81)*. Has richness of flavor and balance; shows promise. Nascig normally keeps his Refosco dal Peduncolo Rosso and Refosco Nostrano separate, but because he had such a small amount of the Nostrano in 1980, he blended them together.★★

1979 Giovanni Dri, Refosco di Ramandolo *(4/81)*. Very dark, inky in fact, purplish color; ripe aroma of black cherries; full, rich and flavorful, recalls black cherries, robust but refined, chewy; a knife-and-fork wine; very long finish.★★★

Tasting Notes

1979 Girolamo Dorigo, Casa Rossa *(twice 4/81).*
Complex aroma recalls cherries, vanilla, and cinnamon,
has a surprising amount of refinement for what is
generally a coarse grape; some tannin, soft and flavorful;
room to improve, but quite good now.★★★ −

1979 Nascig, Refosco dal Peduncolo Rosso *(4/81).*
Expansive, richly concentrated aroma with suggestions
of cherries; cherrylike flavor fills the mouth; young,
but quite enjoyable now; long aftertaste.★★(★)

**1978 Ronchi di Cialla, Refosco dal Peduncolo
Rosso** *(3 times 11/82; 4000 bottles from 5200 vines).*
Richly fruited aroma, black cherries, strawberries, oak,
herbaceous, and spicy notes; some oak, nice acidity
adds zest, a mouthful of nice flavor, smooth-textured;
very long.★★★

SCHIOPPETTINO *(Friuli Venezia Giulia).* Schioppettino, known also as ribolla nera, can
produce wines of real quality, especially in the area around Prepotto in Colli Orientali del Friuli.
There are perhaps ten to fifteen producers who make a Schioppettino, but in our experience no
one produces finer ones than Paolo Rapuzzi.

Rapuzzi began producing wines at his Ronchi di Cialla estate in 1977. His wines are very
fine, and because of his severe selection the quantity is always very limited. When we asked him
why he pruned so closely when mother nature restricted production for him every year, he
responded with a question. "And what if one year mother nature didn't prune for me? I really
don't have a choice if I want to produce top-quality wines." Which he obviously does. Rapuzzi's
yield averages 25 percent of that allowed by DOC for the wines of this zone.

Rapuzzi has 7.4 acres (3 hectares) of schioppettino, from which he produces about 1500
bottles a year. From the 1978 harvest he got only 1400 bottles from his 3500 vines, one bottle of
wine from two and a half vines. Like all his wines, the Schioppettino is aged in new *barriques*
of Slavonian oak, six to eight months for the schioppettino.

The Schioppettinos of Giuseppe Toti and Giorgio Rieppi, also from Prepotto, have received
some favorable reviews in the Italian press. Rating ★★★ −

Tasting Notes

1978 Ronchi di Cialla *(4 times 1/83; 1400 bottles,
3500 vines).* Aroma of cherries and black pepper,
spicy, raspberry, walnut, vanilla, and cassis notes; richly
intense, a nice mouthful of flavor, firm; very long and
very nice.★★★

1977 Ronchi di Cialla *(7/80).* Lovely nose, spice
and flowers, black pepper and fruit; soft, though some
tannin remains, firm acidity; long.★★ +

TAZZELENGHE *(Friuli Venezia Giulia).* The tazzelenghe, tacelenge, or tazzalenga variety is
planted in the area around Buttrio in Udine. There are four or five producers who make a
Tazzelenghe wine.

The most important producer, and the only one whose wine we've tasted, is Cantine Florio.
Florio's tazzelenghe vines are more than thirty years old. Tazzelenghe makes up only a small part
of their annual production, 1100 cases out of 14,500. But that's not so little, depending on how
you look at it; we understand the other producers make only about 250 to 400 bottles in a year.

Florio ages the Tazzelenghe, like all their reds, for about one year in fifty-year-old casks of
185 to 1320 gallons (7 to 50 hectoliters). The Florio Tazzelenghe is a wine reminiscent of a
Cabernet, though with somewhat higher acidity.

Girolamo Dorigo, a very fine producer, and Brava have gotten some good press for their
Tazzelenghes. Rating ★★

Tasting Note

1978 Tenuta Maseri Florio, di Buttrio *(4/81).* Herbaceous aroma, cherry note; tart, some tannin, interesting flavor, needs some age.★★

UCCELLONE *(Piemonte).* Why did we include a Barbera in a discussion of Italy's noble
reds? How could we, in fact, include a Barbera? The truth is we couldn't, up until last winter.
In January, we went to VI.PI.85, a very good new fair of Piemontese wines. And there we
discovered a Barbera unlike any we had tasted before—Giacomo Bologna's Bricco dell'Uccellone.

We were, of course, familiar with his La Monella, which is a very good Barbera. But, good as it is, we could not have included it in the book. The Bricco dell'Uccellone is another story.

When we tasted this wine at the dinner where it had its debut (before it was actually released on the market), we had already tasted it at Giacomo's stand at the fair, and our initial impressions were confirmed. It really was that good. We went over to Giacomo's table to offer our compliments. Giacomo introduced us to his friends at the table and said, "Here is the man responsible for the creation of my Uccellone, Sheldon." What was that? Giacomo is the creator of Bricco dell'Uccellone. "The idea," he said, "came from you. Remember a few years ago, you poured me some very good California Barbera that was aged in *barrique?*" Vaguely, now that he mentioned it. "It put the idea in my mind: Barbera in *barrique. Grazie mille,* Sheldon." "*Mille grazie,* Giacomo." Here was a doubly pleasant surprise—to discover this remarkable wine and to learn that this winelover had played a part, however small in its creation.

—photo by Sheldon Wasserman   *Giacomo Bologna and Pauline Wasserman*

Giacomo's regular Barbera is very good, superb for its type, just as his Moscato is—in fact, the platonic form for a moscato. But Giacomo, a man who values quality in all of its forms, wanted to do something more.

Those of you who have had the opportunity to dine at Giacomo's now defunct and much lamented Trattoria Braida, will know what we are talking about. Giacomo has an eye for beauty, and his palate is as discriminating. Is it any wonder that when we visit him and his wife, the essential Anna (less outgoing and enthusiastic than Giacomo but no less good-hearted and sincere), we discover not only excellent wines, such as the rare Malvasia, Vigna Sotto La Rocca Bernarda from the exceptionally fine Friulian producer Leonardo Specogna, but also elegant gourmet treats—the dishes produced by Anna and by Mama (ex-chef at Braida), olive oil from all over the country, tuscan for the salad, ligurian for the bread, and new specialties, or new to us, like the excellent goose products of the genial Gioacchino Palestro (delivered in person through the snow and fog to his friend Giacomo and Giacomo's friends)—the best of whatever there is.

It's no surprise that Giacomo also had a desire to offer the best Barbera he could find, and he found it in the Bricco dell'Uccellone vineyard and his own cantina, where he turned the grapes into a wine that does no less than create a whole new category of Barbera.

The Bricco dell'Uccellone vineyard has a southern exposure which allows the grapes to ripen fully. In 1982, a very fine vintage, the grapes were harvested in October at 22 percent sugar and .85 percent total acidity. Giacomo fermented the wine in stainless steel, *cappello sommerso,* with a submerged cap, at 25° C. The finished wine was aged in *barrique* for about one year, from February 1983 until March 1984, and given a further year of aging in bottle before release.

Bricco dell'Uccellone has 13.7 percent alcohol. And for the Californians among us who like statistics, 5.8 percent total acidity, 0.4 percent volatile acidity, and 3.5 pH—all surprising figures for Barbera.

This Barbera is so good that as soon as we began to put words to paper, we felt the need to have a glass to accompany them.

Tasting Note

1982 *(11 times, 7/85).* Typical barbera cherries plus oaky vanilla notes on bouquet, rich and expansive; well balanced and supple, with a lot of fruit and the complexity and extra dimension from the oak; long, lingering finish; displays real style and a lot of quality.★★★

Notes

1. Renato Ratti. *Guida ai Vini del Piemonte.* Torino: Edizioni Eda, 1977. We have relied quite heavily on this book and many articles and discussions with Renato Ratti for much, but not all, of the historical information in this chapter.

2. Based on 1982 statistics supplied by Regione Piemonte.

3. Based on 1980 statistics supplied by Regione Piemonte.

4. A. D. Francis, *The Wine Trade.* New York: Harper & Row, 1973.

5. Raymond Flower, *Chianti—The Land, the People, and the Wine* (New York: Universe Books, 1979), p.131.

6. E. Repetti. *Dizionario geografico fisico storico della Toscana.* Firenze, (1833–1846), quoted by Alessandro Boglione in *Flower,* op. cit., appendix 6.

7. S. Pieri, *Toponomastica della Valle dell'Arno* (Roma, 1919), Alessandro Boglione, op. cit.

8. Flower, op. cit., photo between pages 40 and 41.

9. Ibid., p. 279–280.

10. Lamberto Paronetto, *Chianti, The History of Florence and Its Wines* (London: Wine and Spirit Publications, 1970).

11. Ibid., p. 65.

12. Ibid., p. 66.

13. A. D. Francis, *The Wine Trade,* (New York: Harper & Row, 1973), p. 45.

14. André Simon, *The History of the Wine Trade in England,* Volume III (London: Holland Press, 1964), p. 35.

15. Paronetto, op. cit., p. 195.

16. Ibid., p. 169.

17. Ibid., p. 45.

18. Statistics supplied by the Italian Wine Center, New York, 1985.

19. Paronetto, op. cit., p. 67.

20. Guglielmo Solci, *Montalcino pleases the eye, Brunello charms the palate,* Italian Wines & Spirits, August 1983, p. 65.

21. Alessandro Bizzarri, *Sulla Importanza dell'Esame del Mosto nel Processo di Vinificazione, Mezzi Facili per Esaminarlo,* (Milano: A. Lombardi, 1871), pp. 12, 13.

22. Emanuele Pellucci, *Brunello di Montalcino* (Fiesole: Ugo Fontana, 1981)

23. Statistics supplied by the Italian Wine Promotion Center, New York, 1985.

24. Emanuele Pellucci, *Vino Nobile di Montepulciano* (Fiesole: Ugo Fontana, 1985).

25. Ibid.

26. William Younger, *Gods, Men, and Wine* (London: The Wine and Food Society, 1966), p. 202.

27. Zeffiro Bocci, *Wines of the Veneto with controlled specifications of origin (DOC)* (Verona: Ente di Sviluppo Agricolo del Veneto, 1980), p. 142.

28. Giovanni Vicentini, *Veneto Verona Valpolicella Masi 6 Generations in the Shade of the Vine* (Gargagnago: Masi Agricola, S.P.A., 1982), p. 42.

29. Bocci, op. cit., p. 143.

30. Vicentini, op. cit., p. 50.

31. Bocci, op. cit., p. 142.

32. Ibid., p. 145.

33. *South Tyrolean Wine Guide* (Bozen: Board of Trade of the Autonomous Province of Bozen).

34. Zeffiro Bocci, *Wines of the Veneto with controlled specifications of origin (DOC).* Verona: Ente di Sviluppo Agricolo del Veneto, 1980.

35. Ibid, p. 42

Bibliography

Books and Pamphlets

Allen, H. Warner. *A History of Wine.* London: Faber and Faber, 1961.

Bizzarri, Alessandro. *Sulla Importanza dell'Esame del Mosto nel Processo di Vinificazione, Mezzi Facili per Esaminarlo.* Milano: A. Lombardi, 1871.

Bocci, Zeffiro. *Wines of the Veneto with controlled specifications of origin (DOC).* Verona: Ente di Sviluppo Agricolo del Veneto, 1980.

Bonacina, Gianni. *Lo Stivale in Bottiglia Piccola Enciclopedia dei 3811 Vini Italiani,* 3 volumes. Brescia: AEB, 1978.

Canessa, G. *Guida del Chianti,* volume 2. Firenze: Arnaud, 1970.

Corato, Riccardo di. *2214 Vini d'Italia Guida Regionale,* edition no. 2. Milano: Sonzogno, 1976.

Flower, Raymond. *Chianti—The Land, the People and the Wine.* New York: Universe Books, 1979.

Francis, A. D. *The Wine Trade.* New York: Harper & Row, 1973.

Galet, Pierre. *Cepages et Vignobles de France,* volume III, Les Cepages de Cuve. Montpellier: Paysan du Midi, 1962.

Garoglio, Dott. Piero. *Enciclopedia Vitivinicola Mondiale,* volume I. Milano: Edizioni Scientifiche UIV, 1973.

O'Toole, Tom. *South Tyrol Wine Guide.* Bozen: Chamber of Commerce, 1983.

Paronetto, Lamberto. *Chianti, The History of Florence and Its Wines.* London: Wine and Spirit Publications, 1970.

Pellucci, Emanuele. *Brunello di Montalcino.* Fiesole: Ugo Fontana, 1981.

Pellucci, Emanuele. *Vino Nobile di Montepulciano.* Fiesole: Ugo Fontana, 1985.

Pieri, S. *Toponomastica della Valle dell'Arno.* Roma, 1919.

Ratti, Renato. *Guida Ai Vini Del Piemonte.* Torino: Edizioni Eda, 1977.

Repetti, E. *Dizionario geografico fisico storico della Toscana.* Firenze, 1833–1846.

Roncarati, Bruno. *Viva Vino Doc Wines of Italy.* London: Wine and Spirit Publications, 1976.

Simon, André. *The History of the Wine Trade in England,* volume III. London: Holland Press, 1964.

Veronelli, Luigi. *Catalogo dei Vini d'Italia.* Torino: Giorgio Mondadori, 1983.

Veronelli, Luigi. *Catalogo dei Vini del Mondo.* Torino: Giorgio Mondadori, 1982.

Veronelli, Luigi. *Vini d'Italia N. 3.* Torino: Giulio Bolaffi, 1974.

Veronelli, Luigi. *Vini d'Italia N. 4.* Torino: Giulio Bolaffi, 1976.

Veronelli, Luigi. *Vini Rossi d'Italia.* Torino: Giulio Bolaffi, 1980.

Vicentini, Giovanni. *Veneto Verona Valpolicella Masi, 6 Generations in the Shade of the Vine.* Garganago: Masi Agricola, 1982.

Vigliermo, Amerigo. *Carema: Gente e Vino.* Ivrea: Priuli & Verlucca, 1981.

Younger, William. *Gods, Men, and Wine.* London: Wine and Food Society, 1966.

Almanacco 1983 dei Vini del Piemonte. Torino: Regione Piemonte, 1984.

Almanacco 1982 dei Vini del Piemonte. Torino: Regione Piemonte, 1983.

Almanacco 1981 dei Vini del Piemonte. Torino: Regione Piemonte, 1982.

Almanacco 1980 dei Vini del Piemonte. Torino: Regione Piemonte, 1981.

Almanacco 1979 dei Vini del Piemonte. Torino: Regione Piemonte, 1980.

Almanacco 1978 dei Vini del Piemonte. Torino: Regione Piemonte, 1979.

Catalogo dei Confezionatori del Chianti Classico Gallo Nero. Firenze: Consorzio Vino Chianti Classico, 1984.

Disciplinari di Produzione Vini A Denominazione di Origine "Controllata," Vol. I, II, and III. Conegliano: Scarpis, 1968, 1971, 1978.

Guida Turistica di Gattinara. Milano: Associazione Culturale di Gattinara, 1981.

I Grandi Vini de l'Albese. Torino: Ordine dei Cavalieri del Tartufo e dei Vini di Alba, 1977.

Il Chianti Classico. Firenze: Consorzio Vino Chianti Classico, 1984.

I. L. Ruffino 1877–1977. Firenze: private publication, 1978.

South Tyrolean Wine Guide. Bozen: Board of Trade of the Autonomous Province of Bozen.

Vignamaggio e Montagliari dal secolo XIV ai giorni nostri. Firenze: Olimpia.

Magazines

Barolo & Co. News of Piedmont's Wines. This magazine contains up to date information on the wines of Piemonte. It is written in Italian, with summaries in English of the highlights. It is worthwhile for those who want to keep abreast of this important region and its wines. For information, write to Barolo & Co., Via C. Fossati 6, 10141 Torino, Italy.

Civiltà del Bere. Civiltà has a lot of interesting and useful articles, all in Italian, written by knowledgeable journalist and experts. They rarely, if ever, venture an opinion about a producer or his wines. This magazine is a good aid in keeping current with the ever-changing world of Italian wines. For information, write to Editoriale Lariana s.r.l., 20129 Milano, Via Giacinto Gallina 8, Italy.

Italian Wines & Spirits. This quarterly edition of Civiltà del Bere has a combination of original English-language articles by English-speaking journalists and translations of some of the more important articles from the Italian edition. For information, write to Editoriale Lariana s.r.l., 20129 Milano, Via Giacinto Gallina 8, Italy; Italian Wines & Spirits, P.O. Box 1130, Long Island City, N.Y. 11101, U.S.A.; or Spotlight Magazine Distributors Ltd., 1 Benwell Road, Holloway, London N77AX, England.

Index